THE SETTLEMENT OF

THE AMERICAN CONTINENTS

A Multidisciplinary Approach to Human Biogeography

EDITED BY C. Michael Barton, Geoffrey A. Clark, David R. Yesner, and Georges A. Pearson

The University of Arizona Press / Tucson

The University of Arizona Press
© 2004 The Arizona Board of Regents
First Printing
All rights reserved
⊗ This book is printed on acid-free, archival-quality paper.
Manufactured in the United States of America

09 08 07 06 05 04 6 5 4 3 2 1

Library of Congress Cataloging-in-Publication Data
The settlement of the American continents :
a multidisciplinary approach to human biogeography /
edited by C. Michael Barton . . . [et al.].
p. cm.
Includes bibliographical references and index.
ISBN 0-8165-2323-1 (cloth : alk. paper)
1. Human beings—Migrations.   2. Human geography—
Western Hemisphere.   3. Human ecology—Western
Hemisphere.   4. Paleo-Indians—Migrations.
5. Land settlement patterns—Western Hemisphere.
I. Barton, C. Michael.
GN370.S66   2004
304.8—dc22   2003025861

CONTENTS

THE SETTLEMENT OF THE AMERICAN CONTINENTS

THE SETTLEMENT OF THE AMERICAN CONTINENTS

1 An Interdisciplinary Perspective on Long-Term Human Biogeography and the Pleistocene Colonization of the Americas

Geoffrey A. Clark, C. Michael Barton, Georges A. Pearson, and David R. Yesner

Humans are found throughout the world today: They occupy not only all of the continental landmasses, but also most islands large enough to support only small populations. Only those places that are harshly inhospitable to most life—such as Antarctica and the Greenland ice cap—are also largely devoid of human inhabitants, although small groups of people nevertheless maintain footholds even in these "photosynthetic deserts." With global population exceeding 6.5 billion, it is hard to imagine a world without people. Even those places popularly regarded as "pristine" wilderness, such as the great woodlands of prehistoric eastern North America or the Amazon rain forest, were long inhabited by humans and were possibly affected by their activities during millennia of human land use (Denevan 1992).

Long-Term Human Biogeography

This was not always the case. Two million years ago, humans were confined to the African continent, where they first arose and where they evolved along with other apes during the last half of the Cenozoic era. However, the dramatic climatic oscillations that marked the last 1.7 million years (technically the Pleistocene and Holocene epochs) offered new opportunities for mobile, adaptable animals. Humans thrived in this more dynamic environment, soon spreading into southwestern Asia and eastern Europe (Vekua et al. 2002). By about one million years ago, human populations had colonized the middle latitudes of the Eurasian landmass and the African continent (Klein 1999). Over this enormous span of time, Old World plant and animal communities coevolved with human ones. Australia and the Americas, however, remained inaccessible to terrestrial, subtropical humans. Until comparatively recent times, their ecosystems evolved unaffected by the human component found in Africa and Eurasia. During the last episode of worldwide glacial advance, lowered sea levels and the increasingly sophisticated technological skills of modern *Homo sapiens* combined to permit humans to

cross the Sunda Strait into Australia and to survive, and perhaps flourish, on the arctic steppes of northeastern Asia and the Bering Land Bridge as they moved into the Western Hemisphere. This late Pleistocene radiation or range extension increased the land area available to humans by nearly 60 percent and was followed shortly thereafter by an explosion of diverse languages, social systems, and economies in the newly inhabited lands. The effect of this range expansion on the biological communities of Australia and the Americas, which had previously evolved in isolation from humans, was very likely equally dramatic and far reaching, but it remains incompletely understood and a topic of considerable controversy.

Certainly humans preyed on the animals—both large and small—that they encountered in the landscapes they came to inhabit, affecting their abundance and perhaps even driving some to extinction (Martin and Klein 1984). They also consumed diverse plant foods, potentially affecting their distribution and dispersal (Chilton, this volume; Rindos 1980). Humans' roles as social carnivores put them in competition with other large predators in these new lands and expanded the food niche of the carnivores themselves (Webb 1998; Whitney-Smith, this volume). Unique to humans, however, was their regular use of fire. The increasing use of fire that accompanied human colonization had the potential to alter vegetation communities at continental scales (Pyne 1998). Each of these potential forms of impact could have had many other ecological repercussions. Even if they are not well understood, the biogeographical consequences of human range extension into the Americas during the late Pleistocene were certainly complex.

Humans have so long inhabited the farthest reaches of the globe that it is difficult to reconstruct terrestrial ecosystems without taking potential human contributions into account. Without a well-understood, high-resolution "prehuman" baseline, it is even more problematic to appreciate the effects of humans on these ecosystems in particular circumstances. These difficulties in assessing the ways in which humans impact their environments have led to several long-running debates, including (1) the role of humans in the extinction of large animals in Australia and the Americas ten millennia ago, and (2) the role of industrial-age humans in the accumulation of greenhouse gases and its effects upon global climate (Bond et al. 1997). The potential we have today for profoundly altering the world around us gives greater currency (and urgency) to the lessons that can be learned from the last time humans encountered a "pristine" ecosystem at a continental scale: the human colonization of the Americas.

Conceptual Frameworks

This book approaches the human settlement of the Americas from a biogeographical perspective in order to gain a better understanding of the mechanisms and consequences of this unique event. The biogeography of human dispersal in the Western Hemisphere took place at a bicontinental scale. The lessons to be learned from the grand scale of this dispersal are much different from those of the local human population movements that are more typical in the human past. The contributors to this book approach their research from equally broad, continental perspectives.

Clearly the colonization of the American continents cannot be understood from the insights gained from a single or even a few archaeological sites, no matter how important those sites might be. Nor is the simple accumulation of "data" sufficient (Clark 1993). If we are to learn something of lasting value from the settlement of the Americas, we must conscientiously organize the data from diverse sources within well-developed theoretical frameworks. Toward this end, the contributions to this book offer synthetic frameworks for building a more comprehensive picture of the processes and outcomes of human range extension in the Americas, assembled from the many tiny pieces provided by archaeological, paleontological, and paleoecological records. The importance of applying diverse research protocols as well as data sources is also expressed in the range of contributors to this volume: They represent molecular genetics, human osteology, linguistics, and vertebrate paleontology as well as archaeology. Because data have no meaning independent of that conceded them by a conceptual framework, well-developed "high" and "middle-range" theory is equally essential for organizing diverse information into a coherent whole. The contributors to this volume employ theoretical concepts drawn from evolutionary biology, behavioral ecology, and historical linguistics to provide this framework.

Two other themes run through the papers assembled here. The first theme is that human settlement of the American continents is a long-term process rather than an event. Whether it is in the multiple origins of the people who came to the New World over the course of millennia or in the cascade of ecological changes to which humans both contributed and adapted, the colonization of continents is a process that is ongoing today. Largely for this reason, there are few references to the Clovis versus pre-Clovis debate or to claims about who first set foot on North American soil. Time is an important reference variable for measuring change attributable to other causes, but it is not *the* critical variable for tracing the long-term dynamics of human biogeography at continental scales.

The second theme, implicit in some papers and more explicit in others, is that how we approach the archaeological record necessarily colors our interpretations of pattern and process in the past. While this is hardly a novel observation, it is one that we should keep in mind if we wish to gain new insights about the colonization process. Although the contributors to this book are (ostensibly at least) modern humans resident in the Americas, there is nothing in our collective experience to compare with that of the first colonists who made their way into these continents. The uniqueness of this experience and its distinctiveness from anything that is commonplace in our daily lives are among the factors that make this book so valuable. Our own lives offer minimal guidance for interpreting the residual evidence of the Pleistocene hunter-gatherers who colonized the Americas; we can benefit by being exposed to and seriously considering various conceptual approaches to this evidence. As editors, we have sought to bring together scholars who represent a diversity of perspectives, data sources, and research protocols. Our hope is that by doing this, we might inspire readers to raise new questions and pursue new lines of research into the lives of America's first pioneers.

Organization of the Book

The First American Settlers

This volume is arranged into three parts, although there is considerable overlap in the topics from different parts because of the broadly synthetic nature of the work. In part I we ask these questions: Who were the Pleistocene settlers of the American continents, and where did they come from? Anthropological geneticist Theodore Schurr (chapter 2) summarizes recent research on nonrecombinant mitochondrial DNA (mtDNA) and the Y chromosome, both of which are characterized by relatively rapid rates of base-pair substitution (hence, they are better suited than nuclear DNA for use as "molecular clocks"). The mtDNA data, inherited matrilineally, suggest that the most broadly distributed ancestral Amerindian mtDNA haplotypes came from southeastern Siberia, although a smaller subset is derived from populations that once lived in the Amur River/Sea of the Okhotsk region to the northwest. The patrilineally inherited Y-chromosome data also indicate a geographical origin in south-central Siberia, although one group appears to have come from East Asia. Whether the distributions of the four ancestral haplogroups (A–D) found in indigenous New World populations reflect the original pattern of American settlement or subsequent genetic differentiation within certain geographical regions remains unclear. Whatever the case, the molecular clocks based on these genomes indicate an initial colonization interval of 35,000 to 20,000 B.P., which is considerably earlier than the time recognized by most archaeologists (after 20,000 B.P.).

In chapter 3, C. Loring Brace, A. Russell Nelson, and Pan Qifeng reconstruct New World population histories using human craniofacial morphology to assess differences and similarities among recent and prehistoric American samples and to compare them with samples drawn from various parts of the Old World. The analysis shows that the various configurations of craniofacial form cluster regionally and are not distributed in a clinal fashion, as might be expected if a single, protracted colonization had taken place. Most of the aboriginal inhabitants of the Americas separate into two macroclusters. The first macrocluster includes people living along the U.S.–Mexico border, the prehistoric inhabitants of the Mississippi Valley, and much of Latin America. It probably represents the first Asian migrants to the New World, who established themselves in the more optimal, resource-rich environments of the Americas and evidently arrived well before the end of the Pleistocene by a route that remains uncertain. The second macrocluster is also of Asian origin and is represented by three distinct "pulses" corresponding to (1) a late Pleistocene (ca. 12,000 B.P.) migration of Japanese origin, (2) a migration originating in Mongolia-Manchuria after about 5,000 B.P., represented linguistically by Eskimo-Aleut speakers, and (3) modern Na-

Dene speaking peoples who, over the last millennium, had penetrated as far as the American Southwest. Their closest ties are with Chinese populations in East Asia.

Jane Hill offers a linguistic perspective on the Pleistocene pioneers in chapter 4, with a critical evaluation of the work of Joseph Greenberg and Johanna Nichols. Both prominent workers of almost paradigmatic status, they differ from one another in the number of historically significant linguistic units they recognize, in the chronology of those units, and in the types of links they propose between American languages and those of the Old World. Both use methods that are controversial within mainstream historical linguistics. Much of the criticism of Greenberg's work centers on his methodology, called multilateral or mass comparison. Hill points out that mass comparison is a hybrid method that depends, on the one hand, on large-scale, coarse-grained samples and gross pattern recognition, and on the other hand, on a subjective capacity to recognize the rare but critical examples essential to the practice of restrictive comparison, the methodological stock-in-trade of most practicing linguists. Nichols's methodology is completely different from that of Greenberg. In an approach reminiscent of cladistics in the life sciences, she draws samples representative of the approximately 250 generally recognized linguistic stocks and characterizes them in terms of the presence or absence of a set of eleven or twelve "population markers": easily identified, stable, independent typological features that are resistant to spread by contact and of low frequency worldwide. Nichols argues that when languages share these population markers, they are probably connected historically, either through an ancient common ancestor or an ancient zone of areal contact. Although both approaches have their pros and cons, the differences between Greenberg and Nichols reflect a wider divide in the linguistic community between uniformitarians, who argue that the rate of language differentiation has been gradual and constant over the long term, and punctuationalists, who argue that the history of language differentiation has been irregular, with certain kinds of events favoring very rapid language change.

Taking an archaeological perspective, Kenneth Tankersley (chapter 5) traces the ways in which the notion of a Clovis culture complex developed historically and has been applied subsequently across North America. He reviews the Clovis literature to identify the criteria used to define Clovis. What emerges is evidence for a great deal of uniformity across enormous distances. However, there is also variation at multiple levels within the Clovis complex. Causes of this variability potentially include functional differences among sites, cultural drift, adaptation to different regional environments, and sampling error due to the relative paucity of excavated sites. Explaining both this overlying consistency and underlying spatial and temporal variation is the challenge of new research on the colonization of the Americas.

Chapter 6, by Kamille Schmitz, constitutes a synthetic overview of bioarchaeological thought on New World origins. Adopting a principle of consilience (Wilson 1998), she examines potential migration routes, numbers of migrations, source areas for immigrants, numbers of migrants, oral traditions related to indigenous views of origins, and linguistic and archaeological evidence. She concludes that there is a substantial consensus that all Native Americans originated in the Old World, most likely from source populations in East Asia, and that they got here via the Bering Land Bridge. There is less agreement on the number and timing of migrations. Transoceanic migration models receive little empirical support. Lithic similarities between Clovis, Solutrean, and other European Upper Paleolithic archaeological assemblages are probably due to formal convergence and similar adaptations rather than historical connectivity (Clark 2001a, this volume; Straus 2000). The scenario that is most consilient across subdisciplinary specializations posits that a few (two to four) waves or pulses of relatively few individuals, who came from source populations in northeastern Siberia and Mongolia-Manchuria, arrived in the New World after about 13,000 B.P.

The Trail to the Americas

Although many of the contributors in part I touch on the route to the New World taken by Pleistocene pioneers, the authors in part II focus especially on this question. In chapter 7, Stuart Fiedel argues that the Clovis colonization took place extremely rapidly, over about a 500-year interval between 13,400 and 12,900 B.P. Some researchers believe that this colonization was unparalleled ethnographically and historically. Fiedel suggests that an appropriate analogue might be the late prehistoric Thule expansion along the Arctic Coast from Alaska to Greenland, during which Thule peoples traversed a distance of about 1,750 miles in less than 150 years and evidently displaced, replaced, or absorbed earlier Dorset populations. The comparison is not a direct one, however, because there were very few, if any, pre-Clovis inhabitants of the New World, and the Thule

expansion was largely by water. Acknowledging the possibility of pre-Clovis colonists, Fiedel suggests that the presence of a thinly distributed earlier population might have facilitated the prime-habitat "leapfrogging" that allowed Clovis bands to populate a continent more rapidly than they could have if they had encountered territory devoid of humans.

Georges Pearson's contribution (chapter 8) focuses on the Costa Rican site of Guardiría and other Central and South American Paleoindian localities that exhibit an extraordinary range of variation in biface morphology. He suggests that, because Clovis points are rare in South America, the Isthmus of Panama might have constituted a geographical bottleneck for north-south movement by humans. Of the two general models invoked in numerous combinations and variations by scholars of New World origins (interior or coastal migration and stylistic diffusion), Pearson opts for a southward demic expansion by Clovis groups as far as the Isthmus of Panama as the most parsimonious way to account for the appearance of lanceolate fluted points in lower Central America. Beyond the Isthmus, however, the presence of fluting on a wide variety of stemmed and lanceolate points might indicate that this technique diffused among a preexisting South American population.

Geoffrey Clark's essay (chapter 9) is concerned with Stanford and Bradley's North Atlantic model for a historical link between Clovis and the Spanish Solutrean. After identifying what he considers to be the major tenets of the model, he shows that supposedly diagnostic features of each of these analytical units are actually very widely distributed in space and time and bear no specific relationship to either of them. A more serious problem is the adequacy of the conceptual frameworks used to address "peopling" issues. Some elements of both Old and New World research traditions involved in Stone Age archaeology are heavily typological. Card-carrying typologists tend to accept without question the reality of the conventional, normative, prehistorian-defined analytical units and assume that they detect pattern at the levels of "cultures" or "technocomplexes," which are seldom defined. Seeing Clovis as a kind of "New World Paleolithic," Clark argues that it is possible to explain pattern similarities in Paleolithic archaeological assemblages without recourse to "history-like" typology- or technology-based toolmaking traditions (Clark 2002).

Carole Mandryk (chapter 10) uses the widely held, although empirically poorly supported, notion of an ice-free corridor through which the earliest immigrants passed as a vehicle to deconstruct what she considers to be some of the major tenets of the prevailing narrative of American origins. The focus here is on the social context, theoretical orientations, preconceptions, and historical contingencies that influence and shape our constructions of past events and processes. She argues that views of the colonization are rooted in national history, politics, and power relations, and that the past is essentially appropriated by the American archaeological establishment in order to promote a view of the colonization that is consilient with contemporary American values and ideals. Thus, the first Americans are no longer simply the earliest inhabitants of the American continents; they are transformed into Americans barely different from ourselves. One of the many implications of this insightful paper is that ideas about the past often remain influential long after the reasoning that led to their development has been rejected and abandoned.

The Land and People Transformed

The papers in part III address the ecological role of the Pleistocene pioneers in the New World and the consequences of colonization. In chapter 11, David Meltzer tackles questions raised by Robert Kelly's (1995) return-rate-maximizing (RRM) model. This model is built on the assumption that Clovis groups were highly mobile big-game hunters who, upon encountering a continent devoid of other people and teeming with naïve faunas, radiated quickly through a process of range extension by targeting gregarious ungulates at a time when North American climates were rapidly changing. Although he agrees with much of it, Meltzer thinks the RRM model does not adequately address the demographic costs associated with high mobility, nor does it accurately model the conservative nature of forager decision making. He proposes instead a colonization model in which the goal was minimizing uncertainty and demographic risk (MUDR). This model involves a complex series of trade-offs that balance several needs: to maintain resource returns, minimize group size, maximize information gain about resource distributions in relatively unfamiliar terrain, and maintain contact among dispersed groups, which was critical to information flow, social relations, and mating networks. Both models are extremely demanding of the archaeological database; subjecting them to any kind of conclusive empirical test will be difficult.

The essay by Michael Barton, Steven Schmich, and Steven James (chapter 12) begins by outlining a set of ecology-derived expectations about regionwide human adaptations to unpopulated landmasses. It then juxtaposes these expectations against pattern change over time measured by fine-grained radiocarbon chronologies from northwestern Europe (as it was repopulated after the Last Glacial Maximum). Using this model, the authors measure the rate of colonization and show how dietary diversity changes in response to colonization. This model is then applied to the much larger, more complex situation in the Americas, which is complicated by a host of factors, including (1) the very different ecosystem in which the first colonizers found themselves once they had emerged on the continent, and (2) an archaeological time-space grid that is much more coarse-grained than that of western Europe. Although they acknowledge the credibility of the few pre-Clovis sites adequately published to date, the authors focus on the Paleoindian data from North America in an effort to track changing patterns of land use and mobility. As in Europe, movement rates declined over time as the initial colonizers "leapfrogged" through the richest biomes, leaving their descendants to gradually populate the rest of the landscape. The analysis also has implications for long-term ecological change, including natural and human-induced continentwide changes in vegetation communities, the alteration of natural population controls due to human competition with large indigenous carnivores, and the introduction of two new carnivores (humans and dogs), with resultant impacts on large herbivores.

Although Paleoindians are usually portrayed in textbooks and in the media as the quintessential big-game hunters, Elizabeth Chilton argues in chapter 13 that this stereotypical vision belies a much more complex reality. She shows that Paleoindian adaptations were regionally and even locally variable in terms of subsistence pursuits, and that an overemphasis on the hunting of large game is not supported empirically. The traditional archaeological focus on the highly visible, bifacial foliate points obscures much lithic evidence for the hunting and processing of small game and the gathering of plants. She also critiques the gender bias implicit in much Paleoindian research. The unconscious projection of contemporary gender roles (or, more accurately, gender roles that are uncritically derived from ethnographies and idealized conceptual frameworks) onto the remote past has led to a pronounced male bias in Paleoindian research. She concludes that by paying closer attention to empirical patterns and by making explicit our preconceptions and assumptions about gender roles, we might be able to move beyond the functionalist interpretive frameworks that have dominated Paleoindian research so far.

The essay by Douglas MacDonald (chapter 14) contrasts a "transient explorer model" (TEM), in which individual foragers move with no regard for territorial boundaries or social ties, with an "estate settler model" (ESM), in which Paleoindians maintain extensive social networks across large territories and seldom migrate as individuals. Ethnographic and archaeological data from recent time frames and the conceptual framework of behavioral ecology all suggest that the TEM is simply too costly and risky to have been viable for the earliest colonists because of the very low population densities and the high probability of social network breakdown. In addition to being more realistic, the ESM also explains the exogamy characteristic of ethnographic foragers.

In chapter 15, community ecologist Elin Whitney-Smith tackles the question of New World megafauna extinctions through a series of simulations that model different aspects of predator-prey relationships. After modeling an equilibrium system that describes the relevant aspects of North American biocommunities prior to the appearance of humans, she proposes what she calls a "second-order overkill" hypothesis, wherein humans reduce the number of herbivores available to the relevant carnivore guild, causing the carnivores to prey on humans. To reduce this competition, humans increasingly prey on the predators, which in turn reduces always much smaller predator populations below the level at which they can control always much larger herbivore populations. Herbivore populations boom. Human populations also expand, even more rapidly than those of the predators they kill. However, humans fail to control herbivore populations as effectively as the now-scarce predators once did, and herbivore populations overgraze the environment, eventually altering the distributions of woodlands and parklands, which shrink along with the grasslands. Without sufficient food, most grassland-dependent herbivore populations crash, and humans increasingly prey on those herbivores with high reproductive rates that can derive the most nourishment from grassland ecotypes. This leads to a proliferation of bison populations, which become key prey elements in many Archaic adaptations.

In the final paper of this section, Larry Agenbroad and India Hesse (chapter 16) focus on the apparent lack of a Clovis occupation on the intensively investigated Colorado Plateau. Drawing together data from radiocarbon chronologies, paleontology, archaeology, and rock art, they show that the region, which has a well-studied ceramic-period occupation, was in fact home to an indigenous megafauna that extended back in time beyond the limits of radiocarbon dating. Mammoths, bison, surface finds of Clovis and Folsom points, and rock art depictions of extinct megafauna co-occur from 12,000 to 6000 B.P.

The book concludes with remarks by the editors (chapter 17) that might best be summarized in five questions, which were originally proposed by Yesner (1996a). These questions center on the timing of human occupation, the human role in Pleistocene megafaunal extinction, dietary diversity and technological change, the use of coastal resources, and seasonality and logistical strategies: (1) To what degree was the colonization process affected by the climatic changes and associated changes in coastlines due to sea-level fluctuations during the ten millennia that bracket the Pleistocene-Holocene transition? (2) How do we model megafaunal extinctions and the human role in this process? (3) How variable was the human food niche in different parts of the Americas during the initial colonization interval and subsequently? (4) How important were marine and coastal resources to the initial colonizers? and (5) What effects did the Holocene substitution of forest for grassland have on Paleoindian adaptations in which grassland ungulates were important?

In one way or another, these questions all articulate aspects of human forager adaptations with paleoenvironmental contexts in Northeast Asia and the Americas. On a continental scale, the impact of Pleistocene-Holocene-boundary change on human populations was highly variable and was determined by a complex nexus of factors: local patterns of climate change, the diversity of plant and animal species available to the first colonists and their immediate successors, the responses of local floras and faunas to the combined effects of climate change and human impact, and constant fluctuations in local and regional human demography.

New Directions in Interdisciplinary Research, Human Ecology, and the Colonization of the Americas

Clearly the peopling of the Americas was a complex process, and a better understanding of it involves not only conceptual advances (i.e., how we model the colonization), but also efforts to rectify empirical insufficiencies and coordinate diverse data sets. The initial colonization of the New World is an interdisciplinary problem that will require improvements in several areas: the stratigraphic evidence of climate change, geoarchaeological data, chronological frameworks, skeletal and genetic evidence for Native American ancestry, and linguistic models. This new information must augment the archaeological data (from late Pleistocene Northeast Asia and from the New World) that have been the main focus of the debate ever since the first credible evidence for an early human presence in the Americas was established in the 1920s.

Important goals for future research include refinement of DNA research protocols, biochemical analysis of blood and other protein residues on artifacts, ongoing refinement of radiocarbon chronologies, and perhaps most important, the discovery, excavation, and publication of more stratified sites. Not generally appreciated is the fact that most allegedly "early" sites are actually isolated surface finds that lack geological context. Because bifacial foliate points (the hallmark of generic "Paleoindianness") are very widely distributed in space and time (Anderson and Faught 1998a,b; Anderson and Gillam 2000) and exhibit no necessary historical connection to one another, a question arises: What does the Paleoindian occupation of the New World mean or represent in behavioral terms? We suggest that the best way to model Paleoindian adaptations, and by extension the colonization process itself, is to look to the conceptual framework of community ecology and, more broadly, neo-Darwinian evolutionary theory. From the standpoint of Western science, (modern) humans are nothing more (or less) than highly intelligent, technologically sophisticated, socially complex animals. They do not differ qualitatively from other social animals, and because of a common evolutionary heritage, they share with their hominoid cousins many aspects of sociality, even more than is commonly recognized (e.g., Stanford 2001). Put another way, we are only unique in the same way that any species is unique: We possess a unique evolutionary history. It is how we go about modeling that history that makes our inferences naïve or sophisticated, our logic of inference more or less secure.

It has not escaped the attention of its critics that much research on New World origins is heavily dominated by pattern searching and by a relatively mechanistic approach to interpretation that lacks any explicit conceptual framework to lend meaning to pattern. The papers in this book are, perhaps, an initial step in redressing that deficiency. Most of its practitioners consider archaeology a "sciencelike" endeavor. Many American archaeologists are now realizing that evolutionary ecology offers a developed conceptual framework for addressing the peopling issues summarized above (Winterhalder and Smith 2000). However, at the level of the highest or most inclusive conceptual framework (the metaphysical paradigm), there is now, and always has been, considerable disunity (Clark 2001b). Put another way, archaeology has no body of grounded theory.

Should we worry about this? Does it matter? Is it important to building secure inference? Will ongoing research and the accumulation of more data eventually resolve questions about New World origins despite a lack of explicit concern with inferential logic? These are questions that go to the very core of what archaeology is or should be. Archaeology has always been very eclectic in exploiting tools and techniques, empirical insights, models, and theories drawn from other disciplines. In some respects, this interaction is its most creative aspect (Wylie 2000). Seen in this light, however, archaeology is essentially reduced to a collection of methods devoid of a unifying metaphysic that might lend meaning to pattern, and power and scope to explanation. Clearly a "sciencelike" archaeology would benefit enormously from a coherent conceptual framework, explicitly defined and defended, even if it were borrowed from another field. The mere acquisition of more data will never resolve anything because data have no existence independent of the conceptual frameworks that define and contextualize them. If there is no consensus on what constitutes "data"; how data should be defined, measured, or classified; or why particular data are relevant to the solution of particular problems and questions, there can be no consensus on what the patterns in those data mean (Clark 1993).

To an important extent, such epistemological issues contribute to the continuing debates over the validity of the earliest evidence for a human presence in the Americas. At present, the several dozen Paleoindian sites constitute the earliest recognizable industrial configurations in the New World. Backed up by more than one hundred radiocarbon determinations, the archaeological evidence for the initial colonists is nevertheless based on only a handful of careful excavations yielding good industrial samples with associated faunas in solid stratigraphic contexts (see Tankersley, this volume). Even this cannot be said of New World sites thought to be older than about 13,000 B.P., which remain plagued by questions over context, authenticity of artifacts, dating (e.g., controversial techniques and bad sample contexts), and most important, lack of agreement among archaeologists over what constitutes reasonable evidence for an ancient human presence in the Americas.

As noted at the beginning of this essay, the human settlement of the American continents marks an important watershed in the human past. Beyond its importance to the human heritage, it also holds valuable lessons for us today. Paleoindian archaeology has developed in many ways since the Pleistocene presence of humans in the Americas was demonstrated over seventy years ago. The dawn of the twenty-first century is a good time to reexamine the adequacy of our conceptual and methodological tools for understanding the colonization of the hemisphere. The human entry into the New World was part of a larger global process. The first great human colonization or range extension began in Africa and spread our genus across Eurasia. The last great radiation began in Asia and spread humans to Australia, the Americas, and eventually the far-flung Pacific islands. Paleoindian research has long been the purview of North American archaeology. As many of the papers in this volume note, we can benefit by extending our vistas to incorporate other parts of the world.

An important characteristic of Paleoindian archaeology from its inception has been its close association with the geosciences. We strongly encourage this multi- and interdisciplinary approach and advocate looking beyond the geosciences to genetics, skeletal morphometrics, linguistics, and paleoecology. Although the contributions to this volume do not yet represent such genuinely interdisciplinary research, we have tried to showcase the potential contributions that different disciplines can make to a better understanding of the colonization process.

We must also recognize that the human settlement of the Americas was an ecological process as much as or more than a social one. The combined socioecological dynamics of the integration of humans into New World ecosystems may hold the most valuable lessons for the present day. As has been long recognized by ecologists and ecological archaeologists (McGlade 1995, 1999; Zimmerer 1994), simple processes of cause and effect are insufficient to model long-term ecology; nonlinear dynamics and agent-based simulations may be necessary to understand the complex interactions of humans and late Pleistocene landscapes in the Americas. The papers in part III especially speak to the ecological nature of the peopling of the New World, as does recent work by others (e.g., Haynes 2002; Steele et al. 1998). The ecological nature of New World colonization underscores the importance of theory to organize disparate data and methods into a coherent whole. As mentioned above, we feel that neo-Darwinian theory—especially its behavioral and ecological variants, which incorporate human agency and decision making into an evolutionary framework—provides the most powerful and general paradigm for modeling the dynamics of "humanizing" the Americas. Although all theory operates at some level of abstraction, we think that neo-Darwinian theory can be more than a metaphor (cf. Bamforth 2002) and can function as an algorithm (cf. Dennett 1995) to explain a wide range of socioecological processes (sensu Bettinger 1991:213–224).

As the twentieth century drew to a close, the "Clovis and Beyond" conference was convened in Santa Fe, New Mexico, "to provide an overview of factual knowledge of this field that can serve as a foundation for all parties interested in America's earliest prehistory" (Bonnichsen 1999). We try here to build on that foundation and look forward to this century's research on human beginnings in the New World. Although we do not claim to be comprehensive in our efforts to do this, we hope to highlight some of the more promising new directions this research can take for studying the first American settlers.

Acknowledgments

The editors thank Margaret MacMinn-Barton (preparing the bibliography), Michelle Fiedler (preparing the index), and Evelyn VandenDolder (copyediting) for their invaluable assistance in the preparation of the manuscript. We also acknowledge the support of the Department of Anthropology at Arizona State University for hosting the "Pioneers on the Land" conference (December 1999), where the idea for the book originated. C. Loring Brace, University of Michigan, organized an important group of papers that substantially improved the breadth of coverage of the volume. The Department of Anthropology at the University of Alaska—Anchorage also provided valuable assistance in manuscript preparation.

The First American Settlers

Part I focuses on the people who first settled the American continents and on their origins through the diverse perspectives of human biology, archaeology, and linguistics. The overall consensus of the contributors here is that the colonizers were of multiple but not innumerable origins. The geography of eastern Asia and western North America ensured that is was possible for humans (at least for modern *Homo sapiens* with Upper Paleolithic technology) to pass between these continents throughout the late Pleistocene and early Holocene. At the same time, the high latitude of the Beringian isthmus and the presence of continental ice sheets between Beringia and the rest of the Americas until the early Holocene constituted a strong environmental filter that restricted such movements.

Theodore Schurr's chapter begins this section by summarizing recent research on mitochondrial DNA and the Y chromosome which, unlike nuclear DNA, do not recombine. These genetic systems thus serve as more interpretable molecular models for tracing movements and ancestor-descendant relationships of the first Americans.

The paper by C. Loring Brace, A. Russell Nelson, and Pan Qifeng also seeks to reconstruct New World population histories, but instead of genetics, it uses human craniofacial morphology to assess the differences and similarities of recent and prehistoric New World samples to each other and to samples drawn from various parts of the Old World (especially Asia).

Can evidence about the languages of the Americas tell us anything about the origin or antiquity of Native American peoples? The essay by anthropological linguist Jane Hill offers a critical evaluation of two major bodies of historical linguistic research that attempt to answer this question.

Until the publication a few years ago of credible arguments for a marginally earlier, pre-Clovis human presence (e.g., Dillehay 1997b), there was a broad consensus that Clovis archaeological sites, dated to the millennium bracketing 11,000 B.P., represented the earliest evidence for humans in the New World. Just what Clovis is, however, and what it means or represents behaviorally has largely gone unexamined. After reviewing the history of Clovis research, Kenneth Tankersley presents a continentwide overview of the nature and significance of Clovis artifact assemblages by contrasting characteristics that unify the Clovis concept with geographic and temporal variation among Clovis assemblages.

The final paper in this section, by Kamille Schmitz, constitutes a synthetic overview of bioarchaeological thought on New World origins. It follows a principle of consilience (sensu Wilson 1998), wherein a convincing explanation of the multifaceted peopling phenomenon requires specialists to weigh their own findings against those in other research areas and to try to reconcile contradictory results.

2 An Anthropological Genetic View of the Peopling of the New World
Theodore G. Schurr

For decades researchers have attempted to explain the origins of the considerable cultural diversity, linguistic complexity, and biological variation of Native Americans. At times this diversity has been attributed to multiple migrations of Asian peoples to the Americas, or to a single migration and in situ differentiation of ancestral Native Americans that occurred after the initial colonization of the New World. The pathway(s) by which ancestral Native Americans first came to the New World has also been vigorously debated (see contributions by Clark, Mandryk, and Schmitz, this volume). Both coastal and interior routes have been proposed based on archaeological, geological, and linguistic data (see Hill, this volume). Similarly the estimated time of arrival of the first migrants has varied widely; several archaeological studies now suggest that the Clovis lithic tradition may not demarcate the initial entry of ancestral populations into the New World. Furthermore, recent studies of craniometric variation have revealed significant biological differences between the earliest settlers of the Americas (the Paleoindians) and populations dating from the Archaic period and later, including modern Native Americans (see Brace et al., this volume). Overall, these data imply that the colonization of the New World was a more complex process than previously thought, and probably one in which multiple expansions of ancient peoples contributed to the genetic diversity observed in Native American populations.

Questions concerning the origins and affinities of Native Americans have also been approached through the molecular genetic analysis of two uniparentally inherited, nonrecombining genomes: the mitochondrial DNA (mtDNA) and Y chromosome. These genomes possess a series of different markers that help to define or identify specific genetic lineages in human groups. By analyzing the sequence variation in these two genomes, one can identify the genetic lineages that are present within populations, characterize the extent of diversity within them, and ascertain the manner in which they have been spread into neighboring groups. Moreover, by measuring the sequence variation that has accumulated within these genomes, one can estimate their approximate ages in different parts of the world.

Because these molecular data sets provide insights into the genetic prehistory of Native American populations, I will explore them in some detail. More specifically, I will examine a set of linked issues related to the peopling of the New World, including the number of founding genetic lineages in Native Americans, the number of distinct founding haplotypes that each lineage contains, the source area(s) for these genetic lineages, the ages of these lineages in the Americas, and the number of migrations that brought them to the New World. In this fashion, it will be possible to present a more nuanced picture of mtDNA and Y-chromosome variation in Siberian and Native American populations.

Mitochondrial DNA Variation in Siberia and the Americas

Founding mtDNA Lineages in Native American Populations

Studies of molecular genetic variation in modern Native American populations have shown that their mtDNAs belong to five different haplogroups,[1] which have been designated A–D and X (Brown et al. 1998; Forster et al. 1996; Schurr et al. 1990; Torroni et al. 1992, 1993a). Each of these haplogroups is defined by a specific set of RFLPs[2] (table 2.1) and HVR1[3] sequence polymorphisms (table 2.2); various studies have created different nomenclatures to describe them. Although most haplogroups exhibit one to three polymorphisms in the HVR1 that distinguish them from the other mtDNA lineages, haplogroup D does not.[4] However, one can infer the haplogroup to which a given HVR1 sequence belongs by noting which combination of these polymorphisms (its "motif") is present in the mtDNA sequence, as well as the RFLPs that are present in that particular mtDNA, because all of these mutations are linked together in a single haplotype.

Haplogroups A–D comprise most of the mtDNAs in modern Native American populations (Bailliet et al.

TABLE 2.1 Proposed Founding Native American mtDNA Haplogroups and Haplotypes

Haplogroup	HR-RFLP Haplotype	LR-RFLP Haplotype	Polymorphic Restriction Sites[a]
A	AM01	A1	+663e
	AM09	A2	+663e, +16517e
B	AM13	B1	COII/tRNA^{Lys} 9-bp Deletion, +16517e
	None	B2	COII/tRNA^{Lys} 9-bp Deletion
C	AM32	C1	+10394c, +10397a, −13259o/+13262a
	AM43	C2	+10394c, +10397a, −13259o/+13262a, +16517e
D	AM88	D1	−5176a, +10394c, +10397a
	AM44	D2	−5176a, +10394c, +10397a, +16517e
X	AM75	?	−1715c, −14465 BstNI, +16517e
M	N.A.	X6	+10394c, +10397a
	N.A.	X7	+10394c, +10397a, +16517e
?	?	E1	+16517e

Note: Haplogroups A–D and X were identified by HR-RFLP haplotype analysis (Brown et al. 1998; Schurr et al. 1990; Torroni et al. 1992, 1993a) and HVR1 sequencing (Brown et al. 1998; Torroni et al. 1993a). Bailliet et al. (1994) and Merriwether et al. (1995) used an LR-RFLP method similar to that employed by Torroni et al. (1993a) to analyze their Native American samples and then assigned a haplogroup designation based on the presence or absence of these polymorphisms. In their schema, the two putative founding haplotypes of haplogroups A–D and X6/X7 differ by the presence or absence of the *Hae*III 16517 site. No comparable founding haplotypes for haplotype E were observed based on HR-RFLP data. However, because it lacks the diagnostic RFLP markers of haplogroups A–D, haplotype E could represent mtDNAs belonging to haplogroup X or to some other haplogroup of either African or Eurasian origin. In addition, haplotypes X6/X7 can be considered generally equivalent to haplogroup M in Asian populations (Chen et al. 1995; Torroni et al. 1994c) because this large macrocluster of mtDNAs is defined by the same RFLPs. HVR1 sequence data indicate that X6/X7 mtDNAs belong to haplogroups C and D (see main text).
[a]Letter codes for restriction enzymes are as follows: a = *Alu*I; c = *Dde*I; e = *Hae*III; o = *Hine*II; and t = *Bst*NI.

1994; Batista et al. 1995; Bert et al. 2001; Easton et al. 1996; Ginther et al. 1993; Green et al. 2000; Horai et al. 1993; Kolman and Bermingham 1997; Kolman et al. 1995; Lorenz and Smith 1996, 1997; Malhi et al. 2001; Merriwether et al. 1994, 1995; Moraga et al. 2000; Rickards et al. 1999; Santos et al. 1994; Schurr et al. 1990; Torroni et al. 1992, 1993a, 1994a,d; Ward et al. 1991). These haplogroups are distributed throughout the Americas; specific patterns of haplogroup frequencies emerge in certain geographic regions (see below). By contrast, the fifth and rarer mtDNA lineage, haplogroup X, has an almost exclusively North American focus, raising intriguing questions about its origins (Brown et al. 1998; Forster et al. 1996; Scozzari et al. 1997; Smith et al. 1999). Overall, these five haplogroups comprise 95–100 percent of all mtDNAs in indigenous populations of the New World.

A similar pattern has emerged in genetic analyses of ancient populations of the Americas. In every study to date, ancient populations have exhibited the same set of mtDNA lineages that are seen in their modern descendants; only a few of these ancient populations have lineages that may not belong to these haplogroups (see below; Carlyle et al. 2000; Fox 1996; Kaestle and Smith 2001; Merriwether et al. 1994; Monsalve et al. 1996; O'Rourke et al. 2000; Parr et al. 1996; Ribeiro-Dos-Santos et al. 1996; Stone and Stoneking 1998). It is thus fair to say that haplogroups A–D and X represent the primary founding mtDNA lineages in Native American populations.

In addition to haplogroups A–D and X mtDNAs, some studies have detected the presence of "other" (non–haplogroup A–D) haplotypes in Native American groups that could possibly represent additional founding lineages (Bailliet et al. 1994; Lorenz and Smith 1996; Merriwether et al. 1994, 1995; Ribeiro-Dos-Santos et al. 1996; Rickards et al. 1999; Smith et al. 1999; Torroni et al. 1993a; Ward et al. 1991). One putative founding lineage has been observed among South American Indians in the form of "X6/X7" haplotypes (Easton et al. 1996;

TABLE 2.2 HVR1 Sequence Cluster Designations

HVR1 Mutations	Torroni et al. (1992)	Ward et al. (1991)	Horai et al. (1993)	Ginther et al. (1993)	Bailliet et al. (1994)
[16111T] 16223T, 16290T, 16319A, 16362C	A	II	III	IV	III
16189C, 16217C	B	IV	I	I	I
16223T, 16298C [16325C], 16327T	C	III	IV	II	IV
16223T [16325C], 16362C	D	III	II	III	II
16189C [16213A], 16223T, 16278T	X	I	—	—	V

Note: The diagnostic HVR1 mutations for each haplogroup (i.e., its motif) are indicated in the far left column, and the cluster designations given to each one in various mtDNA studies appear in the other five columns. The brackets indicate that the specified polymorphisms distinguish American from Asian or Eurasian mtDNAs belonging to each haplogroup. In the Ward et al. (1991) study, haplogroup C and D were placed in the same cluster, III, because they could not be clearly distinguished from each other. Both Horai et al. (1993) and Ginther et al. (1993) did not observe any HVR1 sequences belonging to haplogroup X; hence, they did not create a category for them. In addition, Bailliet et al. (1994) originally indicated that haplogroup D was defined by the 16187T and 16325C mutations. This definition was made because some South American haplogroup D mtDNAs have the 16187T-16223T-16325C-16362C sequence motif (Ginther et al. 1993; Horai et al. 1993; Moraga et al. 2000), whereas this motif is rare outside of this region.

Merriwether et al. 1994, 1995).[5] X6/X7 haplotypes have the +*Dde*I 10394 and +*Alu*I 10397 sites (+*Dde*I/+*Alu*I sites) that define Asian haplogroup M (Ballinger et al. 1992; Kivisild et al. 1999; Passarino et al. 1996a,b; Schurr et al. 1999; Torroni et al. 1993a, 1994a), but otherwise lack the diagnostic RFLPs of haplogroups C and D (table 2.1). However, subsequent analysis of HVR1 sequences from X6/X7 mtDNAs showed that they clustered within haplogroups C and D (Schurr 1997; Schurr and Wallace 1999; Stone and Stoneking 1998). This result suggested that they are autochthonous haplotypes that derived from haplogroup C and D mtDNAs after the peopling of the Americas.

Rickards et al. (1999) claimed to have identified another founding lineage in the Ecuadorian Cayapa. Their analysis indicated that this group of HVR1 sequences did not belong to haplogroups A–C and had an unusual 16223T-16241G-16291T-16342C-16362C motif, but they did not employ RFLP analysis to confirm these findings. This was an important oversight because both Green et al. (2000) and Moraga et al. (2000) observed the same HVR1 sequences in the Mexican Indians and Chilean Yaghan and Mapuche, respectively, and used RFLP analysis to show they belonged to haplogroup D.

Most of the remaining "other" mtDNAs are likely to have been acquired through historical non-native gene flow. Several studies have revealed slight but nonnegligible European admixture in North American Indian groups by the presence of haplogroups H, J, and K (Scoz-

zari et al. 1997; Smith et al. 1999; Torroni et al. 1993a). There is also increasing evidence of historical African gene flow into Amerindian populations, as evidenced by the presence of African haplogroup L mtDNAs in native populations from North and Central America (Huoponen et al. 1997; Smith et al. 1999; Torroni et al. 1994a).[6] Based on these findings, it is reasonable to expect that nearly all of the "other" mtDNAs in Native American populations belong to one of these non-native haplogroups.

Even after we eliminate haplotypes originating in African or European populations, a few "other" mtDNAs in Native American populations have not yet been assigned to a known haplogroup. Most of them have been identified in ancient populations (Bailliet et al. 1994; Hauswirth et al. 1994; Merriwether et al. 1994; Parr et al. 1996; Ribeiro-Dos-Santos et al. 1996). However, the limited data from these "other" mtDNAs make it difficult to determine their exact genealogical status.[7]

Founding mtDNA Haplotypes in the Americas

Over the past decade, there has been considerable debate not only about the number of founding mtDNA lineages, or haplogroups, present in Native Americans, but also about the number of founding haplotypes[8] from each haplogroup that were brought to the Americas. Based on RFLP data, there appear to be only five founding haplotypes for haplogroups A–D and X (table 2.1).

TABLE 2.3 Founding HVR1 Sequences for Native American Haplogroups

Haplogroup	Haplotype	HVR1 Mutations	Asians	Amerindians	Na-Dene	Eskimos	Aleuts
A	A1	16223T, 16290T, 16319A, 16362C	X	X			
	A2	16111T, 16223T, 16290T, 16319A, 16362C		X	X	X	X
B	B1	16189C, 16217C, 16519C	X	X			
C	C1	16223T, 16298C, 16327T	X	X	X	X	X
	C2	16223T, 16298C, 16325C, 16327T	*	X			
	D0	16223T, 16362C	X	X	X	X	X
D	D1	16223T, 16325C, 16362C	*	X			
	D2	16223T, 16271C, 16362C			X	X	X
X	X1	16189C [16213A], 16223T, 16278T	*	X			

Note: The haplotype designations follow those of Forster et al. (1996), with C2 and D0 being new founding haplotypes proposed in this paper. The asterisk (*) indicates that the demarcated haplotypes are rarely seen in Asian and Siberian populations and, when present, only in specific populations (see text).

Haplotypes AM01 (A), AM13 (B), AM32 (C), and AM88 (D) are the most widely distributed HR-RFLP haplotypes[9] in the Americas and are central to the diversification of their respective haplogroups (Torroni et al. 1992, 1993a, 1994a,d). The three remaining putative founding haplotypes, AM09 (A), AM43 (C), and AM44 (D), differ from these nodal haplotypes by the presence or absence of the hypervariable *Hae*III 16517 site (Torroni et al. 1992, 1993a, 1994a,d). A comparison of Native American and Asian mtDNA data supports these findings because the same founding haplotypes from haplogroups A–D appear in Asian populations (Ballinger et al. 1992; Schurr et al. 1999; Torroni et al. 1993b, 1994c). The last founding haplotype, AM75 from haplogroup X, is very similar to HR-RFLP haplotypes from the same lineage in European populations (Macaulay et al. 1999; Torroni et al. 1996, 1998).

Other investigators using LR-RFLP analysis[10] have suggested that there were two founding haplotypes from haplogroups A, C, and D among the original set of founding Native American mtDNAs; these two haplotypes differed from the nodal haplotypes by the presence or absence of the *Hae*III 16517 site (Bailliet et al. 1994; Easton et al. 1996; Merriwether et al. 1994, 1995; table 2.1). In addition, Bailliet et al. (1994) identified mtDNAs in South American populations that lacked the defining RFLPs of haplogroups A–D; they designated these as belonging to "haplotype E." Based on these LR-RFLP data, a different set of founding haplotypes for Native American populations was proposed, namely A1, A2, B1, C1, C2, D1, D2, and E1 (Bailliet al. 1994; Merriwether et al. 1994; table 2.1). If X6 and X7 are accepted as being additional founding haplotypes for a sixth mtDNA lineage (Easton et al. 1996; Merriwether et al. 1994, 1995), then the total number of founder haplotypes for Native Americans could number as many as ten.

None of these studies, however, provided additional RFLP or HVR1 sequence data to confirm that these LR-RFLP haplotypes were actually the same founding haplotypes defined in HR-RFLP studies of Native American mtDNA variation (table 2.1). This is an important distinction because many Native American and Siberian mtDNAs from haplogroups A–D are identical at the RFLP level, except for the presence or absence of the hypervariable *Hae*III 16517 site, including both putative founding and derived haplotypes in Siberian and Native American populations (Schurr et al. 1999; Starikovskaya et al. 1998; Torroni et al. 1992, 1993a,b).[11] Based on this information, the frequency distributions of LR-RFLP haplotypes defined in this manner, such as A1 and A2, cannot provide sufficient information to discriminate "founding" from "derivative" haplotypes, or to assess the frequency of founding RFLP haplotypes in Native American groups.

Subsequently, Forster et al. (1996) suggested another nomenclatural system for mtDNA haplotypes that relates both RFLP and HVR1 sequence information from single mtDNAs.[12] In this nomenclatural system, founding haplotypes from haplogroups A–D and X are called A1 and A2; B1; C1 and C2 (proposed); D0, D1, and D2 (proposed); and X1. This means that, for Amerindian populations, there are potentially two founding HVR1 sequences for haplogroups A and C, three for D, and only one for haplogroups B and X (table 2.3).

Not surprisingly, the HVR1 sequences indicated as being the founders in the Americas are the most common sequences for each haplogroup among Native American populations and are also the stem types from which most other HVR1 sequences have evolved (Batista et al. 1995; Easton et al. 1996; Ginther et al. 1993; Horai et al. 1993; Kolman and Bermingham 1997; Kolman et al. 1995; Lorenz and Smith 1997; Moraga et al. 2000; Rickards et al. 1999; Santos et al. 1994; S. E. B. Santos et al. 1996; Torroni et al. 1993a; Ward et al. 1991, 1993, 1996). However, only half of these putative founding HVR1 sequences are detected in Eskimo, Aleut, and Na-Dene Indian populations (table 2.3). This pattern highlights the genetic differences between circumarctic and Amerindian populations that have been noted in previous studies (Rubicz et al. 2003; Schurr and Wallace 1999; Schurr et al. 1999; Shields et al. 1993; Starikovskaya et al. 1998).

Some researchers have also detected haplotypes that apparently possess diagnostic RFLP markers from two different haplogroups (Bailliet et al. 1994; Malhi et al. 2001; Martinez-Crusado et al. 2001; S. E. B. Santos et al. 1996; Torroni et al. 1993a). Because of their unique mutational composition, these so-called compound haplotypes have been proposed to represent additional founding haplotypes in Native American populations (Bailliet et al. 1994; S. E. B. Santos et al. 1996). However, careful comparison of the RFLP data and HVR1 sequences from these mtDNAs reveals that they are actually haplogroup A or D mtDNAs that have accumulated RFLPs appearing in other haplogroups (e.g., the Region V 9-bp deletion), possess mutations that appear similar to diagnostic haplogroup RFLPs (e.g., the *Hinc*II 13259 site loss),[13] or have lost diagnostic RFLPs for a particular haplogroup (e.g., *Hae*III 663 site). For this reason, compound haplotypes cannot be considered additional founding mtDNAs in Native American populations.

All other mutations in the HVR1 sequences appear to have arisen in either Asian/Siberian or Native American populations after their shared ancestral population(s) separated. There are some instances of recurrent mutations appearing in both sets of mtDNAs; these occur as parallel mutations in different haplogroups (e.g., Torroni et al. 1993a,b).[14] A number of HVR1 sequences are also shared among geographically adjacent or linguistically related populations, such as the Chibchan-speaking populations of Costa Rica (Batista et al. 1995; Kolman and Bermingham 1997; Kolman et al. 1995). These sequences may represent founding mtDNAs for the expansion of a particular cultural or linguistic tradition but are not pan-Amerindian in nature.[15]

Therefore, the total number of confirmed founding RFLP haplotypes for haplogroups A–D and X is still only five rather than ten or more, contrary to other claims (Bailliet et al. 1994; Bianchi and Rothhammer 1995; Easton et al. 1996; Merriwether et al. 1994, 1995; S. E. B. Santos et al. 1996). Nevertheless, there may be five definitive founding RFLP haplotypes and, at the same time, twice as many associated founding HVR1 sequences among New World populations because of the different evolutionary rates of the coding (slower) and noncoding (faster) portions of the mtDNA genome. Both data sets show a limited number of founding mtDNAs in Native American populations, which indicates that either genetic diversity declined during colonization of the New World or a geographically specific subset of mtDNAs was brought to the Americas by ancient Asian populations.

Distribution of Founding Lineages in the Americas

Upon reviewing published mtDNA data, one notes several major trends in the distribution of haplogroups A–D and X in the Americas. First, the four major founding mtDNA lineages appear in North, Central, and South American populations as well as the three proposed Native American linguistic groups (Amerind, Na-Dene, and Eskimo-Aleut) (Greenberg 1987; Greenberg et al. 1986; Hill, this volume; fig. 2.1). This pattern implies that the four haplogroups were present in the original migration(s) to the New World. However, it is not certain that all four were originally present in ancestral Na-Dene Indians and Eskimo-Aleuts because these populations lack haplogroup B, and usually haplogroup C, mtDNAs (Rubicz et al. 2003; Schurr et al. 1999; Shields et al. 1992, 1993; Starikovskaya et al. 1998; Torroni et al. 1992, 1993a).

Second, among Amerindian populations, there are broad intercontinental patterns of haplogroup distribution. Haplogroup A shows a decreasing north-to-south frequency cline, whereas haplogroups C and D show an increasing north-to-south frequency cline. In contrast, there is no clear clinal distribution for haplogroup B, aside from being virtually absent in north-

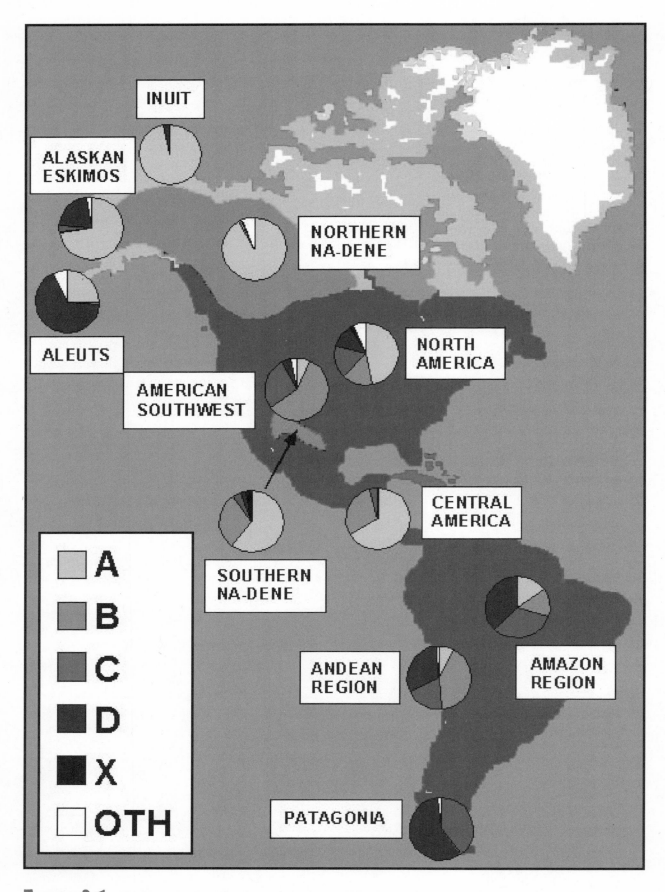

FIGURE 2.1 Haplogroup distribution in Native American populations. The key provides a color code for the different haplogroups. The sequence of haplogroups shown in each pie chart begins with haplogroup A and starts at the twelve o'clock position of the circle.

ern North America (Fox 1996; Lorenz and Smith 1996; Merriwether et al. 1994, 1995; Schurr et al. 1990; Torroni et al. 1992, 1993a, 1994a,d).[16] These distributions may reflect the original pattern of settlement of the Americas, the subsequent genetic differentiation of Native American populations within certain geographic regions, or aspects of both processes.

Haplogroup frequencies also vary in Na-Dene Indian populations. Virtually all northern Na-Dene Indian mtDNAs belong to haplogroup A, whereas the southern Na-Dene Indians (Navajo and Apache) have some mtDNAs from haplogroups B–D (Lorenz and Smith 1996; Merriwether et al. 1994; Shields et al. 1993; Torroni et al. 1992, 1993a). This finding is consistent with the idea that southern Na-Dene populations have become admixed with neighboring Amerindian populations since their arrival in the American Southwest some 500 to 1,000 years ago.

Third, although haplogroup A–D mtDNAs often appear together in single populations, many tribes lack haplotypes from at least one of these lineages (Schurr et al. 1990; Torroni et al. 1992, 1993a,b, 1994a,d). This pattern probably reflects the extent to which genetic drift and founder events have influenced the stochastic extinction and fixation of mtDNA haplotypes. Such an interpretation is also supported by the high frequency of "private haplotypes" in different Amerindian tribes (e.g., Torroni et al. 1993a), which are analogous to the "private polymorphisms" detected in nuclear genes for many of these same populations (e.g., Neel 1978). The general congruence of mitochondrial and nuclear genetic data supports the idea that early geographic isolation and founder effects led to the divergence of regional or tribal gene pools (Neel and Thompson 1978), although not all researchers concur on this point (e.g., Lorenz and Smith 1997).

Along these same lines, researchers have been actively exploring whether there has been genetic continuity between ancient and modern groups within the same geographic region. Genetic drift, population movements, or other stochastic processes may have altered the haplogroup frequencies of the populations that inhabited the same area over a long period of time. For example, based on haplogroup frequency data, the ancient Stillwater Marsh population is not ancestral to any modern Amerindian population from the Great Basin region (Kaestle and Smith 2001). Conversely, ancient Eskimo and Aleut samples have haplogroup frequencies that are nearly identical to those of their modern descendants (Lorenz and Smith 1996; Merriwether et al.

1994; O'Rourke et al. 2000; Rubicz et al. 2003; Saillard et al. 2000; Shields et al. 1993); the same is true for the ancient Anasazi and Fremont cultures compared with modern Puebloan Indian groups (Carlyle et al. 2000; Parr et al. 1996), and for ancient and modern Patagonians and Fuegians (Fox 1996; Moraga et al. 2000). These data suggest that, after they became genetically distinctive from surrounding groups, many regional Amerindian populations maintained their genetic integrity over a considerable length of time.

Origins of mtDNA Haplogroups in East Asia and Siberia

Based on the presence of haplogroups A–D in populations from the Siberian region, some researchers have suggested that Mongolia represents the source area for ancestral Native Americans (Kolman et al. 1996; Merriwether et al. 1996). Haplogroup A–D mtDNAs, however, are also found together in populations that originate as far west as the Altai Mountain region and as far east as Japan and Korea; Mongolia and the Lake Baikal region fall in the middle of these two locations (Ballinger et al. 1992; Derenko et al. 1998; Horai et al. 1996; Kolman et al. 1996; Merriwether et al. 1996; Schurr et al. 2000; Sukernik et al. 1996; Torroni et al. 1994c). As a result, the range of possibilities for the potential source area(s) of ancestral Native Americans has been expanded beyond Mongolia.

Haplogroups A–D actually represent a minority of mtDNA lineages in many Siberian and East Asian populations (fig. 2.2).[17] In fact, most Siberian populations have only haplogroups A, C, and D (Derenko et al. 1998; Schurr 2003; Schurr et al. 1999; Starikovskaya et al. 1998; Sukernik et al. 1996; Torroni et al. 1993b). Haplogroup A is absent or at low frequencies in most Siberian populations, but it rises in frequency in Tuvan, Buryat, and Mongolian groups and appears at its highest frequency in northeastern Siberia (Derenko et al. 1998, 2000; Schurr et al. 1999; Starikovskaya et al. 1998; Sukernik et al. 1996; Torroni et al. 1993b). Haplogroup C and D mtDNAs are found at significant frequencies in every eastern Siberian population, from the Yenisey River in the west to the Bering Sea in the east (Schurr et al. 1999; Starikovskaya et al. 1998; Sukernik et al. 1996; Torroni et al. 1993b), and also appear in many East Asian populations (Ballinger et al. 1992; Horai et al. 1996).

In contrast, almost all Siberian groups lack haplogroup B mtDNAs. Those that do possess these mtDNAs inhabit the southern margin of Siberia adjacent to

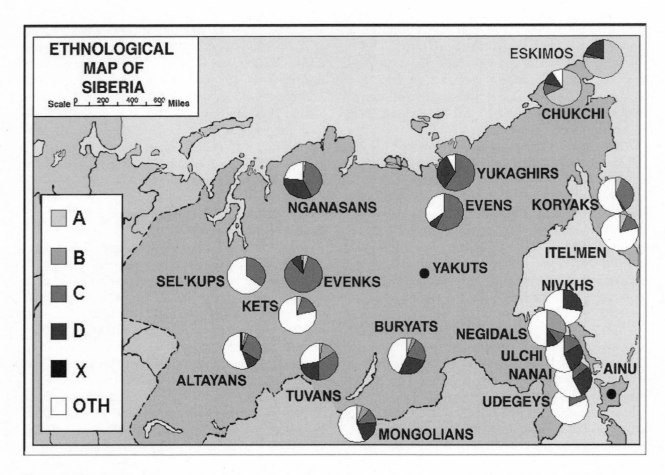

FIGURE 2.2 mtDNA haplogroup distribution in Siberian populations. The key provides a color code for the different haplogroups.

Mongolia and northern China (Derenko and Shields 1998; Kolman et al. 1996; Petrishchev et al. 1993; Schurr et al. 1999; Shields et al. 1992, 1993; Starikovskaya et al. 1998; Sukernik et al. 1996). The frequency of this mtDNA lineage is relatively low in these Siberian/Asian populations, but it increases as one moves into East and Southeast Asia (Ballinger et al. 1992; Harihara et al. 1992; Horai and Matsunaga 1986; Horai et al. 1996; Melton et al. 1995; Redd et al. 1995). This distribution suggests that haplogroup B arose somewhere in East Asia rather than southeastern Siberia, where haplogroups A, C, and D probably evolved, or that haplogroup B has been lost through genetic drift.

Siberian and East Asian populations also appear to lack haplogroup X mtDNAs (Horai et al. 1996; Schurr et al. 1999; Starikovskaya et al. 1998; Sukernik et al. 1996; Torroni et al. 1993b). These haplotypes appear at low frequencies in a number of European and West

Asian populations (Brown et al. 1998; Comas et al. 1996, 1998; Macaulay et al. 1999; Richards et al. 1996; Torroni et al. 1996, 1998), but they are virtually absent in Asian populations east of Kazakhstan (Derenko et al. 2000; Horai et al. 1996; Kolman et al. 1996). The only exceptions are Altayan populations, which exhibit about 3–5 percent haplogroup X mtDNAs (Derenko et al. 2000). This fact, plus the presence of haplogroup A–D mtDNAs in these same populations, led some researchers to suggest that the Altay Mountain region could be the ancestral source area for Native Americans (Derenko et al. 2000).

Antiquity of mtDNA Haplogroups in Siberia and the Americas

One of the most hotly debated questions concerning the origins of Native Americans is the antiquity of the ancestral populations who entered the New World. This

TABLE 2.4 Ages of Haplogroups in Siberia and the Americas

Haplogroup	Geographic Region	Schurr et al. (1999) Coalescence Time (B.P.)	Coalescence Time (B.P.)	(1998) Coalescence Time (B.P.)
A	Siberia	12,727–9655	—	—
	America	35,909–27,241	41,014–28,163	57,000–27,000
B	Asia*	30,454–23,103	—	—
	America	17,727–13,448	39,017–26,791	41,000–16,000
C	Siberia	19,545–14,828	—	—
	America	55,545–42,069	40,680–27,933	41,000–13,000
D	Siberia	50,455–38,276	—	—
	America	25,909–19,655	46,778–32,121	51,000–19,000
X	America	17,000–13,000^	n.d.	n.d.

Note: The abbreviation "B.P." means "before present," and "n.d." means "not determined." The asterisk (*) indicates that the estimate for Asian haplogroup B was obtained by Ballinger et al. (1992); it is consistent with the estimate for haplogroup B obtained from HVR1 sequence data by Lum et al. (1994). The caret (^) denotes that an older time range (36,000–23,000 B.P.) can be obtained for haplogroup X if one uses HVR1 sequence data (Brown et al. 1998).

question has been approached in molecular studies by examining the antiquity and pattern of diversity of the five founding haplogroups in Native American populations. Based on RFLP data, the ages for haplogroups A–D and X in the Americas have been estimated at between 30,000 and 23,000 B.P. (Brown et al. 1998; Torroni et al. 1992, 1993a, 1994d; table 2.4). Note that the divergence estimates for haplogroups B and X in the New World (17,000–13,000 B.P.) are considerably younger than those for haplogroups A, C, and D (table 2.4). These findings suggest that haplogroups B and X could possibly have been brought to the Americas in one or more later and separate migration(s) from the earlier one(s) that brought haplogroups A, C, and D.

The antiquity of most mtDNA haplogroups has also been noted in recent studies of HVR1 sequence diversity in Native American populations. Most of these studies have also provided ages for the five founding haplogroups between 45,000 and 23,500 B.P. (Bonatto and Salzano 1997; Brown et al. 1998; Forster et al. 1996; Stone and Stoneking 1998). In contrast to RFLP studies, however, these estimates argue that haplogroup B was present in the New World by at least 30,000–20,000 B.P. (Bonatto and Salzano 1997; Lorenz and Smith 1997; Stone and Stoneking 1998). This earlier date is consistent with those estimated for haplogroup B in Asia based on both RFLP and HVR1 se-

quence data (30,000–23,000 B.P.; Ballinger et al. 1992; Lum et al. 1994; Redd et al. 1995; table 2.4). Haplogroup B, therefore, may have arrived in the Americas at about the same time as haplogroups A, C, D, and X.[18]

Comparably ancient dates have also been obtained for these mtDNA lineages in both Asia/Siberia (A, C, and D; Schurr et al. 1999; Starikovskaya et al. 1998; Torroni et al. 1993b) and Europe (X; Richards et al. 1998; Torroni et al. 1996, 1998). In fact, it seems that Native American and Siberian populations have no mtDNAs in common, not even those that appear to have identical RFLP haplotypes due to their having different HVR1 sequences (Schurr et al. 1999; Starikovskaya et al. 1998; Torroni et al. 1993b). These findings imply that the haplogroup age estimates reflect the genetic diversity that has accumulated in the American branches of these mtDNA lineages and, hence, the approximate time at which modern humans first entered the Americas.

Other investigators have argued that the 25,000–20,000 B.P. age for these mtDNA lineages represents the age of haplogroup divergence in Asia, not the initial migration to the Americas (Shields et al. 1993; Ward et al. 1991). Working from this premise, Shields et al. (1993) estimated a "late" entry time (14,000–12,000 B.P.) for ancestral Amerindians into the New World, a date that falls within the lower bounds of other age estimates for Native American haplogroups (Bonatto and

Salzano 1997; Stone and Stoneking 1998; Torroni et al. 1993a, 1994d). However, this estimate is based on data taken from mostly Northwest Coast and circumarctic populations that have primarily haplogroup A mtDNAs and that share several HVR1 sequences from haplogroups A, C, and D (Lorenz and Smith 1997; Schurr et al. 1999; Shields et al. 1993; Starikovskaya et al. 1998; Ward et al. 1993). As a consequence, these dates may underestimate the antiquity of human populations in the New World.

Some researchers have suggested that the older colonization dates are inflated because they ignore the fact that multiple founding haplotypes from haplogroups A–D were brought to the Americas by ancestral Amerindian populations (i.e., haplotypes A1/A2, B1/B2, C1/C2, and D1/D2; Bailliet et al. 1994; Easton et al. 1996; Merriwether et al. 1994, 1995; table 2.1). In this view, the older haplogroup ages are overestimates because the genetic diversity that accumulated within each of the two founding haplotypes was combined and not analyzed separately. If the estimates were made separately from each founder haplotype, then the overall age for these mtDNA lineages would be less than 30,000–20,000 B.P., and the colonization date for the Americas would be consistent with a "late" entry model. However, the hypermutability of the *Hae*III 16517 site used to delineate these haplotypes (see above) raises serious questions about their validity as founding mtDNAs. Although this interpretation has merit, the data on which it is based are insufficient to support it.

Number of mtDNA Migrations to the New World

Based on these Siberian and Asian mtDNA data, several models for the peopling of the New World have been proposed. Most investigators have suggested a region extending from the Altai Mountains to southeastern Siberia and northern China as the potential source area(s) for ancestral Native American populations. However, they do not completely agree on the numbers of migrations that left this region and entered the New World. Some researchers have suggested that ancestral Amerindian populations brought at least haplogroup A, C, and D mtDNAs from Siberia during the initial colonization(s) of the New World; haplogroup B may represent a second independent migration from East Asia to the Americas (Starikovskaya et al. 1998; Torroni et al. 1993a,b). It has also been suggested that haplogroup X could represent a separate migration from somewhere in Eurasia because of this

haplogroup's absence in Siberia and much of the Americas (Brown et al. 1998). Other researchers have even argued that each haplogroup represents a separate migratory wave to the New World (Horai et al. 1993).

The majority of investigators assert that haplogroups A–D were brought to the New World in a single migratory event (Forster et al. 1996; Kolman et al. 1996; Lorenz and Smith 1997; Merriwether et al. 1994, 1995, 1996). In their view, the pattern of mtDNA variation seen in modern Amerindian populations is largely attributed to in situ differentiation and population movements that occurred after the initial colonization of the New World.[19] Statistical and pairwise mismatch analyses of HVR1 sequences from haplogroups A–D generally show a single demographic expansion into the New World (Bonatto and Salzano 1997; Stone and Stoneking 1998). However, if multiple expansions of human groups occurred within a limited period of time, the demographic signals of these events may not be detectable by this method (Marjoram and Donnelly 1994).

Based on HVR1 sequence data, it appears that populations originating in both south-central and far eastern Siberia may have brought ancestral haplotypes to the New World. The two most common founding HVR1 sequences from haplogroups C and D in the Americas—C2 and D0 (tables 2.2 and 2.3)—are rarely encountered in Asia and Siberia, but they occur at the highest frequencies in Amur River and East Asian populations (Horai et al. 1996; Schurr et al. 2000). In contrast, HVR1 sequences with the most common motif for haplogroup C (C1) and D (D1) in Asia and Siberia (table 2.2) are not very frequent, if present at all, in most Native American mtDNAs from these haplogroups (Batista et al. 1995; Easton et al. 1996; Ginther et al. 1993; Horai et al. 1993; Kolman and Bermingham 1997; Kolman et al. 1995; Lorenz and Smith 1997; Moraga et al. 2000; Rickards et al. 1999; Santos et al. 1994; S. E. B. Santos et al. 1996; Torroni et al. 1993a; Ward et al. 1991, 1993, 1996). If they were brought to the New World with ancestral Amerindian populations, these two sets of founding mtDNAs may have come from different regions of northern Asia and perhaps at different times.

Y-Chromosome Variation in Siberia and the New World

In characterizing NRY[20] variation in Native Americans, researchers have used several SNP[21] and STR[22] loci to define the paternal lineages within them. However,

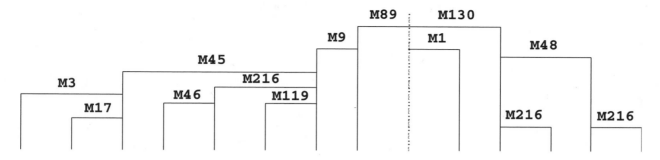

FIGURE 2.3 Y-chromosome SNP phylogeny of haplogroups in Siberian and Native American populations. The SNPs that define each haplogroup are indicated above each branch. The vertical dashed line indicates a branch that extends back to ancestral haplogroups that are not shown in the figure but correspond to the "Null" column in table 2.5. The nomenclature of SNPs follows that provided in Underhill et al. (1996, 1997, 2000) and Y Chromosome Consortium (2002).

most laboratory groups have not used the same combination of these markers in their analyses, leading to alternative nomenclatures for Y haplotypes and haplogroups. In this discussion, I will describe NRY variants in terms of the nomenclature developed by Underhill et al. (1996, 1997, 2000). Through the use of a dHPLC method,[23] Underhill et al. (2000) have identified ten different haplogroups of NRY haplotypes (I–X) in world populations; these haplogroups are defined by specific sets of SNPs.[24] For example, haplogroup V is defined by the M130 (RPS4Y) SNP (Bergen et al. 1999), haplogroup IX is defined by the M173 SNP, and haplogroup X is defined by the M74 SNP (Underhill et al. 2000; fig. 2.3). Haplogroups IX and X also share the M89 and M9 SNPs—two mutations that define a deep branch of the NRY phylogeny from which haplogroups VI–VIII arose—whereas haplogroup V lacks these SNPs.

The NRY haplotypes present in Native American populations represent a subsample of these haplogroups; the majority come from haplogroups V, IX, and X (Underhill et al. 2000). Most of these haplotypes, however, have not been screened for the complete set of haplogroup-defining SNPs identified by Underhill et al. (2000). As a result, it is simpler to refer to these haplotypes in terms of a basic set of informative SNPs for which the majority of them have been analyzed. Using these designations, one can assign these SNP haplotypes to a single paternal "lineage" or a set of related "lineages," some of which correspond to haplogroups I–X (Underhill et al. 2000), and others of which correspond to branches of those haplogroups. Each lineage will be referred to by the last SNP that occurred along that branch of a particular haplogroup. For example, the

M3 mutation occurs within the M45 branch or lineage, which, in turn, is a subbranch of the M74 lineage, a.k.a. haplogroup X, but will be called the M3 lineage.

With this shorthand nomenclature in mind, I will return to the NRY haplotype data for Asian and Native American populations. Various genetic studies have indicated that a variety of Y-chromosome lineages are present among Native American populations. These include the M1, M3, M9, M17, M45, M46 (Tat-C), M89, and M130 lineages, all of which are present in northern Asian populations at various frequencies (fig. 2.3). Not all of these Y lineages were disseminated into the Americas as part of its initial colonization, and, as will be discussed, those that were may not have been brought to the New World through a single population expansion. To draw these distinctions more clearly, I will describe each lineage and its distribution first in Asia and Siberia and then in the Americas.

The M9 lineage defines one of the two major branches in human Y-chromosome lineage evolution. It essentially divides all non-African Y chromosomes from African chromosomes, which, in turn, are defined by either the M1 polymorphism or other SNPs (Hammer et al. 1997; Underhill et al. 1997, 2000). In Siberians the M9 lineage comprises a small minority of their NRY haplotypes (Hammer et al. 1997; Karafet et al. 1999; Lell et al. 1998, 1999, 2000, 2002; Underhill et al. 1997; table 2.5). Most East Asian and Siberian groups exhibit derived M9 haplotypes (i.e., those that evolved from ancestral M9 African haplotypes); the same general pattern is seen in Native American populations (Hammer et al. 1997; Karafet et al. 1999; Lell et al. 1998, 1999, 2000, 2002; Underhill et al. 1997; table 2.5). In Asian,

TABLE 2.5 Y-Chromosome SNP Haplogroup Distribution (in Percentages) in Siberian and Native American Populations

Population	N	M3	M17	M45	M46	M216	M119	M9	M89	Null	M1	M130	M48
Southwest Siberia													
Tuvan	40	—	7.5	15.0	17.5	27.5	—	—	—	—	2.5	10.0	20.0
Tofalar	19	—	5.3	—	47.4	36.8	—	—	—	—	—	10.5	—
Buryat	13	—	—	—	23.1	15.4	46.1	—	7.7	—	—	—	7.7
Yenisey Evenk	31	—	9.7	—	9.7	19.3	3.2	—	—	—	—	—	—
Okhotsk/Amur													
Okhotsk Evenk	16	—	—	—	37.5	—	—	—	—	—	—	—	62.5
Ulchi/Nanai	63	—	—	3.8	9.4	—	3.8	15.1	—	—	—	30.2	37.7
Upriver Negidal	10	—	—	—	—	—	—	—	—	—	—	—	100.0
Downriver Negidal	7	—	—	60.0	—	—	—	—	—	—	—	20.0	20.0
Udegey	20	—	5.0	10.0	—	—	—	25.0	—	—	—	—	60.0
Nivkh	17	—	—	35.3	—	—	5.9	11.8	—	—	—	11.8	35.3
Kamchatka													
Koryak	27	—	—	18.5	22.2	—	—	—	—	—	—	25.9	33.3
Itel'men	19	—	22.2	—	11.1	—	—	—	—	—	—	27.8	38.9
Chukotka													
Chukchi	24	12.5	4.2	20.8	58.3	—	—	—	—	—	—	—	4.2
Siberian Yupik	33	21.2	—	18.2	60.6	—	—	—	—	—	—	—	—
North America													
Navajo	30	63.3	—	33.3	—	—	—	—	—	—	—	3.3	—
Seminole	23	39.1	—	43.5	—	—	—	—	—	13.1	4.3*	—	—
Zapotec/Mixtec	29	75.9	—	17.2	—	—	—	—	—	—	6.9*	—	—
Central America													
Boruca	23	69.6	—	26.1	—	—	—	—	—	—	—	—	—
Guaymi	21	85.7	4.8	9.5	—	—	—	—	—	—	—	—	—
Bribri/Cabecar	13	84.6	—	—	—	—	—	—	—	7.7	—	—	—
Cuna	3	100.0	—	—	—	—	—	—	—	—	—	—	—
South America													
Yanomama	30	26.7	—	73.3	—	—	—	—	—	—	—	—	—
Makiritare	25	68.0	—	32.0	—	—	—	—	—	—	—	—	—
Kraho	7	85.7	—	—	—	—	—	—	—	14.3	—	—	—
Piaroa	6	100.0	—	—	—	—	—	—	—	—	—	—	—
Panoa	5	100.0	—	—	—	—	—	—	—	—	—	—	—
Macushi	4	100.0	—	—	—	—	—	—	—	—	—	—	—
Wapishana	2	50.0	—	50.0	—	—	—	—	—	—	—	—	—

Source: Data are from Lell et al. (2002).

Note: The SNPs that define each haplogroup are indicated above each column of the table. The M216 (DYS7C) mutation also occurs in three other SNP haplogroups (M46, M130, and M48) because it is a recurrent mutation. For this paper, the deletion associated with the M46 SNP is the most important one because these two branches are genealogically related (see fig. 2.3). The M48 SNP appears in a significant number of Siberian M130 haplotypes and defines a major subbranch of this lineage. However, it does not appear in Native American M130 haplotypes. The "null" haplotypes in the Seminoles and Zapotec/Mixtecs denoted with an asterisk (*) contain other markers that indicate they are of African origin.

Siberian, and Native American Y haplotypes, the M9 mutation is associated with the M3, M17, M45, and M46 lineages but not the M130 lineage (fig. 2.3).

Haplogroup M45 is observed in populations throughout Siberia, including those that inhabit Chukotka, Kamchatka, the Amur/Okhotsk region, and central Siberia (table 2.5). This haplogroup, however, is almost completely absent in East Asian populations (Su et al. 1999), which suggests that it arose in northern Asia and has not been widely disseminated into regions farther south. M45 haplotypes also include the most recent ancestors of the M3 lineage that, on the basis of other SNP and STR markers,[25] are found in the central Siberian Kets, Sel'kups, and Altayans (Lell et al. 2000, 2002; Santos et al. 1999). The M3 lineage is the major paternal lineage observed in Native American populations, but in Siberia, it is found only in the Chukchi and Siberian Eskimos (Bianchi et al. 1997, 1998; Karafet et al. 1997, 1999; Lell et al. 1997, 1998, 1999; Santos et al. 1999; Underhill et al. 1996; table 2.5).

The M1 lineage defines a major branch of the human Y-chromosome phylogeny that originated in Africa. The M1 lineage appears at intermediate to high frequencies (46–78 percent) in African populations and at low frequencies (0–11 percent) in European populations (Hammer 1994; Lahermo et al. 1999; Spurdle et al. 1994). It has also been detected at low to moderate frequencies in Central and East Asian populations, such as the Japanese (Hammer and Horai 1995), Koreans (Kim et al. 2000), Tibetans, Mongolians, Yakuts, Altayans, and Tuvans (Hammer et al. 1997; Karafet et al. 1997, 1999; Lell et al. 1997, 1998, 1999, 2000, 2002). The Asian M1 haplotypes, however, differ from those in African populations by having longer 3' oligo (dA) tails on the *Alu* element and by lacking the DYS271 (M2) SNP, which has been found only in African M1 chromosomes (Seielstad et al. 1994).

Recent studies suggest that the M46 lineage arose in southeastern Siberia because this is where its ancestral haplotypes appear (Karafet et al. 1999; Lell et al. 1998, 1999; Zerjal et al. 1997). This SNP occurs in a larger lineage defined by the DYS7C (M216) SNP (deletion), which is seen in Y chromosomes across Eurasia (Zerjal et al. 1997). Populations bearing M46 haplotypes later influenced the Kets, Altayans, and Buryats, as well as the Mongolians, Yakuts, and Chinese Han populations (Karafet et al. 1999; Lell et al. 1998, 1999; Santos et al. 1999; Zerjal et al. 1997). Furthermore, the M46 SNP appears at polymorphic frequencies in north-

ern European populations, such as the Finns and Saami, as well as in the Uralic speakers of western Siberia (Jobling et al. 1996; Karafet et al. 1999; Lahermo et al. 1999; Lell et al. 1998, 1999; Santos et al. 1999; Zerjal et al. 1997). These data imply that Asian populations have significantly genetically influenced these Eurasian gene pools.[26]

Only a few Siberian populations exhibit the M119 lineage. It occurs at moderate frequencies in Buryats and is absent elsewhere in eastern and northern Siberia, but it occurs at significant frequencies in various ethnic Chinese populations (Su et al. 1999). Its presence in these Siberian populations is consistent with the northward migration of this haplogroup from East Asia (Su et al. 1999, 2000). Siberian populations, however, lack the M122 lineage (Lell et al. 2002), which represents a large proportion of northern Chinese and East Asian Y chromosomes (Su et al. 1999, 2000). These findings indicate that the M122 lineage was not brought to Siberia through northern expansions of ethnic Han Chinese groups.

Unlike some of its counterparts, the M130 lineage appears to be quite ancient and widespread in East and Southeast Asia. It appears in populations as far apart as South India, Australia, and Chukotka (Bergen et al. 1999; Karafet et al. 1999; Lell et al. 1998, 1999, 2000, 2002). Based on the diversity of STR alleles associated with Siberian haplotypes, the M130 lineage either arose or diversified in East Asian populations (Bergen et al. 1999; Lell et al. 1998, 1999, 2000, 2002) rather than in the Altai-Sayan/Baikal region, where nearly all other Y lineages are thought to have evolved. This lineage has since spread westward from East Asia into the Lake Baikal region, where it now appears at significant frequencies in Central Asian and central Siberian populations (Bergen et al. 1999; Karafet et al. 1999; Lell et al. 1998, 1999, 2000, 2002).

The remaining Siberian Y chromosomes belong to less frequently occurring lineages. The first of these is defined by the M89 SNP. M89 is one of the most ancient SNPs in human Y chromosomes and occurs in all Y haplotypes, except those that belong to the M1 lineage or other ancestral haplotypes. Among Siberian populations, M89 haplotypes appear only in the Buryats. By contrast, the M17 lineage has arisen recently in Siberia. It appears at low frequencies in a small, but not insignificant, number of Siberian populations; it occurs at the highest frequency among the Itel'men but is absent from the neighboring Koryaks (Lell et al. 1998, 1999, 2002).

Founding Y-Chromosome Lineages in Native Americans

Two paternal lineages encompass the great majority of Native American Y chromosomes, M3 and M45 (table 2.5). The M3 lineage appears at significant frequencies in most Native American populations and is distributed in an increasing north-to-south cline within the New World (Bianchi et al. 1997, 1998; Karafet et al. 1997, 1999; Lell et al. 1997, 1998, 1999; Santos et al. 1999; Underhill et al. 1996). However, it has yet to be found in any African or European populations (Karafet et al. 1999; Santos et al. 1999; Underhill et al. 1996, 1997). The STR data from M3 Y chromosomes also reveal significant differences in haplotype distribution between North/Central and South American Amerindian populations, which suggests different population histories in the two major continental regions (Bianchi et al. 1998; Karafet et al. 1999; Lell et al. 1998, 1999, 2002; Ruiz-Linares et al. 1999; F. R. Santos et al. 1996a,b, 1999).

Among Siberian and Asian populations, the M3 lineage has been observed only in the Siberian Eskimos and the Chukchi (Karafet et al. 1997, 1999; Lell et al. 1997, 1998, 1999; Underhill et al. 1996) and in a single Even individual (Karafet et al. 1997, 1999). The absence of the M3 lineage in nearly every Siberian and Central Asian population and its presence in all major linguistic subdivisions of Native Americans implies that it evolved in the ancestral Native American population(s) after leaving this part of northern Asia, either in Beringia or in the Americas.[27]

The second most frequent Y-chromosome lineage observed in the Americas is M45. The M45 lineage is widely distributed among Native American populations; approximately 29 percent of their Y chromosomes belong to this paternal lineage. Other researchers using different sets of SNPs and STRs to characterize their Y chromosomes have also noted the presence of a second major paternal lineage in the Americas that is analogous to the M45 lineage (Ruiz-Linares et al. 1999; Santos et al. 1999). In addition, phylogenetic analysis of M45 haplotypes revealed two distinct sets in Native American populations. One set appeared only in North and Central American groups, whereas the other was more broadly distributed in populations in North, Central, and South America (Lell et al. 1999, 2000, 2002).

All other Native American Y chromosomes belong to one of several different lineages that are also found in Asian/Siberian populations. DYS7C (M216) haplotypes are completely absent in Native American populations, with the exception of the Navajo (Karafet et al. 1999; Lell et al. 1998, 1999; Santos et al. 1999; Zerjal et al. 1997). The M130 lineage has been seen only in the Na-Dene–speaking Tanana and Navajo and in the Amerindian Cheyenne (Bergen et al. 1999; Karafet et al. 1999; Lell et al. 1998, 1999, 2000, 2002). The M17 lineage is completely absent from Native American populations, with the exception of the Guaymi (Ngöbe), a Chibchan tribe from Costa Rica (Lell et al. 1998, 1999, 2000, 2002). Because the STR alleles in all of these Native American Y haplotypes are consistent with those in Siberian groups, they appear to have been brought to the Americas through a secondary expansion of ancient Asian peoples rather than with the initial immigrants to the New World (Lell et al. 1998, 1999, 2000, 2002).

The M1 lineage has also been observed in several Native American populations. These include the Mixe in southern Mexico (Karafet et al. 1999; Lell et al. 1997), the Seminoles in Florida (Huoponen et al. 1997), and several Central and South American populations (Karafet et al. 1999). However, the two Mixe M1 haplotypes also exhibited other Y markers that appear in non-native populations (Lell et al. 1997), and the Central and South American Indian groups exhibited additional SNPs that typically occur in African M1 haplotypes. Therefore, these Native American populations acquired their M1 haplotypes through intermarriage with persons with African ancestry.

A few Y haplotypes found in Native American populations do not belong to any of these paternal lineages; hence, they were placed into a "null" category (Lell et al. 2000, 2002).[28] These are likely to have been acquired through non-native admixture because of the higher frequencies of such haplotypes in African populations (Hammer et al. 1997, 1998; Underhill et al. 1997). Additional screenings for newly discovered SNPs will further define the origins and affinities of these haplotypes and, thus, their source region.

Founding Y-Chromosome Haplotypes

As seen with the mtDNA data, Native American populations show a limited number of founding haplotypes for the major Y lineages present within them. The proposed founder haplotype of the M3 lineage is the most frequent haplotype in Native American populations and is widely distributed throughout the New World and in Chukotka (Lell et al. 2000, 2002). In light of this distribution, the presence of the M3 founder haplotype in Chukotka could be the result of recent backflow across the Bering Strait, as suggested by Karafet et al. (1999). However, the existence of Chukotkan-specific M3 haplotypes that are differentiated from related Native American haplotypes on the basis of STR allelic variation suggests that haplogroup M3 arose in a Beringian population ancestral to both Native Americans and northeastern Siberians (Lell et al. 2000, 2002).

The M45 haplotype that is directly ancestral to the M3 founder haplotype (M45a) contains the same array of STR alleles as its M3 derivative (Lell et al. 2000, 2002). In fact, M45a haplotypes have the widest geographic distribution of all M45 haplotypes, being present in populations from central Siberia to South America.[29] Another set of M45 haplotypes (M45b) is shared between eastern Siberian populations in Kamchatka and the Amur River region and North and Central American groups. However, none of these M45b haplotypes are seen in central Siberia or South America (Lell et al. 1999, 2000, 2002).

Age of Y-Chromosome Haplogroups in Siberia and the Americas

Not surprisingly, considerable effort has been made to estimate the age of the M3 lineage because it apparently signals the entry of ancestral populations into the New World. An initial study estimated the age of this lineage at 30,000–2150 B.P.[30] (Underhill et al. 1996). Whereas the former age is consistent with an early entry into the New World, the latter clearly underestimates the time of this colonization event, although it raises the possibility that the M3 marker arose in an ancestral Beringian or American population after, rather than before, the initial entry of human populations into the New World. Using different methods, Hammer et al. (1998) and Karafet et al. (1999) arrived at a similar conclusion; their estimates provided an age for the M3 lineage at 10,000–7600 B.P. By contrast, Bianchi et al. (1998) and Forster et al. (2000) estimated a 22,270–20,000 B.P. age for the M3 lineage. Thus, the analyses of Y-chromosome variation in Native American populations do not favor an early entry over a late entry of ancestral populations into the New World.[31]

The M45 lineage has not yet been firmly dated, although insights into its evolution can be gleaned from its STR allelic diversity. As noted above, the STR data indicate that two different sets of M45 haplotypes are present in Native Americans: a central Siberian set (M45a), which is shared with all Native American populations; and an eastern Siberian set (M45b), which is shared with Native Americans from only North and Central America (Lell et al. 2000, 2002). Interestingly, M45a haplotypes showed a greater diversity in and

more varied frequencies of STR alleles than the M45b haplotypes from North and Central American populations. This striking difference in STR allele frequencies among populations in the Americas was not observed in M3 haplotypes (Lell et al. 2000, 2002). Thus, it appears that M45 haplotypes have been introduced at least twice in the New World as part of its initial settlement.

Other researchers have attempted to date the Y lineages present in Siberia and the Americas. Two of the older lineages in Siberia, M1 and M9, have been dated at about 50,000 B.P. (Karafet et al. 1999). The M1 lineage is clearly ancient because of its frequency and diversity in African populations (Hammer et al. 1997), but it may not have reached Central Asia by that time because of its more limited distribution and diversity in Central and East Asia (Hammer and Horai 1995; Hammer et al. 1998; Lell et al. 1997, 1998, 1999). The antiquity of the M9 lineage, however, is consistent with the presence of the M9 mutation in a sizable majority of Siberian Y chromosomes (Karafet et al. 1999; Lell et al. 1999, 2000, 2002; Santos et al. 1999). The age of the oldest SNP in the Y phylogeny, M89, has not yet been estimated, although it must certainly predate the occurrence of the M9 lineage because it appears in all haplotypes bearing the M9 mutation (fig. 2.3).

The M130 lineage appears to be somewhat younger than the M89 or M9 lineages, having been dated at about 25,000 B.P. (Karafet et al. 1999). This date is generally consistent with its broad distribution in East Asia, where it appears to have originated, and with its considerable haplotypic diversity in eastern Siberian and Asian populations (Lell et al. 1999, 2002; Su et al. 1999, 2000). The age of this lineage will probably increase as more STR data from M130 haplotypes are obtained.

The widely distributed M46 lineage is much younger than the other Y haplogroups. It appears to have expanded in Siberia between 4800 and 2400 B.P. (Karafet et al. 1999), a date that is somewhat younger than that estimated for the accompanying DYS7C (M216) mutation (Zerjal et al. 1997). This shallow time depth is consistent with the limited diversity of M46 haplotypes in Siberian populations (Lell et al. 1998, 1999, 2000, 2002). These data also suggest that the M46 lineage arose in Siberia after the initial settlement of the New World, perhaps with the expansion of the reindeer-herding culture in northern Asia and Eurasia (Zerjal et al. 1997).

One of the major lineages present in northern Chinese and East Asian populations, M122, has been dated at about 60,000 B.P. (Su et al. 1999, 2000). As indicated above, M122 haplotypes have not yet been detected in Siberian populations. Despite its antiquity in East Asia, this lineage does not appear to have been brought to Siberia, even in recent times. However, the M119 lineage, which is not yet clearly dated, must be old enough to have been disseminated into some Siberian populations through a northward migration from East Asia.

Number of Migrations Based on Y-Chromosome Variation

At least six different paternal lineages have been identified in Siberia and the Americas using SNP markers (M1, M3, M9, M17, M45, M46, and M130), but only two of these (M3 and M45) fundamentally contributed to the initial peopling of the New World, through either single (Bianchi et al. 1998; Santos et al. 1999; Underhill et al. 1996) or multiple (Karafet et al. 1999; Lell et al. 1998, 1999, 2000, 2002) migration events. A later secondary expansion(s) of human groups into the Americas brought with it a different set of M45 haplotypes and the M17 and M130 lineages, possibly from the Amur River region (Karafet et al. 1999; Lell et al. 1999, 2000, 2002; Su et al. 2000). The high frequency, broad distribution, and relative homogeneity of the M45b haplotypes make it probable that they had a Siberian origin that was temporally or geographically distinct from that bringing the earlier M45a haplotypes that are shared between Native American and central Siberian populations. All of the other Y lineages present in Siberia, such as M46, either arose after the colonization of the New World or originated outside of the geographic region from which ancestral Native American populations left. Some of these lineages became widely dispersed throughout Siberia and Eurasia during Neolithic times. The M1 haplotypes present in Native American populations were acquired through non-native admixture; they were not contributed by founding Asian populations.

Overview of Molecular Data

From these molecular genetic data, what general patterns of biological affinities and origins for Native Americans can be ascertained? All of these studies support the Asian origin of Native American populations. Most of them have suggested a region that extended from central Siberia to the Altai Mountains to southeastern Siberia and northern China as the potential source area(s) for ancestral Native American populations. The

mtDNA data also suggest a possible Eurasian genetic influence because of the presence of haplogroup X in North America, and Y-chromosome data suggest both south-central and eastern Siberia as the source area(s) for ancestral Y lineages brought to the New World. Other researchers have suggested that Polynesian populations may have genetically contributed to ancestral Native American groups (Cann and Lum 1996; Lum et al. 1994), but these putative contacts have not been supported by other genetic data (Bonatto et al. 1996). Various data sets reveal post-Columbian (historical) admixture with peoples of European and African descent (e.g., Huoponen et al. 1997; Rodriguez-Delfin et al. 1997; Scozzari et al. 1997; Smith et al. 1999; Torroni et al. 1994a), but these data cannot be used to reconstruct the prehistory of the New World.

Although these genetic studies show a growing consensus about the general source area for ancestral Amerindian populations, they disagree about the number of migrations that brought these populations to the New World. Most researchers believe that the Na-Dene Indians and Eskimo-Aleuts were part of the most recent expansion of human groups into North America, whether or not they represent separate migrations or a remnant of the ancestral Beringian population that gave rise to all other Native Americans. Researchers, however, disagree on the number of migrations that gave rise to Amerindians: one (Bianchi et al. 1997, 1998; Kolman et al. 1996; Merriwether et al. 1994, 1995; Stone and Stoneking 1998), two (Karafet et al. 1999; Lell et al. 1998, 1999, 2000, 2002; Santos et al. 1999), three (Brown et al. 1998; Torroni et al. 1993a,b), or four (Horai et al. 1993). Because most molecular data sets now suggest that multiple migrations contributed to the genetic diversity of Amerindian populations, the "Amerind" linguistic category probably should no longer be viewed as valid (see Hill, this volume). Regardless of the number of migrations, all of these data sets show the haplotypic distinctiveness between members of the so-called Amerind linguistic group and those of the Eskimo-Aleut and Na-Dene groups; thus, the ancestral Amerindians clearly migrated to the New World before the Eskimo-Aleut and Na-Dene populations.

Perhaps the most controversial aspect of recent molecular studies is the early colonization date that they suggest. Although no one disagrees that the colonization of the New World represents the terminal expansion of modern humans bearing Upper Paleolithic technologies, there has been considerable debate about when this expansion occurred. In particular, researchers have noted the incongruity between the apparently late (15,000–12,000 B.P.) archaeological visibility of the early colonizers of the Americas and the seemingly greater antiquity (35,000–20,000 B.P.) of the genetic lineages that they brought to these regions. The same problem arises when scholars try to reconcile the genetic and geological data. Human groups could have arrived in the New World before, during, or after the Last Glacial Maximum, depending on which genetic lineage ages are used, but glacial barriers would apparently have prevented human movements into the Americas between 25,000 and 18,000 B.P.

Because of the increasingly earlier dates for pre-Clovis archaeological sites in the Americas, the potential entry time and the ages of the genetic lineages are slowly drawing closer together. Ongoing analyses of the mutation rates of mtDNA and Y-chromosome loci may narrow this time range and may even push the initial entry time closer to the dates associated with the oldest archaeological sites in the Americas (16,000–14,000 B.P.). Irrespective of the initial entry time, however, all genetic studies date the emergence of the Eskimo-Aleuts and Na-Dene Indians at between 10,000 and 5000 B.P., well after ancestral Paleoindians arrived in the New World.

The mtDNA and Y-chromosome data have shown that settlement of the Americas after their initial colonization was not a static process. Although most studies show a general genetic division between North and Central America and South America, there is also evidence for both north-south and south-north population contact as well as gene flow between these regions (see also Pearson, this volume). Underlying these broader patterns is considerable evidence for fairly long-term regional and tribal differentiation of populations in the major continental regions of the New World, particularly in South America. These patterns have undoubtedly been shaped by geographic isolation, linguistic differentiation, and genetic drift.

Acknowledgments

The author would like to acknowledge Drs. Jeffrey T. Lell, James V. Neel, Rem I. Sukernik, Yelena B. Starikovskaya, Antonio Torroni, and Douglas C. Wallace for their contributions to multiple studies of Siberian and Native American genetic variation, on which this paper is based. Many thanks are also due to all of those persons who assisted with field research in Siberia, including the medical personnel from local hospitals, and especially the native persons who participated in this work. The research described in this paper has been supported by grants from the Wenner-Gren Foundation for Anthropological Research, the National Science Foundation, the Leakey Foundation, Sigma Xi, the International Science (Soros) Foundation, INTAS, the Russian Fund for Basic Research, the J. Worley Brown Fellowship Fund, the National Institutes of Health, and the Emory Clinical Research Center.

3 Peopling of the New World
A COMPARATIVE CRANIOFACIAL VIEW
C. Loring Brace, A. Russell Nelson, and Pan Qifeng

Thoughtful observers—from Fray José de Acosta in the late sixteenth century to Thomas Jefferson in the eighteenth century to researchers in the present—have realized that East Asia was a prime possibility as the locus of New World human origins (Little 1987). According to the interpretation of Greenberg and colleagues, the distribution of linguistically identifiable groups in the Western Hemisphere may be the result of separate prehistoric population movements into the New World (Greenberg 1987; Greenberg et al. 1986; Hill, this volume). The earliest entrants into the New World would have had uncontested access to both continents and could therefore be expected to have expanded their occupation to the continents' southernmost extent (Barton et al., this volume; Meltzer, this volume; Pearson, this volume).

Because the first inhabitants were few in number, traces of their presence have been hard to locate and date. From the sparse archaeological evidence and complementary molecular genetic data from living populations, an initial date of at least 15,000 B.P. or earlier can be postulated (Dillehay 1999), although the most recent assessment suggests that it may well have been somewhat later than that (Goebel et al. 2003). Whether the first colonists traveled by land or sea does not alter the nature of the interpretation presented here. However, the very old dates of some South American coastal sites require that researchers give serious attention to the coastal-route hypothesis (Anderson 1968; Fladmark 1978, 1979, 1983; Keefer et al. 1998; Meltzer 1993b; Moseley 1975, 1992; Sandweiss et al. 1998). Most of the evidence suggests that the first entrants into the hemisphere focused on the resources that were available in the continental interiors rather than confining themselves to the coastal strip at the western edge (Barton et al., this volume; Frison 1998b; Meltzer 1993b, this volume).

Questions concerning the initial human settlement of the New World have focused on several issues: the initial entry date; the access route; the number and composition of migrations (i.e., one population versus several dissimilar populations); and the genetic relationship between the initial colonists and living American Indian groups, Asian and Pacific populations, and other Old World peoples (Merriwether et al. 1995; Roosevelt et al. 1996; Schurr, this volume; Schurr et al. 1990). Issues of geology, archaeology, and legal ownership are also involved (Denton and Hughes 1981; Hopkins et al. 1982; Morell 1998; Preston 1997; West 1996b). In this chapter, we will summarize and interpret craniometric data in an attempt to answer these questions.

Materials and Methods

Researchers have recently investigated these types of questions by comparing patterns of geographical distributions of human genetic and morphological features (Brace and Tracer 1992; Brace et al. 1993, 2001; Howells 1990; Jantz and Owsley 1998; Lahr 1995; Neves and Pucciarelli 1991; Schmitz, this volume; Schurr, this volume; Steele and Powell 1992; Wallace and Torroni 1992; Ward et al. 1993). Metric variables record inherited differences in cranial and facial form by documenting minor variations in suture placement, suture length, and other details in the construction of the cranial vault and face. The various configurations of craniofacial form cluster regionally and are not distributed in clinal fashion related to the intensity of different selective force gradients. Furthermore, once established, configurations of facial form appear to remain relatively stable over considerable spans of time (Brace and Tracer 1992; Brace et al. 1993, 2001).

Although details of facial form are distributed in regional groupings that may be viewed as implying levels of biological relationship, these considerations must be made at a level well below that of species in a taxonomic sense. The human genotype web is a subspecific, and therefore genetically open, system. None of the earlier human groups sampled in our data set, if they were all alive at the same time, would have been reproductively isolated in a fashion analogous to that of different species in a cladistic scheme. Because of this, the relationships depicted here—although they are of heuristic value in examining similarities and differences between groups of people across regions and over time—do not constitute a taxonomy in the strict sense of the term (Brace 1988).

In this chapter, we attempt to integrate the results of an analysis of craniometric data gathered on prehistoric and recent samples of New World, East Asian, Pacific, and other Old World populations. Our analysis is based on a set of 21 craniofacial measurements made on collections of human crania that represent these samples. The samples are listed in table 3.1. In order to extract more information from our measurement set, we used a series of transforms and trigonometric calculations (Brace and Hunt 1990; Nelson 1998) to increase our list of variables to 36. The complete roster of these variables is recorded in table 3.2.

For the purposes of analysis and comparison, we have followed the procedures for the treatment of variables as described by Howells (1986). These procedures attempt to minimize the effects of major size differences when diverse populations are being compared. The first step is to convert individual unweighted measurements into sex-specific Z-scores, where each Z-score represents the number of standard deviation units by which the value in question departs from the grand mean for each separate dimension of all the samples used in a given analysis. This can be represented as follows:

$$Z_{ij} = \frac{(X_{ij} - \overline{X_i})}{\sigma_i} \tag{1}$$

where i = value of the variable of that number (e.g., 1 ... 36); j = number of the individual; X_{ij} = value of variable i for individual j; X_i = overall sex-specific average value for variable i; and σ_i = overall sex-specific standard deviation for variable i.

The use of Z-scores by themselves does not eliminate the problem of size. In order to obtain relative proportions, or "shapes," for the craniofacial features that we analyzed, we needed some kind of proportional transformation. We followed Howells's pioneering use of the C-score statistic to accomplish this goal (Brace and Hunt 1990; Howells 1986). C-scores are similar to ratios because they are both measures of relative size. The advantage of a C-score over a simple ratio is that the C-score reflects the relative size of a given feature in comparison to the size of all of the other analyzed traits, whereas a ratio reflects the relative size in comparison to only a single referent. C-scores are calculated as the difference between the Z-score of a single variable for a

TABLE 3.1 Samples and *N*s Used in the Analysis

No.	Sample	N
1	Central Valley Woodland, United States	98
2	Mississippian Horizon, Southeastern United States	56
3	Central Valley Archaic, United States	93
4	Puebloan, Southwestern United States	76
5	Australo-Melanesia	25
6	Sub-Saharan Africa	107
7	Windover, Early Archaic Florida, United States	37
8	Europe (Pan-European composite)	346
9	Mexico, Historic	31
10	Ecuador, Peru, Protohistoric	75
11	Southern Great Lakes, Late Woodland, United States	65
12	Nevada Great Basin, Archaic, United States	25
13	Northeast Woodland, Late Woodland, United States	109
14	Northern Plains, Late Prehistoric to Historic, United States	138
15	Northern Great Lakes, Late Woodland, United States	62
16	Northern Archaic, United States	42
17	Inuit, Protohistoric	117
18	Chukchi, Protohistoric	21
19	Ainu, Japan, Historic	68
20	Polynesia, Pacific Basin, Prehistoric to Historic	207
21	Micronesia, Pacific Basin, Prehistoric to Historic	109
22	Haida, Northwest Coast, Historic, Canada	51
23	Patagonia, Prehistoric, South America	28
24	Jōmon, Japan, Prehistoric	53
25	Athabaskan, Prehistoric to Historic, Yukon River Drainage	48
26	Liuwan, Neolithic, Western China	24
27	Aleut, Protohistoric, Aleutian Islands	18
28	Yangshao, Neolithic, Central China	42
29	Anyang, Bronze Age, China	34
30	Henan Province, Modern, China	70
31	Japan, Modern	136
32	Doigahama Yayoi, Prehistoric, Japan	44
33	Buryat, Historic, Siberia	21
34	Mongol, Modern, Mongolia	20
35	Hebei Province, Modern, China	64
36	Manchu, Modern, Heilongjiang Province, China (formerly Manchuria)	18
37	Northeast China, Modern	44
38	Korea, Modern	17
Total		2,639

TABLE 3.2 Craniofacial Measures and Computed Variables in the UMMA Data Set

Var. No.	Description
1	Nasal height
2	Nasal bone height
3	Piriform aperture height
4	Nasion prosthion length
5	Nasion basion
6	Basion prosthion
7	Superior nasal bone width
8	Simotic width
9	Inferior nasal bone width
10	Nasal breadth
11	Simotic subtense
12	Inferior simotic subtense
13	FOW subtense at nasion
14	MOW subtense at rhinion
15	Bizygomatic breadth
16	Glabella opisthocranion
17	Maximum cranial breadth
18	Basion bregma
19	Basion rhinion
20	Width at 13 (FMT-FMT)
21	Width at 14
22	Computed (transformed variable): 16/18
23	Computed (transformed variable): 16/17
24	Computed (transformed variable): 17/18
25	Computed (transformed variable): 13/21
26	Computed (transformed variable): 6/19
27	Cosine angle nasion-prosthion-basion
28	Cosine angle nasion-basion-prosthion
29	Cosine angle prosthion-nasion-basion
30	Angle base—MOW (14)
31	Cosine angle FMT—nasion (13)
32	Angle base—FMT (13)
33	Cosine angle simotic width—simotic subtense (8)
34	Angle base—simotic width (8)
35	Cosine angle inferior nasal bone width—inferior simotic subtense (9)
36	Angle base—inferior nasal bone width (9)

Note: UMMA is an acronym for the University of Michigan Museum of Anthropology.

given individual and the mean Z-score of that individual for all of the measures used in the analysis.

The mean Z-score for a single individual is calculated as follows:

$$\bar{Z}_j = \frac{\sum_{i=1}^{N} Z_{ij}}{N} \tag{2}$$

where Z_{ij} = average Z-score for all variables i ($1 \ldots N$) for individual j; and N = number of variables used (e.g., 36 if all of the variables used here are represented).

The C-score for variable i for individual j is therefore as follows:

$$C_{ij} = Z_{ij} - \bar{Z}_j \tag{3}$$

Other researchers have used multiple-regression procedures to interpolate missing variables, but we decided against this. In our analysis we used up to 21 measurements (table 3.2), but instead of calculating an average Z-score for only the individuals with all 21 measurements and their derived figures, we calculated average Z-scores if 15 or more measurements and their derived variables were present on any one individual. This method allowed us to base our average Z-scores on samples that were larger than those we would have had if we had restricted our usage to only those individuals that had complete data for all the measurements in our roster. We then used these average Z-scores to compute the C-scores for each individual, as shown in equation 3. Then we calculated a mean C-score for each variable by sex and by population and used these sex-specific mean C-scores to generate the male-female mid-sex mean C-scores that served as the basis of our group-by-group comparisons.

More formally, this procedure is as follows:

$$\bar{C}_{iJ} = \frac{\dfrac{\sum_{j=1}^{N_{Jf}} C_{ijJf}}{N_{Jf}} + \dfrac{\sum_{j=1}^{N_{Jm}} C_{ijJm}}{N_{Jm}}}{2} \tag{4}$$

where i = value of the variable; j = number of the individual; J = population sample (e.g., Ainu, Inuit, or Jōmon Japanese); J_f = females only from population J; J_m = males only from population J; N_{Jf} = number of females in population J; and N_{Jm} = number of males in population J. Therefore, C_{ijJf} represents the C-score for the ith variable for the jth individual among the females of the Jth population. $\bar{C}_{iJ}$, then, is the mean C-score for variable i in population J.

We then divided the sum of the mean C-scores for all of the variables by the number of variables that we used in order to generate a population C-score, or $\bar{C}_{Jmf}$, as follows:

$$\overline{C}_{J_{mf}} = \frac{\sum\limits_{i=1}^{N} \overline{C}_{ij}}{N} \qquad (5)$$

where $\overline{C}_{J_{mf}}$ = midsex mean C-score for population J; i = i^{th} variable; and N = number of variables (e.g., 36 if all were present).

We used the sample midsex mean C-scores ($\overline{C}_{J_{mf}}$) to generate a matrix of Euclidean distances, which we, in turn, treated by Ward's method to produce hierarchically organized clusters (Nelson 1998; Romesburg 1984; Ward 1963). Figure 3.1 depicts the clusters produced by applying this procedure to the C-scores generated for the samples listed in table 3.1. Similar clusters were also produced using Mahalanobis D^2 values. The complete set of D^2 values is presented in table 3.3. The D^2 procedure produces greater separation between the terminal twigs and is somewhat less useful in depicting ties between the branches. D^2 figures, however, do have the advantage of yielding typicality probability values. The figure can be checked against a χ^2 table for the appropriate degrees of freedom ($N - 1 = 35$, if all 36 variables were used). This method makes it possible to determine the probability that a given individual will be found in any of the populations against which it is tested (Albrecht 1992).

Results

Researchers previously used this approach to depict the relationships among the peoples of East Asia and the Pacific (Brace and Tracer 1992) and among the original inhabitants of the Western Hemisphere (Nelson 1998). For figure 3.1, we used the larger groupings of those two separate hemispheric sample sets to generate a single dendrogram. For both hemispheres, we used the prehistoric samples that were available. The Chinese Neolithic samples, which represent a time span from well over 7000 to just under 4000 B.P., are approximately contemporary with the Archaic in the New World. The Chinese Bronze Age from Anyang, which dates to about 3000 B.P., is approximately contemporaneous with the Early Woodland of North America. In both hemispheres, the later people clearly appear to be the direct descendants of their immediate temporal predecessors in place. To gain a worldwide perspective, we also included samples from Africa, Australia-Melanesia, and Europe. We should note that their apparent linkage to one specific macrocluster in figure 3.1

would be substantially reduced if we were to include all of the separate samples representing those continentally distinct populations.

The first obvious pattern in figure 3.1 shows that most of the aboriginal inhabitants of the Western Hemisphere were separated into two macroclusters. One cluster includes the peoples along the U.S.-Mexican border (with a tongue of prehistoric samples running up the main course of the Mississippi River) and those in Mexico and South America. This macrocluster has no close ties to populations represented in our samples of prehistoric and recent East Asians. Its links to Africa, Australia-Melanesia, and Europe appear to be just a general reflection of a pan–*Homo sapiens* identity. Figure 3.1 suggests that the attempts to derive all but the northernmost New World populations from a single entering group (Greenberg 1987; Greenberg et al. 1986; Merriwether et al. 1995) have been overly inclusive. Our conclusion is consistent with those of recent studies on Amerind linguistics (Hill, this volume; Nichols and Peterson 1996).

The second major macrocluster in the New World runs west to east along the U.S.-Canadian border and then south to where it meets the first macrocluster. This group includes the Northern Archaic and subsequent Woodland samples and runs from the Haida on the Northwest Coast to the Atlantic seashore and down the East Coast. The morphological continuity from the Archaic across the north to the Windover site in Florida indicates that this configuration has been in place in the New World since 9000 B.P.

The Patagonian samples from southern Chile, Argentina, and Tierra del Fuego are also tied to this macrocluster. Unlike the first macrocluster, this one has a clear-cut Asian link: to the early Holocene Jōmon of Japan and their living descendants, to the Ainu of the northern island of Hokkaidō, and to the Polynesians and Micronesians of Oceania (Brace et al. 1989). Because the Jōmon were in place in the Japanese archipelago much earlier than any of the other representatives of this macrocluster (Brace and Tracer 1992), it seems appropriate to call it the Jōmon-derived cluster.

The remaining macrocluster in figure 3.1 is clearly rooted in the East Asian mainland. Its oldest representatives in the Chinese Neolithic are closely tied to the peoples in the subsequent Bronze Age and to recent Chinese, Korean, and Japanese populations. Our Athabaskan sample from the Yukon drainage in Alaska is also tied to the core of this cluster. The northern and northeastern samples from Mongolia, Heilongjiang

TABLE 3.3 D^2 Matrix for the Samples Used in Figure 3.1

	1	2	3	4	5	6	7	8	9	10	11	12	13	14	15	16	17	18
1																		
2	1.3																	
3	5.7	6.5																
4	4.2	3.7	7.2															
5	26.3	26.9	25.8	25.6														
6	23.6	25.0	22.3	22.4	9.4													
7	25.7	24.9	21.3	22.2	35.2	28.9												
8	18.8	18.3	14.3	16.8	26.3	27.1	24.5											
9	14.9	14.5	10.6	13.0	15.4	14.4	18.0	8.0										
10	19.9	18.9	14.7	16.1	21.1	20.6	21.7	8.9	2.6									
11	8.6	10.3	12.0	9.9	27.0	23.7	25.0	14.8	14.4	21.8								
12	8.2	10.1	10.1	9.0	29.8	25.5	28.4	17.3	16.8	20.9	5.9							
13	4.8	6.5	6.9	10.4	26.8	20.2	21.4	16.5	11.9	18.4	8.5	10.4						
14	10.4	11.1	12.5	10.4	26.6	24.5	24.4	9.6	11.0	13.0	8.0	8.2	11.4					
15	10.1	11.3	14.2	12.1	30.4	31.8	30.2	13.2	17.7	22.0	7.0	7.5	12.2	6.7				
16	13.3	15.3	14.7	15.1	29.1	29.3	33.4	18.0	18.9	22.7	12.3	9.9	14.3	12.5	7.1			
17	23.7	25.8	14.8	26.6	32.1	29.3	18.6	21.9	17.9	23.9	23.0	21.0	20.4	21.4	25.6	25.5		
18	25.1	26.2	18.3	23.4	34.0	31.5	17.7	20.7	18.5	23.4	21.6	19.0	22.5	18.4	24.8	25.2	5.6	
19	25.8	27.8	20.3	27.6	26.7	19.5	16.8	19.2	12.6	18.6	20.3	25.5	19.1	24.0	27.5	26.2	11.8	16.1
20	15.1	14.6	12.0	17.1	17.9	18.6	13.4	13.1	8.8	14.2	14.5	18.7	17.9	15.8	17.9	18.9	10.2	13.1
21	15.8	16.6	11.0	17.3	22.2	21.8	16.2	23.0	15.4	21.7	19.4	20.1	16.3	21.1	21.4	22.0	10.5	14.1
22	19.1	18.7	13.0	15.7	28.1	18.8	18.7	16.2	10.2	12.7	17.3	17.7	16.7	13.6	22.4	22.5	13.9	11.9
23	19.5	17.9	14.9	20.1	27.4	21.7	20.9	15.3	7.6	9.1	21.2	23.6	16.8	16.0	23.1	24.8	18.5	20.9
24	21.2	22.3	16.1	21.5	29.3	21.9	22.0	15.4	11.2	13.0	21.6	21.0	20.3	18.4	22.8	23.7	16.0	20.8
25	15.2	15.6	9.4	14.4	23.7	18.5	12.6	14.1	10.3	14.3	16.5	14.2	12.1	11.6	18.7	19.5	6.6	6.1
26	22.8	24.5	17.3	22.9	32.1	25.9	9.9	24.9	18.6	25.3	19.7	23.5	20.0	21.0	28.0	30.2	14.0	17.5
27	26.1	27.3	17.6	23.4	33.9	29.7	17.6	19.0	16.8	19.7	23.6	20.0	23.5	17.1	21.8	22.5	9.1	5.9
28	25.2	25.0	20.0	26.6	36.7	32.6	9.1	29.2	23.0	29.7	27.4	30.6	24.9	28.9	32.9	35.8	12.6	15.7
29	15.3	15.3	10.0	14.7	22.0	19.8	9.0	17.7	11.7	17.1	15.4	18.1	14.8	16.9	20.6	21.6	10.9	13.7
30	15.6	16.0	9.9	14.8	26.9	23.4	10.5	16.8	13.0	19.4	12.9	14.3	12.4	13.8	16.3	20.0	8.9	10.4
31	19.3	19.4	12.4	18.1	27.3	21.6	5.1	16.8	12.1	16.0	19.0	21.5	15.4	18.8	24.2	24.5	10.7	12.4
32	23.7	25.0	17.9	20.9	32.7	24.5	7.4	22.0	17.5	22.0	20.7	22.4	19.9	18.3	22.7	24.4	13.0	12.3
33	28.2	28.3	21.6	23.5	35.3	36.1	11.3	19.9	19.5	23.6	23.2	26.3	25.7	18.2	22.3	25.6	16.0	11.4
34	37.8	38.2	31.8	32.8	46.5	45.8	18.8	26.1	28.1	32.7	29.6	33.6	33.7	27.0	27.5	33.1	21.6	15.6
35	21.6	21.0	17.0	19.0	31.6	30.3	5.2	19.4	16.4	20.8	19.9	24.3	18.6	19.0	23.9	28.5	14.3	11.7
36	30.9	32.4	24.5	32.1	42.0	39.2	10.5	33.0	28.3	36.1	27.0	32.4	27.9	28.8	33.3	36.4	16.5	19.1
37	24.2	23.6	19.3	22.4	34.2	29.5	5.9	23.4	18.2	22.9	25.0	25.4	20.3	21.8	28.9	31.0	12.5	12.2
38	7.3	8.6	4.6	9.3	22.1	18.4	21.1	17.5	12.1	17.8	10.8	7.6	6.7	14.2	14.4	13.3	17.0	17.3

Note: The names for the numbered samples and their Ns are listed in table 3.1.

in northeastern China, and the Chukchi Peninsula just west of Alaska all eventually tie with the Chinese-dominated cluster; however, they tie more closely with each other. The Inuit (Eskimos) tie first with the Chukchi and Manchu and second with Mongols from Ulaan Baator, Buryats, Aleuts, and the Yayoi rice agriculturalists, who moved into Japan from the tip of the Korean Peninsula just before 2000 B.P.

Measurements were made on three individuals who lived right on the temporal border between the New World Archaic and the preceding Paleoindian periods: the Buhl, Idaho, woman of 10,675 B.P. (Green et al. 1998) and the slightly younger Spirit Cave and Wizard's Beach, Nevada, males (Edgar 1997). As with specimens older than 10,000 years from other parts of the world (Brace 1998; Brace and Tracer 1992), the Buhl specimen

19	20	21	22	23	24	25	26	27	28	29	30	31	32	33	34	35	36	37
7.6																		
14.5	6.5																	
14.4	12.9	15.4																
14.6	11.3	16.3	8.9															
10.9	11.7	15.3	12.1	13.8														
11.4	7.1	9.0	8.3	14.0	12.2													
18.4	16.8	19.5	19.2	25.4	24.9	12.8												
16.5	14.0	13.0	12.2	19.9	17.9	6.7	16.2											
18.1	14.3	12.1	19.4	24.5	22.1	13.7	8.9	14.4										
12.9	7.2	7.8	11.5	16.4	16.6	8.2	5.4	10.6	5.6									
15.8	8.3	8.0	11.7	16.6	19.6	6.5	7.8	9.9	11.6	4.4								
10.2	8.0	12.0	12.5	14.7	13.7	8.2	9.8	13.6	10.0	6.9	10.1							
13.2	13.8	13.7	11.6	20.6	18.4	9.5	10.3	7.6	12.3	9.6	7.4	7.3						
20.1	16.1	17.9	16.8	25.7	25.7	12.5	12.4	6.9	12.3	9.1	10.5	11.2	6.1					
27.1	23.7	26.0	22.3	32.3	34.4	21.8	19.0	11.8	18.7	15.9	14.6	19.8	11.7	4.6				
17.0	10.2	18.3	17.0	20.2	22.0	9.3	9.9	14.6	10.4	8.6	7.8	6.8	11.1	8.6	13.9			
21.7	18.7	18.3	24.5	31.9	29.1	17.7	7.9	16.8	7.1	9.2	10.6	14.6	8.7	12.1	18.4	13.0		
16.9	13.0	17.4	17.2	21.0	22.8	10.7	10.2	16.8	12.3	11.3	9.5	6.1	10.4	12.2	18.5	5.0	14.3	
18.0	11.2	9.0	15.3	17.9	17.2	10.0	20.5	16.8	21.2	11.1	10.0	15.0	16.8	22.6	31.5	19.5	24.1	21.5

does not have a typicality probability higher than 50 percent for inclusion within any of the samples against which she was tested. The Wizard's Beach specimen does not fare much better, although it does achieve an 80 percent chance of inclusion in the Nevada–Great Basin sample. The Spirit Cave specimen also ties to the Nevada–Great Basin sample at a better than 95 percent level.

Discussion

Of the two macroclusters in the penultimate linking in figure 3.1, the first includes the New World groups from the southern parts of the United States on down through Mexico and South America. This grouping displays no particular link to any given Asian population, but it does show remote connections to other, more widely

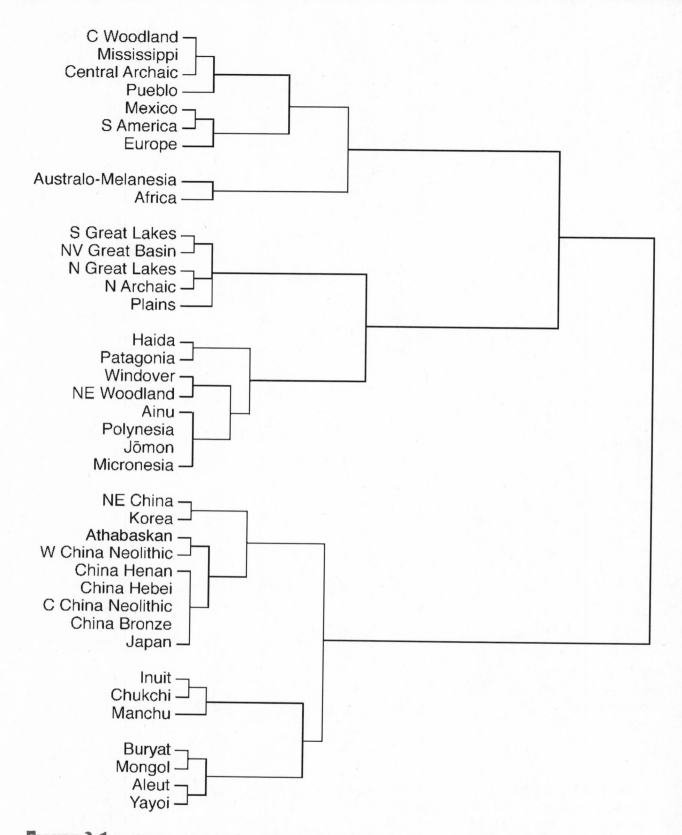

FIGURE 3.1 Euclidean distance dendrogram based on the C-scores from a sampling of pre-European Western Hemisphere groups run against a comparable distribution of samples representing East Asia, Oceania, Africa, and Europe. Ward's method was used to produce the clustering (Nelson 1998; Ward 1963).

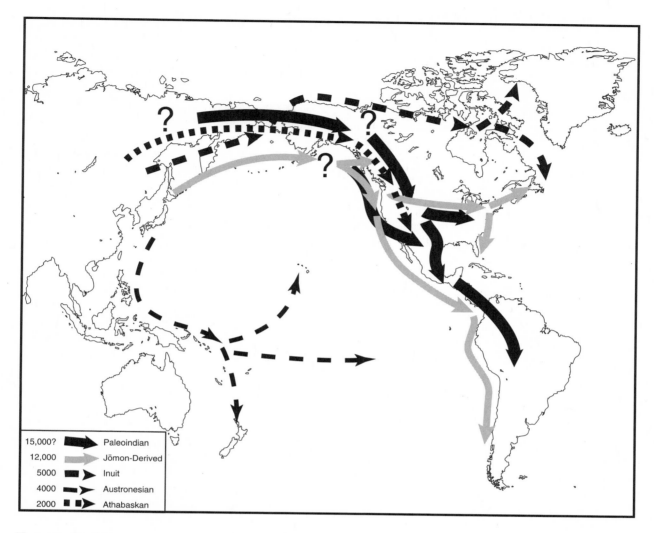

15,000?	Paleoindian
12,000	Jōmon-Derived
5000	Inuit
4000	Austronesian
2000	Athabaskan

FIGURE 3.2 Hypothetical routes and entry times (B.P.) for the four separate groups that initially populated the Western Hemisphere.

separated, Old World regions, such as Africa, Australia, and Europe. These connections suggest only an ancient pan–*Homo sapiens* identity. This conclusion is consistent with the idea that these New World groups are the descendants of the first Asian entrants into the Western Hemisphere during the late Pleistocene but well before the end of the last glaciation. The earliest occupants, the Paleoindians, would have established themselves in the more optimal resource-rich areas (Barton et al., this volume). The solid black arrows in figure 3.2 suggest the access route of the Paleoindians. Several questions remain, however, concerning their Asian origin(s) and their path into North America (i.e., did they travel along the West Coast or through the peri-

odically "ice-free corridor" between the Laurentide and Cordilleran glacial masses; Denton and Hughes 1981; Hopkins et al. 1982; Mandryk, this volume). Subsequent entrants would have avoided direct competition and pursued alternate subsistence strategies (Fiedel, this volume; Meltzer, this volume).

The second major New World cluster shown in figure 3.1 has evident Northeast Asian roots; its oldest representatives are in Jōmon Japan (Pearson et al. 1986). The strength of the Old World ties to these New World groups is consistent with the probability that the ancestors of this macrocluster arrived in the Western Hemisphere more recently than those of the first macrocluster. The intensive focus on aquatic resources that developed near the end of the Pleistocene (12,000 B.P.) along the Northeast Asian coast (Pearson et al. 1986) may have enabled these groups to exploit the marine and littoral resources of the Northwest Coast of North America and to extend that strategy southward along the coast. This focus is evident in the links between the Haida on the Queen Charlotte Islands off the Canadian coast just south of Alaska and the peoples of Washington and northern California. Nothing impeded further movement down the coast by the ancestors of these New World groups. The possibility that they did travel farther south is suggested by their ties with groups as far south as Patagonia and Tierra del Fuego. Their suggested path of movement is shown by the gray arrows in figure 3.2.

Because that southernmost New World sample clearly belongs in the Jōmon-derived cluster, one can ask whether these groups came straight across the Pacific, as did the settlers of Easter Island (Pawley and Green 1975). In order to produce typicality probabilities that would allow us to compare the groups in table 3.1 and the Paleoindian specimens, we had to reduce our variable list to 19, giving us 18 degrees of freedom. The D^2 values comparing the Patagonian sample with the Polynesian and Micronesian sample would not preclude its derivation from such a source, but the values for highland South America and Mexico were even lower, and the figure comparing them to the Haida is the lowest of all at 3.54. This value puts the South American and Mexican samples in the Haida category at more than a 99.5 percent probability. When these samples are compared with those of Australia, the D^2 figure is 14.93, which lowers the typicality probability to about 50 percent, a value that simply indicates they all qualify as human beings.

The aquatic subsistence strategy of the Jōmon-derived entrants at the northwest edge of the New World preadapted them to exploit the rivers, lakes, and marshlands that had opened by the end of the Pleistocene. These aquatic areas were created along what is now the U.S.-Canadian border as the glacial margins melted. An aquatic subsistence strategy would have allowed the entrants to survive without directly competing with the prior arrivals, the descendants of the initial megafauna hunters (Neves and Pucciarelli 1991). The focus on marine resource exploitation had also enabled another Jōmon-derived branch at the northwest edge of the Pacific Basin to move southward from the Japanese archipelago and then eastward into the Pacific

within the last 4,000 to 5,000 years. Figure 3.1 supports the craniofacial analyses that demonstrated that Jōmon Japan was the most likely source for the peoples of Polynesia in Remote Oceania (Brace and Tracer 1992; Brace et al. 1989). The suggested route of their movement into the Pacific is shown in figure 3.2 by the dashed-line arrows (Austronesian) going south from the Japanese archipelago.

The remaining New World populations to consider are those that occupied the northern edge and the northwestern interior of North America: the Aleuts, Inuit, and Na-Dene–speaking peoples. Their location and specialized lifestyle suggest recent entry into the hemisphere. They also tie convincingly with continental Asian populations, as shown in figure 3.1, which suggests that genetic drift has not operated long enough for them to have undergone significant differentiation from their presumed Asian ancestors (Dumond 1987; Park 1998).

The Inuit, who pursue an arctic lifestyle long noted for its adaptive sophistication (Dumond 1987), may represent an arctic adaptation by neighboring Manchu-related people, who may have used the Jōmon-derived aquatic subsistence strategies, enabling them to spread across the northern part of the Western Hemisphere during the last 5,000 years or more (Boas 1921; Fiedel, this volume; Park 1998). The Inuit craniofacial pattern retains its unity all the way from the westernmost parts of Alaska across the northernmost inhabited edge of the continent to Greenland and down the East Coast as far as Labrador (Nelson 1998). As shown in figure 3.1, the Inuit craniofacial pattern resembles that of the Mongol and related samples; it ties most closely to the Chukchi and Manchu pattern at the northeastern edge of Asia and latterly to those of other mainland Asian groups. Ties between the Siberian Chukchi, the Aleuts, and the North American Inuit illustrate the recency of a split between these groups of people, many of whom still speak mutually intelligible dialects and maintain communication across the channel separating the two continents.

The Na-Dene speakers are represented by the Athabaskans in the Alaskan interior, in the Yukon, and southward just inland of the coast at the northwestern edge of the continent. Linguistically these speakers have been called a "shallow family," with a time depth of only 2,000 years (Hill, this volume; Nichols 1997). Their southernmost constituents are represented by the Apache and Navajo, whose forebears had moved south from the Yukon and had reached the American Southwest only within the last 1,000 years (Agostini et al. 1997).

The Na-Dene–speaking peoples employed a subsistence strategy that involved pounding, leaching, grinding, and other plant-processing and nutrient-extracting methods characteristic of a Mesolithic lifestyle. Often derided as an illustration of trivial pointlessness, that extraordinary collection of "recipes"—published by Franz Boas (1921), who is otherwise honored as a founder of American anthropology—displays astonishing ingenuity. By focusing on the most unobvious aspects of the plant and animal worlds, their users could gain sustenance without coming in conflict with those whose focus was on marine resources or products of the chase. This ingenuity may be why the Athabaskan (Na-Dene)–speaking entrants into the northwest corner of North America were able to spread southward just inland of the coast but not extending out into the interior Plains.

Near the end of his career in the late 1930s, the noted linguist Edward Sapir looked to China for linguistic ties to Na-Dene languages (Darnell 1990). As shown in figure 3.1, the Yukon Valley Athabaskan (Na-Dene) speakers tie with Neolithic, Bronze Age, and recent China rather than New World groups. This link is consistent with research that shows the shared presence of the Type 2A manifestation of the JC virus (Agostini et al. 1997). Other genetic work illustrates relationships between Inuit and Na-Dene peoples and suggests that this link may be the result of common origins, although it could also be the consequence of more recent interchange (Szathmáry 1994). Analysis of mitochondrial DNA suggests Central Asia (Mongolia) as the likely origin of these recent New World entrants (Merriwether and Ferrell 1996; Schurr, this volume). Although the location of the Mongol samples in figure 3.1 does not seem to corroborate these findings, the considerable population diversity in present-day and ancient Mongolia suggests that further sampling is necessary before any solid conclusions can be made (Tumen 1994).

In comparisons with a series of Asian samples (Brace and Hunt 1990; Brace and Tracer 1992; Brace et al. 1989), the Na-Dene (Athabaskan), the Inuit (Eskimo-Aleut), the Haida–southern Canada–northern United States, and the Patagonia samples were the New World groups that most clearly displayed ties with recent Asians (fig. 3.1). Na-Dene speakers are the ones who tie most tightly and unequivocally to prehistoric and recent Chinese samples on the Asian mainland, a link that suggests they may represent the most recent entrants into the Western Hemisphere.

A similar picture is drawn when other clustering techniques are used. The neighbor-joining method, which used many of the same samples, as well as other prehistoric and recent samples from Europe to Mongolia, produced comparable clusters (Brace et al. 2001). Although this method has been declared to be superior to the Euclidean distance procedure (Omoto and Saitou 1997), the dendrograms produced by both are strikingly similar. Differences in assessments of group affinities, such as the apparent presence or lack of Jōmon and Ainu ties to the peoples of Oceania (Pietrusewsky and Ikehara-Quebral 2001), are due to the choice of comparison samples rather than the choice of clustering techniques.

Conclusions

However one may choose to interpret the relationships depicted in the craniofacial data presented here, the broad picture that these data illustrate is one of considerable diversity among prehistoric inhabitants of the New World. This concurs with genetic observations made on a more geographically circumscribed database (Merriwether et al. 1995; Schurr, this volume; Schurr et al. 1990). This prehistoric diversity is analogous to the variation observed across Asia (Brace and Hunt 1990; Brace and Tracer 1992; Brace et al. 1989), where a complex population history as demonstrated morphologically is supported by complex patterns of genetic microsatellite distribution (Chu et al. 1998).

Figure 3.2 depicts the probable entry dates and access routes for the groups discussed above. The first entrants into the New World, the Paleoindians, date back to the late Pleistocene, possibly to 15,000 B.P. or earlier. Their descendants now live in the region that extends from the southern United States through Mesoamerica to South America. The next group of entrants can reasonably be traced to Jōmon Japan just as the Pleistocene was coming to an end about 12,000 B.P. This group can usefully be described as the Jōmon-derived group. Their descendants are still demonstrably present along the Northwest Coast of North America, with offshoots down the coast as far as the southern tip of South America. About 7000 B.P., one major branch of the Jōmon-derived group extended eastward along the U.S.-Canadian border as far as the East Coast and then southward as far as Florida (Doran et al. 1986; Tuck

1976). The Inuit and Aleut may represent a later arctic incursion of a Manchu- and Mongol-related group within the last 5,000 years. The last New World entrants, the Athabaskan (Na-Dene)–speaking peoples, were evidently an offshoot of a Chinese-related population in Asia. Using the resources that lay inland from the coast, they entered via Alaska and spread into northwestern Canada; some reached the American Southwest within the last 1,000 years.

This project has clearly documented the magnitude of diversity among recent American Indian populations. It has also provided evidence for multiple migrations into the New World from diverse Old World sources. The results of this project provide enough reasons for questioning the generalization of the eighteenth-century Spanish traveler, Don Antonio de Ulloa, who is often quoted to the effect that "if you have seen one Indian, you have seen them all" (Stewart 1973:55). The evidence presented here shows that this is an unwarranted oversimplification.

Acknowledgments

C. Loring Brace received support for this project from the Committee on Scholarly Communication with the People's Republic of China (1980, 1985), the L. S. B. Leakey Foundation (1986), the National Science Foundation: BNS-9616298 (1986–1988), and the University of Michigan Museum of Anthropology (UMMA) Research Fund (1986, 1990, 1991, and 1992). A. Russell Nelson collected additional data for this research with support from the Rackham School of Graduate Studies and the Office of the Vice President for Research at the University of Michigan, the UMMA James B. Griffin Fund, the UMMA NAGPRA Fund, and an Acorn Grant from the American Academy of Forensic Sciences. The National Science Foundation: INT-9107991 (1992–1993) provided funding to C. Loring Brace and Pan Qifeng. J. M. and M. R. Boyle gave private backing to the project. We gratefully acknowledge these sources of support and collective tolerance.

We are also indebted to Professors S. M. Garn, J. Nichols, and J. M. O'Shea for critical readings of drafts of this chapter. Finally, we express our gratitude for the cooperation and help of Han Kangxin of the Institute of Archaeology in Beijing and of the literally dozens of collection managers and curators, who provided the access and working space that enabled us to collect the data used here.

4 Evaluating Historical Linguistic Evidence for Ancient Human Communities in the Americas
Jane H. Hill

Mainstream historical linguistics on the languages of the Americas during the last century has been very much a matter of fits and starts. A small and underfunded cadre of specialists has simultaneously confronted the need to document an enormous number of languages, including sorting out the structure of grammars and sound systems of otherwise unattested types and classifying the languages genetically and areally.

During the last 30 years, the classification of the languages of the Americas has been dominated by "splitters." If one considers only the languages of North America, most of the genetic units ("language families"[1]) in the six-part classification of North American languages advanced by Sapir (1929) in the 1920s and 1930s were reevaluated in the 1970s and rejected as being inadequately supported (Campbell and Mithun 1979). Efforts at long-range comparison and unification of the languages into very large-scale genetic groups by Matteson (1972) and Swadesh (1971) did not meet a positive reception. Since the publication of Campbell and Mithun's survey of Native American languages in 1979, which listed 62 families for North America, only one new proposal—that of Callaghan (1997) to combine Miwokan and Costanoan into Utian, and Utian and Yokutsan into Yok-Utian—has been more or less universally accepted. To the 60 families that are widely accepted by historical linguists for North America and Mesoamerica we must add at least 82 for Central and South America (Campbell 1997a), for a total of 142. Campbell (1997a) lists a total of 194 language families and isolates for the Americas.

Every Americanist knows that there cannot have been 194 separate entries into the Americas. Nor is it likely that the Pleistocene colonizers, however many groups there were, were large multilingual speech communities. The observable linguistic diversity in the New World must have developed from the radiation of only a few founder languages. An important goal of Americanist historical linguistics must be to retrace the steps of this radiation in order to form hypotheses about the

nature and affiliation of those pioneer linguistic communities. This retracing would take the form of reshaping the 194 families and isolates recognized by Campbell (1997a) from an enormous flat structure into a deeply nested hierarchy of linguistic groups that would model the differentiation from a small number of pioneer groups. However, work on reducing the number of families using standard historical-linguistic methods—the Comparative Method as described in, for instance, Anttila (1972) or Fox (1995)—has been discouragingly slow. Scholars are understandably eager to develop new methods that will give us a clearer picture of the linguistic situation at the dawn of New World prehistory.

In the last few years, two major models of this situation have appeared in the literature: Joseph Greenberg's (1987) three-family classification and Johanna Nichols's quite different four-part system (Nichols 1990, 1998, 1999). These proposals differ from each other in several ways: (1) the number of historically significant linguistic units, (2) the chronology, and (3) the links between American languages and those of the Old World. Both proposals use methods that are controversial within historical linguistics and that are difficult for nonlinguists to evaluate. My purpose here is to clarify these proposals and the methods that underlie them and to provide a critical evaluation. I neglect questions on whether these proposals are supported by data from archaeology or physical anthropology (see other contributions in this volume), and I consider only the kinds of questions that linguists themselves have been raising.

Foundational Concepts in Linguistic Classification

Probably the first principle that is taught in historical linguistics is the following: We can never prove that two languages are *not* related to each other! We can, however, muster better and worse evidence in favor of historical relationship. Linguists recognize four different sources of resemblances between languages. Briefly these are as follows (see table 4.1 for more detail):

TABLE 4.1   **Reasons Why Languages May Resemble Each Other**

Type of Resemblance	Reason for Resemblance	Test for Type
Genetic	Descent from a common ancestral community	Regular sound correspondences, shared aberrancies
Areal	Contact between distinct ancestral communities	Lexical resemblances, phonological and syntactic convergence, discourse convergence
Typological	Limited number of possible expressions of constraints on language form	No historical significance, so test not relevant (involves predictions of typological theory)
Chance	Statistical likelihood of accidental resemblances in components of complex systems	No historical significance (problem is to evaluate probability that resemblances are due to chance)

1. genetic: due to the descent of two or more languages from a common ancestral community,
2. areal: due to contact between two or more languages because of geographic association,
3. typological: due to the limited number of parameters for expression of the constraints on the human capacity for language, such that languages will inevitably share many common properties even in the absence of historical association,
4. chance: due to the likelihood of accidental resemblances in components of complex systems.

Only genetic and areal relationships are of historical significance. Two major methods are used to detect "genetic" relationship, or relationship due to descent from a common ancestor: identifying regularity of sound correspondence between two or more languages and identifying "shared aberrancies" between two or more languages. Regular sound correspondence can be exemplified by one element of the famous set of correspondences known as Grimm's Law in Indo-European. The sounds /f/, /θ/², /h/ in Germanic languages correspond with great regularity to /p/, /t/, /k/ in Latin, Greek, and Sanskrit, with the exceptions characterized by a small set of derived laws. Thus, if we know that a word starts with /p/ in Latin, we can predict that the "cognate" form in Germanic will start with /f/. An example is the Latin *'piscis'* and English 'fish.'

A classic example of a "shared aberrancy" is the suppletion (phonologically unlike forms that mean the same thing) in the system of comparatives and superlatives in English and German, where we find, respectively, 'good, better, best' and *'gut, besser, best.'* It is unlikely that the suppletion /gut ~ bɛs/ would have arisen

independently by chance in both languages, so we postulate that these forms must be inherited from the common ancestral language, Proto-Germanic.

The traditional test for areal, or contact, relationship is the identification of lexical items that have been loaned from one language to another. Dakin and Wichmann (2000:55) observe that such borrowings should exhibit the following properties: "(1) morphological transparency in one language, but not in the others; (2) the ability to reconstruct words to an earlier language stage in the linguistic family of one language, but not of others; (3) phonological and grammatical anomalies, in which non-native forms can be seen to be in conflict with the patterns of native words." Similar phenomena may be identified in morphology, syntax, and discourse. In many cases of language contact, several lines of evidence can be developed.

Advances in linguistic typology have greatly refined our ability to distinguish between historically significant resemblances among languages and those that merely reflect parallel typological developments. A very good example is the typology of word order. Word-order properties tend to hang together as a "suite" of syntactic features. Thus, if a language is "verb final," it will also tend to exhibit the following properties: It will have "postpositions" instead of prepositions to express location, it will have adjective-noun and determiner-noun order, possessed nouns will follow possessor nouns, and head nouns will follow relative clauses that modify them (Greenberg 1966; Hawkins 1983). If these were independent properties, the simultaneous occurrence of all of them in two or more languages might tempt us (and in fact did tempt previous generations) to propose that the languages were somehow historically con-

TABLE 4.2 Greenberg's Proposal

Most Ancient Taxa	Methods	Critique
Eskimo-Aleut	Comparative Method	Uncontroversial
Na-Dene	Comparative Method	Case for inclusion of Haida not considered demonstrated by some specialists
Amerind	Multilateral/Mass Comparison	1. Method cannot distinguish among resemblance types 2. Too much latitude permitted to admit resemblance 3. Errors of fact and execution 4. Poor statistical reasoning in arguments against likelihood of chance resemblance 5. Hypothesis represented as conclusion

nected. We now know, however, that these are not independent properties but count typologically as only one phenomenon, "head finality," which has been determined to be rather randomly distributed among the languages of the world.

Our understanding of what constitutes a "chance resemblance" among languages is more in dispute today than it was only a few years ago. Cases that 20 years ago would have been considered uncontroversial and canonical examples of chance resemblances—for example, Nahuatl *ma-* 'hand', Latin *manus* 'hand'; and Nahuatl *te:o-tl* 'divinity', Latin *deus* 'god'—are now being claimed by some advocates of long-range comparison to be traces of ancient genetic relationship. However, most mainstream historical linguists agree that it is quite easy to find chance resemblances, especially in the relatively short words of basic vocabulary. The reason for this lies in the following facts: (1) common words tend to be short (by Zipf's Law), (2) the number of sounds produced in the languages of the world is by no means infinite, and (3) different sounds have different likelihoods of showing up in different positions in the syllable. Thus in most languages, almost any consonant can initiate a syllable, but fewer can appear as syllabic "codas." The "nucleus" of the syllable is relatively restricted in nearly all languages to vowels and vowel-like, highly "sonorous" consonants, such as nasals. Although most scholars agree that chance resemblances are common, determining their likelihood is surprisingly technical. Linguistics does not have a history of quantitative methods. Several competing algorithms for determining the likelihood of chance resemblances under varying conditions are currently in circulation (e.g., Manaster Ramer and Hitchcock 1996; Oswalt 1998; Ringe 1992, 1999) in a community that is generally poorly qualified to choose

among them. It is important to emphasize that most mainstream historical linguists believe that a single convincing instance of a shared aberrancy of the good-better-best type or a series of solid sound correspondences is superior to any statistical method as evidence for relationship.

The Greenberg Classification and the Method of Mass Comparison

Against the brief background on standard methodology in historical linguistics outlined above, I turn now to recent proposals that use innovative methods. I first review the well-known classification advanced by Joseph Greenberg (1987; Greenberg et al. 1986). The major features and criticisms of this classification are outlined in table 4.2.

Greenberg proposed that the languages of the Americas include three major taxonomic components: Eskimo-Aleut, Na-Dene, and Amerind. Eskimo-Aleut is uncontroversial and represents the last colonization of the New World before the European invasions in the fifteenth and sixteenth centuries. Na-Dene is said to represent the descendants of a second colonization of the Americas. One of the six North American macro-families proposed by Sapir (1929), Na-Dene consists of three major components: Haida, Tlingit, and Eyak-Athabaskan. Some members of the very small community of specialists who are competent to evaluate this proposed affiliation argue that resemblances between Haida and the other languages are more likely due to areal contact than to common genetic inheritance. (Campbell [1997a] offers a useful, if opinionated, review of this controversy.) Amerind is the unit descended from the first colonizers and consists of all American languages not included in Eskimo-Aleut or Na-Dene. Amerind has been more or less categorically rejected by the Americanist linguistic community. Greenberg divides Amerind into 13 families; these are also generally rejected by practicing Americanists. By "rejected," I mean that most Americanists consider Greenberg's proposals as only hypotheses, which will never be substantiated.

The method Greenberg used to establish Amerind and its constituent families is known as "multilateral" or "mass" comparison (henceforth, MC). It consists of the following techniques. Word lists are assembled for as many languages as possible on a continental or even global scale. The lists should include only those lexical items and morphological elements believed to be particularly resistant to borrowing. (Such lists are themselves controversial but would include so-called "basic vocabulary," or the words for items that are part of common human experience rather than associated with specific cultures.) The linguist then searches the matrices constituted by the rows (lexical items) and columns (languages) for patterns of resemblances in sound and meaning. Seeing "resemblances" is as much a matter of art as of science, although certain rules of thumb concerning likely phonological and semantic developments are taken into account.

The tests of sound correspondence and shared aberrancy are not inherently part of the MC method, although they can be applied to its results. For this reason, most historical linguists believe that MC cannot, on its own, distinguish between genetic, areal, and chance resemblances. Greenberg argued that the scale of a multilateral comparison is pivotal: the more languages that are involved, the more likely it is that distinctive patterns of resemblance and nonresemblance unrelated to chance will emerge. In a classic example (to be discussed further below), Greenberg held that a pattern in the phonological form of pronouns, in which the first-person pronoun includes the consonant /n/ and the second-person pronoun includes /m/, argues in favor of Amerind because it is far more likely in those languages than in any other, and because it contrasts with other patterns, such as the one seen in Eurasia, in which /m/ is found in the first person and a consonant such as /t/ or /s/ appears in the second person. Indeed, Greenberg (1997, 2000) believed that the Amerind /n-m/ pattern and its Eurasiatic /m-t-s/ counterpart constituted "shared aberrancies" that prove genetic unity.

The MC method is problematic precisely because of its scale; it is very difficult to present in a convincing way the gestalt that is visible to an investigator. For example, Ruhlen (1996) shows what the experience of pattern recognition is like, on a very small scale, by using data for the major language families of Africa. The obvious method for testing for patterns in the matrices used by multilateral comparativists is cluster analysis. Indeed, Ruhlen (1991) presents a cluster analysis of the relationships of subfamilies within Amerind. In Greenberg's *Language in the Americas* (1987), however, the evidence for Amerind is presented not as a statistically established cluster that contrasts with other clusters, but as a list of sets of resemblances, which is exactly the format used for cognate sets in conventional comparative historical linguistic monographs and articles. Specialists examining these lists thus apply to them the criteria that they would apply to the publication of a genuine cognate set, and they object to the failure of Greenberg's lists to meet the standard of regular sound correspondence. They find that Greenberg was too permissive about semantic resemblance. They identify other methodological errors as well, such as the inclusion of primary kin terms and other words known to be prone to sound symbolism (such as words for concepts like "suck"), the inclusion of Spanish loan words that would have been obvious to an experienced Americanist, and the erroneous analyses of the morphology of individual lexical items. (See Campbell 1988 for a wide-ranging critique of Greenberg 1987.) Specialists have also identified problems in data management. Poser (1992) examined Greenberg's handwritten word lists, which are archived in the Stanford University library, and found many mistakes that were the result of copying errors, the transposition of items in lists, inadvertent shifts of a row or column, mislabeling of columns (where a column is a language), and the like.

Greenberg (1996) argued that the sheer scale of the comparison (his lexical lists were compiled by hand before computer database technology became available) makes such errors inevitable, and that on balance they constitute mere statistical noise that does not substantially undercut his basic conclusion. The difficulty of showing the large-scale patterning that he claims to see, however, not only makes the material vulnerable to specialists who are searching for mistakes, but also leaves the impression that there is a very high probability of finding chance resemblances. One reason for this high probability is that, although MC is implicitly a quantitative method, as pointed out above, there is no controlled sample. Multilateral comparativists seem to cherry-pick, searching through dozens or even hundreds of languages until a suitable set of resemblant forms is found. This search strategy is entirely appropriate in the mainstream comparative method, with which Greenberg was thoroughly familiar. In this method, a serendipitously discovered esoteric item of vocabulary in an obscure language, with only a metaphorical connection to the main semantic thrust of a lexical set, may provide the necessary evidence for refining a particular reconstruction. In the comparative method, however, the investigator is constrained by having to establish regular sound correspondences. In contrast, MC, as currently practiced, seems to accept neither this constraint nor the constraints of statistical methods, such as principled sampling.

The relatively uncontrolled techniques of MC, which permit several degrees of phonological and semantic latitude, make highly likely the occurrence of "false positives" in the form of chance resemblances masquerading as historical evidence. The poor quality of the data increases the problem. In this respect, Greenberg has been criticized for neglecting modern grammars and dictionaries, with reliable transcriptions and morphological analyses conducted according to contemporary standards, in favor of colonial-era sources (Campbell 1988). Greenberg and his collaborators (see Greenberg and Ruhlen 1992) have made very simple statistical arguments, stating that it is highly unlikely that the resemblances they identified are due to chance. Their quantitative arguments, however, are made, not on the totality of the multilateral comparison, but on individual sets of resemblances that are claimed to be historically significant. These statistical arguments against the possibility of chance resemblance have been rejected—in my view, properly—because Greenberg had no sampling strategy, nor did he have a rigorous quantitative characterization of trends in the population that he examined (for instance, the frequency of sounds in particular positions or the frequency of words of certain lengths). It is as if we were throwing dice without restricting the number of faces a die can have, the markings on each face, or the number of dice being thrown at one time; were allowed to continue throwing the dice until the winning set of faces appeared; and were then encouraged to remark on how very unlikely, and therefore probative of our skill or good luck, such a win was.

In summary, MC as practiced by Greenberg is a hybrid and ambiguous method. On the one hand, it depends on large-scale samples and gross pattern recognition, but without statistical controls. On the other hand,

it requires the artful capacity for recognition of rare, yet critical, examples that is essential to the successful practice of the comparative method, but without the control of regular sound correspondence. For these reasons, most linguists judge the MC as useful for generating hypotheses (for which it has been informally used for two centuries, as Greenberg noted), but not useful for yielding results that constitute strong evidence for genetic relationship.

Nichols's Methods and Classification

Nichols (1990) believes that multilateral comparison cannot reveal traces of historical events at the time depth of the original peopling of the Americas. This failure is due to the relentless effects of language change, which are likely to erase all phonological and semantic traces of a common ancestor within 8,000 to 10,000 years of the original radiation.[3] Her alternative method, which is described in detail in Nichols (1992), is to draw a predetermined sample of languages, consisting (where evidence is available) of one language from each of the world's approximately 250 linguistic "stocks," Nichols's term for those taxonomic units that enjoy general acceptance among linguists as being genuinely phylogenetic. In a few cases where stocks are known to be exceptionally "deep," her sample includes daughter languages from each major branch. The number of languages in her sample for each of her studies is carefully enumerated. Each language is categorized by the presence or absence of each member of a set of 11 (Nichols 1998) or 12 (Nichols 1999) "population markers." These are typological features characterized as being easy to identify in a decent grammatical description, relatively stable (that is, likely to endure for a very long time in a language), independent of one another, relatively resistant to spread by contact except under very favorable conditions, and of low frequency worldwide. Thus, when languages share population markers, it is likely to be of historical significance, indicating either an ancient common ancestor or an ancient zone of areal contact. (Nichols believes that, at this time depth, we cannot distinguish between the two.)

Nichols looks for two kinds of patterns in the distribution of population markers. The first involves statistically significant differences in the frequencies of individual markers among geographic areas. The second is the "clumping" of markers. The idea here is that, because population markers are typologically independent of one another, they should eventually distribute

TABLE 4.3 Nichols's Proposal

Most Ancient Taxa	Methods	Critique
"Eastern/Interior" colonization event	Population marker frequency in sample, no clumping of population markers	Validity of clumping and population-marker frequency as indexes of relative chronology or historical association not well established
"VS" languages, first Pacific Rim colonization event	Population marker frequency in sample, clumping of VS and numeral classifier markers	Ditto
"M" languages, second Pacific Rim colonization event	Population marker frequency in sample, clumping of (a) /m/ in second person and (b) identical stems for singular and plural pronouns	Ditto
Eskimo-Aleut	Comparative Method	Uncontroversial

more or less evenly over the globe, mixing randomly one with the other. The clumping of markers within groups of languages should represent the trace of some historical event, such as the descent of all from a common mother tongue or contact among those languages.

In Nichols's most recent proposals (1998, 1999), she argues for four major colonization events in the peopling of the Americas (table 4.3). Nichols argues that the trace of the first colonization event in the history of the Americas can be seen in a sample of 31 languages in eastern North America, where there is no "clumping" of population features. This, she believes, suggests the antiquity of these languages in the region. The second and third colonization events are represented in her sample by 45 languages of the Pacific Coast, the Gulf Coast, Central America, and the Upper Amazon in South America. The population markers in these languages "clump," dividing them into two mutually exclusive groups. Twenty-eight of these languages are "M" languages. In these languages, there is a strong association between one marker, the presence of /m/ as the initial consonant in the second-person pronoun, and another marker, the presence of identical singular and plural pronoun stems. The remaining 17 languages are the verb-initial ("VS") types, which are characterized by two population markers that often co-occur: verb-initial word order and numeral classifiers. Note that although the population markers themselves occur elsewhere in the world, these particular clumps of markers are found only in the Americas. The fourth population event is Eskimo-Aleut, a well-established genetic unit. For Nich-

ols, the languages of Greenberg's Na-Dene phylum are represented in the sample (at the family level), but they have no special status as a necessarily "late" entry into the New World.

Thus far, Nichols has presented the work summarized above only in conference papers, so no body of criticism can be summarized here. Furthermore, Nichols's methods are sufficiently innovative that evaluating them is somewhat challenging. Her samples are clearly defined. Her population markers are rigorously characterized, and identifying their presence or absence in a language is easy and replicable. The major critique thus far published on her work on American languages is Campbell's (1997b) reply to Nichols and Peterson's (1996) study on the distribution of the population markers /n-/ in first person and /m-/ in second person. Nichols and Peterson (1996) argue against Greenberg's claim that the /n-m/ pattern reflects the pattern in the common ancestor, Amerind. Instead they propose that the /n-m/ marker has what they call a "Pacific Rim" distribution, rather than being a specifically American phenomenon. (See Brace et al., this volume for comparable interpretations of skeletal morphometrics.) Campbell (1997b) argues that Nichols and Peterson have not shown that the pattern they found is due to anything more than chance. Nichols and Peterson (1998) replied in turn and criticized Campbell as being unfamiliar with statistical reasoning and consequently introducing inappropriate anecdotal evidence.

Despite the points that Nichols scores in her exchange with Campbell, her methods rely on certain as-

TABLE 4.4 Issues in Chronological Theory

Chronological Approach	Greenberg's View	Nichols's View
Uniformitarian: Language change proceeds such that at continental scales we can predict average rates of change	Lexical items will be replaced in basic vocabulary at a relatively slower rate than elsewhere	1. Lexical replacement eliminates ability to distinguish genetic vs. areal resemblances after 8–10,000 years 2. Fissioning of ancestral stocks into subfamilies occurs at a regular rate (1.6/6,000 years) 3. Population marker distribution will gradually approach the random in a geographic area 4. Similar frequencies of population markers index historical connections
Punctuationalist: Long periods of equilibrium are interrupted by episodes of very rapid language change	Admitted enormous diversity within Amerind is consistent with a very rapid colonization event involving the peopling of an empty continent, even at a date as late as Clovis	Generally rejects relevance of punctuation events at this time scale; enormous diversity of American languages thus argues for very ancient dates of original colonizations

sumptions, made prior to her statistical analyses, that definitely deserve challenge. For instance, she argues that her sampling strategy controls for time depth, so that all the entities in her sample are differentiated from one another by more or less the same spans of time. It is not obvious that this assumption can be sustained, so I will turn now to issues of chronology.

Uniformitarian and Punctuationalist Approaches to Chronology

The issue of chronology in historical linguistics has evolved over the last several years into a battle between uniformitarians and punctuationalists. Uniformitarians argue that the rate of differentiation among languages has been gradual and constant for the entire history of modern human languages. *Ceteris paribus*, the more language diversity there is in a region, the more ancient is the human habitation of that region. Punctuationalists (see Dixon 1997; Nettle 1999b) argue that the history of human linguistic differentiation has been irregular, with certain kinds of events favoring very rapid radiation of languages.

Most Americanists have been uniformitarians and have, like Nichols, argued in favor of a long chronology for the peopling of the Americas because of the very high level of diversity among American languages. Nichols is explicitly uniformitarian and is a long-chronology person, believing that the colonization of the Americas

began before the onset of the last glaciation (Nichols 1990). Greenberg's work includes both uniformitarian and punctuationalist elements. He is a short-chronology person, suggesting that Amerind is the linguistic trace of the Clovis colonization (table 4.4).[4]

The most extreme uniformitarian claim in linguistics, the glottochronological constant, has been largely abandoned. (I do not believe that either Nichols or Greenberg currently support it.) Uniformitarians, however, are still likely to believe that basic vocabulary is relatively resistant to borrowing and that lexical items will thus generally be lost from basic vocabulary at a slower rate than from other parts of the lexicon. Greenberg, one of the founders of lexicostatistical method, certainly believed this. Nichols does not compare basic vocabulary lists. However, based on an analysis of the number of subdivisions in the world's known language stocks, she argues that the fissioning of ancestral stocks into new subfamilies occurs at a relatively regular rate: approximately 1.6 new divisions every 6,000 years (Nichols 1990). This is why she believes that her sample exhibits a "controlled time depth": Each language in her sample is differentiated from its nearest genetic neighbor by about 6,000 years. Thus she claims to have mooted the accusations of anachronism that have plagued the mass comparativists, who, for example, may use resemblances between the forms reconstructed for Proto-Indo-European at 6500 B.P. and the forms collected from a Chukchi speaker in the nineteenth century to suggest a relationship between the two languages.

Nichols's idea about the rate of loss of "clumpiness" is also uniformitarian. We must imagine that at some point an ancestral community exhibited a "clump" of population markers, the result of some historical event. Over time, members of this clump will be lost and replaced by others. Verbs will shift from initial to final position, numeral classifiers will be lost, ergative-absolute marking will shift to nominative-accusative alignment, etc. If we assume that this process of loss and replacement of population markers proceeds at a relatively uniform rate, then we can imagine that "clumpy" regions of the world exhibit relatively young systems of linguistic diversity, whereas the linguistic diversity of regions where the distribution of population markers is more random is relatively ancient.

The punctuationalist position is so labeled and best summarized in Dixon's *The Rise and Fall of Languages* (1997). Dixon claims that we can make no uniformitarian assumptions about language change. Instead rates of linguistic change can be substantially altered by major cultural innovations that favor rapid expansion of groups possessing the innovation at the expense of others who lack it, or by environmental events, such as sea-level changes, glaciation, and volcanic eruptions. Long periods of relative stability can be interrupted in unpredictable ways by events that trigger periods of very rapid change. Dixon's views are adopted by Nettle (1999b) in a paper criticizing Nichols (1990). Nichols argued for a very long chronology in the peopling of the Americas, based on the very high number of language stocks and her proposed fissioning rate of 1.6 new stocks per 6,000 years. Nettle, however, argued that there was no reason to accept Nichols's uniformitarian assumption. Instead he suggested that the colonization of a virgin continent was a punctuational event par excellence (see Barton et al., this volume; Fiedel, this volume), which would precipitate the very rapid formation of new language stocks as the colonizing populations grew and spread through the new lands. Using standard archaeological dates for the first human colonizations of the world's major landmasses, Nettle found a rough global generalization: Linguistic differentiation (measured by stock density) and the age of first colonization are inversely correlated! Africa, the continent that has been inhabited the longest, has the lowest stock density[5], whereas the Americas, the most recently colonized continent, has the highest.

There are other reasons to doubt Nichols's chronology. Relatively few of the stock time-depths of the world can be tied to absolute dates. This is particularly true of New World stocks. We thus have no way of being sure about the chronological properties of Nichols's sample. This means that we also cannot be sure whether the "clumps" that she sees represent the traces of single events or multiple historical events that occurred over a long span of time. For example, Nichols states that her "VS" clump of languages exhibits a combination of verb-initial word order and numeral classifiers, and she suggests that the "VS" languages represent the trace of one of the original colonization events in the New World. These same markers are cited by Campbell et al. (1986) as important markers of the Mesoamerican linguistic area, a historical formation that is probably not more than about 4,000 years old because the verb-final Uto-Aztecan languages found in the Southwest and associated with the arrival there—between 4000 and 3500 B.P.—of cultivated maize must have left the zone of Mesoamerican influence before this areal formation developed (Hill 2001). If this is the case, these features cannot mark the trace of a Pleistocene colonization event.

Nichols's view of eastern North American languages is consistent with Dixon's idea of "equilibrium," that over a very long period a relatively random distribution of features might be produced. The linguistic landscape of the eastern United States, however, does not look like that of Australia, the focus of Dixon's research. There are a few large and several relatively small language families and isolates, but the genetic differences are well defined. This is in sharp contrast to the picture presented by the Pama-Ngyungan system in Australia, where hundreds of languages share many common features. Some Australian linguists claim that Pama-Ngyungan is a genetic unit, which either is of enormous age or is the result of a relatively recent linguistic discontinuity in which most of the original language stocks of Australia became extinct (see Evans and Jones 1997). Others, such as Dixon, believe that it is a very ancient areal formation. In contrast, Americanists specializing in the interior and eastern areas of their continent have not disagreed on the basic structure of the language families in the region.

It should be noted that Nichols is not 100 percent uniformitarian. She distinguishes between the relative conservatism of what she calls "residual zones" and the tendency to innovation in "spread zones" (Nichols 1992). She has argued that the kind of microdifferentiation of ecological zones found in some areas, such as

TABLE 4.5 External Affiliations

Greenberg	Nichols
Amerind: Sister to Eurasiatic (northern Eurasia)	1. Eastern/Interior: Population marker frequencies most like Australasia, "hardly any" affinity for northeast Eurasia
Na-Dene: Sister to Yeniseian within Dene-Caucasian (midlatitude Eurasia)	2, 3. Pacific Rim ("VS" and "M" colonization events): Population marker frequencies align with Australasia, coastal Asia, Siberia
Eskimo-Aleut: Daughter of Eurasiatic	4. Eskimo-Aleut 5. (Na-Dene, considered as genetic unit: No special affinities with Siberia shown by population marker frequencies in Na-Dene languages in sample; no reason to believe Na-Dene is necessarily late arrival)

the Pacific slope of the Americas, is conducive to the formation of linguistic "residual zones," where population markers are very stable and archaisms abound. The ecologies of the Pacific slope make this region of the globe particularly conducive to forms of ethnogenesis that favor very highly marked linguistic features, so that "stability" of relatively rare features is enhanced. However, this does not explain the "clumping" of features among the "M" languages.

Nichols (1998, 1999; Nichols and Peterson 1996) follows Gruhn (1988) in arguing that linguistic evidence supports a colonization event that involved expansion along the Pacific Coast of the Americas. However, unlike Gruhn, Nichols does not believe that this was the first or only colonization, nor does she suggest that the relatively low linguistic diversity of the North American interior and east is the result of geographic spread from an area of higher diversity. Instead Nichols argues that it is the trace of a separate, more ancient colonization.

Greenberg's proposal for Amerind is consistent with a punctuationalist view. If Dixon (1997) and Nettle (1999b) are correct, then the expansion into a new continent by a small founding population of hunter-gatherers could create enormous linguistic diversity in a relatively short period. Compared with the Old World, the New World contains relatively few examples of language spreads that erased this original diversity. Diamond (1997) has pointed out that the north-south orientation of the American continents, separated by the narrow Panamanian isthmus, restricted the spread of new domesticated plants; it could have also restricted language spread (Uto-Aztecan and the Arawakan languages are probably the exceptions). Thus a sizable sample of what may be primordial diversity was still visible after the European conquest.

Greenberg, Nichols, and the Question of Language Affiliations beyond the Americas

Finally I briefly review the question of affiliations of the languages of the Americas with those outside the continent, as proposed by Greenberg and his followers and by Nichols (table 4.5). Greenberg (1997, 2000) believes that the affiliations of the languages of the Americas are found in northern Eurasia. He argues that Amerind is a sister to Eurasiatic, a proposed genetic unit that includes Indo-European, Uralic-Yukaghir, Turkic, Mongolian, Tungus, Korean, Japanese, Ainu, Gilyak, Chukchi-Kamchatkan, and Eskimo-Aleut. Greenberg supports the claim that Na-Dene is a member of the Dene-Caucasian family, which includes North Caucasian, Sino-Tibetan, Yeniseian, and Na-Dene (Shevoroshkin 1991). Ruhlen (1998) recently proposed that the closest sister of Na-Dene within Dene-Caucasian is Yeniseian.[6]

Most historical linguists consider the proposals for Eurasiatic and Dene-Caucasian to be highly speculative. One problem that these constructs face is resolution with the theory of punctuated equilibrium: What events in the history of humanity could have produced a language family the size of Eurasiatic or Dene-Caucasian at the time depth that such families presumably represent? Greenberg (1997, 2000) believed that the Eurasiatic homeland is somewhere in eastern Eurasia. One possibility is that Eurasiatic is the trace of the expansion of modern humans into newly inhabitable areas at the end of the last glaciation, and that Eurasiatic and Dene-Caucasian are the only lineages that survive from the (presumably many) ancestral linguistic groups who lived in the periglacial regions of the Old World and who succeeded in this colonization effort.

Nichols's view contrasts sharply with that of Greenberg. She finds that the population marker frequencies for her first colonization event (in eastern North America) are most like those of Australasia and have "hardly any" affinity to those of northeastern Eurasia. She also finds that her American Pacific Coast languages constitute part of a larger Pacific Rim distribution, with affinities to Siberia, coastal Asia, and Australasia (especially the languages of the Australia–New Guinea interior as opposed to their northwest edges). She maintains that similarities to Siberia do not increase in the north and specifically states that there is no reason to believe that Na-Dene has any affinities in Siberia. She does not propose large multibranched genetic units. In fact, she does not propose any genetic units, holding that both genetic and areal phenomena are involved in the units that her method uncovers. She does, however, need a model for why people would spread around the Pacific Rim in two distinct waves, probably at a pre-Clovis date.

Conclusions

We are today confronted with two very different proposals by respected linguists about the peopling of the Americas. Neither is likely to be testable in the near term by conventional historical linguistic methods. Instead they must be evaluated on their own terms, according to the internal logic of their methods and the realism of their underlying assumptions. Both proposals are, of course, flawed. However, both could certainly be refined, especially by improvements in quantitative methods. In the work that Greenberg has begun, refinements of the database seem especially important. In Nichols's work, her formulations about the relatively uniform rates of language change require refinement, as does the addition, along principled lines, of new languages and linguistic markers to her sample.

I am convinced that conventional methods in historical and comparative linguistics, for all their utility in reconstructing the history of the last 8,000 years, are unlikely to be of much help in identifying the nature of late Pleistocene linguistic diversity in the Americas or the affiliations of American language groups with possible Old World cousins. Thus innovation in method, with all of its problems, is the only course open to us; both Greenberg and Nichols have unquestionably made important contributions to this project.

5 The Concept of Clovis and the Peopling of North America
Kenneth B. Tankersley

During most of the twentieth century, many North American archaeologists accepted Clovis as the oldest (ca. 11,600–10,800 uncal B.P.), unambiguous cultural complex in North America. At the same time, Paleoindian specialists inconsistently attached to Clovis such integrative terms as "culture," "pattern," "stage," "tradition," "assemblage," "category," "period," and "horizon" (Hester 1972:88, 92). Because of suggestions of cotraditions and archaeological sites that predate 12,000 uncal B.P., the spatial definition of the Clovis cultural complex is now being questioned (Frison and Bonnichsen 1996).

A major problem confronting our understanding of Pleistocene population movements in North America is an overly generalized interpretive framework for the Clovis cultural complex. Paleoindian specialists have tended to assume that the archaeological record for Clovis is totally homogeneous, that is, it does not vary in time or space (Ellis 1994:415). Spatially the Clovis cultural complex has been loosely defined as being widespread over North America (fig. 5.1), lying south of the area covered by the late Wisconsin ice sheets, and displaying a remarkable coarse-grained similarity in the artifact assemblage (Willig 1991:92). However, some archaeologists feel that the continentwide features of Clovis assemblages may be more apparent than real (Meltzer 1993a:295).

Clovis in Eastern North America

There is a long-standing debate about whether the term "Clovis" should be applied to eastern artifact assemblages that resemble those from western North America (Smith 1990:231). The geographic focus of Clovis studies has remained the Plains and Southwest regions, where the type sites and type specimens were first defined (Tankersley and Isaac 1990b). This focus, however, is not restricted to the West. In volumes 1–14 (1984–1997) of *Current Research in the Pleistocene*, 40 percent (40 out of 101) of the references to archaeo-logical investigations of Clovis sites and artifacts were about eastern North America, the region from the Mississippi River to the Atlantic Ocean and from the tip of Florida to Hudson Bay. In a recent comprehensive synthesis on the Paleoindian period of the southeastern United States (Anderson and Sassaman 1996), 83 percent (20 out of 24) of the chapters discuss Clovis sites or artifacts. Furthermore, major synthetic volumes covering the late Pleistocene archaeology of North America discuss the presence of Clovis in the East (e.g., Soffer and Praslov 1993; Straus et al. 1996, 1998).

Early Finds

Our geographic perspective of the Clovis cultural complex might have been eastern- rather than western-centric if the importance of Clovis artifacts had been recognized during the early excavation of three late Pleistocene sites in Kentucky, Missouri, and Wisconsin. Perhaps the earliest excavation of Clovis artifacts was made by William Goforth, a pioneer doctor. He excavated in several areas at Big Bone Lick, Kentucky, between 1803 and 1807 in search of an articulated mastodon skeleton. Goforth failed to find a complete specimen, but he did recover an extensive collection of mastodon bones, teeth, and three fluted projectile points, two of which are Clovis points. Although the significance of the artifacts was not recognized at that time, some of them may have been directly associated with the mastodon remains (Freeman et al. 1996:392). Additional Clovis artifacts were recovered from the site during later paleontological and archaeological investigations (Tankersley 1985, 1990a, 1996). Unfortunately, all of the artifacts have come from secondary contexts.

A similar excavation was conducted at a site in eastern Missouri (Freeman et at. 1996:392). In May 1839 Albert C. Koch traveled to what he called "Sulphur Springs," a few kilometers south of St. Louis. The locality in Jefferson County, Missouri, is known today as the Kimmswick site (McMillan 1976:84). Koch excavated several mastodon bones and a Clovis projectile

FIGURE 5.1 Geographic distribution of Clovis sites. See table 5.1 for site names.

point (Graham et al. 1981). The association between Clovis points and mastodons at this site has been subsequently verified (Graham and Kay 1988).

Another tantalizing discovery, but one less publicized, was made in 1897. The skeletal remains of a mastodon were found eroding from a stream bank in Richland County, Wisconsin, near the town of Boaz. A Clovis point manufactured from Hixton silicified sandstone was found in close association with the bones (Mason 1981:101; Palmer and Stoltman 1976).

The Northeast

Many archaeologists feel that the Clovis category should not be applied to any of the early Paleoindian artifact assemblages in the Northeast or Great Lakes region (see Howard 1990; McKenzie 1970:356; Ritchie 1957:11; Roosa 1962:263, 1965:98; H. T. Wright 1996: 431). Although the Clovis cultural complex was initially defined on nontechnological criteria, such as the hunting of certain types of game (Deller and Ellis 1992:131), it came to be viewed as part of a time-sequential complex. Thus, some archaeologists have even suggested that the use of the term "Clovis" should be restricted to

sites that have a direct cultural association with mammoth remains, fluted points, and uncalibrated radiocarbon ages greater than 11,000 B.P. (see Cox 1986). They caution that the use of the term "Clovis" in northeastern North America is unwise unless there is proof of contemporaneity with western Clovis (Spiess and Wilson 1987:50).

A significant problem in using the term "Clovis" in the Northeast is that most of the chronometric dates obtained from early Paleoindian sites are post-Clovis in age (MacDonald 1983:100). On the basis of radiocarbon dating, the artifact assemblages from Bull Brook and Wapanucket, Massachusetts; Debert, Nova Scotia; Vail, Maine; Templeton, Connecticut; and Whipple, New Hampshire appear to be the same age as Folsom sites on the Great Plains (Haynes 1977:166, 1983:25). On the basis of lithic technology, they are neither Clovis nor Folsom (Haynes 1987:86). In fact, most of the fluted points in the Northeast with more deeply indented bases display significant morphological deviations from Clovis (Haynes 1983:25; Howard 1990:259).

The early Paleoindian archaeological record of the Great Lakes region is recognized as the Gainey cultural complex or phase based on the work of Shott (1993). The artifact assemblages are believed to represent a Clovis-related people (Storck 1997:252). The Gainey complex is partly characterized by a Clovis-related fluting technology, but it is assumed to be post-Clovis in age (Deller and Ellis 1992:131; Shott 1993:1; Storck 1997:253). Gainey points are often referred to as Clovis because they are comparable to western bifaces in terms of size and outline. However, they notably differ from the classic western Clovis points by having a well-defined medial ridge, longer flutes, and deeper basal concavities and by displaying the removal of a broad, short flake over the primary flute scar on both faces. This flaking pattern is referred to as the "Barnes finishing" technique (Deller and Ellis 1988:254, 1992:28; Roosa 1965:97). Differences are also apparent in the artifact assemblages. Clovis assemblages lack backed bifaces, offset endscrapers, proximal endscrapers and sidescrapers, and backed and snapped unifaces. These artifacts have been found on Gainey complex sites in the Great Lakes region (Deller and Ellis 1992:132; Mason 1981:86).

The Midwest and Southeast

Unlike the Northeast and Great Lakes region, some of the flaked-stone artifacts in the Midwest and Southeast designated as Clovis resemble those from the Plains of North America closely enough to be incorporated into the type-site assemblage (Anderson 1990:164; Daniel and Wisenbaker 1989:326; Goodyear et al. 1990; Smith 1990:231). The densest concentrations of Clovis sites and artifacts have been found along the major rivers in the central portion of the United States (Anderson 1996). Based on the distribution analysis of Clovis fluted points, major concentrations have been identified in the Ohio, Tennessee, and Cumberland river valleys (Anderson 1996). More Clovis points have been found in three southeastern states than in all the stratified western sites combined (Haynes 1966). Mason (1962:235) argued that Clovis fluted points are so concentrated near these rivers that the southeastern United States could be considered the homeland of the Clovis complex.

Fluted points are more common east of the Mississippi River than west of it, and their range in size, form, and fluting technique is also greater in the East (Mason 1981:86; Morse et al. 1996:327). The great quantity of fluted points in the East may be the result of collector bias (Roberts 1962:263), a longer residence (Dincauze 1993a:286–288), a longer persistence of the technology in this region (Haynes 1977:165), or a higher replacement rate for these points. Some of the early Paleoindian sites in the Midwest and Southeast include split-bone and ground-ivory artifacts and evidence of an extensive blade industry (Dunbar and Webb 1996:331). Because these traits are characteristic of Clovis sites in the Plains of North America, it is plausible to suggest that some of the early Paleoindian sites in the Southeast and Midwest predate those in the Northeast–Great Lakes region (Barton et al., this volume; Deller and Ellis 1992:131).

Development of a Lexicon

The archaeological term "Clovis" is derived from a town in New Mexico near Blackwater Draw Locality No. 1, the type site of the Clovis culture. Although Dent, Colorado, is often heralded as the first documented site with Clovis artifacts in a late Pleistocene context (Figgins 1933), Ridgley Whiteman found a fluted biface along with mammoth bone at Blackwater Draw in 1929, three years before the discovery and excavation of Dent (Stanford et al. 1990:105).

Ultimately the significance of Blackwater Draw was found in its geologic contexts. In 1934 Ernst V. Antevs determined that the Clovis-artifact-bearing sediments were late Pleistocene in age (Haynes 1992). Fifteen years later, Elias H. Sellards and Glen L. Evans demonstrated that Clovis artifacts similar to those recovered from the Dent site in Colorado were included in a deposit that was below a stratum containing artifacts like those found at the Folsom and Lindenmeier sites (Haynes 1992; Stanford et al. 1990:105). This stratigraphic superposition provided the first unequivocal relative age for the Clovis culture, and one that was older than Folsom.

"Fluted Projectile Points"

With a limited database from a handful of recently excavated late Pleistocene sites, the archaeological community quickly noted morphological similarities among the bifacial flaked-stone artifacts recovered from the Dent, Blackwater Draw, Folsom, and Lindenmeier sites. In 1936 Shetrone proposed the locution "Fluted Flint-Blade Culture Complex" as an archaeological designation for sites that produced these distinctive bifaces. Griffin (1965:655) later modified Shetrone's wording to "Fluted-Point Hunters" to avoid the word "blade" which has a specific connotation in Old World archaeology. Shetrone's (1936) term "fluted point" was quickly adopted as a reference to any biface showing fluting or "grooving" on one or more of its faces (Griffin 1965: 655; Wormington 1949:33). Since its inception, the term "fluted point" has been applied to bifacial flaked-stone artifacts recovered from late Pleistocene and early Holocene deposits across the Western Hemisphere.

"Paleoindian"

In 1940 Roberts introduced the term "PaleoIndian" in a paper titled "Developments in the Problem of the North American PaleoIndian." Roberts (1940) used "Paleo-Indian" as a designation for artifact assemblages that appeared to be old on the basis of geologic, faunal, or typological evidence and for prehistoric cultures that were adapted to conditions unlike those of modern times. Initially "Paleoindian" was used in a cautious nonclassificatory sense (Whitthoft 1952). Griffin (1946: 40–43) extended Roberts's (1940) usage of "Paleo-indian" as an economic contrast to "Neo-Indian" (i.e., a Neolithic economic pattern). Griffin's Paleoindian assemblages included what are now known as Archaic assemblages of eastern North America (Whitthoft 1952:1). Like Griffin, Whitthoft (1952:1) viewed "Paleoindian" as a technological stage and equated it with a time horizon that lacked pecked and ground stone tools. Wormington (1957:3) modified Roberts's (1953) later definition of "Paleoindian" to specifically refer to the earliest inhabitants of the New World. Her definition included people who hunted extinct animals, occupied the western United States before 6,000 years ago, and made fluted points in the eastern United States (Frison 1998a:620).

For the most part, modern researchers use "Paleoindian" to describe one or more of the following: (1) the earliest well-documented culture in North America; (2) the characteristics of sites and artifact assemblages; and (3) a particular economic livelihood (Ellis and Deller 1990:37). Although most authors admit that there are problems with the term "Paleoindian," they have adopted its widespread usage in addressing North American cultures that predate 8000 B.P. (Frison 1998a:621). However, there is still no unanimity among researchers on how the term should be specifically applied or, for that matter, spelled (e.g., "Paleo-Indian" vs. "Paleoindian").

"Clovis Fluted Projectile Points"

Within a decade after the discovery and excavation of the Dent site, it had become obvious that more than one human group was present in North America during the late Pleistocene, and an archaeological means of separation was necessary. Typology thus became a fundamental part of Paleoindian studies (Frison 1973:155). In 1941 a symposium on Paleoindian terminology was held in Santa Fe, New Mexico, sponsored by the University Museum of Philadelphia and the Laboratory of Anthropology to attempt to bring some order to the typology of bifacial flaked-stone artifacts excavated from late Pleistocene and early Holocene contexts (Holliday and Anderson 1993:80).

The participants of the symposium decided that the term "Clovis fluted" would include projectile points that displayed the characteristics of bifaces recovered from the Dent and Blackwater Draw sites (Frison 1973:155–156; Wormington 1949:33–34). Although Krieger (1947) is often cited as the first publication containing the term "Clovis fluted point," Howard (1943) was actually the first person to publish the results of the Santa Fe conference and use the name.

The early definitions of "Clovis fluted projectile points" were based on several limited and generalized criteria (Deller and Ellis 1992:131). Clovis points were described as resembling Folsom points but larger, less finely flaked, with more rudimentary grooves but no earlike projections at the base (Wormington 1949:160). Subsequent Clovis point descriptions are more motley (Howard 1990). They range from simple discussions of morphology to complex morphometric attributes and detailed bifacial reduction techniques (e.g., Bradley 1991, 1993; Frison 1991a,b; Haynes 1980, 1983, 1993; Hester 1972; Tompkins 1993; Wormington 1957).

From a functional perspective, Clovis bifaces have a sharp point for initial penetration, sharp blade edges to cut a hole to allow penetration of the projectile, haft bindings, and a shaft (Frison 1989, 1993). The use of a foreshaft combined with basal fluting reduced the total hafting mass and its negative influence on projectile penetration (Frison 1989; Howard 1995). The lenticular cross section of the biface adds structural strength, and the overall symmetry allows the biface to be mounted in perfect alignment, which is absolutely necessary for withstanding the thrust needed to penetrate the hide of a large mammal (Frison 1993:241).

"Clovis Cultural Complex"

Initially Sellards proposed the name "Llano complex" for the assemblage of artifacts found in association with extinct animals at sites on the Plains, such as Dent, Blackwater Draw Locality No. 1, and Miami, Texas

(Wormington 1957:43). Artifacts of the Llano complex included hammerstones, a Clovis fluted projectile point, smaller nonfluted points, scrapers, and split-bone implements (Sellards 1952:17–18). Although many archaeologists subsequently emphasized the Clovis point, Sellards (1952:42) considered the split-bone tool industry to be more important in defining the complex. At the type site, split-bone artifacts are more abundant than any specific flaked-stone tool type, with the exception of sidescrapers (Hester 1972:92–118).

Sellards (1952:41–42) considered Clovis fluted points to be significant because they had been picked up on the surface at various places across North America (e.g., California, Wisconsin, Kentucky, Ohio, Indiana, Virginia, Mississippi, and Tennessee), indicating a wide geographic distribution of this type of artifact. However, fluted points were not the only distinctive Clovis artifacts found outside of the Plains (Byers 1962:249). Projectile points of split-bone and ivory have been found in mammoth-bearing deposits in central Alaska, southeastern Saskatchewan, southern Oregon, and northern Florida (Cressman 1942; Jenks and Simpson 1941; Rainey 1940; Simpson 1948; Wilmeth 1968). Several sites in the Southeast, including the Ichetucknee Springs locality, produced carved ivory artifacts similar to those manufactured from split bone at Blackwater Draw. Like the Clovis type site, the southeastern assemblage was deemed to be late Pleistocene because the ivory had been worked while it was still fresh and resilient, and proboscideans were extinct by the end of the Pleistocene (Dunbar 1991:186; Dunbar and Webb 1996:331).

As the inventory of artifacts from the Clovis type site grew in number and diversity, many archaeologists found Sellards's definition of the Llano complex to be too narrow. It also became increasingly apparent that artifacts recovered from Paleoindian sites in eastern North America closely resembled those from the Plains. In his landmark essay "The Paleo-Indian Tradition in Eastern North America," Mason (1962:235) used the term "Clovis complex" to refer to any site that produced Clovis artifacts. Hester (1972:118) later emphasized that the term "Llano" was geographically too restricted to be useful. He and others considered Clovis to be a continentwide complex, representing a single, pervasive, archaeological culture spread over an immense area (Dragoo 1990:3; Haynes 1964:1408, 1970:77; Hester 1966, 1972:178; MacDonald 1971:38; Purdy 1983:29; West 1983:377).

Most of the confusion in nomenclature is directly related to an overemphasis on minor attribute differences among projectile points (Dincauze 1993a:286–288; Hester 1972:118). We cannot assume a priori that early Paleoindians worked by blueprint specifications or that any deviation from a "standard" has typological significance (Mason 1962:273). The variations in individual collections of Clovis points from single component sites are as stylistically diverse as the variations between collections (Haynes 1964:1408). The historical prominence of typological discussions of projectile points is undoubtedly related to the relative paucity of Clovis material (Frison and Todd 1986:136).

Clovis is now recognized as a clearly defined Pleistocene cultural complex in North America (Haynes 1993:219; Wilke et al. 1991:242). The definition of the Clovis culture has been developing and expanding ever since Sellards's (1952) description of the Llano complex (Willig 1991:92). The Clovis culture is most fully defined in a series of essays by C. Vance Haynes Jr. (1980, 1982, 1987, 1993). Chronometrically the Clovis culture correlates with the Bölling-Alleröd Interstadial of the late Pleistocene. In terms of human activities, the Clovis culture is represented by a variety of sites, including big-game kills, habitations, quarries, mines, workshops, caches, and burials (Tankersley 1998a).

The Clovis culture is archaeologically indexed by a group of distinctive tools that include robust, lanceolate-shaped, bifacially flaked, fluted projectile points; large beveled bifaces used for a variety of tasks as well as for projectile point preforms; large blades and blade cores; cutting and scraping tools made on blades and large primary thinning and shaping flakes (e.g., knives, notches, raclettes, beaks, sidescrapers, concave scrapers, endscrapers, single and multiple gravers, burins, perforators, and combinations thereof); large crescents; and split-bone and ivory tools (Agenbroad 1988:63; Bradley 1993:254; Frison 1991a:322; Goebel et al. 1991: 72; Haury et al. 1959:22; Haynes 1982:388, 1993:219; Hester 1972:92–118; Jelinek 1971:16; Stanford 1991:2; Tankersley 1991).

Formal split-bone and ivory tools include a shaft wrench (Haynes and Hemmings 1968); a burnisher-billet (Saunders et al. 1991); awls or punches; a bone bead; semifabricate (mammoth tusk chopped around the circumference and snapped in two at a point halfway between the tip and alveolar sheath; Hester 1972; Saunders et al. 1990); and beveled, cross-checked base compound points and foreshafts (Frison and Stanford

1982; Gramly 1993; Haynes 1966, 1980, 1982; Hester 1972; Lahren and Bonnichsen 1974; Mehringer 1988; Sellards 1952; Stanford 1991; Tankersley 1997). Other bone and ivory artifacts consist of both expedient and carefully shaped rib segments with rounded and polished ends, scrapers, fleshers, flakers, and inscribed objects (Bradley 1997; Hannus 1990a:86; Haynes 1980: 116–117, 1982:388–389, 1993:219).

For cross-dating, ivory, split-bone, and stone projectile points are the most reliable (Frison 1983:111). The sharp gravers and boring tools of the Clovis complex are quite distinctive, but even some of these are found in later Paleoindian assemblages (Frison 1991b: 125–126). Other artifacts, such as large butchering tools, are not temporally distinct because similar types were retained over long periods of time. Although some individuals or groups preferred one tool type or assemblage over another, the basic process of butchering large animals changed little over a period of 11,000 years (Frison 1991b:311).

Clovis Technology

Bradley (1993) shows that there has been a major change in the way Paleoindian specialists view Clovis artifacts. These artifacts are no longer just classified and compared. The days of simple morphofunctional typologies are gone (but see Clark, this volume). Clovis artifact assemblages are now analyzed with the understanding that they became part of the archaeological record as a result of dynamic behavioral systems (e.g., manufacture, use, reuse, and discard) and natural site-formation processes. This approach to the study of Clovis artifacts has led to a substantial amount of information on the complex nature of Clovis technologies (e.g., Bradley 1993:251; Kelly and Todd 1988; T. M. Morrow 1996).

Stone- and Bone-Tool Manufacture
The material culture of Clovis is best viewed in terms of a technocultural complex or technological system (Hannus 1990a:86; Saunders 1990:137–138). Major elements of Clovis tool technology include a distinctive and sophisticated percussion biface reduction technology and an industry of split-bone and ivory objects (Frison 1990:101–102, 1991b:39–41; Frison and Bonnichsen 1996:312; Goebel et al. 1991:72; Huckell 1979). Clovis bone and ivory technologies include expedient tools and preforms manufactured by chopping, splitting, and flak-ing large, long mammal bones and ivory (Hannus 1990a; Saunders et al. 1990). Formal tools and weaponry were completed by carving, grinding, scoring, incision, drilling, and polishing (Bradley 1997; Hester 1972; Saunders et al. 1991; Sellards 1952; Tankersley 1997).

Clovis lithic technology is well known for its selection of high-quality tool stone, excellence in percussion flaking, and production of a highly efficient tool and weaponry assemblage (Bradley 1991; Frison 1991b; Gardner 1983; Goodyear 1989; Haynes 1982). Clovis flaked-stone technology was wholly integrated as a fail-proof reduction strategy with minimal loss of high-quality stone (Wilke et al. 1991:245). It included the production of prismatic blades that were struck from both ends of large, prepared cores using indirect or direct soft hammer percussion. Platforms were rejuvenated by the removal of core tablet flakes (Collins 1990: 73–74).

Biface Technology
Clovis flaked-stone technology is also characterized by bifacial tool and flake manufacture. Most Clovis tools are either bifaces or the products made from large flakes created during the biface-manufacturing process (Bradley 1991:370). Bifaces served as fully functional implements and as highly portable flake cores (Bradley 1991; Goebel et al. 1991:72; Huckell 1979; Kelly and Todd 1988). Bifacial cores are a popular theme in models of lithic technology constructed for mobile hunter-gatherers (Sassaman 1996:78).

The technology of biface manufacture is as much the signature of Clovis as is the morphology of its characteristic projectile point (Frison and Todd 1986:136–137). This argument was first made in 1962 with the cultural assessment of artifacts excavated from the Union Pacific Mammoth site in Wyoming. This area was designated a Clovis site in the absence of a single fluted projectile point. The artifact assemblage consisted of two bifacial knives and a graver found in direct association with mammoth bones. Union Pacific was included in the Clovis site inventory because the bifacial flaked-stone artifacts were consistent with Clovis technology (Haynes 1992:363; Irwin et al. 1962). The same assertion was later made for other sites, such as Colby, Wyoming. The projectile points were stylistically outside the Clovis norm, but the technology was unmistakable (Frison 1983:111).

Although some Clovis bifaces were made on large flakes, most were the result of several stages of reduction (Tankersley 1998b). They were typically made from a bifacial preform in a reduction sequence that included platform preparation and distinctively spaced, large, percussion flake removal. Early-stage bifaces were fashioned with minimal platform preparation and relatively few flake removals. Platforms were produced by roughly flaking a bevel along the biface edge and were not subsequently ground (Collins 1990:74). Large, deliberately spaced, bifacial thinning flakes were removed in sequence from prepared platforms. Broad flakes extending completely or nearly the width of the biface were removed in a "controlled" *outrepassé* flaking technique (Bradley 1982, 1991, 1993; Frison 1991b). The base was beveled with a few flake removals to serve as the first fluting platform. Subsequently the opposite face was beveled to accommodate the second fluting (Collins 1990). The end of the flute was removed, after which flakes were sometimes removed from the lateral margins, thus intruding on the flute scars (Bradley 1991; Collins 1990:74). A Clovis point outline was maintained through all but the earliest stages of bifacial flaking (Collins 1990). Final trimming was often accomplished by pressure flaking, resulting in even edges and symmetrical outlines centered on the flutes (Collins 1990:74).

A finished Clovis point is a well-designed piece of flaked-stone weaponry. It was the first piece of such weaponry in the world that was designed well enough to allow hunters a dependable and predictable means of pursuing and killing a large mammal on a one-on-one basis (Frison 1993:241).

Interregional Variation

With the tremendous increase in early Paleoindian research comes the realization that the composition of Clovis assemblages varies greatly between sites (Willig 1991:92). Clovis tool kits vary from site to site, and regional technological differences have been noted between artifact assemblages (table 5.1; Haynes 1982: 385; Johnson 1996:197; Shott 1997; Tankersley 1998c: 9). Furthermore, tool-kit composition seems to vary in distinct geographic regions (Bonnichsen 1977:200).

Blades and Blade Cores

True blades are an important cultural trait of the Clovis cultural complex. They were first identified in the Green cache ($n = 17$) at the Clovis type site, Blackwater Draw, New Mexico (Green 1963). Retouched blades were later

reported from the habitation portions of the site (Hester 1972). Since their initial discovery, blades have been found on Clovis sites in both western and eastern North America (table 5.1).

In addition to Blackwater Draw, blades have been reported from the Richey-Roberts cache in Washington (Gramly 1993); the Murray Springs site in Arizona (Goebel et al. 1991; Haynes and Hemmings 1968); the Fenn cache in Wyoming (Frison 1991a,b); the Kevin-Davis cache (Young and Collins 1989), Kincade Rockshelter (Collins et al. 1989), and Aubrey sites in Texas (Ferring 1989, 1990; Stanford 1991); the Busse cache (Hofman 1995) and Sailor-Helton sites in Kansas (Mallouf 1994); and the Domebo site in Oklahoma (Leonhardy 1966). In eastern North America, blades have been described and illustrated from the Bostrom site in Illinois (Tankersley 1995, 1998c; Tankersley and Morrow 1993; Tankersley et al. 1993); the Wells Creek Crater (Dragoo 1973) and Carson-Conn-Short sites in Tennessee (Broster and Norton 1992, 1993, 1996; Broster et al. 1994; Nami et at. 1996); the Cactus Hill (McAvoy and McAvoy 1997) and Williamson sites in Virginia (Haynes 1972; McCarey 1983); the Little River complex (i.e., the Adams, Boyd-Ledford, Ezell, Roeder, and Coombs sites) and Big Bone Lick site in Kentucky (Freeman et al. 1996; Gramly and Yahnig 1991; Sanders 1988, 1990; Smith and Freeman 1991; Tankersley 1985, 1989a,b, 1990a, 1996); and the northern Florida site cluster (Dunbar 1991; Dunbar and Waller 1992).

Clovis blades are an important cultural trait because they are seemingly similar and widespread over North America (fig. 5.2). There is, however, a significant caveat: It is extremely difficult to distinguish between true blades struck from large prepared cores, bladelike flakes struck from bifacial cores, and bladelike flakes fortuitously produced during the early stages of bifacial reduction. They all display minute platforms, almost no bulbs, minimal ripple marks on the interior surface, and a strong curvature. It is quite probable that the Richey-Roberts, Fenn, and Domebo artifacts are bladelike flakes struck from bifaces rather than true blades.

At this juncture, prepared blade cores are the only unequivocal evidence for a Clovis blade-and-core industry. The distribution of Clovis blade cores is restricted to the Plains, Midsouth, and Southeast (fig. 5.3). The morphology and manufacture of blade cores vary between regions. On the Plains, blade cores are unidirectional or bidirectional, polyhedral, and conical (Collins 1990:73–74). In the Midsouth and Southeast, most Clovis blade

TABLE 5.1 Presence (+) or Absence (−) of Key Artifacts at Forty Clovis Sites in the Contiguous United States

Site	Blades	Blade Cores	Split-Bone Points & Foreshafts	Ivory Points & Foreshafts	Red Ochre	Flute Abrasion & Crescents
1. Anzick, Montana	−	−	+	−	+	−
2. Dietz, Oregon	−	−	−	−	−	+
3. Richey-Roberts, Washington	+	−	+	−	+	+
4. Simon, Idaho	−	−	−	−	+	−
5. Blackwater Draw, New Mexico	+	−	+	−	−	−
6. Escapule, Arizona	−	−	−	−	−	−
7. Lehner Ranch, Arizona	−	−	−	−	−	−
8. Murray Springs, Arizona	+	−	−	−	−	−
9. Naco, Arizona	+	−	−	−	−	−
10. Aubrey, Texas	+	+	−	−	−	−
11. Busse, Kansas	+	−	−	−	+	−
12. Colby, Wyoming	−	−	−	−	−	−
13. Crook County, Wyoming	−	−	+	−	+	−
14. Dent, Colorado	−	−	−	−	−	−
15. Domebo, Oklahoma	+	−	−	−	−	−
16. Drake, Colorado	−	−	−	−	−	−
17. Fenn, Wyoming	+	−	−	−	+	+
18. Kevin-Davis, Texas	+	+	−	−	−	−
19. Kincade Rockshelter, Texas	+	+	−	−	−	−
20. Lange-Ferguson, South Dakota	−	−	−	−	−	−
21. Lubbock Lake, Texas	−	−	−	−	−	−
22. Miami, Texas	−	−	−	−	−	−
23. Powers II (Sunrise Mine), Wyoming	−	−	−	−	+	−
24. Sailor-Helton, Kansas	+	−	−	−	−	−
25. Sheaman, Wyoming	−	−	−	+	+	−
26. Union Pacific, Wyoming	−	−	−	−	−	−
27. Bostrom, Illinois	+	−	−	−	−	−
28. Kimmswick, Missouri	−	−	−	−	−	−
29. Ready, Illinois	−	−	−	−	−	−
30. Hiscock, New York	−	−	−	−	−	−
31. Shawnee Minisink, Pennsylvania	−	−	−	−	−	−
32. Sheriden Cave, Ohio	−	−	+	−	−	−
33. Big Bone Lick, Kentucky	+	−	−	−	−	−
34. Cactus Hill, Virginia	+	+	−	−	−	−
35. Carson-Conn-Short, Tennessee	+	+	−	−	−	−
36. Little River Complex, Kentucky	+	+	−	−	−	−
37. Northern Florida Site Cluster, Florida	+	−	−	+	−	−
38. Thunderbird, Virginia	−	−	−	−	−	−
39. Wells Creek Crater, Tennessee	+	+	−	−	−	−
40. Williamson, Virginia	+	+	−	−	−	−

Sources: References for each site are as follows: (1) Frison and Bonnichsen 1996; Jones and Bonnichsen 1994; Lahren and Bonnichsen 1974; Wilke et al. 1991; (2) Willig 1990; (3) Gramly 1993; Mehringer 1988; (4) Butler 1963; Titmus and Woods 1991:120; Woods and Titmus 1985; (5) Green 1963; Hester 1972; Johnson 1991; Saunders et al. 1990, 1991, 1994; Sellards 1952; Warnica 1966; (6) Hemmings and Haynes 1969; (7) Haury et al. 1959; (8) Goebel et al. 1991; Haynes and Hemmings 1968; (9) Haury et al. 1953; (10) Ferring 1989, 1990; Stanford 1991; (11) Hofman 1995; (12) Frison and Todd 1986; (13) Tankersley 1998a; (14) Figgins 1933; (15) Leonhardy 1966; (16) Stanford and Jodry 1988; (17) Frison 1990, 1991a,b; (18) Young and Collins 1989; (19) Collins et al. 1989; (20) Hannus 1985, 1990a,b; (21) Holliday and Johnson 1990:30–31; Johnson 1991:222–223; (22) Holliday et al. 1991, 1994; Johnson 1991; Sellards 1952; (23) Stafford 1990; (24) Mallouf 1994; (25) Frison 1982a,b; (26) Haynes 1992; Irwin et al. 1962; (27) Tankersley 1995, 1998c; Tankersley and Morrow 1993; Tankersley et al. 1993; (28) Graham and Kay 1988; Graham et al. 1981; (29) J. E. Morrow 1995, 1996; Tankersley 1998c; Tankersley and Morrow 1993; (30) C. V. Haynes Jr. 1991a,b; Laub 1990, 1994, 1995, 1996; Laub and McAndrews 1997; Laub et al. 1988, 1994, 1996; (31) McNett 1985a,b; McNett et al. 1977; (32) Tankersley 1997; Tankersley and Landefeld 1998; (33) Tankersley 1985, 1989a,b, 1990a,b, 1996; (34) McAvoy and McAvoy 1997; (35) Broster and Norton 1992, 1993, 1996; Broster et al. 1991, 1994; Nami et al. 1996; (36) Freeman et al. 1996; Gramly and Yahnig 1991; Sanders 1988, 1990; Smith and Freeman 1991; Tankersley 1989a,b, 1990a,b, 1996; (37) Dunbar 1991; Dunbar and Waller 1992; (38) Gardner 1974, 1977, 1983; Gardner and Verrey 1979; (39) Dragoo 1973; (40) Haynes 1972, 1985; McCarey 1983.

FIGURE 5.2 Geographic distribution of Clovis blades. See table 5.1 for site names.

cores are conical, but some are spherical, turtleback shaped, or hoof shaped. Southeastern blade cores are also unidirectional. Although bidirectional cores have been found in the Southeast, they are block flake cores rather than prepared polyhedral blade cores.

Beveled Split-Bone Points and Foreshafts

Split-bone points and foreshafts have been found in both western and eastern North America (fig. 5.4; table 5.2). They have been reported from the Anzick burial in Montana (Lahren and Bonnichsen 1974), the Richey-Roberts cache in Washington (Gramly 1993), Blackwater Draw in New Mexico (Saunders et al. 1994), and Sheriden Cave in Ohio (Tankersley 1997). In the Far West (i.e., Anzick and Richey-Roberts), split-bone foreshafts are cylindrical or subangular and have double-beveled ends and a cross-hachured surface. Incisions are also present along the lateral margins of the beveled ends. Other specimens from the Anzick burial are cylindrical, with one end conically tapered and the opposite end beveled and cross-hachured (Frison 1991a:323). In the Southwest and Great Lakes region (i.e., Blackwater Draw and Sheriden Cave), split-bone points have

a single-beveled end that is cross-hachured and an opposite end that is tapered to a point. Like Anzick, the Sheriden Cave specimens are notched behind the cross-hachured bevel and display a small notch in the center of the beveled end. However, it differs from the Blackwater Draw points because circuit incisions cover the entire exterior of the base.

Decorative motifs or embellishments appear on three split-bone foreshafts from the Richey-Roberts site and on one of the two split-bone points from Sheriden Cave. Two of the Richey-Roberts specimens exhibit a zipperlike design incised into their interior surfaces along the centers of the artifacts (Bradley 1997; Gramly 1993). The third specimen shows a series of small curved incisions on the outside of the bevel. The Sheriden Cave split-bone point displays a diagonal ladderlike design along the lateral margin (Tankersley 1997).

Beveled Ivory Points and Foreshafts

Although ivory points and foreshafts have also been found in both western and eastern North America (fig. 5.5), their distribution is quite different from that of split-bone artifacts. Compare figure 5.4 to figure 5.5.

FIGURE 5.3 Geographic distribution of Clovis blade cores. See table 5.1 for site names.

TABLE 5.2 Presence (+) or Absence (–) of Bone and Ivory Artifacts at Clovis Sites in the Contiguous United States

Site	Raw Material		Beveling		Incisions		Damage		
	Bone	Ivory	Single	Double	Margin	Circuit	Tip	Bevel	Motif
1. Anzick, Montana	+	–	+	+	+	+	+	+	–
3. Richey-Roberts, Washington	+	–	–	+	+	–	–	+	+
5. Blackwater Draw, New Mexico	+	–	+	–	–	–	+	+	–
25. Sheaman, Wyoming	–	+	+	–	–	+	–	–	
32. Sheriden Cave, Ohio	+	–	+	–	+	+	+	+	+
37. Northern Florida Site Cluster, Florida	–	+	+	+	+	+	+	+	+

Sources: See Table 5.1 for site references.

Carved and polished ivory foreshafts and points have been discovered on the northern Plains and in the Southeast (table 5.2). Twenty-one ivory points and foreshafts have been recovered from a cluster of inundated karst sites (e.g., the Aucilla-Wacissa Rivers, Itchtucknee River, Santa Fe River, and Steinhatchee River) in northern Florida (Dunbar 1991:193–210; Dunbar and Waller 1992:293). A single specimen was excavated from the Sheaman site in Wyoming. The proximal end is terminated with an angular bevel that is 75 millimeters long and perfectly straight. Like the split-bone specimens, the Sheaman specimen exhibits a pattern of double cross-hachures on its proximal end (Frison 1982b:144–147).

Although the Sheaman site specimen is identical in cylindrical cross section and overall dimensions to the

FIGURE 5.4 Geographic distribution of Clovis split-bone points and foreshafts. See table 5.1 for site names.

Florida specimens (approximately 203 × 14 × 12 mm), it differs in that incisions are absent along the lateral margins of the base. The Florida ivory points and foreshafts typically display deep circuit incisions that cover the entire exterior of the base. Decorative motifs or embellishments also appear on two of the carved and polished ivory points from northern Florida. One has a zigzag pattern, and the other has a series of parallel lines that transverse the long axis of the artifact (Bradley 1997; Haynes 1982).

Red Ochre

Red ochre (i.e., hematite) has long been recognized as an element of the Clovis complex (Roper 1987, 1989, 1996). It is most strongly associated with the cultural context of the Anzick burial in Montana (Frison and Bonnichsen 1996; Jones and Bonnichsen 1994; Lahren and Bonnichsen 1974; Wilke et al. 1991) and with caches of bifaces, such as Richey-Roberts in Washington (Gramly 1993; Mehringer 1988), Simon in Idaho (Butler 1963; Titmus and Woods 1991:120; Woods and Titmus 1985), Fenn and Crook County in Wyoming

(Frison 1990, 1991a,b; Tankersley 1998b), and Busse in Kansas (Hofman 1995). Red ochre was also found as a coating on artifacts and a living surface at the Sheaman site in Wyoming. The Clovis cultural component at Sheaman contained an oval area stained with red ochre (2.5 × 3 m and 5–8 cm thick). The ochre included small particles, lumps, and coverings on bison bones, both inside and out (Frison 1982b).

Presently the only known Clovis red ochre mine is the Powers II site (also known as 48PL330 and the Sunrise Mine site) in the Hartville Uplift region of southeastern Wyoming (Frison 1991a). The mine is located at a spot where a distinctive variety of specular and earthy hematite is exposed at the surface. Clovis points, bifaces, flake tools, hammerstones, anvil stones, and debitage have been recovered from in situ deposits of tailings, implying that some of these tools were used in the mining process (Stafford 1990; Tankersley et al. 1999).

Red ochre has been recovered from Clovis sites in only the Far West and northern Plains (fig. 5.6). The Busse cache in extreme northwest Kansas is the south-

FIGURE 5.5 Geographic distribution of Clovis ivory points and foreshafts. See table 5.1 for site names.

easternmost appearance of ochre in a Clovis context (Roper 1996:41). Red ochre has not been recovered from a single Clovis site in eastern North America. This is significant because red ochre is prevalent in later Archaic assemblages in eastern North America and because enormous deposits of red ochre are found in the Lake Superior region of northern Michigan, Wisconsin, and Canada. Large quantities of red ochre are also present in New York, eastern Tennessee, and northern Alabama (Vanders and Kerr 1967:191). Despite these vast high-grade hematite deposits, red ochre is conspicuously absent in Clovis sites that lie east of the Plains.

Flute Abrasion and Crescents

Some of the Clovis points manufactured from obsidian on the western High Plains and Great Basin display longitudinal scratching or abrasion on the flute scars (Frison 1991b:48; Tankersley 1994a,b; Wormington 1957:61) Large bifacial crescents have also been reported from a few Clovis sites in this region (Frison 1991a:330, 1991b:48). It is significant that neither flute

abrasion nor large bifacial crescents are known from Clovis sites east of the Plains (fig. 5.7).

Tool Stone

The complexity and diversity of Clovis tool kits may vary more by the distance to tool-stone sources than by any other analytical dimension (Dincauze 1993a). Clovis lithic assemblages dominated by nonlocal tool stones have been documented on the Plains. For example, 85 percent ($n = 11$) of the Drake cache in Colorado is manufactured from Alibates chert (Stanford and Jodry 1988), and 89 percent ($n = 8$) of the Crook County cache in Wyoming is manufactured from large flakes of a Green River Formation, silicified sediment known as Tiger chert (Tankersley 1998b). The principal sources of these materials are more than 500 kilometers from the cache sites (Miller 1991:467).

In the Midwest, exotic tool stone has also been found in Clovis sites. Indeed, Knife River flint has been recovered from the Bostrom site in Illinois and on sites in adjacent St. Louis County, Missouri (Tankersley 1991, 1998c). The source of this material is in southwest-

FIGURE 5.6 Geographic distribution of Clovis red ochre. See table 5.1 for site names.

ern North Dakota, more than 1,500 kilometers from the findspot. Unlike the Crook County and Drake caches, the Bostrom site includes only trace amounts of exotic stone (i.e., less than 1 percent; *n* = 1).

Variability within the Clovis Complex

It is quite possible that regional variability in Clovis artifact assemblages may be due to sampling error. Blackwater Draw is the only known site with an ivory semifabricate and billet (Saunders et al. 1990, 1991, 1994), and Murray Springs is the only known site with a shaft wrench (Haynes and Hemmings 1968).

The variation within site assemblages appears to be as great as the variation among sites (Haynes 1964: 1408). Much of this intra-assemblage variation may be explained by idiosyncratic behavior, differences in raw material, and tool rejuvenation (Stanford 1991:2). In other words, some of the typological disparity may be due to site function and specific resharpening, use, and discard behaviors (Bradley 1991:370; Dincauze 1993a: 286; Haynes 1982:385; Judge 1973:256; Tankersley

1998c:7). Although certain Clovis artifacts are recognizable in pristine form, specific characteristics that enable researchers to discriminate types may be obliterated from the reworked form of an artifact (Frison 1991b:17; Justice 1987:17). It seems equally possible, however, that regional variations are temporally or culturally based (Willig 1991:94).

Variations in Clovis assemblages may be due to driftlike behavioral divergence across space. As in Mason's (1981:86) analogy from linguistics, some of the variations may be linked to habits of local speech. Some of the relatively small variations tend to be concentrated in local regions. These variations may be thought of as technological and stylistic dialects peculiar to people in two widely separated regions. Thus, technological variations may be the result of local, functional, or stylistic variations on a general theme (Mason 1981:86).

Temporal and cultural differences are alternative explanations for regional variation (Willig 1991:93). Assemblage variation may represent distinct regional but contemporary cultural and technological adapta-

FIGURE 5.7 Geographic distribution of Clovis-point flute abrasion and large bifacial crescents. See table 5.1 for site names.

tions by different social groups (Willig 1991:93). However, the co-occurrence of distinct regional adaptations must be validated with chronometric dating. Unfortunately radiocarbon dating does not presently contain the temporal resolution that is needed to show that Clovis variability is distributed as contemporaneous geographic differences (Deller and Ellis 1992:131; Taylor et al. 1996).

Variation may be the result of design experimentation in response to continuous changes in environmental conditions. Variation may be viewed as points on a continuum of ongoing behavioral adaptation (Howard 1995:291). Regrettably the very definition of an artifact type renders time as an artificial series of discrete segments and the cultural process that operates through it as a series of artificial episodic changes (Clark, this volume; Shott 1993:101).

Regional variation in the technological attributes of Clovis artifacts may be the result of enculturation or acculturation (Collins 1990:74). Researchers usually explain Clovis cultural radiation as the product of a colonizing or migrating culture, and the resulting ar-

chaeological horizon as the product of the rapid movement and growth of human populations that encountered a pristine resource-rich landscape (see chapters 11–15). An alternative explanation is that the Clovis radiation may have been the result of a technological advance that conferred an adaptive advantage (Anderson 1996; Pearson, this volume).

Regardless of whether we look to Europe, Asia, or somewhere in between for a cultural progenitor, Clovis artifact assemblages represent a generalized Upper Paleolithic tool kit (Jelinek 1971:20). The Clovis cultural complex has at least ten traits in common with Upper Paleolithic sites in Europe and Asia: an ivory semifabricate; ivory billet large blades and blade cores; endscrapers; burins; a shaft wrench; split-bone and ivory points; flaked-bone, unifacial flake tools; and red ochre (Haynes 1987:85–86; Saunders et al. 1990, 1991). All of these artifacts have been found on the Plains of western North America. Traits that are missing in the East, such as red ochre, can be traced northward to Alaska (e.g., the Broken Mammoth site) and westward to Siberian Upper Paleolithic sites (Yesner 1996b:261).

If we assume that cultural traits diminish with increasing distance from their source area, then the Clovis cultural complex likely spread from the north to the south and from the Plains eastward to the Southeast. There are, however, geographic discontinuities. If these distributions are real and are not the result of archaeological visibility, then other cultural mechanisms, such as independent invention and more localized technological adaptations in response to changes in Pleistocene environmental conditions, must be considered.

Acknowledgments

Research for this essay was partially supported by a grant from the National Science Foundation (Grant SBR 9707984). The generous help and cooperation of the World Lithics Institute, Lithics Casting Lab, and Pete Bostrom are greatly appreciated. Discussions with Jim Dunbar, Forest Fenn, George Frison, C. Vance Haynes, Calvin Howard, Dennis Stanford, and David Webb were invaluable. I also want to express my sincere gratitude to Michael Barton, Geoffrey Clark, Georges Pearson, and David Yesner for the opportunity to contribute to this volume.

6 A Review of Bioarchaeological Thought on the Peopling of the New World

Kamille R. Schmitz

Notions about the nature of the original human colonization of the Americas have long been prevalent in the popular and professional literature. New World migrations have been linked in popular accounts to the wanderings of the lost tribes of Israel, to people from the continents of Atlantis and Mu, and to various groups of transoceanic travelers from Europe and Asia. In 1781 Thomas Jefferson speculated that the Americas might have been colonized by boatloads of Old World migrants. (The existence of the Bering Land Bridge was uncertain at the time.) He thought Asia was a more likely source than Europe because of geographic proximity and because of some appreciation of the physical features shared by Native Americans and East Asians (Stewart 1973:70).

Fairly consistently since the 1930s, the professional literature has identified the Asian-Alaskan route (i.e., the Bering Land Bridge, a 1,000-kilometer-wide subcontinent during the Last Glacial Maximum) as the most likely itinerary for the initial and any subsequent colonists up to historical times. It is now well established that the initial colonization took place many millennia before any sailing craft of the sort envisioned by Jefferson had evolved. Unlike some Native Americans who believe in special creation (e.g., Joe Watkins, as reported by Hall [1998]), most professional anthropologists and archaeologists agree that the ancestors of American Indians and Eskimo-Aleuts were modern humans *(Homo sapiens)* and that they originated in the Old World, where all human macroevolution took place. Modern humans are members of a single species; no fossil or living New World primates are ancestral to, or closely related to, *H. sapiens*. During the two centuries that have elapsed since Jefferson offered his prescient remarks, developments in chronometry, typology, geochronology, physical anthropology, linguistics, genetics, and related fields, as well as archaeological excavations at numerous sites, have vastly increased our knowledge about the first Americans. Although there is a broad consensus about Native American origins, several fascinating issues have yet to be fully resolved. Among them are details concerning the (1) routes, (2) number of migrations, (3) geographical source area(s) of the earliest colonists, (4) chronology of migration events or processes, (5) kinds of technologies that would have facilitated immigration, (6) numbers of migrants, (7) existence (or not) of residual ethnographic traditions, and (8) inferences about the nature of the languages spoken by the first immigrants.

Routes to the New World

Although there are several scenarios for the peopling of the Americas, six models of quite different inferential credibility are found in most modern anthropological literature. Two involve transoceanic voyages, two envision coastal drifts, one proposes an interior migration, and one combines coastal and interior migration.

The Transpacific Route

Perhaps the least plausible route proposed by a professional anthropologist is Rivet's (1957) theory of rafting from Australia to South America by way of Antarctica. Based largely on statistical comparisons of South American and Oceanic cranial and linguistic data, Rivet envisioned Southeast Asians sailing to Australia, then following the coastline of Antarctica, and eventually landing on the southern coast of South America. With the discovery of relatively credible evidence for 60,000-year-old archaeological sites in Australia (e.g., Roberts et al. 1994a,b), the settlement of which would have required watercraft, modern workers have now revisited this theory and have proposed dates as early as 40,000–15,000 years ago. Although humans were almost certainly present in Australia by 40,000 years ago, there is no empirical support for a colonization this early in the New World. Transoceanic voyages of adventurers, such as Thor Heyerdahl, using primitive balsa rafts and reed boats demonstrate the possibility of such colonizations, but the probability is another matter altogether.

The Transatlantic Route

Linked to formal similarities in bifacial foliate projectile points, a second transoceanic model resuscitates an old idea that originated with Hibben (e.g., 1941). In the version proposed most recently by Stanford and Bradley (2000), the first American colonists made a transoceanic voyage across the North Atlantic rather than the Pacific. Spanning a distance of some 5,000 kilometers, Upper Paleolithic Solutrean people from northern Iberia crossed the Atlantic in skin boats at the time of the Last Glacial Maximum (21,000–15,000 years ago). Instead of following the icy Antarctic Coast, the migrants traveled along the southern border of the North Atlantic pack ice that probably extended more or less continuously from northwestern Europe to northeastern North America during the late Pleistocene. In this model, Spanish Solutreans are seen as the source population of colonists who arrived in Virginia and Pennsylvania sometime between 17,000 and 14,000 years ago, bringing with them their distinctive projectile point technology, the putative source of Clovis. There is some technological and typological support for this perspective, but formal similarities are more likely due to convergence than historical relationships (see Clark, this volume).

The Pacific Coast Route

The third model, invoked to explain "early" South American sites and the absence of Clovis or Clovis-like points on that continent, is the Pacific Coast route. This model proposes the following scenario: The founding population, which originated in Northeast Asia, had a maritime adaptation in its Asian homeland and leapfrogged southward along the Pacific Coast of North America, where ice-free refugia existed. The migrants eventually reached the southern tip of South America by around 12,000 years ago (Fladmark 1978; but see Pearson, this volume). More a process than an event, this migration is thought to have occurred between 30,000 and 15,000 years ago. There is substantial archaeological, chronological, and contextual evidence for this scenario at the site of Monte Verde in Chile (Dillehay 1989, 1997b), although this evidence has been questioned by some workers (e.g., Carlson 1996).

The Land-Bridge/Interior Route

The fourth model proposes that big-game hunters crossed the Bering Land Bridge from their homeland in Northeast Asia between 15,000 and 12,000 years ago and headed south through western Canada via an ice-free corridor that existed between the Laurentide and Cordilleran ice sheets, which covered much of North America during the Wisconsin glaciation (Rutter 1980). Once through the inland corridor, they rapidly radiated throughout the rest of North and South America, leaving traces of their passage in the form of megafaunal kill sites associated with Clovis projectile points. There is abundant chronological, paleoenvironmental, and archaeological evidence for this scenario, most importantly in the interiors of Alaska and northeastern Siberia (Hoffecker et al. 1993; West 1996b).

The Land-Bridge/Coastal Route

The fifth model was proposed by Laughlin (1986), who believed that all Native Americans are derived from Northeast Asian migrants who entered the New World along the southern coast of the Bering Land Bridge. Once in the Americas, they quickly developed adaptations that are manifested in several distinctive technological traditions, which are linked archaeologically, ethnographically, and historically to several distinct populations. This view is partly based on the idea (developed in the 1950s by paleobotanists but now largely abandoned) that the Beringian subcontinent was largely a polar desert that was incapable of supporting human populations (Guthrie 1990).

The Land-Bridge/Interior and Coastal Route

The sixth model combines the late Pleistocene, land-bridge/interior, big-game-hunting model with one that postulates coastal drift by a different group of maritime coastal-adapted foragers, who were followed by a forest- and riverine-adapted group (Dikov 1993; Greenberg et al. 1986; Orekhov 1987; Turner 1971). This model is supported by chronological, spatial, morphogenetic, linguistic, genetic, and archaeological evidence in Alaska and Siberia.

Discussion

From the brief description of these models, it is evident that discovering the probable route for the peopling of the Americas involves refining aspects of the Siberian-Alaskan Bering Land Bridge transit. To assist in this refinement, I will use four primary lines of diachronic evidence: (1) the timing of initial entry, (2) the source of the parent population(s), (3) the number of migrations, and (4) the technological inventory of the migrants.

The two transoceanic routes are the least parsimonious because they depend upon the largest number of unwarranted assumptions. Both the Spanish Solutreans and the Australians are assumed to have had boat-building technologies capable of sustaining long voyages on the open sea. Although the Australians must have had such technologies, there is no evidence that the Solutreans did (Straus 2000). The migrants presumably had already developed a maritime adaptation, complete with the aspects of material culture that would seem to be prerequisite for these voyages (e.g., fishing nets, spears, harpoons, fishhooks, and fuel to cook food). In Stanford and Bradley's (2000) North Atlantic model, the Solutrean seems to be equated with a "culture" (i.e., an identity-conscious group of people), a notion that has been contested by other researchers (e.g., Clark 1999a, this volume). If South America had been colonized by Southeast Asians via Australia, one would expect to find evidence of their passage in Polynesia. No sites of the antiquity proposed for this migration have been discovered in that region. Although fraught with problems, the transpacific theory has captured the imagination of the general public and, according to Auel (1998:1675), "makes a better story."

Although its existence and its "permanency" have been questioned over the years (e.g., Mandryk, this volume), the ice-free corridor, which was about 100 kilometers wide and extended 2,400 kilometers from north to south, apparently existed because the Cordilleran and Laurentide ice sheets did not fully coalesce. The corridor would have run from the 49th parallel to the Arctic Ocean, between the Western Interior Plains and the Rocky Mountains (Reeves 1973). Reeves (1973) found no evidence that the Laurentide and Cordilleran ice sheets had fully coalesced, and he concluded that these continental glaciers would have presented no real barrier to population movement. Fladmark (1979) contested this conclusion, however, and noted two major problems with it: (1) the sparse palynological evidence fails to support the existence of the corridor; and (2) glacial lakes, outwash plains devoid of vegetation, extremely severe winter temperatures, and lack of evidence for any significant biotic communities (a "photosynthetic desert") would have precluded use of the corridor for migration. The outwash streams, ponds, and lakes might have served as a better flyway for migratory waterfowl than one that crossed the endless miles of continental ice. Birds could have been one source of food in the corridor during their biannual migrations in the spring and fall. An analysis of faunal re-

mains from Bluefish Caves by the Canadian Museum of Civilization and the Canadian Museum of Nature (1999) identified bones of migratory birds that lived in the region from 25,000 to 10,000 years ago. Based on cut marks and other evidence, these researchers believe that migratory fowl were exploited by humans as the birds passed along their habitual flyways. Although the Alaskan interior was once thought to be a polar desert during glacial maxima, recent evidence has cast doubt on this assumption. Elias (1997) found no evidence for steppe tundra biomes on preserved fragments of the land bridge. He believed that the land bridge was dominated by mesic-shrub tundra associations throughout the Last Glacial Maximum. During the tardiglacial around 14,000 years ago, summer temperatures on Beringia were apparently comparable to those of today; a gradual warming trend followed until about 9700 B.P. (Elias 1997).

In addition to the uncertainty surrounding the duration and existence of the ice-free corridor and the flora and fauna that it might have sustained, critics of this theory often note that very few archaeological sites have been found along the corridor. Haynes (1971) identified five isolated Clovis-point findspots within the putative boundaries of the corridor. Recently a Plainview spear point, which was geologically dated to about 11,000 B.P., was recovered in a well-stratified site in the Lake Minnewonka area of Alberta, Canada (Simon 1999). This site lies in what would have been the ice-free corridor.

The coastal migration route also makes the assumption that the founding population exhibited a maritime adaptation and possessed boats. However, because the pack ice extended farther south than its present location, an open-sea voyage was actually unnecessary. Fladmark (1979) proposed that a chain of large sea-level refugia would have enabled a human migration southward along the Pacific Coast. Invoking linguistic data, Gruhn (1988) argued that the great number of language isolates, subdivisions of language phyla, and diversity of languages along the entire Pacific Coast was the result of one or several coastal migrations. Meltzer (1989), however, noted that the number of languages in an area is a function not only of time but also of the history of interaction (see also Hill, this volume).

Some researchers (e.g., Moss and Erlandson 1995; Sandweiss et al. 1999) have claimed that early sites, particularly those in South America, might have arisen from a coastal migration. Irving (1985) thought that the pre-Clovis sites in South America were the product of a coastal migration by boat. In a recent study, Surovell (1999) constructed a model simulation of a coastal migration from Seattle, Washington, to Monte Verde, Chile. Regardless of the parameter values, Surovell could not get his "migration" to arrive at Monte Verde within the proposed time frame. Although the coastal migration route that Fladmark (1978) suggested has gained some attention recently (e.g., Dixon et al. 1997), there is no archaeological evidence to support this route because Holocene sea-level transgression has inundated the Pleistocene coastline.

Number of Migrations

Although migrations numbering in the hundreds have occasionally been proposed, the professional consensus revolves around a much smaller number: between one and four migrations, depending upon the kind(s) of evidence invoked to support them. Researchers have used various independent lines of evidence to identify the number of migrations: archaeology, osteology, dental morphology, linguistics, and genetics, including DNA analysis.

One Migration

A single-migration hypothesis is supported by the genetic studies of Stone and Stoneking (1998), Bonatto and Salzano (1997), and Merriweather et al. (1995) on mitochondrial DNA (mtDNA); Hammer (1999) on Y chromosomes; and Williams (1999) on human leukocyte antigens. Stone and Stoneking (1998) based their arguments on the fact that the few founding Native American haplotypes, although of Asian origin, are rare today in Asian populations. Thus, the probability that these same haplotypes would have repeatedly been introduced into the Americas is low. Bonatto and Salzano's (1997) conclusions were based on similar diversity levels among the founding haplotypes, which also suggests expansion from a single founding population. They further proposed that this population underwent a severe bottleneck, followed by a reexpansion of Eskimo-Aleut and Na-Dene people. Although Merriwether et al.'s (1995) analysis did not support a genetic bottleneck, these researchers did recognize that the prevalence of lineage A throughout the New World supported the single-wave hypothesis (and that the lineage varied independently of language group). Using "intraspecific phylogeography," Hammer (1999) concluded

that about 80 percent of all genetic variation in Native American populations could be traced to a single founding population that lived around the Lake Baikal region of Siberia. Williams et al. (1985) originally concurred with the three-wave model of Greenberg et al. (1986) but recently changed their position, arguing that their evidence could support either a single migration or multiple migrations from the same source population (Williams 1999).

Laughlin (1986), commenting on the Greenberg et al. (1986) three-wave hypothesis, argued that both the dental and linguistic evidence supported a single wave rather than multiple migrations because of the overall similarity among Native American populations. This viewpoint is strikingly at odds with many of Laughlin's previous publications, in which he argued for a minimum of two migrations: Eskimo-Aleut and "Indian." His revised theory seems to be based largely on a misinterpretation of paleoenvironmental evidence. Mosimann and Martin (1975) and Haynes (1966, 1971, 1980, 1987) asserted that a single migration of relatively few individuals (from 30 to 100) is all that would be required to cause the extinction of North American megafauna. Haynes, reviving the "Dawkins approach" (Laughlin 1988), further correlated a single migration to the overwhelming predominance of a single tool type: the Clovis point. These workers gave no attention to the Eskimo-Aleut entry, presumably because it is considered late, nor did they address the microblade issues of Siberia, Alaska, and the northwestern coast (Carlson 1996; Yi and Clark 1985).

Two Migrations

Two migrations (ancestral Indian followed by Eskimo-Aleut) have long been the physical anthropological favorite, even after the Greenberg et al. (1986) multidisciplinary hypothesis was launched. Lahr (1995), Starikovskaya et al. (1998), and Torroni et al. (1992) favor a two-migration hypothesis mostly based upon the same evidence. They each recognize the four founding haplotypes common in Native Americans, but they calculate a significant time divergence between the appearance of haplotypes A, C, and D on the one hand and haplotype B on the other. The B haplotype common in most Na-Dene speakers represents a much later, and hence separate, migration (Torroni et al. 1992). Like Williams, Zegura recently amended his original position on the number of migrations. Based upon analyses of Y-chromosome data inherited through the paternal line,

Zegura (1999) uncovered traces of two migrations, both of which emanated from the same parent population in the Lake Baikal region.

Three Migrations

The three-wave hypothesis proposed by Greenberg et al. (1986) was initially met with skepticism but remains in the mainstream due to its multidisciplinary nature and to its being (arguably) the most parsimonious of the four migration hypotheses considered here. This scenario was the first to be based on combined evidence from linguistics, dental morphology, genetics, and Siberian-American archaeology. It proposed three distinct Native American populations: Amerind, Na-Dene, and Eskimo-Aleut. These three populations were thought to have arisen from separate, relatively discrete migrations: Amerinds were the initial colonizers, followed by the Na-Dene or the Eskimo-Aleuts, whose order is unclear.

Linguistic critics of the three-wave theory faulted Greenberg's linguistic methodology of mass comparison (Campbell 1986; Nichols 1990), although both Greenberg (1990) and Ruhlen (1996) mounted a vigorous defense (Hill, this volume). Skeptics of the biological (genetic and dental morphological) evidence for a three-fold grouping of New World founder populations (Fox 1986; Laughlin 1986; Szathmáry 1986; Weiss and Woolford 1986) did not find fault with methodology. Instead each had his or her previously proposed settlement scenario based on a single line of evidence or reasoning that differed in varying degrees from the scenario that Greenberg et al. (1986) proposed on multiple lines of evidence.

Although challenges to the three-wave theory continue to emerge, support for it also continues to be invoked (e.g., Powell 1993; Rogers 1986a). For example, Rogers (1986a; Rogers et al. 1990, 1991) believed that Beringia, the northwestern coast, and the southern refugia correlate with present-day biological and linguistic divisions. The isolating mechanisms of the refugia are thus responsible for the diversity present in Native Americans today. In support of Turner's (1986) dental analysis, Powell (1993) performed two different statistical analyses on Turner's data. His resulting trees paralleled those of Turner, lending credence to the division of Native Americans into three groups based on dental morphology. Cavalli-Sforza et al. (1988, 1994) analyzed massive amounts of genetic data, which, in combination with multivariate analyses, supported the linguistic and dental morphological interpretations of three colonization events. With respect to archaeological evidence, West's (1996b) previously mentioned interpretations of Siberian and Alaskan prehistory support the three-migration model.

Four Migrations

Four migration waves are implied by the immunoglobin GM and KM allotype analysis of Schanfield (1992), the mtDNA analysis of Horai (1993) and Wallace et al. (1985), and the linguistic evidence of Nichols (1990). Schanfield identified four distinct Native American populations: (1) non–Na-Dene South American, (2) non–Na-Dene North American, (3) Na-Dene, and (4) Eskaleut. Schanfield arrived at these groups based on timing differentials, and he traced them to four separate parent populations, as did Horai (Horai 1993; Schanfield 1992). Wallace and Torroni (1992) also proposed a four-migration model: (1) two migrations of people ancestral to Amerind speakers, (2) a later Na-Dene migration, and (3) a final Eskimo-Aleut migration coupled with a severe founder effect (see Brace et al., this volume, and Schurr, this volume, for additional discussion of skeletal and genetic evidence). Employing a rigid adherence to uniformitarian assumptions, Nichols (1990) analyzed linguistic diversity in the New World, which she divided into four groups: (1) Eastern/Interior, (2) Pacific Rim, (3) Eskimo-Aleut, and (4) Na-Dene. She hypothesized that these groups could have arisen only from separate migrations of distinct people. Criticisms of Nichols center on the validity of her "clumping" method, her use of population marker frequencies as an index of relative chronology, and her arguable assumptions about glottochronology (Hill 1999, this volume). All of these biological and linguistic inferences are synchronically based and have not yet been correlated with archaeologically identified populations.

Origins of the Parent Population(s)

One issue receiving much attention lately has been the source of the parent population(s). Renewed interest in this subject centers around such finds as the Kennewick man, Spirit Cave man, Gordon Creek remains, and Arlington Springs woman. All of these remains have, at some time, been characterized as "non-Mongoloid" for one reason or another (Rensberger 1997), although the most recent study of Kennewick challenges this contention (Powell and Rose 1999). Generally four geographical source areas for the founder populations have been identified: (1) Australia/Polynesia, (2) Europe, (3) Southeast Asia, and (4) Northeast Asia.

Genetic, skeletal, and dental morphological evidence overwhelmingly identify Asia as the homeland of the first Americans. Just exactly where in Asia, however, is still a matter of debate. Haeussler (1996), Haeussler and Turner (1992), and Turner (1985, 1998, 2002) have concentrated their dental and archaeological search for proximate origin(s) in the region embracing the upper reaches of the Ob, Yenisey, and Amur Rivers. They argue that late Pleistocene small-group differentiation took place, due to river basin isolation and peripheral location, from a central and more generalized sinodont population, such as the one suggested by the skeletal and dental remains found in the Zhoukoudian (Choukoutien) Upper Cave near Beijing (Turner et al. 2000). Interestingly Karafet et al. (1999) have recently proposed the same region for Native American origins on the basis of diachronic Y-chromosome distributional studies (see also Brace et al., this volume; Schurr, this volume).

Australia/Polynesia
The Australian (and African)/Polynesian origin scenario is based solely upon cranial remains, there being no well-accepted supportive genetic, dental, archaeological, or linguistic evidence. Neves and Pucciarelli (1991) and Neves et al. (1999) found that certain Paleoindian crania (e.g., the 11,500–11,000-year-old Lapa Vermelha IV skull from the state of Minas Gerais, Brazil) exhibit a craniometric resemblance to Australians, Africans, and Polynesians. They proposed that a "pre-Mongoloid" race in northern China was the parent population for Australians and later for South Americans. Lahr (1995) concurred with this analysis after her own investigation of human remains from South America. She characterized her skeletal population as lacking "typical" Mongoloid features, and thus agreed with Neves and Pucciarelli's (1991) hypothesis of a pre-Mongoloid colonization.

In their analysis of the 10,675-year-old Buhl cranium from Idaho, Jantz and Owsley (1999) proposed that Buhl had Pacific affinities, specifically with Polynesians. Alternatively Neves and Blum (2000) found that the Buhl skull resembled modern American Indian and East Asian crania. Unfortunately they used this finding as a basis to declare that the Lapa Vermelha IV skull, being vastly different from Buhl, indicated a pre-Paleoindian migration into the New World just a few years before the "Mongoloids" arrived. One cannot help but wonder what would happen to Neves's, Lahr's, and other "pre-Mongoloidist" views if Lapa Vermelha IV and

other purportedly early South American crania turned out to have incorrect age assignments due to faulty associations or dating. For younger readers who may be unfamiliar with the older archaeological literature, I should note this long tradition: claiming greater antiquity for human skeletal remains and artifacts in South America than for anything known from North America or even Siberia. Almost all of these claims have been refuted. Furthermore, such Australian-like or African-like crania have not been identified among any late Pleistocene North American, Siberian, or northern Chinese remains. Even less convincing is the Arlington Springs woman, represented by two femora and one patella, which ostensibly exhibit Polynesian or Southeast Asian affinities (Associated Press 1999). Although I am not well versed in postcranial metric trait variation, I do not understand how a "racial" identification can be based on two femora and one patella.

Europe
The hypothesis of a European source population combines evidence from archaeological complexes with idiosyncratic interpretations of human skeletal remains. C. Vance Haynes Jr., in the tradition of Hansjürgen Müller-Beck (who has since changed his mind), hypothesized a European origin for the first Native Americans. He did not base this idea on skeletal remains, but on technological and typological similarities in artifact forms, such as blades, antler "wrenches," and red ochre (Haynes 1980, 1987). According to Haynes, Caucasoids with Upper Paleolithic technologies migrated across Europe eastward into Asia, where they interbred with the indigenous Asian population, who "swamped" them genetically, so that sinodonty became the dominant dental configuration in these Caucasoid folk. After being "dentally enhanced," they continued across the Bering Land Bridge and traveled down the ice-free corridor into what is now the United States. Once south of the ice sheets, these "Caucasoids" invented the Clovis point, enabling them to exploit the abundant and naïve megafauna that awaited them in the unpopulated continent. Haynes saw no antecedents to Clovis in Asia but identified nine traits common to both eastern European and Clovis artifact types (Haynes 1987). Especially problematic in this theory are the assertions that sinodonty has a dominant genetic expression and that this genetic expression can be correlated with broadly defined racial groups. If anything, genetic mixing between Europeans and East Asians produces an intermediate dental pattern, as seen in such groups as the Samoyeds and Finns

(Adler 1999; Haeussler 1996; Scott and Turner 1997; Zubov and Khaldeeva 1979).

Another version of the European origin scenario is based on similarities between Clovis and Spanish Solutrean projectile points (Jelinek 1971; Stanford and Bradley 2000). Jelinek (1971) explained these resemblances as being due to convergent adaptations to similar climates. Stanford and Bradley (2000), however, thought that the Solutrean (as identified by the distinctive points) represented an identity-conscious social unit and that Solutrean people migrated to the New World, bringing with them the technical elements responsible for the Clovis culture. These researchers noted that Solutrean and Clovis points are both bifacially flaked, whereas Upper Paleolithic Eurasian tool complexes are mainly unifacial. They emphasized that caches of tools with red ochre have been found in both Clovis and Solutrean sites (Stanford 1999a). They also noted that the oldest Clovis sites are found in the southern and southeastern United States, a pattern that fits a migration from east to west, but not from north to south (i.e., it is not consistent with migration through the ice-free corridor). Because only sinodonty has been documented in North America (including Greenland), how the very different European dental pattern came to be the one uniformly typical of Asia is difficult to explain without the hybridization scheme of Haynes. Large collections of late Pleistocene and Holocene teeth that C. G. Turner (personal communication, 2000) has personally examined from France, England, the Netherlands, Denmark, Estonia, the Ukraine, and Russia all exhibit the simplified European dental pattern that is virtually the opposite of sinodonty. Hence, there is no dental support for the Stanford and Bradley proposal.

In an unfortunate lapse of "population thinking," the modern human skeleton known as Kennewick man, which was recovered from a Columbia River bank in eastern Washington and radiocarbon dated to 8410 B.P., was initially identified by Chatters (2000) as that of a "Caucasian." This characterization was based on a cursory assessment of skull form and dentition, which he claimed to be sundadont. The skeleton was that of a 45- to 55-year-old man, who had a Cascade phase projectile point dated to about 9000–4500 B.P. embedded in his pelvis (Slayman 1997). Although Kennewick man is embroiled in a legal repatriation dispute, Powell and Rose (1999) have studied the skeleton and have concluded that it exhibits more Asian than European affinities.

Jantz and Owsley (1997) studied 9,400-year-old skeletal remains from Spirit Cave, Nevada, and concluded that they were "non-Mongoloid," noting their European or Archaic Caucasoid affinities reminiscent of the Ainu of Japan or a Norse population. Although Rensberger (1997) also listed the Gordon Creek, Colorado, and the Browns Valley, Minnesota, remains as being "non-Mongoloid," he provided no convincing evidence to substantiate his claim. Writing about prehistoric southwestern Indian burials, Breternitz et al. (1971) emphasized repeatedly the difficulties inherent in making an "ethnic" or "racial" determination based on a single skull, the near-total absence of comparative skeletal material, and the wide range of cranial variation present in the New World. The Browns Valley skeletons, which were analyzed by A. E. Jenks in the late 1930s, were robust and had "primitive" aspects, yet Jenks (1936) concluded that they were not morphologically distinct in any important way from those of modern Native Americans.

Southeast Asia

Evidence for a Southeast Asian source population comes solely from the analysis of skeletal remains. After performing both qualitative and bivariate quantitative analyses on skeletal remains, Steele and Powell (1992) concluded that the first colonizers were not classically sinodont but were closer to southern Asians and Europeans than to other American Indian populations. Turner (1994a) believed that the dental pattern studies of Steele and Powell (1992) were problematic because they failed to give due consideration to the extensive occlusal surface wear common in these early dentitions.

Powell (1993) and Haydenblit (1996) both traced the parent population of the earliest New World immigrants to Southeast Asia. Powell (1993) determined that the Native skeletal remains in his study were biologically distinct from those of Northeast Asians and had more affinities with Southeast Asians and Europeans than with other Native Americans. Haydenblit (1996) concluded from her study of South American dentitions that the Native population was typically sundadont rather than sinodont. Unfortunately her sample size was small and recent and was derived largely from a single cemetery, where family or lineage effects might "swamp" other, more general patterns.

Northeast Asia

The hypothesis that Northeast Asians were the parent population of Native Americans is supported by genetic, archaeological, and skeletal analyses. More than a dozen genetic studies postdating 1984 demonstrated a Northeast Asian origin for Native Americans (Bonatto and Salzano 1997; Brace et al., this volume; Merriwether et al. 1995; Schurr, this volume; Starikovskaya et al. 1998; Stone and Stoneking 1998; Tokunaga and Juji 1993; Torroni et al. 1992; Wallace et al. 1985; Williams et al. 1985). Hammer (1999), Turner (1983, 1985, 1986), and Zegura (1999) all traced the source population to the region of Lake Baikal in southeastern Siberia. Turner's global research on human dentition conclusively showed that shovel-shaped incisors and several other dental crown and root traits that are common in Asian and Native American populations are uncharacteristic of Europeans (Turner 1983, 1985, 1986). Analyses of the skeletal affinities of Eskimos, Aleuts, and Siberians have been numerous, consilient, and conclusive (e.g., Alekseyev 1979; Anderson 1979; Crawford et al. 1981; Powers 1973; Powers and Hoffecker 1989).

Further support for a Northeast Asian origin comes from archaeology, especially retouched stone-tool types. Borden (1969), Dumond (1980, 1982), Fladmark (1979), West (1975, 1996b), and Yi and Clark (1985) all discerned antecedents to Paleoindian tool types in Northeast Asia. Hoffecker et al. (1993) thought that the Clovis and Nenana complexes shared many technological and typological similarities and that Clovis could easily have been derived from Nenana. Brantingham (1999) interpreted the Clovis phenomenon as microlithic technologies amplified to a larger, macrolithic scale. Tomenchuk and Storck (1997) traced single- and double-scribe compass and coring gravers found in the New World to the Eurasian Upper Paleolithic and Siberian Neolithic traditions.

Timing of Initial Entry

The issue of timing rests mainly with direct chronological findings from dated archaeological excavations. However, some indirect and largely synchronic evidence can be derived from osteological sources. For example, Hrdlicka (1925) convincingly argued that claims for very early humans in the New World were unsupported by the degree of "primitiveness" manifested in prehistoric cranial variation in the Old World. Although all issues regarding theories on the peopling of the New World are to some extent contentious, the issue of timing is perhaps the most hotly debated. For example, James Adovasio, who excavated the Meadowcroft Rockshelter in Pennsylvania, referred to the defenders of "Clovis-first" perspectives as the "Clovis Mafia" (Begley and Murr 1999:53), which, in my view, is a bit over the

top (i.e., the epithet implies that those who differ with Adovasio regarding the credibility of the Meadowcroft dates are not sufficiently committed to scientific rigor).

The timing question can be partitioned into three broad categories, each of which is dependent upon supposedly time-sensitive and diagnostic tool forms: (1) pre–projectile point (200,000–60,000 B.P.), (2) pre-Clovis (60,000–12,000 B.P.), and (3) Clovis (11,500 B.P.). Unfortunately these categories have all been defined in reference to the Clovis projectile point, which first showed up in the Americas around 11,500 B.P. A pre-Clovis designation implies a continuity in tool form through time, which is yet unproven. As suggested by Meltzer (1989), replacing "pre-Clovis" with "pre-12,000 B.P." better defines this category and skirts the sticky problem of rigid formal continuity and its questionable implications. Much of "pre-Clovis" is only marginally earlier, is not very different typologically, and would be better termed "non-Clovis" (see Clark, this volume). One must also keep in mind the recent recalibration of radiocarbon dates, which pushes the Clovis interval back to about 13,250–12,950 cal B.P. (Fagan 1999; Fiedel 1999b).

The Pre-Projectile-Point Era

Few workers have claimed an antiquity for New World sites in the 200,000–60,000 B.P. range because it would entail the presence of archaic forms of humans for which there is no evidence. I mention only the two most controversial sites here because I assume that the rest are even less credible. The Old Crow site, located in the Yukon Territory, has lost much of its credibility following the death of its staunchest defender (Irving 1985). Always highly problematic, the case for great antiquity rested on an elk tibia "flesher" that was originally radiocarbon dated to 27,000 B.P. Later analysis by the AMS method determined the date to be only about 1,350 years old (Nelson et al. 1986).

The Calico Hills site in California's Mojave Desert was dated to 200,000 B.P. by uranium series (Schlemon and Budinger 1990). Discovered and excavated by Ruth Ann Simpson and endorsed as being genuine by Louis Leakey, thousands of primitive-looking stone tools resembling Acheulean bifaces were recovered during the 1960s. Although the formal similarity of the tools was acknowledged, the U-series dates (on flowstones) could not be directly related to the artifacts (some of which are genuine). Most workers now interpret the resemblances as being due to formal convergence rather than great antiquity (Schlemon and Budinger 1990).

The Pre-12,000 B.P. Era

Proponents of a pre-12,000 B.P. settlement of the Americas base their arguments on several lines of reasoning: (1) sites they believe are well dated and archaeologically sound; (2) the fact that Clovis points have not been found in solid stratigraphic contexts in Alaska or in areas south of Panama (Meltzer and Dillehay 1999; Pearson, this volume); (3) evidence supporting a diverse subsistence strategy (Chilton, this volume; Dillehay 1984); and (4) the apparent speed with which Clovis people supposedly spread (Barton et al., this volume; Whitley and Dorn 1993). Butzer (1988), recognizing that both spatial and temporal discontinuities are common in the Old World, proposed a "marginality" or "risk-minimization model" to explain similar gaps in the New World.

Recently a few sites in both North and South America have been dated to the pre-12,000 B.P. era. The newest site to join that rank is the Topper site in South Carolina (Rose 1999). Geologically dated to 18,000 B.P., this site has yielded microblades and a scraper underlying a level with Clovis points (*Discovering Archaeology* 1999). Although as yet not well documented, the Topper site would represent the earliest presence of microblades in the New World. Depending upon the credibility of the early stages of Mochanov's Dyuktai culture, the Topper site may be coeval with the well-stratified, late Dyuktai sequence at Dyuktai Cave, which has been dated to about 18,000 B.P. at the earliest (Yi and Clark 1985). Excavation of the Topper site continues today. Pendejo Cave in New Mexico has produced human fingerprints and hair preserved in clay dating to 37,000–12,000 B.P. (Chrisman et al. 1996). An early human presence, however, has not been generally accepted at Pendejo Cave because of doubts about its stratigraphic integrity (Dincauze 1997).

Although sites claimed to be older than 12,000 B.P. are too numerous to be discussed in their entirety here, I will describe the best known and perhaps most problematic: Pedra Furada Rockshelter, Taima-Taima, Monte Verde, Meadowcroft Rockshelter, and Bluefish Caves.

Guidon and Delibrias (1986) described the Franco-Brazilian excavations at the Pedra Furada Rockshelter in Brazil. They claimed that the oldest level at Pedra Furada, dating to about 32,000 B.P., yielded very primitive-looking quartz flakes and hearths near the base of a seasonal waterfall. When active, this waterfall deposits thousands of cobbles at the bottom of a 30-meter-high cliff, into which the rockshelter is cut. The rockshelter was used sporadically over the late prehistoric period by people who built fires under the overhang. After visiting the site and examining the artifacts, Meltzer and Dillehay (1999) thought that the "choppers" were actually naturally broken pebbles that were selectively removed from the millions of unmodified pebbles and cobbles that had accumulated over millennia at the base of the waterfall. Researchers also disagree on whether the hearths were man made (Marshall 1990).

Gruhn (1987) supported the 13,000 B.P. date for the Taima-Taima open site in Venezuela. This site contained mastodon bones associated with projectile points. Taima-Taima, however, is located at a spring. The likelihood of animal wallowing and trampling, combined with periodic fluctuations in the water table and discharge volume, raises concerns that the bones and artifacts were mixed later (Lynch 1990).

The best documented site and the one that has received the most attention in recent years is Monte Verde in Chile. Excavated by Tom Dillehay, the upper component of this site dates to 13,000 B.P. (Dillehay 1984). Following publication of the massive Monte Verde monographs (Dillehay 1989, 1997b) and endorsement of the site's stratigraphic and contextual integrity by professional archaeologists who visited it (Meltzer et al. 1997), this site is now generally accepted by most workers as the best claimant in the pre-12,000 B.P. category. Recently, however, Fiedel (1999a) identified what he thought were serious problems: the provenience of key artifacts, the lack of photographs of these artifacts in situ, and inconsistencies in the mapping and labeling of artifacts. He also noted that the "site" of Monte Verde had already been destroyed when the team of archaeologists went to South America to inspect it. Responses by Dillehay et al. (1999b) and Collins (1999b), among others, attempted to reconcile these discrepancies and provide explanations for them. Although only marginally earlier than Clovis, the dates for Monte Verde may well be valid. However, at least some of the issues raised by Fiedel should be addressed.

The Meadowcroft Rockshelter in Pennsylvania is one of the few pre-12,000 B.P. sites that has exhibited a certain amount of "pre-Clovis shelf life." Dating between 14,000 and 12,000 B.P., Meadowcroft has yielded stone tools, faunal remains, and charcoal. The dates may be suspect, however, due to possible contamination of the charcoal by groundwater that was permeated with ancient carbon derived from nearby deposits of anthracite (Marshall 1990). For those who retain some confidence in the value of typological systematics, I note that the tools are Archaic rather than Paleoindian.

Perhaps the most credible objection to Adovasio et al.'s (1990) claims for a tardiglacial age is the Meadowcroft fauna, which is exclusively composed of extant species (Dincauze 1981a; C. V. Haynes Jr. 1991a). About 13,000 years ago, Meadowcroft would have been located in the glacial outwash plain or very close to the glacier's edge. One would expect to find species adapted to glacial environments in the faunal assemblage. However, no such forms were found. Meadowcroft may be of near-Clovis antiquity and may simply represent the material remains of a human occupation that involved activities that had nothing to do with the production of big foliate points (i.e., an activity facies, or "structural pose" of an adaptation that produced Clovis points elsewhere; Binford 1981; G. A. Clark, personal communication 2002).

Bluefish Caves in the Yukon region of Alaska have yielded mammoth bone, bird bone, and stone "tools." The dates for Bluefish Caves range from 13,000 to 10,000 B.P. Unfortunately the artifacts are not associated with indisputable hearths, unmistakable tools, or other kinds of demonstrably "cultural" features (e.g., pits; Marshall 1990). Wolves might have denned in these rockshelters; thus bone that appears to be modified would be expected. Taphonomic research should be able to identify the sources of bone modification and accumulation.

As noted above, skeletal evidence for a pre-12,000 B.P. occupation of the Americas is controversial. Taylor et al. (1985) redated several pre-12,000 B.P. skeletal remains by ^{14}C accelerator mass spectrometry. None of the redated human remains were older than 11,000 B.P.

The Clovis Era

The date for the Clovis era is generally uncontroversial: about 11,500 B.P. Although many artifacts are undated isolated finds, Clovis points are numerous and radiometrically well dated throughout North and South America. A few examples of Clovis-age sites are Domebo, Aubrey, Dietz, Anzick, Monte Algre, and Lapa dos Bichos. The main contested issue is whether the Clovis phenomenon corresponds to the initial human *entrada* into the New World. Clovis-first advocates are often accused of unreasonable conservatism and of trivializing the scientific process (Irving 1985). They respond by pointing out that intensive surveys of Alaska related to the construction of the Alaskan pipeline uncovered no sites older than 11,500 B.P. A recent ecological model predicting the movement and impact of first colonizers on a landscape supplied further evidence for the Clovis-first hypothesis (Barton et al. 1999, this volume). This model, which took into account many different variables, showed that Clovis people acted in a manner consistent with that of first colonizers. These researchers concluded that, within the limits of existing theory, people making Clovis points were the first people to colonize the New World.

Technology

I limit my remarks here to two general climatic and geographic considerations as these are mediated by technology. First, workers unfamiliar with Alaskan and Siberian winters find it hard to imagine the harshness of the late Pleistocene interior Siberian climate north of the Arctic Circle, as well as climatic conditions along the northeastern Siberian coast and the southern margins of the Bering Land Bridge. No environment in the world was more demanding for human occupation than the "greater Beringian realm" during late Pleistocene glacial pulses (Turner 1994b). Hence, it is virtually impossible that technologically unsophisticated people managed the Beringian passage. Turner has argued that the people responsible for Calico Hills, Monte Verde, and technologically similar, "simple and primitive" sites could not have survived in the greater Beringian realm. Elsewhere he has suggested that the transit to Alaska was dependent upon the domestication of the Asian wolf for use in hunting, transportation, camp defenses, and, in emergencies, food (Turner 1999). Windproof, tailored fur clothing could not have been manufactured without the innovation of the small-eyed needle, which has been well documented only in post-20,000 B.P. sites in the Eurasian Upper Paleolithic.

Second, any transit along the coasts of the Okhotsk Sea, North Pacific, and Bering Sea would probably have required some kind of watercraft. Because of the probable year-round sea ice in these northern waters during the late Pleistocene (Hopkins 1979), little if any driftwood for dugout boats would have been available from the Kurile Islands to southern British Columbia. Even the much smaller amounts of wood required for framing skin boats would have been problematic and were probably concentrated near the now-submerged mouths of the Anadyr, Yukon, and Kuskokwim Rivers. These rivers drained interior regions that contained arctic steppe vegetation and possibly small microclimatic refugia that contained willow or conifers. On either the interior route or the coastal route to Alaska, sophisticated means of transportation (dogs or watercraft), tailored clothing, weaponry, and numerous skills that are not reflected in stone or bone artifacts would have been absolutely essential.

Numbers of Migrants

Because of the limited amount of genetic and dental morphological variation in North and South America, one can reasonably infer that the original band(s) of colonists contained few members, that these bands were very closely related, or both. The same might be said for the apparent cultural uniformity represented in stone artifacts from late Pleistocene sites in Siberia and Alaska (Dikov 1993; Hoffecker et al. 1993). If we use arctic populations at or around the time of European contact as rough guides to environmental carrying capacity and make allowances for the more severe climates in late Pleistocene times, then numbers of migrants in the low hundreds, spread out over thousands of square kilometers, seem plausible. Although it is presently almost impossible to model the demography of the Beringian realm, all interpretations of genetic, morphological, and cultural variation, including language, must eventually address population size, dispersal, structure, and related considerations that affect microevolution (see MacDonald, this volume; Meltzer, this volume).

Residual Ethnographic Traditions

Perhaps the most strongly held Native American view on cultural affiliation issues is that professional archaeologists and anthropologists give very little credence to the specifics of oral tradition. There are several obvious problems with using oral tradition for historical reconstructions: memory mutability, intentional alterations (like book burning by conquerors and ongoing political correctness), a lack of temporal regularity or clockwork (Mason 2000), and the sheer implausibility of transmitting such traditions over thousands of years and square kilometers (Clark 2001b). However, some aspects of the oral traditions of southwestern Pueblo Indians have a temporal depth of several centuries and have been verified by empirical evidence. Hence, it is a possibility, although a remote one, that aspects of oral traditions can be identified as having their origin in late Pleistocene Siberia or Alaska. These aspects may include shamanistic lore, animal sacrifice, burial considerations, and possibly stories involving great heroes or monumental events. Although its universal character has been questioned, the oral tradition that is common to much of

the Americas—emerging on the earth from the underground realm—might reflect the horrors that accompanied the transit through the ice-free corridor. I suggest that more might be done with oral traditions to develop archaeologically testable inferences about the peopling of the New World.

Language

I end this review with a line of evidence for the peopling of the New World that has been successfully pursued by linguists, such as Joseph Greenberg and Merritt Ruhlen. That these and other contemporary linguists have proposed no New World linguistic connections to the Old World except through northern Eurasia speaks for itself (Hill, this volume). These researchers contend that languages do not readily diffuse and that their distribution in both the present and the past is due almost entirely to having been carried by migrants.

Like dental and genetic traits, language characteristics point to a Northeast Asian origin for Native Americans. Ruhlen (1998) suggested that the Na-Dene language family shared an origin with the Yeniseian family, whose sole remaining language is Ket, which is spoken by a small group of Native Siberians living along the Yenisey River. He also noted that the family is distinct from the Amerind and Eskimo-Aleut families, indicating a separate migration of ancestral Na-Dene speakers. These linguistic approaches tend to assume that language has a fairly direct correlation with physical type, identity consciousness, and the archaeologically identifiable material remains of identity-conscious groups of people. However, that correlation has been questioned for more than 35 years (e.g., Owen 1965).

Conclusions

This paper reviews diachronic and synchronic evidence relevant for evaluating several aspects of inquiry into the initial human colonization of the Western Hemisphere. There is near consensus among scientists that all Native Americans, past and present, had their origin in the Old World. There is less agreement, however, on the migration routes: Six models are prevalent in the contemporary literature. Both transoceanic migrations have little empirical support. Y-chromosome, mtDNA, blood serum, dental morphology, and GM and KM allotype analyses provide no evidence of Austronesian or European genetic contributions to the founding populations of Native Americans. Although studies based on cranial morphology have shown some affinities between Australian/Polynesian and South American populations, most skeletal analyses do not support these hypothetical relationships. Cranial form in the founding population may have varied widely, and craniological studies often do not consider developmental and genetic factors. The lithic similarities between Clovis, Solutrean, and other European tool types probably just represent formal convergence and similar adaptations (Clark 1999a, this volume; Straus 2000).

There is genetic support for both the coastal and the land bridge models. Although some evidence shows that a coastal migration was possible, no evidence has indicated that it actually occurred. The time frame for this model is dependent on the acceptance of pre-12,000 B.P. sites.

The model proposing a land-bridge/interior route through an ice-free corridor is supported by the preponderance of evidence. Pre-12,000 B.P. advocates often complain about the intense scrutiny with which Clovis-first adherents evaluate early sites, yet the fact remains that Clovis is empirically well documented. Although Clovis-first is the most parsimonious of the theories in light of current evidence, new evidence in the form of archaeology, linguistics, physical anthropology, genetics, or geology might lead to the acceptance of other theories or to the merging of theories to create a clearer picture of the events leading to the peopling of the Americas.

I hope that what has emerged from this discussion is the realization that investigations on the colonization of the New World require a holistic approach. We can no longer afford to ignore research conducted in different fields, nor can we allow implicit bias to color our interpretation, evaluation, and validation of new evidence. For the moment, our interpretation of the large body of literature on the peopling of the New World leads us to accept a multifactoral model of a small number of migration waves, representing very few individuals, who came from ancestral stocks that had evolved in northeastern Siberia and Mongolia somewhat earlier than the earliest dates for the human occupation of Alaska (i.e., very late in the Pleistocene). These migrants were dependent on highly sophisticated lithic and organic technologies. Transportation and hunting were likely dependent upon domesticated dogs and perhaps skin-covered boats like the Eskimo-Aleut *bidarki*. The traditions of these early peoples almost certainly included shamanistic practices, mortuary ritual, animal sacrifice, and other cultural features common to nearly all Native Siberians and Native Americans today.

II The Trail to the Americas

In spite of a broad consensus that the first settlers of the Americas were ultimately of East Asian origin, there has remained an active debate over the routes that these colonists followed in populating the two continents of the Western Hemisphere. These debates have recently been restated in the models of Anderson and Gillam (2000, 2001) and Fix (2002) and have reemerged in the discussion of the possibility of European colonization via the North Atlantic (Stanford 1999a).

Probably the most generally accepted model and the one that is best supported empirically—the Bering Land Bridge model—proposes that big-game hunters with Upper Paleolithic technologies walked across a subcontinent-sized land bridge between Siberia and Alaska in what is now the Bering Strait near the end of the last ice age. They passed between the Laurentide and Cordilleran ice sheets in what is today western Canada and headed into the continental interior, eventually winding up at the southern tip of South America by about 10,000 B.P. Their artifacts, first found in the 1920s at a site near Clovis, New Mexico, have turned up at many North American sites dated around 11,000 B.P.

According to a modified version of the Bering Land Bridge model, which could be called the Pacific Coast model, the land bridge might not have existed early enough to account for terminal Pleistocene sites in South America that have produced no evidence of Clovis-type artifacts. This alternative theory suggests that people migrated from Siberia along the western coast of the Americas, on foot and in skin-covered boats like Eskimo kayaks, about a millennium earlier than Clovis. Although this model is plausible based on current knowledge of temporal changes in coastal geomorphology, there is actually very little archaeological evidence to support it. Subsequent Holocene sea-level transgressions would have effectively "drowned" any sites associated with terminal Pleistocene shorelines.

A third model might be called the Australian Route. This idea, presented long ago by Rivet (1957), ultimately derives the first Americans from Southeast Asia. Traveling by large, ocean-going boats like those found in Polynesia, they migrated first to Australia, subsequently took advantage of the trade winds to cross the Pacific Ocean, and eventually arrived at various points along the western coast of South America at a considerably later time than proposed by the first two models. The Australian Route has some rather equivocal archaeological support, mostly in the form of isolated stylistic similarities in ceramic vessel shapes and decorative motifs from both sides of the Pacific. Most scientists consider this model highly conjectural (see Schmitz, this volume), although it enjoys much popular support.

Finally, there is the North Atlantic model, revived recently by Dennis Stanford and Bruce Bradley. These workers propose that America's first inhabitants were the descendants of northern Spanish Solutreans who, traveling in boats, followed the edges of the pack ice surrounding modern Iceland and Greenland during the Last Glacial Maximum. They arrived in North America before Clovis but eventually gave rise to it. This model is based almost entirely on typological similarities in particular classes of retouched stone artifacts (i.e., big, bifacial, foliate points made on blades) found on both sides of the Atlantic Ocean. Whether formal similarity in stone tools can be explained by, or even linked to, historical connectivity is deeply problematic.

Building on evidence presented in the first section of this volume, the chapters in part II examine the routes taken by the first American pioneers and the evidence for their dispersal. Because the initial colonization of "pristine" continents has no parallel in the ethnographic record, we must rely on models developed from theory and tested against the archaeological record to understand this process. If we are not theoretically explicit, however, implicit biases can lead us to treat models as facts and build broad explanations from a small part of the available evidence. In this respect, the chapters in this section also use the record of colonization to examine how we assign meaning to pattern in Paleoindian research and, by extension, how we model the earliest human settlement of the Americas.

Stuart Fiedel's paper begins the section with a discussion of the Paleoindian colonization of the Americas, an apparently very rapid expansion across two continents. Because there is no direct ethnographic analogy for such a rapid, long-distance migration, he uses the late prehistoric Thule (ancestors of recent Inuit or Eskimo groups) expansion across the northern Arctic as a means to explore potential social and environmental causes of Clovis colonization and the mechanisms of migration.

After reviewing early Central and South American archaeological assemblages containing large foliate bifaces, most of which are undated surface finds, Georges Pearson considers some of the key issues surrounding the possible relationships among those assemblages and between them and Clovis colonists. Clovis points sensu stricto have not been found in South America, although morphologically similar forms have been noted. The space-time distributions of these diverse biface forms have implications for how we model the peopling process across the Western Hemisphere.

Geoffrey Clark evaluates Dennis Stanford's and Bruce Bradley's North Atlantic model on chronological criteria and on the composition of the analytical units that constitute consensus views of Solutrean and Clovis. There appears to be little empirical support for the model. A more serious problem, however, is the adequacy of the conceptual frameworks used to address "peopling" issues.

Carole Mandryk frames her discussion of Clovis and the Bering Land Bridge model in terms of a "hero legend" or narrative account, which focuses on the social context, theoretical orientations, bias factors, and other historical contingencies that shape (re)constructions of past events and processes. In challenging us to acknowledge the conceptual biases inherent in the Americanist Paleoindian research tradition (and, indeed, in any research tradition), she encourages us to critically reevaluate the adequacy of late Pleistocene archaeological and environmental data sets for modeling the colonization of the Americas.

7 Rapid Migrations by Arctic Hunting Peoples
CLOVIS AND THULE
Stuart J. Fiedel

The Paleoindian colonization of America was incredibly rapid. The earliest dates obtained for Clovis come from the Aubrey site in Texas (Ferring 1995, 2001): about 11,600–11,550 B.P. (or ca. 13,400 cal B.P.; Hughen et al. 2000). Clovis was everywhere in North America by the time of the Younger Dryas onset at about 12,900 cal B.P. (or ca. 11,000–10,700 B.P.; Fiedel 1999b, 2000a). Soon after its initial expansion, the Clovis complex underwent regional diversification, as Folsom developed in the West and Mid-Paleoindian forms, such as Debert and Cumberland, appeared in the East. Dates of about 11,000–10,700 B.P. from Cerro la China and Cueva del Medio show that Paleoindian hunters making fishtail points had reached the southern tip of South America by about 12,900 cal B.P. (Flegenheimer and Zarate 1997; Nami 1994, 1996). The stylistic and technological derivation of these points from the Clovis tradition is clear (Morrow and Morrow 1999; Pearson, 1998a, this volume) and indicates that these people were Clovis descendants.

It apparently took no more than 500 years for Clovis hunters to fill North America, and in the same time span, an offshoot population trekked some 4,000 miles to Tierra del Fuego. Some archaeologists (e.g., Whitley and Dorn 1993) have expressed incredulity about this remarkable event. They argue that there is no known analog for such rapid population growth and movement by hunter-gatherers; even farmer-pastoralists (e.g., the Bantu) who invaded and occupied new territories moved more slowly (but see Barton et al., this volume). The diagnostic artifacts and their associated dates, however, are staring us in the face; either Paleoindians did expand rapidly, or else a peculiar suite of fluted points, spurred endscrapers, etc. was borrowed by a preexisting population inhabiting a wide range of diverse habitats across the continent. Such wholesale borrowing seems very unlikely (Storck 1991). Only the site of Monte Verde in Chile (Dillehay 1997b), and perhaps Meadowcroft in Pennsylvania (Adovasio et al. 1990, 1999) and Cactus Hill in Virginia (McAvoy and McAvoy 1997), hint at the presence of earlier populations. If we

accept, on the basis of still exiguous and disputable archaeological evidence, that these barely visible precursors really existed, I would argue that they were entirely replaced by Clovis.

Hunter-Gatherer Expansion in the Ethnohistoric Record

There are, in fact, several well-known cases of rapid hunter-gatherer expansion and migration that might be usefully compared to the Clovis spread: for example, the Numic migration into the Great Basin and adjacent regions between about A.D. 1000 and 1500 (Madsen and Rhode 1994), and the migration of Athabaskans from the Yukon to the Southwest (Opler 1983) during the same period. (See also Barton et al., this volume for comparable data on European forager expansion.) Unfortunately archaeologists cannot agree on the timing and process of Numic migration, and the Athabaskans left virtually no archaeological record during their long march to the south. I will focus instead on a migration that is archaeologically well documented so there will be no disagreement concerning either the dates or the cultural processes involved.

The Thule culture, which is ancestral to recent Inuit or Eskimo groups, developed on the west coast of Alaska and spread by a swift coastal migration from northern Alaska to Greenland and Labrador (McGhee 1984). Thule people traversed this distance of about 1,500 to 2,000 miles in less than 150 years, between A.D. 900 and 1050 (fig. 7.1). In the process, they replaced a long-resident precursor population of the Dorset culture, which had occupied the Arctic Coast for 1,500 years. Whether there was face-to-face competitive contact between Dorset and Thule, or whether Dorset collapsed suddenly due to environmental change and Thule moved into the vacuum, remains uncertain (Park 1993).

The main point to be emphasized here is the rapidity of movement in each case. Thule people covered more than 1,500 miles in 100 to 150 years, sloughing

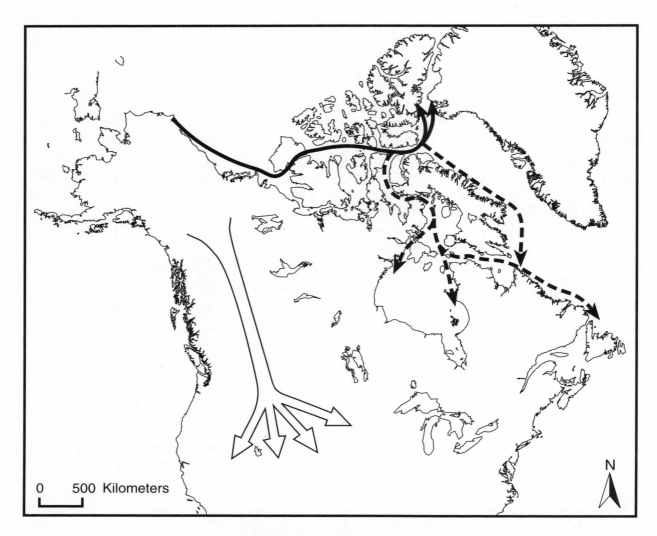

ARCTIC MIGRATION ROUTES

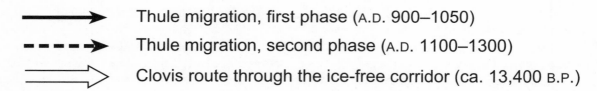

Thule migration, first phase (A.D. 900–1050)

Thule migration, second phase (A.D. 1100–1300)

Clovis route through the ice-free corridor (ca. 13,400 B.P.)

FIGURE 7.1 Migration routes: Ancestral Paleoindians through the ice-free corridor (ca. 13,400 cal B.P.) and Thule Eskimo along the Arctic Coast (ca. A.D. 900–1300).

off sufficient populations along the migration route to fill the intervening territory and to create a visible archaeological record. By the most direct route, Clovis ancestors would have covered about 1,300 miles traveling from Alberta to New Mexico. They could have done this in less than 100 years. In fact, they previously may have trekked through the ice-free corridor in a matter of months, leaving no archaeological record (but see Mandryk, this volume). At a reasonable pace of 15 miles per day, it would have taken 80 days to walk the 1,200 miles through the corridor. (Despite much current speculation, there is no evidence of migration along the alternative hypothetical coastal route [Fiedel 2000a; Yesner 1998].)

Comparison of Clovis and Thule Expansion

If Clovis ancestors undertook their journey at 11,600 B.P., the recently deglaciated corridor was not yet hospitable to big game. (Alaskan bison seem to have migrated south much later, around 10,000 B.P. [Wilson 1996].) Paleoindians appear to have trekked rapidly and intentionally through the corridor (West 1996a:556) to get to the superior hunting grounds beyond it. Initial Thule migration may have also been a directed migration from Alaska to the whale-rich area of Lancaster Sound, northwest of Baffin Island. "To get to Lancaster Sound they had to cross many hundreds of kilometres of essentially uninhabitable wasteland. How early Thule hunters learned what lay on the other side of that wasteland, and how they and their families successfully crossed it, will never be known in detail, but it is one of the great accomplishments of human history" (Morrison 1999:139). One could say the same about the Paleoindian discovery of North America beyond the ice sheets. In the case of Clovis, I have suggested recently (Fiedel 2000b) that central Alaskan Paleoindians realized, through observation of the seasonal southward migrations of waterfowl, that there must be suitable lacustrine habitats somewhere to the south. Initial far-ranging reconnaissance by small parties to confirm this inference and map out the route might have been followed by wholesale migration of entire macrobands (see also Meltzer, this volume).

Causes of Migration

In both cases, migration seems to have begun as a response to ameliorating climate, although social factors may also have played a role. Initial Thule movement occurred during the Medieval Climatic Optimum, but a second phase of migration, with expansion into more interior environments, followed as the climate cooled after A.D. 1200. Emigration of Clovis ancestors from Beringia probably occurred in the latter part of the Bölling-AllERÖD period, a dramatic warming (Elias 2000) that began about 14,700 cal B.P. (12,600 B.P.). Maximal Clovis expansion within North America, however, occurred at a time of climatic stress, during the Intra-Alleröd Cold Period (13,250–13,100 cal B.P.) and the ensuing 200-year warm period that created a drought in the Southwest (C. V. Haynes Jr. 1991a).

In a recent analysis of the late prehistory of the Bering Sea region, Mason (1998) suggests that the west Alaskan Birnirk culture, which is ancestral to Thule, had become marginalized in competition with Old Bering Sea, Ipiutak, and Punuk groups over access to whaling sites and other vital resources. This social pressure may have caused their movement to the Point Barrow area around A.D. 800–900 and was also conducive to further migration. It is likely, however, that occasional collapses of local resources at Point Barrow were a more immediate spur for Thule migration (Mason 1998).

Recent data from Northeast Asia may imply that Clovis ancestors experienced similar social pressure. New radiocarbon dates show that pottery was spreading through the Amur Basin at 13,000–12,000 B.P. (Kuzmin et al. 1997; Kuzmin and Orlova 2000). The New World record shows that Clovis ancestors had accepted neither ceramics nor an earlier innovation, microblade technology. Neither Clovis nor its possible Alaskan ancestor, the Nenana culture, used microblades. But the Denali culture, which entered central Alaska by 10,700 B.P. or earlier (West 1996b), was an offshoot of the microblade-based Dyuktai culture of Siberia. The apparent cultural diversity of terminal Pleistocene Alaska raises the possibility of intersocietal conflict that could have precipitated the southward migration of marginal groups once the ice-free corridor had opened.

Clovis and Thule Demography

Presumably, both in the Thule and Clovis cases, the colonizing population was thinly scattered across the landscape. Historical Eskimo densities are sometimes on the order of one person per 100–200 mi^2 (e.g., ca. 500 people within ca. 60,000 mi^2, or 1 person per 120 mi^2, for the Netsilik in 1888 [Balikci 1984:429]; and ca. 500 within ca. 90,000 mi^2, or 1 person per 180 mi^2, for the Caribou Eskimo in the 1920s [Arima 1984:460]). Cree and Athabaskan hunters of the subarctic forests maintained densities of about one person per 80 mi^2 (e.g., ca. 4,000 Montagnais-Naskapi within ca. 300,000 mi^2 [Helm 1968; Rogers and Leacock 1981:173]). In view of recent reconstructions of eastern Paleoindian environment and economy, such subarctic analogies seem appropriate (Custer and Stewart 1990). At a density similar to that of recent subarctic hunters, it would have taken about 125,000 Paleoindians to fill North and South America below the ice front. If one assumes doubling per generation (every 20 years), an initial population of 500 could have reached this size in 160 years.

In radiocarbon time, this process would unfold within a one-sigma time frame; that is to say, it would appear instantaneous (Barton et al., this volume).

Subsistence and Hunting Technology

The Thule-Clovis analogy can be pushed further. Both cultures specialized in hunting giant mammals: Thule hunted whales, Clovis hunted mammoths (but see Chilton, this volume). Both cultures possessed sophisticated weapons systems for these tasks. Some archaeologists have even suggested that the Clovis point and foreshaft assembly may represent a technology transfer from an original harpoon design used for hunting sea mammals (Boldurian and Cotter 1999; Dixon 1999). Thule people made stylistically distinctive carved harpoon heads of the Sicco type; Clovis fluted points appear to have been similarly emblematic of an ethnic identity (G. Haynes 1991:315; Tankersley, this volume). Thule harpoons were tipped with inset points made of meteoric iron, which was transported through an extensive trade network far beyond its source in Greenland (Pringle 1997b). Similarly Clovis points were made of highly prized cherts that were carried over great distances. Movement of chert points over 300 miles was not uncommon, and a few cases of transport across some 500 miles have been demonstrated in the Plains (Holen 2002). In the Clovis case, it is more likely that the raw material was obtained by direct procurement rather than exchange. It is interesting that Sicco harpoon heads, carried by the initial Thule migrants all the way to Greenland, were replaced by the Thule 3 type within less than 200 years (McGhee 1984). Similarly the classic Clovis form gave way to regional stylistic variants (Folsom, Debert, Barnes, and Fell fishtail) about 300 or 400 years after the initial pulse of expansion.

Hunting giant mammals is a dangerous business, and success brings commensurate social standing. Historical Alaskan Eskimo whaling captains, or *umialiks*, enjoyed high status; similar high-status roles probably already existed in prehistoric Thule whaling societies (Grier 1999; Sheehan 1985). There are hints in the archaeological record, such as the elaborate burial of the Anzick child accompanied by dozens of finely crafted bifaces (Lahren and Bonnichsen 1974), that Clovis society may have contained more status differentiation than we usually assume. Among their other perquisites, Alaskan Eskimo chiefs and successful hunters often had two or more wives (Ray 1984:286). If Clovis hunters were also polygynous, this practice might help to account for the high birth rate that must be assumed in explaining the rapid colonization process.

Migrating whales were most efficiently intercepted by Thule hunters setting out from large centrally positioned villages. Park (1998), however, notes that 35 percent of the 259 archaeologically attested winter villages consisted of only three or fewer houses, with perhaps 15–20 inhabitants. He observes further that some of the larger villages may be repeatedly occupied sites spanning several centuries, so that the apparent population may be inflated. There is a similar problem in interpretations of large Paleoindian sites, such as Gault, Aubrey, Debert, and Bull Brook. Were these sites palimpsests created by repeated visits by the same small band; were they seasonal rendezvous loci, where normally dispersed families or microbands camped together to intercept migrating herds and to exchange goods, mates, and information; or were they one-time marshaling camps or staging areas (Anderson 1990; Dincauze 1993b) occupied by the first groups exploring an unknown territory (Meltzer, this volume)?

When the Little Ice Age set in around A.D. 1400, Thule hunters shifted from their former whaling focus to new strategies with a more interior aspect (McGhee 1984). Northern areas were depopulated, whereas settlement of the Low Arctic expanded. In the eastern Arctic, these adaptive changes mark the transition from Classic to Modified Thule (Whitridge 2001). This process resulted in the diverse seal- and caribou-hunting adaptations of the various historical Eskimo groups. Similarly, after mammoths were killed off during the drought at the end of the Alleröd period, Clovis hunters diversified during the Younger Dryas cold period (12,900–11,570 cal B.P.), shifting to bison, caribou, and deer in varied environmental settings across the continent.

Differences between Clovis and Thule

Some scholars might object to this emphasis on similarities, citing the profound differences between the Clovis and Thule migrations. The Inuit ancestors had several types of watercraft that allowed them to move much faster than people on foot, and they may have already developed dogsleds for terrestrial travel. Thus, their movement through coastal waters could have been much more rapid than the overland trek that Clovis people undertook. However, there is no reason to preclude Paleoindian use of skin-covered boats, perhaps similar to the Mandan bull boats (Engelbrecht and Seyfert 1994). Using hides to cover pole frames was presumably a common method of house construction in Upper Paleolithic Eurasia. The same technique would have sufficed for constructing simple boats. Although these boats might not have been adequate for long coastal voyages (Clark, this volume), they would have been useful for exploring major rivers, such as the Missouri. Watercraft must have been used to reach the Channel Islands off the southern California coast, where a human presence is now documented at about 10,950 B.P. by the redating of Arlington Springs Woman (Stafford et al. 2002).

Gramly's (1993) interpretation of bone rods from the East Wenatchee cache in Washington as sled runners seems far-fetched, and there is no other ostensible evidence of Paleoindian sleds. However, the use of dog-drawn travois by Paleoindians cannot be precluded. Based on skeletal morphology (Olsen and Olsen 1977) and DNA analysis (Leonard et al. 2002; Vila et al. 1997), the New World dog appears to be descended from Old World wolves, so Paleoindian ancestors probably already had domesticated dogs when they left Asia. Evidence of early dogs in western Beringia has been found at Ushki 1 in Kamchatka, where a dog burial dates to about 10,800 B.P. (Dikov 1996). Possible evidence of Paleoindian dogs at the same date has been reported from a Fell I (fishtail point) occupation at Tagua Tagua, Chile (Palma 1969).

Another objection to the Clovis-Thule analogy is that Thule people simply expanded their range into a familiar environment, for which they already possessed sophisticated technological and social adaptations; in contrast, Paleoindians had to adjust repeatedly to unfamiliar terrain and climate as they moved southward (Barton et al., this volume; Meltzer 1995:26, this volume). There are several rejoinders to this objection. The Arctic coastal regions do not, in fact, constitute a uniform environment. Thule material culture and social organization changed rapidly as the migrants encountered new local conditions. Whale-hunting techniques used in northern Alaska had to be altered in the eastern Arctic, which resulted in a new settlement pattern (McGhee 1984:371). Localized adaptations, sometimes entailing abandonment of whaling and a shift to caribou, fish, and seal, emerged during the second phase of Thule expansion, before around A.D. 1200–1300 (McGhee 1984:371; Whitridge 2001). It should be emphasized that these significant changes in basic subsistence patterns had been adopted less than 300 years after the Thule migration started.

If Paleoindians were similarly flexible and opportunistic, we should not be surprised to find evidence of major subsistence reorientation only a few centuries after initial colonization, an adaptation that may be exemplified by marine-focused sites on the southern coast of Peru, which were recently dated to about 11,000–10,700 B.P. (de France et al. 2001; Sandweiss et al. 1998, 2000). The Paleoindians traversed late Pleistocene environments that may have been less sharply differentiated than those of the Holocene, particularly with respect to faunal distributions (Barton et al., this volume; Meltzer, this volume; Whitney-Smith, this volume). Paleontologists often note in fossil assemblages the association of animals that are not sympatric today (e.g., FAUNMAP Working Group 1996). More importantly, the well-documented Paleoindian focus on hunting large migratory animals, such as mammoths, bison, and horses, would have permitted and even compelled wide-ranging movement across environmental boundaries (Kelly and Todd 1988). If they had stuck to the familiar mountain-edge environment as they moved south, Paleoindians could have reached New Mexico without having to change their lifeways; the Athabaskans did the same thing around A.D. 1400.

Preexisting Human Populations

Finally we must consider the most important ostensible difference between Thule and Clovis. Thule people were intruding into an environment that had already been occupied for more than 2,500 years; the resident Dorset population had been there for 1,500 years. Although Thule people evidently collected and sometimes imitated Dorset artifacts, there is no clear indication that they actually encountered living inhabitants in Dorset settlements, nor is there linguistic or cultural evidence of the absorption of Dorset people into Thule culture (Park 1993). Whether Thule expansion or environmental catastrophe was responsible, the Dorset people seem to have disappeared from the landscape abruptly and totally. In contrast to this Arctic situation, most of us have assumed, at least until recently, that Clovis people or their immediate ancestors entered a truly New World with no humans in it. If so, the Thule migration might be a less appropriate analog than the expansion of the Arctic Small Tool Tradition into the same region centuries earlier (ca. 4250–3650 B.P.), when the Arctic was an uninhabited terra incognita (Ellis 1998; Fiedel 1992:151; Maxwell 1976). That earlier migration was also very rapid; initial occupation of northern Labrador may have been as early as 4000 B.P. (Fitzhugh 1976).

Now we must consider Monte Verde. If this Chilean site is really a locus of human occupation, as some scholars have claimed (Dillehay 1997b; but see Fiedel 1999a for a skeptical critique), it seems that some people got into America centuries before Clovis, perhaps at the beginning of the Bölling warming at about 14,700 cal B.P. These supposed precursors were well organized, hunted proboscideans with finely crafted stone points (but may have butchered and skinned them using expediently collected, unmodified cobbles), and had a broad-spectrum foraging economy (Dillehay 1997b). Yet the fishtail points that are ubiquitous from Panama to Tierra del Fuego are derived from Clovis (Pearson, this volume), not from the lithic industry attributed to Monte Verde and perhaps also attested at Taima-Taima in Venezuela (Bryan et al. 1978). If we pursue my analogy, the role of Monte Verde could be compared to that of Dorset. Perhaps the Monte Verdeans were unable to cope with environmental changes brought on by the Antarctic Cold Reversal around 14,000 cal B.P. (Blunier et al. 1997), although these changes apparently were not drastic. More likely, fishtail-point makers and Monte Verdeans were in direct competition for the same habitats and resources (e.g., gomphothere meat), and the intruders succeeded in displacing the residents. Fishtail-like points have been found at Salto Chico, only six miles south of Monte Verde (Dillehay 1997b:50).

Discussion

We might consider whether the presence of an earlier population facilitated leapfrogging from one prime habitat to another, which would have allowed Clovis bands to fill the continent more rapidly than they might have if they had explored virgin territory (but see Barton et al., this volume; Meltzer, this volume). If we accept that a precursor population was already in place when Clovis expansion occurred, the fluted points must be seen in a new light. Fluting may have assured secure fastening of the point to the spear or foreshaft; it may have also taken on magical significance (Bradley 1993) as a cru-

cial prelude to hunting success. We must now wonder, however, if it also served an important social function as a stylistic marker by which Clovis people distinguished themselves from ethnically distinct competitors.

Even if it is ultimately proven (as I suspect it will be) that the few remaining pre-Clovis candidates are fatally flawed and that no other people were south of the ice sheets when the Clovis culture arrived, this explanation of fluting as a socially significant trait may still be valid. The development of fluting would be transposed, however, in Alaska, as two or more culture complexes (ethnic groups?) competed during their expansion into eastern Beringia: Nenana, Dyuktai-Paleoarctic, and early Clovis (north of the Brooks Range, where fluted points have been discovered as undated surface finds [Kunz and Reanier 1994]).

If Clovis people ventured into a landscape devoid of other humans, their rapid expansion may have resulted primarily from the quest for selected habitats (Barton et al., this volume; Meltzer, this volume). They may have been looking for lakes. Clovis migration appears to have coincided with a widespread drought in the Southwest, which probably corresponded to the warm spike that is evident in Greenland ice cores at the end of the Alleröd period about 13,100 cal B.P. Potable water may have been a major determinant of the Clovis settlement pattern (Haynes et al. 1999). Lakes would have also provided a suitable habitat for fish and waterfowl (Fiedel 2000b) and might have been magnets for thirsty megafauna. Paleoindians could have followed the obvious tracks of mammoth herds from one such oasis to the next (G. Haynes 1991 and personal communication, 2000), perhaps moving several hundred miles with each shift of their base camp to a new hunting ground. Thus, there may be a processual similarity in the island hopping of the early Polynesian Lapita people (ca. 3500 cal B.P.; Bellwood 1987), the leapfrogging of Linearbandkeramik people between patches of arable soil in central Europe (ca. 7000 cal B.P.; Fiedel and Anthony 1979, 2003), and the Clovis migration between dispersed mammoth refugia. This similarity would explain the seemingly explosive character of all three population movements.

8 Pan-American Paleoindian Dispersals and the Origins of Fishtail Projectile Points as Seen through the Lithic Raw-Material Reduction Strategies and Tool-Manufacturing Techniques at the Guardiría Site, Turrialba Valley, Costa Rica

Georges A. Pearson

Current New World colonization models must rely on implicit or explicit assumptions as well as key bridging arguments to consolidate the often meager and geographically spotty empirical evidence. Historically archaeologists have traced the expansion of early colonizers across the Americas through the recovery of fluted projectile points, which are considered to be unmistakable signs of the passage of Paleoindians through a region (Tankersley, this volume). Although many points of entry may have been used by early migrants "traveling" to the New World (Dixon 1993, 1999; Greenman 1963; Hall 2000; Rivet 1957; Robledo 1954), most scenarios start in the Bering region, where initial human movements followed a general north-to-south and west-to-east direction (Anderson and Gillam 2000; Barton et al., this volume; Kelly and Todd 1988; Lothrop 1961; Martin 1973; Sauer 1944; Steele et al. 1998; Tankersley 1991). This radiating "wave" is believed to have spread all the way to the tip of South America, culminating in a continentwide human saturation of unglaciated territories (Martin 1973). In situ technocultural changes, local economic specialization, demographic growth, and linguistic diversification followed. These time-dependent processes have often been used to support alternative migration routes into the Americas. For example, a common assumption equates high geographic density and variability of fluted points with length of occupation in a region. This assumption has led some researchers (Mason 1962; Stanford 1991; Williams and Stoltman 1965) to suggest that the Clovis culture originated in the southeastern United States because this area contains a high number of fluted points. (See Clark, this volume, for a discussion on the Clovis-Solutrean connection.) However, geomorphological variables (Ferring 1994), urban development, the availability of resources, or the carrying capacity of late Pleistocene–early Holocene environments (Barton et al., this volume; Steele et al. 1998) could easily explain this phenomenon.

Although the antiquity of fluted points was first recognized in North America (Cotter 1937; Figgins 1927, 1931; Howard 1935; Nelson 1933; Tankersley, this volume), more examples were later discovered farther south between Mexico and Tierra del Fuego (Aschman 1952; Bird 1938, 1988; Di Peso 1955; Sander 1959; Swauger and Mayer-Oakes 1952). Nevertheless, lanceolate forms, which are similar to North American Clovis examples, have been found at very few sites south of Panama (fig. 8.1c; Ardila Calderon and Politis 1989; Carluci 1963; Dillehay 2000:159; Jackson 1995; Jaimes 1997, 1999; Seguel and Campaña 1975). Beyond the isthmian junction, other fluted and nonfluted point types dominate the early record of South America.

In this paper, I present an overview of the current models proffered to explain the presence of Clovis-like points and fishtail projectile points (FTPPs) in Mexico, Central America, and South America. In light of these hypotheses, I also discuss the results from a technological analysis of the lithic assemblage from the Guardiría (Turrialba) Paleoindian site (Snarskis 1979) in Costa Rica. Guardiría is a key site because of its axial location between the continents and because its lithic assemblage contains Clovis-like points as well as FTPPs. I compare the information gathered from this analysis with North American Clovis technology to determine whether the presence of fluted points in lower Central America can be attributed to a population expansion or to a spread of ideas and how these new data might help us understand the origin of FTPPs. All radiocarbon dates presented below are uncalibrated unless otherwise indicated.

Early South American Lithic Industries

Before we can discuss the possible technological influences or connections between North and South America, an overview of early South American lithic industries is necessary. Presented below are some of the better-known and well-defined late Pleistocene–early Holocene complexes of South America.

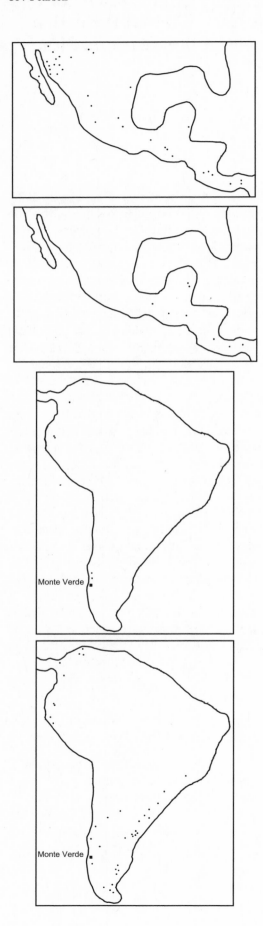

Fishtail Projectile Point Tradition

FTPPs were first discovered in 1937 at Fell's and Pali Aike Caves in Chile (Bird 1938, 1969; Empéraire et al. 1963). At the time, Bird was able to establish the antiquity of FTPPs based on their association with extinct horse and giant-ground-sloth remains (Bird 1988). Since then, many more FTPPs have been found throughout South America (fig. 8.1d; Bell 1965; Chauchat and Quiñones 1979; Flegenheimer 1980; Flegenheimer and Zarate 1989; Martínez 2001; Mayer-Oakes 1986b; Mazzanti 1997; Miotti 1995; Nami 1985, 1987a,b; Ossa 1976; Politis 1991; Schobinger 1971, 1973; Suárez 2000) and in Central America (Bird and Cooke 1978; Bullen and Plowden 1963; MacNeish et al. 1980; Pearson and Bostrom 1998; Ranere and Cooke 1991; Santamaria 1981; Snarskis 1979). Although detailed descriptions and context of find are not available for all South American FTPPs (Politis 1991), many reported examples have unmistakable fluted bases.

Most Central and South American FTPPs differ technologically from Clovis-like points because they were made by thinning large, flat flakes (Bird and Cooke 1978; Ranere and Cooke 1991) as opposed to being the end products of multistage bifacial reduction (Bradley 1982, 1991, 1993; Callahan 1979). Blades on Central American FTPPs were bifacially thinned by removing a series of large expanding flakes from opposing margins. These flakes overlapped at the points' midlines and effectively flattened their central surfaces. Final shaping was accomplished through bimarginal percussion and pressure (Pearson and Bostrom 1998; Ranere and Cooke 1991). Many South American FTPPs were fashioned on flake blanks that required only minimal shaping, leaving large, intact, pseudofluted surfaces on their ventral sides (Bird 1969; Mayer-Oakes 1986b:52). Radiocarbon dates from South American FTPP sites range between 12,400 and 7900 B.P. (table 8.1).

El Jobo Complex

First defined in the late 1950s (Cruxent 1956, 1957; Jackson 1999), the El Jobo complex of Venezuela is characterized by willow-leaf-shaped points with biconvex cross sections that are typically manufactured from

FIGURE 8.1 Geographic distribution of Clovis-like point and FTPP sites: *(a)* Clovis-like point sites in Central America; *(b)* FTPP sites in Central America; *(c)* Clovis-like point sites in South America; and *(d)* FTPP sites in South America.

TABLE 8.1 Radiocarbon Dates from South American FTPP Sites

Country	Site	Lab No.	^{14}C Date	Material	Reference
Ecuador	El Inga	R-1070/2	9030 ± 144	Soil org.	Bell 1965
Ecuador	El Inga	R-1073/3	7928 ± 132	Soil org.	Bell 1965
Argentina	Cerro la China 1	AA-8953	10,804 ± 75	Charcoal	Flegenheimer and Zarate 1997
Argentina	Cerro la China 1	AA-1327	10,790 ± 120	Charcoal	Flegenheimer and Zarate 1997
Argentina	Cerro la China 1	AA-8952	10,745 ± 75	Charcoal	Flegenheimer and Zarate 1997
Argentina	Cerro la China 1	I-12741	10,730 ± 150	Charcoal	Flegenheimer and Zarate 1997
Argentina	Cerro la China 1	AA-8954	10,525 ± 75	Charcoal	Flegenheimer and Zarate 1997
Argentina	Cerro la China 2	AA-8955	11,150 ± 135	Charcoal	Flegenheimer and Zarate 1997
Argentina	Cerro la China 2	AA-8956	10,560 ± 75	Charcoal	Flegenheimer and Zarate 1997
Argentina	Cerro la China 3	AA-1328	*10,610 ± 180	Charcoal	Flegenheimer and Zarate 1997
Argentina	Cerro el Sombrero	AA-4765	10,725 ± 90	Charcoal	Flegenheimer and Zarate 1997
Argentina	Cerro el Sombrero	AA-4767	10,675 ± 110	Charcoal	Flegenheimer and Zarate 1997
Argentina	Cerro el Sombrero	AA-5220	10,480 ± 70	Charcoal	Flegenheimer and Zarate 1997
Argentina	Cerro el Sombrero	AA-4766	10,270 ± 85	Charcoal	Flegenheimer and Zarate 1997
Argentina	Cerro el Sombrero	AA-5221	8060 ± 140	Charcoal	Flegenheimer and Zarate 1997
Argentina	Piedra Museo	LP-949	9230 ± 105	Bone	Miotti 1999
Argentina	Piedra Museo	LP-859	9710 ±105	Bone	Miotti 1999
Argentina	Piedra Museo	AA-8428	10,400 ± 80	Bone	Miotti 1995
Argentina	Abrigo los Pinos	—	9570 ± 120	Charcoal	Mazzanti 1997
Argentina	Cueva Tixi	AA-12130	*10,375 ± 90	Charcoal	Mazzanti 1997
Argentina	Cueva Tixi	AA-12131	*10,045 ± 95	Charcoal	Mazzanti 1997
Argentina	Paso Otero 5	AA-19291	10,190 ± 120	Burned bone	Martínez 2001
Argentina	Paso Otero 5	AA-39363	10,440 ± 100	Burned bone	Martínez 2001
Chile	Cueva del Medio	PITT-0343	12,390 ± 180	Burned bone	Borrero et al. 1998
Chile	Cueva del Medio	NUTA-1737	11,120 ± 130	Bone	Borrero et al. 1998
Chile	Cueva del Medio	NUTA-2197	11,040 ± 250	Bone	Borrero et al. 1998
Chile	Cueva del Medio	NUTA-2330	10,960 ± 150	Bone	Borrero et al. 1998
Chile	Cueva del Medio	NUTA-2331	10,860 ± 160	Bone	Borrero et al. 1998
Chile	Cueva del Medio	NUTA-1812	10,850 ± 130	Bone	Borrero et al. 1998
Chile	Cueva del Medio	NUTA-2332	10,710 ± 190	Bone	Borrero et al. 1998
Chile	Cueva del Medio	NUTA-1811	10,710 ± 100	Bone	Borrero et al. 1998
Chile	Cueva del Medio	NUTA-1735	10,450 ± 100	Bone	Borrero et al. 1998
Chile	Cueva del Medio	Beta-52522	10,430 ± 80	Charcoal	Nami 1996
Chile	Cueva del Medio	NUTA-1734	10,430 ± 100	Bone	Borrero et al. 1998
Chile	Cueva del Medio	Gr-N 14913	10,310 ± 70	Charcoal	Nami 1996
Chile	Cueva del Medio	Beta-39081	10,930 ± 230	Charcoal	Nami 1996
Chile	Cueva del Medio	Gr-N 14911	10,550 ± 120	Bone	Nami 1996
Chile	Cueva del Medio	Beta-58105	10,350 ± 130	Burned bone	Menegaz and Nami 1994
Chile	Cueva del Medio	Beta-40281	9770 ± 70	Bone	Nami 1996
Chile	Cueva del Medio	PITT-0344	9595 ± 115	Charcoal	Nami 1996
Chile	Tres Arroyo	Beta-20219	11,880 ± 250	Charcoal	Nami 1996
Chile	Tres Arroyo	Beta-101023	10,600 ± 90	—	Borrero 1999
Chile	Tres Arroyo	DIC-2333	10,420 ± 100	Charcoal	Nami 1996
Chile	Tres Arroyo	DIC-2732	10,280 ± 110	Charcoal	Nami 1996
Chile	Fell's Cave	I-3988	11,000 ± 170	Charcoal	Bird 1969
Chile	Fell's Cave	W-915	10,720 ± 300	Charcoal	Bird 1969
Chile	Fell's Cave	I-5146	10,080 ± 160	—	Saxon 1976
Chile	Pali Aike	C-485	8639 ± 450	Bone	Bird 1951
Chile	Tagua Tagua 1	GX-1205	11,380 ± 320	Charcoal	Montané 1968
Chile	Tagua Tagua 1	—	11,320 ± 300	—	Núñez et al. 1994
Chile	Tagua Tagua 1	—	11,000± 170	—	Núñez et al. 1994
Chile	Tagua Tagua 2	Beta-45518	9700 ± 90	Charcoal	Núñez et al. 1994
Chile	Tagua Tagua 2	Beta-45519	9900 ± 100	Charcoal	Núñez et al. 1994
Chile	Tagua Tagua 2	Beta-45520	10,190 ± 130	Bone	Núñez et al. 1994

*No diagnostic tools but believed to be FTPP occupations.

quartzite (Nami 1993). Although initial discoveries of El Jobo points were commonly associated with the remains of extinct mammals (Cruxent 1970), mixing and other contextual problems at the El Jobo, Muaco, Taima-Taima, and Cucuruchu sites cast doubt on the alleged antiquity of the points (Haynes 1974; Lynch 1974, 1990). Subsequent excavations at the Taima-Taima site in 1976 (Ochsenius and Gruhn 1999) exposed the midsection of an El Jobo point within the remains of a juvenile *Haplomastodon* (Gruhn and Bryan 1984). Based on a series of radiocarbon assays on wooden twigs believed to be part of one animal's stomach contents, the investigators assigned an age of about 13,000 B.P. for this kill site (Bryan and Gruhn 1999:57).

The El Jobo complex is believed to represent a unique South American pre-Clovis bifacial industry with no cultural affiliation with Clovis Paleoindians (Bryan 1973, 1983). This interpretation has been challenged by critics, who maintain that these artifacts may not be of pre-Clovis age and could have migrated downward through the soft sediments. In addition, upwelling springs may have contaminated the remains with older carbon (Haynes 1974; Lynch 1974, 1994). More recently, an AMS date (B-95602) of 10,710 ± 60 B.P. was obtained on bone collagen from a giant-ground-sloth kill site at El Vano in the Venezuelan Andes (Jaimes 1998). Despite a technological analysis of El Jobo points (Nami 1993), which demonstrated marked differences in reduction strategies when compared with Clovis, new discoveries of fluted examples from the Los Planes site (Jaimes 1997, 1999) might indicate a previously unsuspected relationship between the bearers of these two industries. Two fragments of possible El Jobo points have also been reported from Panama but remain undated (Pearson 2000a,b; Ranere and Cooke 2003). Interestingly El Jobo points show some resemblance to projectiles discovered at Monte Verde, where gomphothere remains were also unearthed (Dillehay 1989, 1997b).

Middle Magdalena/Monte Alegre Complex

The unfluted stemmed projectile points belonging to the Middle Magdalena and Monte Alegre complexes share many similarities (Roosevelt 1998) and are grouped here as a single category. Both point types are characterized by straight bifacially flaked blades shaped by the removal of small parallel pressure flakes, which gives them isosceles or equilateral triangular outlines, depending on their degree of resharpening (Cooke 1998; López Castaño 1989; Roosevelt et al. 1996;

Simões 1976). Shoulders are inversely tapered, and stem shapes range from sharply contracted to pointed. The Middle Magdalena complex of Colombia is dated between 10,400 ± 90 (Beta-40855) and 10,230 ± 80 (Beta-40854) B.P., based on radiocarbon assays from the La Palestina site (López Castaño 1989, 1995, 1999). Projectile points with similar attributes were also discovered at the undated or later sites of Peñones de Bogotá, Puerto Berrío (Ardila Calderon 1991; López Castaño 1990, 1994, 1995), Yondó (Cooke 1998), Mahates, Bentanci (Reichel-Dolmatoff 1965), and Santander (Robledo 1954).

The Monte Alegre complex of Brazil contains comparable triangular stemmed points manufactured from hyaline quartz, such as those discovered at the Tapajós River (Simões 1976) and Caverna da Pedra Pintada (Roosevelt et al. 1996). Radiocarbon dates associated with this Amazonian complex range from 11,145 ± 135 (GX17413) to 10,110 ± 60 (GX19532CAMS) B.P. (Roosevelt 1998) and average approximately 10,500 B.P. (Gibbons 1995). Optically stimulated luminescence and thermoluminescence analyses on sediments and burned lithic artifacts from Caverna da Pedra Pintada provided additional dates ranging from 12,000 to 11,500 B.P. and from 17,500 to 11,900 B.P., respectively (Michab et al. 1998). Faunal and macrobotanical remains recovered from Caverna da Pedra Pintada indicate that these early hunter-gatherers were well adapted to tropical rain forests and subsisted on fruits, nuts, and fish (Roosevelt 1998). Like El Jobo assemblages, the Monte Alegre complex is believed to have derived from a pre-existing culture unrelated to North American Clovis industries. It is also worth mentioning that an undated projectile point with characteristics similar to those of the Middle Magdalena/Monte Alegre specimens was discovered off the Venezuelan coast on the present island of Trinidad (Harris 1991).

Restrepo and Sipaliwini Complexes

Restrepo points from Colombia form a loose ensemble of fluted and unfluted stemmed points that share a basic outline. Restrepo points are unlike FTPPs in overall shape and were manufactured from bifacial preforms (Ardila Calderon 1991; Cooke 1998; Correal Urrego 1993; Reichel-Dolmatoff 1965). Their blades vary between straight and excurvate; at least one displays a serrated edge (see Correal Urrego 1993:fig. 9). Shoulders are variable, and bases are usually straight to slightly concave (Ardila Calderon 1991; Reichel-Dolmatoff 1965), with flute scars extending past the stem and into the blade. Only a single example has been recovered from controlled excavations (Correal Urrego 1983). Radiocarbon dates are still lacking for this complex. Other stemmed examples that may be related to Restrepo points were found in Guyana (Evans and Meggers 1960; Roth 1924; Williams 1998) and in Surinam (Boomert 1977, 1980; Versteeg 1998).

Abriense and Tequendamiense Traditions

The Abriense and Tequendamiense tool traditions of Colombia were first identified at the El Abra and Tequendama type-site rockshelters (Correal Urrego and van der Hammen 1977; Hurt et al. 1977). Abriense assemblages are characterized by small retouched flakes grouped under the Edge-trimmed Tool Tradition (Gruhn and Bryan 1998; Hurt 1977; Nieuwenhuis 1998). Tequendamiense assemblages show a higher degree of workmanship and include formal tool types and bifaces (Cooke 1998; Gruhn and Bryan 1998). Both industries are believed to have been used by groups of transhumant hunter-gatherers, who moved between the highlands of the Sabana de Bogotá and the Magdalena Valley.

The earliest Abriense flake tools at El Abra 2 are associated with a date of 12,400 ± 160 B.P. (GrN-5556), whereas assemblages at the Tequendama 1 rockshelter range in age between 10,920 ± 260 (GrN-6539) and 10,460 ± 130 (GrN-6731) B.P. (Cooke 1998; Correal Urrego and van der Hammen 1977). Abriense and Tequendamiense tools were also found in association with proboscidean remains dated to 11,740 ± 110 B.P. (GrN-9375) at the Tibitó site (Correal Urrego 1981). Other unifacial industries were discovered at the Nemocón 4 and Sueva 1 rockshelters (Correal Urrego 1979). A charcoal date of 10,090 ± 90 B.P. (GrN-8111) was obtained above Abriense-like tools at Sueva 1, providing a minimum age for the occupation (Correal Urrego 1986; Dillehay 2000:123). Despite these results, the Edge-trimmed Tool Tradition is still considered to be ill defined and equivocally dated (Cooke 1998; Lynch 1990, 1994). Moreover, the apparent absence of bifacial flaking in the Abriense industry might reflect a sampling problem (Dillehay 2000:118).

El Inga and Río Cauca Stemmed Points

The El Inga site was discovered in 1956 in the Andean highlands of Ecuador near Quito (Bell 1960, 1965, 2000; Mayer-Oakes 1966; Mayer-Oakes and Bell 1960a,b). El Inga is just one of many localities near the capital where both fluted and unfluted bifacial projectile points have been discovered (Carluci 1963; Mayer-Oakes 1982; Santiana and Carluci 1962). These include Clovis-like, fishtail, Ayampitin-like (teardrop- and laurel-leaf-shaped), Paiján-like, and various stemmed and pentagonal specimens. Among this last category were points described as "Broad Stemmed" (Bell 1965; Mayer-Oakes 1986a,b) and "Shouldered Lanceolate" (Mayer-Oakes 1986a,b) or "Arenal" (Lynch and Pollock 1980). El Inga Broad Stemmed points have triangular outlines and straight to slightly contracted stems. Shoulders are horizontal or slightly tapered above straight or concave bases. Many examples were manufactured on flat flakes that typically exhibit unretouched portions of the original blanks, giving some a pseudofluted appearance. El Inga Shouldered Lanceolate points are pentagonal or rhomboidal in shape. Their technological and typological attributes suggest that they may, in fact, be subtypes (knife?) or preforms for broad-stemmed projectiles (Mayer-Oakes 1986b:151).

Five radiocarbon dates ranging from 9000 to 3900 B.P. were obtained from soil samples at El Inga (Bell 1965). Subsequent comparisons between radiocarbon results and obsidian hydration rinds, measured on artifacts from known stratigraphic proveniences, suggested that the earliest dates of 9030 ± 144 (R-1070/2) and 7928 ± 132 (R-1073/3) B.P. were the most reliable (Bell 1977). Radiocarbon dates derived from soil samples from the nearby site of San José ranged between 3470 and 1480 B.P., whereas obsidian hydration dates from the same locality clustered between 11,300 and 9300 B.P. (Mayer-Oakes 1982, 1986b; Mayer-Oakes and Portnoy 1986, 1993). Another pentagonal point was recovered at Chobshi Cave in the Ecuadorian province of Azuay and was bracketed between 10,010 ± 430 (Tx-1133) and 8480 ± 200 (Tx-1132) B.P. (Lynch and Pollock 1980).

Additional broad-stemmed and shouldered lanceolate points were discovered at the La Elvira and Alto Cauca sites in the Popayán Valley of Colombia (Gnecco and Illera 1989; Illera and Gnecco 1986; Mayer-Oakes 1986b:205; note that Dillehay 2000:123–125 incorporates the Popayán and Middle Magdalena points in the Restrepo complex). One example, found on the surface at La Elvira, is fluted on one side (see Gnecco 1994:fig. 2d) and is estimated to date between 10,000 and 9000 B.P. (Gnecco 1994:39). Pentagonal bifaces associated with radiocarbon dates of 10,050 ± 100 (B-

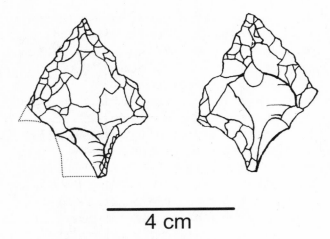

FIGURE 8.2 El Inga–like stemmed point from Lake La Yeguada, Panama.

4 cm

65878), 10,030 ± 60 (B-93275), and 9530 ± 100 (B-65877) B.P. were unearthed at the San Isidro site, located approximately 30 kilometers downstream from Popayán on the Cauca River (Gnecco and Bravo 1994; Gnecco and Mora 1997).

Excavations in the Orinoco Valley of Venezuela recovered another pentagonal point estimated to date between 9000 and 6000 B.P. (Barse 1990). The geographic range of broad-stemmed points may also extend into Panama, where a similar projectile point was discovered at a quarry and workshop near Lake La Yeguada (Hall 1999; Pearson 2000a,b). This specimen was fashioned from a flat jasper flake and displayed flutelike basal-thinning removal on one side of its broken base (fig. 8.2).

Paiján Complex

The Paiján complex is found on the northern coast of Peru. Paiján sites include La Cumbre, the Quirihuac Shelter (Ossa 1978; Ossa and Moseley 1971), and several open-air workshops, campsites, and burials in the Cupisnique desert (Chauchat 1975, 1978, 1992). Paiján sites in the Pampa de los Fosiles date between 10,640 ± 260 (GIF-9403) and 8730 ± 160 (GIF-5159) B.P. (Hall 1995). Most Paiján stemmed points were manufactured from bifacial preforms reduced by direct percussion and shaped by pressure flaking (Pelegrin and Chauchat 1993). Blades are slender, vary morphologically from straight to excurvate to parallel-sided, and are often characterized by acuminated distal tips. Shoulders are horizontal to slightly inversely tapered, and

their narrow unfluted stems are straight to incurvate. Paiján points have been found associated with fish-bone middens, suggesting to investigators that these delicate implements served primarily, although not exclusively, as tips for fishing spears (Chauchat and Briceño 1998). Most importantly, both Paiján and FTPPs were found at La Cumbre (Ossa 1976) and Quebrada Santa María (Chauchat and Pelegrin 1994), indicating that both types may have been used concurrently by the same groups. Based on this evidence, Chauchat and Briceño (1998) believe that Paiján points were ultimately derived from FTPPs, which represent an ancestral bifacial industry. According to this scenario, Paiján points were a technological adaptation by Andean hunters, following an economic diversification or shift from interior to coastal resources. Dillehay (2000:150), however, believes that Paiján and FTPPs represent coexisting but culturally different populations. It should also be noted that Paiján points from the Peruvian coast exhibit some of the same characteristics as the Middle Magdalena specimens (López Castaño 1999:112), suggesting a possible link between these two regions.

The complexes and traditions described above demonstrate that the Paleoindian record of South America is quite intricate and, like that of North America, incorporates many varieties of point types (Dillehay 2000; Gnecco 1990). To this already complicated picture we must now interpose the controversial evidence from Monte Verde (Adovasio and Pedler 1997; Dillehay 1997a; Dillehay et al. 1999a; Fiedel 1999a, 2000c; Meltzer et al. 1997), which has pushed back the initial peopling of the New World by about 1,000 to 500 radiocarbon years. A perplexing outcome of this paradigmatic reshuffling continues to be an absence of similar early sites in North and Central America (but see Barton et al., this volume) and a need to explain the cultural distinctions between Monte Verdeans and Clovis populations. This situation has forced archaeologists to reevaluate the position and role of Clovis groups and to reconsider alternate early migration routes, such as the Pacific Coast (Dillehay 1999; Dixon 1999; Fladmark 1979, 1983; Gruhn 1988, 1994). A coastal migration could explain how the interior of the continent was bypassed while still accounting for the presence of humans in South America (Dillehay 1999). Early maritime sites are well documented on the Pacific side of the Americas and may represent descendants of ancient communities that occupied these shores before the Holocene marine transgression (Chauchat 1992; de France et al. 2001; Dixon et al. 1997; Fedje and Christensen 1999; Keefer et al. 1998; Llagostera 1979; Orr 1962; Sandweiss et al. 1989, 1998; Stothert 1985, 1988; Wisner 1999). One thing is certain: Monte Verde has raised more questions about the peopling of the Americas than it has answered.

To this day, there is no consensus on whether South American fishtail and stemmed points were a result of technological modifications by Clovis groups expanding south (Faught and Dunbar 1997; Lynch 1978; Morrow and Morrow 1999; Ranere 1980, 1997; Ranere and Cooke 1991; Schobinger 1988; Snarskis 1979) or were an independent South American invention carried north by a separate population (Bryan 1973; Politis 1991; Rouse 1976). The historical, technological, and biological relationships between these various industries and the humans who manufactured them are still a matter of conjecture. The ongoing debates over the origin of early South American fluted and unfluted points and their possible connection to Clovis have yet to provide definite answers to some basic questions about the peopling of Central and South America. These problems have inhibited the development of models that integrate both hemispheres of the Americas into a "unified theory" of the peopling of the New World (see Barton et al., this volume). Monte Verde has created a new challenge in the effort to formulate Paleoindian colonization models at a continental scale because it must now be incorporated with the North and South American fluted-point data. Archaeologists must address the current arguments over the relationships between Clovis and other early complexes in South America before they can advance to new levels of model building and hypothesis testing (Bonnichsen and Schneider 1999). The current problem is summarized by Dillehay et al. (1992:186), who state, "Until a secure north-to-south migratory linkage is established between the two continents, it is just as likely that South Americans with flutes and stemmed points migrated north."

The Fluting Technique in Central America

The presence of such a specialized reduction strategy as the fluting technique in both North and South America can be explained either by a pan-continental expansion of related populations or by contact between flute-using groups and other Paleoindians. The idea that fluted points appeared during the same general time period in both North and South America as a result of independent technological convergence (Mayer-

Oakes 1986a; Politis 1991) seems an improbable stretch of coincidence (Lynch 1978; O'Brien et al. 2001:1117). Although most archaeologists would agree with this assessment, the nature and direction of this undeniable interaction still fuel debates (Bonnichsen 1991). In general, the disputes over the origins of South American fluted points (including FTPPs) oppose two main viewpoints: technological diffusion versus human migrations with or without replacement. The early record of Central America could hold the key to answering many of these lingering questions (Dillehay and Meltzer 1991; Meltzer 1995:36).

Mexican and Central American Lanceolate Fluted Points

Diagnostic Paleoindian points have been recovered in all Central American countries except Honduras, El Salvador, and Nicaragua. At least 81 Clovis-like points have been discovered between the Río Grande and the Darien province of Panama (fig. 8.3). Later Paleoindian points, such as Folsom, Plainview, Golondrina, and possibly Meserve/Dalton, have also been found in Mexico (Epstein 1969; MacNeish 1958; Muller 1961) and perhaps Belize (MacNeish et al. 1980). Unfortunately all but a few were surface finds with no means of direct dating. Many specimens are similar to the "classic" straight-based Clovis points from the western United States, whereas others vary technologically and morphologically. For example, many Central American fluted lanceolate points have constricting, or "waisted," bases (Morrow and Morrow 1999; Snarskis 1979). Flaking scars on some specimens (Hester et al. 1980a,b; Ranere and Cooke 1991; Snarskis 1979) indicate that they were manufactured by removing a series of large transverse thinning flakes from opposite margins that traveled beyond the preform's midline. Bimarginal retouch was then used to shape the points; it also removed the initiation and termination scars of the large lateral thinning flakes. Because co-medial flaking (Bradley 1982, 1993) was not used in the final stages of the reduction process on these particular specimens, the blades are often characterized by broad transverse concavities surrounded by small parallel flake scars at their edges (Hester et al. 1980a,b; Ranere and Cooke 1991; Snarskis 1979). Interestingly these points recall Ross County (Prufer and Baby 1963:16), Simpson, and similar Clovis-related types from the eastern and Gulf Coast states, suggesting a possible connection along the Atlantic coastline (Faught and Anderson 1996; Faught and Dunbar 1997).

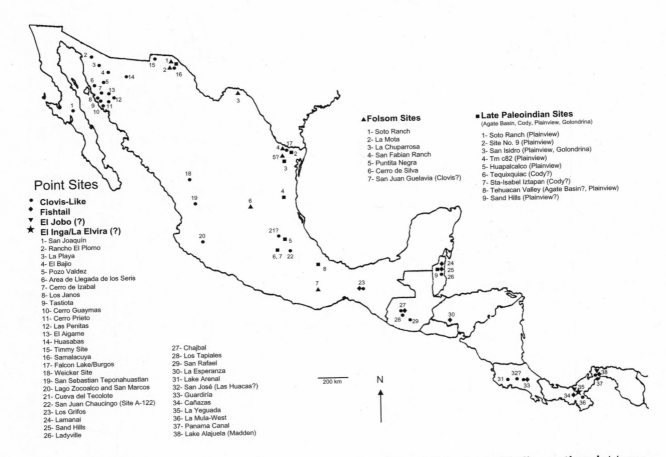

Point Sites
- ● Clovis-Like
- ◆ Fishtail
- ▼ El Jobo (?)
- ★ El Inga/La Elvira (?)

1- San Joaquín
2- Rancho El Plomo
3- La Playa
4- El Bajío
5- Pozo Valdez
6- Area de Llegada de los Seris
7- Cerro de Izabal
8- Los Janos
9- Tastiota
10- Cerro Guaymas
11- Cerro Prieto
12- Las Penitas
13- El Aigame
14- Huasabas
15- Timmy Site
16- Samalacuya
17- Falcon Lake/Burgos
18- Weicker Site
19- San Sebastian Teponahuastlan
20- Lago Zocoalco and San Marcos
21- Cueva del Tecolote
22- San Juan Chaucingo (Site A-122)
23- Los Grifos
24- Lamanai
25- Sand Hills
26- Ladyville

27- Chajbal
28- Los Tapiales
29- San Rafael
30- La Esperanza
31- Lake Arenal
32- San José (Las Huacas?)
33- Guardiría
34- Cañazas
35- La Yeguada
36- La Mula-West
37- Panama Canal
38- Lake Alajuela (Madden)

▲Folsom Sites

1- Soto Ranch
2- La Mota
3- La Chuparrosa
4- San Fabian Ranch
5- Puntita Negra
6- Cerro de Silva
7- San Juan Guelavia (Clovis?)

■ Late Paleoindian Sites
(Agate Basin, Cody, Plainview, Golondrina)

1- Soto Ranch (Plainview)
2- Site No. 9 (Plainview)
3- San Isidro (Plainview, Golondrina)
4- Tm c82 (Plainview)
5- Huapalcalco (Plainview)
6- Tequixquiac (Cody?)
7- Sta-Isabel Iztapan (Cody?)
8- Tehuacan Valley (Agate Basin?, Plainview)
9- Sand Hills (Plainview?)

200 km

N

FIGURE 8.3 Geographic distribution of Central American Paleoindian sites with diagnostic point types.

Mexican and Central American Fluted Stemmed Points

Approximately 15 possible FTPPs have been discovered in Mexico and Central America (fig. 8.3), with an additional 13 reportedly found in Belize (Zeitlin 1984). Although some specimens are questionable (Bullen and Plowden 1963; MacNeish et al. 1980), FTPPs seem to have spread between the isthmuses of Tehuantepec and Panama. As with Clovis-like points, most Central American FTPPs were recovered from undatable open-air sites. All Mexican and Central American FTPPs that have an intact base (n = 14) are fluted. (Note: The base fragment recovered from Los Tapiales could represent an additional FTPP because it displays a "slight shoulder"; Gruhn and Bryan 1977:246).

The northernmost examples of FTPPs were discovered at the Los Grifos site in Mexico (García-Bárcena 1979; Santamaria 1981). Two complete specimens have also been reported from Belize (MacNeish et al. 1980;

Pearson and Bostrom 1998). Other purported FTPPs have come from the La Esperanza site in Honduras, where two fluted stemmed points were discovered (Bullen and Plowden 1963). Two additional FTPPs were also recovered at the Guardiría site in Costa Rica (Ranere and Cooke 1991; Snarskis 1977, 1979). Of potential significance is the fact that most of the FTPPs from Central America have come from Panama. Six were discovered along the exposed shoreline of Lake Alajuela/Madden (Bird and Cooke 1977, 1978; Ranere and Cooke 1991; Sander 1959, 1964), and another was found in a cave in Cañazas (Ranere and Cooke 2003).

Shoulders on Central American FTPPs are slightly broader and more angular than those on classic South American Fell I types, which tend to taper more gradually toward the stem (Bird 1969; Bird and Cooke 1978; Politis 1991; Schobinger 1973). However, these morphological variations could be attributable to different degrees of resharpening. Belizean and Panamanian

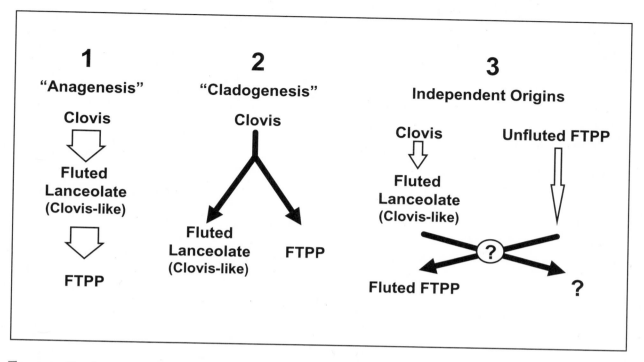

FIGURE 8.4   Models of hypothetical origins of FTPPs.

FTPPs are similar to Restrepo points from Colombia (Ardila Calderon 1991; Bray 1984; Correal Urrego 1983; Reichel-Dolmatoff 1965) and some Sipaliwini points from Guyana and Surinam (Boomert 1977; Evans and Meggers 1960; Williams 1998). This similarity might indicate that Central American and northern South American so-called FTPPs were used by culturally distinct human groups, who were unrelated to populations from the southern cone (Politis 1991). Alternatively northern and southern FTPPs could represent separate moments in a single evolutionary continuum. Other technological similarities, such as those between waisted Clovis-like points from Florida and Panama (Faught and Dunbar 1997), might indicate that population movements along the eastern seaboard of the Americas were widespread and bidirectional and may have even given rise to a circum-Caribbean Paleoindian culture area (Pearson and Bostrom 1998). Although the geographic distributions of FTPPs and Clovis-like points clearly overlap in lower Central America (fig. 8.1a,b; Bird and Cooke 1978; Ranere and Cooke 1991; Snarskis 1979), none of the Costa Rican and Panamanian examples have been dated.

The Origins of South American Fishtail Points

At least three models (fig. 8.4) have been proposed to explain the origins of South American FTPPs and their relationship to Clovis (Bryan 1973; Faught and Dunbar 1997; Lynch 1978; Morrow and Morrow 1999; Politis 1991; Ranere 1980, 1997; Rouse 1976; Schobinger 1988; Snarskis 1979). Each of the hypotheses presented below carries its own set of assumptions and predictions, but all share the idea that the fluting technique was a northern innovation that first appeared and spread with Clovis populations.

Model 1: Anagenesis

FTPPs were the end product of a single evolutionary lineage, starting with parallel-sided Clovis points, changing to waisted forms, and ending with fishtail and other fluted stemmed types (Lynch 1978; Morrow and Morrow 1999; Ranere 1980, 1997; Snarskis 1979). This first model predicts that FTPPs can never be as old as the oldest North American Clovis points. Under this scenario, point assemblages will display a mixture or continuum of morphological and technological traits spread over time (O'Brien et al. 2001). Clear-cut distinctions between individual specimens based on common typological classifications may not be obvious. Observable variations are expected to overlap geographically, perhaps over large areas, with the most significant differences found at geographical and temporal extremities. Morphological and technological changes could be attributed to stochastic drift or selective pressures. The expected pattern for this model predicts that FTPPs will diverge technologically, typologically, or both over chronological and geographical clines. In other words, the similarities between Clovis points and FTPPs will decrease through time and space; the farther south FTPPs are found, the less they will resemble Clovis points, if we assume that a return migration did not occur (Anthony 1990).

Model 2: Cladogenesis

FTPPs were the result of a single or multiple cultural speciation(s) that split Clovis into a new fishtail or stemmed industry and one or more contemporaneous Clovis-like industry(ies). The chronological prediction of this second model is the same as the first: FTPPs can never be as old as the basal Clovis culture. We might expect less geographic overlap between these projectile points, if we assume that morphological and technological differences (i.e., speciation events) are reflections of distinct environmental pressures, economic niches, or local raw-material quality and availability. Greater divergence is also expected with time and distance, but, unlike the first model, transitional projectile forms may be short-lived and limited due to more rapid selection or extinction.

Model 3: Independent Origins

South American bifacial stemmed points (including FTPPs) were the product of one or more independent invention(s) associated with a single or multiple non-Clovis migration(s). These first South Americans later came into contact with Clovis-related groups, from whom they borrowed the fluting technique (Bryan 1983; García-Bárcena 1979; Gruhn and Bryan 1977).

Although the nature of this encounter and its biological ramifications are speculative, it is considered responsible for the exchange of ideas that led to the application of the fluting technique to FTPPs. This is the only model that allows, but does not necessarily require, FTPPs to be as old or older than the oldest Clovis points. Geographical predictions are difficult to assess, but some degree of overlap is expected because con-

tact is posited by this model. Technological similarities between Clovis points and FTPPs would also decrease farther south or, more precisely, closest to the FTPP center of origin. Unlike the other models, a separate origin for FTPPs predicts that the youngest examples will share the most technological traits with Clovis points (e.g., fluted versus unfluted bases).

Because the predictions and the expected archaeological signatures for these three models are not mutually exclusive and because our data are still deficient, no model can be completely rejected at present. This situation is compounded by the particular geographical characteristics of lower Central America, which undoubtedly fractured "waves" of humans migrating south. The narrow Isthmus of Panama funneled populations into South America, and the Colombian coast, which formed a major crossroads, must have separated groups and accelerated cultural differentiation (Dillehay 1999). Consequently Martin's (1973; Mosimann and Martin 1975) radiating "bow waves" model breaks down at the doorstep of South America and must be reevaluated in light of these geographic variables. The peopling of South America must be envisioned as if it were an island, and the dynamic of its colonization must be approached accordingly (Beaton 1991; Bowdler 1977; Rindos and Webb 1992; Webb and Rindos 1997). Regardless of the initial route(s) taken, be it via the interior, the Atlantic Coast, or the Pacific Coast, the constriction of the Isthmus of Panama would have focused the point of entry into South America within a narrow area, mimicking a maritime landing.

Figure 8.5 presents four migration scenarios that illustrate the complexity of the situation created by the geographical characteristics of the Isthmian region and northern South America. These are basic models that allow many permutations. They assume a constant rate of dispersal and are used here simply to illustrate the problem. Furthermore, they do not factor in topography or hydrography, which would add to this complexity (Anderson and Gillam 2000; Faught and Anderson 1996; Steele et al. 1998).

Clearly, geographical and chronological data associated with the expansion of the first South Americans may not be obviously patterned across that continent. Due to the paucity of radiocarbon dates in Central America, we must rely on detailed technological analyses to help unravel the nature of the relationship between Clovis points and FTPPs. Because both types overlap in lower Central America, this region represents a key area in which to conduct such research.

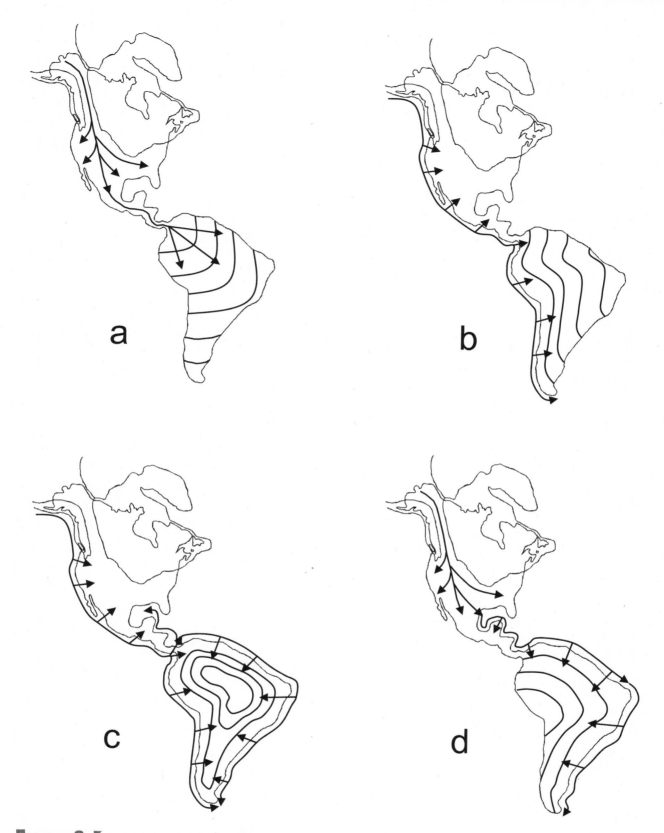

FIGURE 8.5 Hypothetical migration routes from North to South America and population expansions in South America: *(a)* interior migration, with north-to-south expansion in South America; *(b)* Pacific Coast migration, with west-to-east expansion in South America; *(c)* bicoastal migration, with centripetal expansion in South America; and *(d)* Atlantic Coast migration, with east-to-west expansion in South America.

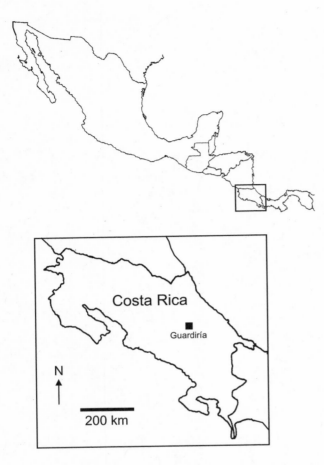

FIGURE 8.6 Location of the Guardiría Paleo-indian site in Costa Rica.

Lithic Reduction Strategies at the Guardiría Paleoindian Site

Guardiría is situated on a low-lying terrace in the Turrialba Valley of Costa Rica (fig. 8.6) and was first excavated by Snarskis in the 1970s (Snarskis 1977, 1979). The site occupies 100,000 m², which includes a point of land at the confluence of the Reventazón and Tuís Rivers, where large chert cobbles abound. Guardiría served as both a camp and a procurement locality for secondary-source lithic raw materials. The available cherts contain many large quartz-crystal inclusions and are best described as "coarse-grained" (Luedtke 1992: 70). They do not compare to the many high-quality lithic raw materials exploited by North American Clovis groups. Nevertheless, the discovery of 18 fluted bifaces in different stages of manufacture attests to substantial workshop activities. The site contains three types of Paleoindian points: parallel sided, waisted, and fish-

tail. Unfortunately Guardiría was discovered on a seasonally plowed and burned sugarcane field, which has precluded the likelihood of obtaining secure radiocarbon dates or stratigraphic contexts for its cultural remains. Presented below are the results of an analysis of the Guardiría lithic collections that I conducted at the Museo Nacional de Costa Rica.

Decortication, Core Reduction, and Flake Production

Reduction of chert nodules at Guardiría began with a transverse blow to one extremity of a cobble to create a striking platform. If this did not remove enough cortex, the cobble was struck again to detach a tablet (fig. 8.7). Bladelike flakes and ridge spalls were then detached from the core's periphery to eliminate the surrounding cortex. The production of large flake blanks for points and other tools followed decortication. Unidirectional flake removals continued until unrecoverable fractures or obtuse angles prevented further reduction. At this point, instead of rejuvenating the original platform, the toolmaker turned over the core and created a second platform by striking off the distal end. This strategy was observed on many pieces in the collection and is diagnostic of lithic reduction at Guardiría. Flake production proceeded from this new platform and made greater use of fortuitous angles as cores shrunk to exhaustion. Both the proximal and distal platform preparation segments were, in turn, used as secondary flake cores or transformed into turtleback scraper-planes (Pearson 1998b).

Manufacturing Techniques and Tool Types

One objective of my study was to compare the technological characteristics and formal tools from the Guardiría collections with North American Clovis assemblages. Some of the more sensitive or diagnostic Clovis technological attributes and tool forms (Bradley 1982, 1991, 1993; Frison and Bradley 1999; J. E. Morrow 1995, 1996; Rogers 1986b; Tankersley, this volume; Wilke et al. 1991) used in my analysis include the following:

1. large overshot (*outrepassé*) bifacial thinning flake and overshot flake scars on bifaces;
2. ground, isolated platforms on the lateral edges of unfinished bifaces;
3. sequences of large, overlapping thinning flakes traveling beyond the midlines of bifaces;
4. ground nipples on bases to facilitate fluting;
5. fluted bifacial preforms;

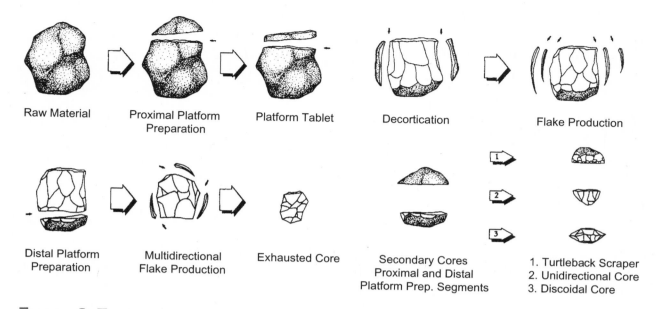

FIGURE 8.7 Reduction sequence of secondary-source lithic raw material at Guardiría, Costa Rica.

6. bifacial bases broken by reverse hinges (i.e., failed fluting attempts);
7. squared edges on bifaces;
8. large bifacial flake cores;
9. blades and blade-manufacturing products (e.g., blade cores and rejuvenation tablets);
10. spurred endscrapers, large scraper-planes, and snubbed-nosed scrapers (limaces).

All of the above were recorded at Guardiría, save the production of blades. Many bifacial preforms were fluted in the early stages of their production (fig. 8.8; Morrow 1995; Ranere 1997), and thinning flake scars showed typical Clovis removal sequences (Bradley 1982) as well as overshots (fig. 8.9). Broken point preforms indicate that flutes were removed from ground nipples.

Diagnostic tools included snub-nosed endscrapers (limaces) and spurred endscrapers. Although formal burins were not identified, numerous snapped and broken pieces had been fortuitously used for the same purpose. A large bifacial flake core was also recovered (fig. 8.10).

Limaces were manufactured using a trihedral flaking technique on thick flakes. First, the bulb and other irregularities on the ventral surface were flattened by ventral retouch. This was accomplished by striking the margins of the tool at low, almost parallel angles in order to detach long straight flakes from the limace's

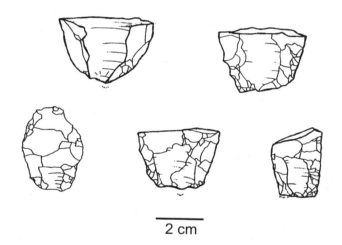

2 cm

FIGURE 8.8 Fluted preforms and points from Guardiría, Costa Rica.

underside. This strategy created step or hinge fractures on the ventral surface, comparable to core-platform rejuvenation techniques. Finally the dorsal keel was shaped by removing flakes from both the ventral face and the dorsal apex.

Despite earlier claims for the presence of blades at Guardiría (Snarskis 1977, 1979), detailed examination of the lithic collection revealed no evidence for this type of industry at the site. Artifacts previously described as blades were either bladelike flakes or ridge spalls,

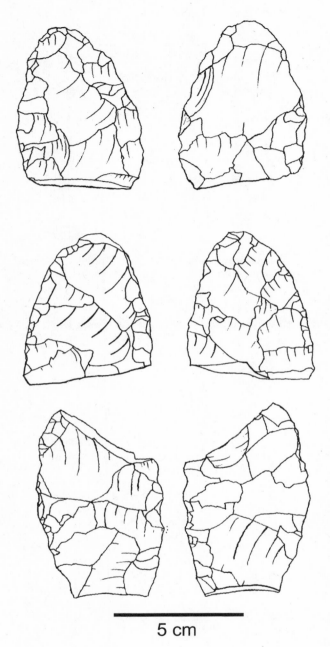

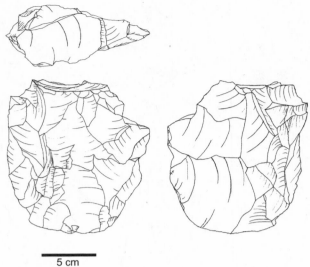

FIGURE 8.10 Large bifacial flake core from Guardiría, Costa Rica.

the absence of blade production at the site, this situation does not apply to other Central American localities where obsidian and high-quality stones were available. Another explanation must therefore be sought to satisfactorily explain why Paleoindians apparently did not manufacture large blades in the Neotropics.

Age of Central American Clovis-Like and Fishtail Points

Thus far, only two sites in Central America—Los Grifos and Los Tapiales—have provided chronometric dates associated with fluted points in buried contexts (table 8.2). The Los Grifos Cave is especially important because both Clovis-like points and FTPPs were found in the same stratigraphic unit, which was bracketed between 9460 ± 150 (I-10761) and 8930 ± 150 (I-10760) B.P. (Santamaria 1981). The relatively close superposition of both point types at Los Grifos suggests that Clovis and FTPP groups occupied the cave consecutively within a short geologic time span, were culturally distinct yet coeval, or were a single group that used both types of bifaces jointly. Nondiagnostic artifacts associated with a radiocarbon date of 9540 ± 150 B.P. (I-10762) and an obsidian hydration date of 9330 B.P. were also discovered below the points.

At Los Tapiales, ten radiocarbon dates were secured on charcoal samples recovered from hearth features and on scattered fragments lying on possible

5 cm

FIGURE 8.9 Bifacial preforms, showing Clovis-like thinning sequences and overshot thinning scars, from Guardiría, Costa Rica.

both common by-products of flake core reduction. Large blade cores and true prismatic blades, such as those found at several North American Clovis sites (Collins 1999a; Tankersley, this volume), were not observed in the Guardiría assemblage. Although one can point to the low quality of the lithic material at Guardiría to explain

TABLE 8.2 Radiocarbon Dates from Mexican and Central American Fluted Point Sites including Earliest Panamanian Dates

Country	Site	Lab No.	^{14}C Date	Material	Remarks	Reference
Mexico	Los Grifos	I-10762	9540 ± 150	Charcoal?	Under fluted points and FTPPs	Santamaria 1981
Mexico	Los Grifos	I-10761	9460 ± 150	Charcoal?	Under fluted points and FTPPs	Santamaria 1981
Mexico	Los Grifos	—	9330	Obsidian	Under fluted points and FTPPs	Santamaria 1981
Mexico	Los Grifos	I-10760	8930 ± 150	Charcoal?	Above fluted points and FTPPs	Santamaria 1981
Guatemala	Los Tapiales	GaK-4885	4730 ± 100	Hearth charcoal	Rejected	Gruhn and Bryan 1977
Guatemala	Los Tapiales	GaK-4886	4790 ± 100	Charcoal		Gruhn and Bryan 1977
Guatemala	Los Tapiales	GaK-4887	7150 ± 130	Hearth charcoal	Rejected	Gruhn and Bryan 1977
Guatemala	Los Tapiales	GaK-2769	7550 ± 150	Charcoal		Gruhn and Bryan 1977
Guatemala	Los Tapiales	GaK-4888	7820 ± 140	Hearth charcoal	Rejected	Gruhn and Bryan 1977
Guatemala	Los Tapiales	Birm-703	7960 ± 160	Charcoal		Gruhn and Bryan 1977
Guatemala	Los Tapiales	Tx-1630	8810 ± 110	Charcoal		Gruhn and Bryan 1977
Guatemala	Los Tapiales	GaK-4890	9860 ± 185	Charcoal		Gruhn and Bryan 1977
Guatemala	Los Tapiales	Tx-1631	10,710 ± 170	Charcoal	Accepted age of site	Gruhn and Bryan 1977
Guatemala	Los Tapiales	GaK-4889	11,170 ± 200	Charcoal		Gruhn and Bryan 1977
Guatemala	Piedra del Coyote	Tx-1633	5320 ± 90	Charcoal	No diagnostics	Gruhn and Bryan 1977
Guatemala	Piedra del Coyote	Tx-1635	9430 ± 120	Charcoal	No diagnostics	Gruhn and Bryan 1977
Guatemala	Piedra del Coyote	Tx-1634	10,020 ± 260	Charcoal	No diagnostics	Gruhn and Bryan 1977
Guatemala	Piedra del Coyote	Tx-1632	10,650 ± 1,350	Charcoal	No diagnostics	Gruhn and Bryan 1977
Panama	La Yeguada	Multiple assays	11,050	Charcoal	Average age for early forest clearing by humans	Piperno et al. 1991
Panama	Corona Rockshelter	Beta-19105	10,440 ± 650	Charcoal	No diagnostics	Cooke and Ranere 1992b:120
Panama	Alvina de Parita	FSU-300	11,350 ± 250	Hearth charcoal		Crusoe and Felton 1974
Panama	Aguadulce Rockshelter	NZA-9622	10,529 ± 184	Phytoliths		Piperno et al. 2000
Panama	Aguadulce Rockshelter	NZA-10930	10,725 ± 80	Phytoliths		Piperno et al. 2000
Panama	Cueva los Vampiros	Beta-5101	8560 ± 650	Charcoal	No diagnostics	Cooke and Ranere 1984

living floors (Gruhn and Bryan 1977). The investigators rejected all hearth dates as being too young and possibly contaminated. Based on the oldest radiocarbon dates and on stratigraphic comparisons with the nearby dated deposits from Piedra del Coyote, Gruhn and Bryan (1977:245) believe that the Los Tapiales occupation is approximately 10,700 B.P.

In Costa Rica, attempts to date the cultural material at Guardiría were also made using the terraces as relative horizontal time markers. The Clovis-like material lay on the highest terrace, whereas an FTPP was found on the lowermost terrace, suggesting that it might be younger (Castillo et al. 1987; Ranere and Cooke 1991).

Although Clovis-like points have not been directly dated in Panama, one discovery is worth noting: Several years before the discovery of the La Mula West fluted-point site (Cooke and Ranere 1992a; Ranere and Cooke 1995, 1996), Crusoe and Felton (1974) found an 11,350 ± 250 B.P. (FSU-300) hearth in the same *albinas* of Parita Bay. The sudden appearance of particulate carbon in Lake La Yeguada's deposits, dated at about 11,050 B.P., has also been interpreted as a sign of early human incursion into the Panamanian highlands (Barton et al., this volume; Bush et al. 1992). The presence of anthropogenic charcoal at Lake La Yeguada suggests that late Pleistocene humans burned the local vegetation to attract game, facilitate the growth of favored plants, or clear areas for camps (Piperno et al. 1990, 1991; Ranere 1992). More recently, dates of 10,725 ± 80 (NZA-10930) and 10,529 ± 184 (NZA-9622) B.P. were obtained on phytoliths associated with a bifacial industry at the Aguadulce Rockshelter (Piperno et al. 2000). Unfortunately it is still impossible to determine if the earliest occupation at Aguadulce is associated with Clovis-like points, FTPPs, or something else altogether.

Discussion

The debates over the presence of fluted points in Central and South America have generally confronted two basic ideas: technological diffusion and human migration. As with many scientific problems that have opposed what were considered mutually exclusive schools of thought, solutions have sometimes been found by reconciling several ideas. The level of difficulty attributed to particular problems might simply be a reflection of the unyielding mental constructs chosen to tackle them. This, in effect, betrays our intellectual limitations. My point is this: Although Clovis groups could have mi-

grated all the way to Panama, this possibility would not have prevented the fluting technique from diffusing farther south via an extant population (cf. Munford et al. 1995; Neves and Pucciarelli 1989, 1991); nor would the initial spread of an idea (i.e., the fluting technique) have stopped Clovis bands from expanding southward.

An important difference between early lithic assemblages from North and South America is the presence of the fluting technique on many stemmed projectile points in the latter. As I described earlier, fluting has been observed on a variety of South American projectile points (Gnecco 1994), such as lanceolate Clovis-like, fishtail, Restrepo, El Inga Broad Stemmed, El Inga Shouldered Lanceolate, and possibly El Jobo points (Jaimes 1997, 1999). Significantly these various technological complexes and accompanying projectile points are concentrated between the Darien province of Panama and the equator in northern South America. The co-occurrence of these point types in this particular region of South America may not be coincidental. Northern South America may have been a zone of contact between northern and southern groups (Bryan 1983), resulting in technological amalgamations akin to a Paleoindian "melting pot." The widespread practice of the fluting technique on such a variety of typologically and technologically different points may be the best evidence supporting the idea that South America was already occupied before the southward expansion of Clovis. Although some researchers have suggested that the rapid, widespread appearance of Clovis-related points and the fluting technique in North America represents in situ technological diffusion within a preestablished population (Bonnichsen 1991; Young and Bonnichsen 1984), this model appears more convincing when applied to South America.

Because the coastal and continental entryways into South America via Panama are extremely narrow, it is conceivable that the first humans to penetrate into Colombia effectively "blocked" or buffered subsequent inflow from the north. South America may have been colonized by fewer "waves" (i.e., inflow from Beringia) and may have experienced very little input from North America once northern Colombia was inhabited. Genetic evidence from the Chibchan tribes of lower Central America shows a "strikingly depauperate mtDNA haplotype diversity" (Kolman et al. 1995:279), which suggests that the isthmus may not have been an active corridor for human interaction and gene flow (Batista et al. 1995; Lorenz and Smith 1996; Torroni et al. 1994d; Ward 1996). If humans did reach South America before the Clovis-related groups, we should not expect much similarity between the archaeological records of both continents. I am not saying that early South Americans were completely isolated from northern influences, both demographic and ideological, but that their overall evolutionary pathways were markedly distinct. We can also surmise that the existence of a "population barrier" in the Isthmian region could have maintained low demographic densities in South America throughout much of its initial prehistory.

Of course, the above hypotheses are just a few possible interpretations based on the available data. Current information has been difficult to thread together in the absence of secure chronometric dates. For example, the copious technological complexes found in northern South America may not have been contemporaneous but could have been the result of several millennia of local evolution. The presence of fluting on such varied points in this region could be a South American counterpart to the fluted-point effervescence that occurred in eastern North America before the Holocene. Perhaps, as Lynch (1998:93) has suggested, the early Holocene environmental conditions of South America maintained an "Epi-Paleoindian" economic component among early Archaic hunter-gatherers. Because Pleistocene megamammals may have been secondary prey species for South American Paleoindians (Borrero et al. 1998), tool kits incorporating fluted points to hunt modern fauna may have persisted longer south of the Isthmus of Panama.

Although I hope that the relative age of FTPPs and Clovis-like points in Central and South America will eventually be resolved by dating future sites, researchers must identify and compare the technological characteristics of these assemblages to understand this relationship beyond mere chronology. This analysis is important because a "classic" Clovis technological yardstick is often used to determine the degree of cultural and, more boldly, biological affinity between early northern and southern Paleoindian populations. This method has both strengths and weaknesses, depending on whether archaeologists recognize and factor in important environmental variables that might explain why incongruities appear between some assemblages. Because reduction processes are influenced by the source and quality of raw materials (Andrefsky 1994), comparisons based on the hallmarks of North American Clovis technology, which are dependent on high-quality stones with predictable fractures, may not be applicable in areas where such materials were absent. Paramount to solving many of these problems is the need to assess

the validity of our assumptions when comparing late Pleistocene–early Holocene assemblages from North, Central, and South America for the purpose of establishing Pan-American Paleoindian cultural relationships. *Interassemblage variability may ultimately say more about an environment and how people were adapting to it than about the identity of the toolmakers.* Because the material at Guardiría has not been dated directly, the antiquity of its lithic remains can be assessed only by comparing their technological and typological attributes to assemblages of secure age. At present, however, very little is known about early-stage Clovis reduction strategies of secondary-source cobbles (Mallouf 1989; Sanders 1990); additional research is needed to detect possible patterns and enable proper comparisons.

Although I acknowledge that evidence usually proffered in support of either human migration or technological borrowing is often subjective, I believe the overall technological similarities between the Guardiría assemblage and North American Clovis industries support a migration model. The mechanisms of this model and the exact migration route(s) of these early colonists, however, are another matter (see contributions by Barton et al., Fiedel, MacDonald, and Meltzer, this volume). Thus far, the data argue against diffusion as the source of Clovis-like material in Central America. If the fluting technique originated in North America, then it is safe to assume that this technological know-how was carried south at least as far as the Isthmus of Panama (Ranere 1997). It is also safe to assume that this population crossed into South America proper. Because radiocarbon dates associated with North American Clovis occupations are, on average, between 1,300 to 400 calendar years older than most FTPP dates from the southern cone (Barton et al., this volume; Fiedel 1999b, 2000a), a Clovis-based origin for FTPPs cannot be completely discounted (Morrow and Morrow 1999). We must concede, however, that if FTPPs were a South American evolutionary offshoot of Clovis, then a return migration (Anthony 1990) or reverse diffusion must have occurred in order to explain the specimens found in Belize and Mexico (Faught and Dunbar 1997; Pearson and Bostrom 1998), if these are indeed related to South American examples.

Conclusions

The geographic distributions of Paleoindian points in Central and South America indicate that considerable overlap exists between Clovis-like points and FTPPs in the region from Mexico to central Chile. Unfortunately our present ensemble of late Pleistocene–early Holocene cultural remains from the midcontinent is composed mainly of surface finds, and only a few radiometric dates are associated with buried Clovis-like and FTPP material. Faced with this dearth of information, archaeologists have yet to untangle the temporal relationship between these two industries.

A technological analysis of the Guardiría lithic assemblage of Costa Rica reveals key similarities and important differences in tool-manufacturing techniques when compared with North American Clovis industries. Bifacial thinning and flute removals at Guardiría followed Clovis reduction strategies. Blade production, however, was not carried out at Guardiría, and most tools were fashioned on large flakes.

Based on the evidence from Costa Rica and Panama, a southward expansion by Clovis groups presents the most parsimonious explanation for the appearance of lanceolate fluted points in lower Central America. However, the application of the fluting technique on a wide variety of lanceolate and stemmed points in northern South America may indicate that regions immediately south of the isthmus were already occupied when Clovis groups entered Panama. Under this scenario, the presence of flutes on some South American projectile points might represent a stylistic statement or a new technological option used to thin bases rather than a functional necessity (Pearson 1999).

Coastal migrations would explain why many parts of the continents' interiors remained unoccupied while humans were already present in South America (Dillehay 1999, 2000). If this hypothesis is true, then the Western Stemmed Point tradition of North America may share a common ancestor with many stemmed point assemblages of South America (Dixon 1999). Technological and typological similarities between Clovis-like points and FTPPs from the Gulf states, Central America, and northern South America form a vast arc along the Gulf of Mexico and the Caribbean, which could represent an ancient Paleoindian interaction sphere (Faught and Dunbar 1997; Pearson and Bostrom 1998).

Acknowledgments

I would like to acknowledge a debt of gratitude to the archaeologists at the Museo Nacional de Costa Rica, whose hospitality and cooperation contributed to the success of this research. Many thanks go to Jack L. Hofman for his guidance and to John W. Hoopes for bringing this project to my attention and paving the way for me. Research in Costa Rica was funded by a Tinker Research Grant from the Center of Latin American Studies of the University of Kansas. Fieldwork in Panama was made possible by a Graduate Student Fellowship from the Smithsonian Institution. Additional help and support were provided by Richard G. Cooke and Dolores R. Piperno of the Smithsonian Tropical Research Institute. Thoughtful comments and suggestions on an early version of this paper were given by an anonymous reviewer. Last but not least, I am especially grateful to Robert A. Beckwith for giving me invaluable physical and mental assistance in and off the field.

9 Deconstructing the North Atlantic Connection
Geoffrey A. Clark

This chapter comprises observations on what might be called the North Atlantic model for the initial colonization of the New World, which was first proposed by Dennis Stanford and Bruce Bradley at the "Clovis and Beyond" conference held in Santa Fe, New Mexico, in October 1999. The essay is divided into two parts. First, I show that there are serious empirical problems with the scenario presented by Stanford and Bradley that preclude its consideration as a New World colonization model. Second, I address what I consider to be conceptual problems with their interpretation of the north Spanish Solutrean, which, in turn, affect the possible relationships between it and the Clovis phenomenon. I also evaluate the epistemology of Americanist Paleoindian research and compare it with that of Paleolithic archaeology in continental (especially Latin) Europe. Despite differences in the preconceptions and biases underlying the conceptual frameworks of the Old and New World research traditions, in both cases the conceptual problems arise from a simplistic, normative, typological view of lithic variability that should have no place in contemporary archaeological systematics.

Readers should keep in mind that, to date, no relatively complete and developed description of the North Atlantic model has been subjected to peer review and published in a refereed journal. Thus the model itself, though it has attracted a lot of attention in the press (e.g., the *New York Times*), in news magazines (e.g., *Newsweek*), and in semipopular science and archaeology periodicals (e.g., *Scientific American* and *Archaeology*), is subject to many interpretations. As I understand the model from newspaper accounts (e.g., Wilford 1999), a report on the conference in the journal *Science* (Holden 1999), and the Smithsonian's web page (Smithsonian Institution 1997), Stanford and Bradley propose that the New World might have been colonized from the east by maritime Solutreans from northern Spain, who emigrated from that area during the Last Glacial Maximum (ca. 18,000 B.P.) in skin boats, skirting the edges of the pack ice that surrounded Iceland and southern Greenland and that covered much of the North Atlantic during

glacial pulses (e.g., Bond et al. 1997; Jöris and Weninger 1998; Pavlov et al. 2001; Svendsen et al. 1999; van Andel 2002). Stanford has felt for a long time that maritime colonization models in general have been overlooked or deemphasized in favor of those focusing on the Bering Land Bridge, the most generally accepted model and the one best supported empirically (e.g., Eriksen and Straus 1998; Straus et al. 1996; West 1996b). However, most of Stanford's previous arguments concerned the peopling of the Pacific Rim (e.g., Stanford 1983, 1997) rather than the American continents per se.

The notion of some kind of Solutrean-Clovis connection goes back to the 1930s with Hibben's (e.g., 1941) long-discredited Sandia culture and to the 1960s with a construct like the North Atlantic model (e.g., Greenman 1963). This connection seems to be based on three things: (1) the apparent lack of technological and typological antecedents to Clovis in North America and Siberia; (2) specific typological similarities between big, foliate, bifacial points made on blades and found in Solutrean and Clovis sites; and (3) what Stanford believes to be a wealth of technological parallels, including *outrepassé* or overshot flaking, particular kinds of endscrapers, bone foreshafts, engraved limestone tablets, and point caches associated with red ochre, all of which are supposedly unique to these two archaeological constructs.

In the space allotted me, I first try to deconstruct the logic of inference underlying the arguments of Stanford and Bradley, and I also offer some observations on the empirical support for them (see also Lepper 1998; Sellet 1998; Straus 2000). Although I know relatively little about Clovis, I do know something about the Solutrean, having excavated several Solutrean sites in northern Spain and having written extensively on the Upper Paleolithic of the region (e.g., Clark 1974; Clark and Cartledge 1973; Straus and Clark 1986). I also know a great deal about epistemology in Old World Paleolithic archaeology (especially as practiced in Latin Europe or the Levant) and how utterly naïve the research traditions of Paleolithic archaeology can sometimes be when making explicit the logic of inference that underlies their knowledge claims (e.g., Clark 1993, 1999b). Although the conceptual issues are by far the more important ones, it is easier to address the empirical problems first. I emphasize that there is absolutely no empirical support for any kind of Solutrean-Clovis connection, however it is construed.

Empirical Problems

A Solutrean-Clovis connection faces three major obstacles. First, there is a time gap of at least 5,000 radiocarbon years (200 human generations) between the latest Iberian Solutrean sites, which have been well dated radiometrically in Catalonia, Valencia, and Andalucia to about 16,500 B.P. (e.g., Straus 2000), and Clovis sites, which have been equally well dated to the 500-year interval bracketing 11,000 B.P. (e.g., Barton et al., this volume; Fiedel, this volume; Taylor et al. 1996). The intervening time interval in Spain is filled with the variously subdivided Magdalenian and Azilian periods, neither of which exhibit much in the way of bifacial flaking, although enough examples of it exist to indicate that their manufacturers could do it when they wanted to. Notice that I avoid calling these prehistorian-defined analytical units "cultures," "technocomplexes," "traditions," or "horizons." There is *absolutely no consensus* about what the basic prehistorian-defined analytical units actually are, mean, or represent behaviorally (e.g., Clark 1997, 2002). I will return to this subject in the second part of this essay.

Second, there is the North Atlantic itself, a not inconsiderable body of water that Stanford thinks could have been crossed by Solutreans in skin boats in as little as two weeks. In this scenario, Solutreans were "pushed toward the coast" by severe glacial conditions, encountered pack ice, and followed it north and west along its southern fringes until they eventually arrived in Nova Scotia. They lived on seabirds, fish, and marine mammals during a voyage that would have covered a distance of at least 5,000 kilometers. We know a great deal about Solutrean adaptations to the coastal environments of northern Spain. There is no evidence whatsoever that the Solutreans exploited marine resources to any great extent, nor is there evidence of any watercraft, any marine species that would imply their presence, or the ability to take 5,000-kilometer cruises (Straus 2000; see Clark and Straus 1983; Straus 1992; and Straus and Clark 1986 for overviews of northern Spanish Solutrean adaptations). There is also the issue

of what the itinerant Solutreans used for fuel during the crossing (unless they ate everything raw) and what provoked these sea voyages. A relatively rapid east-to-west crossing of the North Atlantic would have had to contend with the Rennell's Current, a very strong west-to-east–trending branch of the Gulf Stream (Houston 1967). The Rennell's Current kept the Cantabrian coast relatively warm and moist throughout the last glacial cycle, ameliorating even the severe cold and aridity of the Last Glacial Maximum (ca. 18,000 B.P.). Cantabria was itself a refugium during glacial pulses, when much of continental Europe was completely devoid of humans (Gamble 1986).

Third, and most problematic, is Stanford and Bradley's normative conception of the Solutrean itself, that is, what they think a Solutrean assemblage "looks like" and how it might be defined technologically and typologically. One would think that these scholars (especially Bradley) would recognize that *there is an enormous amount of formal convergence in lithic reduction*; technology and typology do not necessarily (and, in fact, seldom) covary directly with one another, and bifacial foliate points are found all over the world and through time, at least since the late Pleistocene. Bifacial foliate artifacts made on flakes and blades that resemble Solutrean points (which themselves vary widely, though none, to my knowledge, are fluted) show up in numerous areas: Mesolithic sites in Russian East Asia, which have been well dated to about 13,000 B.P. (e.g., Kononenko 1996); central European Mousterian sites and European Russia (the famous *blattspitzen*; Bordes 1968; Freund 1952); Paleolithic sites in China (e.g., Yi and Clark 1983, 1985); the Middle Stone Age in South Africa (e.g., Clark 1982); pre-Dynastic Egypt (e.g., Butzer 1978); various post-Clovis Paleoindian assemblages (e.g., Folsom, Midland, Agate Basin, Hell Gap, and Cody Complex) in western North America (e.g., Tompkins 1993:appendix A); and northern South America (Borrero 1996; Pearson, this volume).

The Upper Paleolithic archaeologist Lawrence Straus has done extensive primary research on the Spanish Solutrean and recently published an empirical critique of the North Atlantic model, which is summarized here as table 9.1. Inspection of the table shows that the similarities between Franco-Cantabrian Solutrean (and Solutrean in general) and North American Clovis sites are confined to the appearance of fairly large bifacial foliate points in both assemblages. This similarity, however, is a formal convergence that is most parsimoniously explained by similar Solutrean and Clo-

TABLE 9.1 Empirical Comparison of Franco-Cantabrian Solutrean and North American Clovis Assemblages

Solutrean	Clovis
Dates 21,000–16,500 B.P.	Dates 11,200–10,900 B.P.
Geographical distribution confined to Iberia and S France (ca. 250,000 km²)	Geographical distribution extends from S Canada to N Mexico (ca. 5.6 million km²)
Defined typologically by a wide variety of unifacial and bifacial foliate stone points, including small shouldered and tanged forms (arrowheads?); some concave-based foliates but no fluting; average length of whole, concave-based foliate points ca. 634 mm; some regional stylistic differences in point forms	Defined typologically by bifacial straight or concave-based fluted foliate points; average length of whole examples is > 100 mm (Collins 1999a: 46); no well-defined regional stylistic differences in point forms
Wide range of other stone artifact types, including various kinds of endscrapers, perforators, knives, and burins; an extensive microlithic component in "modern era" excavations	Very restricted range of other stone artifact types (few endscrapers and burins); no microliths or tanged or shouldered points
A rich organic technology, with beveled bone and antler points, eyed needles, punches, awls, spear throwers, "wands" and "shaft wrenches"	An extremely impoverished organic technology, limited to a few bone and ivory points, foreshafts, and one "shaft wrench" (Haynes and Hemmings 1968)
Extensive evidence for parietal (e.g., Altamira and Cosquer) and portable "art" (e.g., El Parpalló); large numbers of beads made on bone and antler blanks, and perforated animal teeth at some sites	No evidence for parietal or portable "art" (but see Agenbroad and Hesse, this volume); no evidence for personal adornment
Good evidence for mass hunting of small and medium-sized ungulates (ibex, red deer, and reindeer)	No evidence for mass hunting of small and medium-sized ungulates (deer or caprids)
No evidence for the exploitation of megafauna (elephants or rhinos)	Evidence for the exploitation of megafauna (elephants and bison)
No evidence for systematic exploitation of marine resources, nor for the boat-building technologies that would imply it	No evidence for systematic exploitation of marine resources

Source: Straus (2000).

vis adaptations (i.e., predation on large and medium-sized animals) and by limitations imposed on the form of all chipped-stone artifacts because of the reductive nature of lithic technology, which is further constrained by the variation in raw-material quality and "package size."

Clearly Solutrean and Clovis points are not technologically or typologically unique, are not confined to a particular time interval, do not conform to rigid design specifications, and cannot be used to document historical connectivity. This conclusion suggests that tracking the prehistoric peregrinations of Solutreans from Iberia to the New World by tracking the formal similarities between Solutrean and Clovis points is simply not a credible thing to do. The other supposedly diagnostic artifacts (endscrapers, foreshafts, *plaquettes*, ochre,

and caches) invoked by Stanford and Bradley to support the North Atlantic model are even less convincing; although they differ in frequency, these artifacts are more or less ubiquitous in the Upper Paleolithic sites of western Eurasia. *Solutrean assemblages as a whole bear no specific resemblance to Clovis.*

Ambiguity in the meaning assigned to conventional analytical units is a characteristic feature of Paleolithic archaeology in both continental Europe and the New World. In my opinion, neither the Solutrean nor Clovis are "cultures" in any anthropological sense of the term because the time-space distributions of their diagnostic artifacts exceed by orders of magnitude the time-space distributions of any real or imaginable anthropological "culture" that might have produced and transmitted them. Instead I suggest that the diagnostic artifacts are the most visible elements of a universal technology related to predation on large and medium-sized game (Fiedel, this volume; Tankersley, this volume).[1] The formal convergence on big foliate points can be explained completely and unambiguously in strictly functional terms. They show up with a certain frequency in times and places where the hunting of large and medium-sized animals was practiced; they make up only part (albeit a highly visible part) of much broader technocomplexes comprising artifacts that bear no specific resemblance to either Clovis or the Solutrean; and they only appear in areas where relatively fine-grained igneous, metamorphic,[2] or cryptocrystalline siliceous rocks are available in large enough chunks to make big blade (and some flake) blanks. The lack of variety in Clovis and its considerable impoverishment compared with any well-studied, Old World, Upper Paleolithic analytical unit support this interpretation and suggest that small bands of highly mobile foragers were spread very thinly over the landscape. Clovis site densities were much lower than those of late Upper Paleolithic Europe (MacDonald, this volume; Meltzer, this volume), which was a geographical cul-de-sac initially colonized by humans 1.6–1.7 million B.P. (e.g., Vekua et al. 2002).

Conceptual Problems

Before we turn to the conceptual issues, we should ask ourselves what the basic archaeological analytical units are and what they represent in behavioral terms. I suggest that, because of "enculturation" in two rather distinct intellectual traditions (historical and anthropological), European and American workers tend to conceptualize the basic analytical units differently. The basic analytical units in the North Atlantic model are the Solutrean and Clovis. European workers inclined toward culture-history approaches (a group that includes many Upper Paleolithic archaeologists) identify the Upper Paleolithic subdivisions (e.g., Aurignacian, Solutrean, and Magdalenian) by the appearance of allegedly time-sensitive stylistic markers (e.g., Solutrean points) and tend to think of those subdivisions as the material expressions of identity-conscious social units analogous to the tribes, peoples, cultures, and nations of history. American workers tend to be more ecologically oriented and typically see pattern as existing *above* the level of identity consciousness (Binford and Sabloff 1982; Clark 2002). Table 9.2 summarizes and compares the anglophone New World and Latin Old World con-

ceptions of "culture." European conceptual frameworks cannot be easily reconciled with those of the anthropological archaeology practiced in the United States. This problem is not just one of content. We have to ask ourselves, what do these units really "mean" (or represent)? Why do we use them? Is there an explicit justification for using them? Are there alternatives?

What I am trying to say here is that implicit biases, preconceptions, and assumptions about what constitutes Clovis in the New World are often different from those about what constitutes Solutrean in the Old World. Consequently explanations for pattern and process that conflate the two intellectual traditions cannot fail to be incommensurate. To be logically consistent, one must look at Clovis from the culture-history perspective of Latin Europe (i.e., archaeology is history projected back into the preliterate past), or one must look at the Solutrean from the broadly ecological perspective of American processual archaeology (i.e., archaeology is paleoecology, and humans are social carnivores). You cannot conflate the two, as Stanford and Bradley have done. Stanford and Bradley are not alone in this, however. A curious aspect of much Paleoindian research is the persistence of a normative, variety-minimizing, typological, essentialist approach long abandoned by Americanists who work in later time periods. "Clovis" is basically "Clovis points," plus anything else associated with them (see Tankersley, this volume). "Clovis" is defined almost entirely by the presence of these artifacts. The possibility (in fact, the likelihood) that "Clovis" might represent only a small part of one or several much broader adaptations, which include sites that lack the points, is seldom considered (Chilton, this volume).[3]

A second conceptual issue concerns whether the analytical units are demonstrably "cultural" in any meaningful sense of the term. In other words, can they be shown to be the material remains of identity-conscious social units? If they are such remains, how can we show that they are? If they are not, what are the implications? As I just noted, I think that formal similarities between Solutrean and Clovis points can be explained entirely and parsimoniously by functional requirements and technological convergence. The same could be said of any of the prehistorian-defined analytical units used in Paleolithic research (e.g., Mousterian and Aurignacian). A typologically inclined European might argue, as Stanford and Bradley do, that formal similarity is due to historical connectivity, but historical connectivity is unlikely because of the time-

TABLE 9.2   Definition of Culture: Metaphysical Paradigms in Prehistoric Archaeology

New World Paradigm	Old World Paradigm
Developed out of cultural area studies	Developed out of European history and nationalism
Received its mandate from cultural anthropology	Received its mandate from natural science (esp. geology and paleontology)
Essentially gradualist; emphasized continuity over space and time	Characterized by punctuated equilibrium; emphasized discontinuity; aspects of material culture were believed to correspond to social, ethnic, and linguistic groups
Led to normative (i.e., variety-minimizing) views of culture manifested in diagnostic artifact types (e.g., projectile points)	Also normative; cultures equated with differentiated packages of diagnostic traits (i.e., archaeological index fossils)
Recognizes some vectored change within temporally and spatially large and vaguely defined analytical units	Essentially static within equally large and vague analytical units
Coherent; cultures equated with trait complexes that cohere over space and time unless or until the physical environment changes	Incoherent; when cultures changed, they changed *en bloc* and relatively abruptly; the principle cause of cultural change is population replacement
Culture existed at a level *above* that of social, ethnic, and linguistic groups	Culture existed *at the level* of social, ethnic, and linguistic groups
Social organization, ethnicity, and language vary independently of one another	Social organization, ethnicity, and language covary directly with one another
Many definitions of culture; some ideational, others phenomenological	Definition of culture essentially ideational; culture comprises a monothetic set of norms and values in people's heads, which are manifest in their material remains

Source: These biases and preconceptions regarding culture, which are held by the anglophone New World and the Latin Old World, are based on Binford and Sabloff (1982) and Clark (1993, 2002).

space distributions of the "marker types" by which the units are defined.

Leaving aside the ambiguous nature of the analytical units, we might want to ask ourselves a third question: Are they "the same thing" whenever and wherever they are found? Clovis in particular covers an awful lot of territory (certainly more than 3 million km^2) and, I gather, about 500–1,000 years of time (Barton et al., this volume; Tankersley, this volume). Whatever Clovis points represent, they manifestly cannot be linked to technological or typological traditions passed down from generation to generation as a consequence of social learning. Based on what we know about the time-space distribution of bifacial technology in the Old World, knowledge of its methods was virtually universal after some point in the middle Pleistocene and was invoked by foragers everywhere when the quality and "package size" of raw materials permitted it and when the circumstances required it. These circumstances were both general and recurring; they created

the pattern of Clovis "big-game hunters" enshrined in textbook generalizations about Paleoindians (see Mandryk, this volume).

The preceding observations lead to a fourth and broader question. How realistic or defensible is it to treat the analytical units as if they were quasi-historical entities, analogous to the social, ethnic, and linguistic groups known to us from history? More generally, is it justifiable to treat process in "deep time" as if it were analogous to process in more recent historical contexts? I can see some (albeit weak) justification for doing this in the shallow time frames with which most New World researchers deal: the tight chronological controls, a likelihood (or at least the possibility) of historical connectivity, and a rich and fine-grained ethnographic record. However, I do not think it is justifiable in Pleistocene research, where patterns detectable in an archaeological record exist at a resolution beyond that of the identity-conscious social units known to us from history and ethnography. In other words, I do not think that either Clovis or the Solutrean can be treated as quasi-historical entities. Identity-consciousness is never bounded or discrete in time and space, not even in ethnographic contexts. It is a fluid property, constantly changing, constantly being renegotiated every time individuals interact with one another. Because of the resolution of the Pleistocene archaeological record, to claim that identity-consciousness is discrete and marked in time and space by diagnostic artifact types that imply or "map onto" ethnicity stretches credulity to the breaking point.

If Clovis and the Solutrean are "assemblage types" or "technocomplexes" (sensu Clarke 1968), we must ask ourselves a fifth question: What was the mode of transmission through time and across space? To call them "technocomplexes" and then treat them as if they were quasi-historical "cultures" contributes nothing to an improved understanding of either pattern or process in the past.[4] This is where the formal convergence, which is underacknowledged by most workers, enters the picture. As Bordes (1969:4, 5) once remarked, there are only a few ways to chip stone (and even fewer ways to make a projectile point). Chipped stone is not a "plastic" medium like pottery or metal, nor is it as malleable as ground stone or bone worked by cutting, grinding, and polishing. This equifinality in form is characteristic of all lithic reduction, regardless of time or space. What effect might it have had on the nature of transmission and on our ability to detect a "tradition" archaeologically? To my knowledge, no one has addressed these questions directly.

What happens to the analytical units in these comparisons if technology is uncoupled from typology (i.e., if typology is shown to vary independently of technology, as we know it does in the Old World Paleolithic; e.g., Marks 1983)? What effect might this realization have on the conventional notion that typology and technology are related to one another in a regular and systematic way? Stanford and Bradley make the assumption that Clovis and the Solutrean are "real" in some fundamental sense, that they exist independently of the archaeologists who created them, and that they are identifiable both technologically and typologically. We have no reason, however, to think that is the case. Stanford and Bradley appear to explain morphological similarity in both hemispheres in terms of murky historical continuity, but they use an index-fossil-based approach that would be quite at home in Latin and central Europe to do it. Readers should keep in mind that our

basic analytical units are "accidents of history": They were created—not discovered—in order to solve particular problems that were deemed to be important at the time in the research traditions in which they arose. In the case of the European Paleolithic, they were created by several generations of French prehistorians between 1880 and 1940 in order to impose a chronological order on retouched stone tools in the years before any form of absolute dating was available.

Finally we must address the implications of migration itself. The scenario proposed by Stanford and Bradley involves Solutreans being "pushed toward the coast" by severe glacial conditions. Franco-Cantabria, however, was itself a refugium and probably the principle one in western Europe during the Last Glacial Maximum (e.g., Jochim 1987). Although crude proxies for population density do indicate demographic changes corresponding to the Solutrean interval (ca. 20,500–18,500 B.P. in Cantabria), there are no indications of the kinds of factors that would cause foragers in the region to pick up and move. I submit that, because of ambiguity, there are general problems with invoking "migration" to explain pattern changes in Pleistocene archaeology (Clark 1994). The basic problems involve what is meant or implied by the term *migration* (e.g., point-to-point movement by individuals or groups, range extension as modeled in biology, leapfrogging from one resource patch to another, or radiation as defined in paleontology) and how migration events or processes are modeled empirically. As presently used, *migration* and *diffusion* lack consensual operational definitions and are therefore analytically problematic as explanatory devices.[5] Moreover, they are concepts derived from history. One could argue that Paleolithic archaeology is not an extension of history and that historical processes are inappropriate analogues for the processes evident in the archaeological record. One could also show that migration and diffusion are density-dependent phenomena in historical and ethnographic contexts, and are thus unlikely to have occurred prior to the relatively high population densities associated with the effective implementation of domestication economies. A brief excursion into epistemology would show that the credibility accorded to migration and diffusion as explanatory devices varies from one national or regional research tradition to the next (see also Mandryk, this volume). In general, these devices have had little importance in the New World research traditions but considerable explanatory potential in those of Europe. The reason for this difference is probably related to the biases and pre-conceptions of the metaphysical paradigms in the Old and New Worlds and how they affect notions on the nature and meaning of pattern (table 9.2). Leaving aside these epistemological issues, I submit that Stanford and Bradley display only a typological understanding of lithic assemblage variability and define both Clovis and the Solutrean primarily on the basis of the distinctive projectile points.

Why Typological Systematics Are Problematic

The literature on Stone Age archaeology in both hemispheres is replete with examples of unwavering commitment to morphological typology[6] and the lengths to which some will go to preserve its shopworn, threadbare, moth-eaten logic of inference (e.g., Goren-Inbar et al. 2000; Zilhão and d'Errico 1999). Card-carrying typologists tend to accept without question the reality of the conventional, normative, prehistorian-defined analytical units and to assume that they detect pattern at the levels of "cultures" or "technocomplexes," which are seldom defined. In the Old World, at least, typologists also exhibit an annoying tendency to correlate typologically defined archaeological assemblages with biological taxonomic units (usually "Neandertals" and "modern humans"), whereas the credibility of this correlation and of the units themselves is never explicitly questioned. To these workers, Paleolithic archaeology is essentially history projected back into the Pleistocene, and patterns are typically explained post hoc by invoking processes (e.g., migrations) that are analogous to those operating in recent historical contexts. The whole approach is predicated on (1) the existence of toolmaking "traditions" manifest through artifacts that are detectable over hundreds of thousands (even millions) of square kilometers; (2) that these "traditions" (ways of making stone tools transmitted in a social context from one generation to the next) persisted unchanged and intact over tens (or, in the case of the Lower Paleolithic, hundreds) of millennia; and (3) that these "traditions" are detectable at points in space (e.g., Europe and the Levant) that are separated by thousands of kilometers.[7] The pattern similarities themselves are uncontested, but what is causing them to occur—historical connectivity over vast geographical areas and time ranges—is, in my view, deeply problematic.

For some years now, I have argued that the culture-history paradigm, though consistent in its logic of inference, cannot be reconciled with an Americanist perspective grounded in evolutionary ecology. I have also made the following assertions:

1. most of the Paleolithic "index-fossil" tool types are ubiquitous (or nearly so), at least in western Eurasia, and carry little temporal and probably no social information whatsoever;
2. chipped-stone artifact form includes only a minimal and generalized learned-behavior component;
3. no correlations whatsoever can be made between particular kinds of hominids and particular kinds of artifact assemblages (a hotly debated issue for the Middle–Upper Paleolithic transition in Europe);
4. the few processes by which humans chip stone result in much formal convergence;
5. this formal convergence is conditioned by recurrent contextual factors (technology; raw-material quality, size, and distribution; etc.), especially as these factors are affected by mobility;
6. these factors override any hypothetical "cultural" component.

In other words, one can explain pattern similarities in Paleolithic archaeological assemblages without recourse to typology-based toolmaking traditions or the historicist preconceptions, biases, and assumptions upon which they are based.

Explaining Pattern Similarities without Invoking Historical Connections

I offer three reasons why these pattern similarities are not historically connected. First, serious logical and conceptual problems plague the notion of a cultural component in the form of (most) Paleolithic artifacts. The time-space distributions of prehistorian-defined analytical units (e.g., Aurignacian, Gravettian, Solutrean, and Clovis) *exceed by orders of magnitude* the time-space distributions of any real or imaginable social entity that might have produced and transmitted them. Unless one resorts to essentialism (e.g., an ineffable "Clovisness" is manifested in the appearance of big bifacial foliate points) and argues that toolmaking proclivities are encoded genetically (see Clark 1989a; Foley 1987), then there is simply no behavioral or cultural mechanism whereby a hypothetical toolmaking tradition could have arisen, remained intact, and been transmitted over thousands of years and millions of square kilometers. Thus, something other than historical connectivity must account for pattern similarities.

Second, we have no guarantees that the basic analytical units are discrete in space and time and are "the same thing" whenever and wherever they are found. In fact, it is highly likely that they are not the same. The Aurignacian is the quintessential example of this problem, although much of what can be said of the Aurignacian also applies to widespread, New World, technologically and typologically defined analytical units, such as Clovis. The French Aurignacian is defined typologically by the presence of carinated endscrapers, blades, blades with scalar retouch ("Aurignacian blades"), strangled blades, Dufour bladelets, split-based bone points, *sagaies*, and other characteristic tool types, as well as by a range of nonlithic criteria (e.g., ornaments, "art," and "well-organized" campsites). The Levantine Aurignacian is a flake industry bearing no resemblance whatsoever to its French counterpart (Coinman 1998; Marks 1983). It almost entirely lacks personal ornaments, bone or antler tools, figurines, portable art, parietal art, burials, and "well-organized" campsites. When these features of "Aurignacianness" do appear together as a package, it is only in the later phases of the epi-Paleolithic, in the Natufian, after about 12,000 B.P. (Marks 1994). Except for a few split-based bone points and carinated scrapers in Levantine Aurignacian levels at K'sar Akil (Lebanon) and Hayonim and Kebara (Israel), the only similarity between the French and Levantine Aurignacians is the name itself, imported from France by several generations of Levantine scholars trained in the francophone tradition. Whatever the Aurignacian is, it is manifestly *not* a "culture" or a "tradition." The same could be said of Clovis.

Third, problems in resolution lead to problems in identifying a tradition "on the ground." No known Paleolithic site sequence or series of sequences is fine-grained enough to allow us to identify the remains of the hypothetical social units that would have been the bearers of these lithic "traditions" (i.e., the assemblage resolution and integrity are far too low). Moreover, the generally acknowledged fluidity of forager territorial boundaries would have quickly and impossibly confounded any stylistic patterns that might have been manifested in stone-tool form in the archaeological context. Even if there were a "cultural" component to the form of stone artifacts, we could not possibly detect it (Clark 1989b). It is not enough to claim, as some

have done, that we cannot yet model paleoculture adequately. In fact, we can model it very well (e.g., Kuhn 1995; Stiner 1994). By invoking identity-conscious "migrants," whose peregrinations are supposedly manifested in timeless, changeless toolmaking traditions, process in the remote past is treated as if it were analogous to process in recent historical contexts. This approach makes little sense from the standpoint of ecologically oriented Americanist archaeology. However, the debate over the relationship (if any) between Clovis and the marginally earlier non-Clovis sites of Monte Verde, Bluefish Caves, Kenosha, Meadowcroft, Cactus Hill, and Topper (Gibbons 2001) suggests that many Paleoindian specialists have reached a certain "comfort level" with this approach.

Clovis is as close as we are likely to get to a New World Paleolithic, so observations on its Old World counterparts are relevant here. If we leave aside the question of whether or not Clovis is a single thing (an "it," as one reviewer put it), what we think of as Paleolithic technology almost certainly included a range of options broadly distributed in time and space, held in common by all contemporary hominids, and invoked differentially according to context. The challenge of future work is to determine the recurrent contextual factors that constrained choice among these options. Such factors probably include the range, quality, size, and location of raw materials; forager mobility strategies (a consequence of resource distribution); anticipated tasks; group size and composition (which changed over seasons, years, generations, and evolutionary time); the habitual seasonal activities of the occupants of a site in an annual round; and the duration of site occupation. Making allowances for natural site-alteration and site-formation processes, I posit that these recurrent factors acted in concert to create material patterns in the archaeological records of both hemispheres. These patterns are, to a considerable extent, ahistorical; they are not linked in any direct way to social learning or to the materially expressed identity consciousness that is so important in the research traditions of Europe.

Conclusions

The Stanford and Bradley scenario for a North Atlantic colonization of the New World is difficult to sustain empirically and suffers from several crippling conceptual problems related to the logic of inference they use to arrive at their conclusions. Their scenario is an example of post hoc accommodative argument, wherein explanations are developed after an analysis has been completed (in this case, a very superficial one) to account for patterns detected in a data set. Post hoc accommodation is a weak form of inference because the research designs that incorporate it lack a deductive component (or, in default of a deductive component, what is called "consilience," the interlocking or coherence of explanations that crosscut multiple problem domains; Wilson 1998). Post hoc accommodative argument sets the agenda for future research, rather than constituting a set of conclusions that can stand or fall on their own merits (Binford 1981; Clark and Lindly 1989). The North Atlantic model is an interesting idea, but it will require a lot more conceptual development and empirical support before it can be taken seriously by most workers.

It is philosophically radical to claim that retouched stone tools record very little "history" and that identity consciousness plays only a minor role in their morphologies. However, on one level or another, everyone recognizes that chipped stone is an intractable medium. The forms that it can assume are much more severely constrained by rock mechanics than by knapping virtuosity; in fact, they are so constrained that a large stylistic component in the overall shape of retouched stone tools seems highly improbable.[8] Ethnographic rock knockers rarely, if ever, produce chipped-stone artifacts according to strict design specifications; there is also marked variation among individuals within a single group and in the output of a single individual over time (e.g., Shackley 2000). Why should we expect Paleolithic rock knockers to have behaved differently? The culture-history approach, as applied to Stone Age foragers in the distant past, essentially treats their lithic outputs as though they were rigidly invariant. At the same time, however, the approach likens those outputs to the more fluid media of design elements painted or incised on pots, which vary more freely according to stylistic canons than do stone tools made by even the most proficient flint knapper.[9] These tendencies are sometimes carried to an extreme in Europe, where the time-space distributions of archaeological "index-fossil" tool types are treated as if they were analogous to those of coins, the only artifact class that would allow us to trace national boundaries there today in the absence of written records (i.e., Europe is now "homogenized" in its material culture).

Two reviewers of this essay considered these observations to be unduly pessimistic. (One even described it as "dyspeptic.") Although they acknowledged the credibility of many of my objections to the North Atlantic model, they essentially considered the culture-history approach to be "the only game in town" and lamented that this volume explored few alternatives. Although no one has ever accused me of being a starry-eyed optimist, I do not believe such pessimism is warranted. Rather than taking the adequacy of the existing systematics for granted, we need to confront the very real possibility that they might not be up to the task of answering many questions deemed important in Paleolithic research. Because we cannot access ethnicity in the Stone Age does not mean that patterns that are meaningful in behavioral terms cannot be elucidated, defined, and explained. We must strategically match the scale of the conceptual framework to the patterns observed archaeologically. It makes little sense to me to treat stone tools as if they were pots or coins when they very clearly were not. There *are* powerful alternative conceptual frameworks, notably those lumped under the rubric of evolutionary ecology (e.g., Winterhalder and Smith 2000), which do not require us to deal with the problematic notion of identity consciousness or the effect that it might have had on Stone Age material culture.

The aims of my paper were more modest than developing an alternative framework. I simply wanted to note the following: (1) despite paradigmatic differences, Old and New World Paleolithic archaeologists share certain implicit assumptions; (2) some of these assumptions are problematic in respect of explanation; and (3) lithic technology includes an enormous amount of unacknowledged formal convergence, far more than most workers are willing to admit. A good example of an approach to lithic technological variation, which is on a scale appropriate for the resolution that characterizes the Paleolithic, is the work of Steven Kuhn (e.g., 1995). His approach is ultimately grounded in a community ecology framework that treats prehistoric foragers as members of a guild of social carnivores and that makes no assumptions about identity consciousness or ethnicity. The community ecology approach is embedded in an overarching neo-Darwinian paradigm of enormous power and generality that has no rivals in the armamentarium of archaeology (e.g., Barton and Clark 1997; Clark 1999c).

It is distressing to me to think that observations like these would be regarded as unduly negative. I place the highest value on paleoanthropology as "ordinary science," with its inherent complexity, mixed motives, and resistance to oversimplification. As Einstein stated, "Things should be made as simple as possible, but no simpler." It is a facile assumption of those who have faith in the adequacy of the existing systematics that we are discovering, via retouched-stone-artifact typology, something very like the remains of identity-conscious social units analogous to the tribes, peoples, and nations of history. This assumption is deeply problematic and should be subjected to critical scrutiny.

10 Invented Traditions and the Ultimate American Origin Myth

IN THE BEGINNING . . . THERE WAS AN ICE-FREE CORRIDOR
Carole A. S. Mandryk

Until relatively recently, long-standing archaeological consensus was that the carriers of Clovis culture were the first inhabitants of the New World, arriving on foot by way of an unglaciated "ice-free corridor" through the Canadian ice sheets. As originally conceived in the 1930s, the corridor was a feature of deglaciation formed by the retreat of the Laurentide and Cordilleran ice masses as a result of postglacial warming. Even though the corridor route—up the Yukon valley, into the Mackenzie watershed, and down the eastern edge of the Rockies (Johnston 1933)—was from the beginning shown to be insufficiently supported by archaeological evidence (de Laguna 1936; Howard 1936; MacNeish 1959; Rouse 1976), it was quickly established as the prevailing paradigm. In the 1960s, when radiocarbon dating placed the opening of a deglaciation corridor well after accepted dates for archaeological sites on the Plains, debate began on the timing, location, and existence of a corridor through the ice sheets during the Last Glacial Maximum. Though most geological evidence did not support the existence of a corridor during that period, it remained the preferred route; by the 1970s, it had become a "myth," as Fladmark (1986:15) explained, "running through the minds of many archaeologists, like a highway beckoning Paleoindians south from Beringia."

This myth is still preferred by many individuals (see Fiedel 1998; West 1996a), despite the lack of supporting archaeological and geological evidence, partly because ideological and theoretical assumptions in academia and the popular press regarding the earliest Americans block consideration of alternative scenarios. Easton (1992:31) argues that the lack of serious investigation of an alternate migration route along the West Coast is not related to the coastal route's merit or to the oft-cited difficulties of locating archaeological sites under water. It is instead a result of "the almost mythological entrenchment of the ice-free corridor within our culture [and a] predilection to envision the first inhabitants of the Americas as stout-hearted, daring, and voracious big-game hunters."

This introduction leads me to the issue I am interested in exploring: *why* we find particular ideas about the past so attractive. Like Gero (1985, 1989, 1993), I am interested in the role of human agency in the making of knowledge and the way the production of the past proceeds from an ideology of the present. How do social context, theoretical orientations, preconceived ideas, and historical contingencies influence our reconstructions? In other papers, I have addressed the history of the concept of the ice-free corridor, but here I am primarily interested in explaining the *appeal* of this concept. What paths led to the mythological entrenchment of this particular story about the North American past?

I will first examine why there was such a remarkable wholesale acceptance of the notion despite a lack of supporting evidence, and why it still resonates so strongly today. I doubt that the answers lie solely in the nature of the archaeological record or in the particulars of the model itself as an explanatory device for an actual past. Instead I believe the explanation lies in the role the ice-free corridor plays as an essential component of the ultimate American origin myth. The peopling of the New World remains an emotional and contentious topic because it does not simply concern past events; it also involves the issue of identity.

Archaeo-Illogical Explanations

The prominence of the ice-free corridor as a concept can be partly explained by unsubstantiated speculation and the acceptance of faulty logic by archaeologists. Dincauze (1984) noted a tendency for basic assumptions to be unexamined, data to be confused with evidence, and linking arguments to be developed poorly, if at all. Arguments may go directly from observation to interpretation without bothering with data analysis. Here is one example: "There are widespread Paleoindian sites on the Plains. If there had been a corridor through the ice, humans could have passed through it; therefore, they did."

The widespread belief in the corridor was abetted

by the use of the possibilist fallacy, or attempting to demonstrate that a statement is true or false by establishing the *possibility* of its truth; that is, "when 'it could be' is followed by an unearned 'therefore it is'" (Dincauze 1984:292). As with many post hoc interpretations, once an ice-free corridor was considered probable or plausible, it quickly became accepted. As Binford (1981:32) argues regarding a comparable instance of myth-building, "[I]ts *very scale of acceptance* [italics mine] gradually became further justification for belief in the myth." Although errors in logic contribute to an explanation of *how* the ice-free corridor myth grew and developed, they are inadequate to explain *why*. For that understanding we must turn to a sociopolitical analysis.

Sociopolitical Analysis

Review of the history of the concept of the ice-free corridor shows that it can be an emotional issue, which is often characterized by unsubstantiated speculation and intense belief in the face of contradictory evidence. A look into the sociopolitics of archaeological research may help to explain such behavior by exposing some of the means by which the political and social present affects the archaeological past, which is, as Tilley (1990: 138) contends, a "socially produced construction."

Critical Approach

In recent years archaeologists have attacked the "myth of objective research" (Gero 1985:342) in their field and have called for self-reflective criticism, debate, and self-examination "as writers in the texts we produce" (Tilley 1990:143). The contention is that our ideas, assumptions, and interpretations regarding the past are not value and context neutral; "an archaeologist's sociopolitical identity and context [have] a determining influence on his or her archaeological analysis" (Wenke 1989:33). Our values, both personal and archaeological, are embedded in, and necessarily reflect, the larger society of which we are a part (Gero 1989, 1993; Handsman and Leone 1989; Tilley 1989; Wylie 1989). Archaeologists, historians, and all other producers of the past are "neither above nor outside societies but integral agents within them" (Bond and Gilliam 1994:2).

Proponents of critical theory ask, "Who owns the past? For what purposes is the past interpreted and created?" They maintain that the state owns the past and interprets it to support and justify its own existence (Gero 1985, 1989, 1993; Handsman and Leone 1989). Gero (1985:342) argues that "it is only the state that can support, and that requires, the services of elite specialists to produce and control the past." This control of the past also legitimizes control of the present (Kohl 1998). Archaeology in the service of the state "consistently misrepresents the past by making it seem a logical precedent for the present; indeed, archaeology suggests the present is an ineluctable and therefore legitimate outcome of the past" (Leone 1984:34, in Gero 1985:343). Thus the past, as constructed per the ideology of the present-day social order, justifies the present as its inevitable and logical outcome.

The use of the word *constructed* is pertinent to this discussion. Critical theorists stress that science is not just influenced but also constituted by social and political context (Wylie 1989). The belief that archaeologists and other scientists "discover" knowledge is an objectivist view. The opposing constructivist view argues that science is not about discovery but about creativity and *construction*; facts are not observed but are crafted out of "a welter of confusing and conflicting observations" and possibilities and are always within a particular social and political context (Gero 1993:32).

For too long, archaeologists have ignored or denied the connections between their work and the society in which they live (Handsman and Leone 1989). As Trigger (1986:18) argues, "[W]hat people believe about the present conditions their understanding of the past. . . . It is therefore unlikely that American archaeology has been uninfluenced by the ideology of American society and more particularly by the values of the more conservative elements of the middle class to whom such studies have particularly appealed."

Writing the Past for *National Geographic*

Gero and Root (1990), in an insightful analysis of the political function of the past in the United States as exemplified by one very popular example of American mass media, *National Geographic*, demonstrate how American ideological themes of expansionism and capitalism are effectively communicated throughout the magazine. Their analysis of 85 years of archaeological articles in *National Geographic* revealed three principal ways that archaeology is used to encourage American nationalism.

First, the magazine focuses on the "thrill" of archaeology as the exploration and discovery of exotic treasures by bold and competitive individuals. "*National*

Geographic's coverage of archaeology never dwells on explanations of prehistory or technical aspects of excavation. Rather, the editorial emphasis is on the *quest*: the quest in which one must be first, and for which one must traverse great distances in order to acquire artifacts, and above all, the *unique artifact*. The most frequent photographic image in its articles on archaeology displays the *unique artifact*, torn from its original production and use context and cleared from its recent archaeological matrix" (Gero and Root 1990:28). Fragmentary artifacts are seldom depicted; the focus is on the finest, the biggest, the best, and the first.

Second, the magazine tends to humanize and homogenize the past into the American mold. "Frequently the past is made more accessible through the lens of contemporary American concepts, categories and social relations, homogenizing all pasts to look like ours, and marking all prehistoric events along a timeline of the rise of Western civilization. . . . Again and again, present-day American values are extended into the past, onto the peoples of the past, appropriated by us to represent us in an earlier state" (Gero and Root 1990:29). Democratic state systems, specifically the United States, are portrayed as the inevitable and normal outcome of the development of Western civilization.

Third, the magazine contains systematic geographical, topical, and chronological biases in archaeological reporting, with the most attention being devoted to the cultural development of Western civilization and the origins of the Judeo-Christian tradition. Such a focus "make[s] the past appear to be like the present and lead[s] the public to believe that the state has always existed and is the norm as well as the most successful form of social organization. This misrepresentation of the past conveniently gives a time-depth to the American state underwriting a logic that portrays this system of governance as *innately* human and intrinsic to the human condition" (Gero and Root 1990:33).

Peopling of the Earth

It is pertinent to this discussion to take Gero and Root's analysis a bit further and include a *National Geographic* issue published after their paper was written. The October 1988 issue of *National Geographic*, titled "The Peopling of the Earth," illustrates many of the ideological influences summarized above. With this issue we can move past a general consideration of the influence of American ideology on archaeology. We can now analyze the American mythos regarding the peopling of the world and perhaps gain insights on the attitudes toward an ice-free corridor's role in the peopling of America.

This *National Geographic* issue amply illustrates support for American nationalism and for the United States as an inevitable outcome of Western civilization. Though the issue is titled "The Peopling of the Earth," the recurrent subject is clearly the peopling of North America and the origins of Americans.

The issue's introduction, titled "Where Did We Come From?", ostensibly refers to the origin of modern humans, but the focus is on a kind of directed migration to the Americas. "Whether driven by fear, hunger, curiosity, sense of destiny, or a mix of all, mankind—then as now—has continually migrated, as if to fill every void on this planet. . . . [M]an drifted north out of Africa to Europe and eastward to Asia. Millennia later, with the appearance of modern *Homo sapiens*, the great migration pushed on to Australia and the Americas" (Garrett 1988:435). Note the choice of words. "Sense of destiny" is hardly a value-free phrase; it clearly suggests an expansionist, imperialistic view of the world. Also note that humans passively "drifted" to Europe and Asia but actively "pushed on" to Australia and the Americas.

As a consummate example of the quest for unique artifacts, the introduction next discusses the article "Weapons Cache of Ancient Americans" and describes the cache as "the most magnificent collection of their spear points ever found" (Garrett 1988:435). Who are "they"?; the "first Americans," of course. A full-page photo of the two largest Clovis points ever found, photographed not in situ but held aloft in human hands, predictably accompanies the article.

Later in the introduction, the migration story is extended through time from the Upper Paleolithic, to the age of European discovery and colonization that began in the fifteenth century, to the present day, when "never before in history have as many humans been on the move as in this century. It is estimated that more immigrants—legal and illegal—will have entered the United States in the 1980s than in any other decade in our history" (Garrett 1988:437). An article on the Hmong in America illustrates these most recent immigrants, thus completing the circle of past as present, present as past. The present-day American concept of America as "the Promised Land," the goal of the world's immigrants, is pushed into the past. Confusing present with past—making the past the logical precedent for the present, and the present the inevitable outcome of the past—leads to the blurring of identities, so that "modern man" equals "first Americans" equals "Americans." This blurring exemplifies Americans' predilection to define others in terms of themselves, if indeed others are considered at all.

This tendency is clearly seen in the lead article of the issue, titled "The Search for Modern Humans." The search is continually described as a journey, in which the "trail" of modern humans is followed worldwide. By definition, a *search* is an act of inquiry or examination that attempts to establish facts or gain knowledge; it does not imply physical movement as does the word *journey*, which is the act of traveling from one place to another (Guralnik 1978:762, 1284).

The journey starts in France, then moves from Europe to Africa, Asia, Australia, and finally the Americas. There is frequent focus on the Americas as the "goal"; for example, "the trail of man's journey from Asia to the Americas" and "man's route to the Americas" (Putman 1988:464). The author writes, "[As] the plane lifted from Little Diomede and my journey approached its end [in the United States], I thought of the beginning, that dark cave in France, and of all I had seen since, and of how often I had seemed almost within touching distance of our prehistoric ancestors" (Putman 1988:475). Though a nonarchaeologist writing for the general public, Putman shares philosophical, cultural, and theoretical presuppositions with those archaeologists (see Fagan 1987), who "have been propelled by an Eurocentric mandate to link us to Upper Paleolithic 'ancestors' [see Clark, this volume]. That is, we seek to find ourselves in this archaeological record" (Conkey 1987:63).

Putman travels from France across the world on a search (journey) for "modern humans." The end point of his journey is the United States, thus validating America as the logical outcome—if not the only outcome and clearly the best outcome—of the development of modern humans. All roads, all migration routes, lead inevitably to us in the present. The Hmong came to America, just as the "first" Americans did about 12,000 B.P.

The three ways in which archaeology serves nationalist ideology (Gero and Root 1990) are evident in the beliefs concerning the first peopling of the New World. The focus is on the quest: the exploration and discovery of exotic lands by bold and competitive individuals. The idea of America as the ultimate goal of immigrants—whether traveling today or 12,000 years ago—illustrates how present-day American attitudes are extended into the past and are assumed to have been held by people of the past, who, regardless of actual cultural or genetic heritage, are "appropriated by us to represent us in an earlier state" (Gero and Root 1990:29). We find the reconstructed past compelling precisely because it resembles present-day attitudes. This representation of the past gives a time depth to the American system that also makes the past appear to be like the present. America has always existed; it is the norm for humanity and the most successful form of social organization.

The first Americans are not simply ancient inhabitants of the American continents; they are Americans barely different from ourselves. The fact that the earliest Americans are of Asian stock, whereas the majority of Americans are not, is irrelevant. We are tracing an invented cultural past of our present selves, not a real past. From this point of view, of what importance is the concept of the ice-free corridor? It is the instrument, the route, for a critical part of the story: the *beginning*. The bold, adventurous, curious, innovative first Americans migrated to their destiny down the ice-free corridor.

The preceding analysis illustrates general trends and tendencies in writing the present into the past to reflect current American values and ideals. It does not, however, explain what these observations led me to ponder: What are the origins of the story?

Nationalist Narratives and Invented Traditions

What do I mean by "the story"? The role of the ice-free corridor (literally as well as conceptually) is only part of a larger story that Bryan (1991:20) calls the "Clovis-first model." Bryan defines the theoretical assumptions of this Paleoindian origin myth: Clovis hunters, who constituted a single cultural group that descended from northern Eurasian mammoth hunters and possessed a specialized Upper Paleolithic level of cold-adapted technology (believed necessary for crossing Beringia), advanced southward through an inhospitable ice-free corridor. The widespread distribution of fluted points made by these Clovis hunters throughout North America indicates their equally widespread specialization in mega-mammal hunting. Despite few actual co-occurrences of fluted points and extinct mammals, the presence of fluted points was assumed to indicate big-game hunting (Gero 1993; Hudecek-Cuffe 1998). Admittedly, these theoretical assumptions do knit together well into a satisfying narrative story.

As Landau (1991) points out, scientists have long been storytellers; we just didn't realize it. Many scientific theories are essentially narratives with a beginning, a middle, and an end, with "heroes and scoundrels, triumphs and defeats, trials and tribulations, conquests and achievements" (Terrell 1990:4). Knitting together a variety of facts, the story of the first Americans migrating through the ice-free corridor fulfills the general requirements of a narrative story: a beginning, a middle, and an end. It especially mirrors Landau's (1991) observations on hero tales: A humble hero (the Clovis ancestors) departs on a journey (across Beringia), receives essential equipment (what else?: the Clovis point), goes through tests and transformations (the trip through the inhospitable corridor), and finally arrives at a higher state (America). As Terrell (1990:7) notes, "[U]sing narrative to build a sense of completeness and admiration into accounts of history or prehistory can also serve to pull facts together into a coherent sense of cause and effect even when existing scientific theory is inadequate to account for the facts reported and the inferences drawn."

These facts, however, are not observed facts; they are created "facts." As Gero (1993) astutely argues, focusing on the similarities rather than the differences in fluted-point sites "flattens" the data and helps create a national paradigm (but see Tankersley, this volume). That this universal, Paleoindian, specialized big-game-hunting stage is *not supported by archaeological evidence* is irrelevant to acceptance of the narrative. The proposed alternative interpretation of the archaeological record—that it reflects generalized foragers adapting to local ecosystems (Bryan 1991; Chilton, this volume; Roosevelt et al. 1996)—did not suit the needs of a national origin story. This conclusion correlates well with the observation that dominant histories tend to be generalized; they work better that way in absorbing divergent interests and interpretations and in reducing "complex and intricate historical and social diversities to a few prominent cultural images" (Bond and Gilliam 1994:16).

Baker (1992) does a compelling deconstruction of a more familiar American origin myth that is instructive for our understanding of our paleo-origin myths. He describes the Pilgrims as one of America's great national symbols and one that plays a more significant role in our contemporary myth than in our actual history. The Pilgrim settlers of Plymouth became symbols of America's origin even though historical facts showed that Virginia was settled earlier and that the Massa-chusetts Bay Colony was more important. Clearly the actual facts "paled before the psychic force of the Pilgrim Story" (Baker 1992:344), as they do in the story of the first Americans, demonstrating that cultural traditions can be historically significant without being true. The strong feelings about the story suggest that "there [is] obviously something more at work than poor historical knowledge" (Baker 1992:345).

Another key aspect of the Pilgrim story is the importance of tangible physical symbols, such as Plymouth Rock, which became a powerful icon in American consciousness. Commanger (1975) notes that nationalist common denominators tend to be pictorial (visualize yet another map of the ice-free corridor) and symbolic (fluted points = first Americans). Baker (1992:347) describes how de Tocqueville on his travels found "cherished fragments, like pieces of the True Cross, treated as sacred relics." It is not too large a leap to compare this to the near reverence accorded Clovis projectile points, particularly in popular culture and among amateur collectors and avocational archaeologists, but also among professional archaeologists.

I find especially compelling Baker's contention that such symbols were critical to validating the origins of the United States as a young nation. The United States, as a new nation, "had no long-standing traditions, no historical memory" (Baker 1992:347). Because states or "nations without pasts are a contradiction in terms" (Rowlands 1994:133) and because history, tradition, and memory are critical to successful nationalism (Commanger 1975), Americans needed to create a past. As Kohl (1998:233) argues, "[C]onstruction of a national identity for a nation of immigrants is a different task from that for a nation whose citizens believe has been theirs since time immemorial."

Invented Traditions and the Acquisition of a Past

How does America, a nation without a past, acquire one? Commanger (1975) lists three possibilities: (1) by asserting that Americans have no need of a past because they are so sure of a future, (2) by asserting that America has a past, the past of all of Europe, and (3) by using what Americans have, that is, by buttressing the details of the short historical record of the earliest settlers, which is how we got the Pilgrim story among others.

A fourth way to acquire a past is to invent one. Hobsbawm (1992a,b) discusses this concept, agreeing with earlier historians that the United States had a problem with national identity and asserting that the basic political problem in the United States after World War I "was how to assimilate a heterogeneous mass . . . , an almost unmanageable influx of people who were Americans not by birth but by immigration" (Hobsbawm 1992b:279). Hobsbawm uses the term "invented tradition" to describe this process of creating history, a process that applies to the Pilgrim story as well as the ice-free corridor. Neither of these are real pasts; they are invented traditions. The particular story that becomes part of the "ideology of the nation, state or movement is not what has been actually preserved in popular memory, but what has been selected, written, pictured, popularized, and institutionalized by those whose function it is to do so" (Hobsbawm 1992a:13).

The story of the first Americans migrating through an ice-free corridor is thus in the same vein as the Pilgrim story. It simply extends further into the ancient past, fulfilling what Hobsbawm (1992a:14) refers to as a "curious, but understandable paradox, that modern nations generally claim to be the opposite of novel, namely rooted in the remotest antiquity, and the opposite of constructed, namely human communities so 'natural' as to require no definition other than self-assertion."

Rowlands (1994:135) identifies the source of this tendency as classic nineteenth-century liberal nationalism, which "aimed to unify and extend the scale of human social and cultural units by inclusion (via language and education primarily) rather than by separation and exclusion." Commager (1975) notes the tremendous speed and lavishness with which Americans provided themselves with a past. The American preoccupation with the "birth of the nation" began with political independence, intensified during the 1800s with debates about "what is an American" (Billington 1975), surged anew to heal the wounds of the Civil War, and continued into the twentieth century to incorporate waves of immigrants (Billington 1975; Hobsbawm 1992a,b; Rowlands 1994). As Commager (1975:195) argues, "[P]roviding themselves with a historical past was particularly difficult for Americans because it was not something that could be taken for granted, as with most peoples, or arranged once and for all. . . . It was something that had to be done over and over again, for each new wave of newcomers, and that had to be kept up to date, as it were, continually reinvigorated and modernized" (an interesting idea, that of needing to *modernize* the past).

Whenever I read a definition of what it means to be an American, whether from this century or the last,

I hear echoes of the first Paleoindian immigrants. Billington (1975:61) discusses Frederick Jackson Turner's (1893) influential "frontier thesis," which argued that American traits of mobility, optimism, inventiveness, willingness to accept innovation, materialism, and exploitative wastefulness were all frontier-induced traits. The pioneer "accustomed to . . . repeated moves . . . viewed the world through rose-colored glasses as he dreamed of a better future [and] constantly devised new techniques and artifacts to cope with an unfamiliar environment" (Billington 1975:61, 66).

The cultural traits developed on the frontier "form the principal distinguishing characteristics of the American people" today (Billington 1975:67). Billington continues (and here I add the Paleoindian echoes in brackets), "[T]o a degree unknown among Europeans, Americans do display a restless energy [rapid migration to the New World], a versatility [coping with variable environmental conditions], a practical ingenuity [the development of fluting], an earthy practicality [the efficient use of high-quality lithic raw materials]. They do squander their natural resources with an abandon unknown elsewhere [mammoth overkill]; they have developed a mobility both social and physical [fanning out over North America within 500 years and spreading farther until Archaic times] that marks them as a people apart."

The Ice-Free Corridor as American Origin Myth

I would argue that the ice-free corridor story was initially written within the nationalistic historical, theoretical, and political strictures discussed above. The story resonates perfectly as the ultimate origin myth; it extends our national history not just to the first European settlers but back to the first human inhabitants of the continent.[1] By echoing more recent descriptions of American identity, the corridor story provides us with an "empathy with the past—not just an intellectual understanding but an emotional bond with [our] nation's story" (Baker 1992:348). The reluctance to let go of this paleomyth relates to its "common-sense rightness" as a story of "our" past. Just like the Pilgrims, the first migrants through the ice-free corridor became the "spiritual ancestors of all Americans" (Baker 1992:357). Rowlands (1994:136) notes that "the objectification of national spirit, and the recognition of the people or races as embodiments of that spirit, [take] on an enduring form that emphasizes long-term continuity" and that makes the present appear like the past. Bryan (1991:18) describes the Clovis-first model as "logically so compelling it must be true." Why was it perceived as so logical and compelling? Partly, of course, because of its explanatory power regarding the known archaeological record. But beyond that, the model appeals to our common sense, our cultural knowledge, and our assumptions about ourselves in the present. This is how the past is made to seem "inevitable, immediate, and familiar" (Handsman and Leone 1989:119).

Baker (1992:354) notes a problem: "[U]nfortunately, myths are not easy to exorcise; therein lies their power. . . . Scholars underestimate the importance of emotion and sentiment in their pursuit of the truth; people are not informed by reason alone." The power of the ice-free corridor story as heroic narrative, American origin myth, and nationalist ideology is compelling. The concept of the ice-free corridor is held onto tenaciously in the face of conflicting evidence because it is a symbol of all that Americans hold important. It was the first way, the best way, the difficult way, the romantic way. Significantly in this narrative, the route—how they (we?) got here—is inseparable from who we are. Asserting that there was no available corridor for these first(?) immigrants would be equivalent to denying the Pilgrims the Mayflower. This framework may also provide another reason to expect the earliest inhabitants to move so quickly through the corridor. This was no random drifting migration; this was directed migration. These were the first American immigrants on their way to America.

Does this analysis mean that we are incapable of recognizing reality? Of course not. It simply suggests that we must work harder to separate what feels so intuitively right from what we can plausibly demonstrate. It is time to deconstruct the "Clovis-first, American, adventurous, terrestrial, ice-free corridor" story (a task that has begun academically but perhaps not emotionally) and replace it with a more complex reality, whatever that reality may be.

Terrell (1990:18) argues that we expect stories to be constructed from a "well-crafted sequence of events and episodes without extraneous characters, useless detail, unexplained happenings, or loose ends." Clovis migration through an ice-free corridor is a well-told and satisfying story that resonates with our presumptions about American identity. No wonder we are uncomfortable about a world filled with Monte Verde, coastal migration routes, generalized foragers, regional adaptations, and the heretical notion that Clovis may have originated in the southeastern United States. The story no longer has a beginning, middle, or end. It is all loose ends.

That is precisely what makes the current situation so exciting. For more than 60 years, we thought we knew the answers. The prevailing paradigm incorporated all the facts, at least those we chose to recognize. But now those facts, along with loose ends old and new, are whirling in a Cuisinart of intellectual chaos. Yet, if we are willing to part with a cherished myth and expand our vision of what is possible, we can harness the pioneering aspect of American identity to pioneer new archaeological paradigms. There is no telling what the result will be when things settle.

Conclusions

This analysis of why the ice-free corridor was inherently more attractive than a coastal migration route and how the corridor story reflects nationalist ideals is not meant to condemn those who hold particular views, but to make their underlying assumptions more transparent.

That a bias appears to be present in interpretations of the American past does not imply that the bias was intentional or that archaeologists were consciously aware of it. Instead I believe it reflects what Tilley (1990:150) labels "the social and political 'unconscious' of archaeology," as well as the historical trajectory of American archaeological discourse. Trigger (1989) contends that in archaeological interpretation, ideas about the past often remain influential long after the reasoning that led to their development has been rejected and abandoned. Furthermore, "once a 'fact' is arrived at, it is quickly freed from the circumstances of its production and loses all historical relevance to the social and contextual conditions of its construction" (Latour and Woolgar 1979:106, in Gero 1993:32).

It is when an interpretation is seen as common sense that we may be most unaware of its implicit assumptions, internal contradictions, and poorly tested explanations. The problem is not that "archaeology is a political discourse, but that its politics largely take place on a tacit or unconscious level" (Tilley 1989:110). We should not be overly critical of ourselves for not being critical enough about our unconscious biases. It is not easy to recognize the political role of our interpretations and reconstructions or the messages they are sending. Sociopolitical assumptions and attitudes are deeply embedded in one's culture. It is hard indeed to unchain oneself from the cave, stop studying the shadows, and turn and face the light of an alternate reality. This is precisely why we need self-reflexive criticism to help us make our assumptions and attitudes explicit.

If nothing else, I am content to finally understand part of the reason for the intense emotion and belief surrounding the issue of an ice-free corridor. Like Landau (1991:xi), "I do not pretend to stand outside the narrative practice I examine." I do not consider myself immune to the charms of an origin story that could speak to me. As Rowlands (1994:130) reminds us, the quest for cultural origins remains a prime focus of much archaeological writing "precisely because of the appeal of collective identity." I find myself acknowledging the attractiveness of a generalizing paradigm, especially in the context of current tensions between academic and Native communities in North America, particularly the United States.[2] Rowlands (1994:130) states that "for cultural heritage to be significant it must [be] unifying and transcendent and be constitutive of a sense of personal and group identity." The appeal of such a cultural heritage is obvious. However, as Kohl (1998:243) argues, "[C]onstruction of one group's national past should not be made at the expense of others." If only we could invent a new tradition that did indeed include all of us. Clearly we must continually reconstruct our American identity and origin myths, as they are mirror images of one another, apart from the archaeological reality we think we may discover.

Acknowledgments

This paper owes much to three talks I attended in the fall of 1998. Listening to Regna Darnell, I was struck by the phrase "culture overrides race and historical circumstance." From Michael Asch I gained the interesting change in perspective from viewing post-contact history in North America as chapter 15 of a story that started in another place (Europe) to chapter 15 of the story of *this* place. At the Chacmool Conference that year, Joe Watkins gave a talk titled "At What Point 'Ours,' at What Point 'Yours.'" I first took this title to be an opposition, but Joe explained that it did not mean "either-or"; "ours" meant "all of us." These talks made me aware of my own "true hunger for wholeness and unity" (Rowlands 1994:139) and my deep desire to find our history: the cultural history of *all of us* here and now, which we write in the present. It is in this spirit, not one of divisiveness or confrontation, that I wrote this paper. I hope I have caused at least one person to see things a little differently.

I thank Reece Michaelson and three anonymous reviewers for their commentary. Judging by the nature of their comments, I see that my desire to facilitate debate, self-reflexivity, dialogue, and discussion has been at least partially successful. I especially wish to thank Chris Tilley (1990:152) for his charge to all of us to "think about what you would like to write and yet know you dare not set down on paper."

III   The Land and People Transformed

The arrival and spread of humans in the ecosystems of North and South America set in motion a complex wave of ecological and social changes, whose ripples spread across the continents and through time to the present (Martin 1967, 1984b). Although this model almost certainly oversimplified human roles in late Pleistocene American ecosystems, it has served as an effective counterpoint to the popular notion of hunter-gatherers as natural conservationists.

The papers in part III address the ecological role of the Pleistocene pioneers in the New World and the consequences of colonization from the perspective of human behavioral ecology. A relatively new discipline, human ecology first appeared in the mid-1970s with the application of optimal foraging theory to hunter-gatherer resource selection and land-use models. Constantly undergoing redefinition (Winterhalder and Smith 2000), this field has subsequently expanded to embrace a wide range of topics that are important to archaeology and to anthropology in general. The conceptual frameworks and methodologies developed by evolutionary ecologists have assumed increasing importance in recent years in the efforts by archaeologists, human paleontologists, molecular biologists, and linguists to model range extensions, radiations, and migrations of various sizes and scales. Many workers now realize that processes analogous to those that are observable ethnographically—those that take place in time frames measured in minutes, hours, days, weeks, months, and years—may be ill-suited to the study of phenomena like those involved in continental-scale colonization. The latter phenomena can transpire over generations, beyond the memories of individuals and the collective memory of a group; they are set against a backdrop of climate and landscape transformations that operate independently of, and at spatial-temporal scales far beyond, the comprehension of human foragers. Papers in this section address a range of issues using conceptual frameworks, variables, and methodologies drawn from the literature of evolutionary ecology. Although our capacity to assess the explanatory potential of these models remains limited by the empirical insufficiencies of the archaeological record, the approaches themselves represent the best current thinking on how we can improve our understanding of the colonization process.

Part III begins with a paper by David Meltzer that extends Robert Kelly's return-rate-maximizing model to address the costs associated with high mobility. Rather than simply maximizing caloric returns, the primary goals of the more complex colonization model that Meltzer proposes are minimizing both the uncertainty about resources and the demographic risk in unknown landscapes. Long-distance logistical forays to gather information, coupled with residential moves within megapatches that contain familiar resources, led to the rapid expansion of Paleoindian groups across North and South America.

C. Michael Barton, Steven Schmich, and Steven James combine aspects of proposed colonization models for pristine environments at continental scales under the aegis of behavioral ecology. Barton and his colleagues test predictions about forager mobility, colonization rates, and diet diversity against deglaciated northern Europe and the Americas at the end of the Pleistocene. They also explore potential impacts of human-caused environmental change and predation on late Pleistocene ecosystems in the Western Hemisphere.

Elizabeth Chilton focuses attention on the diversity in Paleoindian ecology that is often obscured by an emphasis on big-game hunting. To understand the complexities of initial human settlement in the

New World, we must account for the critical roles of women and children, as well as men, in economic decisions and resource acquisition. We must also recognize the potential importance of small game and plants to Paleoindian subsistence.

From an analysis of forager mobility and mating networks based in evolutionary ecology, Douglas MacDonald suggests that Paleoindian settlement more closely matches an "estate settler" model than a "transient explorer" model (cf. Beaton 1991). Because of very low population densities and the potential for high rates of social network breakdown, groups of early Paleoindians probably traveled mostly locally, and individuals tended to settle on the edges of already colonized lands, thus maintaining reproductive and social ties with larger groups with whom they were related by kin ties.

Megafaunal extinction has most commonly been attributed either to human overexploitation or to climatic change that affected the range and types of forage available to megafauna. In contrast, community ecologist Elin Whitney-Smith proposes a more complex "second-order overkill" scenario. Humans initiate a cascade of ecological changes that involve competition with large carnivores and end with the population collapse of large herbivores and the expansion of grasslands.

The final chapter in this section, by paleontologist Larry Agenbroad and archaeologist India Hesse, examines the evidence for the coexistence of humans and megafauna on the Colorado Plateau, a region long thought to be incapable of supporting either during the late Pleistocene.

11 Modeling the Initial Colonization of the Americas

ISSUES OF SCALE, DEMOGRAPHY, AND LANDSCAPE LEARNING

David J. Meltzer

Those of us who work on the peopling of the Americas think we see in the archaeological record of that colonization processes that are analogous to those that ethnographers observe in *real time*; that is, processes measurable in minutes, hours, days, weeks, etc., such as prey selection and patch choice, demic expansion, group fissioning, and the like. Accordingly, we (I include myself here) readily apply models rooted in foraging theory, for example, or attempt to understand the colonizers' fertility and reproductive tactics in light of modern hunter-gatherers (e.g., Anderson 1995; Barton et al., this volume; Beaton 1991; Kelly 1996, 1999; Kelly and Todd 1988; MacDonald 1999, this volume; Meltzer 1995, 1998; Moore 2001; Steele et al. 1998; Surovell 2000). Some of these models (for modesty's and honesty's sake, I now exclude myself) are clever, some are elegant, and some may even be right. But by constructing models of this continental- and millennial-scale process using variables that specify and even demand real-time values and currencies, we face several critical questions.

First, are ethnographically based models appropriate for understanding this colonization process? We are dealing with a dispersal that took place on an empty landscape, one devoid of other people and undergoing geologically rapid change. Ethnographies record minimal movements over brief periods of time (Fix 1999: 150); even highly mobile groups do not disperse on the scale in which we are interested. All ethnographically known hunter-gatherers have neighbors, near or distant, on whom they can rely for information, resources, and potential mates and against whom they compete or whose presence otherwise affects the decision-making calculus of moving about the landscape and utilizing its resources. Moreover, modern hunter-gatherers have substantial knowledge of their landscape: not complete knowledge (no group ever has [Smith 1983, 1988:250]), but knowledge sufficiently deep that it can reduce forager uncertainty, make it possible to gamble on risky strategies for higher stakes, and generally maximize returns (Smith 1988:231–232).

Second, the colonization of the Americas stretched over thousands of kilometers and played out over centuries (if not millennia). It involved cultural (and genetic) drift of style and technology across space and through time. It also led to continentwide horizon markers and style zones and ultimately to regional adaptations and large-scale patterns of cultural diversity, which, by about 10,000 B.P., suggest fundamental changes in the cultural (and genetic) landscape. Are these larger patterns merely the sum of continuous small-scale (real-time) processes, or are there processes of range expansion that transcend these and that are visible and explicable only at much larger temporal and spatial scales? As Fitzhugh (1997:389) put it, "Are biogeographic and evolutionary processes cumulative with increasing geographic scale; or are they transformative under these conditions, introducing complexities that obscure cause and effect?"

Third, can we link observable real-time processes to the archaeological record? That record is a static contemporary phenomenon composed of samples of past activities that occurred in a bounded space (commonly a site) but often represent unbounded (or at least unknown, varying, and sometimes "averaged") amounts of time. Does it (can it) record real-time actions, such as a forager's prey choice? Kelly (1995:340) argues that "archaeology may not be able to see the . . . cultural musings of a lone forager . . . , [but] coarse as it may be, the archaeological record was nevertheless produced by the behavior of individuals" (see also Boone and Smith 1998:S169; Foley 1992:131; Mithen 1993). But is the behavior of individuals (on which models are based) detectable in the archaeological record, or do the static archaeological patterns exist in unknown (and unknowable) relationship to the dynamic processes that produced them?

Fourth, if the archaeological record does record the variables and currencies of interest, do we possess the methodological tools to detect them? Can we measure, for example, resource abundance and rank from a late Pleistocene fauna that may have accumulated in an archaeological site over an unknown period of time representing an unknown (and potentially biased) fraction of a larger subsistence strategy? Can we do so with sufficient precision to provide empirical tests of the models? It is not enough to show a model can accommodate data; one must also be able to test and falsify it.

We have in the late Pleistocene archaeological record of the Americas a population dispersal of modern humans the likes of which has never been recorded ethnographically, and which also was a relatively rare event in the grand sweep of the prehistory of modern humans. This is not to say rare events are beyond the explanatory pale. I would argue the opposite: All idiographic events have nomothetic undertones, and these processes must have unfolded within broad principles of human adaptation.

The application of uniformitarianism does not demand that the present and past be identical in *substantive* terms, or that the present serve as a direct model of the past. (It's a good thing, too, because no ethnographic analogues exist for this colonization process.) Rather, it provides us with a *methodological* warrant for using processes observable in the present (in ethnographic or ecological real time) as a key to explaining the past (Meltzer 2001; see also Fix 1999:151). Thus, any explanation for that dispersal process must begin with (and not violate) what we know of, for example, the boundaries of human behavior or "the limits of human mobility or demography" (Fix 1999:150). It must also be at the appropriate scale.

Let me frame this discussion, therefore, around two models that purport to accomplish this task: one developed by Kelly and Todd (1988; see also Kelly 1996, 1999); the other, a more recent one I formulated (originally in Meltzer 1998; parts in Meltzer 2001, 2002). My model derives from a foundation that is similar to that of Kelly and Todd, but it attempts to fill in critical gaps in their model. I will use this discussion to illustrate more fully some of the aforementioned concerns about scale and archaeological testability.

A caveat: I address only Clovis. Although I accept evidence of a human presence in the Americas prior to Clovis time (Dillehay 1997b; Meltzer et al. 1997), that population—at least in North America—was apparently insubstantial. Indeed, the expansion of Clovis groups occurred so quickly across such a wide area (archaeologically speaking) that it appears they encountered few (if any) other people along the way (Meltzer 2002). This begs two questions: (1) what was the historical relationship between Clovis and the apparently

earlier migratory pulse into and through North America by ancestral Monte Verdeans; and (2) why was North America effectively an empty landscape by the time Clovis groups arrived (Barton et al., this volume). These, however, are questions I cannot answer.

For reasons that will become obvious, I refer to Kelly and Todd's model as the "return-rate-maximizing model" and mine as the "minimizing-uncertainty-and-demographic-risk model." Because Kelly and Todd's model is by far the better known and better developed of the two, I will start with it.[1]

Return-Rate-Maximizing Model

The return-rate-maximizing model (hereafter RRM) seeks to explain migration throughout the entire Western Hemisphere and assumes that South American Paleoindians were descendants of the same migration as Clovis. Because of the archaeological differences now apparent between North and South American Paleoindians (Dillehay et al. 1992; Lynch 1991; Politis 1991; cf. Kelly 1996:237), that assumption may no longer be justified (but see Pearson, this volume). Moreover, it was North American archaeological data from which the RRM model was derived and that the model attempted to accommodate (indeed, Kelly and Todd [1988] make little mention of any South American data or evidence). For the purposes of this discussion, I will consider the RRM model only in terms of North America. It should also be noted that Kelly and Todd (1988) subsume several distinct Paleoindian traditions in their model, from Clovis to later Paleoindian groups on the Plains, as well as early and late eastern North American Paleoindians. Doing so necessarily combines potentially different adaptive strategies, and not all of these archaeological groups could, strictly speaking, represent colonizers of empty lands.

The RRM model rests on the observation that Clovis groups were highly mobile and radiated quickly throughout the continent, at a time when North American climates and environments were rapidly changing. Among the changes that Kelly and Todd cite are the shift from patchy to zonal environments, a decline in faunal biomass, the extinction of megafauna, and a change from equable to more seasonal/continental climates (e.g., Kelly 1996:231, 1999:150, 152; Kelly and Todd 1988:232–233). Assuming that Clovis groups were "preadapted to hunting," coming as they did from the Arctic, the model further presumes that these groups compensated for their lack of knowledge about the unknown and highly varied habitats of North America by exploiting the same niche—terrestrial game hunting—throughout every habitat they entered (Kelly 1996:231; Kelly and Todd 1988).

According to the model, this made it possible, even necessary, to move swiftly over long distances. Kelly and Todd argue that game populations would have quickly declined or become more wary in the face of hunting pressure and rapid late Pleistocene climatic and environmental change. Faced with diminishing returns, Paleoindians would choose to move to unoccupied patches where familiar game animals were present, rather than stay in the original patch and expand their diet (see also Barton et al., this volume). In doing so, they would be following the Marginal Value Theorem, which holds that foragers stay in a patch as long as return rates are above the average return rate for the entire environment. When the foragers believe that return rates in another patch will be better than those in the current patch, and after factoring in the cost in time and energy to move to the next patch, they will make the move (Stephens and Krebs 1986:94–95). Staying would require experimenting with or using less familiar, lower-ranked, animal and plant resources. If one assumes that the contemporary landscape was rich in animal resources and relatively homogeneous, the costs of moving would have been offset by the higher return rates in the new patch.

The RRM model assumes that colonizing groups were entering a "world undergoing rapid climatic change, from a non-seasonal to a seasonal environment and in which many species of fauna were going extinct" (Kelly 1999:152). Yet extinctions must be irrelevant to the model because it explicitly disavows the notion that Clovis groups relied on Pleistocene megafauna (Kelly 1996:238; Kelly and Todd 1988:233), which, of course, were the fauna that went extinct. There was, however, almost certainly local extirpation of individual species in many areas as they adjusted their ranges to changing climatic and ecological conditions in terminal Pleistocene times.

But how quickly were climates and environments changing, and were the changes rapid enough to be detectable to human foragers?

Climate change occurs at several temporal scales, from large-scale orbitally triggered (Milankovitch) changes, to those occurring on millennial or even (as are apparent in the climates of today) decadal scales (e.g., Alley 2000; Alley et al. 1999; Bond et al. 1997; Mayewski et al. 1993, 1994; Meese et al. 1994; Severinghaus

and Brook 1999; White 2000). The decadal changes would obviously have the most impact on human foragers. There is evidence from Greenland ice cores that atmospheric temperature over the ice sheet changed as much as 10°C or 20°C in less than 50 to 80 years in the terminal Pleistocene (Severinghaus and Brook 1999; Steig 2001; White 2000; cf. Shemesh and Peteet 1998). In the geographically marginal and ecologically unstable High Arctic, where there are relatively few species, such rapid climate change (with attendant changes in temperature, storminess, moisture patterns, etc.) can trigger dramatic resource failure (Fitzhugh 1997:393–395).

Yet it is not certain that climate change in *temperate* North America was as dramatic or rapid as it was over Greenland (Grimm et al. 1993; Peteet 1995). How these changes played out globally remains of considerable but unresolved interest (Alley and Clark 1999; Robdell 2000; Shackleton 2001; Steig 2001). It is difficult, moreover, to detect in the terrestrial paleoecological record even millennial-scale climate changes, not to mention decadal ones, so if changes played out at that scale, they might not be visible (Grimm et al. 1993; Hostetler and Bartlein 1999; Whitlock and Grigg 1999).

Even if climate change in temperate North America was rapid, there still would have been a lag before that change would have affected the biotic communities on which foragers relied, and the effects would certainly not have triggered uniform (or uniformly rapid) responses among plant and animal species and communities. Instead each species would have responded according to its own adaptive tolerances and strategies, moving in different directions and at different rates and times (FAUNMAP Working Group 1996:1601–1602; Graham and Mead 1987:371). Thus, it cannot be assumed that late Pleistocene climatic and ecological change in temperate North America—*if* it was rapid (and it is not certain that it was)—necessarily affected all or even most of the species on which human foragers may have depended. It also cannot be assumed that change occurred at a scale that was visible to or had an impact on human foragers.

The RRM strategy is said to have required Clovis groups to "move constantly into new territory—and thus they were pulled south throughout the Americas" (Kelly 1996:231). The model does not explain why Paleoindian movement would necessarily have been southerly or even unidirectional (cf. Kelly and Todd 1988:234; see also Anthony 1990:901). Indeed, it is difficult to conceive of a reason why the movement should have been southward. Even declining return rates and the realization that the unknown landscape had the potential for higher return rates would not presuppose southerly movement, unless one simultaneously invoked a continentwide wave-front advance (Martin 1973) of a large and expanding population, for whom the only open landscape was to the south. The RRM model also envisions high mobility with only brief residence in a single area. Yet within a few hundred years, the continent was extensively occupied. The model is unclear on how—with mobility that is not driven by demic expansion (see below)—long-term settlement results.

As a consequence of this highly mobile, "technology-oriented" (and prey-oriented) strategy, Paleoindians were not "place-oriented." This does not imply that they were ignorant of the landforms around them, but it does mean that they did not spend sufficient time in different areas to identify the features of a specific area (Kelly and Todd 1988:237, 239).

The model holds that Clovis groups were able to transfer hunting skills from one animal to another, on the assumption that, although prey types vary, foragers harvesting different and perhaps unfamiliar species in the same size class (large game, in this instance) could bring their customary weaponry, hunting skills, and tactics to bear on all (Kelly and Todd 1988:234). In effect, the niche stays constant while patch and prey shift. That premise might be questioned (Frison 1988:100–101), but it seems reasonable for the sake of the model (as does the related point that transferring hunting skills is easier than transferring knowledge of plant resources [Kelly and Todd 1988:234]).

Yet even if foragers harvested in the same size class, different animals almost certainly behaved differently across the landscape. Locating prey required knowledge of the spatial and temporal landscape behavior of the animals. Such behavior varies by age, sex, group size, species composition, season, competitive relationships, available water, physiological stage (breeding, pregnancy, or lactation), grazing sequences, heterogeneity of the vegetation community, topography, and exposure to predation, among other factors (Van Dyne et al. 1980:285–298; see also Frison 1991b:141; Johnson et al. 1992; Winterhalder et al. 1988). Herbivore foraging and food selection are "highly variable from animal to animal, season to season, and place to place," which, to be understood, require "extended periods of [observation] with several animals to average out the variability" (Van Dyne et al. 1980:286, 320). To be successful, Paleoindians either had to have more knowl-

edge of their landscapes than the RRM model assumes; *or* the late Pleistocene landscape had to be extremely rich relative to humans (and thus, search time would have been low); *or* their foraging strategies were less systematic and more encounter based.

The RRM model envisions colonization as a rapid process, in which groups with a relatively narrow diet breadth move quickly through unfamiliar environments and successfully hurdle ecological boundaries by latching on to "similar" prey (large game). The RRM model can thus explain rapid movement without invoking demic expansion as the primary motor driving colonization. This aspect of the model is a virtue because human populations were almost certainly smaller at this time than at any subsequent time in American prehistory, and it is highly unlikely that demographic pressures would have driven colonization. Colonizing groups traveled much farther and faster than they had to if they were just looking for new land (Barton et al., this volume; Kelly 1996; Mandryk 1993).

On Demographics and Landscape Learning

There is an unfortunate gap between those of us who focus on food and those of us who focus on reproduction. (Harpending 1999:517)

Although the RRM model does not require demic expansion to drive colonization, it also does not fully account for demographic questions raised by the model. There are many costs to moving, including the differential payoff of foraging further afield versus expanding the diet to include local, lower-ranked resources; the distance to the next patch; the difficulty of traversing the intervening terrain; the time it takes to break down housing; and the size and composition of the group (Kelly 1995:136–141). To this list we must add a cost specific to the late Pleistocene American landscape: that of moving away from other people, be they kin or unrelated groups. Colonizers must maintain a "critical mass" of population to ensure reproductive viability while living (initially) in relatively small numbers, spread thinly over large areas lacking other people (MacDonald, this volume; Meltzer 1995).

These demographic demands would have been more or less severe depending on the size of the deme, age and sex composition, kin structure and marriage proscriptions, recruitment rate, and environmental uncertainty (and the inverse: knowledge of the landscape), as well as on the rate at which the group was moving from its geographic homeland or parent group and the environmental constraints on group size and population densities (Moore 2001; see also Borgerhoff Mulder 1992:341–342; Fix 1999:48; Lahr and Foley 1998:146; MacArthur and Wilson 1967:78, 80, 88; MacCluer and Dyke 1976; Whallon 1989:434–435). Timing is everything. The most severe demands would likely have occurred as groups traversed the harsh arctic and subarctic environments, which would have selected for rapid movement (Mandryk 1993), thus increasing demographic stress on the populations.

Small groups of highly mobile foragers who disperse rapidly, who go great distances but do not maintain ties or have only attenuated ties to distant home groups, and who have no nearby populations from which to seek mates cannot easily maintain exogamy (Fix 1999:211; Moore 2001; Wobst 1975). Such groups run the risk of population contraction, potentially leading to isolation, higher levels of inbreeding, and drift (genetic and cultural). MacDonald and Hewlett (1999:521; see also MacDonald 1999) suggest that high levels of inbreeding and extinction "are unknown to extant foragers," but this is not correct (Durham 1991:286ff., 1992; Fix 1999). Late Pleistocene colonists were operating under circumstances unknown to extant foragers. When they became geographically isolated and were unable to maintain long-distance contacts or relations, incest taboos might have become a luxury, and groups may have suspended barriers to hybridization or narrowed the bandwidth of what was considered incest (Beaton 1991:224; Durham 1992:333; Fix 1999:98; Wobst 1975:79).

Such groups also have an increased probability of extinction, owing to the stochastic nature of birth and death rates and sex composition (Moore 2001; see also Black 1978; Keegan and Diamond 1987:78; Lahr and Foley 1998:146–147; MacArthur and Wilson 1967:69–80; McArthur et al. 1976; Wobst 1975). Because founding events are often strongly kin structured or can become that way quickly (Moore 2001), extinction events are nonrandom with respect to demes and can potentially operate at the level of groups (Fix 1999:137–142).

The risk of extinction is greatest soon after dispersal, when population numbers and growth rates tend to be low and when small groups are vulnerable to environmental perturbations. Higher growth rates (resulting from increasing birth rates or decreasing mortality) reduce the risk of extinction, but the circumstances under which this can occur with a highly mobile population are somewhat limited, depending to a large degree on the structure, patchiness, and predictability of resources (Cashdan 1992:244–249). Fertility is a product of many factors, including foraging practices, the contributions of others to subsistence, and the availability of alternative caretakers, all of which in some measure reflect ecological differences (Blurton Jones et al. 1989; Borgerhoff Mulder 1992:347).

At the same time, groups moving across increasingly unfamiliar landscapes had to identify and locate vital resources. Foraging theory assumes that a forager has relatively complete information about resource distribution and yields, by which decisions can be made about how long to stay and when to leave a patch (Kaplan and Hill 1992:186; Kelly 1995:96–98; Smith 1983, 1988; Stephens and Krebs 1986:75). Clearly this was not the case for the very first Americans (cf. MacDonald and Hewlett 1999:521), who likely could not anticipate much beyond a seasonal or annual basis when or where resources would be available (and who had no neighbors to ask about such matters). Decisions about patch choice and mobility must take into account the foragers' assessment of the available resources, which will change over time with experience and observation (sampling the environment) within the habitat (Smith 1983:638–639; Stephens and Krebs 1986:95).[2]

Of course, the first Americans were not completely naïve. (No group is thrown rapidly and headlong into a completely novel setting, although English colonists in seventeenth-century America came close and nearly perished as a result [Blanton 2000].) They possessed well-honed hunting strategies, a general knowledge of animal behavior, tool kits adaptable to various contingencies and, in all likelihood, a long history (by virtue of the vast and empty northern landscapes they had traversed en route) of flexible social organization, rapid mobility, long-distance kin relations, and information sharing (Fitzhugh 1997:396–397). What they lacked was geographic information, the ability to predict weather patterns, and specific knowledge about the time/space patterning of potential foods and the location and availability of critical nonfood resources (e.g., water, stone, and wood; Meltzer 2003).

In some situations or with some resources, learning could be rapid. Outcrops of stone suitable for artifact manufacture, for example, are spatially and temporally permanent. Such sources are often extensive, and even if they are limited, finding them may have entailed little more than following alluvial gravel trains upstream to the outcrop. Once those sources were located, they became known and predictable points on a landscape. In fact, I have argued recently (Meltzer 2002) that the distinctive record of stone caches in Clovis (but not later) Paleoindian times marks the discovery of these outcrop sources as well as the subsequent transport of stone (in the form of caches) into areas where stone sources had not yet been located. The cache thus became a fixed and predictable spot on the landscape, where a resupply of stone could be obtained without a long return trip to the quarry, and that would make it possible to venture farther into unknown terrain and explore it in greater depth.

Impermanent resources (plants and animals) in unfamiliar settings had to be identified, initially to determine whether resources that were not in the diet should be added. Their properties or behaviors, habitat, location, and short- and long-term patterns of abundance and distribution as these varied over time and space also had to be learned. For some resources, learning almost certainly required observation and experimentation. Just how much, no one knows, but there are more than 20,000 species and varieties of plants in North America alone. It would have been impossible for each new generation to sample their properties anew. Hence, there must have been a considerable advantage to maintaining that knowledge, as attested by the similarity in medicinal plant use across different areas and the folk taxonomies that identify plants at the genus rather than species level (Daniel Moerman, personal communication, 1999).

The slope of the learning curve and the magnitude of the learning process would have been contingent on several factors, including the nature of the climate and environment, the ecological diversity, rates of climatic and environmental change, and the scale of expansion. Initial conditions—the adaptive strategies and information brought to the process and place—are critical. Even on the least familiar landscape, humans can anticipate and mitigate unfamiliarity by extending outward from known ecological or social contexts and can acquire, process, and spread information rapidly, at least on a generation scale (Gamble 2000; Rockman 2003).

Landscape learning has costs in time and energy. Those expenses, however, can be amortized over other activities (such as logistical hunting forays) and thus can be offset by the benefits of information, notably, reducing environmental uncertainty and increasing foraging stability. The latter benefit assumes that one's knowledge of the environment and ability to predict resource availability and abundance increase with time spent on the landscape. Such information enhances hunter-gatherer survival and success because it provides knowledge of when and where to move as conditions become unfavorable (Binford 1983:34; Kelly 1995: 150–151; Smith 1983).

Kaplan and Hill (1992:186–187; see also Kelly 1995:151; Smith 1983; Stephens and Krebs 1986:103) argue that the greatest effort in information acquisition should occur in extensive, patchy, and temporally variable environments and during times when population numbers are low and groups are most vulnerable to extinction. This is the situation in which colonizers initially found themselves; it would change over time as descendants accumulated knowledge of the landscape. On an unknown landscape, selection would conceivably favor rapid and extensive exploration. That information is gathered by individuals in real time and for small areas, but its contents and utility can extend over longer periods and encompass larger areas if information is shared widely within the group and if it pertains to more permanent or predictable resources (Gamble 1994:98, 106–107, 109).

Forager decision making varies from individual resources to hunt types to habitat patches (Kelly 1995: 94). Yet initial colonizers in a new world have a relatively low level of resource and landscape resolution (see also Barton et al., this volume). The late Pleistocene fossil record shows that, at a gross scale, faunal communities were more heterogeneous and patchy than those of the Holocene (FAUNMAP Working Group 1996:1603–1604). That would have heightened the challenge of niche shifting, and resources would have appeared patchy and out of phase to the colonizers, likely leading to larger range sizes (Cashdan 1992:260).

Because of their larger settlement ranges and the attendant limitations on their ability to track changes in resource availability (a result of their relatively small population numbers and low density on the landscape), colonizing groups would likely track gross habitat types; Beaton (1991) calls them "megapatches." These are ecological features on the order of coasts, plains, mountains, or forests (Beaton 1991:220–221). Thus, the first occupants of the Great Plains (a likely megapatch), would have seen large game animals on a vast grassland. They would not have known and would have to learn that there was variability in the grasses on which those animals grazed, which would have implications for the differential abundance and distribution of game across time and space.

Demography and landscape learning are tightly linked. The decision to stay in a patch or move between patches is partly based on the suitability of a new patch relative to the current one, after factoring in the costs of moving (Baker 1978:43). Foragers who can better calculate those costs (by having more knowledge of available patches) will increase their odds of survival. By gaining information about a landscape, one reduces mortality and thus increases population growth rates (MacArthur and Wilson 1967:88). Of course, "behavioral innovation [a by-product of learning] will sometimes be random with respect to fitness gain, particularly in novel ecological and social settings" (Boone and Smith 1998:S149), but on balance successful colonists (and Clovis groups were clearly successful in the end) will ultimately learn behaviors that will enhance fitness. In addition, long-distance travel to find mates is itself a way of gaining landscape knowledge. The sharing of information becomes another strong incentive to maintain links among dispersed groups (Cashdan 1992:256; see also Smith 1981). Minimizing uncertainty helps maximize demographic success (Fix 1999:68, 206).

Minimizing-Uncertainty-and-Demographic-Risk Model

Consider, then, a colonization process in which the goal was minimizing uncertainty and demographic risk (hereafter MUDR). As with the RRM model, the MUDR model assumes that (1) colonizers arriving south of the ice sheets initially preyed on familiar, high-return resources: large game animals, but not the largest because, for several reasons tied to hunting risk, prey rank declines with extremely large-bodied animals (Broughton 1994:374–375); (2) mobility was more logistical than residential, reflecting the role of hunting (Kelly 1995:130–131); (3) return rates of high-ranked resources declined in the face of hunting pressure (Broughton 1994; Charnov et al. 1976; Grayson and Cannon 1999:147; Winterhalder et al. 1988); and (4) the environments were relatively rich in the number and abundance of species. Because the prey had not previously experienced human predation, one can assume that the fauna was naïve, at least initially.

I do not assume that the colonizers' primary motive was to maximize return rates, or that colonization

washed across the continent in a uniformly expanding wave, however handy the latter assumption may be for models of Pleistocene overkill (cf. Martin 1973) or for simulation models using a random diffusion constant (e.g., Young and Bettinger 1995; cf. Steele et al. 1998).

I do assume that colonization involved trade-offs between multiple competing demands:

1. *maintaining resource returns*, particularly as preferred or high-ranked resources declined or fled due to hunting pressure and when knowledge of the landscape was limited;
2. *minimizing group size* to buffer environmental uncertainty and risk (group size should be large enough to minimize division of labor for task groups and decrease daily variance in return rates; recent compilations suggest a range of 15 to 19 individuals [Binford 2001, and personal communication, 1998; Kelly 1995:213]);
3. *maximizing (logistical) mobility* to learn as much as possible, as quickly as possible, about the landscape and its resources to reduce environmental uncertainty in space and time;
4. *maximizing residential time* to lengthen the period of observation and thus enhance knowledge of local, seasonal, and other changes in resource abundance, availability, and distribution (one learns more by staying longer);
5. *maintaining contact between dispersed groups* to sustain information flow, social relations, and especially demographic viability.

Colonizers had to balance the equation between *moving* to learn and explore and *staying* to observe.

Kelly (1995:151) has argued that "where resources are dense and return rates high, hunter-gatherers may be very mobile initially." I agree. Yet, though I see movement as critical, I do not see it being driven solely by decline in return rates. I would argue that resource depression would not play out in precisely the same fashion or, more correctly, with the same timing, as it does among contemporary hunter-gatherers. Among modern hunter-gatherers, it is often depletion of plant foods within a foraging radius that triggers movement (Kelly 1995:141). To the degree that late Pleistocene colonizing groups relied more heavily on hunting rather than gathering, residence time in a particular patch could be extended. Similarly, logistical reliance on game increases the effective foraging radius (resources can be taken at greater distances from camp and brought back), which in turn makes it possible to prolong residence in a particular patch and minimize residential mobility (Kelly 1995:130–131, 135). Finally, the presumably richer environments of temperate North America would have allowed considerably longer residence before reaching the point of diminishing returns on the resource-harvest curves (the point at which the Marginal Value Theorem applies [Kaplan and Hill 1992; Kelly 1995:92–93]).

Wide-ranging logistical mobility would be important, not just for acquiring food, but also for acquiring information. There is, of course, ample evidence that hunter-gatherers place a premium on gathering and maintaining knowledge of the current and potential state of resources (Kelly 1995:150; Smith 1988:249–250). Under circumstances where the landscape was unknown and lacked "local informants," that premium would have been even greater. Such information, of course, would be critical to determining when and to where a residential move should occur: it would enable an estimation of the risks and costs of travel.

For practical purposes, a curvilinear relationship exists between length of observation and amount of information acquired. Limited observation of a landscape will provide in relatively short order a great deal of information about which large game animals are present, where water is located, and whether stone is available in river and stream gravels (and thus whether there is a potential for upstream outcrops). Longer residence is required, however, to learn what behaviors those game species exhibit under different conditions (as specified above), how reliable those water sources are over the long term, and whether suitable outcrops are present in an area. Hence, the longer the stay and the greater the degree of exploration, the less the uncertainty and the better the information returns.

The parameters and flow of colonization under the MUDR model are shown in figure 11.1. The process begins with a group of colonists arriving in northern North America south of the ice sheets. How large a group is not critical, nor can that figure be inferred with any confidence, depending as it does on a host of unknown (and likely unknowable) variables (Black 1978:65–66; Keegan and Diamond 1987; McArthur et al. 1976). In general and all other things being equal (although they rarely are), the larger the initial group, the greater its chance of demographic success, but there are no guarantees (Moore 2001; Wobst 1975). For the sake of discussion, I also assume that colonists traveled from

Alaska in a single migratory pulse, and upon arriving south of the ice sheets, dispersed into multiple subgroups.

The MUDR model assumes that colonizers had no precise knowledge of the North American landscape or habitats but could recognize or were familiar with species of animals, which would ease entrée into an area. They also may have been familiar with some classes of northern small animals and plants or possibly could recognize them as being related to resources seen elsewhere. As a consequence, the resources of the landscape—the megapatch—would be perceived as discontinuous and unpredictable (Beaton 1991:220). The megapatch would be broad, but the realized niche would be narrow. Environmental uncertainty also would be high, particularly as colonists moved south. Selection would therefore favor rapid exploration, likely within the megapatch, which might be done by the entire group or more efficiently by the smaller (likely family or kin-based) subgroups or scouting parties (see Gamble 1994: 109–110).

Within the separately foraging subgroups, the MUDR model presumes a bifurcation of task groups. Hunting parties could exploit large game and other resources over a wide area within the megapatch, while the remaining members explored and mapped more immediate areas nearer residential bases (Chilton, this volume). The net result would be information on the landscape and resources at the scale of the residential core area and daily foraging radius as well as across the larger logistical foraging radius (sensu Binford 1983: 34).

Initially, of course, the temporal resolution and predictability of resource abundance, behavior, and distribution would be relatively coarse (except for permanent resources), owing to the short knowledge base. Foragers have to repeatedly "sample" a habitat to assess the effects of temperature, topography, time of day, season, etc., on its resources (Smith 1983; Stephens and Krebs 1986:87, 103). Such knowledge obviously improves over observation time.

It is generally posited that hunting large game had high survivorship costs and thus was primarily done by men, and that women, being risk-aversive, avoided such activities (Borgerhoff Mulder 1992:363; Foley 1988:218–220; Hames 1992:226–228; Kelly 1995: 269; there may be other reasons why, in general, women do not hunt). If this were the case, one can speculate that much of the "local" knowledge of resources, especially plants and small animals, may have been

T1 - Colonizing group enters new habitat (megapatch). Antecedent conditions:
- all habitats and most resources are unknown and mostly unpredictable (in time and space)
- landscape is coarse grained and patchy relative to human foragers
- initial subsistence is primarily hunting, with larger game the most highly ranked resource
- subsistence and foraging systems are relatively unstable owing to resource unpredictability
- selection favors rapid information acquisition and landscape learning
- potentially low rate of population growth (owing to environmental uncertainty)

T1.1 - Adaptive responses:
- Colonizers disperse into small, kin-based subgroups. Within subgroups:
  - logistical hunting parties (primarily men) exploit large game over a wide area, locating additional resources and exploring landscape
  - remainder of group (women, elderly, and children) collect small game & plants in a smaller (local) area, identifying and experimenting with unknown resources
- Kin-based subgroups maintain long-distance mating networks or aggregate
  - to share information on newly identified permanent and impermanent resources (utility, location, abundance, behavior, distribution, etc.)
  - to increase effective breeding pool and exchange mates
  - for cooperative hunting (aggregation sites ought to be in productive localities)

T1.2 - New conditions / continued processes:
- high-ranked resources in local areas decline due to resource depression (the result of hunting or increased wariness or abandonment of the area by prey species)
- large- & small-scale landscape/resource "maps" assembled, environmental uncertainty decreases
- new (potentially high-ranked) resources identified, information acquired on utility and current location & abundance, possibly leading to temporary increases in carrying capacity
- mortality rates decrease, overall population increases

T1.3 - Adaptive responses:
- short-term expansion of hunting radius, long-term identification of new foraging areas
- broadening of diet breadth utilizing newly identified resources (small game, plants)
- redundant use of relatively predictable resources (e.g., stone outcrops, springs)
- movement to different areas within megapatch, exploiting now-familiar resources
- development of new technologies to exploit new resources
- continued seasonal / annual aggregation of subgroups, from increasingly distant areas

T1.4 - New conditions / continued processes:
- patch size decreases (megapatch is progressively partitioned into smaller patches); edges and boundaries of megapatch explored
- resources become better mapped and more predictable in space and time (latter being roughly proportional to the duration of the period of observation and occupation)
- niche breadth increases (realized niche becomes larger)
- foraging systems become more stable, less susceptible to environmental perturbations
- continued increase in population, leading to increased numbers of subgroups (demic expansion)

T1.5 - Adaptive responses:
- subgroups on edges of original megapatch explore adjoining megapatch(es), and ultimately – once comparable return rates are established – shift into those new megapatch(es) and repeat landscape-learning process (above)

FIGURE 11.1 Hypothesized parameters of colonization within a megapatch over time (time runs from top to bottom) under the minimizing-uncertainty-and-demographic-risk (MUDR) model. The uppermost box (time = T1) suggests possible antecedent conditions at initial entry into the megapatch. Subsequent boxes (T1.1 through T1.4) indicate possible adaptive processes (foraging, landscape learning, and demographic "maintenance") as groups map onto the new landscape; the boxes also show the cumulative effects of those processes. The lowermost box (T1.5) marks the point when foragers would jump to the next megapatch, at which time the preceding processes would be repeated (to a degree, depending on initial conditions, structure of the landscape, etc.). The temporal scale is arbitrary and relative.

acquired by women and children (Chilton, this volume). More regional landscape maps would result from men's more extensive, long-distance, logistical hunting forays across the area (see also Binford 1983:40).

To survive in the short term, smaller groups would have to be larger than the absolute minimum deme size necessary for reproduction, which, of course, varies depending on the age, sex, and kinship composition of the group, the bandwidth of incest taboos, and similar factors (Black 1978:72; Fix 1999:96; Kelly 1995:209–213; MacDonald, this volume; McArthur et al. 1976:313–314). As Fix (1999:97) notes, "The cultural prescriptions and proscriptions in terms of kinship and age defining a suitable mate interact with the kind and age structure of the population to delimit the potential mate pool of an individual." To survive over the longer term, subgroups would need to participate in the larger effective population (the "metapopulation"; Fix 1999:137; Levins 1970). Small groups would thus attempt to stay connected to others to maintain gene flow; failing to do so would leave them vulnerable to extinction (Fix 1999:137).

Maintenance of links to the metapopulation can be accomplished in several ways, not the least of which are long-distance mating and occasional aggregation of subgroups (Anderson 1995:8–11; Fix 1999:96; Hofman 1994:345–346; MacDonald 1999; MacDonald and Hewlett 1999; Wobst 1975). Among contemporary hunter-gatherers, the smaller the group and the lower the overall density of the population, the greater the area network that is maintained (Lewis R. Binford, personal communication, 1998). The extent of the mating network and the frequency of aggregations among Paleoindians are not known. Ethnographic figures on the former (e.g., MacDonald and Hewlett 1999:fig. 3) are necessarily dampened by the fact that all groups for whom data are available have neighbors. Aggregation among known hunter-gatherers occurs at different intervals, with smaller events taking place on a seasonal or annual basis and larger ones on a multi-year basis (Binford 2001). Because of the distances that groups may have had to travel to aggregate, it would have been difficult to carry large stores of food, so aggregation sites were likely selected for their resource richness rather than other factors, such as the presence of abundant lithic raw materials (Anderson 1990:187, 1995:13). Sufficient food would offset the costs of aggregation and allow communal foraging (Kelly 1995:219–221).

Over time, high-ranked resources would decline due to harvesting or as animals became more wary and fled the area (Broughton 1994:391–392). Foragers can respond to those declines by expanding the foraging and logistical radii, by moving into other newly identified areas within the megapatch, or by expanding the diet breadth. The last two responses reflect the payoff in the investment in landscape learning. Kelly and Todd (1988:234) rightly argue that it is "easier to locate, procure, and process the faunal as opposed to floral resources of a region." Yet it is also true that the location of animals is ephemeral and contingency bound (Kelly 1995:98), whereas some plant resources, such as a grove of nut-bearing trees, can have *relatively* greater predictability. Knowledge of the locations of productive plant habitats can be stored more or less indefinitely, depending on the time scale of biotic change and the capacity of the group to store information.

Expanding the diet breadth would not entail, per force, the exploitation of lower-ranked resources. By having simultaneously identified and acquired information on the utility, exploitability, current location, and abundance of previously unknown resources within the patch, groups could identify new and potentially high-ranked resources. This process could lead to changes in ranking and return rates that would be analogous to the changes in the rank of a food item following technological innovations (e.g., the *atlatl*) or the advent of new foraging techniques (Grayson and Cannon 1999:149–150; Lahr and Foley 1998:147; Winterhalder and Goland 1997:148). Resources that were initially low ranked because they were unknown could rapidly move up in rank, not owing to changes in the resource, but owing to information acquired about that resource. These now higher-ranked resources could produce temporary increases in food gain, a change in diet, an expansion of the diet breadth, or an expansion of the niche breadth (Keegan and Diamond 1987:75; Winterhalder et al. 1988). All of these changes would produce a somewhat distinctive return function: Instead of the gain curve appearing humped (a rise in return rates, followed by decline owing to resource depression), it would appear more sigmoidal, reflecting return rates that increased with time spent in the patch (e.g., Stephens and Krebs 1986:26). Expanding the diet would also help stabilize subsistence, thus reducing mortality rates and increasing population, without any necessary change in birth rate. As populations increased, group sizes might have stayed relatively constant, while the number of groups increased (Binford 1999).

Similarly, over time the extent of dispersal should

change. Initially, mobility and dispersal distances would have been relatively low, simply because the knowledge base was small and information required over the short term was high. Shorter dispersals would make it possible to rapidly gain information on the landscape and its resources (everything at that point is new, after all). At the same time, these forays would minimize the distances and costs of travel to find mates, thus maintaining critical social and reproductive alliances and reducing risk and uncertainty (see also MacDonald, this volume).

As information on the landscape was acquired, new areas and resources were identified and became more predictable. With the attendant decrease in environmental uncertainty, return rates would increase and foraging systems would stabilize and provide greater subsistence security (Binford 1999), making it possible to venture further afield. Groups can space themselves at greater distances and can have larger ranges if they possess better knowledge of available resources, not to mention better maps of the landscape. In fact, it might be advantageous to maximize the distance between groups (while still maintaining contact) to ensure enough new territory for a potential move if local resources decline (Lewis R. Binford, personal communication, 1998).

Under the MUDR model, early in the colonization process, the boundary of the megapatch serves as the boundary and guide to group movement; group members "map" it in all directions but stay within areas that reflect their knowledge of the resource base. Having invested time and energy in identifying the location and character of resources within a megapatch, and lacking (at least in the early stages) demographic pressures to move outside the known area, natural selection would favor staying within that megapatch. The spatial and temporal features of the landscape and its resources would over time "come into focus," and the megapatch would be partitioned into smaller patches between which groups would move (fig. 11.2).

Ultimately, of course, populations would increase, and the extended ranges of groups on the edges of the megapatch would incorporate habitats in adjoining patches or megapatches. Once the information that was gathered on resources in the new region was enough to reduce the risk of moving outside the better-known home range, groups would jump to new megapatches. Because some resources in this new megapatch were known prior to entry, initial niche breadth would be broader, the next megapatch would be smaller, and

it would likely be partitioned into component patches more rapidly.

In effect, movement *within* a megapatch would be less a product of demic expansion and more a result of selection for rapid information acquisition and landscape learning; movement *between* megapatches might well be a by-product of demic expansion. In a repeat of the process of expansion into the first megapatch, foraging strategies within the new megapatch would initially focus on familiar high-ranked resources and later broaden in both diet and range. Colonization would not be a steady movement through the Americas but instead a stutter-step, with relatively longer periods of residence within megapatches separated by rapid movements between patches. This process might look slow in human time (multiple generations), but it would look rapid in archaeological time, which readily encompasses those generations.

A series of trends should mark colonization under this model. The following factors should *increase* over time: information on landscape resources; diet breadth and niche breadth (Barton et al., this volume); utilization of smaller animals and plants (Chilton, this volume); subsistence stability; birth rates and relative population density; spacing between groups (as population increases and the amount of information critical to survival decreases, groups can venture farther from one another); and, of course, overall extent of settlement range. Concurrently, there should be an overall *decrease* in (mega)patch size; the proportion of unknown habitats and resources; environmental uncertainty; mortality rates and the incidence of infanticide; and probability of extinction.

A series of archaeological implications also follows from this model. Different megapatches should be occupied at different times and for different lengths of time. The oldest sites should be in the same megapatch (Beaton 1991:221). Early in colonization, movement should be random with respect to megapatch boundaries, but perhaps nonrandom with respect to topographic features, drainages, etc. Within the megapatches there should be an increase in diet breadth, a depletion of higher-ranked resources, and an increase in the redundancy of use of particular localities, especially the more predictable resource localities, such as stone sources. Aggregation and exchange should take place within the boundaries of the megapatch. Finally, stylistic variability should be more pronounced between megapatches than within them; however, within the megapatches, differentiation should increase over time

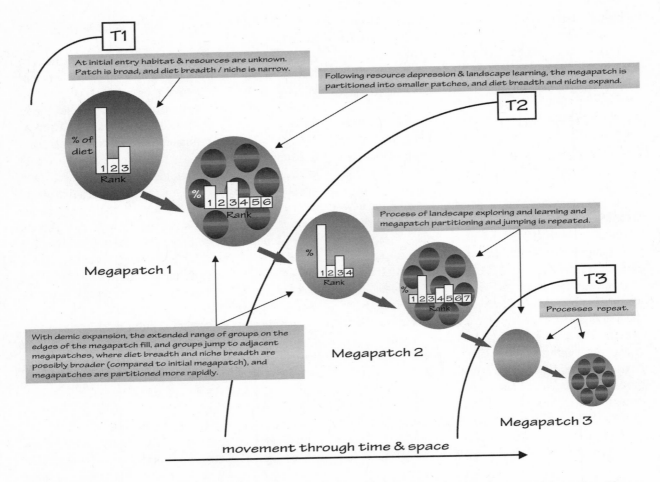

FIGURE 11.2 Schematic depiction of the hypothesized processes detailed in figure 11.1, as they play out in multiple megapatches over time and space. The figure is time-transgressive from upper left to lower right. This figure is intended to convey the serial changes in megapatch and patch size, diet breadth, and relative percentage of prey resources in the diet. Both the temporal and spatial scales are arbitrary and relative.

as the initial "founder styles" diverge and diversify (see Tankersley, this volume).

A Tale of Two Models

Kelly and Todd argue that the RRM model can account for many facets of the Clovis archaeological record, including the apparent homogeneity (relative to later times) of Clovis projectile points and lithic assemblages (Haynes 1982:384–393; Kelly and Todd 1988; Tankersley, this volume). They explain this homogeneity as being the by-product of a closely related, fast-expanding population, whose members share the same adaptation:

terrestrial hunting. They note that the apparent conservatism in tool kits could also be the result of a cultural "founders' effect," in which a familiar technology was carried across the landscape by the same historically related group (Kelly 1996:237–238, 1999:147). They further observe that the model fits the land-use patterns of Paleoindian groups: notably, high settlement mobility, a lack of territorial ranges, an absence of caches or storage facilities, redundant but short-term site use, and the absence (owing to their unfamiliarity with the landscape) of occupations in caves (Kelly 1996:232–236; Kelly and Todd 1988:236–237).[3]

The MUDR model can equally accommodate the

same positive archaeological evidence. It also anticipates the stylistic and functional variability in the Clovis-age tool kit based on the hypothesized differences in divergence times, landscape use, and occupational periods of different megapatches. It can also better account for why and how, within just a few centuries (fast in real time *and* archaeological time), later Paleoindians (e.g., Dalton) acquired knowledge of their landscape. That process presumably unfolded in different ways (possibly at different rates, though that remains to be seen) in different areas of the continent. Thus, the Great Plains, with its relatively treeless, more monotypic, lower-diversity environments and its less complex biotic communities and trophic patterning, would have been more easily and rapidly explored. However, because of the size of the territory needed to support human groups, the Great Plains would ultimately produce comparatively larger realized niches. In contrast, the model predicts that the eastern woodlands, a far more complex and heterogeneous environment with greater resource diversity, would have been explored more slowly, but by the end of Paleoindian time, groups would have been exploiting relatively smaller ranges, at apparently higher densities, with more residential mobility.[4] This evolutionary patterning across space and through time may be archaeologically "visible," as I have argued elsewhere, in the development and differentiation of distinct "style zones" in later Paleoindian projectile points (Meltzer 2002). Precisely how those stylistic phenomena relate to adaptive strategies (let alone on-the-ground social units) is not known.

It is clear, however, that Paleoindian populations (in the aggregate) increased substantially during colonization and learned a great deal about the landscape, more than might be expected of the hurried radiation envisioned in the RRM model. Indeed, the RRM model cannot well explain the trends visible in the Late Paleoindian record. The MUDR model can better account for both Early and Late Paleoindian adaptive trends.

Yet in the end, neither model is very satisfying. Showing a model can accommodate the archaeological record (as Kelly and I have done), or criticizing its logic (as we also have done; see also Anderson 1990) is not the same as providing an archaeological test of the model. In fact, such a test has never been conducted of either model and, given the presently available data, that's no surprise. Both are largely based on real-time variables and processes—individual forager decisions—that we cannot see in the late Pleis-

tocene archaeological record. Not yet, anyway (but see Meltzer 2002).

In order to test the RRM model, we would need to demonstrate that late Pleistocene climate and environmental change was occurring at a scale detectable to humans—which we have not. For both the RRM and MUDR models, we would need to provide precise data on resource ranking relative to Paleoindian technology and the mode and circumstances of procurement (Bettinger 1993:52; Grayson and Cannon 1999) and on resource abundance and distribution across space and through time—which we cannot. Such data would allow us to examine and measure, among other things, energetic return rates by prey taxa (an especially poorly known quantity for now-extinct fauna or fauna and flora in now-extinct biotic communities); taxa and return rates by habitat, megapatch, or patch; changing distribution and abundance of potential resources; risk factors attached to particular prey types; the relative costs (time and energy) and rates of acquiring information and learning those resources; and the order and speed with which new resources were added to the diet. We would need to show whether mobility tended toward a logistical strategy or a residential one.

We would need to do all this with paleoecological and archaeological records by detecting within them subtle temporal changes in resource distribution and abundance due to human predation, by showing that changes in prey are not a function of environmental change unrelated to humans (Grayson and Cannon, 1999:149), and by linking these changes to mobility decisions made by Clovis foragers. And we would need to do this over many sites, all of which had fine-grained chronologies. In effect, we need to take concepts from real time and translate them into archaeological time, making them detectable with variables measurable in the archaeological record (Grayson and Delpech [1998] discuss the complications of such a task and offer an example of tracking changing diet breadth archaeologically in early Upper Paleolithic, large-ungulate faunal assemblages). We need linkage.

That has not been done here or elsewhere (e.g., Surovell 2000). As a result, neither model has any particular advantage over the other merely by virtue of its apparent ability to accommodate aspects of the data. We are left promoting the merits of each model, based largely on our ability to make it sound plausible and fend off criticisms, perhaps while criticizing alternatives (adopting what Wilson [1975] calls an "advocacy

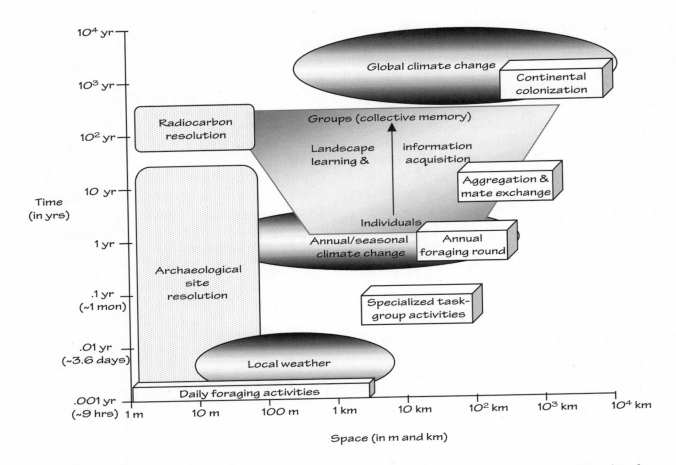

FIGURE 11.3 Various processes and patterns in space (horizontal axis, in meters and kilometers) and time (vertical axis, in years). As noted in the text, *weather and climate* (shown here as ovals) occur at various scales, from local weather, which affects only a relatively small area for a brief period of time, to global climate change, which impacts a very large area over a relatively long period and is likely to be undetectable to foragers, who lack written records or instrumentation. The *expansion and colonization processes* (the three-dimensional rectangles) similarly incorporate activities that extend from very local temporal and spatial scales to cross-continental (10^2 to 10^4 km) and millennial (>10^2 to 10^3 years) scales. Our *archaeological and radiocarbon resolution* of those processes (rounded rectangles) is based on artifacts and sites that represent relatively limited windows of space (1 to 10^2 m) and time, which can usually be resolved within only a narrow span (~10^2 years). The *landscape learning process* (vertical trapezoid) begins with individuals in relatively short time frames (<1 year) in relatively small areas. At the individual level, the process extends from the area one person can cover in a year to the area one can cover in a lifetime, which may reach $N \times 10^3$ km^2 or even $N \times 10^4$ km^2. If individual knowledge is shared and becomes part of the collective memory, the corporate knowledge can encompass information about even larger areas and may include resolution of climatic and environmental change with periodicity on the order of >10^2 years (but likely <10^3 years).

approach"). The RRM model might be right and the MUDR model might be wrong, but we do not and will not know which is true until we can endanger both against real archaeological data at the scale in which we have defined them.

Colonization (fig. 11.3; discussed in more detail in Meltzer 2001) played out at multiple levels, from the daily foraging activities of colonizing groups over the space of a few meters to several kilometers; to aggregation events that may have occurred at multiple-year intervals at a specific locality but involved actions across hundreds of kilometers; to the colonization of the continent itself, which took place over the course of centuries and tens of thousands of kilometers. All of this occurred in an environmental context that itself ranged from local weather patterns lasting days or weeks and affecting only a small area; to interannual, decadal, and millennial climatic variability; to global climate change. Layered atop all of that was landscape learning, which assuredly began locally (in space and time). Through long-term residence, mobility, and observation, however, such knowledge accumulated and was enhanced via information sharing across the group and down through the generations. This process ultimately enabled knowledge of resources and landscapes over large segments of space and time.

What complicates matters is that all of these variables are viewed through the narrow window of an archaeological site, in which the finest level of spatial resolution is still coarser than all but the coarsest of past dynamic processes (Meltzer 2001). An archaeological site normally covers just one spatially circumscribed part of a regional system but may represent a period of time ranging from a single rapid event to a "time-averaged" palimpsest of separate events that occurred over a century or more. Moreover, even under ideal circumstances, the resolution of a site's age is generally no better than a century or two (see Beaton 1991:224; Blackwell and Schwarcz 1993; Dean 1993). Although such large temporal units can potentially be subdivided in later prehistory among archaeological complexes in which stylistic "signaling" is more complex and detailed, such is not the case with the coarser stylistic record of Paleoindians.

The best chance of providing an archaeological test of the MUDR model would be to assess whether the oldest sites are in the same megapatch, whether there was "serial" megapatch use and resource depression within each, and whether stylistic differentiation occurred more slowly between megapatches than within them. We may ultimately be forced to conclude that, whether our models of colonization are fast or slow in "real-time," all of these processes may have played out in the hidden "wink of a radiocarbon eye" (Beaton 1991:224). Coupled with the plateaus in the terminal Pleistocene radiocarbon curves, this may make it impossible for us to tease apart the needed chronology of colonization, movement within and between megapatches, and so on.

To understand the problem in archaeological terms, we must develop models that can be structured at that scale but do not violate what we know of demography, adaptive strategies, etc., in real time, and then we must test those models against the archaeological evidence. We have our work cut out for us.

Acknowledgments

My thoughts on the matters raised in this paper have benefited from the advice and ideas of many colleagues, among them James Adovasio, Lewis R. Binford, Tom D. Dillehay, William Durham, Donald K. Grayson, Jason M. LaBelle, Daniel Moerman, John Moore, and especially Robert L. Kelly. My work has been supported by the Potts and Sibley Foundation and the Quest Archaeological Research Program. The writing of this paper was made possible by a Faculty Research Fellowship leave from Southern Methodist University during the fall of 2000, for which I am most grateful.

12 The Ecology of Human Colonization in Pristine Landscapes
C. Michael Barton, Steven Schmich, and Steven R. James

The peopling of the Western Hemisphere was one of the most significant biogeographic phenomena in modern human history prior to the development of agriculture. Humans spread into two new continents and into the last continental-scale "pristine" ecosystem on the planet. The first colonizers of the Americas were successful arctic hunter-gatherers who were adapted to the rigorous environments of Siberia and Beringia and possibly to the frigid coasts that bordered these areas. As they entered the Americas, they found themselves in a truly new world: a world of forest and woodland instead of steppe and tundra, a world with a new flora and naïve fauna, some of which were similar to the taxa they knew but many of which were unfamiliar.

Such circumstances have happened only two other times for modern humans on a continental scale: the colonization of Sahul (the New Guinea–Australia continent during low Pleistocene sea levels) and the colonization of the land areas exposed by retreating ice sheets at the end of the Pleistocene. These settings provide the only baselines for evaluating the effects of preagricultural humans on pristine ecosystems and the effects of any humans on continental-scale pristine ecosystems. These settings also allow us to view aspects of human behavioral ecology that are not readily apparent in populated landscapes. Certainly the later human expansion to islands of the Pacific Ocean, Indian Ocean, and Mediterranean Sea also provides valuable examples for study. However, the limited geographic size and biological isolation of most of these islands, coupled with the fact that most of the colonizer societies were agriculturalists, make them special cases that are distinct from the initial colonization of the terrestrial ecosystems that characterize continental landmasses.

In the last decade, research into the peopling of the Americas and other landmasses has started to move away from simply documenting the earliest human presence or detailing the activities of single sites and has begun to look more broadly at the processes and effects of colonization behavior from an ecological perspec-tive. This change in focus is exemplified by many of the chapters in this volume, and Anderson and Gillam (2000) provide an excellent review of such studies else-where. One such pioneering work is Kelly and Todd's (1988) article on the peopling of the Americas. Subse-quent treatments by Amick (1996), Anderson and Gil-lam (2000), MacDonald (1999, this volume), Meltzer (2002, this volume), and Steele et al. (1998) build on this work in the New World. Studies by Housely et al. (1997) exemplify similar contributions on Europe, and those by Beaton (1991) and Webb (1998; Webb and Rindos 1997) focus on the colonization of Australia.

These studies model different aspects of the initial colonization of the continental regions and the behav-iors of their first inhabitants. Our objective here is not to propose another new model for the first Americans, but to synthesize from these more specific works a gen-eral model of initial human colonization of empty land-masses. Several other writers have proposed general first-colonization models, most notably Beaton (1991) and Webb and Rindos (1997).

Beaton proposed two modal strategies for first colo-nists: "transient explorer" and "estate settler." Tran-sient explorers are highly mobile and constantly on the lookout for landscape patches with a familiar theme, such as a river valley. Estate settlers establish them-selves in territories and colonize continents by split-ting off into adjacent regions as populations grow. They colonize as small groups essentially drop off along the way. Beaton's two concepts are not mutually exclusive; foraging groups can operate in either mode depending on social and ecological contexts. However, he char-acterizes the initial colonization of Australia and the Americas as more of a transient explorer phenomenon, whereas the subsequent spread throughout the land-scape is better characterized in terms of estate settlers.

Webb and Rindos take a somewhat different per-spective. They note that initial colonizers encounter ecosystems that are different from those from which they came and have scant information about resource availability and distribution. This leaves the first colonizers poorly adapted to the new lands. With only a coarse perception of the new landscape and its resources, these colonizers can most readily recognize, and hence make use of, only the most obvious resources. "Skimming the cream" from the top of an ecosystem, they focus primarily on large animals and the most apparent, most easily processed plant foods. However, this strategy gives the new landscape a low effective carrying capacity: resources are quickly exhausted locally, forcing these poorly adapted colonizers to move to new locales. The result is an extremely rapid spread of initial colonizers, all of whom use a similar restricted set of resources throughout their range.

Although simple and appealing, both models leave unanswered questions about initial colonists. For example, rather than moving to new locales, why don't first colonists simply build on their knowledge of their home territory? Isn't movement to yet another unknown place riskier than staying put? What happens when there is no place left to move to? What processes actually drive the switch from transient explorer to estate settler?

Evolutionary Ecology and Colonization Models

The general models described above can be recast in terms of the concepts of evolutionary ecology. By focusing on individual decisions that are ultimately based on cost-benefit analysis, evolutionary ecology can address some of the unanswered questions and make these models more inclusive. Two now classic ecological models for explaining forager behavior with respect to resource availability and distribution are diet breadth and patch choice. These models are described in detail by Bettinger (1991:83–110), Foley (1985), Kelly (1995:65–160), and Smith and Winterhalder (1992; Winterhalder and Smith 2000). Diet breadth models predict that potential resources can be ranked according to caloric returns minus procurement and processing costs. They predict that, when possible, foragers will tend to take higher-ranking resources. As high-ranking resources become unavailable, they will not be replaced by just lower-ranking resources, but by an increasing diversity of lower-ranking resources. Conversely as higher-ranking resources become more available, diet breadth will decrease as diverse lower-ranking resources are replaced by fewer higher-ranking ones.

Patch choice models describe forager spatial responses to variation in resource availability and dis-

tribution. As humans forage in a particular landscape patch, resources become depleted and their procurement costs rise as they become more difficult to find. At some point, procurement costs in one patch exceed the costs of moving to a new patch where resources have not been depleted. Note that foragers are not expected to exhaust resources within a patch; they only deplete them enough to make moving to a new patch less costly than continuing to forage in the current patch.

Both diet breadth and patch choice models make several simplifying assumptions about the environment and the distribution of resources. Furthermore, the actual costs of caloric benefits are difficult to calculate accurately. These and other pragmatic concerns make these models difficult to apply among modern foragers, whose behavior can be observed, and virtually impossible to use in any quantitative sense for archaeological foragers (Kelly 1995:333–334). Nevertheless, the concepts embodied in these models can be usefully applied qualitatively in a heuristic manner to better understand the behavior of prehistoric foragers.

In this chapter, we combine concepts of both diet breadth and patch choice to develop a general model for initial human colonizers of empty landscapes. Arguably these humans fill an empty niche, although there may be some overlap with other animals, primarily large carnivores and scavengers (see Whitney-Smith, this volume) and the few large omnivores. The absence of other human competition and especially the lack of prior human predation increase the effective availability of large herbivores. Access to large prey would be particularly important to the first colonizers of the Americas, who were almost certainly High Arctic foragers. Foragers in high latitudes, by necessity, derive most of their caloric intake from large terrestrial herbivores and marine fauna (Kelly 1995; Speth and Spielmann 1983). These colonizers are thus preadapted to take advantage of large herbivores in the unoccupied human niche. The same would be true of the hunter-gatherers who first recolonized northern Europe as the Scandinavian ice sheet retreated northward at the end of the Pleistocene. Even tropical foragers can rapidly become big-game hunters under the same ecological circumstances (Webb and Rindos 1997). Furthermore, large animals would be easily identified food sources for colonizing foragers who lacked detailed information about the new land, making their procurement costs lower than those of less obvious resources (Kelly and Todd 1988). These characteristics combine with high caloric values to give these taxa a high dietary ranking, causing humans initially to forego many other potential food sources. Although animal bones (along with stone artifacts) are among the best-preserved residues of the resources used by humans, the same overall pattern of use should apply to other classes of materials. Hence, the most obvious, most easily procured and processed, and highest-quality resources—be they plants, lithic raw materials, or wood—should be the most commonly used resources by initial colonizers.

At any given locale, as humans filled their niche, competition for large herbivores would increase as their numbers declined due to successful hunting. Simultaneously these animals would learn to avoid humans. These factors would decrease the effective availability of large herbivores. Faced with a loss of such high-ranking foods, humans would diversify their diet and include foods that incur higher costs in procurement or processing or that provide fewer calories per unit.

This scenario, however, ignores the possibility of movement as described in patch choice models. Although the depletion of high-ranking resources could lead to increased dietary diversity, patch choice models suggest that foragers will move to a new locality when faced with resource depletion, as long as the costs associated with movement are less than the costs of resource procurement in the original locale. As high-ranking resources become more difficult to procure, foragers would simply move to another locality rather than change their diet. Movement is generally costly, especially movement beyond a group's territory or home range, because the new landscape may be already occupied by other humans. Movement into an area already used by others increases competition for resources, incurs social debts, and may even provoke territorial defense measures, all of which raise the costs of long-distance movement. Movement within a home range is less costly; it incurs only the costs that are directly associated with moving people and their belongings and with building new facilities (e.g., residential structures, nonportable processing equipment, and storage facilities; Kelly 1983, 1995:120–148). In a populated landscape, however, home ranges are generally too small for human movement alone to permit depleted herds of large herbivores to recover.

In an unpopulated landscape, long-distance movement incurs the same physical costs as movement within a home range but does not incur the social costs garnered in a populated landscape. For first colonizers, diet breadth models predict that foragers entering an empty human niche will focus their subsistence on high-ranking large herbivores. Patch choice models predict that when human population growth or herbivore population decline increases procurement costs, foragers will move to new locales where large herbivores are more easily obtained. An important aspect of patch choice models is that they predict foragers will move when procurement costs exceed movement costs, not when resources in a patch are exhausted. For initial colonizers, this threshold would be rapidly crossed because of the lack of other humans in the area. Rather than diversifying their diet by eating more costly foods, humans would move frequently after only modest depletion of herbivore populations.

Expectations and Testing

By applying the ecological models described above, we can propose some general expectations about the nature of settlement systems for the first human colonizers of a landmass. We would expect them initially to focus their subsistence on high-ranking resources, that is, those offering the greatest caloric return for the lowest procurement and processing costs. In terminal-Pleistocene, temperate-latitude, continental environments (and probably subtropical savannahs; Foley 1982), such resources would be best represented by large mammalian herbivores. Although marine mammals offer significant caloric returns, their procurement is generally more costly than that of terrestrial mammals (Bleed 1986; Torrence 1989). If plants contribute to the diet, first colonizers would place the greatest emphasis on those that require the least processing relative to caloric return. This focus would tend to exclude those plants whose processing would require special equipment, such as grinding stones or graters, that would need to be produced, transported, or curated, thus adding to the overall procurement cost. Diet breadth would also be restricted due to the focus on high-ranking resources.

Because mobility costs are generally limited to the physical costs of movement during initial colonization (i.e., there are no social costs as in populated landscapes), declines in availability of high-ranking resources would lead more to settlement shifts than to increased diet diversity. Also, because humans are colonizing a new landmass and moving frequently, landscape knowledge would be almost as limited for the location of a planned move as for an existing settlement. Furthermore, the focus on large, usually wide-ranging, mammalian herbivores and the lack of social or informational impediments to movement would tend to encourage long-distance moves over shorter ones.

In the archaeological record, manifestations of the first human colonizers would include a predominance of large mammals in faunal remains, a lack of plant-processing equipment, widely spaced settlements, and a rapid spread across large areas. As pointed out by Webb and Rindos (1997), the spread of first colonizers could be so rapid as to appear "instantaneous" within the range of error of radiocarbon dates (see also Fiedel 1999b).

We can also apply foraging models to examine how this pattern might shift over time. As the landscape becomes more populated and the social costs of movement increase, movement rates should slow down. As movement becomes more restricted, large herbivores should become more depleted and, hence, more costly to procure. With increased procurement costs for large herbivores and higher movement costs, human groups would find it cost-effective to collect and process a wider diversity of smaller fauna to assuage subsistence shortfalls. Although large herbivores might become depleted earlier due to their more extensive habitat requirements, other high-ranked resources should suffer similar local depletion and replacement. For example, people may shift to small seed plants that are abundant but costly to process.

Colonizers entering populated landscapes would be more complicated to model, but several general predictions can be made. In some cases, these colonizers may possess a competitive advantage—either technological or organizational—that would permit them to use resources more efficiently (i.e., that would support more people per square kilometer) than extant populations or to access resources that extant populations cannot use. Established farmers moving into areas occupied by foragers represent examples of such colonization and may be seen archaeologically in the Iron Age Bantu expansion in sub-Saharan Africa and in the Neolithic LBK expansion in Europe, although aspects of both cases remain open to discussion (Bogucki and Grygiel 1993; Diamond 1997:376–402; Ehret 1984; Phillipson 1993; Thorpe 1996; Vansina 1995; Whittle 1996). Although such colonization could result in population replacement when profound technological or organizational differences are involved, it is difficult to conceive of sufficient competitive differences between two populations of modern human foragers that would lead to similar replacement (but see Fiedel, this volume).

In the more likely case, extant populations would have considerable advantages over immigrants in terms of accumulated information and organizational strategies adapted to a landscape over the long term. In such circumstances, colonizers would be relegated to marginal habitats and niches that are comparatively costly to occupy and exploit for extant populations. The results and archaeological manifestations of such colonization would vary according to the nature of the marginal niches and the success with which they were occupied. One result simply would be absorption of colonizers into extant populations. Emulation of successful behaviors of extant populations and intermarriage to gain access to less marginal habitats would lead to the disappearance of archaeological evidence for immigrants. Alternatively selection might favor the evolution of specialized technologies and organizations that allow colonizers to exploit a niche that would be marginal for extant populations. This would be the behavioral equivalent of character displacement. In such cases, we might expect to find a specialized technology within a fairly narrow environmental range. Such cases might also show rapid spread within a narrow habitat range as colonizers skip over extant populations to fill the new niche. The initial LBK expansion can also be viewed in perspective, as can the late prehistoric Thule expansion across the High Arctic of North America (see Fiedel, this volume).

Most of Eurasia was populated by humans prior to the late Pleistocene, making these models difficult to test both because of the potential for taphonomic alteration and loss of the archaeological record over such a long period, and because of the unknown degree to which mid-Pleistocene humans differed behaviorally from modern ones. During the late Pleistocene, however, modern humans had several opportunities to colonize large landmasses: Sahul, the Americas, and the regions that had been covered by continental glaciers but were reexposed during deglaciation. In this chapter, we compare the model of first colonizers outlined above to archaeological data in glacial Europe and the Americas, and we refer to the colonization of Sahul/Australia.

Northwestern Europe

Northwestern Europe enjoys several advantages as a locale for testing models of initial human colonization of empty landscapes. Foremost is the certainty that humans were colonizing unoccupied landscapes. Unlike Australia and the Americas, northwestern Europe was undoubtedly unoccupied prior to late Pleistocene colonization; the area had been covered by thousands of

TABLE 12.1 European Sites Used for Age-Distance Analysis

European Site	Region	Uncalibrated Radiocarbon Years B.P.*	Calibrated Years B.P. (1 Sigma Range)	Reference
Gönnersdorf	N. Germany	12,828 ± 164	15,721–14,480	Street 1998
Etiolles	Paris Basin	12,634 ± 143	15,526–14,351	Gowlett et al. 1986
Andernach-Martinsberg	N. Germany	12,644 ± 87	15,517–14,377	Street 1998
Slotseng	Denmark	12,520 ± 190	15,471–14,262	Holm 1991
Pincevent	Paris Basin	12,153 ± 109	15,171–13,863	Housley et al. 1997
Køge Bugt Solrød	Denmark	12,140 ± 100	15,154–13,860	AAR-1036 (University of Aarhus Radiocarbon Lab, Denmark)
Poggenwisch	N. Germany	12,500 ± NA	14,759–14,361	Fischer and Tauber 1986
Meiendorf	N. Germany	12,360 ± NA	14,752–14,270	Fischer and Tauber 1986
Stellmoor (Lower)	N. Germany	12,170 ± NA	14,385–14,052	Fischer and Tauber 1986
Klein-Norden	N. Germany	12,035 ± NA	14,106–13,840	Street 1998
Miesenheim II & IV	N. Germany	11,178 ± 104	13,190–13,013	Street 1998
Trollesgave	Denmark	11,100 ± NA	13,158–13,004	Fischer 1989
Fensmark	Denmark	10,810 ± 120	12,983–12,655	Hedges et al. 1993
Kartstein Rockshelter	N. Germany	10,500 ± 113	12,825–12,178	Fischer and Tauber 1986
Lundby Moor	Denmark	9938 ± NA	11,337–11,257	Museum of South Zealand 2002
Lake Fløyrlivatn	SW Norway	9750 ± 80	11,204–11,143	Bang-Andersen 2003
Lake Myrvatn	SW Norway	9610 ± 90	11,166–10,743	Bang-Andersen 1990
Vig	Denmark	9510 ± 115	11,092–10,582	Hedges et al. 1993
Barmose I	Denmark	9176 ± 47	10,401–10,238	Hedges et al. 1992
Lavringe Mose	Denmark	6860 ± NA	7684–7669	Sørensen 1987

*Multiple ^{14}C dates from same stratigraphic context were averaged using Calib 4 (S. Stuiver, University of Washington) prior to calibration.

meters of the Scandinavian ice sheet. The region also has a long history of archaeological study and, hence, a comparatively fine-grained archaeological record, with numerous sites and a well-established chronological framework. However, the dynamics of the retreating ice sheet, rising sea levels in the Baltic and North Seas, and isostatic rebound make characterization of the landscape—and even the extent of available land area—complicated. Furthermore, the retreating ice simply expanded the area of the European subcontinent that was available for human habitation. No physical barrier (such as a seaway, narrow land isthmus, or ice sheet) precluded bidirectional movement between the newly available landmass and the Pleistocene refugia for human populations in Europe. Also, the differences

between the environments of the source region and the colonized area appear to have been minimal. Fauna recolonizing the deglaciated zones would have had a long history of adaptation to (and avoidance of) humans. Colonization processes may have been different than in the continents of Australia and the Americas, which were separated from source populations by oceanic or ice barriers, had flora and fauna that differed from those of the colonists' homelands, and had naïve faunas. With these caveats in mind, we examine the archaeological data for the colonization of northwestern Europe after the Scandinavian ice sheet retreated north of the Baltic Sea by 13,000 B.P.

Figure 12.1 shows the earliest radiocarbon dates for occupation of sites in northwestern Europe (see

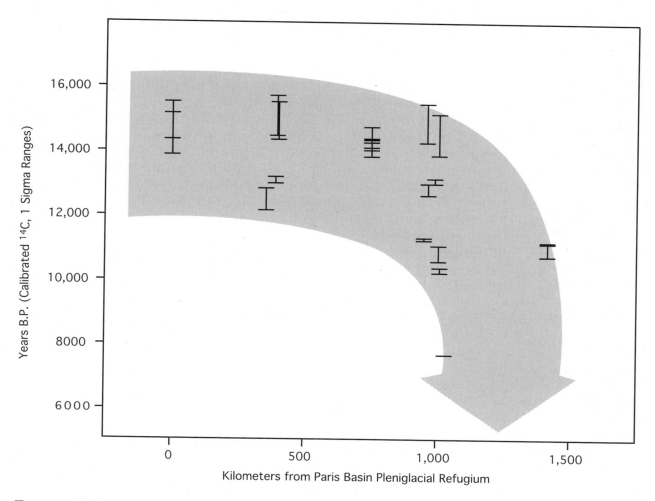

FIGURE 12.1   Calibrated dates (1 sigma ranges) versus distance from Paris Basin pleniglacial refugium for earliest sites in deglaciated northwestern Europe.

table 12.1) and the distance of those sites from one of the Pleistocene refugia in northern France. (We use calibrated dates throughout this paper except as explicitly indicated.) The initial rate of colonization is high at 0.9 km/yr but is considerably lower than the rate of 2–3 km/yr predicted by Webb and Rindos (1997). This is not surprising given the ecological similarities between the source and colonized areas and the smaller region compared with the continent-wide scale mentioned by Webb and Rindos. The rate of colonization, however, slows rapidly as this much smaller area becomes populated by foragers, dropping to 0.3 km/yr by the early Holocene.

Diet diversity (fig. 12.2) also shows patterns that follow those predicted by the behavioral ecology models discussed above (see tables 12.2 and 12.3). The measure of diversity used here is based on the reciprocal of Simpson's index (James 1990; Simpson 1949) and combines values for richness and evenness. In Pleistocene refugia (fig. 12.2A), diet diversity is initially moderate for European foragers in the Early Glacial and drops to low values during the Pleniglacial in the European steppe-tundra. As climate changes at the end of the Pleistocene and the landscape is covered initially by pine-birch woodland and subsequently by deciduous forest, gregarious large herbivores of the steppe-tundra become more difficult to procure; diet diversifies accordingly in these populated areas (Simek and Snyder 1988). Contemporaneously in the recently deglaciated regions (fig. 12.2B), however, movement is a less costly alternative to diet diversification as a means of dealing with increasing risk of scarcity in high-ranking faunal resources. In these areas, diet diversity remains low until

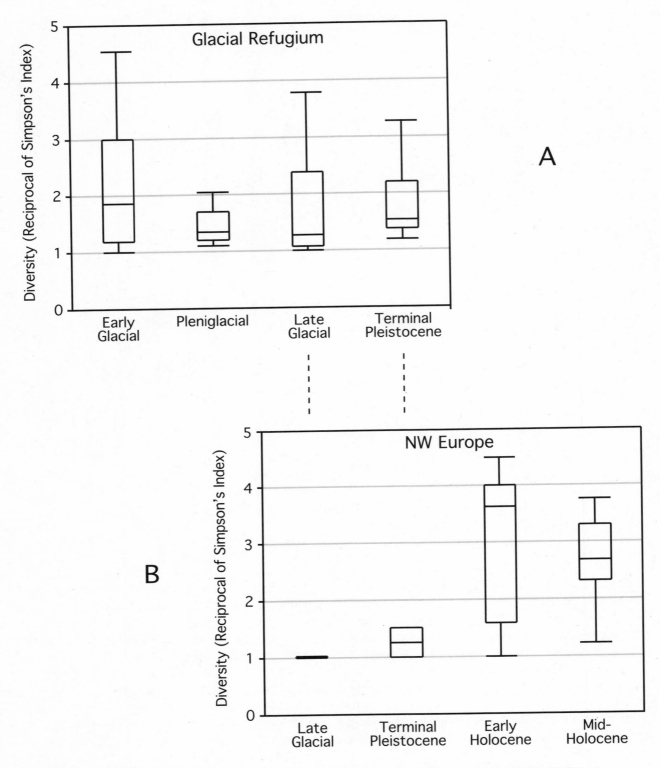

Figure 12.2 Diet diversity (reciprocal of Simpson's index of NISP for fauna) for *(A)* pleniglacial refugia and *(B)* deglaciated northwestern Europe.

TABLE 12.2 European Sites Used for Diet Diversity Analysis: Refugia in Southwestern and Central France and Central Germany

Refugia Site	Period	Phase	Diversity Index	Reference
Baerenkeller	Late Glacial	Hamburgian Bromme	1.03	Eriksen 1996
Lausnitz	Late Glacial	Hamburgian Bromme	1.21	Eriksen 1996
Oelknitz	Late Glacial	Hamburgian Bromme	1.19	Eriksen 1996
Teufelsbruecke 3–4	Late Glacial	Hamburgian Bromme	2.81, 1.60	Eriksen 1996
Blassac	Terminal Pleist.	Azilian	3.27	Boyle 1990
Bois Ragot 3–4b	Terminal Pleist.	Azilian	1.35, 1.62	Boyle 1990
Campalou	Terminal Pleist.	Azilian	1.38	Boyle 1990
Grotte du Tai SN SX, C'1, C"1	Terminal Pleist.	Azilian	2.45, 1.95, 1.86	Boyle 1990
La Faurelie II 2–3	Terminal Pleist.	Azilian	1.19, 1.27	Boyle 1990
Pages	Terminal Pleist.	Azilian	1.41	Boyle 1990
Pont d'Ambon 2–4	Terminal Pleist.	Azilian	1.24–3.22	Boyle 1990
Roc d'Abeilles	Terminal Pleist.	Azilian	2.86	Boyle 1990
Bergerie	Late Glacial	Late Magdalenian	1.19	Boyle 1990
Bois Ragot 5b–6	Late Glacial	Late Magdalenian	2.46, 1.70	Boyle 1990
Bruniquel	Late Glacial	Late Magdalenian	1.13	Boyle 1990
Cap Blanc	Late Glacial	Late Magdalenian	3.22	Boyle 1990
Faustin	Late Glacial	Late Magdalenian	3.62	Boyle 1990
Fongaban 2–6	Late Glacial	Late Magdalenian	1.03–2.39	Boyle 1990
Fontarnaud	Late Glacial	Late Magdalenian	2.95	Boyle 1990
Gabillou	Late Glacial	Late Magdalenian	1.34	Boyle 1990
Gare de Couze (B–H)	Late Glacial	Late Magdalenian	1.27	Boyle 1990
Grotte des Fees	Late Glacial	Late Magdalenian	1.12	Boyle 1990
La Madeleine 2–16	Late Glacial	Late Magdalenian	1.00–2.71	Boyle 1990
La Mairie	Late Glacial	Late Magdalenian	2.39	Boyle 1990
La Mege	Late Glacial	Late Magdalenian	2.39	Boyle 1990
Le Flageolet IX	Late Glacial	Late Magdalenian	1.28	Boyle 1990
Le Morin AI–AIV, B1–BII	Late Glacial	Late Magdalenian	1.04–3.63	Boyle 1990
Marcamps	Late Glacial	Late Magdalenian	1.81	Boyle 1990
Montmorillon	Late Glacial	Late Magdalenian	3.70	Boyle 1990
Reignac	Late Glacial	Late Magdalenian	2.14	Boyle 1990
Roc d'Abeilles	Late Glacial	Late Magdalenian	5.43	Boyle 1990
Rond du Barry D–E	Late Glacial	Late Magdalenian	2.24, 3.78	Boyle 1990
Ste. Eulalie I, III	Late Glacial	Late Magdalenian	1.35, 1.35	Boyle 1990
Combe Cullier 4–5, 8–9, 11–16	Pleniglacial	Middle Magdalenian	1.16–1.56	Boyle 1990
Lachaud	Pleniglacial	Middle Magdalenian	1.86	Boyle 1990
Laugerie Haute Est	Pleniglacial	Middle Magdalenian	1.18, 1.19	Boyle 1990

TABLE 12.2 Continued

Refugia Site	Period	Phase	Diversity Index	Reference
Cottier n II–III	Pleniglacial	Early Magdalenian	1.92	Boyle 1990
Fritch 3–6	Pleniglacial	Early Magdalenian	1.32–1.98	Boyle 1990
Laugerie Haute Est	Pleniglacial	Early Magdalenian	1.10, 2.05	Boyle 1990
Abri Pataud 7	Early Glacial	Late Aurignacian	2.01	Boyle 1990
Caminade Est D	Early Glacial	Late Aurignacian	4.41	Boyle 1990
F4–F1 fr. Ga–Ge sag.	Early Glacial	Late Aurignacian	2.22	Boyle 1990
Font de Gaume	Early Glacial	Late Aurignacian	1.92	Boyle 1990
G0 fr. G0 & F sag.	Early Glacial	Late Aurignacian	1.82	Boyle 1990
G1 sag. G1–G3 fr.	Early Glacial	Late Aurignacian	4.23	Boyle 1990
La Chevre	Early Glacial	Late Aurignacian	2.80	Boyle 1990
La Ferrassie J & K1–3, L1–H1	Early Glacial	Late Aurignacian	3.07, 4.54	Boyle 1990
Maldidier 5–6	Early Glacial	Late Aurignacian	3.30–3.89	Boyle 1990
Pair-non-Pair K	Early Glacial	Late Aurignacian	3.22	Boyle 1990
Roc de Combe 5–6	Early Glacial	Late Aurignacian	1.17, 1.42	Boyle 1990
Abri Pataud 11–14	Early Glacial	Early Aurignacian	1.00–1.91	Boyle 1990
Battus 3	Early Glacial	Early Aurignacian	1.97	Boyle 1990
Bourgeois-Delauny	Early Glacial	Early Aurignacian	2.18	Boyle 1990
Fontaury C2–C3	Early Glacial	Early Aurignacian	2.02, 1.81	Boyle 1990
La Chevre	Early Glacial	Early Aurignacian	1.54	Boyle 1990
La Ferrassie	Early Glacial	Early Aurignacian	1.55	Boyle 1990
La Gravette	Early Glacial	Early Aurignacian	1.11	Boyle 1990
Pair-non-Pair KD	Early Glacial	Early Aurignacian	3.34	Boyle 1990
Roc de Combe 7a–7b	Early Glacial	Early Aurignacian	1.13–1.24	Boyle 1990

population packing again limits movement in the early Holocene. At that time, diet diversity in the deglaciated zone rises dramatically. Overall the available archaeological data for deglaciated northwestern Europe at the end of the Pleistocene fit the model of initial colonizers based on the general principles of evolutionary ecology.

The Americas

For almost all archaeologists, the colonization of Western Hemisphere continents was a late Pleistocene phenomenon that involved completely modern humans, although debate remains over whether the initial colonization took place in the middle or near the end of the late Pleistocene. The Americas encompass a much larger land area than northwestern Europe, potentially affecting the total time span of colonization and the rate of change in subsistence and settlement organization. Unlike in northwestern Europe, there were (and still are) much more pronounced physiographic restrictions to human movement between the Americas and source population areas in northeastern Asia, and another bottleneck exists between North and South America. Even though temperate North America and temperate Eurasia share many aspects of a Holarctic flora and fauna, they do differ, especially in the South American taxa that spread northward after the two American continents collided in the late Tertiary. The initial colonizers of the Americas were almost certainly High Arctic foragers, whether they focused on marine resources, terrestrial resources, or some combination of

TABLE 12.3 European Sites Used for Diet Diversity Analysis: Deglaciated Northwestern Europe

NW European Site	Period	Phase	Diversity Index	Reference
Aamølle	M. Holocene	Mesolithic	3.04	Bay-Petersen 1978
Ageröd I (B, D, HC) & V	M. Holocene	Mesolithic	1.63–3.48	Mithen 1990
Bredasten	M. Holocene	Mesolithic	1.81	Mithen 1990
Dyrholmen	M. Holocene	Mesolithic	3.41	Bay-Petersen 1978
Eretebølle	M. Holocene	Mesolithic	2.90	Bay-Petersen 1978
Faareville	M. Holocene	Mesolithic	2.38	Bay-Petersen 1978
Hallebygaard	M. Holocene	Mesolithic	1.23	Bay-Petersen 1978
Havnø	M. Holocene	Mesolithic	3.76	Bay-Petersen 1978
Kildegaard	M. Holocene	Mesolithic	2.13	Bay-Petersen 1978
Klintesø	M. Holocene	Mesolithic	2.52	Bay-Petersen 1978
Lavringe mose	M. Holocene	Maglemose	5.46	Sørensen 1987
Magleø	M. Holocene	Mesolithic	2.57	Bay-Petersen 1978
Segebro	M. Holocene	Mesolithic	2.88	Mithen 1990
Skateholm	M. Holocene	Mesolithic	2.81	Mithen 1990
Tingbjerggaard	M. Holocene	Mesolithic	2.38	Bay-Petersen 1978
Bedburg	E. Holocene	Early Mesolithic	1.59	Street 1998
Hesselbjgaard	E. Holocene	Early Mesolithic	4.50	Bay-Petersen 1978
Holmegaard	E. Holocene	Early Mesolithic	3.63	Bay-Petersen 1978
Øgaarde	E. Holocene	Early Mesolithic	3.43	Bay-Petersen 1978
Stellmoor (Upper)	E. Holocene	Ahrensburgian	1.00	Eriksen 1996
Svaerdborg	E. Holocene	Early Mesolithic	3.65	Bay-Petersen 1978
Vinde Helsinge	E. Holocene	Early Mesolithic	4.00	Bay-Petersen 1978
Bromme	Terminal Pleist.	Bromme	1.52	Street 1998
Klein-Nordende	Terminal Pleist.	Bromme	1.00	Street 1998
Meiendorf	Late Glacial	Hamburgian	1.03	Eriksen 1996
Poggenwisch	Late Glacial	Hamburgian	1.00	Eriksen 1996
Stellmoor (Lower)	Late Glacial	Hamburgian	1.00	Eriksen 1996

the two. America south of the ice sheets, however, was comparatively mesic and vegetated in a heterogeneous open woodland (Barton 1979; Chilton, this volume; Guilday 1984; Guthrie 1984; Meltzer, this volume; Steele et al. 1998), which was a dramatically different landscape from the steppe-tundra of unglaciated Alaska and northeastern Asia. In contrast with the people who recolonized northwestern Europe, the first colonizers of the Americas found themselves largely isolated from their original homelands and in a very different ecosystem from the one to which they were accustomed but also one rich in easily procured resources.

With this background in mind, we compare the archaeological evidence for the earliest occupants of the Americas with the predictions of the behavioral ecology model described above. We have chosen to use Paleoindian data for this comparison for a variety of reasons. The claimed pre-Clovis localities are few and widely dispersed, and their dates are highly variable (see Meltzer, this volume; Schmitz, this volume). These consider-

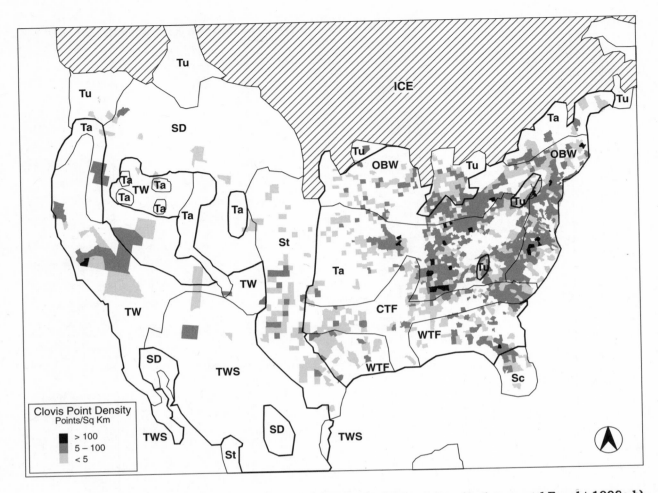

FIGURE 12.3 Distribution of Clovis and morphologically similar points (Anderson and Faught 1998a,b) and North American biomes at 15,600 cal B.P. (13,000 uncal B.P.; Adams and Faure 1998). Heavy line indicates resource-rich woodland and open-forest biomes. CTF = cool temperate forest, OBW = open boreal woodland, Sc = scrub, SD = semidesert, St = steppe, Ta = taiga, Tu = tundra, TW = temperate woodland, TWS = temperate woodland/scrub, WTF = warm temperate forest.

ations, along with the many questions about the reliability of the data from these localities and their interpretation, make it difficult to test the applicability of the ecological model we propose. Furthermore, analysis of the Paleoindian data set from the perspective of this model can shed light on the nature of the Paleoindian colonization, including its relationship to any prior colonization.

Land Use and Mobility

Figure 12.3 shows the distribution of early Paleoindian (i.e., Clovis and morphologically similar) projectile points and reconstructed contemporaneous biomes. Areas of higher densities of discarded projectile points probably indicate zones of more intensive use by these foragers—that is, repeated reoccupation or use by larger social groups than were typical—and, hence, represent major foci of Paleoindian land use. Early Paleoindian points accumulated most densely in the mixed temperate woodlands and open forests of North America. Although the data are much more limited, the same pattern seems to hold true for South America, with the earliest known sites concentrated in late Pleistocene forest-savannah mosaic in northern Brazil, Columbia, and Venezuela and in open forests of the Andean uplands along the western continental margin (Barton et al. 1999). Perhaps the closest modern analog of these communities is the savannah of subtropical Africa

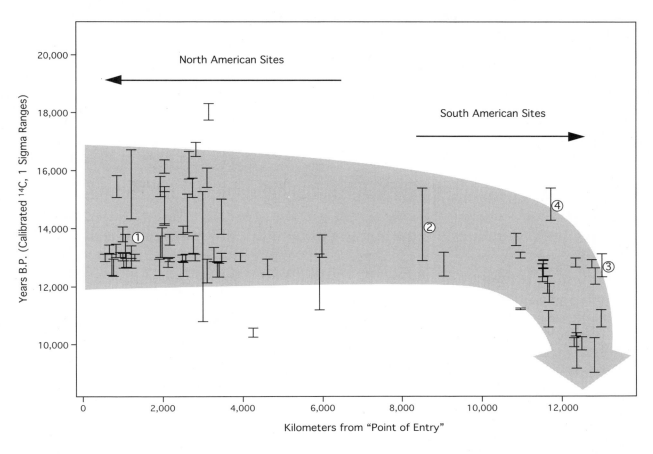

FIGURE 12.4 Calibrated dates (1 sigma ranges) versus distance from entry point for earliest Paleo-indian sites in North and South America. Sites mentioned in text: *(1)* Union Pacific (UP) Mammoth, United States; *(2)* Pachamachay, Peru; *(3)* Fell's Cave, Chile; and *(4)* Monte Verde, Chile.

(Foley 1982; Marean 1997). Like the African savannah, these biomes supported rich and diverse plant communities, many of whose members are no longer found in association with one another. They also seem to have supported an extremely rich array of large gregarious herbivores and the large carnivores and scavengers that preyed upon them (Guilday 1984; Guthrie 1984; Steele et al. 1998). These earliest Paleoindian sites are notably scarcer in completely open steppe and closed dense forest. This pattern suggests an economic emphasis on the most productive biomes, especially those that supported the richest assemblages of large herbivores.

Figure 12.4 shows radiocarbon dates (see tables 12.4 and 12.5) for the earliest Paleoindian sites in the Americas and their linear distances from a hypothetical point of entry at the southern terminus of the late Pleistocene corridor between the Cordilleran and Laurentide ice sheets. (The graph changes very little if an alternate

entry point along the northwestern coast is chosen.) At this bicontinental scale, it is clear that initial movement rates were extremely high, perhaps averaging as much as 10–20 km/yr. This is an order of magnitude greater than the rates discussed above for northwestern Europe and higher than those predicted by Webb and Rindos (1997). In terms of radiocarbon dates, this would appear almost instantaneous (see also Fiedel 1999b). However, it is also apparent that, as in northwestern Europe, movement rates declined over time as the hemisphere became populated; the final colonization of southern South America took nearly as long as the colonization of the rest of the hemisphere. For example, the overall colonization rate from the Union Pacific (UP) Mammoth site in north-central North America to Fell's Cave in the southern tip of South America is about 8 km/yr, whereas the rate from Pachamachay in Peru to Fell's Cave is only 0.4 km/yr (fig. 12.4). Interestingly, when

TABLE 12.4 North American Sites Used for Age-Distance Analysis

N. American Site	Region	Uncalibrated Radiocarbon Years B.P.*	Calibrated Years B.P. (1 Sigma Range)	Reference
Ester Creek	Far NW	12,051 ± 78	15,006–13,841	Dixon 1999; Rainey 1939
Mesa	Far NW	11,660 ± 80	13,824–13,465	Gal 1982; Kunz and Reanier 1996
Tuluaq	Far NW	11,191 ± 87	13,190–13,021	Rasic and Gal 2000
Charlie Lake Cave	Far NW	10,538 ± 82	12,835–12,344	Driver 1988; Driver et al. 1996; Fladmark 1996; Fladmark et al. 1988
Fort Rock Cave	Northwest	13,200 ± 720	16,730–14,367	Bryan and Tuohy 1999; Gilsen 2000; Willig and Aikens 1988
Wasden, Owl Cave	Northwest	12,930 ± 150	15,831–15,086	Bryan and Tuohy 1999
Cooper's Ferry	Northwest	11,370 ± 70	13,457–13,164	Bryan and Tuohy 1999; Davis and Sisson 1998
Connley Cave	Northwest	11,200 ± 200	13,424–12,994	Gilsen 2000; Willig and Aikens 1988
Marmes Rockshelter	Northwest	10,810 ± 300	13,140–12,392	Lyman 2000; Willig and Aikens 1988
Lake Abert	Northwest	10,810 ± 120	12,983–12,655	Gilsen 2000; Pettigrew 1985
Lind Coulee	Northwest	10,680 ± 190	12,951–12,370	Galm and Gough 2000; Lyman 2000
Buhl Burial	Northwest	10,675 ± 95	12,915–12,632	Green et al. 1998; Neves and Blum 2000
Agate Basin	N. Central	11,840 ± 130	14,061–13,565	Haynes et al. 1992; Stanford 1999b
UP Mammoth	N. Central	11,360 ± 350	13,808–13,000	Taylor et al. 1996
Colby	N. Central	11,200 ± 220	13,433–12,987	Frison and Todd 1986; Taylor et al. 1996
Lange/Ferguson	N. Central	11,140 ± 140	13,186–12,992	Hannus 1990; C. V. Haynes Jr. 1991a; Taylor et al. 1996
Casper	N. Central	11,190 ± 50	13,183–13,026	Frison 2000; Stanford 1999b
Jim Pitts	N. Central	11,033 ± 101	13,151–12,904	Stanford 1999b
Hell Gap	N. Central	10,919 ± 206	13,145–12,668	Haynes et al. 1984, 1992
Dent	N. Central	10,980 ± 90	13,136–12,891	Taylor et al. 1996
Anzick	N. Central	10,940 ± 90	13,121–12,882	Taylor et al. 1996
Mud Lake	Midwest	13,440 ± 60	16,381–15,918	Overstreet 1993; Overstreet and Stafford 1997
Hebior	Midwest	12,501 ± 203	15,464–14,184	Overstreet 1993; Overstreet and Stafford 1997
Schaefer Mammoth	Midwest	12,310 ± 60	15,295–14,134	Overstreet 1993; Overstreet and Stafford 1997
Eppley Rockshelter	Midwest	12,185 ± 130	15,207–13,876	Brush 1993; Lepper 1999; Maslowski et al. 1995
Paleo Crossing	Midwest	10,981 ± 95	13,137–12,891	Brose 1994; Fiedel 1999b; Lepper 1999; Maslowski et al. 1995; Tankersley and Holland 1994
Sheriden Cave	Midwest	10,930 ± 89	13,115–12,880	Tankersley 1997; Tankersley and Redmond 1999; Tankersley et al. 1997
Big Eddy	S. Central/SW	12,940 ± 120	15,822–15,134	Hajic et al. 2000; Lopinot et al. 1998, 2000
Johnson	S. Central/SW	11,980 ± 110	14,107–13,825	Broster and Norton 1996; Fiedel 1999b
Domebo	S. Central/SW	11,480 ± 450	14,036–13,007	Haynes 1967; Stafford et al. 1990; Taylor et al. 1996

TABLE 12.4 Continued

N. American Site	Region	Uncalibrated Radiocarbon Years B.P.*	Calibrated Years B.P. (1 Sigma Range)	Reference
Aubrey	S. Central/SW	11,570 ± 70	13,802–13,435	Ferring 1995; Taylor et al. 1996
Blackwater Draw	S. Central/SW	11,300 ± 240	13,753–13,014	Taylor et al. 1996
Lehner	S. Central/SW	10,940 ± 40	13,015–12,887	Haynes 1967; Taylor et al. 1996
Murray Springs	S. Central/SW	10,890 ± 50	12,995–12,685	Haynes 1967; Taylor et al. 1996
Rodgers Shelter	S. Central/SW	10,700 ± 200	12,966–12,378	Ray et al. 2002
Dust Cave	S. Central/SW	10,570 ± 60	12,848–12,365	Driskell 1996
Cactus Hill	Central East	15,070 ± 70	18,307–17,753	McAvoy and McAvoy 1997
Saltville	Central East	13,950 ± 70	16,983–16,492	McDonald 2000
Enoch Fork Shelter	Central East	13,480 ± 350	16,656–15,731	Tankersley 1990b
St. Albans	Central East	12,910 ± 60	15,755–15,092	Brashler et al. 1994
Baucom	Central East	11,100 ± 1530	15,307–10,787	Goodyear 1999
Page-Ladson	Southeast	13,130 ± 200	16,107–15,435	Goodyear 1999
Little Salt Springs	Southeast	12,030 ± 200	15,049–13,822	Anderson et al. 1996; Clausen et al. 1979
Warm Mineral Springs	Southeast	10,980 ± 160	13,150–12,880	Tesar 2000
State Road Ripple	Northeast	11,385 ± 140	13,761–13,158	Herbstritt 1988; Lepper 1999
Lamb	Northeast	11,400 ± 100	13,758–13,167	Gramly 1999
Whipple	Northeast	11,050 ± 300	13,363–12,862	Bonnichsen and Will 1999; Curran 1984; Haynes et al. 1984
Debert	Northeast	10,011 ± 90	13,170–12,874	MacDonald 1966, 1968; Stuckenrath 1964; Stuckenrath et al. 1966; Wilmeth 1978
Hiscock	Northeast	11,004 ± 45	13,136–12,902	C. V. Haynes Jr. 1991a; Laub and Haynes 1998; Laub et al. 1988
Shawnee-Minisink	Northeast	10,625 ± 289	12,971–12,132	McNett 1985b
Vail	Northeast	10,530 ± 103	12,837–12,335	Bonnichsen and Will 1999; Gramly 1982; Haynes et al. 1984; Levine 1990
Hedden	Northeast	10,526 ± 81	12,829–12,340	Spiess and Mosher 1994; Spiess et al. 1995
Alvina de Parita	Mesoamerica	11,350 ± 250	13,779–13,030	Crusoe and Felton 1974
Corona Rockshelter	Mesoamerica	10,440 ± 650	13,132–11,197	Cooke and Ranere 1992b; Gruhn and Bryan 1977
Los Tapiales	Mesoamerica	10,710 ± 170	12,958–12,427	Gruhn and Bryan 1977
Los Grifos	Mesoamerica	9233 ± 108	10,559–10,239	Santamaria 1981
Cueva los Vampiros	Mesoamerica	8560 ± 650	10,397–8651	Cooke and Ranere 1992b

*Multiple ^{14}C dates from same stratigraphic context were averaged using Calib 4 (S. Stuiver, University of Washington) prior to calibration.

TABLE 12.5 South American Sites Used for Age-Distance Analysis

S. American Site	Region	Uncalibrated Radiocarbon Years B.P.*	Calibrated Years B.P. (1 Sigma Range)	Reference
Pachamachay	Northern	11,800 ± 930	15,413–12,910	Gruhn 1997; Rick 1980
Pedra Pintada	Northern	10,531 ± 50	13,183–12,349	Roosevelt et al. 1996
Monte Verde	Southern	12,200 ± NA	15,419–14,307	Dillehay 1989, 1997b; but see Fiedel 1999b
Quereo	Southern	11,600 ± 190	13,829–13,406	Gruhn 1997; Núñez et al. 1994
Tagua Tagua 1	Southern	11,115 ± 146	13,180–12,979	Núñez et al. 1987, 1994
Tres Arroyos	Southern	10,523 ± 84	13,134–12,338	Borrero 1995
Piedra Museo	Southern	10,831 ± 107	12,988–12,662	Miotti 1995; Miotti and Cattaneo 1997
Cerro la China 2	Southern	10,735 ± 97	12,944–12,644	Flegenheimer and Zarate 1997
Cueva del Medio	Southern	10,659 ± 56	12,919–12,633	Borrero 1995
Cerro la China 1	Southern	10,654 ± 66	12,900–12,631	Flegenheimer and Zarate 1997
Cerro la China 3	Southern	10,610 ± 180	12,899–12,331	Flegenheimer and Zarate 1997
Cerro el Sombrero	Southern	10,457 ± 66	12,795–12,170	Flegenheimer and Zarate 1997
Fell's Cave	Southern	10,743 ± 120	12,642–12,089	Bird 1969; Empéraire et al. 1963; Nami 1985; Schobinger 1972
Paso Otero 5	Southern	10,305 ± 87	12,351–11,774	Martínez 2001
Cueva Tixi	Southern	10,144 ± 78	12,092–11,444	Mazzanti 1997
Tagua Tagua 2	Southern	9844 ± 62	11,256–11,195	Núñez et al. 1987, 1994
Marazzi	Southern	9590 ± 200	11,197–10,581	Borrero 1995
Abrigo los Pinos	Southern	9570 ± 120	11,158–10,601	Mazzanti 1997
Cueva de los Manos	Southern	9310 ± 90	10,668–10,291	Borrero 1995
Los Toldos	Southern	8750 ± 480	10,402–9164	Borrero and McEwan 1997; Roosevelt et al. 2002
Pali Aike	Southern	8639 ± 450	10,224–9033	Bird 1951
El Verano	Southern	8960 ± 140	10,222–9774	Borrero 1995, 1999
Cueva del Arroyo Feo	Southern	8952 ± 72	10,211–9919	Borrero 1995

*Multiple ^{14}C dates from same stratigraphic context were averaged using Calib 4 (S. Stuiver, University of Washington) prior to calibration.

Monte Verde, Chile, is plotted in this way, it appears as only a modest outlier to the overall curve.

Although the graph of figure 12.4 provides a useful overview of the colonization process, it is unlikely that humans actually spread southward across the Americas in a consistent wave, such as the "blitzkrieg" schematically portrayed by Martin (1967, 1973, 1984b; Mosimann and Martin 1975). Although the biomes of unglaciated North and South America probably differed less during the late Pleistocene than in the Holocene, the floral and faunal communities still varied geographically (Chilton, this volume). Some biomes would have been more pro-ductive for initial colonizers than others. Based on the model we outline here, we would expect initial colonizers to move first into the most productive biomes, that is, those that produced the highest return for foraging effort (see also Steele et al. 1998). Subsequently, as people accumulated more knowledge of the landscape (lowering the procurement costs associated with uncertainty) and the area became more populated (increasing movement costs while making some resources scarcer), the people would begin to occupy less desirable biomes. In effect, the initial colonizers would leapfrog through the richest biomes, and their descendents would back-

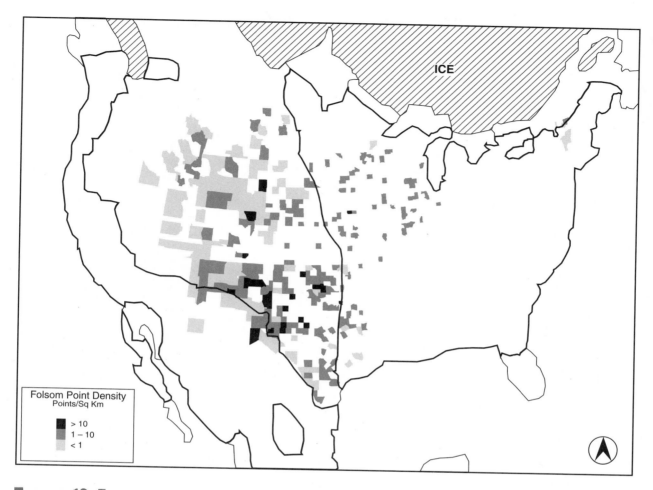

FIGURE 12.5 Distribution of Folsom and morphologically similar points (Anderson and Faught 1998a,b) and North American biomes at 12,000 cal B.P. (11,000 uncal B.P.; Adams and Faure 1998). Heavy line indicates resource-rich woodland and open-forest biomes.

fill the rest of the landscape (see also Meltzer, this volume). The overall distribution of Clovis and Folsom points (Anderson and Faught 1998a,b), as shown in figures 12.3 and 12.5, also supports this model. Although Clovis points are most concentrated in the rich open woodlands (fig. 12.3), Folsom points are found in biomes that people carrying Clovis points seemed to bypass (fig. 12.5).

We model such a process in figure 12.6. We use the earliest Paleoindian sites in each of the potentially richest biomes to represent the initial colonization of highly productive regions and the surrounding Paleoindian sites to represent the backfill effect. Replotting distance versus age using this model offers a different perspective on colonization (fig. 12.7). The "effective colonization distance" to a site is no longer the straight-line distance from an entry point; it is the distance from an entry point to a hypothetical initial colonization "center" in the richest regional biome and then the distance from this "center" to the site. Within each region, "effective colonization distance" correlates well with the age of each site; r^2 values are comparatively high for these chronologically coarse-grained archaeological data. Although the movement rates within any given region are much lower than the overall rates at a continentwide scale (about 2 km/yr), they are much closer to those predicted by Webb and Rindos (1997) for initial colonizers. These patterns lend support to our model of initial colonizers moving extremely rapidly across a landscape at a large scale, as well as the subsequent regional dynamics of peopling the American continents.

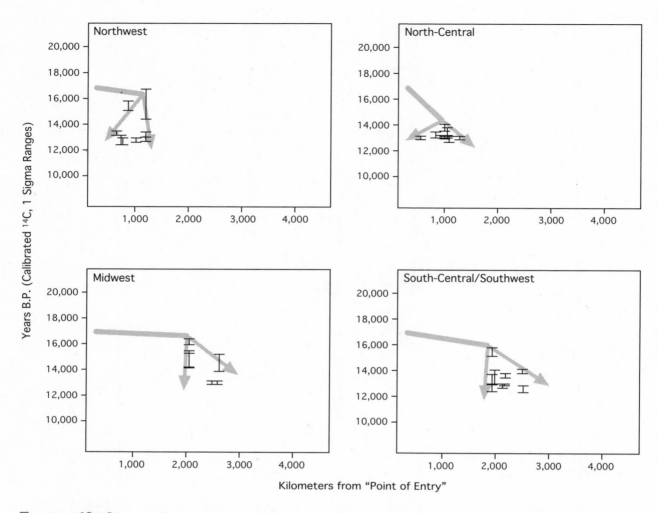

FIGURE 12.6 Modeling initial and regional "backfill" colonization in North America in four regions (see text). Example regions are from the date series shown in figure 12.4.

Demography

The land-use patterns modeled here would lead to low population densities and large use areas or ranges. Such demographic patterns have been suggested for North America on the basis of other evidence, including research by Amick (1996), Anderson and Gillam (2000), Fiedel (this volume), and MacDonald (1999, this volume). Recent population estimates by Amick (1996) and MacDonald (1999, this volume) suggest population densities of 0.002–0.006 persons/sq km for Folsom and regular use areas of 115,000–135,000 sq km per minimal social unit or band. Our modeling suggests that earlier Clovis densities would be even lower. The numbers for Folsom translate into 200–250 bands for the entire unglaciated hemisphere. At around 25 individuals per band, this represents only 5,000–7,000 people.

Furthermore, this population assumes that *all* unglaciated lands were equally occupied, a situation we feel was unlikely (Meltzer, this volume).

These figures seem extremely low for maintaining a viable biological population (MacDonald, this volume; Meltzer, this volume); the actual population of the Americas in the late Pleistocene may have been higher. However, these calculations do offer a baseline for assessing Paleoindian demography and give some idea of the demographic differences between the earliest occupants of the Americas and recent hunter-gatherers. These estimates also underscore the effects of initial colonization on patterning in the archaeological record. Few people are needed to leave lithic debris in South America very shortly after their initial entry into the hemisphere. Because of the rapidity at which humans

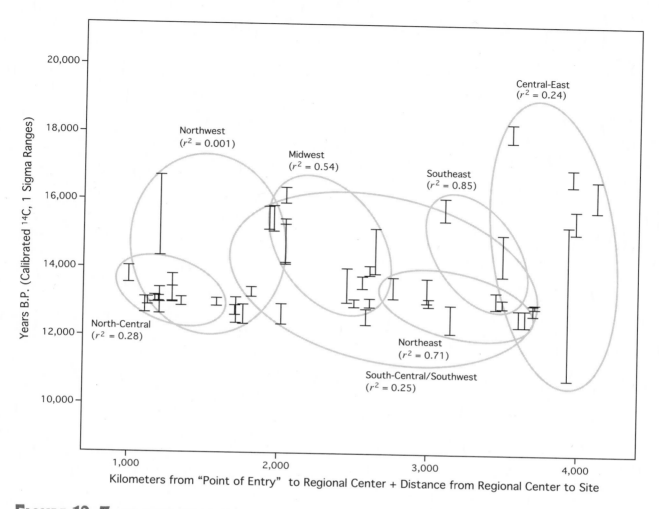

FIGURE 12.7 Modeling initial and regional "backfill" colonization in North America (see text). Correlation values refer to adjusted distances, using calibrated mean ages.

may spread under these circumstances, their wide and patchy dispersal, and the effects of more than 12,000 years of taphonomic processes, early sites could appear virtually anywhere in the hemisphere, including South America (see also Anderson and Gillam 2000). Only by looking at the entire suite of sites can we hope to see even limited evidence of the direction of colonization.

Resource Use

The ecological models discussed here predict low diet diversity for initial colonizers and increasing diet diversity as the landscape becomes populated and high-ranking resources become more costly to procure. Unfortunately many early Paleoindian "sites" are surface accumulations that lack associated faunal remains, and the archaeofauna from many excavated sites have not

been reported in a way that permits quantitative assessment of diversity. Of the sites for which published data are available, however (table 12.6), it appears that diet diversity is very low for Clovis sites (fig. 12.8). In fact, diversity values for the suite of Clovis sites with relevant data are very similar to those for the initial colonizers of northwestern Europe. Also paralleling the northwestern European case study, diet diversity rises after the Clovis period as the landscape becomes more populated (fig. 12.8). This is seen most dramatically in the broad-spectrum foraging that characterizes the late Archaic, as exemplified in a suite of sites from the southwestern United States with relevant published archaeofaunal data (fig. 12.8; table 12.6).

TABLE 12.6 American Sites Used for Diet Diversity Analysis

American Site	Period	Phase	Diversity Index	Reference
Agate Basin	Late Glacial	Clovis	3.77	Frison 1982a; Walker 1982
Colby	Late Glacial	Clovis	1.08	Walker and Frison 1986
Domebo	Late Glacial	Clovis	1.00	Leonhardy 1966
Escapule	Late Glacial	Clovis	1.00	Hemmings and Haynes 1969
Lange-Ferguson	Late Glacial	Clovis	1.00	Hannus 1990b
Lehner	Late Glacial	Clovis	1.27	Haury et al. 1959; Saunders 1977
Mill Iron	Late Glacial	Goshen	1.00	Kreutzer 1996; Todd et al. 1996; Walker and Frison 1986
Monte Verde	Late Glacial		1.09	Casamiquela and Dillehay 1989
Naco	Late Glacial	Clovis	1.00	Haury et al. 1953
Agate Basin	Terminal Pleist.	Folsom	1.58	Frison 1982a; Walker 1982; Zeimens 1982
Bull Brook	Terminal Pleist.	Bull Brook	1.20	Spiess et al. 1985
Hanson	Terminal Pleist.	Folsom	1.00	Ingbar 1992
Horner	Terminal Pleist.	Folsom	1.01	Frison and Todd 1987
Lindenmeier	Terminal Pleist.	Folsom	1.36	Wilmsen and Roberts 1978
Michaud	Terminal Pleist.	Bull Brook	1.00	Spiess and Wilson 1987
Stewart's Cattle Guard	Terminal Pleist.	Folsom	1.00	Jodry and Stanford 1992
Whipple	Terminal Pleist.	Bull Brook	1.00	Spiess et al. 1985
Agate Basin	E. Holocene	Agate Basin	1.01	Frison 1982a; Walker 1982; Zeimens 1982
Agate Basin	E. Holocene	Hell Gap	1.19	Frison 1982a; Walker 1982; Zeimens 1982
Ventana Cave 6–8	E. Holocene	Early Archaic	2.24–2.75	Bayham 1982; James 1990
Coffee Camp	L. Holocene	Late Archaic	2.16	James 1993
Donaldson	L. Holocene	Late Archaic	3.52	Huckell 1995
Tator Hills	L. Holocene	Late Archaic	3.02	James 1993
Ventana Cave 3–5	L. Holocene	Late Archaic	3.86–6.01	Bayham 1982; James 1990

Implications and Discussion

Timing of Initial Colonization

Scholars have argued that the circumstances of late Pleistocene ecosystems and the social and demographic organization of contemporaneous human populations were sufficiently different from those of modern foragers that the latter are poor analogs for understanding the relevant socioecological dynamics in this distant past. In fact, there is no reason to expect inherent behavioral uniformitarianism for any human society, regardless of their mode of subsistence. This is even more the case with modern foragers, who have long been relegated to the few habitats that are inhospitable to agriculture and who have coexisted (often mutualistically) with agriculturalists for millennia. Evolutionary ecology, however, is not based on uniformitarian ethnographic analogy, except for the fundamental assumption that, due to long-term selection, people act to maximize the returns for their efforts (however they may perceive those maximum benefits) within the constraints of the social and ecological contexts in which they find themselves. Evolutionary ecology also assumes that decisions are ultimately made by individuals. Modern societies, including modern foragers, are often used to test models developed in evolutionary

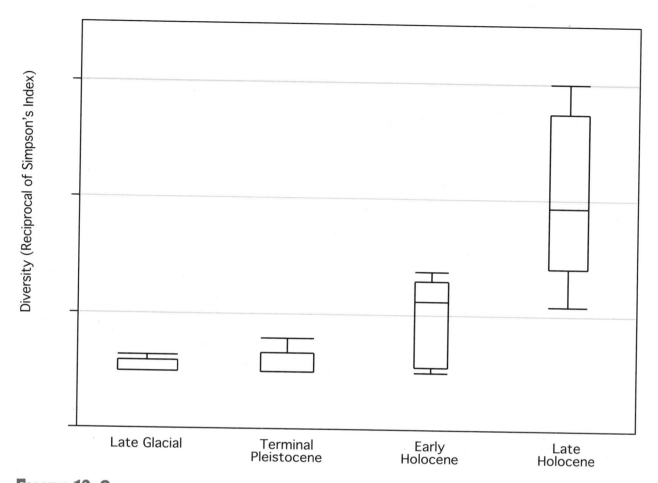

FIGURE 12.8 Diet diversity (reciprocal of Simpson's index of NISP for fauna) for Paleoindian and Archaic sites in North America.

ecology, but analogy with modern peoples is not the source of these models. Hence, we feel that such models are especially relevant for understanding the dynamics of past humans whose socioecological circumstances were much different from any that may be observed today.

In the Americas, the late Pleistocene Paleoindian occupation appears to closely match our proposed model for initial colonizers of empty landscapes. Moreover, critical aspects of the Paleoindian occupation closely parallel the recolonization of northwestern Europe after deglaciation. The late Paleolithic foragers who colonized this part of Europe were clearly entering a landscape devoid of humans. This strongly suggests that the people whose material residues we term "Paleoindian" were behaving *as if* they were initial colonizers of a landscape empty of other humans (see also Fiedel, this volume; Meltzer, this volume). Any prior

colonists also would have had to pass through the Northeast Asian and Alaskan ecological filter before entering the Americas. Successfully living in and passing through this arctic environment would have required sophisticated technological and social skills equal to those of Paleoindian colonizers (see Schmitz, this volume). Furthermore, prior colonists would have had ample opportunity to populate the landscape and accumulate information about the spatial and temporal distribution of resources. Hence, any pre-Paleoindian occupants of the Americas should have been highly effective competitors to subsequent Paleoindian occupants. Note that in the two reasonably well-documented colonizations of the Americas after the late Pleistocene, the immigrants were relegated to narrow niches (the mountain margin zone for the Na-Dene/Athabaskans and the High Arctic coastal zone for the Thule) and have never represented more than a tiny fraction of the previously established Amerind populations of the Western Hemisphere (see Hill, this volume; Schmitz, this volume).

If humans were present in the Americas prior to the Paleoindian entry, they proved to be such ineffective competitors that Paleoindian colonizers behaved as if they did not exist. This seems highly atypical of humans with generally equivalent technological, economic, and social organizations. It is possible, of course, that one or more pre-Paleoindian colonizations failed, and prior human populations had existed but were extinct by the time of the Paleoindian arrival. Such phenomena probably did happen in the past but are not generally recognized because relevant populations failed to reach a level that would achieve archaeological visibility. Although individual populations may have died out, more general colonization failures—in which humans were successful enough to spread across two continents and leave visible residues at a handful of widely dispersed locales but then decline to extinction—seem largely atypical of the spread of modern humans across the globe. The more parsimonious interpretation of the data currently available is that the Paleoindian entry into the New World was the initial colonization of the continents of the Western Hemisphere. The rapidity of this initial human dispersal, its patchy distribution in the most productive environments, and the taphonomic roulette of the 12,000-year-long archaeological record could account for the handful of sites that seem "out of order" with respect to their age and location (see also Anderson and Gillam 2000; Fiedel 1999b).

Human Impacts on Pleistocene Ecosystems

As stated at the beginning of this chapter, the initial colonization of the Americas was a momentous biogeographical phenomenon, as much for American ecosystems as for the first Americans. It would not be an exaggeration to compare it to the impact of the joining of North and South America in the late Tertiary after the two continents had been separated and had developed their own very different ecologies over tens of millions of years. Most scientific study of the ecological impacts of human entry into the New World has focused on the late Pleistocene extinction of large herbivores (see Martin and Klein 1984 and the references therein). In fact, a cursory reading of our model might lead one to the conclusion that it substantiates the human role in the evolutionary demise of late Pleistocene megafauna. In reality this is not the case. If one looks beyond the simplistic view of humans as predators to their role as members and shapers of ecosystems, it becomes apparent that human impacts were likely more far-reaching and considerably more complex than this, and that hunting of large herbivores may well have been among the lesser impacts on faunal and floral communities.

In another case of continental colonization—Australia (or Sahul)—human predation has also been proposed as the primary cause of extinction of large fauna (Martin 1984b). Webb (1998) takes a more sophisticated look at the ecological dynamics of the introduction of humans into Australia. Webb points out that Australia, prior to human colonization, could support only a few large carnivore taxa. The first and foremost ecological impact of humans was as competitors of these large carnivores. Although paleontological data are difficult to read at the resolution desired, it appears that large carnivores became extinct or very rare before the large herbivores did. Webb suggests that by outcompeting large carnivores and driving them to extinction, humans upset a delicate predator-prey relationship between these carnivores and large herbivores. Because their predation patterns differed considerably from those of large marsupial carnivores, humans did not simply replace them in Australian ecosystems. This left large herbivores without the predator-dependent population controls to which they had become adapted over millions of years, sending their populations into boom-bust cycles. According to Webb, this loss of population control combined with large-scale vegetation changes due to human-caused burning and increasing climatic variability during the late Pleistocene were probable primary causes of large herbivore extinctions, though the new human predation patterns may have contributed.

In other words, the introduction of humans into American ecosystems is not simply a matter of rapacious hunters slaughtering naïve animals. Human social and economic behaviors are complex and have diverse and far-reaching environmental consequences (Redman 1999). It is useful to conceive of the overall effect of human entry into the Americas as one in which the hemisphere was transformed into a socioecosystem in which humans became not just members or exploiters, but also active shapers of the new American ecology. Although it is not possible to explore herein the many ramifications of such a perspective, it is valuable to point out some of the most notable potential impacts as directions for future study.

An important component of Webb's model for the impact of humans on Australian megafauna is the low carrying capacity of that continent for large fauna and the inherent fragility of the ecosystem to perturbation. To the best of our knowledge, this is *not* the case for American ecosystems. Late Pleistocene vegetation communities were both richer and more diverse than those of contemporaneous Australia. Furthermore, the landmass of the two American continents is much larger than Australia and extends over a tremendous latitudinal range. As a consequence, large animals were also much more numerous and diverse. In contrast to the three large carnivores that Webb lists for Australia, the Americas supported a diversity of large felids, canids, and ursids (Anderson 1984; Mead and Meltzer 1984; Whitney-Smith, this volume). With these differences, can Webb's models apply to the American context as well?

The entry of humans into the Western Hemisphere brought two large carnivores: humans and their dogs, which were descended from Eurasian wolves (Schwartz 1997:15–18). If humans behaved as predicted by the ecological models discussed above, and as supported by at least some of the archaeological evidence, they and their dogs would have been in direct competition with other large American carnivores. Despite the comparative richness of American ecosystems, large carnivores by necessity exist in much lower numbers than their prey species, making them potentially more vulnerable to extinction when faced with competition for resources. (See Klein 1992 for a discussion of humans and carnivore extinction in early Pleistocene Africa.) If the primary impact of human entry into the Americas was overpredation of large herbivores, the extinction of large carnivores should follow on the heels of herbivore extinction (or be contemporaneous with it) as their food sources were eliminated by humans. However, if initial human impact represented a more subtle form of competition with carnivores, they might become extinct before the large herbivores, as Webb has suggested for Australia. A review of the extinction dates for American fauna compiled by Mead and Meltzer (1984) suggests that carnivores may have become extinct before large herbivores. Although several caveats must be raised in determining extinction dates (J. I. Mead, personal communication 1999; Webb 1998), this reference remains the most comprehensive data set available for late Pleistocene American extinctions. An ANOVA indicates that large carnivore extinctions did precede those of large herbivores overall (N of carnivores = 4, N of herbivores = 19, F = 3.30, p = .08). Computer modeling of human-carnivore competition by Whitney-Smith (this

volume) has produced results analogous to those suggested by us for the late Pleistocene Americas and by Webb for Pleistocene Australia.

The ecological models outlined above predict comparatively modest direct human impacts on large herbivores (but see Haynes 2002 for sophisticated modeling of an alternative view). Patch choice models suggest that initial colonizers would move to new unpopulated locales long before they eliminated large game in a region. Only when movement became more restricted due to the geographic spread of humans did they increase their procurement efforts within a region. By that time, large intelligent herbivores would have become behaviorally adapted to human predation, further increasing their procurement costs. Diet breadth models predict that, when faced with increased procurement costs for large herbivores, humans diversify their diet rather than intensify their efforts to hunt scarcer large game. Although human predation certainly would have affected large herbivore populations, as would any other new predator, humans would be no more likely to expend the increasing effort to eliminate megafauna than would dirk-toothed felids or dire wolves.

To date, there has been little scientific study of the role of human-caused fire in the late Pleistocene ecosystems of the Americas. However, such research elsewhere (Anderson 2002; Bush 1988; Dods 2002; Kershaw et al. 1997; Pyne 1998; Pyne and Goldammer 1997; Webb 1998) indicates that humans dramatically alter the "natural" fire regimes (including temporal and spatial distribution and intensity) of the landscapes they inhabit, with far-reaching consequences for plant communities at regional or even continental scales. In these studies, pollen cores and other sediment samples in which microcharcoal particles have been counted provide evidence for the frequency and extent of burning. Although fires are also caused by lightning or more rarely by volcanic eruptions (James 1989, 1996), human-related burning tends to produce a distinctive signature. Even if humans do not intentionally burn the landscape (though there is considerable ethnohistoric evidence that they do so regularly, as summarized in the studies mentioned above), they build and maintain fires on a daily basis throughout the year. This alone greatly increases the chances of unintentional landscape burning outside the season of natural fires (Pyne 1998; Pyne and Goldammer 1997).

The available data for landscape fires during the late Pleistocene of the Americas are few but suggestive. Relevant pollen and microcharcoal studies are available from Lake La Yeguada, Panama (Bush et al. 1992; Kershaw et al. 1997), southern Wisconsin and Massachusetts (Winkler 1997), and the western slopes of the Sierra Nevada in California (Anderson and Smith 1997). There are dramatic spikes in the amount of microcharcoal coincident with the Paleoindian occupation of each of these regions: at 12,000 cal B.P. in Panama, 14,700–14,100 B.P. in southern Wisconsin, 12,000 B.P. in Massachusetts, and 10,200 B.P. (and possibly as early as 11,400 B.P.) in the Sierra Nevada. Notably the dates vary geographically and seem to better fit our model for spreading human populations more than the synchronous, continentwide climatic changes. In this respect, the Sierra Nevada cores, in an initially less-optimal montane area that we predict would have been populated by backfill rather than initial colonization, show a microcharcoal spike more than 2,000–4,000 years later than the spikes in the other regions.

Viewed from the perspective of evolutionary ecology, the initial colonization of the Americas did not loose a "blitzkrieg" of human predation that led to the extinction of numerous large animal taxa during the late Pleistocene. The entry of humans, however, must have had a significant impact on American ecosystems. It is now apparent that the climatic changes that initiated the early Holocene took place extremely rapidly, with major temperature increases within a few decades (Fiedel 1999b; Taylor 1999). These climatic changes interacted with the large-scale alterations in floral communities due to hemisphere-wide anthropogenic burning and produced the much more fragmented habitats that characterize the Holocene. These continentwide changes in vegetation communities, the loss of predator-based population controls due to human competition with large carnivores, and the introduction of two new carnivores (humans and dogs) probably pushed many large animal taxa beyond the point where they could no longer maintain viable breeding populations. The loss of even some of these large herbivores (proboscideans, for example) would have additional effects on vegetation communities, which were adapted to herbivores as much as the animals were adapted to the plants. The resulting cascade of changes dramatically and permanently altered American ecosystems.

Humans, as participants in the new socioecosystems, were equally affected by these long-term changes that they themselves helped to initiate. Habitat fragmentation due to a combination of climatic changes,

anthropogenic burning, and loss of large herbivores encouraged geographic specialization among humans in social, economic, and technological realms. At the same time, the loss of wide-ranging, high-ranking, large fauna encouraged diet diversification and reliance on a variety of local resources. The result is seen in the regionally diverse material residues of Holocene humans that archaeologists term the Archaic (Barton 1979; Meltzer, this volume).

Conclusions

Although many gaps remain in our study, as well as in those of others who have attempted to understand the dynamics of the colonization of the Americas, data alone will not lead to better understanding (see also Meltzer, this volume). We hope we have shown that ecological modeling based on well-developed evolutionary theory and the extant data compiled by decades of dedicated archaeological research can provide insights into the peopling of the Americas and into the general processes of human colonization. This kind of study can also reveal the type of data that can best develop our understanding of the first Americans. Although more and better dated sites would certainly be helpful, other data may be even more useful. For example, we still lack many systematic surveys and geoarchaeological studies that can tell us where the earliest humans were *not* as well as where they were. We also need a better understanding of the environments in which early Americans lived and more comprehensive information about their diet and the resources (both subsistence and other) that they used (see Chilton, this volume). Finally, there is little direct evidence for the role that the first colonizers played in reshaping American ecosystems into the socioecosystems that characterized the rest of the world. We were surprised to find that, despite decades of research on late Pleistocene environments, microcharcoal analysis (a comparatively simple procedure) is lacking in most studies.

Colonization is not an event but a process that varies dynamically across space and time. The human colonization of "pristine" landscapes offers unique opportunities to understand the full extent of the human role on Earth. Until humans colonize other planets, the only way we can study the long-term consequences of human colonization is through archaeology. In this sense, the peopling of the New World is not simply a long-past event; it is also the beginning of an ongoing process that remains highly relevant to our identity and our future on this planet.

Acknowledgments

We would like to thank Chris Newman of the Conservation and Recreation Lands Archaeological Survey, Florida Bureau of Archaeological Research; Anders Fischer, Skov- og Naturstyrelsen, Denmark; Sveinung Bang-Andersen of the Arkeologisk Museum i Stavanger, Norway; and Agneta Åkerlund of the Department of Archaeology, Stockholm University, Sweden, for their generous help with radiocarbon dates at crucial points in our research. We also would like to acknowledge the Canadian Archaeological Association Radiocarbon Database, compiled by Dr. Richard E. Morlan, Canadian Museum of Civilization, Gatineau, Quebec (http://www .canadianarchaeology.com/radiocarbon/card/card.htm). This is an extremely valuable compilation of radiocarbon dates for North America.

13 Beyond "Big"

GENDER, AGE, AND SUBSISTENCE DIVERSITY IN PALEOINDIAN SOCIETIES
Elizabeth S. Chilton

Despite recent advances in our understandings of the complexity of the peopling of the New World, much of the Paleoindian literature still conjures up conventional notions of Paleoindians as decidedly masculine or, as Michael Barton put it when he invited me to contribute to this volume, "big men with big spears hunting big animals." Even if the hunting of large game was, in fact, part of the diverse array of Paleoindian lifeways, we are surely missing important aspects of these societies by limiting ourselves to this rather narrow—and in many ways unrealistic—way of looking at the colonization and initial settlement of the New World.

Michael Barton and Geoffrey Clark invited me to participate in this volume because of a paper that I published in 1994, "In Search of Paleo-Women: Gender Implications of Remains from Paleoindian Sites in the Northeast" (Chilton 1994). In this paper I argued that an overemphasis on hunting—and, by implication, the activities of men—has severely limited a more anthropological understanding of what was certainly a complex and variable set of adaptations. My 1994 paper was "womanist" in the sense that it was "concerned with the actions, status, or simply presence of women" in the past (Joyce and Claassen 1997:1). In retrospect, this paper was flawed because it focused only on "finding women" in the archaeological record; it did not provide an in-depth discussion of what can be gained simply by *looking* for women and by considering gender as a general structuring principle in our analyses (Joyce and Claassen 1997:2). It is through the conscious and explicit consideration of gender (as well as other aspects of social agency) in our interpretations that we are able to "see differently" (Dobres 1999). By bringing aspects of interpersonal agency into the foreground, "as if people mattered," archaeologists can make substantial changes to their research questions and methodologies, which in turn will profoundly affect the way they interpret the archaeological record (Dobres 1999).

In this chapter I review the current state of Paleoindian research with respect to gender: I trace the roots of a strong emphasis on hunting, big game, and projectile points in Paleoindian research; I outline some of the implications of these biases for understanding the peopling of the New World; and I suggest potentially fruitful avenues of research and ways to move "beyond big." The goal of this review is not the womanist goal of "finding women." Instead my goal is to explore the diversity and idiosyncrasies of both Paleoindians and the archaeological record, so that we may come to more fruitful understandings of what people—women, men, young, old, and middle aged—were doing in North America at the end of the Pleistocene.

Gender Bias in Paleoindian Research

The topic of gender in archaeological inquiry has been discussed in detail elsewhere (e.g., Claassen and Joyce 1997; du Cros and Smith 1993; Gero and Conkey 1991; Kent 1998; Nelson 1997; Walde and Willows 1991; R. P. Wright 1996). Although gender has become an increasingly prevalent topic in archaeological research over the past decade, very little attention has been paid to issues of gender or sex roles in Paleoindian research (see Gero 1993 and Hudecek-Cuffe 1998 for notable exceptions). Relatively few scholars have investigated Native American sex roles for times prior to the adoption of maize agriculture (Claassen 1997:81). In fact, gender is often not studied for hunter-gatherers in general because their adaptations are thought to be determined by the environment (Duke 1991:280). For Paleoindians in particular, social life and individual agency are almost completely ignored. Instead Paleoindians tend to be viewed as adapting to their environment in mechanistic and purely "functional" ways (Hudecek-Cuffe 1998:1). Some archaeologists may argue that we can never hope to understand Paleoindian gender dynamics or even the sexual division of labor because we lack written records and because of the great antiquity of Paleoindian societies. However, if gender is left implicit in our interpretations, if our interpretations are thought to be "gender neutral," we leave the door open for a broad range of assumptions about men's and women's activities and motivations. One of the most problematic assumptions about hunter-gatherer societies is that they recognized only two genders—male and female—and that labor was strictly divided along these lines.

While gender attribution in Paleoindian studies is most often implicit, for many reasons the outcome is decidedly masculine. As Joyce and Claassen (1997:5) point out, "[T]he default gender in much conventional prehistory is not neuter but male." For Paleoindians, gender roles are often "uncritically derived from ethnographies and idealized models . . . that view men hunting and in charge of the political realm and women gathering and relegated to the domestic realm" (Hudecek-Cuffe 1998:1). These types of assumptions have led to a pronounced male bias in Paleoindian research. Some of the reasons for this bias include the following: (1) a view of Paleoindians as heroic explorers, (2) an overemphasis on hunting activities, with the assumption that it was primarily men who hunted, (3) a focus on stone tools, with the assumption that it was primarily men who made and used such tools, and (4) a sexual division of labor within the field of archaeology itself. I discuss each of these in turn.

Paleoindians as Heroic Explorers

Paleoindians are often viewed as heroic, somewhat akin to historic explorers, such as Columbus or Lewis and Clark, moving into uncharted territories with only the crudest of technologies (Chilton 1994:10; Mandryk, this volume). Feder (2000:232) likens the spread of humans into the western Pacific and the Americas to Neil Armstrong's historic walk on the moon. Nowhere is the human global expansion more romanticized than it is for Paleoindians: "No matter how it happened, you have to look at these people as explorers . . . probably young guys who were really bent on what's over the next hill" (C. V. Haynes Jr., quoted in Parfit 2000:46).

This last quote demonstrates one of the drawbacks of viewing Paleoindians as explorers or adventurers: Because many of our historic explorers were men, Paleoindians come to be viewed as men ("guys") as well. Furthermore, with their reliance on stone tool technologies, Paleoindians are viewed as a kind of "earliest common denominator, a base-line of American technological prowess and ecological efficiency" (Gero 1993:35).

What is overlooked in these romantic explorer models is the more mundane daily life of Paleoindians. Unlike Neil Armstrong or Columbus, Paleoindians most certainly did not realize the historical nature of their actions. Instead the first people to enter what we now

call North America consisted of groups of families who were likely more concerned with making supper, finding a good marriage partner, deciding whether the group should split up, or curing the baby's cough. Contrary to models that seek to determine whether Paleoindians "could have made it" to South America by a certain date or whether they "could have" colonized North America within a given period of time (e.g., Surovell 2000), it may be more fruitful to ask, "Why would they have wanted to?" Why, within a person's lifetime, would the goal be to "push on"? Certainly we will come to more realistic understandings of the peopling of the New World when we come to see Paleoindians as not only courageous, curious, and adventurous, but occasionally complacent, conservative, and illogical as well.

Overemphasis on Hunting

Another way that bias has been introduced into Paleoindian research is through an overemphasis on hunting, including the assumption that it was primarily men who hunted. Before the advent of radiocarbon dating, Paleoindian research focused on kill sites on the Plains because the presence of extinct fauna in stratigraphic association with Paleoindian artifacts helped to demonstrate the antiquity of these early sites (Bruhns and Stothert 1999:27; Tankersley, this volume). On the Plains, Clovis artifacts were (and are) often found with mammoth and bison remains and date to approximately 11,000 B.P. (Haynes 1993). This association and the apparent scarcity of nonkill sites led researchers to believe that Paleoindians were first and foremost mobile hunters (see discussions in Meltzer 1988, this volume). The extinction of megafauna seemed to be roughly coincident with the peopling of North America, further contributing to the stereotype of Paleoindians as big-game hunters (see Martin 1973).

The paleohunter ideal lived on long after the invention of radiocarbon dating. Until fairly recently, North America was presumed to have been a rather harsh environment during the late Pleistocene. Many of the ethnographic analogies were thus taken from areas where hunting presumably played a major role in subsistence (i.e., marginal environments that are poor in plant foods). For Paleoindians in eastern North America, these ethnographic analogies consisted of present-day arctic and subarctic hunters (Barton et al., this volume; Levine 1997; Meltzer, this volume). However, contrary to the assumption that Paleoindians were greeted by a treeless tundra in eastern North America, paleoenvironmental data indicate that during the eleventh millennium B.P., much of the region was forested (Dincauze 1981b, 1988; see also discussion in Levine 1997).

Another reason for an overemphasis on hunting by archaeologists studying the Paleoindian period is that sites from this period are most often identified by their diagnostic fluted projectile points. Because stone artifacts are often the only materials that are preserved on sites of this antiquity, our sample of human behavior is severely limited (see discussion in Clark, this volume). Although many archaeologists recognize that the numerous unifacial tools found on Paleoindian sites most likely represent bone-, wood-, and hide-working industries, lithic remains are still given primacy in interpretations of settlement and subsistence for Native peoples (Funk 1972; Gardner 1974; Lacy 1979; MacDonald 1985). Paleoindian sites are often identified on the basis of a single fluted point or on "stray finds." However, at many large Paleoindian sites (especially in eastern North America) projectile points and bifacial tools constitute the *minority* of finished stone tools that have been found (e.g., Funk and Wellman 1984; Gramly 1982). Paleoindian sites without the diagnostic fluted points may go (or may have gone) unnoticed or understudied. Eastern North America contains numerous examples of mobile foragers who used a combination of bifacial and expedient core technologies, perhaps in cases of local raw-material abundance (see discussion in Sassaman 1992:256; see also an example from the Gulf of Maine Archaic in Robinson 1992). Thus, the availability of lithic raw materials could have affected what types of tools were made *and whether or not* a bifacial tool industry was in place.

Because of the presumed emphasis on Paleoindian hunting, contrary evidence is often overlooked or explained away. For example, MacDonald (1985) reported that projectile points constitute just over 2 percent of the total artifact assemblage at the Paleoindian Debert Site in Nova Scotia. Using rather circular reasoning, he concluded that "hunting is definitely underrepresented among a population that existed by hunting" (MacDonald 1985:110). Similarly, Gramly (1982) assumes a priori that Vail, a Paleoindian site in Maine, is a hunting camp. Although endscrapers are nearly ten times more numerous than fluted projectile points at this site, they are afforded only one-fourth as much text. Even though projectile points constitute the minority of finished tools at most Paleoindian sites, they are often allotted the lion's share of research and interest (see Clark, this volume).

What is the current archaeological evidence for Paleoindian hunting in North America? Because the techniques used to study past environments have become more sophisticated in the last twenty years, we now know that late Pleistocene North America contained a diverse array of microenvironments: some rich in animals, others rich in plants, but patchy and, in many cases, unpredictable (see Frison 1993:247). It has become increasingly evident that Paleoindians on the Plains and elsewhere were not dependent on large animals for their survival. According to Lepper and Meltzer (1991:177), "Evidence for Paleoindian exploitation of Pleistocene megafauna as a specialized system of widespread, systematic, intense predation does not exist." Groups on the Plains were more likely versatile foragers who used a wide variety of subsistence strategies and depended on "local resources, preferences, and available technology and knowledge" (Hudecek-Cuffe 1998:68). For example, Johnson's (1991) evaluation of (1) the Clovis data from the southern Plains, (2) climatic and physiographic data, and (3) archaeological theory for hunter-gatherers led her to conclude that Paleoindians in this region were broad-spectrum, generalist foragers who hunted and scavenged a variety of animals on an opportunistic basis.

Bryan (1991) provides an intriguing explanation for the hunting of large game by some groups on the Plains. He suggests that the fluted point tradition developed in the southeastern United States, after which some proto-Clovis eastern foragers started to exploit bison and mammoths on a seasonal basis on the Plains. He further argues that elsewhere, in ecosystems with a greater diversity of plants and animals, people continued their general foraging and hunted large game opportunistically (Bryan 1991:23). According to Bryan (1991), bison hunters on the Plains experimented with more effective hunting techniques, including new projectile point forms. Regardless of whether Clovis technology moved from east to west, from west to east, or otherwise, the great variability in both shape and technology in fluted points, as well as the rest of the Paleoindian artifact assemblages, suggests the adaptation by different groups to different environmental zones (Bonnichsen 1991:315; Tankersley, this volume). We should therefore expect that Clovis peoples exploited a wide variety of plants and animals depending on the environmental zone, the season, and perhaps the particular group.

Better preservation of the bones of large animals (as opposed to small animals) has fueled the focus on the hunting of megafauna. Until recently our methodologies have not been adequate to recover evidence for the exploitation of plants and small animals for such ancient times (Frison 1993:247). In recent years the thorough analysis of remains from key archaeological sites and the creative approaches to archaeological interpretation have gone a long way toward understanding the possibilities for Paleoindian subsistence beyond large game. In the central United States, archaeologists have long known that Paleoindians exploited small animals. For example, at the site of Pelican Rapids (Minnesota), the burial of a fifteen-year-old girl (dated to approximately 11,000 B.P.) was found with a conch shell pendant and fragments of turtle carapace (Jenks 1936; Redder and Fox 1988). More recent excavations of archaeological sites in Texas have revealed diverse subsistence and material culture for Paleoindians. For example, at Horn Shelter (Texas), two interred males were found with items that included five separate turtle carapaces, four deer-antler tools, perforated coyote-sized canine teeth, and a small-eyed bone needle, possibly a net-weaving needle (Redder and Fox 1988). Radiocarbon dates on wood charcoal and shell from the same substratum ranged from about 10,400 to 9300 B.P. (Redder and Fox 1988). Also found in association with the burials were bird claws, eighty marine shell beads, and a sandstone slab for grinding beads. Numerous faunal remains were also recovered from the burial fill, including fish, frog, snake, turtle, rabbit, probably deer, and small rodents (Redder and Fox 1988). Although this particular site most likely dates to the late Paleoindian period, it still presents us with possibilities for earlier adaptations. The presence of turtle carapace, conch shell, bird claws, and the like does not directly suggest that these animals were eaten, especially because in many burial contexts they are used for ornamental purposes. Nevertheless, I would assume that if one part of a turtle, shellfish, or bird was used by Paleoindians, then the animal was probably also part of the subsistence economy. Their appearance in graves also suggests that these animals may have held importance in the lives of these people beyond ornamentation.

The Clovis Aubrey site in north-central Texas is one of the few sites where a diverse fauna provides evidence of a more generalized foraging adaptation for Paleoindians, despite the lack of direct association (Ferring 1995). More than forty taxa were identified in pond sediments at the site and appear to represent natural accumulation; the faunal material is bracketed by radiocarbon ages of about 12,330 and 10,940 B.P. (Ferring 1995:277). Due to some evidence for the butchering of bison, the site appears to represent a possible bison kill. It is likely, however, that other animals were exploited as well; other faunal remains include deer, squirrel, lemming, muskrat, and a variety of rabbits, fishes, and birds (Ferring 1995). There is clear evidence of turtle procurement and processing at this site; further taphonomic analysis may demonstrate that other animals were exploited by Paleoindians as well (Ferring 1995:280).

In eastern North America the notion of Paleoindians as big-game hunters is even less well supported than it is on the Plains. In the past, the Paleoindian construct that was developed on the Plains was overlain in eastern North America without considering its vastly different forested, mountainous terrain (Gero 1993:38). Evidence for the human exploitation of mammoth and mastodon in the East is scarce, suggesting megafauna were hunted or scavenged as part of a larger subsistence system (Meltzer 1988:24).

For the Northeast, Dincauze (2000:38) reports that archaeological sites have "yet to yield evidence of the dramatic herd-kills that point to big game hunting." Instead Paleoindians in the Northeast were apparently "generalized foragers exploiting a wide variety of environments" (Dincauze 1993a:285). Pronounced seasonal variability during the late Pleistocene meant that food resources were less predictable in distribution and quantity than they are in modern temperate forests (Dincauze 1993a:285). Because the environment was much different from what they had experienced in the West and because of seasonal dynamism and resource unpredictability, the adaptations of Paleoindian peoples in the Northeast would necessarily have been swift and opportunistic (Dincauze 1993a:285).

One Northeast site that has been particularly important for offering alternatives to big-game-hunting models is the Shawnee Minisink site in Pennsylvania. The remains of numerous plant species, including Acalypha sp., hackberry, blackberry, hawthorn plum, grape, and Chenopodium, were found in the Paleoindian level of the site and suggest a fall occupation (Dent and Kauffman 1985). According to McNett (1985a:322), most of the resource procurement and processing centered around the plants mentioned above, as well as fish.

Detailed analyses of the stone tools from Shawnee Minisink also support the interpretation of a diverse foraging base at this site. The diversity of tool types and the edge wear and edge angles of the tools suggest that they were used for a wide variety of activities, from working on soft materials, such as fish, game, and animal skins, to working on hard materials, such as wood, bone, and antler (Marshall 1985:195). The edge angles of most of the endscrapers suggest that they were used in the manufacture of wood and bone implements (McNett 1985a). This observation is extremely important because such perishable implements rarely survive in the archaeological record. The next most common types of endscraper apparently were used for skinning, hide scraping, processing sinew and fibers, shredding, heavy bone-working, and similar activities (McNett 1985a). Paleoindian inhabitants of the Shawnee Minisink site may have been using and repairing fishing implements and perhaps were harvesting salmon; overall, it is clear that they were primarily foragers and not specialized hunters (McNett 1985a:322).

Some intriguing and creative interpretations have recently come to the fore concerning the possible importance of birds in the peopling of North America. Fiedel (2000b:5) suggests that it is possible that the first people to enter the New World sustained themselves by "netting injured or fatigued migrating birds on the shores of the proglacial lakes" (see also Schmitz, this volume). Birds would have been a reliable and easily collected food source because about 20 percent of any given population of migrating birds typically dies during migration (Fiedel 2000b). Fiedel further supports this avian model by citing Yesner's (1998) late Pleistocene data from the interior of Alaska. At the Broken Mammoth site, mammoth remains are present in the earliest portion of the site in the form of tusk sections and fragments; however, nearly 40 percent of the meat (by weight) was apparently derived from birds, such as swans, brants, geese, and ducks (Yesner 1998:208). Game species represented at this site include bison, elk, caribou, wild sheep, and a variety of small mammals, such as marmot, hare, river otter, arctic fox, and ground squirrel, as well as fish (Yesner 1998:208).

Dincauze and Jacobson (2001) propose that the first peoples to enter the Northeast may have moved east along the southern shores of the Great Lakes and then northeast along the shores of the Champlain Sea. A major attraction for this entry point into New England would have been the summer nesting birds of the Atlantic flyway, as well as fish and fur-bearing predators (Dincauze and Jacobson 2001). Although their model is not currently supported by direct evidence, it provides a nice fit with the eastern fluted-point typology and chronology, as well as the apparent movement of lithic raw materials during the Paleoindian period. Even

though both Fiedel's (2000b) and Dincauze and Jacobson's (2001) models are based largely on speculation at this point, it is apparent that the authors' intentions are to stimulate research on subsistence practices and colonization models for northeastern Paleoindians.

An Old World precedent exists for the netting of birds. Recent research on microscopic fiber impressions on clay fragments dated between 29,000 and 22,000 B.P. suggests the use of nets by Gravettian peoples from Spain to southern Russia (Pringle 1997a:1203; see also Soffer et al. 1998). It is therefore not far-fetched to suggest that these and other fiber technologies were available to the people who first colonized the New World. Paleoindians likely used nets to capture birds, rabbits, foxes, and other animals. The identification of the use of nets offers an alternative to what are typically spear-centric and adult-male-centric views of hunting: "Net hunting is communal and it involves the labor of children and women" (Olga Soffer quoted in Pringle 1997a:1203; Soffer et al. 1998; see also Hewlett 1992 for an example of the involvement of women and children in net hunting among the Aka).

Are Sex Roles Carved in Stone?

Paleoindians participated in subsistence activities that included, but were not restricted to, the hunting of game, both large and small. The presence of high-quality flaked-stone spear points in Paleoindian sites provides evidence for the hunting of game with spears. The common assumption is that hunting was undertaken predominantly by men. There is a long history to this assumption in the United States. A particularly striking example comes from the Archaic Indian Knoll site, where researchers insisted that it was unlikely that women hunted with spears, despite the fact that many of the female burials from that site contained spear-thrower weights (Webb 1946; Winters 1968; see also discussion in Doucette 2003).

Many archaeologists apparently believe there was a fairly strict sexual division of labor among Paleoindians, as well as other hunter-gatherers. In modeling the peopling of North America, for example, Surovell (2000:497) assumes what he calls a "classic" division of labor: "[M]en hunt, women gather." Although most researchers refer to "hunters" instead of "men" in their discussions of Paleoindians, most archaeologists apparently consider the words to be synonymous. For example, in one of the few published reports on Paleoindian sites in the Northeast, Gramly (1982:65) writes, "For young hunters the thrill of the hunt left them wandering, full of emotion. The older men, however, immediately set about preparing carcasses for transport. . . . Two men were required to skid a caribou as far as the edge of the river, where they were cleverly trussed up enabling them to be floated to the other shore."

Even in my own discussion of Paleoindian division of labor (Chilton 1994), I did not question the assumptions that it was primarily men who hunted and took part in special tasks away from the home base, and that women's activities were centered around the "domestic" site. The division of labor is often treated by archaeologists as if it were a given (Nelson 1997:85). Rather than assuming (or imposing) a so-called classic division of labor, archaeologists should view the distribution of social roles by gender as "a problem worthy of exploration in its own right" (Bird 1993:22).

Ethnographic and ethnohistoric data from the last few hundred years suggest that much of the "maintenance work" in any given society *is* done by women: preparing food, cleaning, making or repairing clothing, caring for children, etc. (Nelson 1997:87). Does this mean, however, that sex roles are carved in stone? In communities that existed before the advent of agriculture, the division of labor was probably less strict than it was in relatively recent societies, for which we have written records or ethnographic data (Claassen 1997:82–83).

The !Kung of south-central Africa are commonly used as an example of quintessential hunter-gatherers. Certainly the environment encountered by Paleoindians differed greatly from the Kalahari environment inhabited by the !Kung. Nevertheless, the !Kung provide a detailed example of a relatively egalitarian group of hunter-gatherers with a small group size and high mobility. Such organizational characteristics may crosscut environmental parameters. In the 1970s, the !Kung demonstrated a lack of rigidity in sex typing many adult activities, including domestic chores and some aspects of child rearing, at least for children who were older than nine or ten months (Draper 1975). Both hunting and gathering kept adults away from camp for up to several days each week (Draper 1975:85). For the !Kung, "a number of factors appear to be working directly and indirectly to insure high autonomy of females and immunity of females to subordination by males" (Draper 1975:105). Draper's (1975) comparison of !Kung groups in the "bush setting" to more sedentary groups demonstrated that sexual egalitarianism is undermined by increasing sedentism. According to Kent (1998:54), "When sociopolitical differentiation begins

to emerge, as with the presence of an informal leader, other realms of culture, including gender, also become differentiated."

For highly egalitarian societies, "the division of labor is extremely flexible and little emphasis is placed on the difference between males and females" (Kent 1999:38). For the central Kalahari G/wi and G//ana, for example, even though hunting is typically referred to as "men's work" and gathering is referred to as "women's work," men and women routinely perform both tasks (Kent 1999:39). It is important to think about not only how various gendered and nongendered tasks may have interdigitated, but also how they may have shifted under particular circumstances (Nelson 1997:88).

Evidence for Women Hunting

Women are often assumed not to have been involved in hunting because of the constraints of motherhood. As Nelson (1997:87) points out, however, not all women become mothers, child care is not necessarily restricted to women, and infant care is not necessarily the sole responsibility of the biological mother. In fact, in many societies child care is a collective activity. Although there are obvious physical limitations during pregnancy, not all women in any given population are of reproductive age. For example, prepubescent and older women may have differentially participated in hunting activities. Ethnographic sources even refer to young mothers riding horses, swimming, and hunting *while carrying their babies* (Maranda 1974; McKell 1993; Turnbull 1981; for a full discussion and further references, see Hudecek-Cuffe 1998:21).

Based on their long-term historical, ethnographic, and archaeological study in northwestern Saskatchewan, Brumbach and Jarvenpa (1997:32) report Chipewyan women hunting without being constrained by motherhood. Their study suggests that prior to European contact, Chipewyan women bore relatively few children and were integrated into the full range of hunting activities (Brumbach and Jarvenpa 1997:32). Women's participation in hunting activities varied with age; young women and adolescents were particularly active (Brumbach and Jarvenpa 1997). As women took on more family responsibilities, they were less likely to take part in distant hunting activities, but they became more involved in hunting closer to home using snares and nets. In later years women often resumed their more distant hunting activities (Brumbach and Jarvenpa 1997).

Wadley's (1998) review of modern ethnographic literature from around the globe (particularly Africa) suggests that, although men generally handle weapons, women are not excluded from playing an active role in the hunt and in the quest for meat in general. Ethnographic reports concerning Aboriginal Australian women indicate that they often hunted small game, but also occasionally hunted kangaroos and participated in communal hunts (see discussion in Bird 1993).

This short review of the ethnographic literature suggests that the role of women in hunting varies greatly from one society to the next, but that women are not usually excluded from hunting. Women should also not be excluded from our models of prehistoric hunting without evidence to support such a conclusion.

Stone Tools Are Forever

Because of the generally poor preservation of organic remains, Paleoindian archaeological sites contain mostly stone artifacts. The traditional emphasis on hunting is thus both a cause and effect of the fixation on fluted points. An overemphasis on stone tools leads to other sources of bias because stone tools are thought to have been mainly manufactured and used by men (Gero 1991a; Nelson 1997:91). As Nelson (1997:91) puts it, "Stone tools above all are regarded as a masculine invention, and stone knapping is presumed to be a male occupation, even when no gender attribution is made." An overemphasis on hunting and stone tools in Paleoindian research parallels the notion in human evolution that "all human progress was due to men hunting animals with tools they themselves had made" (Bruhns and Stothert 1999:28). Because it is often presumed that only males hunted and that hunting separates humans from other primates, "we are forced to conclude that females are scarcely human" (Kephart 1970:5, quoted in Slocum 1975:38).

Gero (1991b:176) states that there is no compelling reason to argue against women making and using all kinds of stone tools. To elucidate the bare minimum of women's participation in stone tool production, Gero proposes that we examine the following: (1) evidence of lithic manufacture and use at habitation sites (since both male and female activities are certainly represented at such sites); (2) the use of local lithic raw materials (to avoid arguments about whether women would stray far from base camp); and (3) the manufacture and use of expedient flake tools (including "utilized flakes") because they comprise most of the tools in the archaeological record, allowing us to "see women" more certainly.

Women must have produced at least some of the stone tools found at archaeological sites, and they certainly were responsible for some of the utilized flakes (Gero 1991b). Schultz (1992:345) observes that scraping a bison hide with an endscraper (which is often assumed to have been women's work) would require one hundred or more resharpening episodes. It seems unreasonable to assume that a woman would have waited for a man to resharpen a stone tool during such a task or to provide the needed tools in the first place, "like a 1950s girl waiting for her date to open the car door" (Nelson 1997:94).

Ethnographic evidence for women as stone-tool makers is not difficult to find (Nelson 1997:92). There are numerous ethnographic and historical references to women making and using both stone and perishable tools in Aboriginal Australia and New Guinea: digging and fighting sticks, flake scrapers, stone knives, stone hatchets, and stone-tipped spears (Bird 1993). More importantly, Bird's (1993) review of the ethnographic literature demonstrates considerable variability in gender relationships and the organization of labor. In some societies, the ax is a vital part of a woman's tool kit and is made by women for their own use. In other communities, men were the makers and owners of stone axes, although women might borrow them and use them as much as or even more than men.

Although some egalitarian societies show little task differentiation by gender, the roles and activities of women and men in these societies were not necessarily undifferentiated. As Sassaman (1992:250) points out, "[I]f we allow that women and men alike used stone tools, we should anticipate that any differences in the productive activities of men and women involving stone tools would contribute to technological variation in the material records of those activities." Such variations might include spatial patterning, distribution of raw materials, discard behavior, work schedules, and scale of production (Sassaman 1992:250). Task differentiation and spatial patterning will serve as important areas of inquiry for future research on Paleoindians (see below). Rather than making assumptions about the role of women in stone-tool manufacture and use, researchers should make the gendered division of labor in any society an explicit area of inquiry.

Bias of the Researchers

As in all archaeological interpretation, one of the most difficult sources of bias to assess in Paleoindian research is that which is introduced by the researchers themselves. To what degree have the agendas, experiences, and interests of archaeologists affected the state of our knowledge about Paleoindians? (see Clark, this volume; Mandryk, this volume)

More men are interested in the earlier part of human prehistory than are women. According to Zeder's (1997:125) analysis of the Society for American Archaeology (SAA) census data, a higher percentage of men are interested in earlier time periods (listed as Paleolithic and Neolithic), whereas a higher proportion of women list their primary research interest as state societies and historical and protohistorical time periods. Similarly, and true to the stereotype, a higher percentage of men are interested in lithics as an analytical tool, whereas a higher percentage of women are interested in ceramics.

Gero (1991b) points out that flint knapping is viewed as a male arena, especially in replicative studies. She notes that a vast majority of such studies are undertaken by men, thus producing a cognitive association between men and flaked stone tools, particularly projectile points. According to Gero (1991b:167), "If male archaeologists are replicating anachronistic stone technologies for purposes other than reiterating an elemental association of males with stone tool projection and use, their reenactments nevertheless project and keep alive as male, the reduction of nature through stone."

Has a sexual division of labor in Paleoindian research produced a "sexual division of knowledge" (Gero 1993:38)? Gero (1993) reported that seventeen of the eighteen major Paleoindian books published between 1965 and 1990 were authored or edited by males or pairs of males. Of the articles contained in the nine edited volumes, only 10 percent were written by women. Likewise, of the papers on Paleoindians that were read at the SAA and regional Plains Anthropology meetings, only 11 percent were presented by women (Gero 1993:33).

Has this gender distribution changed in the last decade? Yes, to some degree. My review of edited and single authored volumes of Paleoindian research published between 1991 and 2000 indicates that approximately 18 percent of the authors were women (in some cases the author's gender was not clear to me from the first name). Of the SAA papers read at organized sessions on Paleoindians from 1990 to 1999, roughly 20 percent were presented by women. Whether this is because Paleoindian research attracts fewer women or because the organizers are usually male (about 71 percent, which could produce inadvertent bias in invitations), the result is the same. These statistics take on addi-

tional significance when compared to the percentage of women in American archaeology as a whole. Zeder's (1997) study reported that 51 percent of the students and 36 percent of the professionals who contributed to the SAA survey were women. Thus, women are not contributing to Paleoindian archaeology proportionally, which undoubtedly affects the kind of research that is undertaken and its methodologies and results.

Turtles, Grapes, and Babies: It's the Little Things That Count

One of the reasons that Paleoindian research has not attracted the interest of a higher proportion of women may be that it has historically focused on the activities of men or on what are often perceived as male activities. Obviously, this becomes a vicious cycle because the lack of women in Paleoindian research partially accounts for the lack of serious attention given to women, children, and other areas of inquiry.

So where should we turn to develop more complex and realistic interpretations of Paleoindians? First, as I discussed earlier, archaeologists need to look beyond an emphasis on hunting to broader understandings of the larger subsistence and settlement systems of the late Pleistocene. To some degree, finding sites where evidence of plant remains have been preserved is simply a matter of taphonomic luck (e.g., deposits at the Shawnee Minisink site were buried in deep alluvium). As Dincauze (1993a:284) suggests, finds such as this may indicate where we should look for similar evidence. Certainly careful searching and innovations in our techniques for finding perishable food remains and artifacts will go a long way toward fleshing out our models of Paleoindians. For example, sandal and cordage fragments found on the California coast indicate a basketry tradition that was previously unknown. These artifacts enhance our understanding of a "richer and more elaborate" material culture for these early Holocene (9900–8600 cal B.P.) peoples (Connolly et al. 1995:316). Blood residue analysis may provide much information on the types of animals exploited by Paleoindian peoples (Morlan 1991:305); phytolith analysis may provide the same information on plants (Kealhofer 1999).

Second, environmental reconstruction is an important avenue of research for understanding the contexts of social choices made by Paleoindians. There are no appropriate modern analogues for the environments and lifestyles of Paleoindian times (Dincauze

1993a; Kelly and Todd 1988:231; Meltzer, this volume; but see also MacDonald, this volume). Attention to environmental parameters will therefore be even more important. As previously discussed, adaptations necessarily took place rapidly and opportunistically, especially when Paleoindians moved between environmental zones (Dincauze 1993a:281; Meltzer, this volume). The mutable nature of the late Pleistocene environment would have required enormous flexibility in the peoples of North America. We are only beginning to understand their resourcefulness and creativity. The recent hypotheses proffered by Fiedel (2000b) and Dincauze and Jacobson (2001) on Paleoindian exploitation of birds will provide creative avenues of inquiry on paleoenvironments, especially if, as Bryan (1991:28) suggests, the southern shore of Beringia and the northwestern coast of North America provide the most reasonable route of entry for the peopling of the New World (see also Gruhn 1988).

Demographic Models and Reproduction

As Paleoindians moved into a landscape previously uninhabited by humans, population size and growth would have been critical factors in their survival (MacDonald, this volume; Meltzer, this volume). Because they did not necessarily have the luxury of "turning to their neighbors" (Kelly and Todd 1988:231), the well-being of both women and children would have been essential for the survival of the population and would have provided important parameters in decisions about habitation duration, division of labor, and the exploitation of resources (Chilton 1994:12).

Reproductive aspects of women's lives in prehistoric times have largely been ignored (Bentley 1996). Reproduction and fertility, however, have important implications for (1) sexual division of labor, and (2) family size, which in turn affects household structure, architectural design, and social organization (Bentley 1996: 24).

Surovell's (2000) recent article, "Early Paleoindian Women, Children, Mobility, and Fertility," provides a refreshing look at women's fertility as it affected the peopling of the New World. Although it is encouraging to see an emphasis placed on the health and activities of paleowomen, this article also demonstrates some of the potential pitfalls in modeling women's fertility and reproduction. Surovell's proximate goal is to evaluate whether high residential mobility is compatible with high fertility. Ultimately, however, his main objective is to determine if it is *possible* that Paleoindians populated

North America within a seven-hundred-year period as, he believes, the archaeological record indicates (ca. 11,500–10,800 B.P.). Surovell necessarily makes a series of assumptions about the Paleoindian population before testing his mathematical model. First, he assumes that in terms of reproduction, the goal of Paleoindians was to maximize reproductive potential. Second, he assumes a "classic division of labor . . . men hunt, and women gather" (Surovell 2000:497). As a corollary to this second assumption, he posits that "males never bring young children on hunting forays, but females must always carry young children the roundtrip distance on foraging trips" (Surovell 2000: 497). Third, the model predicts that for any "homogenous environment," people can maximize their reproductive output by moving residential camps frequently, thus minimizing child-related transport costs.

Using the extant demographic literature for hunter-gatherers, Surovell (2000:497) concludes that high mobility (defined as frequent movements of residential camps) is *not* incompatible with high fertility, given the assumptions listed above. But how realistic are these assumptions, and what does the evaluation of this model really tell us?

The first assumption, that Paleoindians wanted to maximize reproductive potential (as measured by fertility), is not well supported. Although a certain level of fertility is important for the survival of a population, infant survival is actually far more important than female fertility for determining population growth, and thus, reproductive success (Jones 2000). Using a diverse sample of human populations, Jones (2000) constructed age-specific population models and calculated fitness sensitivities. He concluded that (1) fitness is always most sensitive to improvements in the survival of young children, and (2) the contribution of fertility to fitness is always less than that of infant survival. Of course, female health and fertility is very important in general, but future demographic models of the peopling of North America should consider the effects of mobility, diet, and general lifestyle on the survival of young children, as well as the welfare of the rest of the population.

I have already discussed at length the problem with assuming a so-called classic division of labor, which is Surovell's second assumption. We can not assume that only men hunted or that only women gathered, nor can we assume that only women of child-bearing age carried children. Surovell's third assumption—that the environment in North America was homogeneous during the late Pleistocene—is also problematic. The environment was apparently patchy and, at times, unpredictable. Demographic models must be based on environmental data at a regional, not continental, scale.

Certainly, even *thinking* about the fertility of women and the survival of infants is a significant improvement in models of Paleoindians. Questions such as "How long did it take populations in North America to reach a certain density?" and "What were the logistics of colonization?" force us to think about decisions and constraints within a human lifetime. For example, several years ago Dincauze (1993a,b) proposed a colonization model for the Northeast that prompted a dialogue about the logistics of the peopling of the region. She proposed that "[m]oving along the rivers, exploring resources, and learning to hunt in the forest . . . [Paleoindians] might have extended their frontiers only on a generational basis as population grew" (Dincauze 1993a:288; see also MacDonald, this volume). For the first time, regional archaeologists are discussing the colonization of New England within human terms. What would one of these initial staging camps or exploratory camps look like? What part of the population would move into a new area first, and how long would it be before more people would join them? How would the various camps communicate with one another and across what distances? Ultimately a thorough consideration of the complex and multifaceted demography of Paleoindians will lead to more humanized interpretations of these first peoples.

Spatial Patterning: Can We "Find" Women?

In 1994 I suggested that the recognition and interpretation of activity areas and spatial patterns would ultimately contribute the most toward determining the social dimensions (including gender) of Paleoindian sites (Chilton 1994). I also suggested, however, that women and children would more often participate in domestic-site-centered activities, whereas men would more often participate in procurement activities, which would have included long-distance travel. Of course, I fell into my own trap by describing an idealized 1950s sexual division of labor.

I still believe, however, that the analysis of site plans has much to contribute. Yellen (1977) suggests that to understand the relationship between an activity and where it occurred within a site, one must distinguish between the areas that were used in common and those that were used by a single family group. Next he suggests "drawing a line" between family areas and areas that were used for special tasks.

Jarvenpa and Brumbach (1998) present a clear model of spatial patterning for a fairly mobile group of foragers in the Canadian subarctic: the Chipewyan. Their research demonstrates that in the early twentieth century, Chipewyan women and men participated in hunting, fishing, trapping, and snaring. Winter hunting camps were the loci of processing tasks, such as preparing hides, drying meat, and producing grease. These camps were composed of nuclear families, older husband-wife pairs, or, less frequently, all-male teams. Even though the camps were inhabited for one to two weeks, Jarvenpa and Brumbach (1998) suggest that, archaeologically, these sites would *not* be highly visible.

Winter "staging" sites, on the other hand, consisted of communities of several dozen people and were reoccupied seasonally for up to a decade (Jarvenpa and Brumbach 1998). These larger residential sites contained a variety of storage and special-purpose features and would be highly visible archaeologically (Jarvenpa and Brumbach 1998:109).

After the 1950s and largely due to outside influences, the Chipewyan hunting pattern shifted from predominantly bush-centered to village-centered hunts. In the latter case, animals are hunted mainly by men. The intact or only roughly butchered carcass is brought back to the village (instead of to a hunting camp, as described above), where most processing takes place. Obviously these behaviors result in fewer but larger and more heavily used archaeological sites and activity areas than does the bush-centered hunt. Jarvenpa and Brumbach (1998:110) suggest that the decision-making processes that result in either a bush-centered or village-centered hunting pattern "are affected more by cultural dimensions of gender and political economy than by factors relating to women's innate abilities."

One of the most important challenges of interpreting Paleoindian site plans is to determine whether a fairly large site is the result of an annual or biannual seasonal camp for a group of mobile foragers, or whether it served as a centralized settlement for a larger, semisedentary group. Jarvenpa and Brumbach's (1998:112) research indicates that the presence of specialized features or activity areas denotes the latter: Central-based settlement patterns are "accompanied by greater investment in special-purpose, gender differentiated storage and processing features."

In order to interpret site plans, we need to evaluate the function of archaeological features, the patterning of tasks, the duration of site occupation, and the relationship among contemporaneous sites in the region. For example, do all sites look pretty much the same in terms of spatial patterning and site function, or is there a hierarchy of site sizes and types? Ultimately the only way we can begin to understand the sexual division of labor or the gender relations of Paleoindians is to determine whether they were highly egalitarian, somewhat egalitarian, or not at all egalitarian peoples. Although there are no contemporary environmental analogues for the late Pleistocene in North America, there may be compelling social analogues if we look at cross-cultural comparisons of egalitarian societies. We should not, however, assume that all Paleoindians were the same; we should not expect the same social analogue to apply equally well across environmental, temporal, and social boundaries. A series of social models are required that are built upon fine-grained analyses and interpretations of site plans, feature patterning, and site hierarchies at a regional level.

If we have any hope of understanding even some of the gendered aspects of Paleoindian society, our research will require more than just "'finding' men and women" (Conkey and Gero 1991:14). We must move away from simply assigning a sex to various items and tasks and focus on the more dynamic aspects of gender relations and decision making (Hudecek-Cuffe 1998:28).

The Bottom Line and the Feminist Critique

> If we include gender in the models, we may begin to account for variation that cannot be fully explained by tool function, raw material constraint, or group mobility. (Sassaman 1992:259)

As I have tried to demonstrate, what is needed in Paleoindian research is more attention to the social parameters of life during the late Pleistocene. Because of the highly variable resources of late Pleistocene environments, Paleoindian groups undoubtedly relied on information shared with other groups (Hudecek-Cuffe 1998:92). The sharing of information would have been an integral part of mating networks, trade and exchange, and social alliances (Hudecek-Cuffe 1998:92; MacDonald, this volume). Communication and informa-

tion exchange are characteristics of all human groups. But in the uncharted social and environmental world of Paleoindians, these factors would have been absolutely critical to survival (Hudecek-Cuffe 1998; Meltzer, this volume).

The ultimate goal is "the recognition . . . of a social and engendered life for Paleoindians" in a world that includes both mega- and microfauna, and with a broad range of material culture that includes more than fluted points (Gero 1993:39). The contribution of the feminist critique to this goal is that it demonstrates that women's domestic and reproductive roles in societies are not naturally given (Moore 1988:53). It also demonstrates that male behavior is often taken as the norm against which "all success and deviance are measured" (Gero 1991a:97).

In response to these critiques, assumptions about the sexual division of labor and gender as a central organizing principle should be made explicit in our research designs, methodologies, and interpretations of Paleoindian societies. As Joyce and Claassen (1997:5) suggest about the papers in their *Women in Prehistory* volume, an examination of women and gender improves our reconstruction of prehistory by prompting us to approach "conventional data sets with more complex, and therefore more realistic, models of social differentiation." When we can imagine a life of smoky campfires, turtle soup, wild grapes, crying babies, dreams of the hunt, and a variety of social tensions and diversions, we have made one small step toward understanding the lives of Paleoindians.

Acknowledgments

I wish to thank Michael Barton and Geoff Clark for inviting me to contribute to this volume. Dena Dincauze inspired me to undertake this topic for a paper written in 1989 and published in a much more primitive form in 1994. Ivy Owens (Research Assistant, Harvard University) collected much of the data on the proportion of women participating in Paleoindian publications and conference papers, and she provided assistance with bibliographic databases. I am thankful to Jamie Jones for very helpful conversations about fertility and fitness. A special thanks to Michael Sugerman, who provided much needed brainstorming sessions and editorial assistance. Any flaws in this paper are solely my responsibility.

14 Early Paleoindians as Estate Settlers

ARCHAEOLOGICAL, ETHNOGRAPHIC, AND EVOLUTIONARY INSIGHTS
INTO THE PEOPLING OF THE NEW WORLD

Douglas H. MacDonald

The methodology of this and other recent papers (MacDonald 1998, 1999; Surovell 2000) supports the contention that we can learn a great deal about early Paleoindian behavior through the study of contemporary foragers and evolutionary theory. This position stands in contrast to that of several other researchers, who have legitimately questioned the validity of ethnographic analogy in the study of early Paleoindians (Amick 1996; Hofman 1994; Tankersley 1998c). These authors suggest that modern foragers are radically different from early Paleoindians because the latter adapted to a world unlike any that humans had encountered before or since (Kelly and Todd 1988; Tankersley 1998c). Early Paleoindians, because of their migration into uninhabited lands, experienced new choices, new environmental mosaics, and new regions in which to hunt and gather (Elias 1997:124; Pielou 1991).

Some researchers posit that, because of the unique colonizing situation of early Paleoindians, no modern group can serve as a model for them (Kelly and Todd 1988:239; Tankersley 1998c:12). Many archaeologists suggest that "we cannot, then, look to Inuit or San hunter-gatherers to theorize on Paleoindian adaptation" (Ingbar 1992:188; but see Fiedel, this volume), or that "to simply accommodate the interpretation of archaeological remains to contemporary hunter-gatherer situations will not inform us about the past" (Hofman 1994:361).

As I have stated elsewhere (MacDonald 1998), there is no direct ethnographic analogy for early Paleoindians. Caution should be exercised when using any cross-cultural analyses in the study of prehistoric populations (Gould 1978; Kelly 1995; Shott 1992). However, the observation of cross-cultural behavioral patterns among foragers can provide data by which we can make reasonable predictions about early Paleoindian behavior as reflected in the various artifacts of the archaeological record. By identifying common behaviors of contemporary foragers, we may infer aspects of prehistoric hunter-gatherer lifeways (Burch 1994; Schiffer 1996). This paper identifies cross-cultural patterns of mobility and settlement that can be applied to a better understanding of early Paleoindian colonization of the Americas.

Cross-Cultural Patterns of Forager Mobility and Settlement

In another paper (MacDonald and Hewlett 1999), Barry Hewlett and I provide an extensive review of forager travel patterns and determine some aspects of forager travel that are likely to be cross-cultural universals. This research suggests that foragers generally organize their movements into three or four levels. Binford (1983:34–42), for example, discusses four levels of Nunamiut mobility: (1) foraging radius, (2) annual range, (3) extended range, and (4) lifetime range. The foraging radius includes the area used during daily subsistence, whereas the annual range is the region used during a year for logistical (subsistence) and residential purposes. The extended range is a "no-man's land," which is used as a resource supply by new groups or by groups extending their annual ranges. The lifetime range is the region "over which they can expect to live during their lifetime" (Binford 1983:39).

Sampson's (1988) concentric zone model also includes four major zones of movement: (1) core range (daily subsistence), (2) annual range (annual subsistence territory), (3) lifetime range (farthest distance traveled in a lifetime), and (4) gift recycling zone (beyond the individual travel realm but infiltrated by down-the-line trading). In Sampson's model, as in Binford's, movement between zones is regulated by responses to resource availability.

Not only do these patterns in travel zones emerge, but population density and size are generally also patterned into such zones. Wobst (1974:173) proposes that Paleolithic hunter-gatherers used "three cultural units of predictable and consistent membership": (1) the maximum band (175–475 people), (2) the minimum band (25 people), and (3) the nuclear family. Within these cultural units, the numbers of 25 and 175–475 are sometimes referred to as "magic numbers" (Wobst 1974:170). The minimum band size of 25 is ideal because it is large enough to maintain reliable cultural transmission between generations. In addition, "there have to be enough members to effectively carry out the daily activities required for the group's survival . . . through mutual food sharing and cooperation" (Wobst 1974:172). The minimum band size is thus regulated by subsistence concerns. The size is also perfect because it is large enough to survive fluctuations in the life histories of individuals, reflecting the important role of reproductive interests. In the maximum band, the group size is a function of two factors: the number of individuals needed for an effective mating pool (Wobst 1974:166–167) and the geographic packing of those bands within a given region.

Mandryk's (1993) model expands upon this concept, suggesting that resource availability controls population density (Birdsell 1953), which, in turn, controls range size (Mandryk 1993:46–47). Thus, the extent of mobility for both reproductive and subsistence concerns is a by-product of environmental productivity. The strong relationship between mating distance and population density, which is presented elsewhere (MacDonald and Hewlett 1999), is consistent with these models of Upper Paleolithic population (Birdsell 1953; Whallon 1989; Wobst 1974; Yengoyan 1968): Magic numbers mirror what it takes to maintain a population. In other words, even forager societies with the lowest population densities incorporate similar numbers of people into their social realm simply by increasing the size of their territories. The lower the population density, the greater the mean mating and socializing range in any given population.

Generally these models, as well as data collected for another study (MacDonald and Hewlett 1999), support the contention that there are three levels of movement among foragers. The first level of the model is called "micromovement" and refers to individual and group mobility for subsistence rounds. This level corresponds to the foraging radius in Binford's model, the nuclear family and minimum band in Wobst's model, and the core and annual ranges in Sampson's model.

The second level of mobility is called "mesomovement" and refers to intermediate distances to visit friends and relatives (often in-laws for males and families of origin for females). Clans with long histories of reciprocal marriage exchange are often found at this intermediate distance. The mean mating distance of a population is likely to fall within this range. Long-term marriage links are the primary feature of this scale of mobility, but in difficult times (e.g., a shortage of resources and social conflicts), families may undertake mesomovements and remain there for long periods. Mesomovement is also likely to represent the mean limit of social knowledge, that is, the mean total number of people one gets to know and learn from during one's lifetime. It is a close approximation to the annual range in Binford's and Sampson's models and the maximum band in Wobst's model.

The final level is called "macromovement" and refers to mobility to explore "exotic" sites for potential or especially scarce resources (Meltzer, this volume), be they reproductive or somatic. This exploratory travel involves more risks, so not everyone participates; however, the benefits are potentially great, especially if things are difficult in the other two mobility ranges. Males with few kin resources or males or females with unusual backgrounds (e.g., problems with sorcery) are likely to travel these long distances. Individuals may explicitly look for mates or find mates along the way. Men will be more likely than women to make these trips, but overall travel to these long-distance sites will likely be infrequent, unless the individual or group decides that the potential resources are better than the existing resources. Macromovement is similar to the extended and lifetime ranges in Binford's model and the lifetime range in Sampson's model.

Cultural Homogeneity and Population Stability

A key point of this three-tier mobility model is that population density, which is affected by a host of environmental factors (Birdsell 1953; Mandryk 1993), controls the intergroup variation in travel distance within each level: the lower the population density, the larger the micromovements, mesomovements, and macromovements. If we accept this logic, we can assume that early Paleoindians, with population densities as low as 0.02–0.05 persons per square kilometer, possessed large territories that likely incorporated hundreds of thousands of square kilometers (Amick 1996:415).

One means to assess the extent of social connectivity between widespread populations is by tracking the distribution of artifacts, or cultural phenotypes, across the landscape. One of the most common phenotypes of the early Paleoindian period in North America is the fluted spear point. Although highly variable in terms of specific reduction strategies, fluted point technologies existed across North America (Tankersley, this volume). Such a wide distribution of common cultural phenotypes suggests interregional contact and transfer of technological and socioreligious ideals between widespread cultural groups (Hayden 1982:115; Kelly and Todd 1988:235; MacDonald 1998; Storck 1991:158–159).

This transfer of what some have called a more than utilitarian projectile technology (see Bradley 1993:255) indicates cultural transmission of knowledge from elders to the young over dozens of generations and across large geographical tracts. The cultural connections of the population, as reflected in tool kits, show a stable population that used established territories rather than frequent large-scale travel to unknown locales.

In support of these statements, archaeological data suggest that in regions of tool-stone abundance, early Paleoindians emphasized the use of local lithic raw materials in tool production (MacDonald 1999; Meltzer 1989; Tankersley 1998c). The majority of early Paleoindians thus used micromovements and mesomovements rather than large-scale macromovements. Although macromovements occurred, as shown in the widespread distribution of common artifacts, such large-scale travel was rare, as exemplified by the minority of nonlocal lithic raw materials at most early Paleoindian archaeological sites in tool-stone-rich landscapes (MacDonald 1999; Tankersley, this volume). The risks and costs of macromovement were likely too great to be popular among Paleoindians, except in cases of resource scarcity, such as the lack of good-quality tool stone in some areas of the North American Plains (Hofman 1991:350; Hofman et al. 1990:248).

Discussion

As discussed here and elsewhere (MacDonald 1999; MacDonald and Hewlett 1999; Surovell 2000), contemporary foragers use predictable patterns of social and territorial organization. This predictability derives principally from the inherent human need to optimize somatic and reproductive success. In these cases, ethnographic analogy is useful in understanding early Paleoindian behavior. Several recent studies propose that some early Paleoindian migrations failed because of low population density and the demise of social cohesiveness with neighboring groups (Rogers and Rogers 1987). This scenario is essentially the "transient explorer" model of early Paleoindian colonization (Beaton 1991:215–216; Meltzer 1995:28), in which individuals

moved frequently and without regard for territorial boundaries or social ties. As Beaton (1991:215) writes, "[S]uch a strategy . . . implies very low social connectivity [and] very high inbreeding coefficients."

In consort with the ethnographic and archaeological data presented here and elsewhere (MacDonald 1999; MacDonald and Hewlett 1999), evolutionary theory indicates that the transient explorer model is simply too costly and risky to have been viable for early Paleoindians. Ethnography supports this conclusion: No known ethnographic precedent exists for this type of forager settlement, nor has any known forager group ever incorporated inbreeding into its reproductive system, regardless of the population density. Incest taboos are a cross-cultural phenomenon and thus are a human universal with origins explained by evolutionary theory (Durham 1991; MacDonald 1997; Thornhill 1990). This paper argues that it is extremely unlikely that early Paleoindians would have abandoned such a fundamental principle of human behavior to explore new lands and discover new territory.

Rather than transiently exploring, early Paleoindians likely founded the Americas in a much more gradual process; recent archaeological data suggest that North and South America were settled by pre-Clovis foragers before 12,000 B.P. (Dillehay 1997b; Meltzer et al. 1997). The model presented here is essentially the "estate settler" model, as originally defined by Beaton (1991:215–216). In this model, trade and cross-cultural linkage not only occurred, but also were a means to legitimize ties between highly mobile regional bands (see Wiessner 1982). Rather than transiently exploring, groups of individuals traveled mostly locally and settled on the edges of already colonized lands. In doing so, individuals maintained reproductive and social ties with larger groups from their previous territory. In this model, exogamy, a common trait of all foragers (Thornhill 1990:113), is the main mode of marriage and reproduction. The widespread distribution of common early Paleoindian cultural phenotypes confirms the high degree of social connectivity between the widely distributed groups.

Conclusions

Because of the high rates of inbreeding inherent in the model, transient exploring is clearly not an optimal settlement pattern and has not occurred among any known foraging culture. In contrast, estate settling has low risk and high benefits for social, somatic, and reproductive needs (Kaplan and Hill 1992). In terms of life history dynamics (Cashdan 1983; Hill and Hurtado 1996), the estate settler model is clearly the most beneficial and logical for maximizing the individual fitness of early Paleoindians. Most early Americans likely lived in one territory for their entire lives, with small families and bands occasionally establishing new homes on the fringes of known hunting and gathering lands. It is altogether possible that this pioneering population knew little of their achievement because the pace of colonization was imperceptibly slow and multigenerational. Nevertheless, it was in those rare fringe colonies that people founded the New World, pushing early Americans from Siberia to Chile over a several-thousand-year period.

15 Late Pleistocene Extinctions through Second-Order Predation
Elin Whitney-Smith

Scholars have tried to explain the migration of *Homo sapiens* into the New World, the spread of Clovis culture across the New World, and the subsequent collapse of that culture into isolated and retrograde pockets. They have worked against the backdrop of evidence of late Pleistocene extinctions and the two major theories—climate change and overkill—that have been proposed to account for that evidence. Neither of these extinction theories has been useful in explaining migration or the Clovis phenomenon. The migration picture has also been made more complex as scholars endeavor to incorporate the pre-Clovis finds into a more general explanation (e.g., see Fiedel, Meltzer, and Pearson, this volume).

A new hypothesis on late Pleistocene extinctions, second-order predation, suggests that other factors drove population circulation patterns in the New World. This hypothesis may also explain the rise and fall of Clovis culture and may indicate new ways of thinking about migration. Recently validated through a system dynamics model, second-order predation is consistent with a wide range of archaeological, biological, and ecological evidence (Whitney-Smith 2001). This chapter presents this new hypothesis in the context of the climate change and overkill theories and briefly considers its implications for Clovis culture and the peopling of the Americas.

Current Theories of Extinction

One school of thought points to climate change as the culprit in Pleistocene extinctions. Over time, the climate change theory has encompassed much more than just a change in annual temperature. It has been expanded to include changes in precipitation and continentality (Axelrod 1967; Bryson et. al 1970; Graham and Lundelius 1984; King and Saunders 1984; Slaughter 1967), changes in growing season length (Hoppe 1978), and changes in vegetation from "plaid" to "striped" environments (Guthrie 1984, 1990).

The primary shortcoming of the climate change theory is that mammoths, ground sloths, mastodons, and other animals that became extinct had survived similarly warm periods during previous interglacials. Though Holocene climate is more continental than Pleistocene climate in the New World, it is not more continental than the Pleistocene climate of Siberia, where these same animals thrived (Flerov 1967; Frenzel 1968). Also, the animals that became extinct were large and hence able to migrate if they found the growing season too short or the vegetation too scarce. Furthermore, New World horses, which became extinct at the end of the Ice Age, are thriving in the Holocene New World climate of today (Pennycuick 1979).

Another main school of thought sees overkill by *H. sapiens* as the major cause of megafaunal extinctions (Martin 1963, 1967, 1984a, 1984b, 1986). Computer models have been created to show how overkill might have led to mass extinctions (Mosimann and Martin 1975; Whittington and Dyke 1984). An important shortcoming of these two computer models is that they use a constant carrying capacity. In modeling, carrying capacity represents the number of organisms a given area can support under *steady-state* conditions. In other words, in a steady-state ecosystem, carrying capacity is used as a shorthand for food, water, space, the ability to find a mate, and other factors. However, it is possible (and indeed likely, as discussed below) that during periods of mass extinction, carrying capacity would have varied over time and varied differently for different taxa. A third computer model (Alroy 2001) avoids this particular problem by tying human recruitment to hunting. One problem that all three simulations share is that they model a particular answer rather than a problem. The answer, as stated in *Time* magazine, is this: "All people had to do was kill slightly more animals than were born" (Nash 2001:64). This is intuitively, or at least arithmetically, obvious. For a model to be useful, it should allow a comparison of competing hypotheses.

Because both the climate and the overkill theories of late Pleistocene extinctions are unsatisfactory in several respects, some investigators hold that extinction must be due to a combination of anthropogenic factors and climatic or other environmental change. However, to state this without specifying the mechanism behind the combination does not allow us to test hypotheses, nor does it allow us to evaluate one hypothesis against another.

An Alternative Model

Temperature change became an inadequate hypothesis to account for extinctions as scientists learned more about climate change. The overkill hypothesis as currently defined is also simplistic. It, too, needs to be expanded. Diamond (1984) has documented several anthropogenic causes for extinctions during the historical period. Modern man has proven versatile as an exterminator, with at least six major methods long at his disposal: overkill, habitat destruction (by logging, fire, introduced browsing and grazing animals, and draining), introduction of predators, introduction of competitors, introduction of diseases, and extinctions secondary to other extinctions. (A seventh method, chemical pollution, has recently been added to man's arsenal.) All six methods were probably effective in prehistoric extinctions as well. (Diamond 1984:839).

It seems reasonable, as suggested by Diamond, to think about extinctions as resulting from a variety of anthropogenically related factors. Many of those mentioned above work through the environment and cause a collapse of one ecosystem into another. This might account for both the extinctions and the differences between the Pleistocene-Holocene transition and previous glacial-interglacial transition periods. A closer examination of the characteristics of an extinction event may yield criteria to use in evaluating these factors.

Based on a comparison of bone marrow and tusk condition from late Pleistocene mammoth remains and modern African elephants that have starved, G. Haynes (1991, 1998) suggests that mammoths may have suffered from dietary stress. Dietary stress is also implicated as a cause of extinction by an isotopic analysis of mammoth and mastodon remains (Koch 1998). However, neither climate change nor overkill by *H. sapiens* should have directly caused conditions of food scarcity during the Pleistocene-Holocene transition. On the contrary, as herbivores were reduced in numbers due to hunting, the competition between them for food would have also been reduced. This, in turn, should have resulted in a net increase in available food. In addition,

the retreat of the ice sheet at this time should have freed up more land for vegetation. In sum, climate change and overkill should have resulted in more plants per remaining animal, not fewer.

Also suggested as evidence of food scarcity among herbivores is a greater ratio of ruminants to nonruminants in the Holocene as compared to the Pleistocene (Graham 1998; Guthrie 1984; Koch 1998). Ruminants extract energy and nutrients from their food more efficiently than do nonruminants. They therefore need less food to survive and reproduce (Guthrie 1984; Janis 1975).

Problematic evidence for each of the two major extinction models provides other clues to what might have happened during this transition. As mentioned above, a problem for the supporters of climate change is that horses can live in Holocene environments today but became extinct during the Pleistocene-Holocene transition. Because of the lack of evidence for sloth hunting, the extinction of the ground sloth presents a problem for the overkill supporters. Analysis of sloth dung suggests that, on the path to extinction, the ground sloth ate less and less globemallow, its preferred food, and more and more mormon tea, an herb generally avoided by other herbivores (Hansen 1978).

Any new hypothesis on late Pleistocene extinctions should address the following: (1) the extinction of horses in North America, (2) the extinction of the ground sloth, (3) the bias in favor of ruminants, and (4) the bias in favor of small mammal size. It also should take into account other characteristics of the Pleistocene-Holocene transition summarized in table 15.1. In addition, the alternative hypothesis should include relevant information and understandings that come from the ecological study of the interactions within and among present-day animal and plant populations and communities.

Pleistocene Extinctions Due to Second-Order Predation

A five-step second-order predation model accounts for the features considered above:

1. After the arrival of *H. sapiens* in the New World, existing predators must share the prey populations with this new predator. Due to this competition, populations of original, or first-order, predators decline. This is represented graphically in figure 15.1.
2. Second-order predation begins as humans begin to kill predators.

TABLE 15.1 Features of the Pleistocene-Holocene Transition

	Pleistocene	Holocene
Climate	Colder, less continental, higher relative humidity, ice sheets	Warmer, more continental, lower relative humidity, ice sheets melted
Vegetation	Mixed woodland-parkland, patchiness in coastal forests, more trees in the center of the country	Unbroken tree cover in the east and west, prairie-grassland in the center of the country
Animals	More genera, large animals, greater nonruminant-to-ruminant ratio	Fewer and smaller animals, a greater percentage of ruminants
Archaeology	Paleo artifacts, stylistic homogeneity, megafauna remains	Archaic artifacts, stylistic heterogeneity, no megafauna remains

3. Prey populations are no longer well controlled by predation. Killing of nonhuman predators by *H. sapiens* reduces their numbers to a point where these predators no longer regulate the size of the prey populations.

4. Lack of regulation by first-order predators triggers boom-and-bust cycles in prey populations. Prey populations expand and consequently overgraze and overbrowse the land. Soon the environment is no longer able to support them. As a result, many herbivores starve. Species that rely on the slowest recruiting food become extinct, followed by species that cannot extract the maximum benefit from every bit of their food.

5. Boom-bust cycles in herbivore populations change the nature of the vegetative environment, with consequent climatic impacts on relative humidity and continentality. Through overgrazing and overbrowsing, mixed parkland becomes grassland, and climatic continentality increases.

The decline in first order predator populations may have led to "man-eating" predators. This occurred in Africa when rinderpest, a pathogen functioning as a predator, was introduced into the wildebeest and buffalo populations. The loss of these animals to rinderpest was so severe that lion populations were deprived of a major source of food. Prior to this time, lions and humans had established a relationship of mutual avoidance. With the severe loss of their traditional prey, however, the lions turned to attacking and eating humans. This threat triggered an anti-lion response among humans. The anthropogenic death of lions contributed significantly to the reduction of their numbers (Schaller 1972; Sinclair 1979).

This scenario would have been even more likely in the Pleistocene. Because nonhuman predators in the New World did not evolve in the presence of humans, they were probably "naïve" and lacked both avoidance and defense behaviors. In addition, humans were hunters who frequently occupied the same territory as nonhuman predators. This propinquity would have allowed humans to recognize the nonhuman predators as actual or potential competitors for prey species. Because human hunters had the opportunity to learn the habits of the nonhuman predators, and because they possibly saw themselves as competing with or preyed upon by these animals, it is reasonable to assume that they eventually began killing them. Also, because humans in cold climates require some kind of clothing, it is likely that they hunted carnivores for their fur. At first, killing the competition would have relieved predatory pressure on the prey, thus allowing the herbivores to regain at least some of their numbers. The increased abundance of prey would have convinced *H. sapiens* that the nonhuman predators were competitors that kept the food supply low; therefore, humans would have continued to kill carnivores. This also accords with what we know of *H. sapiens* populations today, in which killing a top predator is associated with manliness.

Impacts on Vegetation and Climate

Under conditions of scarcity in edible plants, mixed feeders, such as mammoths and mastodons, would have been forced to eat less grass and more browse (tender twigs and leaves of trees and shrubs). They would have pushed over and destroyed many trees in their efforts to get at the tender shoots at the tops of the trees. In current ecosystems, under scarcity conditions elephants have turned mixed woodland/grassland into grassland in less than fifty years (Anderson and Walker

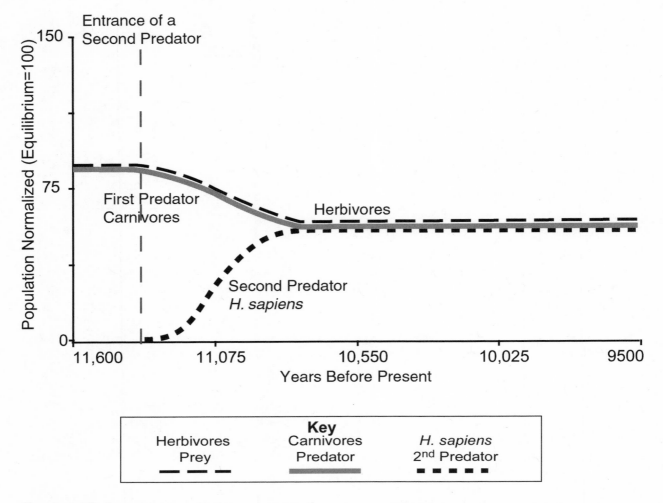

FIGURE 15.1 Effects of the arrival of a new predator on the populations of North American prey and predators.

1974; Barnes 1985; Laws 1970; Leuthold 1977; Short 1981; van Wyk and Fairfall 1969; Walker et al. 1987; Yoaciel 1981).

Loss of tree cover would have favored the grazers and selected against those animals that needed mixed food. This shift in vegetation would have put additional competitive pressure on animals that were exclusively browsers. Together the mixed feeders and browsers, by virtue of their eating habits, would have had a profound impact on trees, eventually turning mixed parkland into prairie or grassland. In a denuded environment, herbivore species that were able to survive on the newest shoots of grass would have received the most nutrition out of poor-quality forage. Within species, smaller animals that reproduce on the least amount of forage would have been selectively favored. Ultimately the

only surviving large herbivore was the bison, a ruminant grazer whose size declined significantly across the Pleistocene-Holocene transition, and which became a member of the stable Holocene prairie ecosystem.

The bust phase of the boom-and-bust cycle would have placed a premium upon efficient use of available energy, and the less efficient nonruminants would have had a lower survival potential than the more efficient ruminants. If *H. sapiens* populations experienced food stress during the time of scarcity, they probably would have strengthened their efforts to kill any remaining nonhuman predators, whom they viewed as even more serious competitors for food. In this way, humans would have unknowingly exacerbated the problems associated with the next boom phase of the cycle.

The loss of tree cover that occurred as a result of

Key

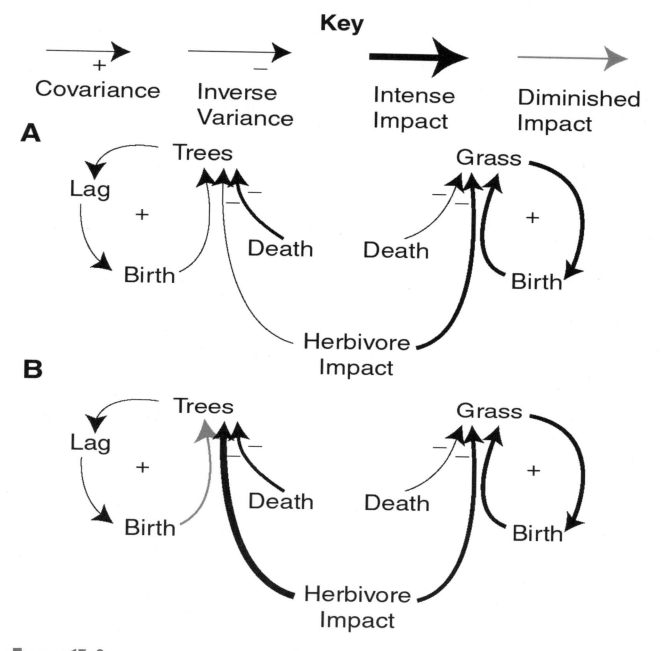

FIGURE 15.2 Roles of trees and grass in climate change: *(A)* trees and grass under normal conditions; *(B)* trees and grass under scarcity conditions.

these ecological boom-and-bust cycles also decreased atmospheric moisture, which, in turn, resulted in a more continental climate. Continentality is largely a factor of the relative aridity of the environment (Deshmukh 1986; Martin 1993). Figures 15.2A and 15.2B show the role of tree cover in this shift in climate. Figure 15.2A shows the vegetative regime under normal conditions.

Trees recruit slowly, and there is a time lag before a lost tree can replace its biomass. The death of an individual tree diminishes the amount of aggregate biomass of the community of trees, but proportionally few trees die from herbivore browsing. The obverse is true of grass. There is little loss of accumulated biomass per individual grass plant, and although many grass plants suffer from herbivore grazing, there is heavy and relatively rapid replenishment of biomass. Figure 15.2B shows that under scarcity conditions, there is an increase in herbivore impact on both trees and grass, but the impact on trees is far greater because large herbivores knock them over to get at the tops. For a small marginal increase in nutrition for the herbivores, a large number of trees are killed.

Computer Simulation of Second-Order Predation

Requirement for a Dynamic Equilibrium Model

If a model is to be a valid test of the link between one or more proposed causes of mass extinctions, model simulations in the absence of those causes must not show extinctions. (Otherwise, it is likely that we have created a simulated environment where extinctions occur willy-nilly: not a useful testing ground for explanations of extinction.) In particular, in the absence of human inmigration and climate change, the model should exhibit a steady state, in which (1) fauna and flora stocks are maintained at the same levels over time, and (2) these levels recover from small random shocks. Modelers term this recovery to a steady state a "dynamic equilibrium."

Real life is not like a laboratory, of course, and real ecosystems are seldom, if ever, in a state of equilibrium. But to isolate the relevant variables in a model of possible causes of late Pleistocene megafaunal extinction in North America, we must assume that prior to the entry of new, or second-order, predators (*H. sapiens* in this case), the plants, herbivores, and original (first-order) predators existed in a state of dynamic equilibrium.

Values Used in Simulations

Whittington and Dyke (1984) created a computer simulation to test the overkill hypothesis. In order to test the second-order predator hypothesis against the overkill hypothesis, I used the same values wherever possible. As in the Whittington and Dyke simulation, the initial population of humans entering the New World has been set to two hundred (see also Budyko 1967, 1974), with an annual growth rate of 0.0443 (see also Birdsell 1957). Additional baseline values used by Whittington and Dyke have been modified to fit the modeling paradigm here. Prey carrying capacity has been reexpressed in terms of plant biomass per square mile, and prey-

biomass replacement rate has been calculated from the following equation: birth rate − (average death rate from predation + "natural" death rate) = 0.25.

The hunting rate used in the simulation presented here is based on the amount of food needed per pound of predator per year. Data from extant predators suggests twenty pounds of food per year per pound of predator (Exotic Feline Breeding Compound, Feline Conservation Center, Rosamond, Calif., personal communication 1996; International Wolf Center 1995; Petersen 1977; Schaller 1972). It is assumed that *H. sapiens* requires half the amount of meat that an obligate predator needs. The ratio of trees to grasses is arbitrarily set at 50 percent initially to represent mosaic parkland communities in late Pleistocene North America.

Modeling Paradigm

All of the models presented in the simulation are organized in a series of sectors, each of which takes a similar form. The amount of animal stock in any sector at any given time is determined by taking the amount of stock in the sector at the previous time and multiplying it by some growth rate (as discussed above), which is modified by the dietary limits of the sector and by the death rate and the hunting or consumption rate. Birth and death rates for each type of animal are modified by the resources that are available. Thus, browsers are limited by the number of trees, times the efficiency rate for browsers. Ruminant grazers are limited by the amount of grass, times the efficiency rate for ruminant grazers. Nonruminant grazers are limited by the amount of grass, times the efficiency rate for nonruminant grazers. Carnivores and *H. sapiens* are limited by the number of herbivores.

Mixed feeder populations are controlled slightly differently because mixed feeder births are limited by the number of trees, and mixed feeder deaths are limited by the amount of grass. This formula is based on research on mixed feeders, which indicates that birth rates are dependent on the availability of nutrients from trees, whereas calories are obtained mainly from grasses. The efficiency of mixed feeders is determined by the balance of grass and trees; a deviation from the norm makes the animals less efficient, increases the death rate, and decreases the birth rate.

Grazers are divided into ruminants and nonruminants. Ruminants are assumed to be more efficient than nonruminants and have a more static recruitment rate. Nonruminants are assumed to have recruitment rates that are more responsive to changes in grass avail-

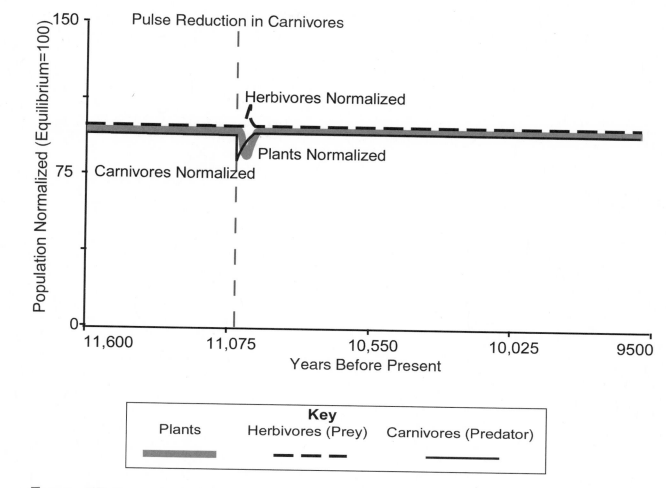

FIGURE 15.3 Equilibrium mode.

ability. Ruminants are assumed to be able to process low-quality grass when the stock of high-quality grass is depleted, though at a much reduced efficiency. The apportionment of grass between ruminant and nonruminant grazers is made according to the proportion of animals in the population.

Grass is divided into high- and low-quality grasses, and trees are divided into small (or new-growth) trees and large trees. Herbivores are assumed to prefer high-quality grass and small trees. If, however, they consume all of the preferred food available, then they will eat the less-preferred food but will need more of it to satisfy their nutritional needs.

For carnivores, the distribution of hunting among prey species is based on relative prey density. The reduction in carnivore populations is a factor of carnivore density and kills by *H. sapiens*. At maximum carnivore density, a one-hundred-pound *H. sapiens* kills 2.5

pounds of carnivore per year. As carnivore densities fall off, kills per pound of *H. sapiens* drop off to zero.

Simulation Results

Establishing a baseline. Before introducing humans into the model, I had to establish a dynamically stable ecosystem and test its stability. An equilibrium among plants (small and large trees, high- and low-quality grass), herbivores (browsers, mixed feeders, ruminant grazers, and nonruminant grazers), and carnivores is shown in figure 15.3. To demonstrate dynamic equilibrium, I perturbed the model with a one-time pulse reduction in carnivore populations and subsequently returned the model to normal.

Modeling the overkill hypothesis. Figure 15.4 shows the impact of a second predator and models the overkill hypothesis. *H. sapiens* enters the New World at 11,500 B.P. as a second predator, one hundred years

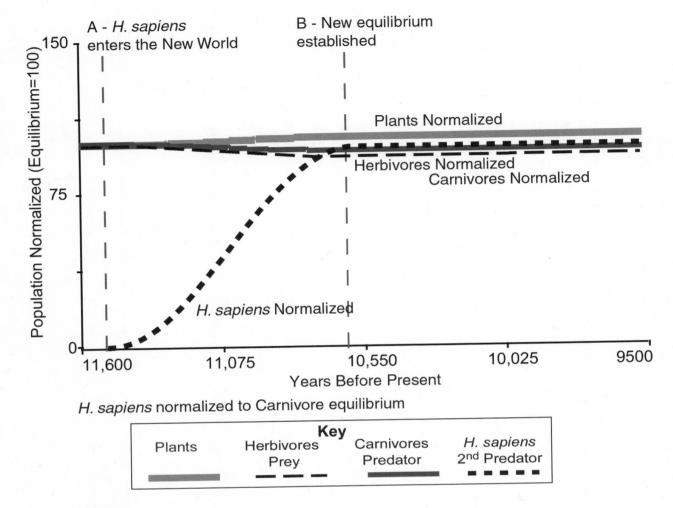

FIGURE 15.4 Overkill model.

after the start of the model (at the first dashed line, A). As *H. sapiens* becomes established (from A to B), there is very little disturbance to any of the sectors. Plants increase as herbivore populations drop in response to the increase in predator pressure. A new equilibrium ecosystem that includes *H. sapiens* starts at point B, when animal populations are within 90 percent of starting values. Carnivore populations are reduced relatively more than herbivores, but only by a fraction of a percent. The sum of all plants increases slightly to 101 percent of its starting value.

Modeling the second-order predation hypothesis. Simulation results are shown in figure 15.5. Second-order predation starts in the same way as overkill, with *H. sapiens* entering the New World about 11,500 B.P. (at A). Predation on carnivores by *H. sapiens* reduces carnivore populations so much that they no longer con-

trol herbivore population levels. This leads to a boom in herbivore populations that peaks at B and a simultaneous decrease in plant populations. This, in turn, results in a major crash in herbivore, carnivore, and *H. sapiens* populations (at C), allowing plant populations to partially recover (between C and D). This partial recovery is followed by a second dip (i.e., extinction event) in herbivore, carnivore, and *H. sapiens* populations (at D) and a second increase in plant populations.

Evaluating the Model Results

To understand the causes of these results, one must study the herbivore population dynamics as shown in figure 15.6. From the initial entry of *H. sapiens* (at A) to the peak in herbivore populations (at B), browser and ruminant grazer populations boom. Mixed feeder populations begin to expand but then slump as they ex-

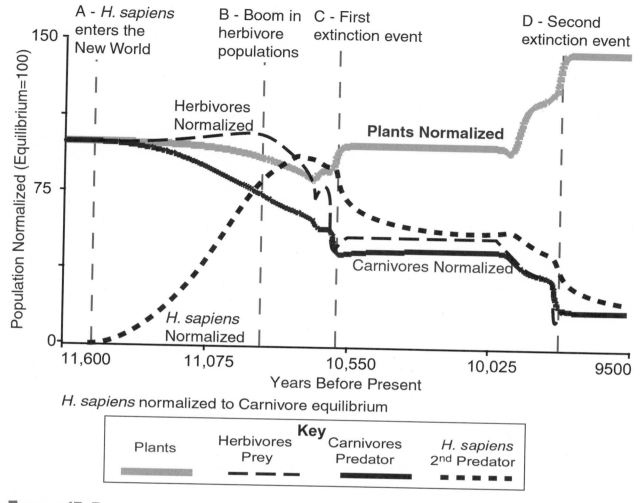

FIGURE 15.5 Second-order predation model, aggregated view.

perience competition from browsers and grazers. Non-ruminant grazer populations also slump. Note that populations of ruminant and nonruminant grazers vary inversely.

During the next time period (from B to C), mixed feeder populations dip more severely, followed by browsers. During that initial extinction event (just after C), ruminant grazers dip severely because they bear all of the pressure of predation from both carnivores and *H. sapiens*. The final time period (from C to D) marks a decrease in ruminant grazers, allowing populations of nonruminants to boom. The latter maintain their population levels for much of the period until ruminants become the dominant herbivores just before the second extinction event (at D), at which point nonruminants decline. Nonruminant grazers subsequently become extinct during the second extinction event (at D).

To understand the dynamics of the herbivore populations, one must also study the vegetation dynamics, as shown in figure 15.7. During the period between the introduction of *H. sapiens* and the first extinction event (from A to C), browsers and mixed feeders eat trees faster than the trees can recover, resulting in a complete crash of small-tree populations (at C). This crash is followed by the near-extinction of large trees as well, allowing grass to take over the area previously occupied by trees. Grass reaches a new level of stability at the first extinction event (at C) and remains stable until just before the second extinction event because of the lack of trees and the competition between the grazer populations. Just before the second extinction event, trees, freed from predation by browsers and mixed feeders, recover and colonize new territory. The end result is a loss of grassland to trees.

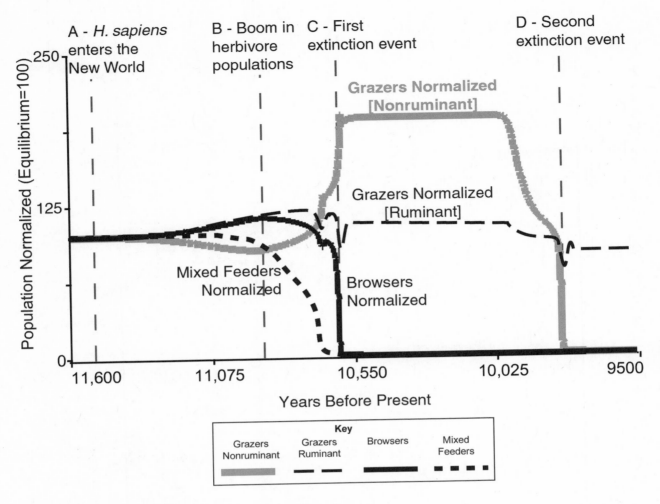

FIGURE 15.6 Second-order predation model, herbivores.

Discussion

Simulation modeling of second-order predation reproduces the late Pleistocene extinction of large mammals and accounts for previously unexplained aspects of the Pleistocene-Holocene transition (see table 15.1). This second-order predation model suggests that trees radically declined during the Holocene due to herbivore overbrowsing. When trees repopulated the landscape, they spread from the mountain refugia where they had survived (due to comparative inaccessibility to large mammalian herbivores). After the late Pleistocene megafaunal extinctions, this in-filling would have created closed-canopy forests because of the lack of large herbivores, such as mammoths and mastodons, that would have knocked down trees and established gaps in the forest. This sequence of events has occurred

in recent times in Australia when Aboriginal fire-stick farming was eliminated in areas where there were no large herbivores (Flannery 1995).

At the same time that trees were spreading from the mountain ranges, bison would have been repopulating the plains. Giant herds of new, smaller, obligate-grazing bison would have assumed a different lifestyle to cope with scarcity conditions. By roaming and foraging over vast areas, they would have maintained grazed prairies and prevented forest encroachment (McNaughton 1979, 1984; McNaughton and Georgiadis 1986). At some point, a balance would have been reached; the plains, maintained by bison, and the closed-canopy forest would have met. Because very few trees grew on the plains, there would have been very little transpiration and hence low relative humidity, which would account for an increase in continentality.

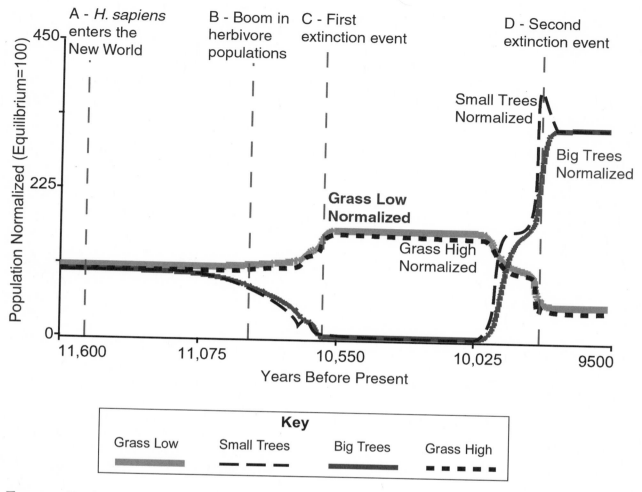

FIGURE 15.7 Second-order predation model, plants. Four-herbivore model.

As stated earlier, to be an improvement, any new hypothesis on late Pleistocene extinctions should address and explain the following: (1) the extinction of horses in North America, (2) the extinction of the ground sloth, (3) the bias in favor of ruminants, and (4) the bias in favor of small mammal size. The second-order predation hypothesis accounts for all four. The extinction of horses would have been caused by the starvation of nonruminant grazers during the boom-and-bust dynamic. The fact that horses currently survive in a Holocene climate is no longer an anomaly. The period of boom-and-bust was an ecological bottleneck, through which some animals, such as horses, were not able to pass. When they were eventually reintroduced in North America, horses successfully adapted to the warmer, more continental climate.

Similar forces can also explain the extinction of the ground sloth. The second-order predation hypothesis posits that herbivores eat nonpreferred food if their preferred food is unavailable. With an increase in all herbivore populations, many more-efficient herbivores competed for high-quality plant food. The change in the composition of ground sloth dung shows a picture of an animal that was increasingly unable to find its preferred food because other animals were eating it. Initially the sloth simply ate more and more of a food that it could tolerate, but one that was not eaten by other animals. Over time, the less desirable food came to dominate the sloth's diet. Because it was unable to process a steady diet of antiherbivory toxins, the sloth ultimately became extinct (Phillips 1984).

Second-order predation also accounts for the apparent ecological bias that favored the survival of ruminants and smaller-sized mammals across the

Pleistocene-Holocene transition, while larger mammals became extinct. In an exhausted environment, animals that are more efficient will prevail over the less efficient ones. All things being equal, ruminants will extract more nutritional value from the same quantity of forage than will nonruminants. Similarly, when there is competition among species, smaller animals will be at an advantage because they require less food to attain reproductive maturity and will therefore leave more offspring.

Archaeological Implications

With the discovery of pre-Clovis sites, previous theories on human migration and its relationship to late Pleistocene extinctions need to be reexamined (e.g., see Fiedel, this volume; Meltzer, this volume). In this regard, the second-order predation hypothesis encourages new ways of thinking about the ecological impacts of human migration. It suggests that the populations of now extinct species followed a cyclical boom-bust pattern in the late Pleistocene rather than declining monotonically from a peak to zero. A boom-bust pattern would have created scattered local abundance and scarcity instead of a more homogeneous pattern. According to Yellen and Harpending (1972; see also Harpending and Davis 1976; Yellen 1976), this kind of environment tends to support group mobility and a networked social structure. The concomitant changes in vegetation modeled here would have created further pressure on people to adopt a mobile lifestyle. It is also possible that *H. sapiens* would have been hunters of animals during booms and scavengers of dying animals during busts. The picture is one of herbivores, vegetation, carnivores, and humans in a continual churn as they searched for sufficient resources. Greater human mobility in these circumstances would further increase the likelihood that groups from different areas would come in contact with each other, producing greater homogeneity in artifact assemblages across vast distances.

In the context of the second-order predation model, the archaeological manifestation known as Clovis may have arisen in three different ways. In the most widely accepted scenario, Clovis people swept into the New World, bringing their hunting way of life and the practice of predator predation. When local herbivore population busts occurred, these people moved on to new territories, until they had spread throughout the New World. Any pre-Clovis people were killed off, or they adopted the Clovis lifestyle and technology. An alternate scenario posits that some pre-Clovis people developed a new way of interacting with herbivores, creating local booms. As herbivores consumed more vegetation, these *H. sapiens* groups were forced to adopt a more migratory lifestyle based on hunting; they developed sophisticated hunting technology that diffused throughout the New World. In the final scenario, as a result of the boom in herbivores, there were fewer plants available for *H. sapiens* to gather, but there were ever more herbivores to hunt. To survive, *H. sapiens* was forced to adopt a life strategy based on following the herbivores. As each group responded to conditions of local but widely scattered herbivore abundance, they moved away from their traditional territories, eventually meeting and interacting with each other. The sophisticated hunting technology known as Clovis is a result of the synergy between interacting groups.

These three scenarios have implications for what we would expect to find in the archaeological record. The first scenario implies that we should be able to trace the origin of Clovis technology to a single geographic source, which represents the point where these people initially entered the New World. The second scenario also suggests a single geographic source for Clovis, but not one that is consistent with entry from another continent. The third scenario implies that Clovis technology originated from more than one geographic location and may have even emerged throughout the continent.

Currently available archaeological evidence is only beginning to reach sufficient resolution to distinguish between these scenarios (see discussions by Barton et al., Meltzer, and Tankersley, this volume). The second-order predation hypothesis, however, provides directions for future research into the possible relationships between Clovis and any earlier human populations in the New World. Although this model necessarily oversimplifies the nature of ecological change during the Pleistocene-Holocene transition, it offers a more sophisticated framework for exploring the complex role of humans in the dynamics of both plant and animal communities. In so doing, it better accounts for the existing record of large animal extinctions and other aspects of late Pleistocene ecological change.

16 Megafauna, Paleoindians, Petroglyphs, and Pictographs of the Colorado Plateau

Larry D. Agenbroad and India S. Hesse

Paleolithic art has long been used as evidence of the contemporaneity of ancient humans and extinct Pleistocene animals in Europe and Asia. The lack of such Paleolithic art has been partly used to discredit the presence of early peoples in large areas of the North American continent (Bain 1976). In particular, the Colorado Plateau has been deemed to be void of the presence of Paleoindian peoples.

The Colorado Plateau, an expanse of some 130,000 mi² (209,170 km²) of parts of Utah, Colorado, New Mexico, Wyoming, and Arizona, has largely been ignored in studies of preceramic prehistory. The archaeological focus on the agricultural ceramic cultural manifestations on the Colorado Plateau has resulted in a near-vacuum of knowledge for the preceding 9,000 years of prehistory in this large area (Agenbroad 1990). As a partial justification for this disinterest in the Paleoindian and Archaic cultural manifestations on the plateau, a "myth" was started: There were no Paleoindians on the Colorado Plateau because there was no megafaunal resource base.

McGregor (1941) was one of the first plateau archaeologists to put the concept in print. While explaining the presence of bison at Ridge Ruin near Flagstaff, he stated, "[B]ison did not range historically west of the Rio Grande" (p. 256). Jesse Jennings, one of the great plateau archaeologists, noted that the "first occupation (Desert Culture–Peripheral big game hunter) began earlier than 11,000 years ago, possibly before the termination of the Pleistocene. Large extinct mammals had already disappeared from the Great Basin by this time" (Jennings and Norbeck 1955:2). He was specifically referring to the Great Basin in the 1955 publication, but he extended the idea to all of Utah in a later publication. "Although he was hunting big game such as mammoth, long-horned bison, horse, and camel in the wide plains east of the Rockies, in Utah and the Great Basin, these animals had apparently become extinct before man's presence" (Jennings 1960:5). A similar view was stated in Jennings (1964).

By 1964 Reed (p. 177) had put flesh on the bones of the myth, and it began to fill out:

In much of the Southwest proper, the Big Game hunters do not seem to have been present in any number. Sandia Cave, and a few isolated finds of single points of known types (occurring scattered from Durango and Baja California northward, but rare within the Southwest proper, except perhaps northern Chihuahua)—this almost exhausts the list. The recent discovery of a fluted-point site in Monument Valley, north of Comb Ridge, in northernmost Arizona or southernmost Utah, has been reported. In addition, there is the unreported (so far as I am aware) surface find in 1950 of a Sandia point on a mesa a few miles northwest of Shiprock, New Mexico.

In the region to the west, a number of important Early Man sites fall within the Greater Southwest, as far north as Danger Cave. But the Big Game hunters—and presumably the big game—were concentrated, it appears, on the Great Plains from eastern New Mexico and the Texas panhandle and eastern Colorado north and eastward. Very possibly the great beasts of the Late Pleistocene did not range normally or in any great numbers into the mountain and mesa country of the central Southwest. But neither are very early Desert Archaic remains known from the central and southern Colorado Plateau, and the preagricultural Basketmaker I period still is a postulated necessary assumption in what theoretically should be its home range.

Marwitt (1969:21) developed the myth further and even stated that most Indian cultures in Utah appear to be less than 4,000 years old.

Probably because of aridity and a dearth of the requisite animals, remains of the classic big game hunters of the Great Plains are rarely encountered in either the Great Basin or the western Colorado Plateau. The Llano complex, associated with the hunting of mammoth, is represented in Utah only by a few surface finds of Clovis or Clovis-like projectile points, which contributed little to our knowledge of the complex. As with the Llano, archaeological evidence fails to show any significant Utah distribution of the slightly later (BC 9,000–7,000) Folsom culture, which was based on the hunting of the now extinct *Bison antiquus*. Most Indian cultures in Utah appear younger than 2,000 BC.

By 1970 the myth had become established and was often repeated. As reported by Hauk (1977:65–66), "The presence of Plano Culture hunters in Utah is not widely acknowledged. . . . The slight Paleoindian utilization of Utah can possibly be tied to the relative scarcity of the large game species in Utah."

Parry and Smiley (1990:51) noted, "Prior to 8,000 B.P. coniferous forests interspersed with grass/sagebrush parklands likely covered much of the area. Such a climatic regime would not be ideal for Pleistocene megafauna, although the presence of bison and mammoth (Hack 1942:29) are documented by a few finds in the region. The apparently sporadic and ephemeral Paleoindian occupation may reflect the inability of the area to sustain large numbers of herbivores that Judge (1982) has suggested were possibly a 'focal' resource of such groups."

Our research (Agenbroad and Mead 1987, 1992; Davis et al. 1984) has indicated that the postulated coniferous forest interspersed with grass-sagebrush parkland was exactly the paleoenvironment that promoted the largest mammoth density on the Colorado Plateau. In this paper, we will shatter the myth and invalidate the justifications for not researching the aceramic cultures of this area. Our attack will be four pronged: paleontological, archaeological, chronological, and artistic (petroglyphs and pictographs). Our focus will be on the documented presence of two genera of megafauna—mammoth and bison—and their known hunters, the Paleoindians (ca. 12,000–6000 B.P.).

Evidence from the Colorado Plateau

When one speaks of the Colorado Plateau, the limits of this physiographic province are usually depicted as shown on the maps in this chapter (figs. 16.1–16.6). The original designation of the Colorado Plateau, made by John Wesley Powell, was even larger and included most

TABLE 16.1 Mammals (Megafauna) of the Colorado Plateau

Pleistocene	Holocene
Camel (*Camelops*)	
Horse (*Equus*)	
Llama (*Llama*)	
Mammoth (*Mammuthus*)	
Mastodon (*Mammut*)	
Mountain Goat (*Oreamnos*)	
Musk Ox (*Symbos*)	
Shrub Ox (*Euceratherium*)	
Sloths (*Glossotherium, Nothrotheriops*)	
Tapir (*Tapirus*)	
Antelope (*Stockoceras*)	Antelope (*Antiocapra*)
Bison (*Bison*)	Bison (*Bison*)
Cats (*Felis, Panthera, Leo*)	Cats (*Felis, Panthera*)
Coyote (*Canis latrans*)	Coyote (*Canis*)
Bear (*Ursus, Arctodus*)	Bear (*Ursus*)
Wolf (*Canis armbrusteri, C. edwardii*)	Wolf (*Canis lupus*)
Humans (*Homo*)	Humans (*Homo*)
	Elk (*Cervus*)
	Deer (*Odocoileus*)
	Bighorn Sheep (*Ovis*)

of the Green River drainage in Wyoming. We will refer to Powell's designation as the Greater Colorado Plateau and the smaller delineation as the Colorado Plateau. In the discussion that follows, some of the archaeological and paleontological locales fall outside the Colorado Plateau proper but are within the Greater Colorado Plateau.

Paleontological Evidence

Table 16.1 lists the large wild mammals found on the Colorado Plateau. The Pleistocene fauna, as recognized in the paleontological record, includes 20 genera of large mammals, whereas the Holocene fauna includes only 10. Two of these genera, *Mammuthus* and *Bison*, were the known prey of early human hunters. By using the record left by these two species, we can estimate the abundance of large mammalian prey species during the late Pleistocene. However, the fossil record includes only a small percentage of the living population of animals at a given time. For each recorded mammal fossil, there were probably 99 more animals of the same species living at the same time in the same area. Maps of known rock art for mammoths and bison closely approximate the distribution of these animals, as known from paleontological locations.

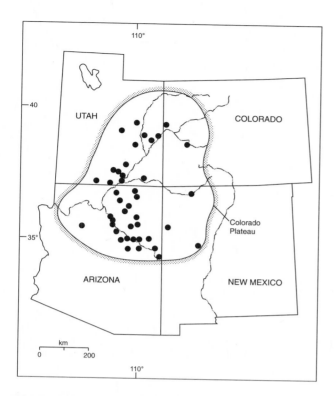

FIGURE 16.1 Reported locations of *Mammuthus* on the Colorado Plateau.

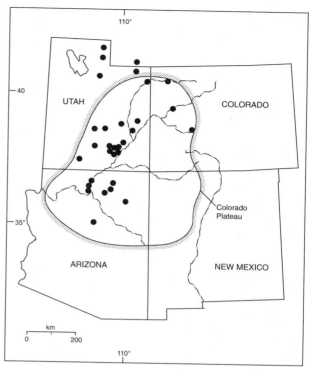

FIGURE 16.2 Reported locations of *Bison* on the Colorado Plateau.

Figure 16.1 shows 42 documented mammoth localities on the Colorado Plateau (see Agenbroad and Mead 1989). These localities cluster along major watercourses. Modern elephants need large quantities of water in their daily routine; mammoths presumably also ranged near water. Radiocarbon dates for reported mammoth localities on the plateau range from 30,800 to 10,350 B.P.

Figure 16.2 shows 31 documented bison localities on the Colorado Plateau (see Agenbroad and Mead 1987; Davis et al. 1984; Gooding and Shields 1985; Hansen 1980; Harris 1985; Madsen 1980; Mead and Agenbroad 1992; Mead et al. 1991; Parry and Smiley 1990; Sharrock 1966; Shields 1968; Stokes et al. 1966). A possible identification bias may exist in reports of bison localities. *Bison* and *Bos* (domestic cattle) are similar enough in postcranial skeletons that most people cannot differentiate between their remains. Because much of the plateau has been grazed by domestic cattle since the mid to late 1800s, the number of *Bison* localities is probably much larger.

Archaeological Evidence

Three prehistoric groups specialized in hunting mammoths and bison. The Clovis culture, defined by large, lanceolate, fluted projectile points, is commonly associated with mammoth remains (as well as smaller animals; see Chilton, this volume). Folsom culture projectile points, which are smaller but have larger flutes than Clovis projectile points, are most commonly associated with *Bison* remains. Plano culture artifacts reflect a variety of stemmed- to indented-base projectile points, which are nearly always associated with *Bison* as a prey animal.

Figures 16.3, 16.4, and 16.5 present maps of Clovis, Folsom, and Plano localities documented on the Colorado Plateau (see Agenbroad 1967; Ayers 1966; Copeland and Fike 1988; Danson 1961; Davis 1985, 1988; Downum 1993; Geib 1995; Gunnerson 1956; Hadlock 1962; Hesse 1995; Huckell 1982; Hunt and Tanner 1960; Jennings 1968; Longacre and Graves 1976; Schroedl 1977, 1991; York 1990). The distribution of the 35 Clovis localities, most of which are surface finds, closely resembles the reported mammoth distribution. In other words, mammoth hunters were where the mammoths

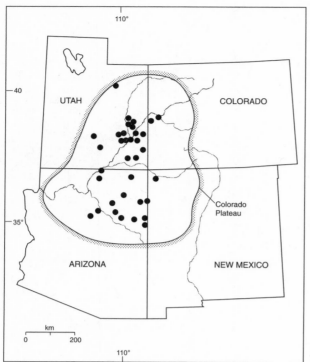

FIGURE 16.3 Reported locations of Clovis culture artifacts on the Colorado Plateau.

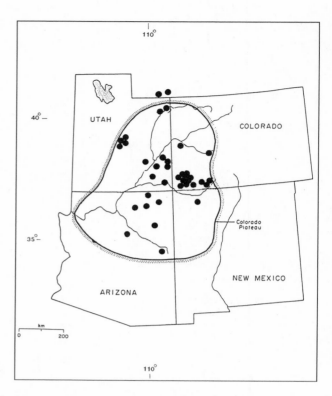

FIGURE 16.5 Reported locations of Plano culture artifacts on the Colorado Plateau.

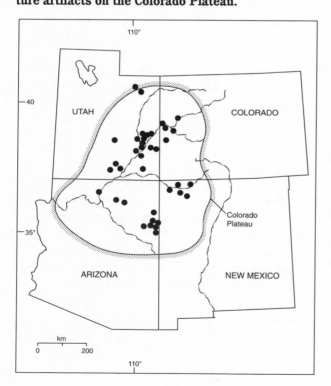

FIGURE 16.4 Reported locations of Folsom culture artifacts on the Colorado Plateau.

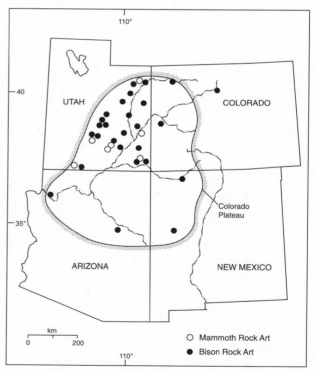

FIGURE 16.6 Rock art of mammoths and bison on the Colorado Plateau.

FIGURE 16.7 Representative mammoth rock art of the Colorado Plateau. The top figure and the third figure from the top on both the left and right sides are pictographs from Ferron Canyon in Utah.

Figure 16.8 Representative bison rock art of the Colorado Plateau.

were. Similarly the distribution of the 38 Folsom localities closely matches the bison distribution, with higher frequencies in the upper San Juan River and Little Colorado River drainages than are suggested by paleontological evidence alone (possibly due to the identification bias against bison). The 38 Plano artifact localities display an even heavier concentration between the Gunnison River and San Juan River drainages, an area that is not well represented in the paleontological record of bison.

Chronological Evidence

Radiocarbon dates are available for some of the reported sites. Only 14 of the 42 documented mammoth sites (33 percent) have been radiocarbon dated. These dates range from 30,800 to 10,350 B.P., with no major temporal absence. The weighted average of the four youngest radiocarbon dates for mammoths is 11,270 ± 65 B.P., which approximates the time of mammoth extinction on the Colorado Plateau (Agenbroad and Mead 1989).

Twenty-seven radiocarbon dates are available for bison localities. These dates range from more than 40,000 to 355 B.P. (the former date is the approximate upper limit of radiocarbon chronology). Six dates are from the protohistoric period, three are from the Archaic period, and 18 are from the late Pleistocene. This information suggests that bison were more abundant on the Colorado Plateau during the late Pleistocene than during most of the Holocene.

Rock Art

Mammoths and bison have been recorded in the rock art on the Colorado Plateau, both in petroglyphs and pictographs (see Castleton 1978, 1979; Cole 1990; Jones and Goodfellow 1988; Liddiard and Liddiard 1993; Patterson 1992; Schaafsma 1963, 1971, 1975; Stokes and Stokes 1980; Thompson 1993; Waur 1965). Because of concerns that some pictographs are modern fakes (L. Marononi, personal communication 1985; Patterson 1992), the petroglyphs are given more credibility. Some of the bison rock art is certainly historical because the bison appear in the same panels as do the mounted hunters. Figure 16.6 shows the known rock-art localities that depict mammoth and bison on the Colorado Plateau. Some

of the mammoth petroglyphs are in the same canyons that contain mammoth skeletal and fecal remains. Figures 16.7 and 16.8 provide examples of mammoth and bison rock art on the plateau.

Maps of paleontological locales and artifacts show that megafauna and Paleoindians were present on the Colorado Plateau. When combined with rock art and a radiocarbon chronology, they provide convincing evidence to dispel the myth that human hunters and their major prey species did not live on the plateau from 12,000 to 6000 B.P. Because of the dearth of preceramic studies in this region, at least 9,000 years of plateau prehistory is not being adequately researched.

Conclusions

Paleontological, archaeological, chronological, and artistic evidence converge to refute the myth about the absence of Paleoindians and Pleistocene megafauna on the Colorado Plateau. Mammoth remains, Clovis artifacts, and mammoth rock art are found across the plateau and are all present in several areas. Chronological information places mammoths on the plateau from 30,800 to 10,350 B.P. Radiocarbon estimates for mammoth extinction on the plateau mirror the temporal span of Clovis hunters.

Bison remains, Folsom and Plano artifacts, and bison rock art are also found on the plateau, and some areas contain all of these. Although some Folsom and Plano artifacts are found in areas of the plateau with no recorded paleontological presence of *Bison*, it is probable that *Bison* remains are often misidentified as *Bos*. Nevertheless, the chronology of documented *Bison* localities on the plateau indicates a greater presence of bison in the late Pleistocene than in the Holocene. The number of bison remains from Folsom and Plano (Paleoindian) sites nearly equals the number from late Archaic and protohistoric sites.

Prehistoric rock art, especially petroglyphs, also lends credence to the presence of Paleoindian hunters on the plateau from 12,000 to 6000 B.P. These people *were* the "Pleistocene pioneers." It is unfortunate that their presence has been denied, overlooked, and unresearched for so long.

17 Peopling of the Americas and Continental Colonization

A MILLENNIAL PERSPECTIVE

David R. Yesner, C. Michael Barton, Geoffrey A. Clark, and Georges A. Pearson

The papers in this book reveal, and to varying degrees shed light on, several critical issues and conundra that continue to plague those interested in the peopling of the Americas. The authors of these papers are united in their insistence on placing these issues in a broader context rather than simply evaluating individual archaeological sites and the artifacts, features, and radiocarbon dates that they exhibit. In doing so, most of the authors have moved away from the finger-pointing and ad hominem attacks that have unfortunately characterized much of the debate concerning not only the peopling of the Americas but also continental colonization worldwide. At the same time, they have eschewed the notion that any individual site, artifact, human skeleton, DNA sample, or vocabulary list should establish or even challenge our understanding of the process of the peopling of the Americas and have favored a truly anthropological, broadly based series of concepts.

Accomplishing this task requires several steps that are largely independent of the different types of data that the authors have marshaled to support their views. These data come from the subdisciplines of prehistoric archaeology, human osteology, anthropological genetics, anthropological linguistics, and paleontology, all of which make important contributions to this volume. The steps include (1) using existing data to model the process of continental colonization; (2) testing implications of the model against a sufficiently large sample of archaeological sites, radiocarbon dates, human remains, genetic assays, or word comparisons to evaluate the data; and (3) using these tests to increase the realism of the models and to suggest the kinds of data needed for further refinement.

This method of multiple working hypotheses, which is more of a tradition in geology than in anthropology, still has too many shortcomings to warrant following it. The method results in mutually exclusive models—coastal migration OR ice-free corridors, human-caused extinction OR death through natural causes, transient explorers OR estate settlers—much of which is anti-

thetic to real scientific discussion of colonization processes. This method also fails to integrate a researcher's work with—or to even consider—the data from other anthropological subdisciplines, a deficiency that is partly due to the researcher's limited knowledge of these other data sets.

Peopling of the Americas and the Method of Multiple Working Hypotheses

Twenty years ago, Dincauze (1984:309–310) argued that a basic body of interwoven, widely accepted, anthropological arguments underlies the process of the peopling of the Americas.

> [H]uman expansion into . . . high-latitude habitats was accomplished only after the achievement and control of fire and . . . after the development of [tailored] skin clothing and artificial shelter. . . . Most of us accept the idea that humans entered the Americas via Beringia, whether on land or in small boat crossings, because there is no other obviously feasible route for peoples with strong North Asian affinities. Given all this, it is reasonable to suppose that pioneer human groups entered the Americas through the "cold filter" of the High Arctic, and that they must have manifested the cultural and physical adaptations appropriate to such a traverse. Given these few postulates, arguments for early human residents in the Americas who lacked elementary material culture, the control of fire, minimum bands of at least 25 people, hunting skills of a high order, and the ability to adapt to changing conditions by rapidly modifying their cultural inventories, are necessarily subject to extreme skepticism. . . .
>
> Evidence for early human occupation of the New World will have to be congruent with the[se] ideas . . . , or the proponent must demonstrate that the new evidence is sufficiently robust to demand

the replacement of some or all of the established concepts. Here again, as in any competition between hypotheses, tests must be devised that will result in the elimination of one or more of the competitors. The burden of devising and making such tests properly rests not with the defenders of disciplinary orthodoxy, but with the challengers. . . . We . . . have respectable canons of disproof at our disposal, and those must be utilized to carry the burden of the argument. . . . Arguments from authority, arguments by assertion, "*ad hoc* accommodative arguments" (Binford 1981), and special pleading lead only to controversy or to "myths."

In other words, models and arguments for the peopling of the Americas must be couched in anthropological terms and must follow well-established paradigms within that discipline, unless those paradigms are being challenged by a significant set of contravening data. These models should offer some explanation for the timing, route, and destination of human migration into northeastern Asia, Beringia, and areas south of the North American ice sheets, including the changing environmental challenges and opportunities and the underlying causes of demic expansion. Such explanations should be consistent with our understanding of earlier human expansions in the Old World, such as Australasia, central Siberia, and the Japanese archipelago, unless we can provide special circumstances. As with all good science, we create a story based on the best evidence at hand but must be willing to give it up in a moment if new contravening evidence becomes available.

When competing paradigms exist, we must clearly specify the levels of proof. As an archaeological example, when we consider the validity of a hypothesized migration route (e.g., a coastal, riverine, glacial margin, grassland, or other expansion pattern), simply showing that several sites of similar (or disparate) age lie along a stretch of coast, river, glacial margin, or open terrestrial environment is clearly insufficient proof. We should specify the degree of overlap between radiocarbon dates (at one or two sigma) that we use to assume contemporaneity. We must consider the levels of similarity between archaeological assemblages from such sites, including not only the diagnostic artifacts and features but also the full range of artifact and feature variability and the subsistence and technoeconomic patterns. We must clearly specify the axes of assemblage variability, which should involve widely accepted variables for char-

acterizing assemblages. Quantitative analysis of inter-assemblage differences is always preferable because it moves the use of archaeological data toward the same level as biological data and thereby avoids the "arm waving" that inevitably results from qualitative assessments. The paradigm should demonstrate that people had enough technology to expand along the hypothesized migration route and that they had the requisite socioeconomic organization to use that technology. For example, as Schmitz indicates in her paper in this volume, evidence for such requisite technological development among hypothetical coastal migrants would include evidence for boats capable of sustaining a long-distance voyage, for fishhooks and nets, and for the actual use of marine resources.

The above comments apply to two recent attempts to derive Paleoindians from seafaring societies. The first attempt concerns Spanish Solutrean expatriates, who theoretically crossed the Atlantic Ocean in some sort of watercraft, and whose descendants became the pre-Clovis occupants of eastern North American sites, such as Topper and Cactus Hill (Stanford and Bradley 2002). As Straus (2000) has noted and as Clark discusses in this volume, this connection cannot be drawn on the basis of technological or typological similarities because nothing like diagnostic Paleoindian fluted points appears in Solutrean contexts, and because supposedly diagnostic Solutrean bifacial foliate points (which do appear in Paleoindian contexts) are distributed worldwide. Other Solutrean characteristics cited by Stanford and Bradley, such as bone and ivory foreshafts and point caches associated with red ochre, were clearly distributed throughout northern Eurasia during Upper Paleolithic times. Because there is no evidence for coastal voyages by Upper Paleolithic Europeans, and because there were serious obstacles to such voyages due to Atlantic currents (as Clark notes in this volume), is it not more parsimonious to draw whatever connections existed between Solutreans and Paleoindians *from the other direction*, across northern Eurasia to North America?

Related but somewhat distinct arguments also apply to hypotheses regarding migrants along the northwestern coast of North America. In this case, positing a coastal migration involves connecting the dots between a few coastal or near-coastal sites dated earlier than 11,000 B.P.—including some sites on the Channel Islands off the California coast and others on the southern Peruvian coast—and then attempting to link these sites to other hypothetical, early coastal sites farther north. (We use uncalibrated radiocarbon dates throughout this chapter.) These early Californian and Peruvian sites suffer from two major problems, however. First, they contain very small artifact inventories that typically consist of nondiagnostic debitage, probably because they are ephemeral or at best short-term seasonal sites, a fact that makes artifact assemblage comparison problematic at best. Second, their use of marine resources can best be characterized as opportunistic strandlooping, reflected in limited use of shellfish, seabirds, and small, nearshore fish and sea mammals, which would not have required the use of boats. Not until Holocene times is more intensive use of marine resources demonstrable. Attempts to link these sites to 10,500 B.P. human remains from southeastern Alaska and artifacts of a similar age found off the British Columbia coast represent more wishful thinking than proof of a late Pleistocene coastal migration (Yesner 1998). As in the Solutrean case, problems with navigating ice-choked coasts, finding sources of driftwood for skin-boat frames, and establishing large base camps for sea-mammal retrieval and butchery make drawing such connections farther north even more tenuous. Again, because of this situation, is it not more parsimonious to suggest that the few examples of pre-11,000 B.P. coastal sites in the Americas represent independent, short-term, seasonal penetrations to the coast by groups who experimented with maritime subsistence in areas with high productivity and locally robust human population densities? Even Erlandson (2002:81), one of the biggest defenders of this idea, noted that "more tangible evidence will be required to prove that such a [coastal] migration actually occurred." Adovasio (2002:280) also noted that "the trouble with coastal routes across either the Pacific or the Atlantic is that at present there is basically no evidence at all that either actually happened."

In this volume, Mandryk takes a somewhat different position. She argues that anthropologically based migration stories can blind us to the reality of how the peopling of the Americas took place:

> Clovis migration through an ice-free corridor is a well-told and satisfying story that resonates with our presumptions about American identity. No wonder we are uncomfortable about a world filled with Monte Verde, coastal migration routes, generalized foragers, regional adaptations, and the heretical notion that Clovis may have originated in the southeastern United States. The story no longer has a beginning, middle, or end. It is all loose ends. That

is precisely what makes the current situation so exciting.

In our view, the excitement comes from rigorously testing each of these alternatives, which are not on the same level of proof. The faunal evidence, for example, clearly shows that generalized foraging occurred at particular times and places (see the discussion below under "Variability in the Paleoindian Record"). The same evidence, however, can also be used to defend basic continuity in the specialized big-game-hunting lifestyle because both caribou hunting and broad-spectrum foraging characterized late Upper Paleolithic subsistence strategies. In contrast, a northwestern North American coastal migration route and a Clovis origin in the southeastern United States, which are mutually exclusive, antithetical notions for the first American colonists, are a long way from proof, based on the criteria listed above; new fluted-point discoveries in the area of the ice-free corridor also keep that issue alive.

In biological anthropology, linking human skeletal remains to extant human populations requires a multivariate approach, which allows quantitative assessment of the "closeness" or similarity of frequency distributions among many variables. When using genetic markers to establish the affinities between living populations and to imply similarity by descent and therefore common origins, researchers must establish freedom from directional selection, a task that may not be possible, even in mtDNA and Y-chromosome analyses (Jobling et al. 1998; see also comments by Schurr, this volume). When using mtDNA or Y-chromosome data to establish the affinities and timing of divergence among living populations, researchers should specify the assumptions of the molecular clock that governs such divergences.

Similarly, in anthropological linguistics, researchers should specify their assumptions in lexical and grammatical analyses that use word lists or grammatical similarities to establish the relationship among groups, and by implication, their origins and divergence. Researchers should also consider multiple hypotheses and indicate linkages with other data sets.

During the past 20 years, several new data sets have emerged that are relevant to the peopling of the Americas. Geological and climatological data that concern the colonization of Beringia, the western margin of the cordillera, the corridor between the Laurentide and Cordilleran ice sheets, and the region south of the ice sheets have increased the specificity of our arguments concerning migration routes. Stable isotope analyses have refined our reconstructions of both paleoenvironments and paleodiets. Refinements in zooarchaeological and paleobotanical analyses have encouraged us to consider subsistence diversity among early New World colonists. New theoretical concerns in archaeology have fostered our interest in gender roles, household organization, and other aspects of early New World sociopolitical systems, which were not even considered 20 years ago.

Most of the significant technological breakthroughs that are relevant to the peopling of the Americas are in the subfield of biological anthropology. New molecular (mtDNA and Y-chromosome) data threaten to revolutionize our understanding of the probable ancestry of New World peoples and add to the data from the more traditional analyses of anthropometrics, discrete osteological and dental traits, and genetic polymorphisms based on red blood cell antigens and serum proteins. Different sets of data, of course, tend to support somewhat disparate conclusions. For example, as Schurr notes in this volume and elsewhere (Schurr 1996), mtDNA data have consistently suggested an earlier date (up to 35,000 B.P.) for the initial colonization of the Americas than is provided by other data sets. Colonization, however, is associated with a huge range (i.e., it could be as late as 20,000 B.P.), and significant variation exists between the data sets of different researchers (cf. Merriwether 2002).

In contrast, osteological and dental data from extant groups do not support occupation of the Americas before about 15,000 B.P., and no human skeletons have been dated before 12,000 B.P. All of these data sets, however, support (as do most interpreters of the archaeological record) the idea that the origin of American colonists was Asia, particularly Northeast and Central Asia. There appears to be a growing consensus, based on all of these data sets, that Central Asia (i.e., the area from the Altai region to central and southeastern Siberia and northern China) is the likely source area for Amerind groups. A later Inuit/Aleut migration is also clearly linked to Northeast Asian groups, possibly from as far south as the region that includes the Amur River mouth, Primorie Province, northern Japan, and northeastern China.

Beyond this agreement, the consensus fades somewhat. Some molecular geneticists see evidence for one or two other migrations, whereas others do not. Some molecular geneticists, as well as the immunoglobin ana-

lyses of Schanfield (1992), tend to support more than one Amerind ancestral group, including different ancestors for North American and South American Amerinds. Most genetic data support a distinctive Na-Dene migration that occurred later than the Amerind migration, as do Brace et al.'s (this volume) osteological data and Turner's (2002) dental data. Brace et al.'s data, based on craniometrics of both recent and prehistoric populations, also show at least three distinctive clusters within Amerind, which may reflect different linguistic groups. One of these three clusters includes coastal groups around the Pacific Rim from Micronesia to Patagonia. Whether this cluster can be considered a meaningful assessment of a coastal migration hypothesis remains problematic. However, it is interesting that the early Holocene skeletal remains from the Americas that are cited as the most "Ainu-like" (i.e., reflecting a more narrow, long-headed, generalized, Paleoasiatic population ancestry) are concentrated in the Pacific Northwest, as reflected in the Kennewick and Spirit Cave individuals. Could these be possible descendants of an early Holocene migration reflected in the microblade assemblages that range from interior Alaska down the Northwest Coast? It has been tempting to suggest that those are Na-Dene peoples, but Brace et al.'s analysis might suggest otherwise. In general, Steele and Powell's (1992, 2002) analyses have shown that Paleoindians as a group were narrower headed and more Ainu (or Jōmon)–like, but they also draw affinities to Southeast Asian groups. As Schmitz (this volume) notes, no matter how many migrations we posit or what their exact Asian affinities might be, we are still left with the central paradox that early New World colonists tend to show an Asian physical type associated with an essentially European Upper Paleolithic technology. How that process evolved is still one of the essential questions in understanding New World origins.

The subfield of anthropological linguistics has had fewer innovations in method that concern the peopling of the Americas. The paper by Hill (this volume), however, suggests that this is the direction in which we may need to move. The methods of Greenberg (1987), based essentially on lexicostatistics using multiple comparisons of vocabulary word lists, and the methods of Nichols (1990, 1992, 2002), based on the "clumping" or association of grammatical "population markers" (which are analogous to genetic markers in biological anthropology), have both produced significant insights into historical reconstructions of Native American groups. They have, however, run out of steam. Both methods have their adherents, but both also have serious problems. Greenberg's methods are particularly affected by subjectivity and lack of rigorous quantitative analysis; they allow too many possibilities of noise (chance associations) to be interpreted as system (valid evidence of group associations and common origins). Nichols's analysis is more rigorous, but it rests on the basic glottochronological assumption of uniform rates of language transformation. As Hill points out, the case of continental colonization is one in which this uniformitarian assumption is least likely to hold because rapid colonization is probably accompanied by higher than "normal" rates of linguistic differentiation.

This problem goes to the core of many of the assumptions about the peopling of the Americas. The idea that linguistic diversity equals time depth has been deeply embedded in anthropological thinking for many decades. It has been used, for example, to defend the notion that Eskimo origins must have taken place in southwestern Alaska because that is where the greatest diversity in Eskimo speech occurs (even though we know that nineteenth-century historical migrations were probably responsible for much of that diversity). A more modern but similar example is the one presented by Gruhn (1988), who argues that the high linguistic diversity in coastal California reflects the greater antiquity of human migration to and occupation of that coastline, despite the fact that this diversity is probably due to late prehistoric and historical movements of groups (especially Algonkian and Athabaskan outliers) into the region. In resource-rich environments, such as ocean and lake shores, population packing is far more likely to take place (Yesner 1980); many groups of disparate backgrounds may move into those areas to take advantage of those resources. This situation is essentially what Wilmsen (1973) argued was reflected in the disparate stylistic types found at the Lindenmeier Paleoindian site in Colorado. In his own work in southern Maine, Yesner similarly argued that the clustering of larger numbers of projectile point styles along large lakes during the late Archaic period represented an opportunistic response, which drew various populations into a single ecosystem that could support such population packing, at least during "good times" (Yesner et al. 1983). Such an analysis could obviously be applied to opportunistic packing in other situations.

The different approaches of Greenberg and Nichols also affect their views on the time depth for the peopling of the Americas. Greenberg's qualitative assessments led him to conclude that the Clovis migra-

tion was the first, or at least the first with Americas-wide impact, which established the Amerind language family. Nichols's assumptions about the rates of language stock changes led her to believe in a much earlier, pre-Clovis settlement of the Americas. Greenberg and Nichols also tend to be language lumpers in different ways. Nichols believes, for example, that American Pacific Coast languages can be separated from Greenberg's larger Amerind construct and that they are more closely affiliated with a larger Pacific Rim group that stretches from the Russian Far East to Australasia. (This finding is particularly noteworthy in light of similar conclusions from some molecular and osteological studies cited above.) Unlike Nichols, Greenberg believes that Na-Dene is a language stock that is separate from other Native American groups but is affiliated with a Dene-Caucasian construct from central-western Siberia. Nichols and Greenberg apparently agree only on the existence of Inuit/Aleut as a separate language stock, although they posit different Old World affiliations for this group.

Despite these disparate conclusions, most of the papers in this volume, which are based on rigorous methodologies, move us toward a truly anthropological approach to the peopling of the Americas, as advocated by Dincauze and others. In doing so, however, they fly in the face of continued advocacy for inductive, intuitive, and possibilist approaches to the question of continental colonization, approaches that are often closer to arm waving than to true science. Some of these approaches appear to be the nineteenth-century assertions of Charles Abbott and Frederick Putnam in modern dressing. Other apparently novel approaches, such as abandoning the concept of "Paleoindian" in favor of "Paleoamerican" and attaching simple racial categories to individual human skeletons, carry more sinister, politically charged messages that can be viewed as disenfranchising Native Americans from their long-term history. In the following discussion, we will identify some of the critical issues that still affect our understanding of the process of the peopling of the Americas and of continental colonization in general. We will also analyze the data sets and models from one or more subdisciplines of anthropology that are related to these issues.

Chronology and Process: Pre-Clovis Sites and the Question of Missing Data

The goal of science, as noted above, is to create the best narratives that we can from the evidence at hand, but to be willing to rewrite those narratives in an instant if and when superior evidence becomes available. We cannot build such narratives from negative or nonexistent data, whether they are coastal sites that have been hypothetically buried by rising sea levels or language groups that have become extinct. The story of the colonization of the Americas must be based on extant archaeological data and their distribution and on the human skeletal remains and surviving human populations. Radiocarbon-dating evidence and its statistical treatment is also a critical part of this exercise. However, currently intractable problems involving the radiocarbon plateau at the Pleistocene-Holocene boundary (see Fiedel 1999b, 2000a) create difficulties in attaching significance to some time frames: for example, the gap between the earliest dates from Beringia (the 12,000 B.P. Nenana complex) and well-accepted dates from southern South America (the 12,500 B.P. Monte Verde site).

In spite of these caveats and the warnings raised by Dincauze and others, let us concede that there may be several sites in the Americas whose radiocarbon dates, technologies, or stratigraphic associations reflect one or more pre-Clovis migrations and occupations. If we accept Monte Verde, Meadowcroft, Cactus Hill, Topper (some of the strongest recent contestants), or any of the few dozen other potential pre-Clovis sites as valid contenders for such status, does this acceptance significantly impact our understanding of the colonization process from an anthropological perspective?

Greenberg et al. (1986) and Meltzer (1989) indirectly tackled this question several years ago when they considered the possibility of pre-Clovis extinctions. Greenberg et al. (1986:477) noted that natural selection may have led to the "reproductive failure of the hypothetical pre-Clovis people," who represented small demographic isolates that failed to survive and adapt to adverse or changing environmental conditions because they did not become large enough to reproduce viably. Meltzer (1989:482–483) presented the following argument:

The possibility that the earliest migration was not a single episode but a multiple series, and that some of those . . . may have failed, has consequences for understanding the origin and variation of modern populations. . . . [S]patial and temporal "gaps" in the Pleistocene archaeological record . . . [may] represent discontinuities following a failed migration. . . . It might further be speculated that if there

were a series of unrelated failed migrations, and if they are detected the various assemblages will not necessarily all look alike. . . . [I]f there was a pre-12,000 yr BP population that reached the size where it was archaeologically detectable, but then failed, that has important implications for understanding the adaptive process of human migration. But what ultimately may have far greater evolutionary significance for North American prehistory is the fact that a group (or groups) came together to comprise Clovis, and survived.

These sentiments are echoed by Barton et al. (this volume), who suggest that it is possible that "one or more pre-Paleoindian colonizations failed, and prior human populations had existed but were extinct by the time of the Paleoindian arrival."

From an anthropological viewpoint, it may matter little if a handful of hypothetical pre-Clovis sites existed as a result of one or more episodic pulses of colonization by highly mobile, transient, peripheral groups. Even if these groups were present, they had little detectable impact on the megafauna of the Americas. This fact places them in strong contrast with later Clovis people and, by analogy, with the earliest Australian immigrants, whose initial presence at around 50,000 B.P. is closely tied to continentwide megafaunal extinctions (see Flannery 1995, 2001). As Barton et al. (this volume) note, if humans were present in the Americas prior to the Paleoindian entry, they proved to be such ineffective competitors that Paleoindian colonizers behaved as if they did not exist. We thus need to construct models and narratives based on the broadly successful Clovis migration, rather than conjuring up elements of earlier migrations that have left little trace in the archaeological record and little impact on their environments or later entrants.

We agree with Meltzer's (1989:483) assertion that we should "abandon the term pre-Clovis as it is used as a generic referent to that time period before Clovis, and use it only in the sense where a historical relation to Clovis is implied." Because the term "Clovis" sensu stricto refers to a technocomplex (Tankersley, this volume) rather than a chronostratigraphic association, the term "pre-Clovis" should be used in the same fashion. In that sense, the term "pre-Clovis" should be applied to the Nenana complex of interior Alaska (see Bever 2001 and Hamilton and Goebel 1999 for recent reviews) because temporal/historical antecedence has been attributed (Yesner 2001, 2004; Yesner and Pearson 2002) and because of strong technological links, including the predominance of macroblade-based industries, unifacial technologies, endscrapers, sidescrapers, gravers, *pièces esquillées* (Goebel et al. 1991), mammoth ivory and bone points, foreshafts, awls, and needles (Yesner 1996b; Yesner et al. 2000). Although Adovasio and Pedler (2001) have argued for a decoupling of the Nenana complex (at sites such as Broken Mammoth, Walker Road, Moose Creek, and Dry Creek) from Clovis Paleoindians based on both time and technology, they provide only two lines of evidence: (1) later dates for the complex (the Nenana complex was, in fact, long lasting, particularly in the Tanana Valley, where it spans the period from 12,000 to 9500 B.P.); and (2) the possibility that the complex may include a few microblades (microblades have been found at only two sites: Swan Point, which has been subjected to relatively small-scale excavation, and Healy Lake, which has serious problems with date reversals and stratigraphic associations). As a result, arm waving ("no amount of imaginative musings could derive or even relate Clovis to [the Nenana complex]"; p. 5) has replaced the statistical treatment of assemblage similarity that Goebel et al. (1991) provided. Although the Nenana complex may not represent the sole ancestor of Clovis Paleoindians (cf. Haynes 1982), they may have been by-products of the same late Pleistocene migratory pulse, which deposited the Nenana complex in eastern Beringia a few hundred years earlier than it deposited the Clovis complex farther south (by whatever route).

Modeling Paleoindian Colonization as Demic Expansion

From an anthropological perspective, it is clear that models for the colonization of the Americas should be based on the main (Clovis) Paleoindian migration, the first of the three major migrations posited by Greenberg et al. (1986) and discussed by Schmitz (this volume). The earliest attempts at modeling the process of Paleoindian colonization on a broad scale can be attributed to Martin (1973) and Mosimann and Martin (1975). Their focus was on demonstrating that rapid initial colonization of the Americas was possible and could be modeled to reflect the actual ages and distributions of archaeological sites, as well as the chronology and pattern of late Pleistocene animal extinction. (These are, of course, not necessarily mutually exclusive paradigms. One can certainly believe in a late chronology for human occupation, or at least Clovis occupation, with-

out megafaunal extinction, although this notion creates serious problems for many researchers.)

Martin's (1973) original model, which expanded on an earlier discussion by Haynes (1964, 1969), had two basic components: (1) a model of human population expansion, based on assumed rates of human population growth in a previously unexploited environment; and (2) a model of the impact of human hunting on large (more than 400 kilograms) animal populations, based on assumed culling rates. The assumptions of the model were based on rates near the maximum of observed human ranges; i.e., human population growth rates of 3.4 percent per annum, and annual removal rates of 26 percent of the megafaunal biomass. These numbers were based, in turn, on the assumption that humans who entered a "virgin" environment would multiply at or near the maximum observed growth rate, based on a Pitcairn Island model, and would engage in "wasteful" consumption of prey, based on a Plains Indian model. (Today we would say that optimal foragers in such unexploited environments, who enjoyed high encounter rates with large biomasses of aggregated preferred fauna, could afford to take only the highest-return cuts of meat before they initiated a new search.) Martin's model also assumed that human occupation of the Americas postdated 15,000 B.P. and that the major wave of demic expansion occurred south of an ice-free corridor, which extended from the southern Yukon to central British Columbia. The outcome of the model was population saturation of North America in 350 years and of the Americas as a whole in 1,000 years; faunal extinction occurred within a decade as a wave of demic expansion passed through each region.

To be fair, we must note that the assumptions of multiple working hypotheses were, in fact, met in the Martin (1973) model. He was able to demonstrate, for example, that the basic outcomes of the model would still hold with lower initial colonizing populations and human population growth rates as low as 1.4 percent per annum (which would produce continental saturation within 800 years), and with megafaunal culling rates as low as 20 percent. Furthermore, he accepted the possibility of "early early" sites in the Americas (i.e., pre-15,000 B.P.), but he believed that such sites would be "scarce." The model was further fleshed out by Mosimann and Martin (1975). Young and Bettinger (1995) accepted a 3 percent-per-annum human-population increase as part of their model of the peopling of the Americas, which would lead to saturation of the New World in 1,500 years. This model was echoed by Webb and Rindos (1997), who accepted a longer saturation time of 3,000 years, which involved demic expansion at the rate of 7–10 km/yr, although they felt that 2–3 km/yr might be more realistic based on the Australian model (Rindos and Webb 1992).

In contrast, Webster (1981) and Hassan (1981) found these rates to be unrealistic, based on "an intrinsic growth rate that is greater than the potential growth rate of hunter-gatherers, even with the child-spacing interval reduced to its natural limits" (Hassan 1981:201). Hassan suggested a revised model based on population growth rates of 0.1 percent per annum, near the lowest end of the observed range for hunter-gatherers. According to this model, population saturation would require 8,000–10,000 years, and thus would also require initial entry into the Americas at 25,000–20,000 B.P. Hassan, however, accepted a non-steady-state population-growth model, with more rapid growth occurring at the end of the Pleistocene, thus leading to greater archaeological site visibility. He also accepted the possibility that the overall population growth rate might have been closer to 0.5 percent, leading to population saturation in 1,200–2,200 years. Although the Martin and Hassan colonization models for the Americas do not overlap, the difference between their lowest and highest values, respectively, is only 0.9 percent population growth per annum and only 400 years in saturation time. As Whittington and Dyke (1984) have demonstrated, simulation models that eliminate the "wave front" and include "prey switching" still lead ultimately to megafaunal extinction.

Some researchers have recently undertaken more sophisticated, GIS-based mathematical modeling of the colonization process (see Krist and Brown 1994). Anderson and Gillam (2000), for example, use physiographic data, including the elevation and location of coasts, rivers, lakes, mountains, and glaciers, to model the colonization process in great detail. They subdivide the North and South American continents into environmental components, within which separate movements and population expansions hypothetically occurred. In Anderson and Gillam's approach, the ice-free corridor (or "western corridor," as it is sometimes called) population-entry model has been replaced by multiple colonization models. These models include a Northwest Coast entry model, which is "currently the alternative model of choice for the introduction of people south of the Canadian ice sheets" (Anderson and Gillam 2000:45) and which posits inland west-to-east penetration beginning at the mouth of the Columbia River.

Anderson and Gillam also consider an additional entry into eastern North America, which begins by crossing the Isthmus of Panama from west to east and then proceeding northward; this entry explains the similarities among fishtail points in the southeastern United States, Central America, and South America. From these entry points, Anderson and Gillam generate least-cost solutions for movement across North and South America, based on Kelly and Todd's (1988) scenarios in which coasts, rivers, and lakeshore routes are the primary points of entry into novel environments (see also Engelbrecht and Seyfert 1994) and in which radial spread occurs across grassland regions. Many of these least-cost solutions seem counterintuitive, including the following: (1) movement from interior Alaska northward to the North Slope and the MacKenzie River drainage before proceeding southward to the ice-free corridor, rather than moving due east toward the southern Yukon; (2) overland movement from the Great Lakes through Illinois and Indiana, rather than through the Ohio River valley; (3) east-to-west rather than west-to-east movement into the central and southern Plains; and (4) entry into South America primarily through the Amazon River basin and only secondarily through the Andean region, with later west-to-east movement toward the Amazon mouth and southwestward movement toward southern Chile and Tierra del Fuego. After assuming that demic expansion is based on these least-cost solutions, Anderson and Gillam proceed by way of multiple working hypotheses. In doing so, they demonstrate that population growth rates of as little as 0.25 percent per annum would produce population saturation of the New World in 4,550 years, of 0.5 percent in 2,275 years, and of about 0.7 percent in 1,700 years, all of which are well within the range of contemporary hunter-gatherers. They note that somewhat longer colonization times would be produced by a "string-of-pearls" population model, which assumes the budding of daughter populations into adjacent territories. Much faster colonization times, even exceeding those of the Martin model, would be produced by a "leapfrog" population model, in which populations disperse more rapidly over large areas, circumventing resource-poor or already occupied areas.

Steele et al. (1996, 1998) have taken the modeling process one step further by considering the likely rates of human population growth in individual habitats along the colonization route (from Beringia to Tierra del Fuego), based on regional vegetational reconstructions at 1,000-year intervals. Following the method of multiple working hypotheses, Steele et al. consider population growth rates that range from around 0.15 percent to as much as 4 percent per annum, but they clearly accept the latter more than the former. They believe that most contemporary hunter-gatherers, for whom lower growth rates have been cited, have population densities that are close to carrying capacity for their habitats, a scenario that is highly unlikely among colonizing populations, especially initial, transient, highly mobile groups. Steele et al. then attempt an actual match with archaeological data in the form of fluted-point distributions from North America (Anderson and Faught 1998a; cf. Morrow and Morrow 1999). The problems of fit—particularly fewer fluted points in western North America than are predicted by the model—are probably the result of deficiencies in data collection rather than in the model. Like Anderson and Gillam (2000), Steele et al. (1998) suggest that we eschew standard, wavelike, random demic expansion models in favor of two other types of models: (1) linear (i.e., "string-of-pearls") population movements along the ice-free corridor, coasts, rivers, and the Andean mountains; and (2) asymmetrical, discontinuous, patchy, nonrandom movements (of which the "leapfrog" would be one type), reflecting assessments by rapidly moving groups of the risks and potential benefits of individual habitats.

Archaeological tests of these demic expansion models are exceedingly difficult to obtain, particularly those of the "blitzkrieg" (rapid population expansion) variety. The plateau in radiocarbon-date calibration for the terminal Pleistocene is one confounding factor. A second problem, as Paul Martin has consistently argued, is the ephemeral archaeological signature expected from a rapidly expanding population. As Barton et al. (this volume) note, "The rapidity of this initial human dispersal, its patchy distribution in the most productive environments, and the taphonomic roulette of the 12,000-year-long archaeological record" create numerous problems in creating definitive tests.

Failure to consider potential impacts on Pleistocene fauna is also a drawback of some of the more recent demic expansion models. However, Whitney-Smith (this volume) has produced a more sophisticated variant on the Pleistocene overkill model than was presented by Whittington and Dyke (1984). In her "second-order" model, she assumes not only that humans hunted herbivorous megafauna, but also that they consciously cut back on predators to reduce the competition for megafaunal prey. This strategy would allow the herbi-

vore populations to expand, overgraze, and decimate the environment, forcing them to adopt less desirable foods and eventually to become extinct. The only surviving herbivores would be those that are not obligate grazers but mixed feeders, such as bison and wapiti. This strategy would favor the evolution of subspecies, such as wood bison, which actually did occur. Whitney-Smith's model is ingenious and gains support from the simulations that she runs. It is also supported by some paleobotanical data from the Great Basin and by the apparent extinction of large carnivores before large herbivores (see Barton et al., this volume). In Whitney-Smith's view, her model also helps to explain the extinction of some megafaunal taxa, especially ground sloths, which she finds difficult to attribute to either climatic change or direct human overharvesting. The model has some problems, however. Whitney-Smith notes that it assumes that North American ecosystems were in equilibrium prior to the arrival of Homo sapiens. It also assumes that this state of equilibrium postdated human arrival, or at least that humans had little direct impact on megafaunal herbivores. Otherwise, one would assume that any expansion of herbivore populations would have been very brief and that predator elimination would not have continued if herbivore populations began to expand.

Whitney-Smith also notes that fire ecology and other factors should be considered in future, more sophisticated demic expansion models. This suggestion is echoed by Barton et al. (this volume), who argue that human-induced fire, either purposeful or accidental, could have been a potent force in Paleoindian transformation of the landscape and possibly in megafaunal extinction. To this scenario they add the potential impacts of dogs accompanying immigrant groups, directly competing with other carnivores, and perhaps hastening large herbivore extinction in the manner described by Whitney-Smith.

Whatever their sophistication, all of these demic expansion models are based on the assumption that the process of colonization of the Americas was a simple density-dependent one. That, however, is an assumption that needs to be seriously questioned.

Beyond Modeling: The Cultural Ecology of Continental Colonization

Descriptive models of New World colonization, no matter how robust or detailed, offer answers to only those questions concerning the antiquity of occupation in specific landforms, the routes of colonization and spread, the relationship between antecedent and descendant populations, and the potential impact of human colonizers on resource populations. To advance beyond such questions of time and place, we need a more detailed cultural ecology of continental colonization. Such an approach has three basic components: (1) explaining the impetus toward migration and colonization on the basis of "push" and "pull" factors; (2) detailing the process by which colonizing human populations interact with novel environments and their resources; and (3) linking archaeological site configurations, including artifacts, features, and faunal inventories, to colonizing populations.

Explaining Late Pleistocene Emigration from Northeastern Eurasia

As Dillehay (1991:231) has noted, "[E]arly human migration in the Americas is generally believed to have been conditioned by such density-dependent processes as resource availability and environmental variability (e.g., Martin 1967, Haynes 1969)." In fact, relatively little attention has been paid to the motivations underlying the early human colonizers of Beringia. This oversight is partially due to disagreements about when colonization of western Beringia initially occurred.

Those who believe in earlier occupation of the region, perhaps along drowned former coastlines, may seek explanations in opportunistic responses to changing environmental conditions. However, the most parsimonious interpretation of existing archaeological data and radiocarbon dates from western Beringia suggest that a major long-term impediment existed between the colonization of the Lena-Aldan river basins to the west and the colonization of the regions of Chukotka and Kamchatka to the east. Although dates ranging back to the beginning of the Upper Paleolithic characterize the former region, no sites in the Chukotka-Kamchatka region apparently predate 14,000 B.P., after the Last Glacial Maximum. The sample size is small, being limited to the Berelekh and Ushki sites; most of the sites in the region represent undated or undatable surface finds from coastal and river terraces (see West 1996b). These data suggest that colonization may have followed hard on the heels of glacial recession and ameliorating late Pleistocene climate and was coeval with human reoccupation of central and northern Europe (Gamble 1986, 1995). Other possibilities include the development of technology that allowed occupation of this extremely cold environment, particularly advances in clothing manufacture, although shelter and food storage may also have been important variables. The nature of the late Pleistocene forest-steppe, with larger populations of bison and wapiti, may also have been a factor. Increased regional populations may have created local expansion pressures. Powers (1990) has suggested that expanding human populations to the west and south may have placed important demographic pressures on Chukotkan and Kamchatkan peoples, giving them greater impetus to seek lands farther east.

The large number of radiocarbon dates from Alaska now make it clear that initial occupation took place sometime around 12,000 B.P. (although the slightly earlier dates from Bluefish Caves in the northern Yukon suggest that colonization of eastern Beringia occurred around 14,000 B.P., or at about the same time as western Beringia). This timing is coincident with the "push" factor of rising late Pleistocene sea levels; retreating human populations may have followed the paleo–Yukon River from its mouth to the more stable inland conditions along its tributaries, such as the Tanana and Nenana Rivers. At the same time, the replacement of the tundra-steppe by an open parkland containing dwarf birch, dwarf willow, and poplar (aspen and cottonwood) would have presented additional sources of fuel and expanding opportunities for hunting wapiti and bison (see Zutter 1989). With reestablishment of the North Pacific flyway across southern Alaska, increased waterfowl populations may have become an attractive resource for netting with Upper Paleolithic technologies. This possibility is suggested by the faunal inventories from the Broken Mammoth site (Yesner 1994, 1996b, 2000), which are dominated by bison, wapiti, and waterfowl; waterfowl are also present in significant numbers at Bluefish Caves. Fiedel (2000b) has even suggested that migrants may have continued to pursue waterfowl from interior Alaska across the ice-free corridor, where lakes may have attracted and provided this resource, even though large game populations were limited. Southward population expansion from Alaska and the Yukon, which was coincident with glacial recession (around 11,500 B.P.; see Jackson and Duk-Rodkin 1996), may have been primarily an opportunistic response to increased resource availability, although population pressure may have also been involved.

Most discussions of environmental factors related to the peopling of the Americas have been possibilist arguments that focus on barriers and limitations to human migration rather than motivating factors (Butzer 1991; Fladmark 1978, 1979, 1983; Mandryk 1990; Reeves 1983; Willig 1996; Wright 1991). This statement is certainly true of Mandryk's (this volume) comments on the ice-free corridor. Other approaches have tried to implicate disease as an impeding or impelling factor in human colonization of the Americas (e.g., Dillehay 1991; Wendorf 1989), but like arguments for late Pleistocene watercraft (Engelbrecht and Seyfert 1994), these approaches are built entirely from circumstantial, not archaeological, evidence. As Lynch (1991) has noted, the "cold filter" hypothesis that reduced, not increased, tropical pathogens during the course of arctic migrations probably lessened disease as a factor in colonization of the Americas and, in fact, may have helped to increase human population densities. Disease would likely have been more of a problem for high-density, warmer-temperature coastal migrants than for interior migrants to the Americas (Lynch 1991).

The Colonization Process: Migration Models

During the heyday of the "New Archaeology," migration as an explanation for culture change was strongly impugned, except for the spread of early human populations, the colonization of some "marginal" regions, such as the Arctic, and the expansion of some agricultural groups. By the late 1980s that situation had changed, and migration models again achieved theoretical acceptability (Anthony 1990; Rouse 1986). This change was partly stimulated by the "Out of Africa" models based on archaeology and molecular genetics, which offered respectability to such discussions (Cavalli-Sforza and Cavalli-Sforza 1995; Gamble 1994).

A clear example of this reacceptance of migration models in culture change theory comes from the Fiedel paper in this volume. Fiedel uses the arctic model—the late prehistoric Thule Inuit migration—as an analogy for the rapid, main (Clovis), Paleoindian migration because this large-scale migration model apparently never disappeared from the radar screen of North American archaeologists. Other analogies are certainly possible, particularly the Numic migration into the Great Basin and the Athabaskan expansion from the western subarctic to the southwestern United States, as Fiedel notes. Fiedel, however, finds several points of analogy between the Thule and Clovis migrations, including their rapidity and their dependence on megafauna (cf. Yesner 1996b; Yesner et al. 1992). The greatest point of divergence is, of course, the fact that the High Arctic

was already occupied by Dorset (Arctic Small Tool tradition) populations; but the distinctiveness of their lifeways and the fact that there was apparently little or no interaction between the Thule and Dorset peoples make the analogy closer. Fiedel also effectively addresses the possible objection that the Thule people moved into a familiar environment, whereas the Clovis people did not: Both groups probably required about the same level of environmental readaptation and technological retooling. The take-away message is this: If the Thule effectively extirpated the Dorset people or forced them to withdraw in the face of competitive pressure, couldn't the Clovis migrants have done the same to the hypothetical small populations of pre-Clovis folks, such as the Monte Verdeans? This scenario would have been especially true in the situations of precarious, rapid climatic change that accompanied both the late prehistoric Thule migration of the Medieval Optimum and the earlier Pleistocene-Holocene transition.

Another clear example of the use of migration hypotheses is Pearson's (this volume) treatment of the relationship between Clovis technologies, which are diagnostically represented by fluted points, and the classical fishtail projectile points (FTPPs) of South America. The Isthmus of Panama appears to be the meeting ground for these technologies. It contains the southernmost Clovis fluted points (with a few possible exceptions in South America) and quarry sites that show reduction strategies and technologies similar to Clovis (large, square, bifacial cores and preforms with ground nipples and platforms; prefluting; hinge fractures; *outrepassé* thinning flakes; limaces; and spurred endscrapers). It is also home to some of the northernmost FTPPs (although a few specimens are known from Mexico and Belize). Pearson, like Fiedel and other researchers cited above, argues for a rapid Clovis migration as far south as Central America. What happened there is not yet clear, but the dating of Clovis and FTPP sites seems to favor the possibility that FTPP evolved from Clovis in Central America and was not the result of a reverse migration or "backwash." If the former did occur, then the FTPP migration from Central America to Patagonia was apparently as rapid as the Clovis migration to Central America!

New theoretical approaches to human migration have drawn from prehistoric cultural ecology. These models are being applied to the problem of the peopling of the Americas, especially subsistence and settlement patterns. One early approach was Kelly and Todd's (1988) now classic discussion of "Coming into the Country." In that model, they argued that Clovis migrants would have been highly mobile colonists, who were highly dependent on megafaunal resources, particularly in the arctic environment from which they presumably emerged. As such, they would have maximized the return rate of resources by moving to new patches, where they could continue to practice their high-return, big-game-hunting way of life rather than increase their dietary breadth to include lower-return resources (small game, birds, fish, shellfish, and plants. Whether this is an accurate characterization of early Paleoindian subsistence is a subject that is tackled below.) The result was the rapid movement of Paleoindian colonists that is apparent in the archaeological record and that is now explainable through a density-independent process differing from the simple demic expansion discussed above. This rapid movement was possible because abundant big game could always be found in the new patch and because no one else was there to exploit that patch! The model assumes that lack of knowledge of newly encountered environments was not a hindrance to this process and that hunting skills were rapidly transferable from one megafaunal taxon to another. It also assumes that the need for groups to shift to the exploitation of new patches was exacerbated both by rapid climatic change at the Pleistocene-Holocene transition and by human impacts on megafaunal resources. In contrast, later Paleoindians would have had a different relationship to the landscape, created by the extinction of megafauna (from whatever cause or causes) and by a change from a more equable to a more seasonal, continental climate. Under those circumstances, a shift to a broader-spectrum diet and a more sedentary (or semisedentary) way of life would have occurred.

Beaton's (1991) comparative discussion of "transient explorers" and "estate settlers" covered much of the same ground. It presented two idealized models of early colonization behavior in the peopling of Australia and the Americas and tried to describe such behavior in socioecological terms (sensu Barton et al., this volume). Perhaps to make the models more viable, Beaton described them in a relatively simplistic, strongly contrastive manner, differentiating between highly mobile foragers and more settled, semisedentary hunter-gatherers. This portrayal has led to some interpretive problems. For example, Beaton (1991) suggested that the earliest colonists (transient explorers) had little or no impact on the Australian megafauna. This statement is now clearly belied by new radiocarbon dates on both

sites and megafaunal extinctions from 60,000 to 50,000 B.P. (Flannery 1995; Webb 1998).

Testing the Beaton Model: The Case of the Broken Mammoth Site

The application of Beaton's (1991) model to a particular case—that of the early Nenana and Denali complexes in interior Alaska—shows some of the strengths and weaknesses of this model.

The Broken Mammoth site (XBD-131) is in some ways a typical bluff-top overlook site in interior Alaska that contains evidence of late Pleistocene and Holocene human occupation established in eolian loess deposits derived from river bars and ultimately from glacial outwash sediments. Broken Mammoth is unique, however, in the following ways:

1. It contains the oldest dates in consistent stratigraphic sequence in Beringia and possibly in the Americas. Three dates of 11,770 B.P. are derived from the basal occupation unit, which is associated with the lowest paleosol stringer lying directly above sterile late Pleistocene sands.
2. It contains well-defined, horizontal paleosols in which occupation units are emplaced (probably representing conflations of paleovegetational surfaces and anthropogenic debris, particularly hearth smears) that can be traced over tens of meters with no evidence of faulting or cryoturbation.
3. The separation of stratigraphic units allows clear discrimination between two main early episodes of occupation at the site, an earlier one at 11,800–11,000 B.P. and a later one at 10,500–9300 B.P.
4. The depth of the loess cap and the calcareous nature of the sediments derived from rocks of the Alaska Range to the south have preserved faunal remains and bone and ivory tools found in the lowest (late Pleistocene and early Holocene) units at the site, in a fashion unique to late Pleistocene–early Holocene sites in interior Alaska (Pearson 1999; Yesner 2000).
5. The analysis of these faunal remains has provided a database on early subsistence and settlement patterns that is unparalleled in interior Alaska.

Together these data offer unique capabilities of testing the Beaton model at the point of initial human colonization of the Americas in eastern Beringia.

Materials from the Broken Mammoth site enable a point-by-point assessment of those aspects of the Beaton model that can be applied to intrasite data. In each case listed below, italics highlight a criterion for differentiating transient explorers from estate settlers in the Beaton model, followed by its application to the Broken Mammoth archaeological data.

1. *Demography: Transient explorers should be characterized by low fecundity, low budding threshold, and high extinction probability, whereas estate settlers should be characterized by high fecundity, high budding threshold, and low extinction probability.* Archaeologically, transient explorers should be reflected by small occupations with relatively little debris, as well as small, shallow hearths and limited evidence for dwellings. In contrast, estate settlers should be reflected by larger occupations with greater amounts of debris, as well as larger, deeper hearths and more substantial evidence for dwellings.

At Broken Mammoth, although the two main early occupations both contain evidence of the Nenana complex (Yesner and Pearson 2002), the earliest occupation dating from 11,800 to 11,000 B.P. is characterized by a much smaller amount of debris, significantly greater distances between hearths and other occupational foci, smaller, shallower hearths, and no evidence of dwellings. In contrast, the overlying occupational unit is characterized by a much larger amount of debris covering a significantly larger percentage of the site area, as well as much larger, deeper hearths. There is also possible evidence of dwellings in the form of lithic remains and small bone fragments distributed radially around hearths, with larger bones and bone fragments distributed a meter or more from the hearths, and a few examples of possible postholes (Stone and Yesner 2003). These data suggest much longer-term occupations associated with the second wave of colonization: perhaps on the order of weeks to months, as opposed to days to weeks for the initial colonists. The nature of these more sedentary occupations strongly supports the Beaton model.

2. *Tool inventories of transient explorers should be generalized and conservative, whereas tool inventories of estate settlers should be specialized and inventive.* At Broken Mammoth, the earliest occupation is characterized by a great deal of uniformity in the lithic assemblage. The assemblage is dominated by large cobble tools (mostly choppers, planoconvex scrapers, and other modified core tools), as well as numerous flake tools (mostly unmodified flakes and some retouched flakes). Most of these lithic remains are made from either quartz ventifacts, which are distributed abundantly throughout the region in association with earlier late Pleisto-

cene sand deposits, or local small river cobbles, as indicated by the high frequencies of round, weathered cortex flakes. This restriction to the use of low-quality but abundantly available local materials may simply be due to the highly transient nature of the occupation. However, it may also be due to these factors: the best local lithic sources—the high-quality cherts found in the Landmark Gap/Amphitheater Mountains area of the Alaska Range and the obsidians found in the Wrangell Mountains—may have still been under ice until after 11,000 B.P., and knowledge of more distant lithic sources, such as the Livengood cherts, may have been very limited. Besides a more limited range of generalized lithic tool types, the earliest occupation contains few examples of organic (bone and ivory) tools.

In contrast, the later occupation contains a much wider range of tool types, including more specialized bifaces, scrapers, and flake knives, as well as some unifacial tools. The stone tools are made from a wider variety of lithic sources, including various cherts as well as obsidians from as far away as the Batza Tena source in the Koyukuk River region hundreds of miles to the northwest. The later occupation also contains a wide variety of organic tools that are unknown from other early Beringian sites, including mammoth ivory rods, eyed needles, and other implements. For both occupations, the Broken Mammoth site may have been critically positioned for access to these resources (quartz ventifacts, river cobbles, and mammoth ivory from eroding contexts at the valley margin).

These data also strongly support the Beaton model. Beaton, however, suggested that one should expect highly curated tool industries to be found in association with transient explorers because mobile groups would have transported these curated materials from point to point. Broken Mammoth contains no real evidence for the transport of such curated tool types, a lack that may be explained by the extreme dearth of high-quality lithic materials as compared with those found in warmer regions, such as Australia.

3. *The range of activities should be repetitive in the occupations of transient explorers but varied in the occupations of estate settlers.* This criterion is clearly demonstrable with the data from the Broken Mammoth site. The functions of the tool assemblages associated with the earliest occupation seem homogeneous and repetitive. Faunal remains associated with the earliest occupation also show less spatial differentiation; a redundant combination of some large mammals (predominantly wapiti and bison), some small mammals, and

a wide variety of birds (predominantly waterfowl) are found in association with virtually all of the occupation loci.

In contrast, the second occupational unit contains evidence of a wide variety of activities, including tool manufacture, resharpening, caching, and discard; scanning for game, primary and secondary butchery, cooking, discard, and probable caching of meat sections; and hide preparation and clothing manufacture or repair. Also in contrast to the lowest unit at the site, the second occupational unit shows a concentrated focus on large game animals, and concentrations of specific animals (bison, wapiti, moose, and caribou) are associated with hearths in different parts of the site. Whether this is the result of butchery practices, caching behavior, nuclear-family-based exploitation patterns, or temporal differences in the hearth deposits is unknown.

4. *The exploitation strategies of transient explorers should be those of foragers/pursuers, whereas the strategies of estate settlers should be those of searchers/collectors. The "colonizing logic" of transient explorers should include a relatively narrow dietary breadth, whereas that of estate settlers should include a relatively wide dietary breadth.* The extensive faunal data from eight field seasons of excavation at the Broken Mammoth site (in excess of 10,000 elements) create some problems for this criterion. The earliest occupation at the site is clearly characterized by a greater diversity of taxa, as noted above. This finding appears to be consistent with a characterization of the early occupants as coarse-grained foragers rather than fine-grained collectors, but it is inconsistent with the notion that they should possess a relatively narrow dietary breadth. Similarly the behavior of later occupants seems to be consistent with fine-grained collectors but is not characterized by a relatively wide dietary breadth. However, the Broken Mammoth data may simply reflect the season of exploitation in each occupational unit. More waterfowl in the earliest occupational unit, for example, may reflect seasonal spring use of the site rather than a broader pattern of regional exploitation of available taxa.

The Broken Mammoth data show that the Beaton model contains both strengths and weaknesses. The data, however, also suggest that the earliest colonists of interior eastern Beringia were different from those who were present 1,000 years later, and that the earliest colonists were more "transient," whereas the later ones were more "settled." This finding may represent a special case in applying the Beaton model, as will be discussed below.

The Colonization Process: Socioecological Models

MacDonald (this volume) is less kind in his assessment of the utility of the Beaton model for understanding the behavior of early Paleoindian colonizers. In his view, they were all estate settlers because transient exploration would have been "too costly and risky to have been viable for early Paleoindians." In MacDonald's view, even the earliest colonists needed to maintain strong reproductive and social ties with larger groups from their previous territory in order to sustain population continuity. In making this assertion, MacDonald appeals to ethnographic models of hunter-gatherer socioecology (cf. MacDonald 1998; Surovell 2000). He concludes that there is an inexorable link between the nature of the colonization process and the chronology of the peopling of the Americas. Because the founding of the Americas must have been a "gradual process," the Americas must have been settled "by pre-Clovis foragers before 12,000 B.P."

Meltzer, in arguably the meatiest article in this collection, arrives at a conclusion strikingly similar to that of MacDonald by using other socioecological models derived from hunter-gatherer foraging theory in his discussion of the colonizing process (see Meltzer 2002 for further development of this theme). He confronts the Kelly and Todd (1988) model head-on, suggesting that maximizing behavior may not have systematically characterized Paleoindian colonists. One particular weakness that Meltzer finds with the Kelly and Todd (1988) model is its assumption of a non-density-dependent process based on the fact that "human populations were almost certainly smaller at this time than at any subsequent time in American prehistory." Whether Paleoindian populations were smaller than succeeding early Archaic or Altithermal groups in various parts of North America could certainly be argued. Meltzer, however, asserts—as does MacDonald—that there would have been a "demographic risk" to such low population densities and interpopulation distances: "Colonizers must maintain a 'critical mass' of population to ensure reproductive viability." The risk of population extinction would have been greatest after dispersal because of the vulnerability of populations entering unknown environments and because of the energy they needed to devote to learning such new environments. This scenario would have been particularly true in the more patchy, heterogeneous environments of the Pleistocene-Holocene transition. The problem would have been exacerbated by the inability to obtain information from other groups, as modern hunter-gatherers do. Those who remained behind with smaller population densities would have been more vulnerable. This vulnerability, however, could have been offset by high fertility at the rates envisioned in the demic expansion models cited above. Meltzer apparently thinks that this level of demographic response would have been impossible or insufficient. He suggests instead that early colonists might have had to temper resource maximization with risk minimization in order to maintain demographic viability. In his model, there would have been trade-offs between acquiring resources, acquiring information, and minimizing extinction risks. Fine-grained resource-exploitation strategies (focusing on high-ranked resources, such as large game) would have been mixed with coarse-grained strategies (taking resources as they are encountered, including some lower-ranked ones), as well as with attempts to learn about previously unknown, but potentially higher-ranked, resources. The settlement patterns of these Paleoindian groups would have been characterized by complex aggregation and dispersal strategies. "Colonization would not be a steady movement through the Americas but instead a stutter-step, with relatively longer periods of residence within megapatches separated by rapid movements between patches. This process might look slow in human time (multiple generations), but it would look rapid in archaeological time, which readily encompasses those generations."

This model of the colonization process brings us to the problem of archaeological testability. As Meltzer himself acknowledges, the small temporal and spatial scales that differentiate models emphasizing resource acquisition on the one hand and risk minimization on the other may make them too difficult to test on the archaeological record. These models are only testable at the level of individual sites and regions, and at that level, local and regional idiosyncratic features are likely to come into play. Such local tests, however, can still provide valuable insights into the colonization process. Meltzer notes that useful data for these tests might include evidence for serial use of patches (whose dates may be differentiated beyond the error margin of radiocarbon assays), as well as changes in resource use and stylistic "signaling." As noted above, these criteria are well met at Broken Mammoth, which may serve as one of the best indicators of the nature of the colonization process.

Many of the same issues are confronted by Barton et al. in their article on "The Ecology of Human Coloni-

zation in Pristine Landscapes" (this volume). Although Kelly and Todd (1988), Steele et al. (1998), Anderson and Gillam (2000), and Meltzer (this volume) have all presented convincing arguments for patch saturation, "stutter-step," or "string-of-pearls" models for characterizing the dynamics of Paleoindian migrations, none have convincingly offered *explanations* for the underlying process. To address this problem, Barton et al. effectively turn once again to socioecological theory, specifically optimal foraging theory, for a demonstration of underlying causes.

According to this theory, a consumer will continue to exploit a landscape patch until the abundance of highly ranked prey (those that offer the highest return for the energy invested in search, pursuit, retrieval, and processing) within the patch falls to the point at which the cost of moving to a new patch is less than the cost of attempting to exploit more of those highly ranked items. Such models have been widely applied to understanding hunter-gatherer foraging behavior. In the case of Paleoindian migrants, Barton et al. assume that those highly ranked resources would have been megafauna, which were being depleted as human migrants continued to fill locales. (Barton et al. agree with Webb and Rindos's [1997] assumption that megafauna would have been the key resource because other resources may have been poorly known by immigrant populations. Kelly and Todd [1988] also assume that megafauna would have been the key resource, although they offer climate change as well as human predation as an explanation for resource decline.)

Under such situations, foragers have a choice: to diversify their diet to include lower-ranked resources or to move to a new landscape patch where higher-ranked resources are more abundant. In general, movement is costly, especially riskier, longer-distance ("leapfrogging") movement into unknown territories. Local movement within a territory is less costly, but if that territory is populated, movement within it still incurs the costs of competition over resources, social debts, and territorial defense. If resources decline enough, undertaking long-distance moves may be advantageous, as long as the new territory is unpopulated. For Paleoindians, this strategy would have resulted in a "leapfrog through the richest biomes," after which "their descendents would backfill the rest of the landscape."

Once again, the critical aspect of this hypothesis is archaeological testability. Citing a lack of abundantly available, uniformly rigorous, zooarchaeological data, Barton et al. use the distribution of Clovis and Folsom projectile points as test data. These data do seem to confirm the "leapfrog" and "backfill" model: Clovis entrants leapfrog between sites that appear to be particularly conducive to proboscidean exploitation, whereas Folsom migrants backfill much of the intervening territory after the proboscideans become extinct.

Another important aspect of this model is raised by Barton et al. but is not addressed because of the lack of available data. "What happens," they ask, "when there is no place left to move to? What processes actually drive the switch from transient explorer to estate settler?" Here they appeal to the broad subsistence changes that accompanied the shift from Paleoindian to early Archaic. The Beringian data, however, may offer a more potent test. Why, for example, does the shift from transient explorer to estate settler seem to come so much earlier in Beringia than in areas south of the ice sheets, and why does the Beaton model apply so poorly in Beringia, as noted above? The answers may be found in some of the unique aspects of Beringian colonization. The rising waters of the Bering Sea to the west and the slow melting of the western corridor may have created a population bottleneck in eastern Beringia around 11,000 B.P. At the same time, human populations (as noted above) were being opportunistically drawn into interior Alaska, with its abundant populations of bison, elk, and other species, during the relatively brief "poplar rise" (12,000–9000 B.P.). This movement would have caused locally dense human populations to develop within an otherwise relatively empty landscape. As a result, the assumptions of an unpopulated landscape would have been violated, and human populations may have opted to stay put more often and intensively exploit local landscape patches. This situation would have been exacerbated by the very early xerothermic maximum (around 9000 B.P.) in interior Alaska, which resulted in proboscidean extinction in that area well before it occurred in the continental United States. One consequence of this development may have been a rapid shift by Paleoindians to higher-cost taxa, such as small mammals, birds, and fish, as is found at the Broken Mammoth site (Yesner 1994).

Variability in the Paleoindian Record

If Tankersley's paper is any indication, Meltzer has much to worry about in the context of local and regional variability in Paleoindian archaeological complexes. The variability may be an artifact of our inability to control the temporal and stratigraphic data

sufficiently, or it may simply be the result of the archaeological visibility of specific facets of assemblages due to preservation or serendipity. However, it is clear that there is significant interregional variation in Clovis tool-kit composition; for example, in the relative importance and form of large blades and blade cores, and in the presence or absence of split-bone points and ivory points and foreshafts. Such variations may be attributed to differences in raw-material availability, tool rejuvenation frequencies, site locations, and targeted species. There is also variation in the frequencies of exotic stone types and caching and storage behavior, which may reflect local differences in approaching the landscape, such as the aggregation-dispersal strategies discussed by Meltzer. The presence or absence of red ochre may be more reflective of ideological differences, which are difficult to pin down from the archaeological record. Tankersley also suggests that some variation may be the result of local "design experimentation in response to continuous changes in environmental conditions," as well as "enculturation or acculturation," presumably between Paleoindian groups. Some axes of Clovis assemblage variability are apparently real; others are simply a function of the archaeological record.

This brings us to one of the most important axes of Paleoindian variability: the socioeconomic organization underlying Paleoindian sites. In spite of the admonitions by Gero (1993), Surovell (2000), and others, researchers have paid little attention to the reconstruction of social dynamics in Paleoindian society. We agree with Chilton's assessment in this volume and in her previous article (Chilton 1994:8–11) that there is "an assumption—most often implicit—that Paleoindians were primarily hunters of large game"; such "an emphasis on hunting and its correlates (i.e., big game and large spears) gives primacy to the role of men in Paleo-societies, if it is assumed that hunting was a masculine undertaking." Meltzer, for example, assumes that, because big-game hunting was a risky activity and women were often busy caring for children, the former activity was predominantly a male one. However, we do not know if men were the exclusive hunters of big game; some modern ethnographic models (e.g., the Agta) suggest that women may have also been involved. Furthermore, we do not know which, if any, contemporary hunter-gatherer models should or could be applied to the very different conditions of the Pleistocene-Holocene transition or to the Paleoindian circumstances of high mobility, which probably required unusually high flexibility in social roles. The tyranny of contemporary ethnographic models is, in any case, something to avoid.

Even if women were not particularly involved in big-game hunting, the importance that big-game hunting held in Paleoindian societies is still questionable. The evidence from the Broken Mammoth site clearly shows that eastern Beringian groups exploited small game, waterfowl, other birds, and fish, as well as bison, wapiti, caribou, and mountain sheep. Approximately 40 percent of the subsistence (by weight) was provided by birds (Yesner 1994). Whether or not this is a special case for Paleoindian migration, as noted above, remains to be seen. Chilton, however, argues that the picture is no different farther south. She notes that an extremely diverse subsistence base is evident at Paleoindian sites in Texas (Aubrey and Horn Shelter), Minnesota (Pelican Rapids), Pennsylvania (Shawnee Minisink), and elsewhere. In fact, a more exclusive, big-game-hunting orientation is defensible only in the classic High Plains sites; ironically, most of the classic, Paleoindian, big-game-hunting models derive from that region. Undoubtedly netting technologies were used to exploit many species, particularly birds, and women were involved in their capture, a practice that, as Olga Soffer has emphasized (in Pringle 1997a), goes back to at least Gravettian (Upper Paleolithic) times. Plants, of course, are nearly invisible in the Paleoindian archaeological record, and even small game, birds, and fish do not preserve nearly as well, or have as great an archaeological visibility, as large animal remains.

Where organic tools are preserved in Paleoindian sites, we have not only the bone and ivory points and foreshafts discussed by Tankersley, but also awls and eyed needles, such as those that were recovered at the Broken Mammoth site. These tools reflect both hunting gear and "maintenance" gear that was used to manufacture and repair clothing, skills that were critical for survival in arctic or late Pleistocene environments. Much of this work was probably done by women, although how much is difficult to say. Even when only stone tools are preserved, as is often the case, researchers tend to overlook the scrapers and gravers—which were probably made and used more often by women for clothing manufacture and repair—and focus on the projectile points, as Chilton notes. In his own work, Yesner has continually argued that the record from the Broken Mammoth site suggests not only the presence and activities of women (e.g., using the sewing gear, for which abun-

dant evidence is found at the site), but also of entire households, including children. This analysis is based on the total picture: diversity in residential activities, length of occupation, and permanence of facilities reflected at the site, as well as regional settlement patterns. In essence, this is what Chilton (this volume) is seeking when she appeals for social models "that are built upon fine-grained analyses and interpretations of site plans, feature patterning, and site hierarchies at a regional level."

There is precious little in these articles to illuminate the ideological aspects of early New World colonists. Highly mobile initial colonists may have had little time to engage in such activities; perhaps if they had done so, they would have low archaeological visibility. For whatever reason, the engraved mobile objects of Upper Paleolithic European societies are extremely rare in Paleoindian sites. Researchers have found a few examples of the decoration and application of red ochre on bone and ivory points and on limestone palettes. Rock art, however, is one of the few widely available items that we can point to as evidence of Paleoindian ideology. Agenbroad and Hesse address that subject in this volume. They show that the presence of mammoths, in particular, in Colorado Plateau art can be used (along with the traditional archaeology) to document the presence of Paleoindians and their prey. In the future, researchers must give more attention to the creation and character of this art as reflections of Paleoindian beliefs.

What Do We Know about Paleoindian Colonization?

Based on the above comments, what would represent a modal view of our knowledge about Paleoindian colonization of the Americas at the beginning of the new millennium? We suggest the following as a synopsis:

1. There may have been several colonization episodes of the Americas. Regardless of the number, each episode involved populations migrating from East Asia rather than Europe.
2. There may have been temporally pre-Clovis population pulses into the Americas. Such pulses were probably swamped by the major wave of Clovis Paleoindian migration in the terminal Pleistocene.
3. The wave of Paleoindian migration may have left daughter populations in interior Alaska and the

area south of the ice sheets, creating the strong statistical assemblage affiliation between the Nenana and Clovis complexes.

4. Fluted points may have been invented by Paleoindians, perhaps to hunt large proboscideans. This technology may have moved southward to Central America, where fishtail points may have also been invented.

5. The process of the Paleoindian peopling of the Americas was probably rapid but did not occur purely through demic expansion; it likely involved "stutters and stops." Colonization probably had significant effects (as did climatic change) on remaining Pleistocene megafauna. In response, colonists both pursued large game in novel environments and broadened their use of smaller game, birds, and fish in some circumstances. They probably combined resource-maximization and risk-avoidance strategies as a part of that process.

6. Initial colonists, who were probably more transient explorers, were followed by a later wave of settlers. This contrast, however, can be overdrawn. Colonization proceeded differently in different sets of environments.

7. Eastern Beringia may have been a special case in the colonization of the Americas. A geographical bottleneck, earlier megafaunal extinction, and opportunistic availability of a rich terrestrial ecosystem in a concentrated area during the terminal Pleistocene may have created regionally dense populations, an earlier focus on a broad spectrum of resources, and more intensive, longer-term regional settlement.

8. A great deal of variability existed in Paleoindian subsistence strategies, technologies, and approaches to the landscape as shown in caching and storage behaviors, all of which are all related to variations in the environments that Paleoindians traversed and occupied.

9. Paleoindian colonization required maximum flexibility, not only in subsistence strategies, but also in social roles and household organization. Researchers must view assumptions about gender roles and other aspects of social organization in this light and must consider the general problem of drawing ethnographic analogies to a world that was very different from the one today.

Paleobiologists are fond of insisting on the lack of homologies between the vegetative environments and faunal associations of the Pleistocene-Holocene transition and those of the present. If that is true, then insights into the socioeconomic organization of Paleoindian peoples will come less from ethnographic analogies than from insights drawn directly from archaeological and paleoenvironmental data.

We would be well served to focus our energies on these potential avenues of research for the near future. This focus will take us far beyond the arm waving about migration routes and assemblage comparisons and even beyond the simplistic modeling of demic population expansion. It will do so by providing broader insights into the details of continental colonization behavior and more generally into the transformations of hunter-gatherer societies under circumstances that are little reflected in the ethnographic record. To achieve these goals, however, we must devote much more attention to the details of Paleoindian site contents and to new avenues for their interpretation.

NOTES

Chapter 2: Anthropological Genetic View

1. A haplogroup (haplotype group) is a set of haplotypes that share a common set of polymorphisms, or mutations, as a consequence of being genealogically related. Individual haplotypes are defined by the combination of RFLPs and HVR1 mutations that are present in them.

2. RFLP stands for "restriction fragment length polymorphism." Because most of these polymorphisms occur in the coding sequences of the mitochondrial genome, they generally reflect the pattern of variation in and the relative evolutionary rate of mtDNA sequences that are under functional constraints.

3. HVR1 stands for "hypervariable region 1" of the mtDNA control region. Direct sequencing provides a nucleotide-by-nucleotide reading of this noncoding segment of the mtDNA genome. The HVR1 also mutates more rapidly than the coding sequences in the rest of the mtDNA genome (Horai et al. 1995; Ingman et al. 2000). Because of this feature, it is possible to obtain a detailed assessment of mutational changes that have occurred within the HVR1.

4. Haplogroup D shares the 16223T (223T) mutation with haplogroups A, C, and X; the 16325C (325C) mutation with haplogroup C; and the 16362C (362C) mutation with haplogroup A.

5. X6/X7 haplotypes should not to be confused with haplogroup X mtDNAs. Haplogroup X was identified in European populations by Torroni et al. (1996) and was named following a nomenclature started in 1992 by the Wallace Laboratory at Emory University. This was the same year that Easton et al. (1996) and Merriwether and Ferrell (1996) published data on the presence of X6/X7 mtDNAs in Native Americans. Thus, the naming of haplogroup X was temporally synchronous with that of X6/X7 mtDNAs in Native American populations, as was the identification of these two kinds of mtDNAs as belonging to putative founding haplogroups in Native Americans.

6. The same is true for admixed populations of the Americas, such as Black Caribs (Monsalve and Hagelberg 1997), Cubans (Torroni et al. 1995), Puerto Ricans (Martinez-Crusado et al. 2000), Mexican Americans (Merriwether et al. 1997), and Afro-Brazilians and Afro-Uruguayans (Bortolini et al. 1997; Bravi et al. 1997).

7. Most of these mtDNAs were screened for only the RFLP markers of haplogroups A–D, not for those of haplogroups L, M, X, or other Eurasian lineages. The expanded screening would have indicated that the other mtDNAs were acquired through nonnative admixture, were related to haplogroup X or so-called X6/X7 mtDNAs, or were acquired through contamination with modern DNA. An additional problem was that the sequenced portion of the HVR1 from ancient samples was not as long as that typically obtained from modern mtDNAs.

8. To be considered a founding haplotype, candidate mtDNAs have to meet several criteria. First, founding haplotypes should be widespread within Amerindians and shared between tribes because they would have preceded tribal differentiation. Second, founding haplotypes should be central (nodal) to the branching of their haplogroup in phylogenetic analyses because all new haplotypes would have originated from them. Third, founding haplotypes should be present in East Asian and Siberian populations because they originated in those geographic regions and have persisted there after the departure of the ancestral Native American population(s). Conversely, mtDNA haplotypes that are derived from these founding haplotypes should have a limited distribution; they should be present only in single populations or be shared between populations that are genetically, linguistically, or geographically proximate.

9. HR-RFLP stands for "high-resolution restriction fragment length polymorphism." HR-RFLP analyses survey individual mtDNAs for sequence variation using a series of restriction enzymes that cleave the mtDNA molecule at different recognition sites (i.e., at locations containing specific combinations of nucleotide bases) within it. Point mutations, the source of most sequence variation in DNAs, either eliminate or create recognition sites in mtDNAs by altering their nucleotide base composition. As a result, HR-RFLP analysis catalogues the sequence changes that have occurred within the recognition sites of these mtDNAs.

10. An alternative to screening the whole mtDNA genome for variation is low-resolution RFLP (LR-RFLP) analysis. This method takes advantage of the ability of RFLP analysis to detect specific maternal lineages in human populations. Because many maternal lineages have specific geographic origins, such as haplogroup L in the African continent (Chen et al. 1995), it is possible to screen mtDNAs from a particular population for the RFLPs that define these maternal lineages and to determine the relative genetic contribution of individuals having differing geographic origins.

11. The *Hae*III 16517 site is known to be hypermutable, being gained or lost through multiple T→C or C→T transitions at np 16519 within the *Hae*III recognition site (GGCC) that begins at np 16517 (Chen et al. 2000; Schurr et al. 1999). As a result, this site should not be considered an RFLP marker for haplogroups A–D in Native Americans, except for haplogroup B, in which, for some reason, the site is far less mutable.

12. This naming system is not comprehensive because of the limited samples that were used to construct the median network on which it is based. It is also of limited resolution compared with

networks based on HR-RFLP haplotypes. The system, however, accurately represents the clusters of haplotypes that one sees when combining both forms of sequence information.

13. This mutation is different from the −*Hinc*II 13259/+*Alu*I 13262 polymorphism that occurs in haplogroup C mtDNAs. The *Hinc*II 13259 site loss is caused by a mutation in the first third of the recognition sequence for this restriction enzyme, whereas the linked −*Hinc*II 13259/+*Alu*I 13262 polymorphism is created by a mutation in the latter third of the *Hinc*II recognition sequence, which overlaps with that of *Alu*I, thereby creating the *Alu*I 13262 site gain.

14. This finding is not surprising because many nucleotide sites are known to undergo mutation more often than others in the HVR1 (Gurven 2000; Hasagawa et al. 1993; Stoneking 2000; Wakeley 1993).

15. The same pattern is also apparent in the RFLP haplotype data (Torroni et al. 1993a, 1994a,d).

16. Haplogroup B, however, does appear at relatively high frequencies in the Andean region of South America (Merriwether et al. 1994; Torroni et al. 1993a), perhaps because of founder effects.

17. Various other Eurasian and Asian haplogroups comprise the rest of the Siberian mtDNAs. This distribution probably reflects population dynamics in Siberia before and after the colonization of the New World, such as the expansion of Paleoasiatic speakers in northeastern Asia (Schurr and Wallace 1999; Schurr et al. 1999; Starikovskaya et al. 1998), the spread of Tungusic-speaking populations throughout eastern and central Siberia (Derenko et al. 2000; Schurr and Wallace 1999; Schurr et al. 1999; Torroni et al. 1993a), the spread of Uralic speakers in northern Asia (Lahermo et al. 1996), and the northward expansion of Turkic speakers into Siberia (Yakuts; Torroni et al. 1998).

18. Because of these contrasting results, the source of the discrepancy between the RFLP and HVR1 divergence estimates is not entirely clear. It may be attributable to differences in the assumptions of the statistical methods used to make these estimates, the sampling of Amerindian populations with high frequencies of closely related deletion haplotypes, or the extent of variation revealed by HR-RFLP versus HVR1 sequence data.

19. None of these studies, however, accounted for the known RFLP haplotype differences between Amerindians, Na-Dene Indians, and Eskimo/Aleuts, which reflect at least two expansions into the New World.

20. NRY stands for "nonrecombining region of the Y chromosome." Because most of this chromosome does not undergo recombination, all of the SNPs within it can be considered to be linked and part of a single haplotype.

21. SNP stands for "single nucleotide polymorphism." SNPs consist of point mutations and small insertions or deletions (indels) in the NRY. Y chromosomes are divided into distinct lineage clusters, or haplogroups, based on the presence or absence of one to several SNPs. Haplotypes belonging to these haplogroups are further assayed for diversity using more variable loci, such as STRs, in which multiple alleles or variants of different sizes are present within a population.

22. STR stands for "short tandem repeat." STRs are composed of multiple copies of short nucleotide sequences, such as GAG or GATA. Each "allele" of an STR marker or locus consists of a certain number of sequence repeats. The number of repeats present at a particular locus is called its "allele size." STR markers usually increase or decrease in allele size over time and typically mutate much more rapidly than the other genetic systems (SNPs and indels), thereby providing a finer resolution of sequence change in the Y chromosome.

23. dHPLC stands for "denaturing high-performance liquid chromatography." This method is described in Underhill et al. (1997).

24. There has been a recent attempt to reconcile these differing nomenclatures (Y Chromosome Consortium 2002), but the resulting compromise has created a nomenclature that is quite complicated and not easily employed to describe NRY haplotypes.

25. Multiallelic STR markers typically subdivide biallelic (SNP) Y-chromosome haplotypes, but not in exactly the same way that HVR1 sequences subdivide RFLP haplotypes in the mtDNA. Unlike HVR1 mutations, STR loci do not provide additional markers that confirm the lineal identity of a paternal lineage. Instead the overall pattern of allelic variation at STR loci gives information about the evolutionary trajectory of a paternal lineage. The same biallelic haplotype may have several different alleles for a particular STR locus because the higher mutation rate of the STR produces a large number of alleles that distinguish otherwise identical SNP haplotypes from each other. In addition, the same STR allele at a particular locus may be observed in different Y SNP haplotypes, either because of the recent increase or decrease in allele size, or because of the convergence of the STR allele sizes in the two haplotypes. For these reasons, many different STR loci are typically analyzed for every SNP haplotype; in this combination of loci, it is possible to see the directionality of allele-size changes occurring within them, and hence, how they have evolved within these paternal lineages.

26. Interestingly, M46 haplotypes are common in northeastern Siberian groups, including the Chukchi and Siberian Eskimos, but are rarer in Amur River groups (Karafet et al. 1999; Lell et al. 1998, 1999). Among Okhotsk/Amur populations, this lineage appears only in the groups that have had recent contact or shared origins with central Siberians, such as the Okhotsk Evenks, Ulchi, Nanai, and downriver Negidals. It is absent, however, in the groups that have maintained greater geographic or linguistic isolation, namely the Udegeys, Nivkhs, and upriver Negidals (Lell et al. 1999, 2000, 2002). These data suggest that the M46 lineage was recently introduced into the Okhotsk/Amur region, probably from south-central Siberia.

27. The M3 lineage also appears to have been maintained in the Beringian populations that were ancestral to modern-day Eskimos, Aleuts, and Chukchi, who show genetic affinities with other circumpolar populations (Forster et al. 1996; Schurr et al. 1999; Shields et al. 1993; Starikovskaya et al. 1998; Torroni et al. 1993b).

28. If these Y haplotypes were to be screened for the array of new SNPs recently detected in African Y chromosomes, they would be placed in known paternal lineages; hence, the haplotypes would not be "null."

29. Unrelated studies of Y-chromosome variation in Siberian and Native American populations have revealed similar patterns of haplotypic variation. Several researchers have defined Y haplotypes by analyzing variation in the alphoid heteroduplex (α) type

II gene, along with additional SNP and STR markers (Bianchi et al. 1997, 1998; Peña et al. 1995; Rodriguez-Delfin et al. 1997; F. R. Santos et al. 1996a, 1999). These studies revealed the presence of a major founding Y haplotype, A0, in Native American populations defined by the combination of the αII/DYS19/M3 markers. This haplotype is synonymous with the M3 lineage; it appears to have originated somewhere in east-central Siberia and occurs at the highest frequencies in South American populations.

30. The reason for the wide-ranging age estimate is that Underhill et al. (1996) used two different mutation rates for autosomal STRs to obtain them.

31. The discrepancies in these Y-haplogroup age estimates may reflect the different mutation rates of the different kinds (tri-, tetra-, and penta-) of Y-chromosome STRs (de Knijff et al. 1997; Kayser et al. 1997) that are used to make them. The mutation rate of a given STR can also vary considerably depending on the size (number of repeats of the variable block) of the founder allele at each STR locus (Carvalho-Silva et al. 1999). However, Heyer et al. (1997) reported that Y STRs have mutation frequencies comparable to those on the autosomes; these frequencies are roughly equal to those originally published by Weber and Wong (1993). Recent work also suggests that STRs have a more rapid mutation rate than previously estimated, meaning that modern human populations may have spread into different parts of the Old and New Worlds later than estimated in earlier genetic studies (Thomson et al. 2000). These data sets show that more focused studies of STR evolution in Amerindian populations are needed to clarify the date(s) of initial colonization of the New World from a Y-chromosome perspective.

Chapter 4: Historical Linguistic Evidence

1. "Language family" is the term used for genetic units in historical and comparative linguistics. Members of a "language family" ("family" for short) are hypothesized to have all descended from a single common ancestral language, which can be reconstructed as a "protolanguage."

2. This symbol represents the sound of orthographic "th" in the English word "thing."

3. Many scholars have noted that the figure of "8,000 to 10,000 years" is a rule of thumb and is not based on quantitative principle. It is conceivable that analytic ingenuity might uncover "shared anomalies" in such sheltered contexts as basic verbs (as in Indo-European), which could provide convincing evidence of genetic units older than 10,000 years.

4. In a discussion at the "Pioneers on the Land" symposium that was held on December 4, 1999, Steve Zegura stated that Greenberg had told him that he did not insist on the equation between Clovis and Amerind.

5. The exact number of linguistic stocks in the various continents remains in dispute, so Nettle's statistics must be approximate. For instance, Nettle's work follows Greenberg (1963) in recognizing only four major linguistic stocks in Africa: Khoisan, Niger-Kordofanian, Nilo-Saharan, and Afro-Asiatic.

6. Nichols (personal communication, 1999) argues that Ruhlen's results do not pass the tests that distinguish the trace of a historical event from resemblance by chance.

Chapter 9: North Atlantic Connection

1. Big stone points are clearly only one of several possible alternative technologies (e.g., bone and antler points, harpoons, stone-tipped arrows, darts, and nets) suitable for the exploitation of large and medium-sized game. Mass hunting drives involving deadfalls are well documented in Paleolithic sites in both hemispheres and required no technology specifically related to killing animals.

2. The elegant Solutrean foliate points from northern Spain that Straus describes (e.g., Straus and Clark 1986) were made almost exclusively from fine- and medium-grained green quartzite.

3. Typologically defined "Archaic" lithic scatters are almost certainly time-transgressive. Some probably extend back to Paleoindian time ranges; some may simply represent limited-activity sites produced by pottery-making people as recently as historical times. Because these sites seldom contain datable material, it is difficult to demonstrate this possibility empirically.

4. This is a significant failing of the *chaîne opératoire* approaches to technological variation that are favored by recent generations of French prehistorians (e.g., Boëda 1991), who were influenced by Leroi-Gourhan (1964, 1965). The *chaîne opératoire*, which resembles Schiffer's (1987) behavior chain, constitutes a descriptive advance over the ad hoc approaches that were used before the 1980s and a desirable shift in emphasis away from the obsession with typology. However, the very few *chaînes* identified so far are explained wholly in terms of social learning (i.e., technological traditions handed down from generation to generation over thousands of years). Formal convergence as a consequence of the constraints imposed by rock mechanics is never considered.

5. The weight of the evidence accumulated so far indicates that modern humans from Asia colonized the New World over a long interval beginning about 15,000 B.P. Just *how* they did this is the subject of this book. No one is denying that people migrated, but we need to model the migration process much more precisely than we have done so far.

6. There are other kinds of typologies, of course, including functional ones. Morphological typologies, however, are the most common ones used historically (and currently) in Paleolithic research; see Bisson (2000) for an excellent discussion of the problems associated with them.

7. In the case of Clovis, these points in space would include the Great Plains, the southeastern United States, and northern Mexico.

8. See the exchange between Barton (1997), Barton and Neeley (1996), Clark (1996), and Neeley and Barton (1994) on the one hand, and Goring-Morris (1996), Henry (1996), and Kaufman (1995) on the other hand, regarding the causes of microlith pattern variation in the epi-Paleolithic (20,000–10,000 B.P.) of the southern Levant.

9. Bordes (1969), certainly one of the most proficient modern flint knappers and a towering figure in midcentury Paleolithic archaeology, provided an excellent discussion of the constraints that operate on the chipping of stone. He nevertheless believed that ethnicity was "writ small" in the form of retouched stone tools, and he could not see the contradictions inherent in the historical cultural approach. He argued to the end of his life that pattern was largely attributed to changeless lithic "traditions" held

in the minds of people long dead and rediscovered by modern archaeologists. When change had occurred in the Paleolithic (and it was exceptionally rare), population replacement was the only mechanism that Bordes invoked to account for it (Binford and Sabloff 1982).

Chapter 10: Ultimate American Origin Myth

1. Kohl (1998:235) relates a somewhat parallel situation in Argentina, where Paleoindian remains from Patagonia are seen as *los primeros argentinos*, who "initiated the national adventure."

2. I exempt Canada and Canadians from much of the above discussion because (1) their issues of national identity are quite different from those of the United States (see Ferguson 1997); and (2) they have (my subjective assessment based on lengthy periods of time spent in both countries) a much less emotional perspective on this issue, even though one could argue that the Canadians "own" the corridor in a physical sense.

Chapter 11: Modeling Initial Colonization

1. I do not attempt to summarize the discussion, pro and con, surrounding this model. For that, see Kelly 1996, 1999, and the references therein.

2. Two prehistoric arctic groups, the Paleoeskimo and (many thousands of years later) the Thule, seemingly provide exceptions to this rule. They traveled rapidly across great distances, hardly stopping to incorporate new food resources into their diet (Dumond 1984; Fitzhugh 1997; McGhee 1984). The analogy, however, is far from perfect because each group relied on one or a few keystone species (musk ox and bowhead whales, respectively), and each group exploited niches with which it was already familiar (Meltzer 2002).

3. Of course, accommodating negative data is not very meaningful because the absence of cave occupations may reflect only methodological shortcomings; even if this absence is real, it may be insignificant. Hopewell groups did not live in caves either; this does not mean they did not know such features existed.

4. Without putting too fine a point on it, I suggest that we compare this process to the Homestead Act of 1862. It provided (if certain requirements were met) free title to 160 acres of land in the public domain. In the well-watered eastern United States, that was enough. But as settlers moved into the semiarid Plains after the Civil War, it quickly became apparent that 160 acres was insufficient to establish a successful homestead. There was simply not enough rainfall to allow successful farming or ranching. In recognition of that climatic reality, the Desert Land Act of 1877 increased the size of western homesteads to 640 acres, but that was still inadequate. J. W. Powell argued that the minimal size should be 2,560 acres. Congress would never go that far (Webb 1931:413–422). The relative scale of late Paleoindian ranges in the eastern woodlands (smaller) compared to the Plains (much larger) makes it clear that they had figured out matters long before the U.S. Congress ever did.

BIBLIOGRAPHY

Adams, J. M., and H. Faure
  1998 Review and Atlas of Palaeovegetation: Prelimi-
       nary Land Ecosystem Maps of the World since
       the Last Glacial Maximum. Electronic document,
       http://www.esd.ornl.gov/projects/qen, accessed
       2002.
Adler, A. J.
  1999 The Dentition of Contemporary Finns. Master's
       thesis, Arizona State University, Tempe.
Adovasio, J. M.
  2002 *The First Americans: In Pursuit of Archaeology's
       Greatest Mystery*. Random House, New York.
Adovasio, J. M., J. Donahue, and R. Stuckenrath
  1990 The Meadowcroft Rockshelter Radiocarbon
       Chronology 1975–1990. *American Antiquity* 55(2):
       348–354.
Adovasio, J. M., and D. R. Pedler
  1997 Monte Verde and the Antiquity of Humankind in the
       Americas. *Antiquity* 71:573–580.
  2001 Pre-Clovis Sites and Their Implications for Human
       Occupation before the Last Glacial Maximum. Paper
       presented at the 66th Annual Meeting of the Society
       for American Archaeology, New Orleans.
Adovasio, J. M., D. R. Pedler, J. Donahue, and R. Stuckenrath
  1999 No Vestige of a Beginning nor Prospect for an
       End: Two Decades of Debate on Meadowcroft
       Rockshelter. In *Ice Age Peoples of North America:
       Environments, Origins, and Adaptations of the First
       Americans*, edited by R. Bonnichsen and K. L. Turn-
       mire, pp. 416–431. Oregon State University Press,
       Corvallis.
Agenbroad, L. D.
  1967 The Distribution of Fluted Points in Arizona. *Kiva*
       32:113–120.
  1988 Clovis People: The Human Factor in the Pleistocene
       Megafauna Extinction Equation. In *Americans before
       Columbus: Ice Age Origins*, edited by R. C. Carlisle,
       pp. 63–74. Ethnology Monographs, No. 12. Depart-
       ment of Anthropology, University of Pittsburgh,
       Pittsburgh.
  1990 Before the Anasazi. *Plateau* 61(2):1–32.
Agenbroad, L. D., and J. I. Mead
  1987 Late Pleistocene Alluvium and Megafauna Dung
       Deposits of the Central Colorado Plateau. In *Geo-
       logic Diversity of Arizona and Its Margins: Excursions
       to Choice Areas*, edited by G. H. Davis and E. M.
       VandenDolder, pp. 68–84. Special Paper, No. 5. Ari-
       zona Bureau of Geology and Mineral Technology,
       Tucson.
  1989 Quaternary Geochronology and Distribution of
       Mammuthus on the Colorado Plateau. *Geology* 17:
       861–864.
  1992 *Quaternary Paleoenvironmental Studies of the Colo-
       rado Plateau: Year IV*. Contract No. CX-1200-4-A062.
       National Park Service, Lakewood, Colo.
Agostini, H. T., R. Yanagihara, V. Davis, C. F. Ryschewsitch, and
G. L. Stoner
  1997 Asian Genotypes of JC Virus in Native Americans
       and in a Pacific Island Population: Markers of Viral
       Evolution and Human Migration. *Proceedings of the
       National Academy of Sciences of the United States of
       America* 94:14542–14546.
Albrecht, G. H.
  1992 Assessing the Affinities of Fossils Using Canoni-
       cal Variates and Generalized Distances. *Human
       Evolution* 7:49–69.
Alekseyev, V. P.
  1979 The Genetic Structure of Asiatic Eskimos and
       Coastal Chukchis Compared to That of American
       Arctic Populations. *Arctic Anthropology* 16:147–163.
Alley, R. B.
  2000 The Younger Dryas Cold Interval as Viewed from
       Central Greenland. *Quaternary Science Reviews* 19:
       213–226.
Alley, R. B., and P. Clark
  1999 The Deglaciation of the Northern Hemisphere.
       Annual Review of Earth and Planetary Science 27:
       149–182.
Alley, R. B., P. Clark, L. Keigwin, and R. Webb
  1999 Making Sense of Millennial-Scale Climate Change.
       In *Mechanisms of Global Climate Change at Millen-
       nial Time Scales*, edited by P. Clark, R. S. Webb, and
       L. Keigwin, pp. 385–394. American Geophysical
       Union, Washington, D.C.
Alroy, J.
  2001 A Multispecies Overkill Simulation of the End–
       Pleistocene Megafaunal Mass Extinction. *Science*
       292:1893–1896.
Amick, D. S.
  1996 Regional Patterns of Folsom Mobility and Land
       Use in the American Southwest. *World Archaeology*
       27(3):411–426.
Anderson, A.
  2002 Faunal Collapse, Landscape Change, and Settle-

ment History in Remote Oceania. *World Archaeology* 33(3):375–390.

Anderson, D. D.

1968   A Stone Age Campsite at the Gateway to America. *Scientific American* 218:24–33.

1979   Archaeology and the Evidence for the Prehistoric Development of Eskimo Culture: An Assessment. *Arctic Anthropology* 16:16–26.

Anderson, D. G.

1990   The Paleoindian Colonization of Eastern North America: A View from the Southeastern United States. In *Early Paleoindian Economies of Eastern North America*, edited by K. B. Tankersley and B. L. Isaac, pp. 163–216. Research in Economic Anthropology Supplement, No. 5. JAI Press, Greenwich, Conn.

1995   Paleoindian Interaction Networks in the Eastern Woodlands. In *Native American Interaction: Multiscalar Analyses and Interpretations in the Eastern Woodlands*, edited by M. Nassaney and K. Sassaman, pp. 1–26. University of Tennessee Press, Knoxville.

1996   Models of Paleoindian and Early Archaic Settlement in the Lower Southeast. In *The Paleoindian and Early Archaic Southeast*, edited by D. G. Anderson and K. E. Sassaman, pp. 16–28. University of Alabama Press, Tuscaloosa.

Anderson, D. G., and M. K. Faught

1998a   The Distribution of Fluted Paleoindian Projectile Points. *Archaeology of Eastern North America* 26:163–187.

1998b   A North American Paleoindian Projectile Point Database. Electronic document, http://www.anthro.fsu.edu/research/paleo/paleoind.html, accessed 2002.

Anderson, D. G., and J. C. Gillam

2000   Paleoindian Colonization of the Americas: Implications from an Examination of Physiography, Demography, and Artifact Distribution. *American Antiquity* 65(1):43–66.

2001   Paleoindian Interaction and Mating Networks: Reply to Moore and Moseley. *American Antiquity* 66(3):530–535.

Anderson, D. G., R. Ledbetter, and L. O'Steen

1990   *Paleoindian Period Archaeology of Georgia*. Laboratory of Archaeology Series Report, No. 28. University of Georgia, Athens.

Anderson, D. G., L. D. O'Steen, and K. E. Sassaman

1996   Environmental and Chronological Considerations. In *The Paleoindian and Early Archaic Southeast*, edited by D. G. Anderson and K. E. Sassaman, pp. 3–28. University of Alabama Press, Tuscaloosa.

Anderson, D. G., and K. E. Sassaman (editors)

1996   *The Paleoindian and Early Archaic Southeast*. University of Alabama Press, Tuscaloosa.

Anderson, E.

1984   Who's Who in the Pleistocene: A Mammalian Bestiary. In *Quaternary Extinctions: A Prehistoric Revolution*, edited by P. S. Martin and R. G. Klein, pp. 40–89. University of Arizona Press, Tucson.

Anderson, G. D., and B. H. Walker

1974   Vegetation Composition and Elephant Damage in the Sengwa Research Area, Rhodesia. *Journal of South African Wildlife Management Association* 4:1–14.

Anderson, R. S., and S. J. Smith

1997   The Sedimentary Record of Fire in Montane Meadows, Sierra Nevada, California, USA: A Preliminary Assessment. In *Sediment Records of Biomass Burning and Global Change*, edited by B. Stocks, pp. 313–327. Springer-Verlag, Berlin.

Andrefsky, W. A.

1994   Raw Material Availability and the Organization of Technology. *American Antiquity* 59:21–34.

Anthony, D. W.

1990   Migration in Archaeology: The Baby and the Bathwater. *American Anthropologist* 92:895–914.

Anttila, R.

1972   *An Introduction to Historical and Comparative Linguistics*. Macmillan, New York.

Ardila Calderon, G. I.

1991   The Peopling of Northern South America. In *Clovis: Origins and Adaptations*, edited by R. Bonnichsen and K. L. Turnmire, pp. 261–282. Center for the Study of the First Americans, Oregon State University, Corvallis.

Ardila Calderon, G. I., and G. G. Politis

1989   Nuevos datos para un viejo problema: Investigación y discusiones en torno del poblamiento de América del Sur. *Boletín Museo del Oro* 23:3–45.

Arima, E. Y.

1984   Caribou Eskimo. In *Arctic*, edited by D. Damas, pp. 447–462. Handbook of North American Indians, Vol. 5. Smithsonian Institution Press, Washington, D.C.

Asch, M.

1998   *From* Terra Nullius *to Affirmation: Reconciling Aboriginal Rights and the Canadian Constitution*. Department of Anthropology, Harvard University, Cambridge.

Aschman, H.

1952   A Fluted Point from Central Baja California. *American Antiquity* 17(3):262–263.

Associated Press

1999   Bones Date First American: Ancient Woman's Thigh Bones Unearthed. Electronic document, http://www.abcnews.go.com/sections/science/DailyNews/humanbones990412.html, accessed 2000.

Auel, J. M.

1998   Early Americans. *Science* 280:1674–1675.

Axelrod, D. I.

1967   Quaternary Extinctions of Large Mammals. *University of California Publications in Geological Sciences* 74:1–42.

Ayers, J. E.
1966   A Clovis Fluted-Point from the Kayenta, Arizona Area. *Plateau* 38:76–78.

Bahn, R., and A. L. Bryan
1991   A Review of Lynch's Description of South American Sites. *American Antiquity* 56:342–348.

Bailliet, G., F. Rothhammer, F. R. Carnese, C. M. Bravi, and N. O. Bianchi
1994   Founder Mitochondrial Haplotypes in Amerindian Populations. *American Journal of Human Genetics* 55: 27–33.

Bain, J. G.
1976   Paleolithic Rock Art: Does It Exist in N. America? *American Indian Rock Art* 2:109–113.

Baker, J.
1992   Haunted by the Pilgrims. In *Art and Mystery of Historical Archaeology. Essays in Honor of James Deetz*, edited by A. E. Yentsch and M. C. Beaudry, pp. 343–358. CRC Press, Boca Raton, Fla.

Baker, R. R.
1978   *The Evolutionary Ecology of Animal Migration.* Holmes and Meier, New York.

Balikci, A.
1984   Netsilik. In *Arctic*, edited by D. Damas, pp. 415–430. Handbook of North American Indians, Vol. 5. Smithsonian Institution Press, Washington, D.C.

Ballinger, S. W., T. G. Schurr, A. Torroni, Y. Y. Gan, J. A. Hodge, K. Hassan, K. H. Chen, and D. C. Wallace
1992   Southeast Asian Mitochondrial DNA Analysis Reveals Genetic Continuity of Ancient Mongoloid Migrations. *Genetics* 130:139–152.

Bamforth, D. B.
2002   Evidence and Metaphor in Evolutionary Archaeology. *American Antiquity* 67(3):435–452.

Bang-Andersen, S.
1990   The Myrvatn Group, a Preboreal Find-Complex in Southwest Norway. In *Contributions to the Mesolithic in Europe: Papers Presented at the Fourth International Symposium, The Mesolithic of Europe, Leuven, 1990*, edited by P. M. Vermeersch and P. Van Peer, pp. 215–226. Studia Preistorica Belgica, No. 5. Leuven University Press, Leuven, Belgium.
2003   Encircling the Living Space of Early Postglacial Reindeer Hunters in the Interior of Southern Norway. In *Mesolithic on the Move*, edited by L. Larsson, H. Kindgren, K. J. Knutsson, D. Loeffler, and A. Akerland, pp. 193–204. Oxbow Books, Oxford.

Barnes, R. F. W.
1985   Effects of Elephant Browsing on Woodlands in a Tanzanian National Park: Measurements, Models, and Management. *Journal of Applied Ecology* 20: 521–540.

Barse, W. P.
1990   Preceramic Occupations in the Orinoco River Valley. *Science* 250:1388–1390.

Barton, C. M.
1979   Terminal Pleistocene Environments and Human Adaptation in North America. Paper presented at the 44th Annual Meeting of the Society for American Archaeology, Vancouver, B.C.
1991   Retouched Tools: Fact or Fiction? Paradigms for Interpreting Chipped Stone. In *Perspectives in Prehistory Paradigmatic Biases in Circum-Mediterranean Hunter-Gatherer Research*, edited by G. A. Clark, pp. 143–163. University of Pennsylvania Press, Philadelphia.
1997   Stone Tools, Style, and Social Identity: An Evolutionary Perspective on the Archeological Record. In *Rediscovering Darwin: Evolutionary Theory in Archeological Explanation*, edited by C. M. Barton and G. A. Clark, pp. 141–156. Archeological Papers of the American Anthropological Association, No. 7. Washington, D.C.

Barton, C. M., and G. A. Clark (editors)
1997   *Rediscovering Darwin: Evolutionary Theory in Archeological Explanation.* Archeological Papers of the American Anthropological Association, No. 7. Washington, D.C.

Barton, C. M., and M. P. Neeley
1996   Phantom Cultures of the Levantine Epipaleolithic. *Antiquity* 70(267):139–147.

Barton, C. M., D. I. Olszewski, and N. R. Coinman
1995   Beyond the Graver: Reconsidering Burin Function. *Journal of Field Archaeology* 23(1):111–125.

Barton, C. M., S. Schmich, and S. James
1999   Colonization Ecology and the Peopling of the New World. Paper presented at the Pioneers on the Land: How America Got Its People Conference, Arizona State University, Tempe.

Batista, O., C. J. Kolman, and E. Bermingham
1995   Mitochondrial DNA Diversity in the Kuna Amerinds of Panama. *Human Molecular Genetics* 4:921–929.

Bayham, F. E.
1982   A Diachronic Analysis of Prehistoric Animal Exploitation at Ventana Cave. Ph.D. dissertation, Arizona State University, Tempe.

Bay-Petersen, J. L.
1978   Animal Exploitation in Mesolithic Denmark. In *The Early Postglacial Settlement of Northern Europe: An Ecological Perspective*, edited by P. Mellars, pp. 115–145. University of Pittsburgh Press, Pittsburgh.

Beaton, J. M.
1991   Colonizing Continents: Some Problems from Australia and the Americas. In *The First Americans: Search and Research*, edited by T. D. Dillehay and D. J. Meltzer, pp. 209–230. CRC Press, Boca Raton, Fla.

Begley, S., and A. Murr
1999   The First Americans. *Newsweek* 26:50–57.

Bell, R. E.
1960   Evidence of a Fluted Point Tradition in Ecuador. *American Antiquity* 26(1):102–106.
1965   *Investigaciones arqueológicas en el sitio de El Inga.* Casa de la Cultura, Quito.
1977   Obsidian Hydration Studies in Highland Ecuador. *American Antiquity* 42(1):68–78.

2000   *Archaeological Investigation at the Site of El Inga, Ecuador*. R. E. Bell Monographs in Anthropology, No. 1. Sam Noble Oklahoma Museum of Natural History, University of Oklahoma, Norman.

Bellwood, P.
1987   *The Polynesians: The Prehistory of an Island People*. Thames and Hudson, London.

Bentley, G. R.
1996   How Did Prehistoric Women Bear "Man the Hunter"? Reconstructing Fertility from the Archaeological Record. In *Gender and Archaeology*, edited by R. P. Wright, pp. 23–51. University of Pennsylvania Press, Philadelphia.

Bergen, A. W., C.-Y. Wang, J. Tsai, K. Jefferson, C. Dey, K. D. Smith, S.-C. Park, S.-J. Tsai, and D. Goldman
1999   An Asian–Native American Paternal Lineage Identified by RPS4Y Resequencing and Microsatellite Haplotyping. *Annals of Human Genetics* 63:63–80.

Bert, F., A. Corella, M. Gené, A. Pérez-Pérez, and D. Turbón
2001   Major Mitochondrial DNA Haplotype Heterogeneity in Highland and Lowland Amerindian Populations from Bolivia. *Human Biology* 73:1–16.

Bettinger, R. L.
1991   *Hunter-Gatherers: Archaeological and Evolutionary Theory*. Plenum Press, New York.
1993   Doing Great Basin Archaeology Recently: Coping with Variability. *Journal of Archaeological Research* 1: 43–66.

Bever, M. R.
2001   An Overview of Alaskan Late Pleistocene Archaeology: Historical Themes and Current Perspectives. *Journal of World Prehistory* 15:125–192.

Bianchi, N. O., G. Bailliet, C. M. Bravi, R. F. Carnese, F. Rothhammer, V. L. Martínez-Marignac, and S. D. J. Pena
1997   Origin of Amerindian Y-Chromosomes as Inferred by the Analysis of Six Polymorphic Markers. *American Journal of Physical Anthropology* 102:79–89.

Bianchi, N. O., C. I. Catanesi, G. Bailliet, V. L. Martínez-Marignac, C. M. Bravi, L. B. Vidal-Rioja, R. J. Herrera, and J. S. López-Camelo
1998   Characterization of Ancestral and Derived Y-Chromosome Haplotypes of New World Native Populations. *American Journal of Human Genetics* 63: 1862–1871.

Bianchi, N. O., and F. Rothhammer
1995   Reply to Torroni and Wallace. *American Journal of Human Genetics* 56:1236–1238.

Billington, R. A.
1975   The Frontier and the American Character. In *Historical Viewpoints: Notable Articles from American Heritage*, 2nd ed., Vol. 1 (to 1877), edited by J. A. Garraty, pp. 58–69. Harper & Row, New York.

Binford, L. R.
1981   *Bones: Ancient Men and Modern Myths*. Academic Press, New York.
1983   Long Term Land Use Patterns: Some Implications for Archaeology. In *Lulu Linear Punctuated: Essays in Honor of George Irving Quimby*, edited by R. C. Dunnell and D. K. Grayson, pp. 27–53. Anthropo-

logical Papers of the Museum of Anthropology, No. 72. University of Michigan, Ann Arbor.
1999   Time as a Clue to Cause. *Proceedings of the British Academy* 101:1–35.
2001   *Constructing Frames of Reference: An Analytical Method for Archaeological Theory Building Using Ethnographic and Environmental Data Sets*. University of California Press, Berkeley.

Binford, L. R., and J. Sabloff
1982   Paradigms, Systematics, and Archaeology. *Journal of Anthropological Research* 38:137–153.

Bird, C. F. M.
1993   Woman the Toolmaker: Evidence for Women's Use and Manufacture of Flaked Stone Tools in Australia and New Guinea. In *Women in Archaeology: A Feminist Critique*, edited by H. du Cros and L. Smith, pp. 22–30. Department of Prehistory, Australian National University, Occasional Papers in Prehistory, No. 23. Highland Press, Canberra.

Bird, J. B.
1938   Antiquity and Migrations of the Early Inhabitants of Patagonia. *Geographical Review* 28(2):250–275.
1951   South American Radiocarbon Dates. In *Radiocarbon Dating: A Report on the Program to Aid in the Development of the Method of Dating*, edited by F. Johnson, pp. 37–49. Memoirs of the Society for American Archaeology, No. 8. Washington, D.C.
1969   Comparison of South Chilean and Ecuadorian "Fishtail" Projectile Points. *The Kroeber Anthropological Society Papers* 40:52–71.
1988   *Travels and Archaeology in South Chile*. University of Iowa Press, Iowa City.

Bird, J. B., and R. G. Cooke
1977   Los artefactos mas antiguos de Panama. *Revista Nacional de Cultura* 6:7–31.
1978   The Occurrence in Panama of Two Types of Paleo-Indian Projectile Points. In *Early Man from a Circum-Pacific Perspective*, edited by A. L. Bryan, pp. 263–272. Occasional Papers, No. 1. Department of Anthropology, University of Alberta, Edmonton.

Birdsell, J. B.
1953   Some Environmental and Cultural Factors Influencing the Structuring of Australian Aboriginal Populations. *American Naturalist* 87:171–207.
1957   Some Population Problems Involving Pleistocene Man. In *Population Studies: Animal Ecology and Demography*, pp. 47–69. Cold Spring Harbor Symposia on Quantitative Biology, Vol. 22. Cold Spring Harbor Laboratory, Cold Spring Harbor, N.Y.

Bisson, M.
2000   Nineteenth Century Tools for 21st Century Archaeology? Why the Middle Paleolithic Typology of François Bordes Must Be Replaced. *Journal of Archaeological Method and Theory* 7:1–48.

Black, S.
1978   Polynesian Outliers: A Study in the Survival of Small Populations. In *Simulation Studies in Archaeology*, edited by I. Hodder, pp. 63–76. Cambridge University Press, Cambridge.

Blackwell, B., and H. Schwarcz

1993   Archaeochronology and Scale. In *Effects of Scale on Archaeological and Geoscientific Perspectives*, edited by J. Stein and A. Linse, pp. 29–58. Special Paper, No. 283. Geological Society of America, Boulder, Colo.

Blanton, D.

2000   The Weather Is Fine, Wish You Were Here, Because I'm the Last One Alive: "Learning" the Environment in the English New World Colonies. Paper presented at the 65th Annual Meeting of the Society for American Archaeology, Philadelphia.

Bleed, P.

1986   The Optimal Design of Hunting Weapons: Maintainability or Reliability. *American Antiquity* 51(4): 737–747.

Blunier, T., J. Schwander, B. Stauffer, T. Stocker, A. Dallenbach, A. Indermuhle, J. Tschumi, J. Chapellaz, D. Raynaud, and J. M. Barnola

1997   Timing of the Antarctic Cold Reversal and the Atmospheric CO_2 Increase with Respect to the Younger Dryas Event. *Geophysical Research Letters* 24(21):2683–2686.

Blurton Jones, N. G., K. Hawkes, and J. F. O'Connell

1989   Modelling and Measuring Costs of Children in Two Foraging Societies. In *Comparative Socioecology: The Behavioral Ecology of Humans and Other Mammals*, edited by V. Standen and R. A. Foley, pp. 367–390. Blackwell Scientific Publications, Oxford.

Boas, F.

1921   Ethnology of the Kwakiutl: Based on Data Collected by George Hunt. In *35th Annual Report of the Bureau of American Ethnology*, pp. 305–601. U.S. Government Printing Office, Washington, D.C.

Boëda, E.

1991   Approche de la variabilité des systèmes de production lithique des industries du Paléolithique inférieur et moyen. *Techniques et Culture* 17/18: 37–79.

Bogucki, P., and R. Grygiel

1993   The First Farmers of Europe: A Survey Article. *Journal of Field Archaeology* 20:399–425.

Boldurian, A. T., and J. L. Cotter

1999   *Clovis Revisited: New Perspectives on Paleoindian Adaptations from Blackwater Draw, New Mexico*. University of Pennsylvania Museum, Philadelphia.

Bonatto, S. L., A. J. Redd, F. M. Salzano, and M. Stoneking

1996   Lack of Ancient Polynesian-Amerindian Contact. *American Journal of Human Genetics* 59:253–256.

Bonatto, S. L., and F. M. Salzano

1997   Diversity and Age of the Four Major mtDNA Haplogroups, and Their Implications for the Peopling of the New World. *American Journal of Human Genetics* 61:1413–1423.

Bond, G., W. Showers, M. Cheseby, R. Lotti, P. Almasi, P. Demenocal, P. Priore, H. Cullen, I. Hadjas, and G. Bonani

1997   A Pervasive Millennial-Scale Cycle in North Atlantic Holocene and Glacial Climates. *Science* 278: 1257–1266.

Bond, G. C., and A. Gilliam

1994   Introduction. In *Social Construction of the Past: Representation as Power*, edited by G. C. Bond and A. A. Gilliam, pp. 1–22. Routledge, London.

Bonnichsen, R.

1977   *Models for Deriving Cultural Information from Stone Tools*. Archaeological Survey of Canada, Mercury Series Paper, No. 60. National Museum of Man, Ottawa.

1991   Clovis Origins. In *Clovis: Origins and Adaptations*, edited by R. Bonnichsen and K. L. Turnmire, pp. 309–329. Center for the Study of the First Americans, Oregon State University, Corvallis.

1999   An Introduction to the Conference Perspective. Paper presented at the Clovis and Beyond Conference, Santa Fe, N.Mex.

Bonnichsen, R., and A. L. Schneider

1999   Breaking the Impasse on the Peopling of the Americas. In *Ice Age Peoples of North America: Environments, Origins, and Adaptations of the First Americans*, edited by R. Bonnichsen and K. L. Turnmire, pp. 497–519. Oregon State University Press, Corvallis.

Bonnichsen, R., and R. F. Will

1999   Radiocarbon Chronology of Northeastern Paleoamerican Sites: Discriminating Natural and Human Burn Features. In *Ice Age Peoples of North America: Environments, Origins, and Adaptations of the First Americans*, edited by R. Bonnichsen and K. L. Turnmire, pp. 395–415. Oregon State University Press, Corvallis.

Boomert, A.

1977   Prehistorie. In *Encyclopedie van Suriname*, edited by C. F. A. Bruijning, J. Voorhoeve, and W. Gordijn, pp. 506–515. Elsevier, Amsterdam.

1980   The Sipaliwini Archaeological Complex of Surinam: A Summary. *Nieuwe West-Indische Gids* 54(2): 94–108.

Boone, J., and E. A. Smith

1998   Is It Evolution Yet? A Critique of Evolutionary Archaeology. *Current Anthropology, Supplement* 39:S141–S173.

Borden, C. E.

1969   Early Population Movements from Asia into Western North America. *Syesis* 2:1–14.

Bordes, F.

1968   *The Old Stone Age*. McGraw-Hill, New York.

1969   Reflections on Typology and Techniques in the Paleolithic. *Arctic Anthropology* 6(1):1–29.

Borgerhoff Mulder, M.

1992   Reproductive Decisions. In *Evolutionary Ecology and Human Behavior*, edited by E. A. Smith and B. Winterhalder, pp. 339–374. Aldine de Gruyter, New York.

Borrero, L. A.

1995   The Archaeology of the Far South of America— Patagonia and Tierra del Fuego. In *Ancient Peoples and Landscapes*, edited by E. Johnson, pp. 207–215. Museum of Texas Tech University, Lubbock.

1996 The Pleistocene-Holocene Transition in Southern South America. In *Humans at the End of the Ice Age: The Archaeology of the Pleistocene-Holocene Transition*, edited by L. G. Straus, B. V. Eriksen, J. M. Erlandson, and D. R. Yesner, pp. 339–354. Plenum Press, New York.

1999 The Prehistoric Exploration and Colonization of Fuego-Patagonia. *Journal of World Prehistory* 13: 321–355.

Borrero, L. A., and C. McEwan

1997 The Peopling of Patagonia: The First Human Occupation. In *Patagonia: Natural History, Prehistory, and Ethnography*, edited by A. Prieto, pp. 33–45. Princeton University Press, Princeton, N.J.

Borrero, L. A., M. Zarate, L. Miotti, and M. Massone

1998 The Pleistocene-Holocene Transition and Human Occupations in the Southern Cone of South America. *Quaternary International* 49/50:191–199.

Bortolini, M. C., M. A. Zago, F. M. Salzano, W. A. Silva Jr., S. L. Bonatto, M.-C. B. O. de Silva, and T. A. Weimer

1997 Evolutionary and Anthropological Implications of Mitochondrial DNA Variation in African Brazilian Populations. *Human Biology* 69:141–159.

Bowdler, S.

1977 The Coastal Colonization of Australia. In *Sunda and Sahul*, edited by J. Allen, J. Golson, and R. Jones, pp. 205–246. Academic Press, London.

Boyle, K. V.

1990 *Upper Palaeolithic Faunas from South-West France: A Zoogeographic Perspective*. BAR International Series, No. 557. British Archaeological Reports, Oxford.

Brace, C. L.

1988 Punctuationism, Cladistics, and the Legacy of Medieval Neoplatonism. *Human Evolution* 3:121–138.

1998 Crô-Magnon Redux. *Anthropology Newsletter* 39:4, 6.

Brace, C. L., M. L. Brace, and W. R. Leonard

1989 Reflections on the Face of Japan: A Multivariate Craniofacial and Odontometric Perspective. *American Journal of Physical Anthropology* 78:93–113.

Brace, C. L., and K. D. Hunt

1990 A Non-racial Perspective on Human Variation: A(ustralia) to Z(uni). *American Journal of Physical Anthropology* 82:341–360.

Brace, C. L., A. R. Nelson, N. Seguchi, H. Oe, L. Sering, Pan Qifeng, L. Yongyi, and D. Tumen

2001 Old World Sources of the First New World Inhabitants. *Proceedings of the National Academy of Sciences of the United States of America* 98:10017–10022.

Brace, C. L., and D. P. Tracer

1992 Craniofacial Continuity and Change: A Comparison of Late Pleistocene and Recent Europe and Asia. In *The Evolution and Dispersion of Modern Humans in Asia*, edited by T. Akazawa, K. Aoki, and T. Kimura, pp. 439–471. Hokusen-Sha, Tokyo.

Brace, C. L., D. P. Tracer, L. A. Yaroch, J. Robb, K. Brandt, and A. R. Nelson

1993 Clines and Clusters versus "Race": A Test in Ancient Egypt, and the Case of a Death on the Nile. *Yearbook of Physical Anthropology* 36:1–31.

Bradley, B. A.

1982 Flaked Stone Technology and Typology. In *The Agate Basin Site: A Record of the Paleoindian Occupation of the Northwestern High Plains*, edited by G. C. Frison and D. J. Stanford, pp. 181–212. Academic Press, New York.

1991 Lithic Technology. In *Prehistoric Hunters of the High Plains*, 2nd ed., edited by G. C. Frison, pp. 369–395. Academic Press, New York.

1993 Paleoindian Flaked Stone Technology in the North American High Plains. In *From Kostenki to Clovis: Upper Paleolithic-Paleoindian Adaptations*, edited by O. Soffer and N. D. Praslov, pp. 251–262. Interdisciplinary Contributions to Archaeology. Plenum Press, New York.

1997 Clovis Ivory and Bone Tools. In *Le travail et l'usage de l'ivoire au Paleolithique superieur*, edited by J. Hahn, M. Menu, Y. Taborin, P. Walter, and F. Widemann, pp. 1–7. Istituto Poligrafico e Zecca Dello Stato Libreria, Dello Stato, Italy.

Brantingham, J.

1999 Late Pleistocene Lithic Technology in Northeast Asia. Paper presented at the Pioneers on the Land: How America Got Its People Conference, Arizona State University, Tempe.

Brashler, J. G., S. J. Kite, and N. Freidlin

1994 Recent Research at the St. Albans Site: 46KA27. In *The First Discovery of America: Archaeological Evidence of the Early Inhabitants of the Ohio Area*, edited by W. S. Dancey, pp. 133–143. Ohio Archaeological Council, Columbus.

Bravi, C. M., M. Sans, G. Bailliet, V. L. Martínez-Marignac, M. Portas, I. Barreto, C. Bonilla, and N. O. Bianchi

1997 Characterization of Mitochondrial DNA and Y-Chromosome Haplotypes in a Uruguayan Population of African Ancestry. *Human Biology* 69:641–652.

Bray, W.

1984 Across the Darien Gap: A Colombian View of Isthmian Archaeology. In *The Archaeology of Lower Central America*, edited by F. W. Lange and D. Stone, pp. 305–338. University of New Mexico Press, Albuquerque.

Breternitz, D. A., A. C. Swedlund, and D. C. Anderson

1971 An Early Burial from Gordon Creek, Colorado. *American Antiquity* 36:170–182.

Brose, D. S.

1994 Archaeological Investigations at the Paleo Crossing Site, a Paleoindian Occupation in Medina County, Ohio. In *The First Discovery of America: Archaeological Evidence of the Early Inhabitants of the Ohio Area*, edited by W. S. Dancey, pp. 61–76. Ohio Archaeological Council, Columbus.

Broster, J. B., D. P. Johnson, and M. R. Norton

1991 The Johnson Site: A Dated Clovis-Cumberland Occupation in Tennessee. *Current Research in the Pleistocene* 8:8–10.

Broster, J. B., and M. R. Norton
  1992 Paleoindian Projectile Point and Site Survey in Tennessee: 1988–1992. In *Paleoindian and Early Archaic Period Research in the Lower Southeast: A South Carolina Perspective*, edited by D. G. Anderson, K. E. Sassaman, and C. Judge, pp. 263–268. Council of South Carolina Professional Archaeologists, Columbia.
  1993 The Carson-Conn-Short Site (408N190): An Extensive Clovis Habitation in Benton County, Tennessee. *Current Research in the Pleistocene* 10:3–5.
  1996 Recent Paleoindian Research in Tennessee. In *The Paleoindian and Early Archaic Southeast*, edited by D. G. Anderson and K. E. Sassaman, pp. 288–297. University of Alabama Press, Tuscaloosa.

Broster, J. B., M. R. Norton, D. J. Stanford, C. V. Haynes Jr., and M. A. Jodry
  1994 Eastern Clovis Adaptations in the Tennessee River Valley. *Current Research in the Pleistocene* 11:12–14.

Broughton, J.
  1994 Declines in Mammalian Foraging Efficiency during the Late Holocene, San Francisco Bay, California. *Journal of Anthropological Archaeology* 13:371–401.

Brown, M. D., S. H. Hosseini, A. Torroni, H.-J. Bandelt, J. C. Allen, T. G. Schurr, R. Scozzari, F. Cruciani, and D. C. Wallace
  1998 Haplogroup X: An Ancient Link between Europe/Western Asia and North America? *American Journal of Human Genetics* 63:1852–1861.

Bruhns, K. O., and K. E. Stothert
  1999 *Women in Ancient America*. University of Oklahoma Press, Norman.

Brumbach, H. J., and R. Jarvenpa
  1997 Woman the Hunter: Ethnoarchaeological Lessons from Chipewyan Life-Cycle Dynamics. In *Women in Prehistory: North America and Mesoamerica*, edited by C. Claassen and R. A. Joyce, pp. 17–32. University of Pennsylvania Press, Philadelphia.

Brush, N.
  1993 Twelve Thousand Years of Human Occupation at the Eppley Rockshelter. *Current Research in the Pleistocene* 10:5–7.

Bryan, A. L.
  1973 Paleoenvironments and Cultural Diversity in Late Pleistocene South America. *Quaternary Research* 3:237–256.
  1983 South America. In *Early Man in the New World*, edited by R. Shutler Jr., pp. 137–146. Sage Publications, Beverly Hills, Calif.
  1991 The Fluted-Point Tradition in the Americas: One of Several Adaptations to Late Pleistocene American Environments. In *Clovis: Origins and Adaptations*, edited by R. Bonnichsen and K. L. Turnmire, pp. 15–33. Center for the Study of the First Americans, Oregon State University, Corvallis.

Bryan, A. L., R. M. Casamiquela, J. M. Cruxent, R. Gruhn, and C. Ochsenius
  1978 An El Jobo Mastodon Kill at Taima-Taima, Venezuela. *Science* 200:1275–1277.

Bryan, A. L., and R. Gruhn
  1999 The Radiocarbon Dates of Taima-Taima. In *Taima-Taima: A Late Pleistocene Paleo-Indian Kill Site in Northernmost South America*, edited by C. Ochsenius and R. Gruhn, pp. 53–58. South American Quaternary Documentation Program. Carl Christian Ochsenius-Siftung Singen am Hohentwiel, Baden-Wèurttemburg, Germany.

Bryan, A. L., and D. R. Tuohy
  1999 Prehistory of the Great Basin/Snake River Plain to about 8,500 Years Ago. In *Ice Age Peoples of North America: Environments, Origins, and Adaptations of the First Americans*, edited by R. Bonnichsen and K. L. Turnmire, pp. 249–263. Oregon State University Press, Corvallis.

Bryson, R. A., D. A. Baerreis, and W. M. Wendland
  1970 The Character of Late-Glacial and Post-Glacial Climatic Changes. In *Pleistocene and Recent Environments of the Central Great Plains*, edited by W. Dort Jr. and J. K. Jones Jr., pp. 54–74. Department of Geology, University of Kansas, Special Publication, No. 3. University of Kansas Press, Lawrence.

Budyko, M. I.
  1967 On the Causes of the Extinction of Some Animals at the End of the Pleistocene. *Soviet Geography Review and Translation* 8:783–793.
  1974 *Climate and Life*. Academic Press, New York.

Bullen, R. P., and W. W. Plowden Jr.
  1963 Preceramic Archaic Sites in the Highlands of Honduras. *American Antiquity* 28(3):382–385.

Burch, E. S., Jr.
  1994 The Future of Hunter-Gatherer Research. In *Key Issues in Hunter-Gatherer Research*, edited by E. S. J. Burch and L. J. Ellanna, pp. 441–455. Berg Publishers, Oxford.

Burney, D. A.
  1987 Late Quaternary Stratigraphic Charcoal Records from Madagascar. *Quaternary Research* 28(2):274–280.
  1993 Recent Animal Extinctions: Recipes for Disaster. *American Scientist* 81(6):530–541.

Burney, D. A., and R. D. E. MacPhee
  1988 Mysterious Island. *Natural History* 97(6):530–541.

Bush, M. B.
  1988 Early Mesolithic Disturbance: A Force on the Landscape. *Journal of Archaeological Science* 15:453–462.

Bush, M. B., D. R. Piperno, P. A. Colinvaux, P. E. de Oliveira, L. A. Krissek, M. C. Miller, and W. E. Rowe
  1992 A 14,300-yr Paleoecological Profile of a Lowland Tropical Lake in Panama. *Ecological Monographs* 62:251–275.

Butler, B. R.
  1963 An Early Man Site at Big Camas Prairie, South-Central Idaho. *Tebiwa* 6:22–23.

Butzer, K. W.
  1978 The People of the River. In *Ancient Egypt*, edited by

J. Billard, pp. 32–72. National Geographic Society, Washington, D.C.

1988 A "Marginality" Model to Explain Major Spatial and Temporal Gaps in the Old and New World Pleistocene Settlement Records. *Geoarchaeology* 3: 193–203.

1991 An Old World Perspective on Potential Mid-Wisconsinan Settlement of the Americas. In *The First Americans: Search and Research*, edited by T. D. Dillehay and D. J. Meltzer, pp. 137–156. CRC Press, Boca Raton, Fla.

Byers, D. S.
1962 Comments. *Current Anthropology* 3:247–250.

Callaghan, C.
1997 Evidence for Yok-Utian. *International Journal of American Linguistics* 63:18–64.

Callahan, E.
1979 The Basics of Biface Knapping in the Eastern Fluted Point Tradition: A Manual for Flintknappers and Lithic Analysts. *Archaeology of Eastern North America* 7:1–180.

Campbell, L.
1986 Comments. *Current Anthropology* 27:488–489.

1988 Review of *Language in the Americas*, by Joseph H. Greenberg. *Language* 64:591–615.

1997a *American Indian Languages: The Historical Linguistics of Native America*. Oxford University Press, New York.

1997b American Personal Pronouns: A Second Opinion. *Language* 73:339–351.

Campbell, L., T. Kaufman, and T. Smith-Stark
1986 Mesoamerica as a Linguistic Area. *Language* 62: 530–570.

Campbell, L., and M. Mithun (editors)
1979 *The Languages of Native America: Historical and Comparative Assessment*. University of Texas Press, Austin.

Canadian Museum of Nature
1999 Bird Bones Indicate Possible Human Presence in Ice Age Yukon. Electronic document, http://www.nature.ca/nature_e.cfm?, accessed 2000.

Cann, R. L., and J. K. Lum
1996 Mitochondrial Myopia: Reply to Bonatto et al. *American Journal of Human Genetics* 59:256–257.

Carlson, R. L.
1996 Introduction to Early Human Occupation in British Columbia. In *Early Human Occupation in British Columbia*, edited by R. L. Carlson and L. D. Bona, pp. 3–10. University of British Columbia Press, Vancouver.

Carluci, M. A.
1963 Puntas de proyectil. *Tipos, tecnica y areas de distribución en el Ecuador andino. Humanitas* 4(1): 5–56.

Carlyle, S. W., R. L. Parr, M. G. Hayes, and D. H. O'Rourke
2000 Context of Maternal Lineages in the Greater Southwest. *American Journal of Physical Anthropology* 113: 85–101.

Carvalho-Silva, D. R., F. R. Santos, M. H. Hutz, F. M. Salzabo, and S. D. Pena
1999 Divergent Human Y Chromosome Microsatellite Evolution Rates. *Journal of Molecular Evolution* 49: 204–214.

Casamiquela, R., and T. D. Dillehay
1989 Vertebrate and Invertebrate Faunal Analysis. In *Monte Verde: A Late Pleistocene Settlement in Chile, Vol. I: Palaeoenvironment and Site Context*, edited by T. D. Dillehay, pp. 205–210. Smithsonian Institution Press, Washington, D.C.

Cashdan, E.
1983 Territoriality among Human Foragers: Ecological Models and an Application to Four Bushman Groups. *Current Anthropology* 24:47–66.

1992 Spatial Organization and Habitat Use. In *Evolutionary Ecology and Human Behavior*, edited by E. A. Smith and B. Winterhalder, pp. 237–266. Aldine de Gruyter, New York.

Castillo, C. D., E. Castillo O., M. Rojas G., and C. Valldeperas A.
1987 *Analysis de la lítica lasqueada del sitio 9-FG-T*. Tesis de licenciatura, Universidad de Costa Rica, Turrialba.

Castleton, K. B.
1978 *Petroglyphs and Pictographs of Utah: Volume 1: The East and the Northeast*. Utah Museum of Natural History, Salt Lake City.

1979 *Petroglyphs and Pictographs of Utah: Volume 2: The South, Central, West, and Northwest*. Utah Museum of Natural History, Salt Lake City.

Cavalli-Sforza, L. L., and F. Cavalli-Sforza
1995 *The Great Human Diasporas: The History of Diversity and Evolution*. Helix Books, Reading, Mass.

Cavalli-Sforza, L. L., A. Piazza, and P. Menozzi
1994 *History and Geography of Human Genes*. Princeton University Press, Princeton, N.J.

Cavalli-Sforza, L. L., A. Piazza, P. Menozzi, and J. Mountain
1988 Reconstruction of Human Evolution: Bringing Together Genetic, Archaeological, and Linguistic Data. *Proceedings of the National Academy of Sciences of the United States of America* 85:6002–6006.

Charnov, R., G. Orians, and K. Hyatt
1976 The Ecological Implications of Resource Depression. *American Naturalist* 110:247–259.

Chatters, J. C.
2000 The Recovery and First Analysis of the Early Holocene Human Skeleton from Kennewick, Washington. *American Antiquity* 65(2):291–315.

Chauchat, C.
1975 The Paiján Complex, Pampa de Cupisnique, Peru. *Nawpa Pacha* 13:85–96.

1978 Additional Observations on the Paiján Complex. *Nawpa Pacha* 16:51–64.

1992 *Préhistoire de la côte nord du Pérou: Le Paijanien de Cupisnique*. Cahiers du Quaternaire, No. 18. CNRS-Éditions, Centre Régional de Publication de Bordeaux, Bordeaux.

Chauchat, C., and J. Briceño
1998 Paiján and Fishtail Points from Quebrada Santa

María, North Coast of Peru. *Current Research in the Pleistocene* 15:10–12.

Chauchat, C., and J. Pelegrin
1994 Le premier peuplement de la côte désertique du Pérou. *Bulletin de la Société Préhistorique Française* 91(4/5):275–280.

Chauchat, C., and J. Z. Quiñones
1979 Una punta en cola de pescado procedente de la costa norte del Peru. *Nawpa Pacha* 17:143–146.

Chen, Y. S., A. Olckers, T. G. Schurr, A. M. Kogelnik, K. Huoponen, and D. C. Wallace
2000 Mitochondrial DNA Variation in the Southern African Kung and Khwe and Their Genetic Relationships to Other African Populations. *American Journal of Human Genetics* 66:1362–1383.

Chen, Y. S., A. Torroni, L. Excoffier, A. S. Santachiara-Benerecetti, and D. C. Wallace
1995 Analysis of mtDNA Variation in African Populations Reveals the Most Ancient of All Human Continent-Specific Haplogroups. *American Journal of Human Genetics* 57:133–149.

Chilton, E. S.
1994 In Search of Paleo-Women: Gender Implications of Remains from Paleoindian Sites in the Northeast. *Bulletin of the Massachusetts Archaeological Society* 55(1):8–13.

Chrisman, D., R. S. MacNeish, J. Mavalwala, and H. Savage
1996 Late Pleistocene Human Friction Skin Prints from Pendejo Cave, New Mexico. *American Antiquity* 61:357–376.

Chu, J. Y., W. Huang, S. Q. Kuang, J. M. Wang, J. J. Xu, Z. T. Chu, Z. Q. Yang, K. Q. Lin, P. Li, M. Wu, Z. X. Geng, C. C. Tan, R. F. Du, and L. Jin
1998 Genetic Relationship of Populations in China. *Proceedings of the National Academy of Sciences of the United States of America* 95:11763–11768.

Claassen, C.
1997 Changing Venue: Women's Lives in Prehistoric North America. In *Women in Prehistory: North America and Mesoamerica*, edited by C. Claassen and R. A. Joyce, pp. 65–87. University of Pennsylvania Press, Philadelphia.

Claassen, C., and R. A. Joyce (editors)
1997 *Women in Prehistory: North America and Mesoamerica.* University of Pennsylvania Press, Philadelphia.

Clark, G. A.
1974 Excavations in the Late Pleistocene Cave Site of Balmori, Asturias (Spain). *Quaternaria* 18:383–426.
1983 *The Asturian of Cantabria: Early Holocene Hunter-Gatherers in Northern Spain.* Anthropological Papers of the University of Arizona, No. 41. Tucson.
1989a Alternative Models of Pleistocene Biocultural Evolution: A Response to Foley. *Antiquity* 63:153–161.
1989b Romancing the Stones: Biases, Style, and Lithics at La Riera. In *Alternative Approaches to Lithic Analysis*, edited by D. O. Henry and G. H. Odell, pp. 27–50. Archeological Papers of the American Anthropological Association, No. 1. Washington, D.C.

1993 Paradigms in Science and Archaeology. *Journal of Archaeological Research* 1:203–234.
1994 Migration as an Explanatory Concept in Paleolithic Archaeology. *Journal of Archaeological Method and Theory* 1:305–343.
1996 Plus français que les Français. *Antiquity* 70:128–130.
1997 The Middle-Upper Paleolithic Transition in Europe: An American Perspective. *Norwegian Archaeological Review* 30:25–53.
1999a Deconstructing the North Atlantic Model for Migration. Paper presented at the Pioneers on the Land: How America Got Its People Conference, Arizona State University, Tempe.
1999b Modern Human Origins: Highly Visible, Curiously Intangible. *Science* 283:2029–2032; 284:917.
1999c Review of *Sociocultural Evolution* (B. Trigger). *American Antiquity* 64:547–548.
2000 Deconstructing the North Atlantic Connection. *Current Research in the Pleistocene* 17:11–14.
2001a Comment on "Tool Standardization in the Middle and Upper Paleolithic: A Closer Look" (A. Marks et al.). *Cambridge Archaeological Journal* 11:32–34.
2001b On the Questionable Practice of Invoking the Metaphysic. *American Anthropologist* 103:43–47.
2002 Neanderthal Archaeology: Implications for Our Origins. *American Anthropologist* 104:50–67.

Clark, G. A., and T. Cartledge
1973 Recent Excavations in the Cave of Coberizas (Province of Asturias, Spain). *Quaternaria* 17:387–411.

Clark, G. A., and J. Lindly
1989 The Case for Continuity: Observations on the Biocultural Transition in Europe and Western Asia. In *The Human Revolution*, edited by P. Mellars and C. Stringer, pp. 626–676. Edinburgh University Press, Edinburgh.

Clark, G. A., and L. G. Straus
1983 Late Pleistocene Hunter-Gatherer Adaptations in Cantabrian Spain. In *Hunter-Gatherer Economy in Prehistory*, edited by G. Bailey, pp. 131–148. Cambridge University Press, Cambridge.

Clark, J. D.
1982 The Cultures of the Middle Paleolithic/Middle Stone Age. In *The Cambridge History of Africa, Vol. 1: From the Earliest Times to c. 500 BC*, edited by J. D. Clark, pp. 248–341. Cambridge University Press, Cambridge.

Clarke, D.
1968 *Analytical Archaeology.* Methuen, London.

Clausen, C. J., A. D. Cohen, E. Emiliani, J. A. Holman, and J. J. Stipp
1979 Little Salt Spring, Florida: A Unique Underwater Site. *Science* 203:609–614.

Coinman, N. R.
1998 The Upper Paleolithic of Jordan. In *The Prehistoric Archaeology of Jordan*, edited by D. O. Henry, pp. 39–63. BAR International Series, No. 705. British Archaeological Reports, Oxford.

Cole, S. J.
　1990　*Legacy on Stone: Rock Art of the Colorado Plateau and Four Corners Region*. Johnson Book, Boulder, Colo.

Collins, M. B.
　1990　Observations on Clovis Lithic Technology. *Current Research in the Pleistocene* 7:73–74.
　1999a　*Clovis Blade Technology*. University of Texas Press, Austin.
　1999b　Reply to Fiedel, Part II. *Discovering Archaeology, Special Report* 1(6):14–15.

Collins, M. B., G. L. Evans, T. N. Campbell, M. C. Winans, and C. E. Mear
　1989　Clovis Occupation at Kincaid Shelter, Texas. *Current Research in the Pleistocene* 6:3–4.

Comas, D., F. Calafell, E. Mateu, A. Perez-Lezaun, and J. Bertranpetit
　1996　Geographic Variation in Human Mitochondrial DNA Control Region Sequence: The Population History of Turkey and Its Relationship to the European Populations. *Molecular Biology and Evolution* 13:1067–1077.

Comas, D., F. Calafell, E. Mateu, A. Perez-Lezaun, E. Bosch, R. Martinez-Arias, J. Clarimon, F. Facchini, G. Fiori, D. Luiselli, D. Pettener, and J. Bertranpetit
　1998　Trading Genes along the Silk Road: mtDNA Sequences and the Origin of Central Asian Populations. *American Journal of Human Genetics* 63:1824–1838.

Commanger, H. S.
　1975　The Search for a Usable Past. In *Historical Viewpoints: Notable Articles from American Heritage*, 2nd ed., Vol. 1 (to 1877), edited by J. A. Garraty, pp. 182–197. Harper & Row, New York.

Conkey, M. W.
　1987　Interpretative Problems in Hunter-Gatherer Regional Studies. In *The Pleistocene Old World: Regional Perspectives*, edited by O. Soffer, pp. 63–77. Plenum Press, New York.

Conkey, M. W., and J. M. Gero
　1991　Tensions, Pluralities, and Engendering Archaeology: An Introduction to Women and Prehistory. In *Engendering Archaeology: Women and Prehistory*, edited by J. M. Gero and M. W. Conkey, pp. 3–30. Basil Blackwell, Cambridge, England.

Connolly, T. J., J. M. Erlandson, and S. E. Norris
　1995　Early Holocene Basketry and Cordage from Daisy Cave San Miguel Island, California. *American Antiquity* 60(2):309–318.

Cooke, R. G.
　1998　Human Settlement of Central America and Northernmost South America (14,000–8,000 BP). *Quaternary International* 49/50:177–190.

Cooke, R. G., and A. J. Ranere
　1984　The "Proyecto Santa María": A Multidisciplinary Analysis of Prehistoric Adaptations to a Tropical Watershed in Panama. In *Recent Developments in Isthmian Archaeology: Advances in the Prehistory of Lower Central America*, edited by F. W. Lange, pp.

3–30. BAR International Series, No. 212. British Archaeological Reports, Oxford.
　1992a　The Origin of Wealth and Hierarchy in the Central Region of Panama (12,000–2,000 BP) with Observations on Its Relevance to the History and Phylogeny of Chibchan-Speaking Polities in Panama and Elsewhere. In *Wealth and Hierarchy in the Intermediate Area*, edited by F. W. Lange, pp. 243–316. Dumbarton Oaks Research Library and Collection, Washington, D.C.
　1992b　Prehistoric Human Adaptations to the Seasonally Dry Forests of Panama. *World Archaeology* 24(1):114–133.

Copeland, J. M., and R. E. Fike
　1988　Fluted Points in Utah. *Utah Archaeology* 1:5–28.

Correal Urrego, G.
　1979　*Investigaciones arqueológicas en abrigos rocosos de Nemocón y Sueva*. Fundación de Investigaciones Arqueológicas Nacionales. Banco de la República, Bogota.
　1981　*Evidencias culturales y megafauna pleistocénica en Colombia*. Fundación de Investigaciones Arqueológicas Nacionales, No. 12. Banco de la República, Bogota.
　1983　Evidencia de cazadores especializados en el sitio de la Gloria, Golfo de Urabá. *Revista de la Academia Colombiana de Ciencias Exactas, Fisicas y Naturales* 58:77–82.
　1986　Apuntes sobre el medio ambiente pleistocénico y el hombre prehistorico en Colombia. In *New Evidence for the Pleistocene Peopling of the Americas*, edited by A. L. Bryan, pp. 115–131. Center for the Study of Early Man, University of Maine, Orono.
　1993　Nuevas evidencias culturales pleistocénicas y megafauna en Colombia. *Boletín de Arqueología* 8(1):3–12.

Correal Urrego, G., and T. van der Hammen
　1977　*Investigaciones arqueológicas en los abrigos del Tequendama: 12,000 años de historia del hombre y de su medio ambiente en la Altiplanicie de Bogotá*. Biblioteca Banco Popular, Bogota.

Cotter, J. L.
　1937　The Occurrence of Flints and Extinct Animals in Pluvial Deposits near Clovis, New Mexico. Part IV: Report on Excavation at the Gravel Pit, 1936. *Proceedings of the Academy of Natural Science of Philadelphia* 89:1–16.

Cox, S. L.
　1986　A Re-Analysis of the Shoop Site. *Archaeology of Eastern North America* 14:101–170.

Crawford, M. H., J. H. Mielke, E. J. Devor, D. D. Dykes, and H. F. Palesky
　1981　Population Structure of Alaskan and Siberian Indigenous Communities. *American Journal of Physical Anthropology* 55:167–185.

Cressman, L.
　1942　*Archaeological Researches in the Northern Great Basin*. Carnegie Institution of Washington Publication, No. 58. Washington, D.C.

Crusoe, D. L., and J. H. Felton
 1974 La Alvina de Parita: A Paleo-Indian Camp in Panama. *Florida Anthropologist* 27:145–148.
Cruxent, J. M.
 1956 A Lithic Industry of Paleo-Indian Type in Venezuela. *American Antiquity* 22(2):172–179.
 1957 Further Comments on the Finds at El Jobo, Venezuela. *American Antiquity* 22:412.
 1970 Projectile Points with Pleistocene Mammals in Venezuela. *Antiquity* 49:223–225.
Curran, M. L.
 1984 The Whipple Site and Paleoindian Tool Assemblage Variation: A Comparison of Intrasite Structuring. *Archaeology of Eastern North America* 12:5–40.
Custer, J. F., and R. M. Stewart
 1990 Environment, Analogy, and Early Paleoindian Economies in Northeastern North America. In *Early Paleoindian Economies of Eastern North America*, edited by K. B. Tankersley and B. L. Isaac, pp. 303–322. Research in Economic Anthropology Supplement, No. 5. JAI Press, Greenwich, Conn.
Dakin, K., and S. Wichmann
 2000 Cacao and Chocolate: A Uto-Aztecan Perspective. *Ancient Mesoamerica* 11:55–75.
Daniel, R. I., and M. Wisenbaker
 1989 Paleoindian in the Southeast: The View from Harney Flats. In *Paleoindian Lithic Resource Use*, edited by C. Ellis and J. Lathrop, pp. 323–344. Westview Press, Boulder, Colo.
Danson, E. B.
 1961 Early Man Points from the Vicinity of Sanders, Arizona. *Plateau* 34:67–68.
Darnell, R.
 1990 *Edward Sapir: Linguist, Anthropologist, Humanist.* University of California Press, Berkeley.
 1998 *An Anthropologist's View of the Canadian Borderlands.* Department of Anthropology, Harvard University, Cambridge.
Davis, L. G., and D. A. Sisson
 1998 An Early Stemmed Point Cache from the Lower Salmon River Canyon of West-Central Idaho. *Current Research in the Pleistocene* 15:12–14.
Davis, O. K., L. D. Agenbroad, P. S. Martin, and J. I. Mead
 1984 The Pleistocene Dung Blanket of Bechan Cave, Utah. In *Contributions in Vertebrate Paleontology: A Volume in Memorial to John E. Guilday*, Vol. 3, edited by H. H. Genoways and R. R. Dawson, pp. 267–282. Special Publication, No. 8. Carnegie Museum of Natural History, Pittsburgh.
Davis, W. E.
 1985 The Montgomery Folsom Site. *Current Research in the Pleistocene* 2:11–12.
 1988 The Lime Ridge Clovis Site. *Utah Archaeology* 1:66–67.
Dean, J.
 1993 Geoarchaeological Perspectives on the Past: Chronological Considerations. In *Effects of Scale on Archaeological and Geoscientific Perspectives*, edited by J. Stein and A. Linse, pp. 59–65. Special Paper,

No. 283. Geological Society of America, Boulder, Colo.
de France, S. D., D. K. Keefer, J. B. Richardson, and A. U. Alvarez
 2001 Late Paleoindian Coastal Foragers: Specialized Extractive Behavior at Quebrada Tacahuay, Peru. *Latin American Antiquity* 12(4):413–426.
de Knijff, P., M. Kayser, C. Caglià, D. Corach, N. Fretwell, C. Gehrig, G. Graziosi, F. Heidorn, S. Herrmann, B. Herzog, M. Hidding, K. Honda, M. Jobling, M. Krawczak, K. Leim, S. Meuser, E. Meyer, W. Oesterreich, A. Pandya, W. Parson, G. Penacino, A. Perez-Lezaun, A. Piccinini, M. Prinz, and L. Roewer
 1997 Chromosome Y Microsatellites: Population Genetic and Evolutionary Aspects. *International Journal of Legal Medicine* 110:134–140.
de Laguna, F.
 1936 An Archaeological Reconnaissance of the Middle and Lower Yukon Valley, Alaska. *American Antiquity* 2:6–12.
Deller, D., and C. J. Ellis
 1988 Early Palaeo-Indian Complexes in Southwestern Ontario. In *Late Pleistocene and Early Holocene Paleoecology and Archaeology of the Eastern Great Lakes Region*, edited by R. Laub, N. Miller, and D. W. Steadman, pp. 251–263. Buffalo Society of Natural Sciences Bulletin, No. 33. Buffalo, N.Y.
 1992 *Thedford II: A Paleoindian Site in the Ausable River Watershed of Southwestern Ontario.* Memoirs of the Museum of Anthropology, No. 24. University of Michigan, Ann Arbor.
Denevan, W. M.
 1992 The Pristine Myth: The Landscape of the Americas in 1492. *Annals of the Association of American Geographers* 82(3):369–385.
Dennett, D. C.
 1995 *Darwin's Dangerous Idea.* Simon & Schuster, New York.
Dent, R. J., and B. E. Kauffman
 1985 Aboriginal Subsistence and Site Ecology as Interpreted from Microbial and Faunal Remains. In *Shawnee Minisink: A Stratified Paleoindian-Archaic Site in the Upper Delaware Valley of Pennsylvania*, edited by C. W. McNett Jr., pp. 55–79. Academic Press, Orlando, Fla.
Denton, G. H., and T. J. Hughes
 1981 *The Last Great Ice Sheets.* Wiley, New York.
Derenko, M. V., B. A. Malyarchuk, I. K. Dambueva, C. Dorzhu, and I. Zakharov
 1998 Buryat and Tuva Populations from South Siberia Exhibit the Highest Percentage of New World mtDNA Haplogroups. *American Journal of Human Genetics, Supplement* 63:A211.
Derenko, M. V., B. A. Malyarchuk, I. K. Dambueva, G. O. Shaikhaev, C. M. Dorzhu, D. D. Nimaev, and I. A. Zakharov
 2000 Mitochondrial DNA Variation in Two South Siberian Aboriginal Populations: Implications for the Genetic History of North Asia. *Human Biology* 72:945–973.

Derenko, M. V., and G. F. Shields
1998 Variability of Mitochondrial DNA in Three Groups of Indigenous Inhabitants of Northern Asia. *Genetika* 34:676–681.

Deshmukh, I.
1986 *Ecology and Tropical Biology*. Blackwell Scientific Publications, Palo Alto, Calif.

Diamond, J.
1984 Historic Extinctions: A Rosetta Stone for Understanding Prehistoric Extinctions. In *Quaternary Extinctions: A Prehistoric Revolution*, edited by P. S. Martin and R. G. Klein, pp. 824–862. University of Arizona Press, Tucson.
1997 *Guns, Germs, and Steel: The Fate of Human Societies*. Norton, New York.

Dikov, N. N.
1993 *Asia at the Juncture with America in Antiquity: The Stone Age of the Chukchi Peninsula*. Nauka, St. Petersburg. Translated by R. L. Bland 1997, Beringia Program, National Park Service, Anchorage.
1996 The Ushki Sites, Kamchatka Peninsula. In *American Beginnings: The Prehistory and Palaeoecology of Beringia*, edited by F. H. West, pp. 244–250. University of Chicago Press, Chicago.

Dillehay, T. D.
1984 A Late Ice Age Settlement in Southern Chile. *Scientific American* 251(4):106–117.
1991 Disease Ecology and Initial Human Migration. In *The First Americans: Search and Research*, edited by T. D. Dillehay and D. J. Meltzer, pp. 231–266. CRC Press, Boca Raton, Fla.
1997a The Battle of Monte Verde. *The Sciences* 37:28–33.
1999 The Late Pleistocene Cultures of South America. *Evolutionary Anthropology* 7:206–216.
2000 *The Settlement of the Americas: A New Prehistory*. Basic Books, New York.

Dillehay, T. D. (editor)
1989 *Monte Verde: A Late Pleistocene Settlement in Chile, Vol. I: Palaeoenvironment and Site Context*. Smithsonian Institution Press, Washington, D.C.
1997b *Monte Verde: A Late Pleistocene Settlement in Chile, Vol. II: The Archaeological Context*. Smithsonian Institution Press, Washington, D.C.

Dillehay, T. D., G. Calderon, G. Politis, and M. Beltrao
1992 Earliest Hunters and Gatherers of South America. *Journal of World Prehistory* 6:145–204.

Dillehay, T. D., and M. B. Collins
1991 Monte Verde, Chile: A Comment on Lynch. *American Antiquity* 56:333–341.

Dillehay, T. D., M. B. Collins, M. Pino, J. Rossen, J. Adovasio, C. Ocampo, X. Navarro, P. Rivas, D. Pollack, A. G. Henderson, J. Saavedra, P. Sanzana, P. Shipman, M. Kay, G. Muñoz, A. Karathanasis, D. Ugent, M. Cibull, and R. Geissler
1999a On Monte Verde: Fiedel's Confusions and Misrepresentations. Electronic document, http://www.uky.edu/Projects/MonteVerde, accessed February 10, 2000.

Dillehay, T. D., and D. J. Meltzer
1991 Finale: Process and Prospects. In *The First Americans: Search and Research*, edited by T. D. Dillehay and D. J. Meltzer, pp. 287–294. CRC Press, Boca Raton, Fla.

Dillehay, T. D., M. Pino, J. Rossen, C. Ocampo, P. Rivas, D. Pollack, and G. Henderson
1999b Reply to Fiedel, Part I. *Discovering Archaeology, Special Report* 1(6):12–14.

Dincauze, D. F.
1981a The Meadowcroft Papers. *Quarterly Review of Archaeology* 2:3–4.
1981b Paleoenvironmental Reconstruction in the Northeast: The Art of Multidisciplinary Science. In *Foundations of Northeast Archaeology*, edited by D. R. Snow, pp. 51–96. Academic Press, New York.
1984 An Archaeological Evaluation of the Case for Pre-Clovis Occupations. *Advances in World Archaeology* 3:275–323.
1988 Tundra and Enlightenment: Landscapes for Northeastern Paleoindians. *Quarterly Review of Archaeology* 9(2):5–8.
1993a Fluted Points in the Eastern Forests. In *From Kostenki to Clovis: Upper Paleolithic-Paleoindian Adaptations*, edited by O. Soffer and N. D. Praslov, pp. 279–292. Plenum Press, New York.
1993b Pioneering in the Pleistocene: Large Paleoindian Sites in the Northeast. In *Archaeology of Eastern North America: Papers in Honor of Stephen Williams*, edited by J. B. Stoltman, pp. 45–59. Archaeological Report, No. 25. Mississippi Department of Archives and History, Jackson.
1997 Regarding Pendejo Cave: Response to Chrisman et al. *American Antiquity* 62(3):554–555.
2000 The Northeast. *Common Ground* (Special Issue, "The Earliest Americans") Spring/Summer 2000:34–43.

Dincauze, D. F., and V. Jacobson
2001 The Birds of Summer: Lakeside Routes into Late Pleistocene New England. *Canadian Journal of Archaeology* 25:121–126.

Di Peso, C. C.
1955 Two Cerro Guamas Clovis Points from Sonora, Mexico. *Kiva* 21(1/2):13–15.

Discovering Archaeology
1999 Breaking the Clovis Barrier: Were the First Americans in South Carolina? *Discovering Archaeology* 1(5):16.

Dixon, E. J.
1985 The Origins of the First Americans. *Archaeology* 38(2):22–27.
1993 *Quest for the Origins of the First Americans*. University of New Mexico Press, Albuquerque.
1999 *Bones, Boats, and Bison: Archeology and the First Colonization of Western North America*. University of New Mexico Press, Albuquerque.

Dixon, J. E., T. H. Heaton, T. E. Fifield, T. D. Hamilton, D. E. Putnam, and F. Grady
1997 Late Quaternary Regional Geoarchaeology of South-

east Alaska Karst: A Progress Report. *Geoarchaeology* 12:689–712.

Dixon, R. M. W.

1997   *The Rise and Fall of Languages*. Cambridge University Press, Cambridge.

Dobres, M. A.

1999   Of Paradigms and Ways of Seeing: Artifact Variability as if People Mattered. In *Material Meanings: Critical Approaches to the Interpretation of Material Culture*, edited by E. S. Chilton, pp. 7–23. University of Utah Press, Salt Lake City.

Dods, R. R.

2002   The Death of Smokey Bear: The Ecodisaster Myth and Forest Management Practices in Prehistoric North America. *World Archaeology* 33(3):475–487.

Doran, G. H., D. H. Dickel, W. E. Ballinger Jr., O. F. Agee, P. J. Lapis, and W. W. Hauswirth

1986   Anatomical, Cellular, and Molecular Analysis of 8,000-Yr-Old Man Brain Tissue from the Windover Archaeological Site. *Nature* 323:803–806.

Doucette, D. L.

2003   Unraveling Middle Archaic Expressions: A Multidisciplinary Approach towards Feature and Material Culture Recognition in Southeastern New England. Ph.D. dissertation, Harvard University, Cambridge.

Downum, C. E.

1993   Evidence of a Clovis Presence at Wupatki National Monument. *Kiva* 58(4):487–494.

Dragoo, D. W.

1973   Wells Creek: An Early Man Site in Stewart County, Tennessee. *Archaeology of Eastern North America* 1:1–55.

1990   *Palaeo-Indian Projectile Points and Tools: Eastern North America*. Institute for Human History, Gloucester, Mass.

Draper, P.

1975   !Kung Women: Contrasts in Sexual Egalitarianism in Foraging and Sedentary Contexts. In *Toward an Anthropology of Women*, edited by R. R. Reiter, pp. 77–109. Monthly Review Press, New York.

Driskell, B. N.

1996   Stratified Late Pleistocene and Early Holocene Deposits at Dust Cave, Northwestern Alabama. In *The Paleoindian and Early Archaic Southeast*, edited by D. G. Anderson and K. E. Sassaman, pp. 315–330. University of Alabama Press, Tuscaloosa.

Driver, J. C.

1988   Late Pleistocene and Holocene Vertebrates and Palaeoenvironments from Charlie Lake Cave, Northeast British Columbia. *Canadian Journal of Earth Sciences* 25:1545–1553.

Driver, J. C., M. Handly, K. R. Fladmark, D. E. Nelson, G. M. Sullivan, and R. Preston

1996   Stratigraphy, Radiocarbon Dating, and Culture History of Charlie Lake Cave, British Columbia. *Arctic* 49(3):265–277.

du Cros, H., and L. Smith (editors)

1993   *Women in Archaeology: A Feminist Critique*. Department of Prehistory, Australian National University,

Occasional Papers in Prehistory, No. 23. Highland Press, Canberra.

Duke, P.

1991   Recognizing Gender in Plains Hunting Groups: Is It Possible or Even Necessary? In *The Archaeology of Gender: Proceedings of the Twenty-Second Annual Conference of the Archaeological Association of the University of Calgary*, edited by D. Walde and N. Willows, pp. 280–283. University of Calgary Archaeological Association, Calgary, Alberta.

Dumond, D. E.

1980   The Archaeology of Alaska and the Peopling of America. *Science* 209:984–991.

1982   Colonization of the American Arctic and the New World. *American Antiquity* 47:885–895.

1984   Prehistory: Summary. In *Arctic*, edited by D. Damas, pp. 72–79. Handbook of North American Indians, Vol. 5. Smithsonian Institution Press, Washington, D.C.

1987   A Reexamination of Eskimo-Aleut Prehistory. *American Anthropologist* 89:32–56.

Dunbar, J. S.

1991   Resource Orientation of Clovis and Suwannee Age Paleoindian Sites in Florida. In *Clovis: Origins and Adaptations*, edited by R. Bonnichsen and K. L. Turnmire, pp. 185–213. Center for the Study of the First Americans, Oregon State University, Corvallis.

Dunbar, J. S., and B. I. Waller

1992   Resource Orientation of Clovis, Suwannee, and Simpson Age Paleoindian Sites in Florida. In *Paleoindian and Early Archaic Period Research in the Lower Southeast: A South Carolina Perspective*, edited by D. G. Anderson, K. E. Sassaman, and C. Judge, pp. 279–295. Council of South Carolina Professional Archaeologists, Columbia.

Dunbar, J. S., and S. D. Webb

1996   Bone and Ivory Tools from Submerged Paleoindian Sites in Florida. In *The Paleoindian and Early Archaic Southeast*, edited by D. G. Anderson and K. E. Sassaman, pp. 331–353. University of Alabama Press, Tuscaloosa.

Durham, W.

1991   *Coevolution: Genes, Culture, and Human Diversity*. Stanford University Press, Stanford, Calif.

1992   Applications of Evolutionary Culture Theory. *Annual Review of Anthropology* 21:331–355.

Easton, N. A.

1992   Mal de Mer above Terra Incognita, or, "What Ails the Coastal Migration Theory?" *Arctic Anthropology* 29:28–42.

Easton, R. D., D. A. Merriwether, D. E. Crews, and R. E. Ferrell

1996   mtDNA Variation in the Yanomami: Evidence for Additional New World Founding Lineages. *American Journal of Human Genetics* 59:213–225.

Edgar, H. J. H.

1997   Paleopathology of the Wizard's Beach Man (AHUR 2023) and the Spirit Cave Mummy (AHUR 2064). *Nevada Historical Society Quarterly* 40:57–61.

Ehret, C.

1984   Historical/Linguistic Evidence for Early African Food Production. In *From Hunters to Farmers: The Causes and Consequences of Food Production in Africa*, edited by S. A. Brandt, pp. 26–33. University of California Press, Berkeley.

Elias, S. A.

1997   New Evidence on the Environments Encountered by Paleoindians in Central and Eastern Beringia. *Current Research in the Pleistocene* 14:123–125.

2000   Late Pleistocene Climates of Beringia, Based on Analysis of Fossil Beetles. *Quaternary Research* 53(2):229–235.

Ellis, C.

1994   Some Unanswered Questions concerning Paleoindian Settlement and Subsistence in Southern Ontario. In *Great Lakes Archaeology and Paleoecology*, edited by R. I. MacDonald, pp. 413–429. Quaternary Sciences Institute, Waterloo, Ontario.

1998   The Fluted Point Tradition and the Arctic Small Tool Tradition: What's the Connection? Paper presented at the 31st Annual Chacmool Conference, University of Calgary, Calgary, Alberta.

Ellis, C., and D. B. Deller

1990   Paleoindians. In *The Archaeology of Southern Ontario to A.D. 1650*, edited by C. Ellis and N. Ferris, pp. 37–63. Occasional Publications of the London Chapter, No. 5. Ontario Archaeological Society, London.

Empéraire, J., A. Laming-Empéraire, and H. Reichlen

1963   La Grotte Fell et autres sites de la région volcanique de la Patagonie Chilienne. *Journal de la Société des Américanistes* (Nouvelle Série) 52:167–254.

Engelbrecht, W. E., and C. K. Seyfert

1994   Paleoindian Watercraft: Evidence and Implications. *North American Archaeologist* 15:221–234.

Epstein, J. F.

1969   *The San Isidro Site: An Early Man Campsite in Nuevo Leon, Mexico*. Anthropology Series, No. 7. Department of Anthropology, University of Texas, Austin.

Eriksen, B. V.

1996   Resource Exploitation, Subsistence Strategies, and Adaptiveness in Late Pleistocene–Early Holocene Northwest Europe. In *Humans at the End of the Ice Age: The Archaeology of the Pleistocene-Holocene Transition*, edited by L. G. Straus, B. V. Eriksen, J. M. Erlandson, and D. R. Yesner, pp. 101–128. Plenum Press, New York.

Eriksen, B. V., and L. G. Straus (editors)

1998   As the World Warmed: Human Adaptations across the Pleistocene/Holocene Boundary. *Quaternary International* 49/50:1–199.

Erlandson, J. M.

2002   Anatomically Modern Humans, Maritime Voyaging, and the Pleistocene Colonization of the Americas. In *The First Americans: The Pleistocene Colonization of the New World*, edited by N. G. Jablonski, pp. 59–92. Memoirs of the California Academy of Sciences, No. 27. San Francisco.

Erlandson, J. M., M. Tveskov, D. Kennett, and L. Ingram

1996   Further Evidence for a Terminal Pleistocene Occupation of Daisy Cave, San Miguel Island, CA. *Current Research in the Pleistocene* 13:13–15.

Evans, C., and B. J. Meggers

1960   *Archaeological Investigations in British Guiana*. Bureau of American Ethnology Bulletin, No. 177. Smithsonian Institution, Washington, D.C.

Evans, N., and R. Jones

1997   The Cradle of the Pama-Ngyungans: Archaeological and Linguistic Speculations. In *Archaeology and Linguistics*, edited by M. Patrick and E. Nicholas, pp. 385–417. Oxford University Press, Melbourne.

Fagan, B. M.

1987   *The Great Journey: The Peopling of Ancient America*. Thames and Hudson, London.

1999   American Origins. *Discovering Archaeology* 1(3): 12–15.

Faught, M. K., and D. G. Anderson

1996   Across the Straits, down the Corridor, around the Bend, and off the Shelf: An Evaluation of Paleoindian Colonization Models. Paper presented at the 61st Annual Meeting of the Society for American Archaeology, New Orleans.

Faught, M. K., and J. Dunbar

1997   Paleoindian Archaeology in Two Regions Exhibiting Waisted Lanceolate Projectile Points: Florida and Panama. Paper presented at the 62nd Annual Meeting of the Society for American Archaeology, Nashville, Tenn.

FAUNMAP Working Group

1996   Spatial Response of Mammals to Late Quaternary Environmental Fluctuations. *Science* 272: 1601–1606.

Feder, K. L.

2000   *The Past in Perspective: An Introduction to Human Prehistory*. Mayfield, Mountain View, Calif.

Fedje, D. W., and T. Christensen

1999   Modeling Paleoshorelines and Locating Early Holocene Coastal Sites in Haida Gwaii. *American Antiquity* 64:635–652.

Ferguson, W.

1997   *Why I Hate Canadians*. Douglas & McIntyre, Vancouver, B.C.

Ferring, C. R.

1989   The Aubrey Clovis Site: A Paleoindian Locality in the Upper Trinity River Basin, Texas. *Current Research in the Pleistocene* 6:9–11.

1990   The 1989 Investigations at the Aubrey Clovis Site, Texas. *Current Research in the Pleistocene* 7:10–12.

1994   The Role of Geoarchaeology in Paleoindian Archaeology. In *Method and Theory for Investigating the Peopling of the Americas*, edited by R. Bonnichsen and D. G. Steele, pp. 57–72. Center for the Study of the First Americans, Oregon State University, Corvallis.

1995   The Late Quaternary Geology and Archaeology of

the Aubrey Clovis Site, Texas: A Preliminary Report. In *Ancient Peoples and Landscapes*, edited by E. Johnson, pp. 273–281. Museum of Texas Tech University, Lubbock.

2001 *The Archaeology and Paleoecology of the Aubrey Clovis Site (41DN479), Denton County, Texas*. Report from Center for Environmental Archaeology, Department of Geography, University of Texas, to U.S. Army Corps of Engineers, Fort Worth, Tex.

Fiedel, S. J.

1992 *Prehistory of the Americas*. 2nd ed. Cambridge University Press, Cambridge.

1998 Rapid Migrations by Arctic Hunting Peoples: Clovis and Thule. Paper presented at the 63rd Annual Meeting of the Society for American Archaeology, Seattle.

1999a Artifact Provenience at Monte Verde: Confusion and Contradictions. *Discovering Archaeology, Special Report* 1(6):1–12.

1999b Older Than We Thought: Implications of Corrected Dates for Paleoindians. *American Antiquity* 64(1): 95–115.

2000a The Peopling of the New World: Present Evidence, New Theories, and Future Directions. *Journal of Archaeological Research* 8(1):39–103.

2000b Quacks in the Ice: Waterfowl, Paleoindians, and the Discovery of America. Paper presented at the 65th Annual Meeting of the Society for American Archaeology, Philadelphia.

2000c Response to Dillehay: Some Preliminary Comments. Electronic document, http://archaeology.about.com/library/excav/blmvfiedel.htm, accessed January 4, 2002.

Fiedel, S. J., and D. W. Anthony

1979 The Diffusion of the Early European Neolithic: A Reconsideration. Paper presented at the 2nd Eastern European Archaeology (Hleb i Vino) Conference, University of Pennsylvania, Philadelphia.

2003 Deerslayers, Pathfinders, and Icemen: Origins of the European Neolithic as Seen from the Frontier. In *Colonization of Unfamiliar Landscapes: The Archaeology of Adaptation*, edited by M. Rockman and J. Steele, pp. 144–168. Routledge, London.

Figgins, J. D.

1927 The Antiquity of Man in America. *Natural History* 27:229–239.

1931 An Additional Discovery of the Association of a Folsom: Artifact and Fossil Mammal Remains. *Proceedings of the Colorado Museum of Natural History* 10:23–24.

1933 A Further Contribution to the Antiquity of Man in America. *Proceedings of the Colorado Museum of Natural History* 12:16–33.

Fischer, A.

1989 A Late Palaeolithic "School" of Flint-Knapping at Trollesgave, Denmark. *Acta Archaeologica* 60: 33–49.

Fischer, A., and H. Tauber

1986 New C-14 Datings of Late Palaeolithic Cultures from Northwestern Europe. *Journal of Danish Archaeology* 5:7–13.

Fitzhugh, W.

1976 Paleoeskimo Occupations of the Labrador Coast. In *Eastern Arctic Prehistory: Paleoeskimo Problems*, edited by M. S. Maxwell, pp. 103–118. Memoirs of the Society for American Archaeology, No. 31. Washington, D.C.

1997 Biogeographical Archaeology in the Eastern North American Arctic. *Human Ecology* 25:385–418.

Fix, A. G.

1999 *Migration and Colonization in Human Microevolution*. Cambridge University Press, Cambridge.

2002 Colonization Models and Initial Genetic Diversity in the Americas. *Human Biology* 74:1–10.

Fladmark, K. R.

1978 The Feasibility of the Northwest Coast as a Migration Route for Early Man. In *Early Man in America from a Circum-Pacific Perspective*, edited by A. L. Bryan, pp. 119–128. Occasional Papers, No. 1. Department of Anthropology, University of Alberta, Edmonton.

1979 Routes: Alternative Migration Corridors for Early Man in North America. *American Antiquity* 44: 55–69.

1983 Times and Places: Environmental Correlates of Mid-to-Late Wisconsinan Human Population Expansion in North America. In *Early Man in the New World*, edited by R. Shutler, pp. 13–42. Sage Publications, Beverly Hills, Calif.

1986 Getting One's Berings. *Natural History* 95:8–17.

1996 The Prehistory of Charlie Lake Cave. In *Early Human Occupation in British Columbia*, edited by L. D. Bona, pp. 11–20. University of British Columbia Press, Vancouver.

Fladmark, K. R., J. C. Driver, and D. Alexander

1988 The Paleoindian Component at Charlie Lake Cave (HbRf-39), British Columbia. *American Antiquity* 53(2):371–384.

Flannery, T. F.

1995 *The Future Eaters: An Ecological History of the Australasian Lands and People*. George Braziller, New York.

2001 *The Eternal Frontier: An Ecological History of North America and Its Peoples*. Text Publishers, Melbourne.

Flegenheimer, N.

1980 Hallazgos de puntas "cola de pescado" en la provincia de Buenos Aires. *Relaciones de la Sociedad Argentina de Antropología* 14(1):169–176.

Flegenheimer, N., and M. Zarate

1989 Paleoindian Occupation at Cerro El Sombrero Locality, Buenos Aires Province, Argentina. *Current Research in the Pleistocene* 6:12–13.

1997 Considerations on Radiocarbon and Calibrated Dates from Cerro La China and Cerro El Sombrero, Argentina. *Current Research in the Pleistocene* 14: 27–28.

Flerov, C. C.

1967 On the Origin of the Mammalian Fauna of Canada.

In *The Bering Land Bridge*, edited by D. M. Hopkins, pp. 271–280. Stanford University Press, Stanford, Calif.

1971   The Evolution of Certain Mammals during the Late Cenozoic. In *The Late Cenozoic Glacial Ages*, edited by K. K. Turekian, pp. 479–492. Yale University Press, New Haven, Conn.

Foley, R. A.

1982   A Reconsideration of the Role of Predation on Large Mammals in Tropical Hunter-Gatherer Adaptation. *Man* 17(3):393–402.

1985   Optimality Theory in Anthropology. *Man* 20:222–242.

1987   Hominid Species and Stone Tool Assemblages: How Are They Related? *Antiquity* 61:380–392.

1988   Hominids, Humans, and Hunter-Gatherers. In *Hunters and Gatherers: History, Evolution, and Social Change*, edited by T. Ingold, D. Riches, and J. Woodburn, pp. 207–221. Berg Publishers, Oxford.

1992   Evolutionary Ecology of Fossil Hominids. In *Evolutionary Ecology and Human Behavior*, edited by E. A. Smith and B. Winterhalder, pp. 131–164. Aldine de Gruyter, New York.

Forster, P., R. Harding, A. Torroni, and H.-J. Bandelt

1996   Origin and Evolution of Native American mtDNA Variation: A Reappraisal. *American Journal of Human Genetics* 59:935–945.

Forster, P., A. Röhl, P. Lünnermann, C. Brinkmann, T. Zerjal, and C. Tyler-Smith

2000   A Short Tandem Repeat-Based Phylogeny for the Human Y Chromosome. *American Journal of Human Genetics* 67:182–196.

Fox, A.

1995   *Linguistic Reconstruction: An Introduction to Theory and Method*. Oxford University Press, New York.

Fox, C. L.

1996   Mitochondrial DNA Haplogroups in Four Tribes from Tierra del Fuego–Patagonia: Inferences about the Peopling of the Americas. *Human Biology* 68:855–871.

Fox, J. A.

1986   Comments. *Current Anthropology* 27:488–489.

Freeman, A. K. L., E. E. Smith, and K. B. Tankersley

1996   A Stone's Throw from Kimmswick: Clovis Period Research in Kentucky. In *The Paleoindian and Early Archaic Southeast*, edited by D. G. Anderson and K. E. Sassaman, pp. 385–403. University of Alabama Press, Tuscaloosa.

Frenzel, B.

1968   The Pleistocene Vegetation of Northern Eurasia. *Science* 161:637–649.

Freund, G.

1952   *Die Blattspitzen des Paleolithikums in Europa*. Quatär Bibliotek, Bonn.

Frison, G. C.

1973   The Plains. In *The Development of North American Archaeology*, edited by J. E. Fitting, pp. 151–184. Anchor Press, Garden City, N.Y.

1982a   Bison Dentition Studies. In *The Agate Basin Site:*

A Record of the Paleoindian Occupation of the Northwestern High Plains, edited by G. C. Frison and D. J. Stanford, pp. 240–260. Academic Press, New York.

1982b   The Sheaman Site: A Clovis Component. In *The Agate Basin Site: A Record of the Paleoindian Occupation of the Northwestern High Plains*, edited by G. C. Frison and D. J. Stanford, pp. 43–157. Academic Press, New York.

1983   The Western Plains and Mountain Region. In *Early Man in the New World*, edited by R. Shutler, pp. 109–124. Sage Publications, Beverly Hills, Calif.

1988   Paleoindian Subsistence and Settlement during Post-Clovis Times on the Northwestern Plains. In *Americans before Columbus: Ice Age Origins*, edited by R. C. Carlisle, pp. 83–106. Ethnology Monographs, No. 12. Department of Anthropology, University of Pittsburgh, Pittsburgh.

1989   Experimental Use of Clovis Weaponry and Tools on African Elephants. *American Antiquity* 54:766–784.

1990   Clovis, Goshen, and Folsom: Lifeways and Cultural Relationships. In *Megafauna and Man: Discovery of America's Heartland*, edited by L. D. Agenbroad, J. I. Mead, and L. W. Nelson, pp. 100–122. Scientific Papers, No. 1. Mammoth Site of Hot Springs, South Dakota, Inc., Hot Springs.

1991a   The Clovis Cultural Complex: New Data from Caches of Flaked Stone and Worked Bone Artifacts. In *Raw Material Economies among Prehistoric Hunter-Gatherers*, edited by A. Montet-White and S. Holen, pp. 321–334. Publications in Anthropology, No. 19. University of Kansas Press, Lawrence.

1993   North American High Plains Paleo-Indian Hunting Strategies and Weaponry Assemblages. In *From Kostenki to Clovis: Upper Paleolithic-Paleoindian Adaptations*, edited by O. Soffer and N. D. Praslov, pp. 237–249. Plenum Press, New York.

1998a   Paleoindian. In *Archaeology of Prehistoric Native America: An Encyclopedia*, edited by G. Gibbon, pp. 620–621. Garland Publishing, New York.

1998b   Paleoindian Large Mammal Hunters on the Plains of North America. *Proceedings of the National Academy of Sciences of the United States of America* 95:14576–14583.

2000   A 14C Date on a Late-Pleistocene *Camelops* at the Casper–Hell Gap Site, Wyoming. *Current Research in the Pleistocene* 17:28–29.

Frison, G. C. (editor)

1991b   *Prehistoric Hunters of the High Plains*. 2nd ed. Academic Press, New York.

Frison, G. C., and R. Bonnichsen

1996   The Pleistocene-Holocene Transition on the Plains and Rocky Mountains of North America. In *Humans at the End of the Ice Age: The Archaeology of the Pleistocene-Holocene Transition*, edited by L. G. Straus, B. V. Eriksen, J. M. Erlandson, and D. R. Yesner, pp. 303–318. Plenum Press, New York.

Frison, G. C., and C. B. Bradley

1999   *The Fenn Cache: Clovis Weapons and Tools*. One Horse Land and Cattle Co., Santa Fe, N.Mex.

Frison, G. C., and D. J. Stanford (editors)
1982 *The Agate Basin Site: A Record of the Paleoindian Occupation of the Northwestern High Plains*. Academic Press, New York.

Frison, G. C., and L. C. Todd
1986 *The Colby Mammoth Site: Taphonomy and Archaeology of a Clovis Kill in Northern Wyoming*. University of New Mexico Press, Albuquerque.
1987 *The Horner Site: The Type Site of the Cody Cultural Complex*. Academic Press, Orlando, Fla.

Funk, R. E.
1972 Early Man in the Northeast and the Late Glacial Environment. *Man in the Northeast* 4:7–39.

Funk, R. E., and B. Wellman
1984 The Corditaipe Site: A Small Isolated Paleoindian Camp in the Upper Mohawk Valley. *Archaeology of Eastern North America* 12:72–80.

Gal, R.
1982 An Annotated and Indexed Roster of Archaeological Radiocarbon Dates from Alaska, North of 68° Latitude. *Anthropological Papers of the University of Alaska* 20(1):159–180.

Galm, J. R., and S. Gough
2000 Site 45KT1362, a c. 10,000 Yr B.P. Occupation in Central Washington. *Current Research in the Pleistocene* 17:29–31.

Gamble, C. S.
1986 *The Palaeolithic Settlement of Europe*. Cambridge University Press, Cambridge.
1994 *Timewalkers: The Prehistory of Global Colonization*. Harvard University Press, Cambridge.
1995 The Earliest Occupation of Europe: The Environmental Background. In *The Earliest Occupation of Europe*, edited by W. Roebroeks and T. V. Kolfschoten, pp. 279–296. University of Leiden, Leiden.
2000 Social and Ecological Knowledge in the Process of Colonization. Paper presented at the 65th Annual Meeting of the Society for American Archaeology, Philadelphia.

García-Bárcena, J.
1979 *Una punta acanalada de la Cueva los Grifos, Ocozocoautla, Chiapas*. Cuadernos de Trabajo, No. 17. Departamento de Prehistoria, Instituto Nacional de Antropología e Historia, Mexico City.

Gardner, W. M.
1974 *The Flint Run Paleoindian Complex: A Preliminary Report 1971 through 1973 Seasons*. Archaeology Laboratory Occasional Papers, No. 1. Catholic University of America, Washington, D.C.
1977 Flint Run Paleoindian Complex and Its Implications for Eastern North America Prehistory. In *Amerinds and Their Paleoenvironments in Northeastern North America*, edited by W. S. Newman and B. Salwen, pp. 251–263. Annals of the New York Academy of Sciences, Vol. 288. New York.
1983 Stop Me If You've Heard This One Before: The Flint Run Paleoindian Complex Revisited. *Archaeology of Eastern North America* 11:49–59.

Gardner, W. M., and R. Verrey
1979 Typology and Chronology of Fluted Points from the Flint Run Area. *Pennsylvanian Archaeologist* 49:13–45.

Garrett, W. E.
1988 Where Did We Come From? *National Geographic* 189:434–437.

Geib, P. R.
1995 Two Fluted Points from the Kaibito Plateau, Northeastern Arizona. *Kiva* 61:89–97.

Gero, J. M.
1985 Socio-politics of Archaeology and the Woman-at-Home Ideology. *American Antiquity* 50:342–350.
1989 Producing Prehistory, Controlling the Past: The Case of New England Beehives. In *Critical Traditions in Contemporary Archaeology: Essays in the Philosophy, History, and Socio-politics of Archaeology*, edited by V. Pinsky and A. Wylie, pp. 96–103. Cambridge University Press, Cambridge.
1991a Gender Divisions of Labor in the Construction of Archaeological Knowledge. In *The Archaeology of Gender: Proceedings of the Twenty-Second Annual Conference of the Archaeological Association of the University of Calgary*, edited by D. Walde and N. Willows, pp. 96–102. University of Calgary Archaeological Association, Calgary, Alberta.
1991b Genderlithics: Women's Roles in Stone Tool Production. In *Engendering Archaeology: Women and Prehistory*, edited by J. M. Gero and M. W. Conkey, pp. 163–193. Basil Blackwell, Cambridge, England.
1993 The Social World of Prehistoric Facts: Gender and Power in Paleoindian Research. In *Women in Archaeology: A Feminist Critique*, edited by H. du Cros and L. Smith, pp. 31–40. Department of Prehistory, Australian National University, Occasional Papers in Prehistory, No. 23. Highland Press, Canberra.

Gero, J. M., and M. W. Conkey (editors)
1991 *Engendering Archaeology: Women and Prehistory*. Basil Blackwell, Cambridge, England.

Gero, J. M., and D. Root
1990 Public Presentations and Private Concerns: Archaeology in the Pages of *National Geographic*. In *The Politics of the Past*, edited by P. Gathercote and D. Lowenthal, pp. 19–37. Unwin Hyman, London.

Gibbons, A.
1995 First Americans: Not Hunters, but Forest Dwellers? *Science* 272:346–347.
2001 The Peopling of the Pacific. *Science* 291:1735–1737.

Gilsen, L.
2000 Listing of Radiocarbon Dates from the State of Oregon. Manuscript on file, State Historic Preservation Office, Salem, Oreg.

Ginther, C., D. Corach, G. A. Penacino, J. A. Rey, F. R. Carnese, M. H. Hutz, A. Anderson, J. Just, F. M. Salzano, and M. C. King
1993 Genetic Variation among the Mapuche Indians from the Patagonian Region of Argentina: Mitochondrial DNA Sequence Variation and Allele Frequencies of Several Nuclear Genes. In *DNA Fingerprinting: State*

of the Science, edited by S. D. J. Pena, R. Chakraborty, J. T. Epplen, and A. J. Jeffreys, pp. 211–219. Berkhauser Verlag, Basel.

Gnecco, C.
1990   El paradigma paleoindio en Suramerica. *Revista de Antropología y Arqueología* 6(1):37–78.
1994   Fluting Technology in South America. *Lithic Technology* 19(1):35–42.

Gnecco, C., and M. Bravo
1994   Análisis sintáctico de la tecnología de resducción bifacial en San Isidro, un sitio de cazadores-recolectores del Holoceno temprano. *Boletín Museo del Oro* 37:77–96.

Gnecco, C., and S. Mora
1997   Late Pleistocene/Early Holocene Tropical Forest Occupations at San Isidro and Peña Roja, Colombia. *Antiquity* 71:683–690.

Gnecco, C. C., and H. M. Illera
1989   La Elvira: Un sitio paleoindio en el valle de Popayán. *Boletín de Arqueología* 4:19–28.

Goebel, F. E., W. R. Powers, and N. F. Bigelow
1991   The Nenana Complex of Alaska and Clovis Origins. In *Clovis: Origins and Adaptations*, edited by R. Bonnichsen and K. L. Turnmire, pp. 49–80. Center for the Study of the First Americans, Oregon State University, Corvallis.

Goebel, T., M. R. Waters, and M. Dikove
2003   The Archaeology of Ushki Lake, Kamchatka, and the Pleistocene Peopling of the Americas. *Science* 301:501–505.

Gooding, J., and W. L. Shields
1985   *Sisyphus Shelter*. Cultural Resources Series, No. 18. U.S. Bureau of Land Management, Salt Lake City.

Goodyear, A. C., III
1989   A Hypothesis for the Use of Cryptocrystalline Raw Materials among Paleo-Indian Groups of North America. In *Eastern Paleoindian Lithic Resource Use*, edited by C. Ellis and J. Lothrop, pp. 1–10. Westview Press, Boulder, Colo.
1999   The Early Holocene Occupation of the Southeastern United States: A Geoarchaeological Summary. In *Ice Age Peoples of North America: Environments, Origins, and Adaptations of the First Americans*, edited by R. Bonnichsen and K. L. Turnmire, pp. 432–481. Oregon State University Press, Corvallis.

Goodyear, A. C., III, J. L. Michie, and T. Charles
1990   *The Earliest South Carolinians: The Paleoindian Occupation of South Carolina*. Occasional Papers, No. 2. Archaeological Society of South Carolina, West Columbia.

Goren-Inbar, N., C. S. Feibel, K. L. Verosub, Y. Melamed, M. E. Kislev, E. Tchernov, and I. Saragusti
2000   Pleistocene Milestones on the Out-of-Africa Corridor at Gesher Benot Ya'aqov, Israel. *Science* 289:944–947.

Goring-Morris, N. A.
1996   Square Pegs into Round Holes: A Critique of Neeley and Barton. *Antiquity* 70:130–135.

Gould, R. A.
1978   *Explorations in Ethnoarchaeology*. University of New Mexico Press, Albuquerque.

Gowlett, J. A. J., E. T. Hall, R. E. M. Hedges, and C. Perry
1986   Radiocarbon-Dates from the Oxford AMS System—Archaeometry Datelist 3. *Archaeometry* 28(1):116–125.

Graham, R. W.
1976   Late Wisconsin Mammal Faunas and Environmental Gradients of the Eastern United States. *Paleobiology* 2:343–350.
1998   Mammals' Eye View of Environmental Change in the United States at the End of the Pleistocene. Paper presented at the 63rd Annual Meeting of the Society for American Archaeology, Seattle.

Graham, R. W., C. V. Haynes Jr., D. L. Johnson, and M. Kay
1981   Kimmswick: A Clovis-Mastodon Association in Eastern Missouri. *Science* 213:1115–1117.

Graham, R. W., and M. Kay
1988   Taphonomic Comparisons of Cultural and Non-cultural Faunal Deposits at the Kimmswick and Barnhart Sites, Jefferson County, Missouri. In *Late Pleistocene and Early Holocene Paleoecology and Archaeology of the Eastern Great Lakes Region*, edited by R. Laub, N. Miller, and D. W. Steadman, pp. 227–240. Buffalo Society of Natural Sciences Bulletin, No. 33. Buffalo, N.Y.

Graham, R. W., and E. L. Lundelius
1984   Coevolutionary Disequilibrium and Pleistocene Extinctions. In *Quaternary Extinctions: A Prehistoric Revolution*, edited by P. S. Martin and R. G. Klein, pp. 223–250. University of Arizona Press, Tucson.

Graham, R. W., and J. Mead
1987   Environmental Fluctuations and Evolution of Mammalian Faunas during the Last Deglaciation in North America. In *North America and Adjacent Oceans during the Last Deglaciation*, edited by W. Ruddiman and H. Wright, pp. 371–402. Geological Society of America, Boulder, Colo.

Gramly, R. M.
1982   *The Vail Site: A Palaeo-Indian Encampment in Maine*. Buffalo Society of Natural Sciences Bulletin, No. 30. Buffalo, N.Y.
1993   *The Richey Clovis Cache: Earliest Americans along the Columbia River*. Persimmon Press Monographs in Archaeology. Persimmon Press, Buffalo, N.Y.
1999   *The Lamb Site: A Pioneering Clovis Encampment*. Persimmon Press, Kenmore, N.Y.

Gramly, R. M., and C. Yahnig
1991   The Adams Site (15Ch90) and the Little River, Christian County, Kentucky, Clovis Workshop Complex. *Southeastern Archaeology* 10:134–145.

Grayson, D. K., and M. Cannon
1999   Human Paleoecology and Foraging Theory in the Great Basin. In *Models for the Millennium: Great Basin Anthropology Today*, edited by C. Beck, pp. 141–151. University of Utah Press, Salt Lake City.

Grayson, D. K., and F. Delpech
1998   Changing Diet Breadth in the Early Upper Paleo-

lithic of Southwestern France. *Journal of Archaeological Science* 25:1119–1129.

Green, F. E.
1963 The Clovis Blades: An Important Addition to the Llano Complex. *American Antiquity* 29:145–152.

Green, L. D., J. N. Derr, and A. Knight
2000 mtDNA Affinities of the Peoples of North-Central Mexico. *American Journal of Human Genetics* 66: 989–998.

Green, T. J., B. Cochran, T. W. Fenton, J. C. Woods, G. L. Titmus, L. Tieszen, M. A. Davis, and S. J. Miller
1998 The Buhl Burial: A Paleoindian Woman from Southern Idaho. *American Antiquity* 63(3):437–456.

Greenberg, J. H.
1963 *The Languages of Africa.* Stanford University Press, Stanford, Calif.
1966 Some Universals of Grammar with Particular Reference to the Order of Meaningful Elements. In *Universals of Language,* edited by H. G. Joseph, pp. 73–113. MIT Press, Cambridge, Mass.
1987 *Language in the Americas.* Stanford University Press, Stanford, Calif.
1990 The American Indian Language Controversy. *Review of Archaeology* 11:5–14.
1996 In Defence of Amerind. *International Journal of American Linguistics* 62(2):128–161.
1997 The Indo-European First and Second Person Pronouns in the Perspective of Eurasiatic, Especially Chukotkan. *Anthropological Linguistics* 39:187–195.
2000 *Indo-European and Its Closest Relatives: The Eurasiatic Family: Grammar.* Stanford University Press, Stanford, Calif.

Greenberg, J. H., and M. Ruhlen
1992 Linguistic Origins of Native Americans. *Scientific American* 267(5):94–99.

Greenberg, J. H., C. G. Turner II, and S. L. Zegura
1986 The Settlement of the Americas: A Comparison of the Linguistic, Dental, and Genetic Evidence. *Current Anthropology* 27:477–497.

Greenman, E. F.
1963 The Upper Paleolithic and the New World. *Current Anthropology* 4:41–66.

Grier, C.
1999 The Organization of Production in Prehistoric Thule Whaling Societies of the Central Canadian Arctic. *Canadian Journal of Archaeology* 23(1):11–28.

Griffin, J. B.
1946 Man in Northeastern North America. *Papers of the Robert S. Peabody Foundation for Archaeology* 3: 37–95.
1965 Late Quaternary Prehistory in the Northeastern Woodlands. In *The Quaternary of the United States,* edited by H. E. Wright and D. C. Frey, pp. 655–667. Princeton University Press, Princeton, N.J.

Grimm, E., G. Jacobson, W. Watts, B. Hansen, and K. Maasch
1993 A 50,000 Year Record of Climatic Oscillations from Florida and Its Temporal Correlation with Heinrich Events. *Science* 261:198–200.

Gruhn, R.
1987 On the Settlement of the Americas: South American Evidence for an Expanded Time Frame. *Current Anthropology* 28:363–365.
1988 Linguistic Evidence in Support of the Coastal Route of Earliest Entry into the New World. *Man* 23(1): 77–100.
1994 The Pacific Coast Route of Initial Entry: An Overview. In *Method and Theory for Investigating the Peopling of the Americas,* edited by R. Bonnichsen and D. G. Steele, pp. 249–256. Center for the Study of the First Americans, Oregon State University, Corvallis.
1997 The South American Context of the Pedra Pintada Site in Brazil. *Current Research in the Pleistocene* 14: 29–32.

Gruhn, R., and A. L. Bryan
1967 The Record of Pleistocene Megafaunal Extinction at Taima-Taima, Northern Venezuela. In *Pleistocene Extinctions: The Search for a Cause,* edited by P. S. Martin and H. E. Wright Jr., pp. 128–137. Yale University Press, New Haven, Conn.
1977 Los Tapiales: A Paleo-Indian Campsite in the Guatemalan Highlands. *Proceedings of the American Philosophical Society* 121:235–273.
1984 The Record of Pleistocene Megafaunal Extinction at Taima-Taima, Northern Venezuela. In *Quaternary Extinctions: A Prehistoric Revolution,* edited by P. S. Martin and R. G. Klein, pp. 128–137. University of Arizona Press, Tucson.
1991 A Review of Lynch's Description of South American Pleistocene Sites. *American Antiquity* 56:342–348.
1998 A Reappraisal of the Edge-Trimmed Tool Tradition. In *Explorations in American Archaeology: Essays in Honor of Wesley R. Hurt,* edited by M. G. Plew, pp. 37–53. University Press of America, Lanham, Md.

Guidon, N., and G. Delibrias
1986 Carbon-14 Dates Point to Man in the Americas 32,000 Years Ago. *Nature* 321(6072):769–771.

Guilday, J. E.
1984 Pleistocene Extinction and Environmental Change: Case Study of the Appalachians. In *Quaternary Extinctions: A Prehistoric Revolution,* edited by P. S. Martin and R. G. Klein, pp. 250–258. University of Arizona Press, Tucson.

Gunnerson, J. H.
1956 A Fluted Point in Utah. *American Antiquity* 21: 412–414.

Guralnik, D. B. (editor)
1978 *Webster's New World Dictionary.* 2nd college ed. William Collins and World Publishing Co., Cleveland.

Gurven, M.
2000 How Can We Distinguish between Mutational "Hot Spots" and "Old Sites" in Human mtDNA Samples? *Human Biology* 72:455–471.

Guthrie, R. D.
1968 Paleoecology of the Large Mammal Community

in Interior Alaska during the Late Pleistocene. *American Midland Naturalist* 79:346–363.

1984 Mosaics, Allelochemics, and Nutrients: An Ecological Theory of Late Pleistocene Megafaunal Extinctions. In *Quaternary Extinctions: A Prehistoric Revolution*, edited by P. S. Martin and R. G. Klein, pp. 259–298. University of Arizona Press, Tucson.

1990 *Frozen Fauna of the Mammoth Steppe: The Story of Blue Babe*. University of Chicago Press, Chicago.

Hack, J. T.
1942 *The Changing Physical Environment of the Hopi Indians of Arizona*. Papers of the Peabody Museum of Archaeology and Ethnology, Vol. 35. Cambridge, Mass.

Hadlock, H. L.
1962 Surface Surveys of Lithic Sites on the Gallegos Wash. *El Palacio* 69:174–184.

Haeussler, A. M.
1996 Dental Anthropology of Russia, Ukraine, Caucasus, Central Asia: The Evaluation of Five Hypotheses for Paleo Indian Origins. Ph.D. dissertation, Arizona State University, Tempe.

Haeussler, A. M., and C. G. Turner II
1992 The Dentition of Soviet Central Asians and the Quest for New World Ancestors. *Journal of Human Ecology* (Special Issue) 2:273–297.

Hajic, E. R., R. D. Mandel, and E. A. Bettis III
2000 Stratigraphic and Paleoenvironmental Investigations. In *The 1999 Excavations at the Big Eddy Site (23CE426)*, edited by M. D. Conner, pp. 26–36. Special Publication, No. 3. Center for Archaeological Research, Southwest Missouri State University, Springfield.

Hall, D. A.
1995 Stone-Tool Tradition Endures Radical Environmental Change. *Mammoth Trumpet* 10(3):1–9.

1999 Where North Meets South: Seeking a "Unified Theory" in Panama. *Mammoth Trumpet* 14:8–11.

2000 The North Atlantic Hypothesis. *Mammoth Trumpet* 15(2):1–7.

Hall, R. L.
1998 Tribal Members Active at SAA Even at Pre-Clovis Symposium. *Mammoth Trumpet* 13:12.

Hames, R.
1992 Time Allocation. In *Evolutionary Ecology and Human Behavior*, edited by E. A. Smith and B. Winterhalder, pp. 203–235. Aldine de Gruyter, New York.

Hamilton, T. D., and F. E. Goebel
1999 Late Pleistocene Peopling of Alaska. In *Ice Age Peoples of North America: Environments, Origins, and Adaptations of the First Americans*, edited by R. Bonnichsen and K. L. Turnmire, pp. 156–199. Oregon State University Press, Corvallis.

Hammer, M. F.
1994 A Recent Insertion of an Alu Element on the Y Chromosome Is a Useful Marker for Human Population Studies. *Molecular Biology and Evolution* 11: 749–761.

1999 The Y-Chromosome as an Anthropological Tool: Native American Founder Haplotypes. Paper presented at the Pioneers on the Land: How America Got Its People Conference, Arizona State University, Tempe.

Hammer, M. F., and S. Horai
1995 Y Chromosomal DNA Variation and the Peopling of Japan. *American Journal of Human Genetics* 56: 951–962.

Hammer, M. F., T. Karafet, A. Rasanayagam, E. T. Wood, T. K. Altheide, T. Jenkins, R. C. Griffiths, A. R. Templeton, and S. L. Zegura
1998 Out of Africa and Back Again: Nested Cladistic Analysis of Human Y Chromosome Variation. *Molecular Biology and Evolution* 15:427–441.

Hammer, M. F., A. B. Spurdle, T. Karafet, M. R. Bonner, E. T. Wood, A. Novelletto, P. Malaspina, R. J. Mitchell, S. Horai, T. Jenkins, and S. L. Zegura
1997 The Geographic Distribution of Human Y Chromosome Variation. *Genetics* 145:787–805.

Hammer, M. F., and S. L. Zegura
1996 The Role of the Y Chromosome in Human Evolutionary Studies. *Evolutionary Anthropology* 5: 116–134.

Handsman, R. G., and M. P. Leone
1989 Living History and Critical Archaeology in the Reconstruction of the Past. In *Critical Traditions in Contemporary Archaeology: Essays in the Philosophy, History, and Socio-politics of Archaeology*, edited by V. Pinsky and A. Wylie, pp. 117–135. Cambridge University Press, Cambridge.

Hannus, L. A.
1985 The Lange-Ferguson Site: An Event of Clovis Mammoth Butchering with Associated Bone Tool Technology: The Mammoth and Its Track. Ph.D. dissertation, University of Utah, Salt Lake City.

1990a The Lange-Ferguson Site: A Case for Mammoth Bone-Butchering Tools. In *Megafauna and Man: Discovery of America's Heartland*, edited by L. D. Agenbroad, J. I. Mead, and L. W. Nelson, pp. 86–99. Scientific Papers, No. 1. Mammoth Site of Hot Springs, South Dakota, Inc., Hot Springs.

1990b Mammoth Hunting in the New World. In *Hunters of the Recent Past*, edited by B. O. K. Reeves, pp. 47–67. Unwin Hyman, London.

Hansen, R. M.
1978 Shasta Ground Sloth Food Habits, Rampart Cave, Arizona. *Paleobiology* 4:302–303.

1980 Late Pleistocene Plant Fragments in the Dungs of Herbivores at Cowboy Cave. In *Cowboy Cave*, edited by J. D. Jennings, pp. 179–189. Anthropological Papers, No. 104. University of Utah, Salt Lake City.

Harihara, S., M. Hirai, Y. Suutou, K. Shimizu, and K. Omoto
1992 Frequency of a 9-bp Deletion in the Mitochondrial DNA among Asian Populations. *Human Biology* 64: 161–166.

Harpending, H.
1999 Comment on "Reproductive Interests and Forager Mobility" by D. MacDonald and B. Hewlett. *Current Anthropology* 40:517.

Harpending, H., and H. Davis
1976 Some Implications for Hunter-Gatherer Ecology Derived from the Spatial Structure of Resources. *World Archaeology* 8:275–286.

Harris, A. H.
1985 *Late Pleistocene Vertebrate Paleoecology of the West.* University of Texas Press, Austin.

Harris, P. O. B.
1991 A Paleo-Indian Stemmed Point from Trinidad, West Indies. Paper presented at the 14th Congress of the International Association for Caribbean Archaeology, Barbados.

Hasagawa, M., A. Di Rienzo, and T. Kocher
1993 Toward a More Accurate Time Scale for the Human Mitochondrial DNA Tree. *Journal of Molecular Evolution* 37:347–354.

Hassan, F. A.
1981 *Demographic Archaeology.* Academic Press, New York.

Hauk, F. R.
1977 *Cultural Resource Evaluation in Central Utah.* Cultural Resource Series, No. 3. U.S. Bureau of Land Management, Salt Lake City.

Haury, E. W., E. Antevs, and J. F. Lance
1953 Artifacts with Mammoth Remains, Naco, Arizona. *American Antiquity* 19:1–24.

Haury, E. W., E. B. Sayles, and W. W. Wasley
1959 The Lehner Mammoth Site, Southeastern Arizona. *American Antiquity* 25:2–42.

Hauswirth, W. W., C. D. Dickel, D. J. Rowold, and M. A. Hauswirth
1994 Inter- and Intrapopulation Studies of Ancient Humans. *Experientia* 50:585–591.

Hawkins, J. A.
1983 *Word Order Universals.* Academic Press, New York.

Hayden, B.
1982 Interaction Parameters and the Demise of Paleo-Indian Craftsmanship. *Plains Anthropologist* 27:109–123.

Haydenblit, R.
1996 Dental Variation among Four Prehispanic Mexican Populations. *American Journal of Physical Anthropology* 100:225–246.

Hayes, M. G., and D. H. O'Rourke
2000 Population Replacement in Human Prehistory as Assessed by Ancient mtDNA. *American Journal of Human Genetics, Supplement* 67:A234.

Haynes, C. V., Jr.
1964 Fluted Projectile Points: Their Age and Dispersion. *Science* 145:1408–1413.
1966 Elephant-Hunting in North America. *Scientific American* 214(6):104–112.
1967 Quaternary Geology of the Tule Springs Area, Clark County, Nevada. In *Pleistocene Studies in Southern Nevada*, edited by H. M. Wormington and D. Ellis, pp. 15–104. Anthropological Papers, No. 13. Nevada State Museum, Carson City.
1969 The Earliest Americans. *Science* 166:709–715.
1970 Geochronology of Man-Mammoth Sites and Their Bearing on the Origin of the Llano Complex. In *Pleistocene and Recent Environments of the Central Great Plains*, 3rd ed., edited by W. Dort and J. K. Jones, pp. 77–92. Department of Geology, University of Kansas, Special Publication, No. 3. University Press of Kansas, Lawrence.
1971 Time, Environment, and Early Man. *Arctic Anthropology* 8(2):3–14.
1972 Stratigraphic Investigations at the Williamson Site, Dinwiddie County, Virginia. *The Chesopiean* 10:107–114.
1974 Paleoenvironments and Cultural Diversity in Late Pleistocene South America: A Reply to A. L. Bryan. *Quaternary Research* 4:378–382.
1977 When and from Where Did Man Arrive in Northeastern North America: A Discussion. In *Amerinds and Their Paleoenvironments in Northeastern North America*, edited by W. S. Newman and B. Salwen, pp. 165–166. Annals of the New York Academy of Sciences, Vol. 288. New York.
1980 The Clovis Culture. *Canadian Journal of Anthropology* 1:115–121.
1982 Were Clovis Progenitors in Beringia? In *Paleoecology of Beringia*, edited by D. M. Hopkins, J. V. Matthews Jr., C. E. Schweger, and S. B. Young, pp. 383–398. Academic Press, New York.
1983 Fluted Points in the East and West. *Archaeology of Eastern North America* 11:24–27.
1985 Introduction. In *The Williamson Site, Dinwiddie County, Virginia*, edited by R. M. Peck, p. vii. Peck Publishing, Harrisburg, N.C.
1986 Mammoth Hunters of the USA and USSR. In *Beringia in the Cenozoic Era*, edited by V. L. Kontrimavichus, pp. 557–570. Russian Translation Series. A. A. Balkema, Rotterdam, Netherlands.
1987 Clovis Origin Update. *Kiva* 52:83–93.
1991a Geoarchaeological and Paleohydrological Evidence for a Clovis-Age Drought in North America and Its Bearing on Extinction. *Quaternary Research* 35:438–450.
1991b More on Meadowcroft Radiocarbon Chronology. *The Review of Archaeology* 12(1):8–14.
1992 Contributions of Radiocarbon Dating to the Geochronology of the Peopling of the New World. In *Radiocarbon Dating after Four Decades*, edited by R. F. Taylor, A. Long, and R. S. Kra, pp. 355–374. Springer-Verlag, New York.
1993 Clovis-Folsom Geochronology and Climatic Change. In *From Kostenki to Clovis: Upper Paleolithic-Paleoindian Adaptations*, edited by O. Soffer and N. D. Praslov, pp. 219–236. Plenum Press, New York.

Haynes, C. V., Jr., R. P. Beukens, A. J. T. Jull, and O. K. Davis
1992 New Radiocarbon Dates for Some Old Folsom Sites: Accelerator Technology. In *Ice Age Hunters of the Rockies*, edited by D. J. Stanford and J. S. Day, pp. 83–100. Denver Museum of Natural History, Denver, and University Press of Colorado, Niwot.

Haynes, C. V., Jr., D. J. Donahue, A. J. T. Jull, and T. H. Zabel
  1984 Application of Accelerator Dating to Fluted Point Paleoindian Sites. *Archaeology of Eastern North America* 12:184–191.

Haynes, C. V., Jr., and E. T. Hemmings
  1968 Mammoth-Bone Shaft Wrench from Murray Springs, Arizona. *Science* 159:186–187.

Haynes, C. V., Jr., D. J. Stanford, M. Jodry, J. Dickenson, J. L. Montgomery, P. H. Shelley, I. Rovner, and G. A. Agogino
  1999 A Clovis Well at the Type Site 11,500 BC: The Oldest Prehistoric Well in America. *Geoarchaeology* 14(5): 455–470.

Haynes, G.
  1991 *Mammoths, Mastodonts, and Elephants: Biology, Behavior, and the Fossil Record*. Cambridge University Press, Cambridge.
  1998 Clovis Diet and Mammoth-Hunting. Paper presented at the 63rd Annual Meeting of the Society for American Archaeology, Seattle.
  2002 The Catastrophic Extinction of North American Mammoths and Mastodonts. *World Archaeology* 33(3):391–416.

Hedges, R. E. M., R. A. Housley, C. R. Bronk, and G. J. Vanklinken
  1992 Radiocarbon-Dates from the Oxford AMS System—Archaeometry Datelist 15. *Archaeometry* 34(2): 337–357.

Hedges, R. E. M., R. A. Housley, C. B. Ramsey, and G. J. Vanklinken
  1993 Radiocarbon-Dates from the Oxford AMS System—Archaeometry Datelist 17. *Archaeometry* 35(2): 305–326.

Helm, J.
  1968 The Nature of Dogrib Socioterritorial Groups. In *Man the Hunter*, edited by R. B. Lee and I. DeVore, pp. 118–125. Aldine, Chicago.

Hemmings, E. T., and C. V. Haynes Jr.
  1969 The Escapule Mammoth and Associated Projectile Points, San Pedro Valley, Arizona. *Journal of the Arizona Academy of Science* 5:184–188.

Henry, D. O.
  1996 Functional Minimalism versus Ethnicity in Explaining Lithic Patterns in the Levantine Epipaleolithic. *Antiquity* 70:135–136.

Herbstritt, J. T.
  1988 A Reference for Pennsylvania Radiocarbon Dates. *Pennsylvania Archaeologist* 58(2):1–29.

Hesse, I. S.
  1995 A Reworked Clovis Point near Chevelon Ruin, Arizona. *Kiva* 61:83–88.

Hester, J. J.
  1966 Origins of the Clovis Culture. Paper presented at the 36th International Congress of Americanists, Barcelona and Seville, 1964.
  1972 *Blackwater Locality No. 7: A Stratified, Early Man Site in Eastern New Mexico*. Fort Burgwin Research Center, Ranchos de Taos, N.Mex.

Hester, T. R., H. J. Shafer, and T. C. Kelly
  1980a Lithics from a Preceramic Site in Belize: A Preliminary Note. *Lithic Technology* 9:9–10.
  1980b A Preliminary Note on Artifacts from Lowe Ranch: A Preceramic Site in Belize. In *The Colha Project Second Season, 1980 Interim Report*, edited by T. R. Hester, J. D. Eaton, and H. J. Shafer, pp. 229–232. Center for Archaeological Research, University of Texas, San Antonio, and Centro Studi e Ricerche Ligabue, Venice, Italy.

Hewlett, B. S.
  1992 Husband-Wife Reciprocity and the Father-Infant Relationship among Aka Pygmies. In *Father-Child Relations: Cultural and Biosocial Contexts*, edited by B. S. Hewlett, pp. 153–176. Aldine de Gruyter, New York.

Heyer, E., J. Puymirat, P. Dieltjes, E. Bakker, and P. de Knijff
  1997 Estimating Y Chromosome Specific Mutation Frequencies Using Deep Rooted Pedigrees. *Human Molecular Genetics* 6:799–803.

Hibben, F.
  1941 *Evidences of Early Occupation in Sandia Cave, New Mexico, and Other Sites in the Sandia Manzano Region*. Smithsonian Miscellaneous Collections, Vol. 99, No. 23. U.S. Government Printing Office, Washington, D.C.

Hill, J. H.
  1999 Evaluating Historical Linguistic Evidence for Ancient Human Communities in the Americas. Paper presented at the Pioneers on the Land: How America Got Its People Conference, Arizona State University, Tempe.
  2001 Proto-Uto-Aztecan: A Community of Cultivators in Mesoamerica? *American Anthropologist* 103(4): 913–934.

Hill, K., and A. M. Hurtado
  1996 *Ache Life History: The Ecology and Demography of a Foraging People*. Aldine de Gruyter, New York.

Hobsbawm, E.
  1992a Introduction: Inventing Traditions. In *The Invention of Tradition*, edited by E. Hobsbawm and T. Ranger, pp. 1–14. Cambridge University Press, Cambridge.
  1992b Mass Producing Traditions: Europe, 1870–1914. In *The Invention of Tradition*, edited by E. Hobsbawm and T. Ranger, pp. 263–307. Cambridge University Press, Cambridge.

Hoffecker, J. F., W. R. Powers, and T. Goebel
  1993 The Colonization of Beringia and the Peopling of the New World. *Science* 259:46–53.

Hofman, J. L.
  1991 Folsom Land Use: Projectile Point Variability as a Key to Mobility. In *Raw Material Economies among Prehistoric Hunter-Gatherers*, edited by A. Montet-White and S. Holen, pp. 335–374. Publications in Anthropology, No. 19. University of Kansas Press, Lawrence.
  1994 Paleoindian Aggregations on the Great Plains. *Journal of Anthropological Archaeology* 13:341–370.
  1995 The Busse Cache: A Clovis-Age Find in Northwest-

ern Kansas. *Current Research in the Pleistocene* 12:
17–19.

Hofman, J. L., D. S. Amick, and R. O. Rose
1990   Shifting Sands: A Folsom-Midland Assemblage from
a Campsite in Western Texas. *Plains Anthropologist*
35(129):221–253.

Holden, C.
1999   Were Spaniards among the First Americans? *Science*
286:1467–1468.

Holen, S.
2002   Clovis Long-Distance Movement of Lithic Materials
on the Central Great Plains. Paper presented at the
67th Annual Meeting of the Society for American
Archaeology, Denver.

Holliday, V. T., and A. B. Anderson
1993   "Paleoindian," "Clovis," and "Folsom": A Brief
Etymology. *Current Research in the Pleistocene* 10:
79–81.

Holliday, V. T., C. V. Haynes Jr., J. Hofman, and D. Meltzer
1991   The Miami Site Revisited: A Clovis Mammoth Kill
in the Texas Panhandle. *Current Research in the
Pleistocene* 8:36–39.

1994   Geoarchaeology and Geochronology of the Miami
Clovis Site, Southern High Plains of Texas. *Quaternary Research* 41:234–244.

Holliday, V. T., and E. Johnson (editors)
1990   *Guidebook to the Quaternary History of the Llano
Estacado*. Lubbock Lake Landmark Quaternary Research Center Series, No. 2. Museum of Texas Tech
University, Lubbock.

Holliday, V. T., and D. J. Meltzer
1996   Geoarchaeology of the Midland (Paleoindian) Site,
Texas. *American Antiquity* 61(4):755–771.

Holm, J.
1991   Settlements of the Hamburgian and Federmesser
Cultures at Slotseng. *Journal of Danish Archaeology*
10(1991):7–19. Odense University Press, Odense,
Denmark.

Hopkins, D. M.
1979   Landscape and Climate of Beringia during Late
Pleistocene and Holocene Times. In *The First Americans: Origins, Affinities, and Adaptations*, edited by
W. S. Laughlin and A. B. Harper, pp. 15–41. Gustav
Fischer, New York.

Hopkins, D. M., J. V. Mathews Jr., C. E. Schweger, and S. B.
Young (editors)
1982   *Paleoecology of Beringia*. Academic Press, New York.

Hoppe, P. P.
1978   Rumen Fermentation in African Ruminants. Paper
presented at the 13th Annual Congress of Game
Biologists, Atlanta.

Horai, S.
1993   Different Waves of Migration to the New World: Implications of Mitochondrial DNA Polymorphism in
Native Americans. *Current Research in the Pleistocene*
10:43–45.

Horai, S., and K. Hayasaka
1990   Intraspecific Nucleotide Sequence Differences in
the Major Non-coding Region of the Human Mitochondrial DNA. *American Journal of Human Genetics*
46:828–842.

Horai, S., K. Hayasaka, R. Kondo, K. Tsugane, and N. Takahata
1995   Recent African Origin of Modern Humans Revealed
by Complete Sequences of Hominoid Mitochondrial DNAs. *Proceedings of the National Academy of
Sciences of the United States of America* 92:532–536.

Horai, S., R. Kondo, Y. Nakagawa-Hattori, S. Hayashi, S. Sonoda, and K. Tajima
1993   Peopling of the Americas, Founded by Four Major
Lineages of Mitochondrial DNA. *Molecular Biology
and Evolution* 10:23–47.

Horai, S., and E. Matsunaga
1986   Mitochondrial DNA Polymorphism. II. Analysis with
Restriction of Four and Five Base-Pair Recognition.
Human Genetics 72:105–117.

Horai, S., K. Murayama, K. Hayasaka, S. Matsubayashi, Y. Hattori, G. Fucharoen, and S. Harihara
1996   mtDNA Polymorphism in East Asian Populations,
with Special Reference to the Peopling of Japan.
American Journal of Human Genetics 59:579–590.

Hostetler, S., and P. Bartlein
1999   Simulation of the Potential Responses of Regional
Climate and Surface Processes in Western North
America to a Canonical Heinrich Event. In *Mechanisms of Global Climate Change at Millennial Time
Scales*, edited by P. Clark, R. S. Webb, and L. Keigwin, pp. 313–327. American Geophysical Union,
Washington, D.C.

Housley, R. A., C. S. Gamble, M. Street, and P. Pettitt
1997   Radiocarbon Evidence for the Late Glacial Human
Recolonization of Northern Europe. *Proceedings of
the Prehistoric Society* 63:25–54.

Houston, J. M.
1967   *The Western Mediterranean World: An Introduction to
Its Regional Landscapes*. F. A. Praeger, New York.

Howard, C. D.
1990   The Clovis Point: Characteristics and Type Description. *Plains Anthropologist* 35:255–262.

1995   Projectile Point and Hafting Design Review. *North
American Archaeologist* 16:291–301.

Howard, E. B.
1935   Evidence of Early Man in North America. *The
Museum Journal* 24(2/3):53–171.

1936   An Outline of the Problem of Man's Antiquity in
North America. *American Anthropologist* 38:394–
413.

1943   The Finley Site: Discovery of Yuma Points, in Situ,
near Eden, Wyoming. *American Antiquity* 8:224–
234.

Howells, W. W.
1986   Physical Anthropology of the Prehistoric Japanese. In *Windows on the Japanese Past: Studies in
Archaeology and Prehistory*, edited by R. J. Pearson,
G. L. Barnes, and K. L. Hutterer, pp. 85–99. Center
for Japanese Studies, University of Michigan, Ann
Arbor.

1990   *Who's Who in Skulls: Ethnic Identification of Crania
from Measurements*. Papers of the Peabody Museum

of Archaeology and Ethnology, Vol. 82. Cambridge, Mass.

Hrdlicka, A.
1925 *The Origin and Antiquity of the American Indian.* Smithsonian Report for 1923. Smithsonian Institution, Washington, D.C.

Huckell, B. B.
1979 Of Chipped Stone Tools, Elephants, and the Clovis Hunters: An Experiment. *Plains Anthropologist* 24:177–189.
1982 *The Distribution of Fluted Points in Arizona: A Review and Update.* Archaeological Series, No. 145. University of Arizona, Tucson.
1995 *Of Marshes and Maize: Preceramic Agricultural Settlements in the Cienega Valley, Southeastern Arizona.* Anthropological Papers of the University of Arizona, No. 59. Tucson.

Hudecek-Cuffe, C. R.
1998 *Engendering Northern Plains Paleoindian Archaeology: Decision-Making and Gender Roles in Subsistence and Settlement Strategies.* BAR International Series, No. 699. British Archaeological Reports, Oxford.

Hughen, K. A., J. R. Southon, S. J. Lehman, and J. T. Overpeck
2000 Synchronous Radiocarbon and Climate Shifts during the Last Deglaciation. *Science* 290:1951–1954.

Hunt, A. P., and D. Tanner
1960 Early Man Sites near Moab. *American Antiquity* 26:110–112.

Huoponen, K., A. Torroni, P. R. Wickman, D. Sellitto, D. S. Gurley, R. Scozzari, and D. C. Wallace
1997 Mitochondrial and Y Chromosome-Specific Polymorphisms in the Seminole Tribe of Florida. *European Journal of Human Genetics* 5:25–34.

Hurt, W. R.
1977 The Edge-Trimmed Tool Tradition of Northwest South America. In *For the Director: Research Essays in Honor of James B. Griffin*, edited by C. E. Cleland, pp. 268–294. Anthropological Papers of the Museum of Anthropology, No. 61. University of Michigan, Ann Arbor.

Hurt, W. R., T. van der Hammen, and G. Correal Urrego
1977 *The El Abra Rockshelters, Sabana de Bogotá, Colombia, South America.* Occasional Papers and Monographs, No. 2. Indiana University Museum, Bloomington.

Illera, C. H. M., and C. Gnecco
1986 Puntas de proyectil en el valle de Popayán. *Boletín Museo del Oro* 17:45–57.

Ingbar, E. E.
1992 The Hanson Site and Folsom on the Northwestern Plains. In *Ice Age Hunters of the Rockies*, edited by D. J. Stanford and J. S. Day, pp. 169–192. Denver Museum of Natural History, Denver, and University Press of Colorado, Niwot.

Ingman, M., H. Kaessmann, S. Pääbo, and U. Gyllensten
2000 Mitochondrial Genome Variation and the Origin of Modern Humans. *Nature* 408:708–713.

International Wolf Center
1995 Frequently Asked Questions (FAQ). Electronic document, http://www.wolf.org/wolves/, accessed 1996 and 1997.

Irving, W. N.
1985 Context and Chronology of Early Man in the Americas. *Annual Review of Anthropology* 14:529–555.

Irwin, C., H. T. Irwin, and G. A. Agogino
1962 Ice Age Man vs. Mammoth in Wyoming. *National Geographic* 121:828–837.

Jackson, L. E., Jr., and A. Duk-Rodkin
1996 Quaternary Geology of the Ice-Free Corridor: Glacial Controls on the Peopling of the New World. In *Prehistoric Mongoloid Dispersals*, edited by T. Akazawa and E. J. E. Szathmáry, pp. 214–227. Oxford University Press, Oxford.

Jackson, L. J.
1995 A Clovis Point from South Coastal Chile. *Current Research in the Pleistocene* 12:21–23.
1999 El Jobo Points: Age, Context, and Definition. *Current Research in the Pleistocene* 16:41–43.

Jacobsen, G. L., Jr., T. Webb III, and E. C. Grimm
1987 Patterns and Rates of Vegetation Change during the Deglaciation of Eastern North America. In *North America and Adjacent Oceans during the Last Deglaciation*, edited by W. F. Ruddiman and H. E. Wright Jr., pp. 277–288 and end maps. Geological Society of America, Boulder, Colo.

Jaimes, A.
1997 The Northwest of Venezuela: A Regional Intersection for the Cultural Dynamics during the Final Pleistocene. Paper presented at the 62nd Annual Meeting of the Society for American Archaeology, Nashville, Tenn.
1998 El Vano, Venezuela: El Jobo Traditions in a Megathere Kill Site. *Current Research in the Pleistocene* 15:25–27.
1999 Nuevas evidencias de cazadores-recolectores y aproximación al entendimiento del uso espacio geográfico en el noroccidente de Venezuela. Sus implicaciones en el contexto suramericano. *Arqueología del Area Intermedia* 1:83–120.

James, S. R.
1989 Hominid Use of Fire in the Lower and Middle Pleistocene: A Review of the Evidence. *Current Anthropology* 30:1–26.
1990 Monitoring Archaeofaunal Changes during the Transition to Agriculture in the American Southwest. *Kiva* 56:25–43.
1993 Archaeofaunal Analyses of the Tator Hills Sites, South-Central Arizona. In *Archaic Occupation on the Santa Cruz Flats: The Tator Hills Archaeological Project*, edited by C. D. Halbirt and T. K. Henderson, pp. 345–371. Northland Research, Tempe, Ariz.
1996 Early Hominid Use of Fire: Recent Approaches and Methods for Evaluation of the Evidence. In *Colloquia of the XIII International Congress of Prehistoric and Protohistoric Sciences, Vol. 5: The Lower and Middle Paleolithic*, edited by M. Piperno, pp. 65–75. ABACO Edizioni, Forlì, Italy.

Janis, C.
　1975　The Evolutionary Strategy of the Equidae and the Origins of the Rumen and Caecal Digestion. *Evolution* 30:757–774.

Jantz, R. L., D. R. Hunt, A. B. Falsetti, and P. J. Key
　1992　Variation among North Amerindians: Analysis of Boas's Anthropometric Data. *Human Biology* 64: 435–461.

Jantz, R. L., and D. W. Owsley
　1997　Pathology, Taphonomy, and Cranial Morphometrics of the Spirit Cave Mummy. *Nevada Historical Society Quarterly* 40:62–84.
　1998　How Many Populations of Early North Americans Were There? *American Journal of Physical Anthropology, Supplement* 26:128.
　1999　Ice Age Humans in Asia and the Peopling of the Americas. Paper presented at the Clovis and Beyond Conference, Santa Fe, N.Mex.

Jarvenpa, R., and H. J. Brumbach
　1998　The Gendered Nature of Living and Storage Space in the Canadian Subarctic. In *From the Ground Up: Beyond Gender Theory in Archaeology*, edited by N. L. Wicker and B. Arnold, pp. 107–123. BAR International Series, No. 812. British Archaeological Reports, Oxford.

Jelinek, A. J.
　1971　Early Man in the New World: A Technological Perspective. *Arctic Archaeology* 8(2):15–21.
　1992　Perspectives from the Old World on the Habitation of the New. *American Antiquity* 57:345–347.

Jenks, A. E.
　1936　Artifacts and Minor Objects Found with the Minnesota Skeleton. In *Pleistocene Man in Minnesota*, edited by A. E. Jenks, pp. 161–169. University of Minnesota Press, Minneapolis.

Jenks, A. E., and H. H. Simpson
　1941　Beveled Artifacts in Florida of the Same Type as Artifacts Found near Clovis, New Mexico. *American Antiquity* 6:314–319.

Jennings, C. H.
　1968　The Paleoindian and Archaic Stages in Western Colorado. *Southwestern Lore* 34:11–20.

Jennings, J. D.
　1960　Early Man in Utah. *Utah Historical Quarterly* 28: 3–27.
　1964　The Desert West. In *Prehistoric Man in the New World*, edited by J. D. Jennings and E. Norbeck, pp. 149–174. University of Chicago Press, Chicago.

Jennings, J. D., and E. Norbeck
　1955　Great Basin Prehistory: A Review. *American Antiquity* 21:1–11.
　1988　*Utah's Ferron Creek Prehistoric Rock Art*. Walks Association, Salt Lake City.

Jobling, M. A., V. Samara, A. Pandya, N. Fretwell, B. Bernasconi, R. J. Mitchell, T. Gerelsaikhan, B. Dashnyam, A. Sajantila, P. J. Salo, Y. Nakahori, C. M. Disteche, K. Thangaraj, L. Singh, M. H. Crawford, and C. Tyler-Smith
　1996　Recurrent Duplication and Deletion Polymorphisms on the Long Arm of the Y Chromosome in Normal Males. *Human Molecular Genetics* 5:1767–1775.

Jobling, M. A., and C. Tyler-Smith
　1995　Fathers and Sons: The Y Chromosome and Human Evolution. *Trends in Genetics* 11:449–456.

Jobling, M. A., G. Williams, K. Schiebel, A. Pandya, K. McElreavey, L. Salas, G. A. Rappold, N. A. Affara, and C. Tyler-Smith
　1998　A Selective Difference between Human Y-Chromosomal DNA Haplotypes. *Current Biology* 8: 1391–1394.

Jochim, M. A.
　1987　Late Pleistocene Refugia in Europe. In *The Pleistocene Old World: Regional Perspectives*, edited by O. S. N. York, pp. 317–332. Plenum Press, New York.

Jodry, M. A., and D. J. Stanford
　1992　Stewart's Cattle Guard Site: An Analysis of Bison Remains in a Folsom Kill-Butchery Campsite. In *Ice Age Hunters of the Rockies*, edited by D. J. Stanford and J. S. Day, pp. 101–168. Denver Museum of Natural History, Denver, and University Press of Colorado, Niwot.

Johnson, A. R., J. Wiens, B. Milne, and T. Crist
　1992　Animal Movements and Population Dynamics in Heterogeneous Landscapes. *Landscape Ecology* 7: 63–75.

Johnson, E.
　1991　Late Pleistocene Cultural Occupation on the Southern Plains. In *Clovis: Origins and Adaptations*, edited by R. Bonnichsen and K. L. Turnmire, pp. 215–236. Center for the Study of the First Americans, Oregon State University, Corvallis.

Johnson, M. F.
　1996　Paleoindians near the Edge: A Virginia Perspective. In *The Paleoindian and Early Archaic Southeast*, edited by D. G. Anderson and K. E. Sassaman, pp. 187–221. University of Alabama Press, Tuscaloosa.

Johnston, W. A.
　1933　Quaternary Geology of North America in Relation to the Migration of Man. In *The American Aborigines: Their Origin and Antiquity*, edited by D. Jenness, pp. 11–45. University of Toronto Press, Toronto.

Jones, J. H.
　2000　Human Evolutionary Demography: The Evolution of the Human Life Cycle. Paper presented at the Human Behavior and Evolution Society, Amherst, Mass.

Jones, R. V., and D. E. Goodfellow
　1988　*Utah's Ferron Creek Prehistoric Rock Art*. Walks Association, Salt Lake City.

Jones, S., and R. Bonnichsen
　1994　The Anzick Clovis Burial. *Current Research in the Pleistocene* 11:42–44.

Jöris, O., and B. Weninger
　1998　Extension of the 14C Calibration Curve to ca. 40,000 Cal BC by Synchronizing Greenland 180/160 Ice Core Records and North Atlantic Foraminifera

Profiles: A Comparison with U/Th Coral Data. *Radiocarbon* 40:495–504.

Joyce, R. A., and C. Claassen
1997 Women in the Ancient Americas: Archaeologists, Gender, and the Making of Prehistory. In *Women in Prehistory: North America and Mesoamerica*, edited by C. Claassen and R. A. Joyce, pp. 1–14. University of Pennsylvania Press, Philadelphia.

Judge, W. J.
1973 *Paleoindian Occupation of the Central Rio Grande Valley in New Mexico*. University of New Mexico Press, Albuquerque.
1982 The Paleo-Indian and Basketmaker Periods: An Overview and Some Research Problems. In *The San Juan Tomorrow: Planning for the Conservation of Cultural Resources in the San Juan Basin*, edited by F. Plog and W. Wait, pp. 5–57. National Park Service, Southwest Region, Santa Fe.

Justice, N. D.
1987 *Stone Age Spear and Arrow Points of the Midcontinental and Eastern United States: A Modern Survey and Reference*. Indiana University Press, Bloomington.

Kaestle, F.
1995 Mitochondrial DNA Evidence for the Identity of the Descendants of the Prehistoric Stillwater Marsh Population. In *Bioarcheology of the Stillwater Marsh: Prehistoric Human Adaptation in the Western Great Basin*, edited by C. S. Larsen and R. L. Kelly, pp. 737–749. American Museum of Natural History, New York. Also in *Anthropological Papers of the American Museum of Natural History* 77:73–80.

Kaestle, F. A.
1997 Molecular Analysis of Ancient Native American DNA from Western Nevada. *Nevada Historical Society Quarterly* 40:85–96.

Kaestle, F. A., and D. G. Smith
2001 Ancient Mitochondrial DNA Evidence for Prehistoric Population Movement: The Numic Expansion. *American Journal of Physical Anthropology* 115(1):1–12.

Kaplan, H., and K. Hill
1992 The Evolutionary Ecology of Food Acquisition. In *Evolutionary Ecology and Human Behavior*, edited by E. A. Smith and B. Winterhalder, pp. 167–202. Aldine de Gruyter, New York.

Karafet, T. M., S. L. Zegura, O. Posukh, L. Osipova, A. Bergen, J. Long, D. Goldman, W. Klitz, S. Harihara, P. de Knijff, V. Wiebe, R. C. Griffiths, A. R. Templeton, and M. F. Hammer
1999 Ancestral Asian Source(s) of New World Y-Chromosome Founder Haplotypes. *American Journal of Human Genetics* 64:817–831.

Karafet, T. M., S. L. Zegura, J. Vuturo-Brady, O. Posukh, L. Osipova, V. Wiebe, F. Romero, J. C. Long, S. Harihara, F. Jin, B. Dashnyam, T. Gerelsaikhan, K. Omoto, and M. F. Hammer
1997 Y-Chromosome Markers and Trans–Bering Strait Dispersals. *American Journal of Physical Anthropology* 102:301–314.

Kaufman, D.
1995 Microburins and Microliths of the Levantine Epi-paleolithic: A Comment on the Paper by Neeley and Barton. *Antiquity* 69(263):375–381.

Kayser, M., C. Caglià, D. Corach, N. Fretwell, C. Gehrig, G. Graziosi, F. Heidorn, S. Herrmann, B. Herzog, M. Hidding, K. Honda, M. Jobling, M. Krawczak, K. Leim, S. Meuser, E. Meyer, W. Oesterreich, A. Pandya, W. Parson, G. Penacino, A. Perez-Lezaun, A. Piccinini, M. Prinz, C. Schmitt, and L. Roewer
1997 Evaluation of Y-Chromosomal STRs: A Multicenter Study. *International Journal of Legal Medicine* 110:125–133.

Kealhofer, L.
1999 Integrating Phytoliths within Use-Wear/Residue Studies of Stone Tools. *Journal of Archaeological Science* 26:527–546.

Keefer, D. K., S. D. de France, M. E. Moseley, J. B. Richardson III, D. R. Satterlee, and A. Day-Lewis
1998 Early Maritime Economy and El Niño Events at Quebrada Tacahuay, Peru. *Science* 281:1833–1835.

Keegan, W. F., and J. Diamond
1987 Colonization of Islands by Humans: A Biogeographic Perspective. *Advances in Archaeological Method and Theory* 10:49–92.

Kelly, R. L.
1983 Hunter-Gatherer Mobility Strategies. *Journal of Anthropological Research* 39:277–306.
1988 The Three Sides of a Biface. *American Antiquity* 53:717–734.
1995 *The Foraging Spectrum: Diversity in Hunter-Gatherer Lifeways*. Smithsonian Institution Press, Washington, D.C.
1996 Ethnographic Analogy and Migration to the Western Hemisphere. In *Prehistoric Mongoloid Dispersals*, edited by T. Akazawa and E. J. E. Szathmáry, pp. 228–240. Oxford University Press, Oxford.
1999 Hunter-Gatherer Foraging and Colonization of the Western Hemisphere. *l'Anthropologie* 37:143–153.

Kelly, R. L., and L. C. Todd
1988 Coming into the Country: Early Paleoindian Hunting and Mobility. *American Antiquity* 53(2):231–244.

Kent, S.
1998 Invisible Gender—Invisible Foragers: Southern African Hunter-Gatherer Spatial Patterning and the Archaeological Record. In *Gender in African Prehistory*, edited by S. Kent, pp. 39–67. AltaMira Press, Walnut Creek, Calif.
1999 Egalitarianism, Equality, and Equitable Power. In *Manifesting Power: Gender and the Interpretation of Power in Archaeology*, edited by T. L. Sweely, pp. 30–48. Routledge, New York.

Kephart, J.
1970 Primitive Women as Nigger, or, the Origin of the Human Family as Viewed through the Role of Women. Master's thesis, University of Maryland, College Park.

Kershaw, A. P., M. B. Bush, G. S. Hope, K.-F. Weiss, J. G. Goldammer, and R. Sanford
1997 The Contribution of Humans to Past Biomass Burning in the Tropics. In *Sediment Records of Biomass*

Burning and Global Change, edited by B. Stocks, pp. 413–442. Springer-Verlag, Berlin.

Kim, W., D. J. Shin, S. Harihara, and Y. J. Kim
2000 Y Chromosomal DNA Variation in East Asian Populations and Its Potential for Inferring the Peopling of Korea. *Journal of Human Genetics* 45:76–83.

King, J. E., and J. J. Saunders
1984 Environmental Insularity and the Extinction of the American Mastodont. In *Quaternary Extinctions: A Prehistoric Revolution*, edited by P. S. Martin and R. G. Klein, pp. 315–345. University of Arizona Press, Tucson.

Kivisild, T., M. J. Bamshad, K. Kaldma, M. Metspalu, E. Metspalu, M. Reidla, S. Laos, J. Parik, W. S. Watkins, M. E. Dixon, S. S. Papiha, S. S. Mastana, M. R. Mir, V. Ferak, and R. Villems
1999 Deep Common Ancestry of Indian and Western-Eurasian Mitochondrial DNA Lineage. *Current Biology* 9:1331–1334.

Klein, R. G.
1992 The Impact of Early People on the Environment: The Case of Large Mammal Extinctions. In *Human Impact on the Environment: Ancient Roots, Current Challenges*, edited by J. Firor, pp. 13–34. Westview Press, Boulder, Colo.
1999 *The Human Career*. 2nd ed. University of Chicago Press, Chicago.

Krieger, A. D.
1947 Certain Projectile Points of the Early American Hunters. *Bulletin of the Texas Archaeological and Paleontological Society* 18:7–27.
1962 Comments. *Current Anthropology* 3:256–259.

Koch, P. L.
1998 Diet Breadth and Home Range of Late Pleistocene Megafauna. Paper presented at the 63rd Annual Meeting of the Society for American Archaeology, Seattle.

Kohl, P. L.
1998 Nationalism and Archaeology: On the Constructions of Nations and the Reconstructions of the Remote Past. *Annual Review of Anthropology* 27:223–246.

Kolman, C. J., and E. Bermingham
1997 Mitochondrial and Nuclear DNA Diversity in the Choco and Chibcha Amerinds of Panama. *Genetics* 147:1289–1302.

Kolman, C. J., E. Bermingham, R. Cooke, R. H. Ward, T. D. Arias, and F. Guionneau-Sinclair
1995 Reduced mtDNA Diversity in the Ngöbé Amerinds of Panamá. *Genetics* 140:275–283.

Kolman, C. J., N. Sambuughin, and E. Bermingham
1996 Mitochondrial DNA Analysis of Mongolian Populations and Implications for the Origin of New World Founders. *Genetics* 142:1321–1334.

Kononenko, N. (editor)
1996 *Late Paleolithic–Early Neolithic: Eastern Asia and Northern America*. Akademia Nauk, Vladivostok.

Kreutzer, L. A.
1996 Taphonomy of the Mill Iron Site Bison Bonebed. In *The Mill Iron Site*, edited by G. C. Frison, pp. 101–143. University of New Mexico Press, Albuquerque.

Krist, F. J., Jr., and D. G. Brown
1994 GIS Modeling of Paleoindian Period Caribou Migrations and Viewsheds in Northeastern Lower Michigan. *Photogrammetric Engineering and Remote Sensing* 65:1129–1137.

Kuhn, S. L.
1995 *Mousterian Lithic Technology: An Ecological Perspective*. Princeton University Press, Princeton, N.J.

Kunz, M. L., and R. E. Reanier
1994 Paleoindians in Beringia: Evidence from Arctic Alaska. *Science* 263:660–662.
1996 Mesa Site, Iteriak Creek. In *American Beginnings: The Prehistory and Palaeoecology of Beringia*, edited by F. H. West, pp. 497–504. University of Chicago Press, Chicago.

Kutzbach, J. E.
1987 Model Simulations of the Climatic Patterns during the Deglaciation of North America. In *North America and Adjacent Oceans during the Last Deglaciation*, edited by W. F. Ruddiman and H. E. Wright Jr., pp. 425–446. Geological Society of America, Boulder, Colo.

Kuzmin, Y. V., A. J. T. Jull, Z. S. Lapshina, and V. E. Medvedev
1997 Radiocarbon AMS Dating of the Ancient Sites with Earliest Pottery from the Russian Far East. *Nuclear Instruments and Methods in Physics Research B* 123:496–497.

Kuzmin, Y. V., and L. A. Orlova
2000 The Neolithization of Siberia and the Russian Far East: Radiocarbon Evidence. *Antiquity* 74:356–364.

Lacy, D.
1979 In Quest of a Paleoindian Bone-Tool Industry: The Missing Dimension in the Northeast. Manuscript on file, Department of Anthropology, University of Massachusetts, Amherst.

Lahermo, P., A. Sajantila, P. Sistonen, M. Lukka, P. Aula, and M.-L. Savontaus
1996 The Genetic Relationship between the Finns and the Finnish Saami: Analysis of Nuclear DNA and mtDNA. *American Journal of Human Genetics* 58:1309–1322.

Lahermo, P., M.-L. Savontaus, P. Sistonen, J. Béres, P. de Knijff, P. Aula, and A. Sajantila
1999 Y Chromosomal Polymorphisms Reveal Founding Lineages in the Finns and the Saami. *European Journal of Human Genetics* 7:447–458.

Lahr, M. M.
1995 Patterns of Modern Human Diversification: Implications for Amerindian Origins. *Yearbook of Physical Anthropology* 38:163–198.

Lahr, M. M., and R. A. Foley
1998 Towards a Theory of Modern Human Origins: Geography, Demography, and Diversity in Recent Human Evolution. *Yearbook of Physical Anthropology* 41:137–176.

Lahren, L. A., and R. Bonnichsen
1974 Bone Foreshafts from a Clovis Burial in Southwestern Montana. *Science* 186:147–150.

Landau, M.
1991 *Narratives of Human Evolution*. Yale University Press, New Haven, Conn.

Latour, B., and S. Woolgar
1979 *Laboratory Life*. Sage Library of Social Research, Beverly Hills, Calif.

Laub, R. S.
1990 The Hiscock Site (Western New York): Recent Developments of Pleistocene and Holocene Interest. *Current Research in the Pleistocene* 7:116–118.
1994 The Pleistocene/Holocene Transition in Western New York State. In *Great Lakes Archaeology and Paleoecology*, edited by R. McDonald, pp. 155–167. Quaternary Sciences Institute, Waterloo, Ontario.
1995 The Hiscock Site (Western New York): Recent Developments in the Study of the Late Pleistocene Component. *Current Research in the Pleistocene* 12:26–29.
1996 Taphonomic Effects of Tree-Falls: Examples from the Hiscock Site (Late Quaternary, Western New York). *Current Research in the Pleistocene* 13:71–72.

Laub, R. S., M. F. deRemer, C. A. Dufort, and W. L. Parsons
1988 The Hiscock Site: A Rich Late Quaternary Locality in Western New York State. In *Late Pleistocene and Early Holocene Paleoecology and Archaeology of the Eastern Great Lakes Region*, edited by R. Laub, N. Miller, and D. W. Steadman, pp. 67–81. Buffalo Society of Natural Sciences Bulletin, No. 33. Buffalo, N.Y.

Laub, R. S., C. A. Dufort, and D. J. Christensen
1994 Possible Mastodon Gastrointestinal and Fecal Contents from the Pleistocene of the Hiscock Site, Western New York State. *New York State Museum Bulletin* 481:135–148.

Laub, R. S., and G. Haynes
1998 Fluted Points, Mastodons, and Evidence of Late-Pleistocene Drought at the Hiscock Site, Western New York State. *Current Research in the Pleistocene* 15:32–34.

Laub, R. S., and J. H. McAndrews
1997 Pleistocene Giant Beaver (*Castoroides ohioensis*) from the Hiscock Site, Western New York State. *Current Research in the Pleistocene* 14:143–145.

Laub, R. S., J. Tomenchuk, and P. L. Storck
1996 A Dated Mastodon Bone Artifact from the Late Pleistocene of New York. *Archaeology of Eastern North America* 24:1–17.

Laughlin, W. S.
1986 Comments on the Settlement of the Americas: A Comparison of the Linguistic, Dental, and Genetic Evidence. *Current Anthropology* 27:489–490.
1988 Continental Crossing. *The Sciences* 28:489–490.

Laws, R. M.
1970 Elephants as Agents of Habitat and Landscape Change in East Africa. *Oikos* 21:1–15.

Lell, J. T., M. D. Brown, T. G. Schurr, R. I. Sukernik, Y. B. Starikovskaya, A. Torroni, L. G. Moore, G. M. Troup, and D. C. Wallace
1997 Y Chromosome Polymorphisms in Native American and Siberian Populations: Identification of Native American Y Chromosome Haplotypes. *Human Genetics* 100:536–543.

Lell, J. T., T. G. Schurr, R. I. Sukernik, Y. B. Starikovskaya, and D. C. Wallace
1998 Identification and Characterization of Siberian and Native American Y-Chromosome Lineages by Microsatellite Analysis. *American Journal of Human Genetics, Supplement* 63:A1234.
1999 Y Chromosome Haplotypes Reveal Distinct Migration Patterns in Siberia and the Americas. *American Journal of Human Genetics, Supplement* 65:A41.

Lell, J. T., R. I. Sukernik, Y. B. Starikovskaya, B. Su, L. Jin, T. G. Schurr, P. A. Underhill, and D. C. Wallace
2000 The Dual Origin and Siberian Affinities of Native American Y Chromosomes. *American Journal of Human Genetics, Supplement* 67:A236.
2002 The Dual Origin and Siberian Affinities of Native American Y Chromosomes. *American Journal of Human Genetics* 70:192–206.

Leonard, J. A., R. K. Wayne, J. Wheeler, R. Valadez, S. Guillen, and C. Vila
2002 Ancient DNA Evidence for Old World Origin of New World Dogs. *Science* 298:1613–1616.

Leone, M. P.
1984 Interpreting Ideology in Historical Archaeology: Using the Rules of Perspective in the William Paca Garden, Annapolis, Maryland. In *Ideology, Power, and Prehistory*, edited by D. Miller and C. Tilley, pp. 25–35. Cambridge University Press, Cambridge.

Leonhardy, F. C.
1966 *Domebo: A Paleo-Indian Mammoth Kill in the Prairie-Plains*. Contributions, No. 1. Museum of the Great Plains, Lawton, Okla.

Lepper, B. T.
1998 The Sinking of Beringia. *Current Research in the Pleistocene* 15:vii–viii.
1999 Pleistocene Peoples of Midcontinental North America. In *Ice Age Peoples of North America: Environments, Origins, and Adaptations of the First Americans*, edited by R. Bonnichsen and K. L. Turnmire, pp. 362–394. Oregon State University Press, Corvallis.

Lepper, B. T., and D. J. Meltzer
1991 Late Pleistocene Human Occupation of the Eastern United States. In *Clovis: Origins and Adaptations*, edited by R. Bonnichsen and K. L. Turnmire, pp. 175–184. Center for the Study of the First Americans, Oregon State University, Corvallis.

Leroi-Gourhan, A.
1964 *Le geste et la parole 1: La technique et la langage*. Michel Albin, Paris.
1965 *Le geste et la parole 2: La mémoire et les rhythmes*. Michel Albin, Paris.

Leuthold, W.
1977 Spatial Organization and Strategy of Habitat Utilization of Elephants in Tsavo National Park, Kenya. *Zeitschrift Saugetierk* 42:358–379.

Levine, M. A.
  1990 Accommodating Age: Radiocarbon Results and
        Fluted Point Sites in Northeastern North America.
        Archaeology of Eastern North America 18:33–63.
  1997 The Tyranny Continues: Ethnographic Analogy
        and Eastern Paleo-Indians. In *Caribou and Reindeer
        Hunters of the Northern Hemisphere*, edited by L. J.
        Jackson and P. T. Thacker, pp. 221–244. Avebury
        Ashgate Publishing Ltd., Hampshire, England.
Levins, R.
  1970 Extinction. *Some Mathematical Questions in Biology*
        1:75–108.
Liddiard, M., and J. Liddiard
  1993 *A Guide to Rock Art in Nine Mile Canyon*. Arrowhead
        Enterprises, Sandy, Utah.
Little, B.
  1987 The Misusable Past: Facts and Fantasies in North
        American Archaeology. *Expedition* 29(2):27–37.
Llagostera, M. A.
  1979 9,700 Years of Maritime Subsistence on the Pacific:
        An Analysis by Means of Bioindicators in the North
        of Chile. *American Antiquity* 44:309–324.
Longacre, W. A., and M. W. Graves
  1976 Probability Sampling Applied to an Early Multi-
        Component Surface Site in East-Central Arizona.
        Kiva 41:277–287.
López Castaño, C. E.
  1989 Evidencias paleoindias en el valle medio del río
        Magdalena (municipios de Puerto Berrío, Yondó y
        Remedios). *Boletín de Arqueología* 4(2):3–24.
  1990 Cazadores-recolectores tempranos en el Magda-
        lena medio (Puerto Berrío, Antioquia). *Boletín de
        Arqueología* 5(2):11–29.
  1994 Aproximaciones al medio ambiente, recursos y ocu-
        pación temprana del valle medio del río Magdalena.
        Informes Antropológicos 7:5–15.
  1995 Dispersión de puntas de proyectil bifaciales en la
        cuenca media del río Magdalena. In *Ambito y ocupa-
        ciones tempranas de la América tropical*, edited by
        I. Cavelier and S. Mora, pp. 73–82. Instituto Colom-
        biano de Antropología, Fundación Erigaie, Santafé
        de Bogotá.
  1999 *Ocupaciones tempranas en las tierras bajas tropicales
        del valle medio del río Magdalena sitio 05-YON-002,
        Yondó-Antioquia*. Fundación de Investigaciones
        Arqueológicas Nacionales, No. 67. Banco de la
        República, Bogota.
Lopinot, N. H., J. H. Ray, and M. D. Conner
  1998 *The 1997 Excavations at the Big Eddy Site
        (23CE426) in Southwest Missouri*. Special Publica-
        tion, No. 2. Center for Archaeological Research,
        Southwest Missouri State University, Springfield.
  2000 *The 1999 Excavations at the Big Eddy Site
        (23CE426)*. Special Publication, No. 3. Center for
        Archaeological Research, Southwest Missouri State
        University, Springfield.
Lorenz, J. G., and D. G. Smith
  1996 Distribution of Four Founding mtDNA Haplogroups
        among Native North Americans. *American Journal of
        Physical Anthropology* 101:307–323.
  1997 Distribution of Sequence Variations in the mtDNA
        Control Region of Native North Americans. *Human
        Biology* 69:749–776.
Lothrop, S. K.
  1961 Early Migrations to Central and South America: An
        Anthropological Problem in Light of Other Sciences.
        *Journal of the Royal Anthropological Institute of Great
        Britain and Ireland* 91:97–123.
Luedtke, B. E.
  1992 *An Archaeologist's Guide to Chert and Flint*. Ar-
        chaeological Research Tools, No. 7. Institute of
        Archaeology, University of California, Los Angeles.
Lum, J. K., O. Rickards, C. Ching, and R. L. Cann
  1994 Polynesian Mitochondrial DNAs Reveal Three Deep
        Maternal Lineage Clusters. *Human Biology* 66:
        567–590.
Lyman, R. L.
  2000 A List of Washington State Radiocarbon Dates.
        Northwest Anthropological Research Notes 34(2):
        155–215.
Lynch, T. F.
  1974 The Antiquity of Man in South America. *Quaternary
        Research* 4:356–377.
  1978 The South American Paleo-Indians. In *Ancient
        Native Americans*, edited by J. D. Jennings, pp.
        445–490. W. H. Freeman and Co., San Francisco.
  1990 Glacial-Age Man in South America? A Critical
        Review. *American Antiquity* 55(1):12–36.
  1991 The Peopling of the Americas: A Discussion. In *The
        First Americans: Search and Research*, edited by T. D.
        Dillehay and D. J. Meltzer, pp. 267–274. CRC Press,
        Boca Raton, Fla.
  1994 L'homme des glaciation en Amérique du Sud: Une
        vision européenne. *l'Anthropologie* 98(1):32–54.
  1998 The Paleoindian and Archaic Stages in South
        America: Zones of Continuity and Segregation. In
        *Explorations in American Archaeology: Essays in
        Honor of Wesley R. Hurt*, edited by M. G. Plew, pp.
        89–100. University Press of America, Lanham, Md.
Lynch, T. F., and S. Pollock
  1980 Chobshi Cave and Its Place in Andean and Ecuador-
        ian Archeology. In *Anthropological Papers in Memory
        of Earl H. Swanson, Jr.*, edited by L. Harten, C. War-
        ren, and D. Tuohy, pp. 19–40. Idaho State Museum
        of Natural History, Pocatello.
Mabry, J.
  2000 Rethinking the Peopling of the Americas. *Archae-
        ology Southwest* 14:1–11.
MacArthur, R. H., and E. O. Wilson
  1967 *The Theory of Island Biogeography*. Monographs
        in Population Biology, No. 1. Princeton University
        Press, Princeton, N.J.
Macaulay, V., M. Richards, E. Hickey, E. Vega, F. Cruciani, V. Guida, R. Scozzari, B. Bonné-Tamir, B. Sykes, and
A. Torroni
  1999 The Emerging Tree of West Eurasian mtDNAs: A

Synthesis of Control-Region Sequences and RFLPs. *American Journal of Human Genetics* 64:232–249.

MacCluer, J., and B. Dyke
1976 On the Minimum Size of Endogamous Populations. *Social Biology* 23:1–12.

MacDonald, D. H.
1997 Hunter-Gatherer Mating Distance and Early Paleoindian Social Mobility. *Current Research in the Pleistocene* 14:119–121.

1998 Subsistence, Sex, and Cultural Transmission in Folsom Culture. *Journal of Anthropological Archaeology* 17:217–239.

1999 Modeling Folsom Mobility, Mating Strategies, and Technological Organization in the Northern Plains. *Plains Anthropologist* 44(168):141–161.

MacDonald, D. H., and B. S. Hewlett
1999 Reproductive Interests and Forager Mobility. *Current Anthropology* 40(4):501–524.

MacDonald, G. F.
1966 The Technology and Settlement Pattern of a Paleo-Indian Site at Debert, Nova Scotia. *Quaternaria* 8: 59–74.

1968 *Debert: A Paleo-Indian Site in Central Nova Scotia.* Anthropology Papers, No. 16. National Museums of Canada, Ottawa.

1971 A Review of Research on Paleo-Indian in Eastern North America, 1960–1970. *Arctic Anthropology* 8: 32–41.

1983 Eastern North America. In *Early Man in the New World*, edited by R. Shutler, pp. 97–108. Sage Publications, Beverly Hills, Calif.

1985 *Debert: A Paleo-Indian Site in Central Nova Scotia.* Persimmon Press, Buffalo, N.Y.

MacNeish, R. S.
1958 *Preliminary Archaeological Investigations in the Sierra de Tamaulipas, Mexico.* Transactions of the American Philosophical Society, Vol. 48, Pt. 6. Philadelphia.

1959 Men Out of Asia: As Seen from the Northwest Yukon. *Anthropological Papers of the University of Alaska* 7:41–70.

MacNeish, R. S., S. J. K. Wilkerson, and A. Nelken-Terner
1980 *First Annual Report of the Belize Archaic Archaeological Reconnaissance.* Robert F. Peabody Foundation for Archaeology, Andover, Mass.

Madsen, D. B.
1980 Fremont/Sevier Subsistence. In *Fremont Perspectives*, edited by D. B. Madsen, pp. 25–33. Selected Papers, No. 16. Antiquities Section, Utah State Historical Society, Salt Lake City.

Madsen, D. B., and D. Rhode (editors)
1994 *Across the West: Human Population Movement and the Expansion of the Numa.* University of Utah Press, Salt Lake City.

Malhi, R. S., B. A. Schultz, and D. G. Smith
2001 Distribution of Mitochondrial Lineages among Native American Tribes of Northeastern North America. *Human Biology* 73:17–55.

Mallouf, R. J.
1989 A Clovis Quarry Workshop in the Callahan Divide: The Yellow Hawk Site, Taylor County, Texas. *Plains Anthropologist* 34(124):81–103.

1994 Sailor-Helton: A Paleoindian Cache from Southwestern Kansas. *Current Research in the Pleistocene* 11: 44–46.

Manaster Ramer, A., and C. Hitchcock
1996 Glass Houses: Greenberg, Ringe, and the Mathematics of Comparative Linguistics. *Anthropological Linguistics* 38(4):601–620.

Mandryk, C. A.
1990 Could Humans Survive the Ice-Free Corridor? Late-Glacial Vegetation and Climate in West-Central Alberta. In *Megafauna and Man: Discovery of America's Heartland*, edited by L. D. Agenbroad, J. I. Mead, and L. W. Nelson, pp. 67–79. Scientific Papers, No. 1. Mammoth Site of Hot Springs, South Dakota, Inc., Hot Springs.

1993 Hunter-Gatherer Social Costs and the Nonviability of Submarginal Environments. *Journal of Anthropological Research* 49:39–71.

Maranda, E. K.
1974 Lau, Malaita: "A Woman Is an Alien Spirit." In *Many Sisters: Women in Cross-Cultural Perspective*, edited by C. J. Matthiasson, pp. 177–202. Free Press, New York.

Marean, C. W.
1997 Hunter-Gatherer Foraging Strategies in Tropical Grasslands: Model Building and Testing in the East African Middle and Later Stone Age. *Journal of Anthropological Archaeology* 16:189–225.

Marjoram, P., and P. Donnelly
1994 Pairwise Comparisons of Mitochondrial DNA Sequences in Subdivided Populations and Implications for Early Human Evolution. *Genetics* 136:673–683.

Marks, A. E.
1983 The Middle to Upper Paleolithic Transition in the Levant. *Advances in World Archaeology* 2:51–97.

1994 In Search of the Neandertals: A Levantine Perspective. *Cambridge Archaeological Journal* 4:104–106.

Marks, A. E., H. J. Hietala, and J. K. Williams
2001 Tool Standardization in the Middle and Upper Paleolithic: A Closer Look. *Cambridge Archaeological Journal* 11:12–30.

Marshall, E.
1990 Clovis Counterrevolution. *Science* 249:738–741.

2001 Pre-Clovis Sites Fight for Acceptance. *Science* 291: 1730–1732.

Marshall, S. B.
1985 Paleoindian Artifact Form and Function at Shawnee Minisink. In *Shawnee Minisink: A Stratified Paleoindian-Archaic Site in the Upper Delaware Valley of Pennsylvania*, edited by C. W. McNett Jr., pp. 165–209. Academic Press, Orlando, Fla.

Martin, P. S.
1963 *The Last 10,000 Years: A Fossil Pollen Record of the American Southwest.* University of Arizona Press, Tucson.

1967 Prehistoric Overkill. In *Pleistocene Extinctions: The Search for a Cause*, edited by P. S. Martin and H. E.

Wright Jr., pp. 75–120. Yale University Press, New Haven, Conn.

1973 The Discovery of America. *Science* 179:969–974.

1984a Catastrophic Extinction and Late Pleistocene Blitzkrieg: Two Radiocarbon Tests. In *Extinctions*, edited by M. H. Nitecki, pp. 153–189. University of Chicago Press, Chicago.

1984b Prehistoric Overkill: The Global Model. In *Quaternary Extinctions: A Prehistoric Revolution*, edited by P. S. Martin and R. G. Klein, pp. 354–403. University of Arizona Press, Tucson.

1986 Refuting Late Pleistocene Extinction Models. In *Dynamic Extinction*, edited by D. K. Elliot, pp. 1073–1030. Wiley & Sons, New York.

1993 Coupling the Atmosphere with Vegetation. In *Vegetation Dynamics and Global Change*, edited by A. M. Solomon and H. H. Shugart, pp. 133–149. Chapman & Hall, New York.

Martin, P. S., and R. G. Klein (editors)

1984 *Quaternary Extinctions: A Prehistoric Revolution.* University of Arizona Press, Tucson.

Martínez, G. A.

2001 "Fish-Tail" Projectile Points and Megamammals: New Evidence from Paso Otero 5 (Argentina). *Antiquity* 75:523–528.

Martinez-Crusado, J. C., G. Toro-Labrador, J. A. Salas-Luciano, M. Estévez-Montero, M. Troche-Matos, E. Gómez-Sánchez, A. Román-Colón, M. Latorre-Estévez, L. Godoy-Muñoz, R. Rivera-Torres, A. Lobaina-Manzanet, H. Sánchez-Cruz, P. Ortiz-Bennúdez, F. Cruz-Guilloty, I. Y. Navarro-Millán, and J. S. Ramírez

2000 Most Puerto Rican mtDNAs Are of Native American Origin and Exhibit Low Genetic Diversity. *American Journal of Human Genetics, Supplement* 67:A236.

Martinez-Crusado, J. C., G. Toro-Labrador, V. Ho-Fung, M. A. Estévez-Montero, A. Lobaina-Manzanet, D. A. Padovani-Claudio, H. Sánchez-Cruz, P. Ortiz-Bennúdez, and A. Sanchez-Crespo

2001 Mitochondrial DNA Analysis Reveals Substantial Native American Ancestry in Puerto Rico. *Human Biology* 73:491–511.

Marwitt, J. P.

1969 Prehistoric Man in Utah: A Summary. *Utah Geological and Mineral Survey Bulletin* 82:21–37.

Maslowski, R. F., C. M. Niquette, and D. M. Wingfield

1995 The Kentucky, Ohio and West Virginia Radiocarbon Database. *West Virginia Archeologist* 47(1/2):1–75.

Mason, O. K.

1998 The Contest between the Ipiutak, Old Bering Sea, and Birnirk Polities and the Origin of Whaling during the First Millennium A.D. along Bering Strait. *Journal of Anthropological Archaeology* 17:240–325.

Mason, R. J.

1962 The Paleo-Indian Tradition in Eastern North America. *Current Anthropology* 3:227–283.

1981 *Great Lakes Archaeology.* Academic Press, New York.

2000 Archaeology and Native North American Traditions. *American Antiquity* 65(2):239–266.

Matteson, E.

1972 *Comparative Studies in Amerindian Languages.* Mouton, The Hague.

Maxwell, M. S. (editor)

1976 *Eastern Arctic Prehistory: Paleoeskimo Problems.* Memoirs of the Society for American Archaeology, No. 31. Washington, D.C.

Mayer-Oakes, W. J.

1966 El Inga Projectile Points: Surface Collections. *American Antiquity* 31(5):644–661.

1982 Early Man in the Northern Andes: Problems and Possibilities. In *Peopling of the New World*, edited by J. E. Ericson, R. E. Taylor, and R. Berger, pp. 269–283. Ballena Press, Los Altos, Calif.

1986a Early Man Projectile Points and Lithic Technology in the Ecuadorian Sierra. In *New Evidence for the Pleistocene Peopling of the Americas*, edited by A. L. Bryan, pp. 133–156. Center for the Study of Early Man, University of Maine, Orono.

1986b *El Inga: A Paleo-Indian Site in the Sierra of Northern Ecuador.* Transactions of the American Philosophical Society, Vol. 76, Pt. 4. Philadelphia.

Mayer-Oakes, W. J., and R. E. Bell

1960a Early Man Site Found in Highland Ecuador. *Science* 131:1805–1806.

1960b An Early Site in Highland Ecuador. *Current Anthropology* 1(5/6):429–430.

Mayer-Oakes, W. J., and A. W. Portnoy

1986 Early Man Lithic Studies at San José, Ecuador. *Current Research in the Pleistocene* 3:31–33.

1993 Paleo-Indian Studies at San Jose, Ecuador. *Lithic Technology* 18(1/2):28–36.

Mayewski, P. A., L. Meeker, S. Whitlow, M. Twickler, M. Morrison, R. Alley, P. Bloomfield, and K. Taylor

1993 The Atmosphere during the Younger Dryas. *Science* 261:195–197.

Mayewski, P. A., L. Meeker, S. Whitlow, M. Twickler, M. Morrison, P. Bloomfield, G. Bond, R. Alley, A. Gow, P. Grootes, D. Meese, M. Ram, K. Taylor, and W. Wumkes

1994 Changes in Atmospheric Circulation and Ocean Ice Cover over the North Atlantic during the Last 41,000 Years. *Science* 263:1747–1751.

Mazzanti, D. L.

1997 Excavaciones arqueológicas en el sitio Cueva Tixi, Buenos Aires, Argentina. *Latin American Antiquity* 8(1):55–62.

McArthur, N., I. Saunders, and R. Tweedie

1976 Small Population Isolates: A Micro-Simulation Study. *Journal of the Polynesian Society* 85:307–326.

McAvoy, J. M., and L. D. McAvoy

1997 *Archaeological Investigations of Site 44SX202, Cactus Hill, Sussex County, Virginia.* Research Report, No. 8. Virginia Department of Historic Resources, Richmond.

McCarey, B. C.

1983 The Paleo-Indian in Virginia. *Quarterly Bulletin Archeological Society of Virginia* 38:43–70.

McDonald, J. N.

2000 An Outline of the Pre-Clovis Archeology of SV-2,

Saltville, Virginia, with Special Attention to a Bone Tool Dated 14,510 Yr BP. *Jeffersonian Contributions from the Virginia Museum of Natural History* 9:1–59.

McGhee, R.
1984   Thule Prehistory of Canada. In *Arctic*, edited by D. Damas, pp. 369–376. Handbook of North American Indians, Vol. 5. Smithsonian Institution Press, Washington, D.C.

McGlade, J.
1995   Archaeology and the Ecodynamics of Human-Modified Landscapes. *Antiquity* 69:113–132.
1999   Archaeology and the Evolution of Cultural Landscapes: Towards an Interdisciplinary Research Agenda. In *The Archaeology and Anthropology of Landscape*, edited by P. J. Ucko and R. Layton, pp. 459–482. Routledge, London.

McGregor, J. C.
1941   *Winona and Ridge Ruin*. Museum of Northern Arizona Bulletin, No. 18. Flagstaff.

McKell, S. M.
1993   An Axe to Grind: More Ripping Yarns from Australian Prehistory. In *Women in Archaeology: A Feminist Critique*, edited by H. du Cros and L. Smith, pp. 115–120. Department of Prehistory, Australian National University, Occasional Papers in Prehistory, No. 23. Highland Press, Canberra.

McKenzie, D. H.
1970   Statistical Analysis of Ohio Fluted Points. *Ohio Journal of Science* 70:352–364.

McMillan, R. B.
1976   Man and Mastodon: A Review of Koch's 1840 Pomme de Terre Expeditions. In *Prehistoric Man and His Environments: A Case Study in the Ozark Highland*, edited by W. Wood and R. McMillan, pp. 81–96. Academic Press, New York.

McNaughton, S. J.
1979   Grassland-Herbivore Dynamics. In *Serengeti: Dynamics of an Ecosystem*, edited by A. R. E. Sinclair and M. Norton-Griffiths, pp. 46–82. University of Chicago Press, Chicago.
1984   Grazing Lawns: Animals in Herds, Plant Form, and Coevolution. *American Naturalist* 124:863–886.

McNaughton, S. J., and N. J. Georgiadis
1986   Ecology of African Grazing and Browsing Mammals. *Annual Review of Ecology and Systematics* 17:39–65.

McNett, C. W., Jr.
1985a   The Shawnee Minisink Site: An Overview. In *Shawnee Minisink: A Stratified Paleoindian-Archaic Site in the Upper Delaware Valley of Pennsylvania*, edited by C. W. McNett Jr., pp. 321–325. Academic Press, Orlando, Fla.

McNett, C. W., Jr. (editor)
1985b   *Shawnee Minisink: A Stratified Paleoindian-Archaic Site in the Upper Delaware Valley of Pennsylvania*. Academic Press, Orlando, Fla.

McNett, C. W., Jr., B. A. McMillan, and S. B. Marshall
1977   The Shawnee-Minisink Site. In *Amerinds and Their Paleoenvironments in Northeastern North America*, edited by W. S. Newman and B. Salwen, pp. 282–

296. Annals of the New York Academy of Sciences, Vol. 288. New York.

Mead, J. I., and L. D. Agenbroad
1992   Isotope Dating of Pleistocene Dung Deposits from the Colorado Plateau, Arizona and Utah. *Radiocarbon* 34:1–19.

Mead, J. I., and D. J. Meltzer
1984   North American Late Quaternary Extinctions and the Radiocarbon Record. In *Quaternary Extinctions: A Prehistoric Revolution*, edited by P. S. Martin and R. G. Klein, pp. 440–450. University of Arizona Press, Tucson.

Mead, J. I., S. E. Sharpe, and L. D. Agenbroad
1991   Holocene Bison from Arches National Park, Southeastern Utah. *Great Basin Naturalist* 51:336–342.

Meese, D. A., A. Gow, P. Grootes, P. Mayewski, M. Ram, M. Stuiver, K. Taylor, E. Waddington, and G. Zielinski
1994   The Accumulation Record from the GISP2 Core as an Indicator of Climate Change throughout the Holocene. *Science* 266:1680–1682.

Mehringer, P. J.
1988   Clovis Cache Found: Weapons of Ancient Americans. *National Geographic* 174:500–503.

Melton, T., R. Peterson, A. J. Redd, N. Saha, A. S. M. Sofro, J. Martinson, and M. Stoneking
1995   Polynesian Genetic Affinities with Southeast Asian Populations as Identified by mtDNA Analysis. *American Journal of Human Genetics* 57:403–414.

Meltzer, D. J.
1988   Late Pleistocene Human Adaptations in Eastern North America. *Journal of World Prehistory* 2(1):1–52.
1989   Why Don't We Know When the First People Came to North America? *American Antiquity* 54:471–490.
1993a   Is There a Clovis Adaptation? In *From Kostenki to Clovis: Upper Paleolithic-Paleoindian Adaptations*, edited by O. Soffer and N. D. Praslov, pp. 293–310. Plenum Press, New York.
1993b   Pleistocene Peopling of the Americas. *Evolutionary Anthropology* 1:157–169.
1995   Clocking the First Americans. *Annual Review of Anthropology* 24:21–45.
1997   Monte Verde and the Pleistocene Peopling of the Americas. *Science* 276:754–755.
1998   Colonizing Empty Continents: Demographic Constraints, Learning Strategies in New Environments, the Geography of Adaptation, and Issues of Scale (Geographic and Temporal). Paper presented at the Entering New Landscapes Conference, Stanford University, Stanford, Calif.
2001   Why We Still Don't Know When the First People Came to North America. In *On Being First: Cultural Innovation and Environmental Consequences of First Peoplings*, edited by J. Gillespie, S. Tupakka, and C. de Mille, pp. 1–25. Proceedings of the 31st Annual Chacmool Conference. Archaeological Association of the University of Calgary, Calgary, Alberta.
2002   What Do You Do When No One's Been There Before? Thoughts on the Exploration and Colonization of New Lands. In *The First Americans: The Pleisto-*

cene Colonization of the New World, edited by N. G. Jablonski, pp. 27–58. Memoirs of the California Academy of Sciences, No. 27. San Francisco.

2003 Lessons in Landscape Learning. In *Colonization of Unfamiliar Landscapes: The Archaeology of Adaptation*, edited by M. Rockman and J. Steele, pp. 222–241. Routledge, London.

Meltzer, D. J., and T. D. Dillehay

1999 The Search for the Earliest Americans. *Archaeology* 52:60–61.

Meltzer, D. J., D. K. Grayson, G. Ardila, A. W. Barker, D. F. Dincauze, C. V. Haynes Jr., F. Mena, L. Núñez, and D. J. Stanford

1997 On the Pleistocene Antiquity of Monte Verde, Southern Chile. *American Antiquity* 62(4):659–663.

Menegaz, A. N., and H. G. Nami

1994 Late Pleistocene Faunal Diversity in Ultima Esperanza (Chile): Further Data from Cueva del Medio. *Current Research in the Pleistocene* 11:93–95.

Merriwether, D. A.

2002 A Mitochondrial Perspective on the Peopling of the New World. In *The First Americans: The Pleistocene Colonization of the New World*, edited by N. G. Jablonski, pp. 295–310. Memoirs of the California Academy of Sciences, No. 27. San Francisco.

Merriwether, D. A., A. G. Clark, S. W. Ballinger, T. G. Schurr, H. Soodyall, T. Jenkins, S. T. Sherry, and D. C. Wallace

1991 The Structure of Human mtDNA Variation. *Journal of Molecular Evolution* 33:543–555.

Merriwether, D. A., and R. E. Ferrell

1996 The Four Founding Lineage Hypothesis for the New World: A Critical Reevaluation. *Molecular Phylogenetics and Evolution* 5:241–246.

Merriwether, D. A., W. W. Hall, A. Vahlne, and R. E. Ferrell

1996 mtDNA Variation Indicates Mongolia May Have Been the Source for the Founding Population for the New World. *American Journal of Human Genetics* 59:204–212.

Merriwether, D. A., S. Huston, S. Iyengar, R. Hamman, J. M. Norris, S. M. Shetterly, M. I. Kamboh, and R. E. Ferrell

1997 Mitochondrial versus Nuclear Admixture Estimates Demonstrates a Past History of Directional Mating. *American Journal of Physical Anthropology* 102:153–159.

Merriwether, D. A., F. Rothhammer, and R. E. Ferrell

1994 Genetic Variation in the New World: Ancient Teeth, Bone, and Tissue as Sources of DNA. *Experientia* 50:592–601.

1995 Distribution of the Four Founding Lineage Haplotypes in Native Americans Suggests a Single Wave of Migration for the New World. *American Journal of Physical Anthropology* 98:411–430.

Michab, M., J. K. Feathers, J. L. Joron, N. Mercier, M. Selos, H. Valladas, C. Valladas, J. L. Reyss, and A. C. Roosevelt

1998 Luminescence Dates for the Paleoindian Site of Pedra Pintada, Brazil. *Quaternary Geochronology* 17:1041–1046.

Michie, J. L.

1992 The Taylor Site: An Early Occupation in Central South Carolina. In *Paleoindian and Early Archaic Period Research in the Lower Southeast: A South Carolina Perspective*, edited by D. G. Anderson, K. E. Sassaman, and C. Judge, pp. 208–241. Council of South Carolina Professional Archaeologists, Columbia.

Miller, J. C.

1991 Lithic Resources. In *Prehistoric Hunters of the High Plains*, 2nd ed., edited by G. C. Frison, pp. 449–476. Academic Press, New York.

Miotti, L.

1999 Quandary the Clovis Phenomenon: A View from South America. Poster presented at the Clovis and Beyond Conference, Santa Fe, N.Mex.

Miotti, L. L.

1995 Piedra Museo Locality: A Special Place in the New World. *Current Research in the Pleistocene* 12:36–38.

Miotti, L. L., and R. Cattaneo

1997 Bifacial/Unifacial Technology c. 13,000 Years Ago in Southern Patagonia. *Current Research in the Pleistocene* 14:62–65.

Mirsky, S.

1999 Bones to Pick. *Scientific American* 280(2):36–37.

Mithen, S.

1993 Individuals, Groups, and the Paleolithic Record: A Reply to Clark. *Proceedings of the Prehistoric Society* 59:393–398.

Mithen, S. J.

1990 *Thoughtful Foragers: A Study of Prehistoric Decision Making*. Cambridge University Press, Cambridge.

Monsalve, J. V., and E. Hagelberg

1997 Mitochondrial DNA Polymorphisms in Carib People of Belize. *Proceedings of the Royal Society of London, Series B* 264:1217–1224.

Monsalve, M. V., F. Cardenas, F. Guhl, A. D. Delaney, and D. V. Devine

1996 Phylogenetic Analysis of mtDNA Lineages in South American Mummies. *Annals of Human Genetics* 60:293–303.

Montané, J.

1968 Paleo-Indian Remains from Laguna de Tagua Tagua, Central Chile. *Science* 161:1137–1138.

Moore, H. L.

1988 *Feminism and Anthropology*. Polity Press, Cambridge, England.

Moore, J. H.

2001 Evaluating Five Models of Human Colonization. *American Anthropologist* 103:395–408.

Moraga, M. L., P. Rocco, J. F. Miquel, F. Nervi, E. Llop, R. Chakraborty, F. Rothhammer, and P. Carvallo

2000 Mitochondrial DNA Polymorphisms in Chilean Aboriginal Populations: Implications for the Peopling of the Southern Cone of the Continent. *American Journal of Physical Anthropology* 113:19–29.

Morell, V.

1990 Confusion in Earliest America. *Science* 248:439–441.

1998 Kennewick Man's Trials Continue. *Science* 280:190.

Morlan, R. E.

1991 Peopling of the New World: A Discussion. In *Clovis:*

Origins and Adaptations, edited by R. Bonnichsen and K. L. Turnmire, pp. 303–308. Center for the Study of the First Americans, Oregon State University, Corvallis.

Morrison, D.
1999   The Earliest Thule Migration. *Canadian Journal of Archaeology* 22(2):139–156.

Morrow, J. E.
1995   Clovis Projectile Point Manufacture: A Perspective from the Ready/Lincoln Hills Site, 11JY46, Jersey County, Illinois. *Midcontinental Journal of Archaeology* 20(2):167–191.
1996   The Organization of Early Paleoindian Lithic Technology in the Confluence Region of the Mississippi, Illinois, and Missouri Rivers. Ph.D. dissertation, Washington University, St. Louis, Mo.

Morrow, J. E., and T. A. Morrow
1999   Geographic Variation in Fluted Projectile Points: A Hemispheric Perspective. *American Antiquity* 64(2): 215–231.

Morrow, T. M.
1996   Lithic Refitting and Archaeological Site Formation Processes: A Case Study from the Twin Dutch Site, Greene County, Illinois. In *Stone Tools: Theoretical Insights into Human Prehistory*, edited by G. H. Odell, pp. 345–373. Plenum Press, New York.

Morse, D. F., D. G. Anderson, and A. C. Goodyear
1996   The Pleistocene-Holocene Transition in the Eastern United States. In *Humans at the End of the Ice Age: The Archaeology of the Pleistocene-Holocene Transition*, edited by L. G. Straus, B. V. Eriksen, J. M. Erlandson, and D. R. Yesner, pp. 319–338. Plenum Press, New York.

Moseley, M. E.
1975   *The Maritime Foundations of Andean Civilization.* Cummings Publishing Co., Menlo Park, Calif.
1992   Maritime Foundations and Multilinear Evolution. *Andean Past* 3:5–42.

Mosimann, J. E., and P. S. Martin
1975   Simulating Overkill by Paleoindians. *American Scientist* 63:304–313.

Moss, M. L., and J. M. Erlandson
1995   Reflections on North American Pacific Coast Prehistory. *Journal of World Prehistory* 9:1–45.

Muller, F.
1961   Tres objectos de piedra de Huapalcalco, estado de Hidalgo. In *Homenaje a Pablo Martínez del Río, en el XXV aniversario de la edición de "Los origenes americanos,"* pp. 319–322. Instituto Nacional de Antropología e Historia, Mexico City.

Munford, D., M. do Carmo Zanini, and W. A. Neves
1995   Human Cranial Variation in South America: Implications for the Settlement of the New World. *Brazilian Journal of Genetics* 18:673–688.

Museum of South Zealand (Denmark; Sydsjællands Museum)
2002   Pre Boreal Elk Bones from Lundby Moor. Electronic document, http://www.aabne samlinger.dk/sydsjaellands/elge/english.htm, accessed 2002.

Nami, H. G.
1985   Excavación arqueológica y hallazgo de una punta de proyectil "Fell I" en la "Cueva del Medio," Seno de Ultima Esperanza, Chile. *Anales del Instituto de la Patagonia* 16:103–109.
1987a   Cueva del Medio: A Significant Paleoindian Site in Southern South America. *Current Research in the Pleistocene* 4:157–159.
1987b   Cueva del Medio: Perspectivas arqueológicas para la Patagonia austral. *Anales del Instituto de la Patagonia* 17:73–106.
1993   Aportes para el conocimiento de técnicas liticas del Pleistoceno final. Analisis de artefactos bifaciales del norte de Venezuela (colección Edmonton, Canada). *Relaciones de la Sociedad Argentina de Antropología* 19:417–450.
1994   Reseña sobre los avances de la arqueología fini-pleistocénica del extremo sur de Sudamérica. *Revista Chungara* 26(2):145–163.
1996   New Assessments of Early Human Occupations in the Southern Cone. In *Prehistoric Mongoloid Dispersal*, edited by T. Akazawa and E. J. E. Szathmáry, pp. 254–269. Oxford University Press, Oxford.

Nami, H. G., M. R. Norton, D. Stanford, and J. B. Broster
1996   Comments on Eastern Clovis Technology at the Carson Conn Short Site (40bn190), Tennessee River Valley. *Current Research in the Pleistocene* 13:62–64.

Nash, J. M.
2001   Who Killed Woolly? New Studies Suggest That Stone Age Hunters May Have Driven Dozens of Huge Creatures to Extinction. *Time* June 18:64.

Neel, J. V.
1978   Rare Variants, Private Polymorphisms, and Locus Heterozygosity in Amerindian Populations. *American Journal of Human Genetics* 30:465–490.

Neel, J. V., and E. A. Thompson
1978   Founder Effect and the Number of Private Polymorphisms Observed in Amerindian Tribes. *Proceedings of the National Academy of Sciences of the United States of America* 75:1904–1908.

Neeley, M. P., and C. M. Barton
1994   A New Approach to Interpreting Late Pleistocene Microlith Industries in Southwest Asia. *Antiquity* 68(259):275–288.

Nei, M.
1987   *Molecular Evolutionary Genetics.* Columbia University Press, New York.

Nelson, A. R.
1998   A Craniofacial Perspective on North American Indian Population Affinity and Relation. Ph.D. dissertation, University of Michigan, Ann Arbor.

Nelson, D. E., R. E. Morlan, J. S. Vogel, J. R. Southon, and C. R. Harington
1986   New Dates on Northern Yukon Artifacts: Holocene Not Upper Pleistocene. *Science* 232:749–751.

Nelson, M. C.
1991   The Study of Technological Organization. *Archaeological Method and Theory* 3:57–100.

Nelson, N. C.
1933 The Antiquity of Man in America in the Light of Archaeology. In *The American Aborigines: Their Origin and Antiquity*, edited by D. Jenness, pp. 87–130. University of Toronto Press, Toronto.

Nelson, S. M.
1997 *Gender in Archaeology: Analyzing Power and Prestige*. AltaMira Press, Walnut Creek, Calif.

Nemechek, S.
2000 Who Were the First Americans? *Scientific American* 283:80–87.

Nettle, D.
1999a *Linguistic Diversity*. Oxford University Press, Oxford.
1999b Linguistic Diversity of the Americas Can Be Reconciled with a Recent Colonization. *Proceedings of the National Academy of Sciences of the United States of America* 96:3325–3329.

Neves, W. A., and M. Blum
2000 The Buhl Burial: A Comment on Green et al. *American Antiquity* 65(1):191–193.

Neves, W. A., J. F. Powell, and E. G. Ozolins
1999 Extra-continental Morphological Affinities of Lapa Vermelha IV, Hominid 1: A Multivariate Analysis with Progress Numbers of Variables. *Homo* 50:263–282.

Neves, W. A., and H. M. Pucciarelli
1989 Extra-continental Biological Relationships of Early South American Human Remains: A Multivariate Analysis. *Ciência e Cultura* 41:586–575.
1991 Morphological Affinities of the First Americans: An Exploratory Analysis Based on Early South American Human Remains. *Journal of Human Evolution* 21:261–273.

Nichols, J.
1990 Linguistic Diversity and the First Settlement of the New World. *Language* 66:475–521.
1992 *Linguistic Diversity in Space and Time*. University of Chicago Press, Chicago.
1997 Modeling Ancient Population Structures and Movement in Linguistics. *Annual Review of Anthropology* 26:359–384.
1998 The First Four Discoveries of America: Linguistic Evidence. Paper presented at the 1998 Annual Meeting of the American Association for the Advancement of Science, Philadelphia.
1999 The Pleistocene Component of the Native American Population: A Linguistic Perspective. Paper presented at the 68th Annual Meeting of the American Association of Physical Anthropology, Columbus, Ohio.
2002 The First American Languages. In *The First Americans: The Pleistocene Colonization of the New World*, edited by N. G. Jablonski, pp. 273–294. Memoirs of the California Academy of Sciences, No. 27. San Francisco.

Nichols, J., and D. A. Peterson
1996 The Amerind Personal Pronouns. *Language* 72:336–371.

1998 The Amerind Personal Pronouns: A Reply to Campbell. *Language* 74:605–614.

Nieuwenhuis, C. J.
1998 Unattractive but Effective: Unretouched Pointed Flakes as Projectile Points? A Closer Look at the Abriense and Tequendamiense Artifacts. In *Explorations in American Archaeology: Essays in Honor of Wesley R. Hurt*, edited by M. G. Plew, pp. 133–163. University Press of America, Lanham, Md.

Núñez, A. L., J. Varela, and R. Casamiquela
1987 Ocupación paleoindio en el centro-norte de Chile: Adaptación circunlacustre en las tierras bajas. In *Investigaciones paleoindias al sur de la línea ecuatorial*, edited by B. Meggers, pp. 27–36. Taraxacum, Washington, D.C.

Núñez, A. L., J. Varela, R. Casamiquela, and C. Villagrá
1994 Reconstrucción multidisciplinaria de la ocupación prehistórica de Quereo, centro de Chile. *Latin American Antiquity* 5(2):99–118.

O'Brien, M. J., J. Darwent, and R. L. Lyman
2001 Cladistics Is Useful for Reconstructing Archaeological Phylogenies: Paleoindian Points from the Southeastern United States. *Journal of Archaeological Science* 28:1115–1136.

Ochsenius, C., and R. Gruhn (editors)
1999 *Taima-Taima: A Late Pleistocene Paleo-Indian Kill Site in Northernmost South America*. South American Quaternary Documentation Program. Carl Christian Ochsenius-Siftung Singen am Hohentwiel, Baden-Wèurttemburg, Germany.

Olsen, S. J., and J. W. Olsen
1977 The Chinese Wolf Ancestor of New World Dogs. *Science* 197:533–535.

Omoto, K., and N. Saitou
1997 Genetic Origins of the Japanese: A Partial Support for the Dual Structure Hypothesis. *American Journal of Physical Anthropology* 102:434–467.

Opler, M. E.
1983 The Apachean Culture Pattern and Its Origins. In *Southwest*, edited by A. Ortiz, pp. 368–392. Handbook of North American Indians, Vol. 10. Smithsonian Institution Press, Washington, D.C.

Orekhov, A. A.
1987 *An Early Culture of the Northwest Bering Sea*. Translated by R. L. Bland. Shared Beringian Heritage Program, Anchorage. Nauka, Moscow.

O'Rourke, D. H., S. W. Carlyle, and M. G. Hayes
1999 Ancient DNA Patterns and the Peopling of the Americas. *American Journal of Physical Anthropology, Supplement* 28:215.

O'Rourke, D. H., M. G. Hayes, and S. W. Carlyle
2000 Spatial and Temporal Stability of mtDNA Haplogroup Frequencies in Native North America. *Human Biology* 72:15–34.

Orr, P. C.
1962 The Arlington Spring Site, Santa Rosa Island, California. *American Antiquity* 27:417–419.

Ossa, P. P.

1976 A Fluted "Fishtail" Projectile Point from La Cumbre, Moche Valley, Peru. *Nawpa Pacha* 13:97–98.

1978 Paiján in Early Andean Prehistory: The Moche Valley Evidence. In *Early Man in America from a Circum-Pacific Perspective*, edited by A. L. Bryan, pp. 290–295. Occasional Papers, No. 1. Department of Anthropology, University of Alberta, Edmonton.

Ossa, P. P., and M. E. Moseley

1971 La Cumbre: A Preliminary Report on Research into the Early Lithic Occupation of the Moche Valley, Peru. *Nawpa Pacha* 9:1–16.

Oswalt, R. L.

1998 A Probabilistic Evaluation of North Eurasiatic Nostratic. In *Nostratic: Sifting the Evidence*, edited by J. C. Salmons and B. D. Joseph, pp. 199–216. John Benjamins, Amsterdam.

Overstreet, D. F.

1993 *Chesrow: A Paleoindian Complex in the Southern Lake Michigan Basin*. Case Studies in Great Lakes Archaeology, No. 2. Great Lakes Archaeological Press, Milwaukee.

Overstreet, D. F., and T. W. Stafford Jr.

1997 Additions to a Revised Chronology for Cultural and Non-cultural Mammoth and Mastodon Fossils in the Southwestern Lake Michigan Basin. *Current Research in the Pleistocene* 14:70–71.

Owen, R.

1965 The Patrilocal Band: A Linguistically and Culturally Hybrid Unit. *American Anthropologist* 67:675–690.

Palma, J.

1969 El sitio de Tagua-Tagua en el ámbito paleo-americano. In *Actos del V° Congreso Nacional de Arqueología*, pp. 315–325. Museo Arqueológico de La Serena, La Serena, Chile.

Palmer, H. A., and J. A. Stoltman

1976 The Boaz Mastodon: A Possible Association of Man and Mastodon in Wisconsin. *Midcontinental Journal of Archaeology* 1:163–177.

Parfit, M.

2000 Hunt for the First Americans. *National Geographic* 98:41–67.

Park, R. W.

1993 The Dorset-Thule Succession in Arctic North America: Assessing Claims for Culture Contact. *American Antiquity* 58(2):203–234.

1998 On the Dorset/Thule Analogy for the Middle/Upper Paleolithic Transition. *Current Anthropology* 39(3):355–356.

Parr, R. L., S. W. Carlyle, and D. H. O'Rourke

1996 Ancient DNA Analysis of Fremont Amerindians of the Great Salt Lake Wetlands. *American Journal of Physical Anthropology* 99:507–518.

Parry, W. J., and F. E. Smiley

1990 Hunter-Gatherer Archaeology in Northeastern Arizona and Southeastern Utah. In *Perspectives on Southwestern Prehistory*, edited by P. E. Minnis and C. L. Redman, pp. 47–56. Westview Press, Boulder, Colo.

Passarino, G., O. Semino, L. F. Bernini, and A. S. Santachiara-Benerecetti

1996a Pre-Caucasoid and Caucasoid Genetic Features of the Indian Population, Revealed by mtDNA Polymorphisms. *American Journal of Human Genetics* 59:927–934.

Passarino, G., O. Semino, G. Modiano, L. F. Bernini, and A. S. Santachiara-Benerecetti

1996b mtDNA Provides the First Known Marker Distinguishing Proto-Indians from the Other Caucasoids: It Probably Predates the Diversification between Indians and Orientals. *Annals of Human Biology* 23:121–126.

Patterson, A.

1992 *A Field Guide to Rock Art Symbols of the Greater Southwest*. Johnson Books, Boulder, Colo.

Pavlov, P., J. Svendsen, and S. Indrelid

2001 Human Presence in the European Arctic Nearly 40,000 Years Ago. *Nature* 413:64–67.

Pawley, A., and R. Green

1975 Dating the Dispersal of the Oceanic Languages. *Oceanic Linguistics* 12:1–68.

Pearson, G. A.

1998a Pan-American Paleoindian Dispersals as Seen through the Lithic Reduction Strategies and Tool Manufacturing Techniques at the Guardiria Site, Turrialba Valley, Costa Rica. Paper presented at the 63rd Annual Meeting of the Society for American Archaeology, Seattle.

1998b Reduction Strategy for Secondary Source Lithic Raw Materials at Guardiria (Turrialba), 9-FG-T, Costa Rica. *Current Research in the Pleistocene* 15:84–86.

1999 North American Paleoindian Bi-beveled Bone and Ivory Rods: A New Interpretation. *North American Archaeologist* 20:117–139.

2000a Archaeological Verification of a Palaeoecological Hypothesis: The La Yeguada Survey, 1999. Paper presented at the 65th Annual Meeting of the Society for American Archaeology, Philadelphia.

2000b New Evidence of Early Bifacial Industries on the Isthmus of Panama. *Current Research in the Pleistocene* 17:61–63.

Pearson, G. A., and P. A. Bostrom

1998 A New Fluted Stemmed Point from Belize and Its Implication for a Circum-Caribbean Paleoindian Culture Area. *Current Research in the Pleistocene* 15:84–86.

Pearson, R. J., G. L. Barnes, and K. L. Hutterer (editors)

1986 *Windows on the Japanese Past: Studies in Archaeology and Prehistory*. Center for Japanese Studies, University of Michigan, Ann Arbor.

Pelegrin, J., and C. Chauchat

1993 Tecnología y función de las puntas de Paiján: El aporte de la experimentación. *Latin American Antiquity* 4:367–382.

Peña, S. D. J., F. R. Santos, N. O. Bianchi, C. M. Bravi, F. R. Carnese, F. Rothhammer, T. Gerelsaikhan, B. Munkhtuja, and T. Oyunsuren
  1995   A Major Founder Y-Chromosome Haplotype in Amerindians. *Nature Genetics* 11:15–16.

Pennycuick, C. J.
  1979   Energy Costs of Locomotion and the Concept of "Foraging Radius." In *Serengeti: Dynamics of an Ecosystem*, edited by A. R. E. Sinclair and M. Norton-Griffiths, pp. 164–185. University of Chicago Press, Chicago.

Peteet, D.
  1995   Global Younger Dryas? *Quaternary International* 28:93–104.

Petersen, R. O.
  1977   *Wolf Ecology and Prey Relationships on Isle Royale.* Scientific Monographs, No. 11. National Park Service, Washington, D.C.
  1995   Wolves as Interspecific Competitors in Canid Ecology. In *Ecology and Conservation of Wolves in a Changing World*, edited by L. N. Carbyn, S. H. Fritts, and D. R. Seip, pp. 315–323. Occasional Publications, No. 35. Canadian Circumpolar Institute, University of Alberta, Edmonton.

Petrishchev, V. N., A. B. Kutuyeva, and Y. G. Rychkov
  1993   Region-V Deletions and Insertions in mtDNAs from Ten Mongoloid Populations of Siberia. *Genetika* 29:1196–1203.

Pettigrew, R. M.
  1985   *Archaeological Investigations on the East Shore of Lake Abert, Lake County, Oregon.* Anthropological Papers, No. 32. University of Oregon, Portland.

Phillips, A. M.
  1984   Shasta Ground Sloth Extinction: Fossil Packrat Midden Evidence from the Western Grand Canyon. In *Quaternary Extinctions: A Prehistoric Revolution*, edited by P. S. Martin and R. G. Klein, pp. 148–159. University of Arizona Press, Tucson.

Phillipson, D. W.
  1993   *African Archaeology.* 2nd ed. Cambridge University Press, Cambridge.

Pielou, E. C.
  1991   *After the Ice Age.* University of Chicago Press, Chicago.

Pietrusewsky, M., and R. Ikehara-Quebral
  2001   Multivariate Comparisons of Rapa-Nui (Easter Island), Polynesian, and Circum-Polynesian Crania. In *Pacific 2000: Proceedings of the Fifth International Conference on Easter Island and the Pacific*, edited by C. M. Stevenson, G. Lee, and F. Morin, pp. 457–494. Easter Island Foundation, Los Osos, Calif.

Piperno, D. R., M. B. Bush, and P. A. Colinvaux
  1990   Paleoenvironments and Human Occupation in Late-Glacial Panama. *Quaternary Research* 33:108–116.
  1991   Paleoecological Perspectives on Human Adaptation in Central Panama, I: The Pleistocene. *Geoarchaeology* 6:201–226.

Piperno, D. R., A. J. Ranere, I. Holst, and P. Hansell
  2000   Starch Grains Reveal Early Root Crop Horticulture in the Panamanian Tropical Forest. *Nature* 407:894–897.

Politis, G. C.
  1991   Fishtail Projectile Points in the Southern Cone of South America: An Overview. In *Clovis: Origins and Adaptations*, edited by R. Bonnichsen and K. L. Turnmire, pp. 287–301. Center for the Study of the First Americans, Oregon State University, Corvallis.

Poser, W.
  1992   The Salinan and Yurumangu Data in Language in the Americas. *International Journal of American Linguistics* 58:202–229.

Powell, J. F.
  1993   Dental Evidence for the Peopling of the New World: Some Methodological Considerations. *Human Biology* 65:799–819.

Powell, J. F., and J. C. Rose
  1999   Report on the Osteological Assessment of the "Kennewick Man" Skeleton (CENWW.97.Kennewick). Electronic document, http://www.cr.nps.gov/aad/kennewick/powell_rose.htm, accessed 2000.

Powell, J. F., and D. G. Steele
  1992   A Multivariate Craniometric Analysis of North American Paleoindian Remains. *Current Research in the Pleistocene* 9:59–62.

Powers, W. R.
  1973   Paleolithic Man in Northeast Asia. *Arctic Anthropology* 10(2):1–106.
  1990   The Peoples of Eastern Beringia. *Prehistoric Mongoloid Dispersals* 7:53–74.

Powers, W. R., and J. F. Hoffecker
  1989   Late Pleistocene Settlement in the Nenana Valley, Central Alaska. *American Antiquity* 54(2):263–287.

Preston, D.
  1997   Cannibals of the Canyon. *The New Yorker* 72:70–81.

Pringle, H.
  1997a   Ice Age Communities May Be the Earliest Known Net Hunters. *Science* 277:1203–1204.
  1997b   New Respect for Metal's Role in Ancient Arctic Cultures. *Science* 277:766–767.

Prufer, O. H., and R. S. Baby
  1963   *Palaeo-Indians of Ohio.* Ohio Historical Society, Columbus.

Purdy, B. A.
  1983   Comments on "A Compilation of Fluted Points of Eastern North America by Count and Distribution: An AENA Project." *Archaeology of Eastern North America* 11:29.

Putman, J. J.
  1988   The Search for Modern Humans. *National Geographic* 1744:439–477.

Pyne, S. J.
  1998   Forged in Fire: History, Land, and Anthropogenic Fire. In *Advances in Historical Ecology*, edited by W. Balée, pp. 64–103. Columbia University Press, New York.

Pyne, S. J., and J. G. Goldammer
  1997   The Culture of Fire: An Introduction to Anthropo-

genic Fire History. In *Sediment Records of Biomass Burning and Global Change*, edited by B. Stocks, pp. 71–114. Springer-Verlag, Berlin.

Rainey, F.
1939   Archaeology in Central Alaska. *Anthropological Papers of the American Museum of Natural History* 36(4):351–405.
1940   Archaeological Investigations in Central Alaska. *American Antiquity* 4:299–308.

Ranere, A. J.
1980   Human Movements into Tropical America at the End of the Pleistocene. In *Anthropological Papers in Memory of Earl H. Swanson, Jr.*, edited by L. Harten, C. Warren, and D. Tuohy, pp. 41–47. Idaho State Museum of Natural History, Pocatello.
1992   Implements of Change in the Holocene Environments of Panama. In *Archaeology and Environment in Latin America*, edited by O. R. Ortiz-Troncoso and T. V. D. Hammen, pp. 25–44. Universiteit van Amsterdam, Amsterdam.
1997   Paleoindian Expansion into Tropical America: The View from Central America. Paper presented at the 62nd Annual Meeting of the Society for American Archaeology, Nashville, Tenn.

Ranere, A. J., and R. G. Cooke
1991   Paleoindian Occupation in the Central American Tropics. In *Clovis: Origins and Adaptations*, edited by R. Bonnichsen and K. L. Turnmire, pp. 237–253. Center for the Study of the First Americans, Oregon State University, Corvallis.
1995   Evidencias de ocupación humana en Panamá a postrimerías del Pleistoceno y a comienzos del Holoceno. In *Ámbito y ocupaciones tempranas de la América tropical*, edited by I. Cavalier and S. Mora, pp. 5–26. Instituto Colombiano de Antropología, Fundación Erigaie, Bogota.
1996   Stone Tools and Cultural Boundaries in Prehistoric Panama: An Initial Assessment. In *Paths to Central American Prehistory*, edited by F. W. Lange, pp. 49–77. University Press of Colorado, Niwot.
2003   Late Glacial and Early Holocene Occupation of Central American Tropical Forests. In *Under the Canopy: The Archaeology of Tropical Rain Forests*, edited by J. Mercader, pp. 219–248. Rutgers University Press, New Brunswick, N.J.

Rasic, J., and R. Gal
2000   An Early Lithic Assemblage from the Tuluaq Site, Northwest Alaska. *Current Research in the Pleistocene* 17:66–68.

Ray, D. J.
1984   Bering Strait Eskimo. In *Arctic*, edited by D. Damas, pp. 285–303. Handbook of North American Indians, Vol. 5. Smithsonian Institution Press, Washington, D.C.

Ray, J. H., N. H. Lopinot, and E. R. Hajic
2002   The Big Eddy Site: A Multicomponent Paleoindian Site on the Ozark Border, Southwest Missouri. Electronic document, http://www.smsu.edu/car/Big Eddy2.html, accessed 2002.

Redd, A. J., N. Takezaki, S. T. Sherry, S. T. McGarvey, A. S. Sofro, and M. Stoneking
1995   Evolutionary History of the COII/tRNA^{Lys} Intergenic 9-Base Pair Deletion in Human Mitochondrial DNAs from the Pacific. *Molecular Biology and Evolution* 12: 604–615.

Redder, A. J., and J. W. Fox
1988   Excavation and Positioning of the Horn Shelter's Burial and Grave Goods. *Central Texas Archaeologist* 11:1–9.

Redman, C. L.
1999   *Human Impact on Ancient Environments*. University of Arizona Press, Tucson.

Reed, E. K.
1964   The Greater Southwest. In *Prehistoric Man in the New World*, edited by J. D. Jennings and E. Norbeck, pp. 175–191. University of Chicago Press, Chicago.

Reeves, B. O. K.
1973   The Nature and Age of the Contact between the Laurentide and Cordilleran Ice Sheets in the Western Interior of North America. *Arctic and Alpine Research* 5:1–16.
1983   Bergs, Barriers, and Beringia: Reflections on the Peopling of the New World. In *Quaternary Coastlines and Marine Archaeology: Towards the Prehistory of Land Bridges and Continental Shelves*, edited by P. M. Masters and N. C. Flemming, pp. 389–412. Academic Press, New York.

Reichel-Dolmatoff, G.
1965   *Colombia: Ancient Peoples and Places*. Frederick A. Praeger, New York.

Rensberger, B.
1997   Putting a New Face on Prehistory. *Washington Post* April 15: A1.

Ribeiro-Dos-Santos, A. K. C., S. E. B. Santos, A. L. Machado, V. Guapindaia, and M. A. Zago
1996   Heterogeneity of Mitochondrial DNA Haplotypes in Pre-Columbian Natives of the Amazon Region. *American Journal of Physical Anthropology* 101: 29–37.

Richards, M., H. Côrte-Real, P. Forster, V. Macaulay, H. Wilkinson-Herbots, A. Demaine, S. Papiha, R. Hedges, H.-J. Bandelt, and B. Sykes
1996   Paleolithic and Neolithic Lineages in the European Mitochondrial Gene Pool. *American Journal of Human Genetics* 59:185–203.

Richards, M., V. A. Macaulay, H.-J. Bandelt, and B. C. Sykes
1998   Phylogeography of Mitochondrial DNA in Western Europe. *Annals of Human Genetics* 62:241–260.

Rick, J. W.
1980   *Prehistoric Hunters of the High Andes*. Academic Press, New York.

Rickards, O., C. Martínez-Labarga, J. K. Lum, G. F. De Stefano, and R. L. Cann
1999   mtDNA History of the Cayapa Amerinds of Ecuador: Detection of Additional Founding Lineages for the Native American Populations. *American Journal of Human Genetics* 65:519–530.

Rindos, D.
1980   Symbiosis, Instability, and the Origins and Spread of Agriculture: A New Model. *Current Anthropology* 21:751–772.

Rindos, D., and E. Webb
1992   Modeling the Initial Human Colonization of Australia: Perfect Adaptation, Cultural Variability, and Cultural Change. *Proceedings of the Australian Society for Human Biology* 5:441–454.

Ringe, D. A.
1992   *On Calculating the Factor of Chance in Language Comparison*. Transactions of the American Philosophical Society, Vol. 82, Pt. 1. Philadelphia.
1998   Probabilistic Evidence for Indo-Uralic. In *Nostratic: Sifting the Evidence*, edited by J. C. Salmons and B. D. Joseph, pp. 153–197. John Benjamins, Amsterdam.
1999   How Hard Is It to Match CVC-Roots? *Transactions of the Philological Society* 97(2):213–244.

Ritchie, W. A.
1957   *Traces of Early Man in the Northeast*. New York State Museum and Science Service Bulletin, No. 358. State University of New York (SUNY), Albany.

Rivet, P.
1957   *Les origines de l'homme américain*. Gallimard, Paris.

Robdell, D.
2000   The Younger Dryas: Cold, Cold Everywhere? *Science* 290:285–286.

Roberts, F. H. H.
1940   Developments in the Problem of the North American PaleoIndian. *Smithsonian Miscellaneous Collection* 100:51–116.
1953   Recent Developments in the Early Man Problem in the New World. *Eastern States Archaeological Federation Bulletin* 12:9–11.
1962   Comments. *Current Anthropology* 3:262–263.

Roberts, R. G., R. Jones, and M. A. Smith
1994a   Beyond the Radiocarbon Barrier in Australian Prehistory: A Critique of Allen's Commentary. *Antiquity* 68(260):611–616.

Roberts, R. G., R. Jones, N. A. Spooner, M. J. Head, A. S. Murray, and M. A. Smith
1994b   The Human Colonization of Australia: Optical Dates of 53,000 and 60,000 Years Bracket Human Arrival at Deaf Adder Gorge, Northern Territory. *Quaternary Science Reviews* 13:575–586.

Robinson, B. S.
1992   Early and Middle Archaic Period Occupation in the Gulf of Maine Region: Mortuary and Technological Patterning. In *Early Holocene Occupation in Northern New England*, edited by B. S. Robinson, J. B. Petersen, and A. K. Robinson, pp. 63–116. Occasional Publications in Maine Archaeology, No. 9. Maine Historic Preservation Commission, Augusta.

Robledo, E.
1954   Migraciones oceánicas en el poblamiento de Colombia. *Boletín del Instituto de Antropología* 1(3):215–234.

Rockman, M.
2003   Knowledge and Learning in the Archaeology of Colonization. In *Colonization of Unfamiliar Landscapes: The Archaeology of Adaptation*, edited by M. Rockman and J. Steele, pp. 3–24. Routledge, London.

Rodriguez-Delfin, L., S. E. B. Santos, and M. A. Zago
1997   Diversity of the Human Y Chromosome of South American Amerindians: A Comparison with Blacks, Whites, and Japanese from Brazil. *Annals of Human Genetics* 61:439–448.

Rogers, E. S., and E. Leacock
1981   Montagnais-Naskapi. In *Subarctic*, edited by J. Helm, pp. 169–189. Handbook of North American Indians, Vol. 6. Smithsonian Institution Press, Washington, D.C.

Rogers, L. A., and R. A. Rogers
1987   Inbreeding and Wisconsin Glacial Barriers. *Current Research in the Pleistocene* 4:45–46.

Rogers, R. A.
1986a   Language, Human Subspeciation, and Ice Age Barriers in Siberia. *Canadian Journal of Anthropology* 5:11–22.
1986b   Spurred End Scrapers as Diagnostic Paleoindian Artifacts: A Distributional Analysis on Stream Terraces. *American Antiquity* 51:338–341.

Rogers, R. A., L. D. Martin, and T. D. Nicklas
1990   Ice-Age Geography and the Distribution of Native North American Languages. *Journal of Biogeography* 17:131–143.

Rogers, R. A., L. A. Rogers, R. S. Hoffmann, and L. D. Martin
1991   Native American Biological Diversity and the Biogeographic Influence of Ice Age Refugia. *Journal of Biogeography* 18:623–630.

Romesburg, H. C.
1984   *Cluster Analysis for Researchers*. Wadsworth Inc., Belmont, Calif.

Roosa, W. B.
1962   Comments. *Current Anthropology* 3:263–265.
1965   Some Great Lakes Fluted Point Types. *Michigan Archaeologist* 11:89–102.

Roosevelt, A. C.
1998   Paleoindian and Archaic Occupations in the Lower Amazon, Brazil: A Summary and Comparison. In *Explorations in American Archaeology: Essays in Honor of Wesley R. Hurt*, edited by M. G. Plew, pp. 165–191. University Press of America, Lanham, Md.

Roosevelt, A. C., J. Douglas, and L. Brown
2002   The Migrations and Adaptations of the First Americans: Clovis and Pre-Clovis Viewed from South America. In *The First Americans: The Pleistocene Colonization of the New World*, edited by N. G. Jablonski, pp. 159–235. Memoirs of the California Academy of Sciences, No. 27. San Francisco.

Roosevelt, A. C., M. Lima da Costa, C. Lopes Machado, M. Michab, N. Mercier, H. Valladas, J. Feathers, W. Barnett, M. Imazio da Silveira, A. Henderson, J. Sliva, B. Chernoff, D. S. Reese, J. A. Holman, N. Toth, and K. Schick
1996   Paleoindian Cave Dwellers in the Amazon: The Peopling of the Americas. *Science* 272:373–384.

Roper, D. C.
  1987 Plains Paleoindian Red Ochre Use and Its Possible
        Significance. *Current Research in the Pleistocene* 4:
        82–84.
  1989 Grinding Stones in Plains Paleoindian Sites: The
        Case for Pigment Processing. *Current Research in the
        Pleistocene* 6:36–37.
  1996 Variability in the Use of Ochre during the Paleo-
        indian Period. *Current Research in the Pleistocene*
        13:40–42.

Rose, M.
  1999 The Topper Site: Pre-Clovis Surprise. *Archaeology*
        52(4):18.

Roth, W. E.
  1924 *An Introductory Study of the Arts, Crafts, and Cus-
        toms of the Guiana Indians*. 38th Annual Report of
        the Bureau of American Ethnology. Smithsonian
        Institution, Washington, D.C.

Rothhammer, F., C. Silva, S. M. Callegari-Jacques, E. Llop, and
F. M. Salzano
  1997 Gradients of HLA Diversity in South American
        Indians. *Annals of Human Biology* 24:197–208.

Rouse, I.
  1976 Peopling of the Americas. *Quaternary Research* 6:
        567–612.
  1986 *Migrations in Prehistory: Inferring Population Move-
        ments from Cultural Remains*. Yale University Press,
        New Haven, Conn.

Rowlands, M.
  1994 The Politics of Identity in Archaeology. In *Social
        Construction of the Past: Representation as Power*,
        edited by G. C. Bond and A. A. Gilliam, pp. 129–143.
        Routledge, London.

Rubicz, R., T. G. Schurr, and M. H. Crawford
  2003 Mitochondrial DNA Diversity in Modern Aleut
        Populations. *Human Biology*, in press.

Ruhlen, M.
  1991 The Amerind Phylum and the Prehistory of the New
        World. In *Sprung from Some Common Source*, edited
        by S. M. Lamb and E. D. Mitchell, pp. 328–350.
        Stanford University Press, Stanford, Calif.
  1996 *The Origin of Language: Tracing the Evolution of the
        Mother Tongue*. John Wiley & Sons, New York.
  1998 The Origin of the Na-Dene. *Proceedings of the Na-
        tional Academy of Sciences of the United States of
        America* 95:13994–13996.

Ruiz-Linares, A., D. Ortiz-Barrientos, M. Figueroa, N. Mesa,
J. G. Munera, G. Bedoya, I. D. Velez, L. F. Garcia, A. Perez-
Lezaun, J. Bertranpetit, M. W. Feldman, and D. B. Goldstein
  1999 Microsatellites Provide Evidence for Y Chromosome
        Diversity among the Founders of the New World.
        *Proceedings of the National Academy of Sciences of the
        United States of America* 96:6312–6317.

Rutter, N.
  1980 Late Pleistocene History of Western Canada Ice-
        Free Corridor. *Canadian Journal of Anthropology* 1:
        1–8.

Saillard, J., P. Forster, N. Lynnerup, H.-J. Bandelt, and S. Nørby
  2000 mtDNA Variation among Greenland Eskimos: The

Edge of the Beringian Expansion. *American Journal
        of Human Genetics* 67:718–726.

Sajantila, A., P. Lahermo, T. Anttinen, M. Lukka, P. Sistonen,
M.-L. Savontaus, P. Aula, L. Beckman, L. Tranebjaerg, T. Gedde-
Dahl, L. Issel-Tarver, A. DiRienzo, and S. Pääbo
  1995 Genes and Languages in Europe: An Analysis of
        Mitochondrial Lineages. *Genome Research* 5:42–52.

Sampson, C. G.
  1988 *Stylistic Boundaries among Mobile Hunter-Foragers*.
        Smithsonian Institution Press, Washington, D.C.

Sander, D.
  1959 Fluted Points from Madden Lake. *Panama Archae-
        ologist* 2:39–51.
  1964 Lithic Material from Panama: Fluted Points from
        Madden Lake. *Actas del XXXV Congreso de Ameri-
        canistas* 1:183–192.

Sanders, T. N.
  1988 The Adams Site: A Paleoindian Manufacturing and
        Habitation Site in Christian County, Kentucky. In
        Paleoindian and Archaic Research in Kentucky, edited
        by C. D. Hockensmith, D. Pollack, and T. Sanders,
        pp. 1–24. Kentucky Heritage Council, Frankfort.
  1990 *Adams: The Manufacturing of Flaked Stone Tools at
        a Paleoindian Site in Western Kentucky*. Persimmon
        Press, Buffalo, N.Y.

Sandweiss, D. H., D. K. Keefer, and J. B. Richardson III
  1999 First Americans and the Sea. *Discovering Archae-
        ology* 1(1):59–65.

Sandweiss, D. H., H. McInnis, R. L. Burger, A. Cano, B. Ojeda,
R. Paredes, M. del Carmen Sandweiss, and M. D. Glascock
  1998 Quebrada Jaguay: Early South American Maritime
        Adaptations. *Science* 281:1830–1832.

Sandweiss, D. H., J. B. Richardson III, E. J. Reitz, J. T. Hsu, and
R. A. Feldman
  1989 Early Maritime Adaptations in the Andes: Prelimi-
        nary Studies at the Ring Site, Peru. In *Ecology,
        Settlement, and History in the Osmore Drainage, Peru*,
        edited by D. S. Rice, C. Stanish, and P. R. Scarr, pp.
        35–84. BAR International Series, No. 545, Pt. 1.
        British Archaeological Reports, Oxford.

Sandweiss, D. H., B. Tanner, D. Sanger, F. Andrus, and
D. Piperno
  2000 Paleoindian-Age Domestic Structure at a Peruvian
        Fishing Site. Paper presented at the 65th Annual
        Meeting of the Society for American Archaeology,
        Philadelphia.

Santamaria, D.
  1981 Preceramic Occupations at Los Grifos Rock Shelter,
        Ocozocoautla, Chiapas, Mexico. In *X Congreso Unión
        Internacional de Ciencias Prehistóricas y Protohistóri-
        cas*, edited by J. García-Bárcena and F. Sanchez
        Martínez, pp. 63–83. Instituto Nacional de Antropo-
        logía e Historia, Mexico City.

Santiana, A., and M. A. Carluci
  1962 El paleoindio en el Ecuador. *Humanitas* 3(2):5–41.

Santos, F. R., T. Gerelsaikhan, B. Munkhtuja, T. Oyunsuren, J. T.
Epplen, and S. D. J. Pena
  1996a Geographic Differences in the Allele Frequencies of

the Human Y-Linked Tetranucleotide Polymorphism DYS19. *Human Genetics* 97:309–313.

Santos, F. R., A. Pandya, C. Tyler-Smith, S. D. J. Pena, M. Schanfield, W. R. Leonard, L. Osipova, M. H. Crawford, and R. J. Mitchell

1999 The Central Siberian Origin for Native American Y-Chromosomes. *American Journal of Human Genetics* 64:619–628.

Santos, F. R., L. Rodriguez-Delfin, S. D. Pena, J. Moore, and K. M. Weiss

1996b North and South Amerindians May Have the Same Major Founder Y Chromosome Haplotype. *American Journal of Human Genetics* 58:1369–1370.

Santos, M. R., R. H. Ward, and R. Barrantes

1994 mtDNA Variation in the Chibcha Amerindian Huetar from Costa Rica. *Human Biology* 66:963–977.

Santos, S. E. B., A. K. C. Ribeiro-Dos-Santos, D. Meyer, and M. A. Zago

1996 Multiple Founder Haplotypes of Mitochondrial DNA in Amerindians Revealed by RFLP and Sequencing. *Annals of Human Genetics* 60:305–319.

Sapir, E.

1929 Central and North American Languages. *Encyclopaedia Britannica* (14th ed.) 5:138–141.

Sassaman, K. E.

1992 Lithic Technology and the Hunter-Gatherer Sexual Division of Labor. *North American Archaeologist* 13(3):249–262.

1996 Early Archaic Settlement in the South Carolina Coastal Plain. In *The Paleoindian and Early Archaic Southeast*, edited by D. G. Anderson and K. E. Sassaman, pp. 58–83. University of Alabama Press, Tuscaloosa.

Sassaman, K. E., and D. G. Anderson

1996 The Need for a Regional Perspective. In *The Paleoindian and Early Archaic Southeast*, edited by D. G. Anderson and K. E. Sassaman, pp. 215–221. University of Alabama Press, Tuscaloosa.

Sauer, C. O.

1944 A Geographic Sketch of Early Man in America. *Geographical Review* 34:529–573.

Saunders, J. J.

1977 Lehner Ranch Revisited. In *Paleoindian Lifeways*, edited by E. Johnson, pp. 48–64. Museum Journal, No. 17. West Texas Museum Association, Texas Tech University, Lubbock.

1990 Immanence, Configuration, and the Discovery of America's Past. In *Megafauna and Man: Discovery of America's Heartland*, edited by L. D. Agenbroad, J. I. Mead, and L. W. Nelson, pp. 136–143. Scientific Papers, No. 1. Mammoth Site of Hot Springs, South Dakota, Inc., Hot Springs.

Saunders, J. J., G. A. Agogino, A. T. Boldurian, and C. V. Haynes Jr.

1991 A Mammoth-Ivory Burnisher-Billet from the Clovis Level, Blackwater Locality No. 1, New Mexico. *Plains Anthropologist* 36:359–364.

Saunders, J. J., E. B. Daeschler, and J. L. Cotter

1994 Descriptive Analyses and Taphonomical Observations of Culturally-Modified Mammoths Excavated at "The Gravel Pit," near Clovis, New Mexico in 1936. *Proceedings of the Academy of Natural Sciences of Philadelphia* 145:1–28.

Saunders, J. J., C. V. Haynes Jr., D. Stanford, and G. A. Agogino

1990 Mammoth-Ivory Semifabricate from Blackwater Locality No. 1, New Mexico. *American Antiquity* 55:112–119.

Saxon, E. C.

1976 La prehistoria de Fuego-Patagonia: Colonización de un habitat marginal. *Anales del Instituto de la Patagonia* 7:63–73.

Schaafsma, P.

1963 *Rock Art in the Navajo Reservoir District.* Papers in Anthropology, No. 7. Museum of New Mexico, Santa Fe.

1971 *The Rock Art of Utah: From the Donald Scott Collection.* Papers of the Peabody Museum of Archaeology and Ethnology, Vol. 65. Cambridge, Mass.

1975 *Rock Art in New Mexico.* University of New Mexico Press, Albuquerque.

Schaller, G.

1972 *The Serengeti Lion: A Study of Predator Prey Relations.* University of Chicago Press, Chicago.

Schanfield, M. S.

1992 Immunoglobin Allotypes (GM and KM) Indicate Multiple Founding Populations of Native Americans: Evidence of at Least Four Migrations to the New World. *Human Biology* 64:381–402.

Schiffer, M. B.

1987 *Formation Processes of the Archaeological Record.* University of New Mexico Press, Albuquerque.

1996 Some Further Comments on the Dalton Settlement Pattern Hypothesis. In *Behavioral Archaeology: First Principles*, edited by J. M. Skibo, pp. 74–87. University of Utah Press, Salt Lake City.

Schlemon, R. J., and F. E. Budinger Jr.

1990 The Archaeological Geology of the Calico Site, Mohave Desert, California. In *Archaeological Geology of North America*, edited by N. Lasca and J. Donahue, pp. 301–313. Centennial Special Volume, No. 4. Geological Society of America, Boulder, Colo.

Schobinger, J.

1971 Una punta de tipo "cola de pescado" de la Crucesita (Mendoza). *Anales de Arqueología y Etnología* 26:89–97.

1973 Nuevos hallazgos de puntas "colas de pescado" y consideraciones en tomo al origen y dispersión de la cultura de cazadores superiores toldense (Fell I) en Sudamérica. *Atti del 40 Congresso Internazionale Degli Americanisti* 1:33–50. Genoa.

1988 *Prehistoria de Sudamérica culturas preceramicas.* Alianza Editorial, Madrid.

Schroedl, A. R.

1977 The Paleo-Indian Period on the Colorado Plateau. *Southwestern Lore* 43:1–9.

1991 Paleo-Indian Occupation in the Eastern Great Basin and Northern Colorado Plateau. *Utah Archaeology* 4:1–15.

Schultz, J. M.

1992   The Use-Wear Generated by Processing Bison
        Hides. *Plains Anthropologist* 37(141):333–351.

Schurr, T. G.

1996   Mitochondrial DNA and the Peopling of the New
        World. *American Scientist* 8:246–253.

1997   The Nature of mtDNA Variation in Native Ameri-
        cans: Founding Lineages, "Other" Haplotypes,
        and Genetic Diversity of Ancestral Populations.
        Paper presented at the 66th Annual Meeting of the
        American Association of Physical Anthropology,
        St. Louis, Mo.

2003   Molecular Genetic Diversity of Siberian Popula-
        tions: Implications for Ancient DNA Studies of
        Archeological Populations from the Cis-Baikal Re-
        gion. In *Prehistoric Foragers of the Cis-Baikal, Siberia:
        Proceedings from the First Conference of the Baikal Ar-
        chaeology Project*, edited by A. Weber, H. McKenzie,
        and R. Bettinger. Canadian Circumpolar Institute,
        Edmonton, Alberta, in press.

Schurr, T. G., S. W. Ballinger, Y. Y. Gan, J. A. Hodge, D. A. Merriwether, D. N. Lawrence, W. C. Knowler, K. M. Weiss, and D. C.
Wallace

1990   Amerindian Mitochondrial DNAs Have Rare Asian
        Variants at High Frequencies, Suggesting They
        Derived from Four Primary Maternal Lineages.
        American Journal of Human Genetics 46:613–623.

Schurr, T. G., Y. B. Starikovskaya, R. I. Sukernik, A. Torroni,
and D. C. Wallace

2000   Mitochondrial DNA Diversity in Lower Amur River
        Populations, and Its Implications for the Genetic
        History of the North Pacific and the New World.
        *American Journal of Physical Anthropology, Supple-
        ment* 30:274–275.

Schurr, T. G., R. I. Sukernik, Y. B. Starikovskaya, and D. C.
Wallace

1999   Mitochondrial DNA Diversity in Koryaks and
        Itel'men: Ancient and Recent Population Expan-
        sions and Dispersals in Okhotsk–Bering Sea Re-
        gion. *American Journal of Physical Anthropology* 108:
        1–40.

Schurr, T. G., and D. C. Wallace

1999   mtDNA Variation in Native Americans and Siberians
        and Its Implications for the Peopling of the New
        World. In *Who Were the First Americans: Proceedings
        of the 58th Annual Biology Colloquium, Oregon State
        University*, edited by R. Bonnichsen, pp. 41–77. Cen-
        ter for the Study of the First Americans, Oregon
        State University, Corvallis.

2003   Genetic Prehistory of Paleoasiatic-Speaking
        Peoples of Northeastern Siberia and Their Links to
        Native American Populations. In *Constructing Cul-
        tures Then and Now: Celebrating Franz Boas and the
        Jesup North Pacific Expedition*, edited by L. Kendall
        and I. Krupnik, pp. 77–93. Smithsonian Institution
        Press, Washington, D.C.

Schwartz, M.

1997   *A History of Dogs in the Early Americas*. Yale Univer-
        sity Press, New Haven, Conn.

Scott, G. R., and I. C. G. Turner

1997   *The Anthropology of Modern Human Teeth: Dental
        Morphology and Its Variation in Recent Human Popu-
        lations*. Cambridge University Press, Cambridge.

Scozzari, R., F. Cruciani, P. Santolamazza, G. Vona,
P. Moral, V. Latini, L. Varesi, M. M. Memmi, V. Romano, G. De
Leo, M. Gennarelli, J. Jaruzelska, R. Villems, J. Parik, V. Mac-
aulay, and A. Torroni

1997   mtDNA and Y-Chromosome-Specific Polymorphisms
        in Modern Ojibwa: Implications about the Origin of
        Their Gene Pool. *American Journal of Human Genetics*
        60:241–244.

Seguel, Z. S., and O. O. Campaña Von

1975   Presencia de megafauna en la provincia de Osorno
        (Chile) y sus posibles relaciones con cazadores
        superiores. In *Actas y trabajos del primer Congreso
        de Arqueología Argentina*, edited by J. Mare, pp.
        237–243. Museo Histórico Provincial, Buenos Aires.

Seielstad, M. T., J. M. Hebert, A. A. Lin, P. A. Underhill,
M. Ibrahim, D. Vollrath, and L. L. Cavalli-Sforza

1994   Construction of Human Y-Chromosomal Haplotypes
        Using a New Polymorphic A to G Transition. *Human
        Molecular Genetics* 3:2159–2161.

Sellards, E. H.

1952   *Early Man in America*. Greenwood Press, New York.

Sellet, F.

1998   The French Connection: Investigating a Possible
        Clovis-Solutrean Link. *Current Research in the Pleis-
        tocene* 15:67–68.

Severinghaus, J., and E. Brook

1999   Abrupt Climate Change at the End of the Last Gla-
        cial Period Inferred from Trapped Air in Polar Ice.
        Science 286:930–934.

Shackleton, N.

2001   Climate Change across the Hemispheres. *Science*
        291:58–59.

Shackley, M. S.

2000   The Stone Tool Technology of Ishi and the Yana
        of North-Central California: Inferences for Hunter-
        Gatherer Cultural Identity in Historic California.
        American Anthropologist 102:693–712.

Sharrock, F. W.

1966   *Prehistoric Occupation Patterns in Southwest Wyoming
        and Cultural Relationships with the Great Basin
        and Plains Culture Areas*. Anthropological Papers,
        No. 77. University of Utah, Salt Lake City.

Sheehan, G.

1985   Whaling as an Organizing Focus in Northwestern
        Alaskan Eskimo Societies. In *Prehistoric Hunter-
        Gatherers: The Emergence of Cultural Complexity*,
        edited by T. D. Price and J. A. Brown, pp. 123–154.
        Academic Press, San Diego.

Shemesh, A., and D. Peteet

1998   Oxygen Isotopes in Fresh Water Biogenic Opal:
        Northeastern US Allerod-Younger Dryas Tem-
        perature Shift. *Geophysical Research Letters* 25:
        1935–1938.

Shetrone, H. C.

1936   The Folsom Phenomena as Seen from Ohio. *Ohio*

State Archaeological and Historical Quarterly 45:
240–256.

Shevoroshkin, V. (editor)

1991 *Dene-Sino-Caucasian Languages.* Brockmeyer,
Bochum, Germany.

Shields, G. F., K. Hecker, M. I. Voevoda, and J. K. Reed

1992 Absence of the Asian-Specific Region V Mitochondrial Marker in Native Beringians. *American Journal
of Human Genetics* 50:758–765.

Shields, G. F., A. M. Schmiechen, B. L. Frazier, A. Redd, M. I.
Voevoda, J. K. Reed, and R. H. Ward

1993 mtDNA Sequences Suggest a Recent Evolution-
ary Divergence for Beringian and Northern North
American Populations. *American Journal of Human
Genetics* 53:549–562.

Shields, W. F.

1968 *The Woodruff Bison Kill.* Miscellaneous Anthropological Papers, No. 21. University of Utah, Salt Lake
City.

Short, J.

1981 Diet and Feeding Behaviour of the Forest Elephant.
Mammalia 45:177–186.

Shott, M. J.

1992 On Recent Trends in the Anthropology of Foragers: Kalahari Revisionism and Its Archaeological
Implications. *Man* 27:843–871.

1993 *The Leavitt Site: A Parkhill Phase Paleoindian Occupation in Central Michigan.* Memoirs of the Museum
of Anthropology, No. 25. University of Michigan,
Ann Arbor.

1997 Activity and Formation as Sources of Variation in
Great Lakes Paleoindian Assemblages. *Midcontinental Journal of Archaeology* 22:197–236.

2000 The Midwest. *Common Ground* (Special Issue, "The
Earliest Americans") Spring/Summer 2000:20–33.

Simek, J. F., and L. M. Snyder

1988 Changing Assemblage Diversity in Perigord Ar-
chaeofaunas. In *Upper Pleistocene Prehistory of Western Eurasia*, edited by A. Montet-White, pp. 321–332.
University Museum, University of Pennsylvania,
Philadelphia.

Simões, M. F.

1976 Nota sobre duas pontas-de-projétil da Bacia do
Tapajós (Pará). *Boletim do Museu Paraense Emilio
Goeldi* 62:1–15.

Simon, T.

1999 An 11,000-Year-Old Spearhead and a Race against
Time. Electronic document, http://www.exn.ca/
stories/1999/06/10/53.asp, accessed 2000.

Simpson, E. H.

1949 Measure of Diversity. *Nature* 163:688.

Simpson, J. C.

1948 Folsom-like Points from Florida. *Florida Anthropologist* 1:11–15.

Sinclair, A. R. E.

1979 Dynamics of the Serengeti Ecosystem: Pattern and
Process. In *Serengeti: Dynamics of an Ecosystem*,
edited by A. R. E. Sinclair and M. Norton-Griffiths,
pp. 1–31. University of Chicago Press, Chicago.

Slaughter, B. H.

1967 Animal Ranges as a Clue to Late-Pleistocene Extinction. In *Pleistocene Extinctions: The Search for a
Cause*, edited by P. S. Martin and H. E. Wright Jr.,
pp. 155–167. Yale University Press, New Haven,
Conn.

2000 Russia. In *Encyclopedia of Human Evolution and Pre-
history*, edited by E. Delson, I. Tattersall, J. A. van
Couvering, and A. S. Brooks, pp. 618–620. Garland
Publishing, New York.

Slayman, A. L.

1997 A Battle over Bones. *Archaeology* 50(1):16–22.

Slocum, S.

1975 Woman the Gatherer: Male Bias in Anthropology. In
Toward an Anthropology of Women, edited by R. R.
Reiter, pp. 36–50. Monthly Review Press, New
York.

Smith, D. G., R. S. Malhi, J. Eshleman, A. Redd, M. I. Voevoda,
J. K. Reed, and R. H. Ward

1999 Distribution of Haplogroup X among Native North
Americans. *American Journal of Physical Anthropology* 110:271–284.

Smith, E. A.

1981 The Application of Optimal Foraging Theory to the
Analysis of Hunter-Gatherer Group Size. In *Hunter-
Gatherer Foraging Strategies*, edited by B. Winter-
halder and E. Smith, pp. 36–65. University of
Chicago Press, Chicago.

1983 Anthropological Applications of Optimal Foraging
Theory: A Critical Review. *Current Anthropology* 24:
625–651.

1988 Risk and Uncertainty in the "Original Affluent
Society": Evolutionary Ecology of Resource-Sharing
and Land Tenure. In *History, Evolution, and Social
Change*, edited by T. Ingold, D. Riches, and J. Wood-
burn, pp. 222–251. Hunters and Gatherers, Vol. 1.
Berg Publishers, Oxford.

Smith, E. A., and B. Winterhalder (editors)

1992 *Evolutionary Ecology and Human Behavior.* Aldine de
Gruyter, New York.

Smith, E. E.

1990 Paleoindian Economy and Settlement Patterns
in the Wyandotte Chert Source Area, Unglaciated South-central Indiana. In *Early Paleoindian
Economies of Eastern North America*, edited by K. B.
Tankersley and B. L. Isaac, pp. 217–258. Research
in Economic Anthropology Supplement, No. 5. JAI
Press, Greenwich, Conn.

Smith, E. E., and A. K. L. Freeman

1991 The Archaeological Investigation of a Series of
Early Paleoindian (Clovis) Sites in the Little River
Region of Christian County, Kentucky. *Current
Research in the Pleistocene* 8:41–43.

Smith, F. H.

1976 The Skeletal Remains of the Earliest Americans: A
Survey. *Tennessee Anthropologist* 1:116–147.

Smithsonian Institution

1997 Northern Clans, Northern Traces: Journeys in the
Ancient Circumpolar World. Electronic document,

http://www.mnh.si.edu/arctic/arctic/html/ancient
.html, accessed January 27, 2002.

Snarskis, M. J.
1977 Turrialba (9-FG-T), un sitio paleoindio en el este de Costa Rica. *Vinculos* 3(1/2):13–25.
1979 Turrialba: A Paleo-Indian Quarry and Workshop Site in Eastern Costa Rica. *American Antiquity* 44: 125–138.

Soffer, O.
1985 *The Upper Paleolithic of the Central Russian Plain.* Academic Press, Orlando, Fla.

Soffer, O., J. M. Adovasio, D. C. Hyland, B. Klíma, and J. Svoboda
1998 Perishable Technologies and the Genesis of the Eastern Gravettian. *l'Anthropologie* 36(1/2):43–68.

Soffer, O., and N. D. Praslov (editors)
1993 *From Kostenki to Clovis: Upper Paleolithic-Paleoindian Adaptations.* Plenum Press, New York.

Sørensen, S.
1987 A Maglemosian Hut at Lavringe Mose, Zealand. *Journal of Danish Archaeology* 6:53–62.

Speth, J. D., and K. A. Spielmann
1983 Energy Source, Protein Metabolism, and Hunter-Gatherer Subsistence Strategies. *Journal of Anthropological Archaeology* 2:1–31.

Spiess, A. E., M. L. Curran, and J. R. Grimes
1985 Caribou (*Rangifer tarandus* L.) Bones from New England Paleoindian Sites. *North American Archaeologist* 6:145–159.

Spiess, A. E., and J. Mosher
1994 Hedden: A Paleoindian Site on the Kennebunk Plains. *Maine Archaeological Society Bulletin* 34(2): 25–54.

Spiess, A. E., J. Mosher, K. Callum, and N. A. Sidell
1995 Fire on the Plains: Paleoenvironmental Data from the Hedden Site. *Maine Archaeological Society Bulletin* 35(1):13–52.

Spiess, A. E., and D. B. Wilson
1987 *Michaud A Paleoindian Site in the New England–Maritimes Region.* Occasional Publications in Maine Archaeology, No. 6. Maine Historic Preservation Commission, Augusta.

Spurdle, A. B., M. F. Hammer, and T. Jenkins
1994 The Y Alu Polymorphism in Southern African Populations and Its Relationship to Other Y-Specific Polymorphisms. *American Journal of Human Genetics* 54:319–330.

Stafford, M. D.
1990 The Powers II Site (48PL330): A Paleoindian Red Ochre Mine in Eastern Wyoming. M.A. thesis, University of Wyoming, Laramie.

Stafford, T., V. S. Sellars, and J. R. Johnson
2002 Chronostratigraphy at Arlington Springs, a Paleoindian Site in Insular California. Paper presented at the 67th Annual Meeting of the Society for American Archaeology, Denver.

Stafford, T. W., Jr., P. E. Hare, L. Currie, A. J. T. Jull, and D. Donahue
1990 Accuracy of North American Human Skeleton Ages. *Quaternary Research* 34:111–120.

Stanford, C.
2001 *Significant Others: The Ape-Human Continuum and the Quest for Human Nature.* Basic Books, New York.

Stanford, D. J.
1983 Pre-Clovis Occupation South of the Ice Sheets. In *Early Man in the New World,* edited by R. Shutler, pp. 65–72. Sage Publications, Beverly Hills, Calif.
1991 Clovis Origins and Adaptations: An Introductory Perspective. In *Clovis: Origins and Adaptations,* edited by R. Bonnichsen and K. L. Turnmire, pp. 1–13. Center for the Study of the First Americans, Oregon State University, Corvallis.
1997 Interview. Electronic document, http://www.mnh.si.edu/arctic/arctic/html/dennis_stanford.html, accessed September 2001.
1999a Alternative Views on the Peopling of the Americas. Paper presented at the Clovis and Beyond Conference, Santa Fe, N.Mex.
1999b Paleoindian Archaeology and Late Pleistocene Environments in the Plains and Southwestern United States. In *Ice Age Peoples of North America: Environments, Origins, and Adaptations of the First Americans,* edited by R. Bonnichsen and K. L. Turnmire, pp. 281–339. Oregon State University Press, Corvallis.

Stanford, D. J., and B. Bradley
2000 The Solutrean Solution: Did Some Ancient Americans Come from Europe? *Discovering Archaeology* 2(1).
2002 Ocean Trails and Prairie Paths? Thoughts about Clovis Origins. In *The First Americans: The Pleistocene Colonization of the New World,* edited by N. G. Jablonski, pp. 255–272. Memoirs of the California Academy of Sciences, No. 27. San Francisco.

Stanford, D. J., C. V. Haynes Jr., J. J. Saunders, G. A. Agogino, and A. T. Boldurian
1990 Blackwater Draw Locality 1: History, Current Research, and Interpretations. In *Guidebook to the Quaternary History of the Llano Estacado,* edited by V. T. Holliday and E. Johnson, pp. 105–128. Lubbock Lake Landmark Quaternary Research Center Series, No. 2. Museum of Texas Tech University, Lubbock.

Stanford, D. J., and M. A. Jodry
1988 The Drake Clovis Cache. *Current Research in the Pleistocene* 5:21–22.

Starikovskaya, Y. B., R. I. Sukernik, T. G. Schurr, A. M. Kogelnik, and D. C. Wallace
1998 Mitochondrial DNA Diversity in Chukchi and Siberian Eskimos: Implications for the Genetic Prehistory of Ancient Beringia. *American Journal of Human Genetics* 63:1473–1491.

Starostin, S.
1999 Historical Linguistics and Lexicostatistics. In *His-*

torical Linguistics and Lexicostatistics, edited by V. Shevoroshkin and P. J. Sidwell, pp. 3–50. Association for the History of Language, Melbourne, Australia.

2000 Comparative-Historical Linguistics and Lexicostatistics. In *Time Depth in Historical Linguistics, Vol. 1*, edited by C. Renfrew, A. McMahon, and R. L. Trask, pp. 223–266. Papers in the Prehistory of Languages. McDonald Institute for Archaeological Research, Cambridge, England.

Steele, D. G., and J. F. Powell

1992 Peopling of the Americas: Paleobiological Evidence. *Human Biology* 64:303–336.

2002 Facing the Past: A View of the North American Human Fossil Record. In *The First Americans: The Pleistocene Colonization of the New World*, edited by N. G. Jablonski, pp. 93–122. Memoirs of the California Academy of Sciences, No. 27. San Francisco.

Steele, J., K. Adams, and T. J. Sluckin

1998 Modeling Paleoindian Dispersals. *World Archaeology* 30:286–305.

Steele, J., T. J. Sluckin, D. R. Denholm, and C. S. Gamble

1996 Simulating Hunter-Gatherer Colonization of the Americas. In *Interfacing the Past: Computer Applications and Quantitative Methods in Archaeology*, edited by H. Kamermans and K. Fennema, pp. 223–227. Analecta Praehistoria Leidensia, No. 28. Publications of the Institute of Prehistory, University of Leiden, Leiden.

Steig, E.

2001 No Two Latitudes Alike. *Science* 293:2015–2016.

Stephens, D., and J. Krebs

1986 *Foraging Theory*. Princeton University Press, Princeton, N.J.

Stewart, T. D.

1973 *The People of America*. Weidenfeld and Nicolson, London, and Scribner, New York.

1981 The Evolutionary Status of the First Americans. *American Journal of Physical Anthropology* 56:461–466.

Stiner, M.

1994 *Honor among Thieves: A Zooarchaeological Study of Neandertal Ecology*. Princeton University Press, Princeton, N.J.

Stokes, W. L., M. Anderson, and J. H. Madsen Jr.

1966 Fossil and Sub-fossil Bison of Utah and Southern Idaho. *Proceedings of the Utah Academy of Sciences, Arts, and Letters* 43(2):37–39.

Stokes, W. M., and W. L. Stokes

1980 *Messages on Stone: Selections of Native Western Rock Art*. Starstone Publishing Co., Salt Lake City.

Stone, A. C., and M. Stoneking

1998 mtDNA Analysis of a Prehistoric Oneota Population: Implications for the Peopling of the New World. *American Journal of Human Genetics* 62:1153–1170.

Stone, D. E., and D. R. Yesner

2003 Spatial Distributions of Activities and Prehistoric Human Behavior at the Broken Mammoth Paleoindian Site, Big Delta, Alaska. In *2001: An (Archaeological) Space Odyssey*, edited by Judith Klassen. Proceedings of the 34th Annual Chacmool Conference. Department of Archaeology, University of Calgary, Calgary, Alberta, in press.

Stoneking, M.

2000 Hypervariable Sites in the mtDNA Control Region Are Mutational Hotspots. *American Journal of Human Genetics* 67:1029–1032.

Storck, P. L.

1991 Imperialists without a State: The Cultural Dynamics of Early Paleoindian Colonization as Seen from the Great Lakes Region. In *Clovis: Origins and Adaptations*, edited by R. Bonnichsen and K. L. Turnmire, pp. 153–252. Center for the Study of the First Americans, Oregon State University, Corvallis.

1997 *The Fisher Site: Archaeological, Geological, and Paleobotanical Studies at an Early Paleo-Indian Site in Southern Ontario, Canada*. Memoirs of the Museum of Anthropology, No. 30. University of Michigan, Ann Arbor.

Stothert, K. E.

1985 The Preceramic Las Vegas Culture of Coastal Ecuador. *American Antiquity* 50:613–637.

1988 *La prehistoria temprana de la península de Santa Elena, Ecuador: Cultura las vegas*. Miscelánea Antropológica Ecuatoriana, Serie Monográfica, No. 10. Museos del Banco Central del Ecuador, Guayaquil.

Straus, L., B. Eriksen, J. Erlandson, and D. Yesner (editors)

1998 *As the World Warmed*. Elsevier Science Ltd., Oxford.

Straus, L. G.

1986 An Overview of the La Riera Chronology. In *La Riera Cave: Stone Age Hunter-Gatherer Adaptations in Northern Spain*, edited by L. G. Straus and G. A. Clark, pp. 19–24. Anthropological Research Papers, No. 36. Arizona State University, Tempe.

1992 *Iberia before the Iberians*. University of New Mexico Press, Albuquerque.

2000 Solutrean Settlement of North America? A Review of Reality. *American Antiquity* 65:219–226.

Straus, L. G., and G. A. Clark (editors)

1986 *La Riera Cave: Stone Age Hunter-Gatherer Adaptations in Northern Spain*. Anthropological Research Papers, No. 36. Arizona State University, Tempe.

Straus, L. G., B. V. Eriksen, J. M. Erlandson, and D. R. Yesner (editors)

1996 *Humans at the End of the Ice Age: The Archaeology of the Pleistocene-Holocene Transition*. Plenum Press, New York.

Street, M.

1998 The Archaeology of the Pleistocene–Holocene Transition in the Northern Rhineland, Germany. *Quaternary International* 49/50:45–67.

Stuckenrath, R. J.

1964 The Debert Site: Early Man in the Northeast. *Expedition* 7(1):20–29.

Stuckenrath, R. J., W. R. Coe, and E. K. Ralph

1966 University of Pennsylvania Radiocarbon Dates IX. *Radiocarbon* 8:348–385.

Su, B., J. Xiao, P. Underhill, R. Deka, W. Zhang, J. Akey,
W. Huang, D. Shen, D. Lu, J. Luo, J. Chu, J. Tan, P. Shen,
R. Davis, L. Cavalli-Sforza, R. Chakraborty, M. Xiong, R. Du,
P. Oefner, Z. Chen, and L. Jin
> 1999   Y-Chromosome Evidence for a Northward Migration
> of Modern Humans into Eastern Asia during the
> Last Ice Age. *American Journal of Human Genetics*
> 65:1718–1724.

Su, B., X. Song, Y. Ke, F. Zhang, J. T. Lell, D. T. Wallace, P. A.
Underhill, R. S. Wells, D. Lu, R. Chakraborty, and L. Jin
> 2000   Genetic Evidence for an East Asian Contribution to
> the Second Wave of Migration to the New World.
> *American Journal of Human Genetics, Supplement*
> 67:A236.

Suárez, R.
> 2000   Paleoindian Occupations in Uruguay. *Current Re-*
> *search in the Pleistocene* 17:78–80.

Sukernik, R. I., T. G. Schurr, Y. B. Starikovskaya, and D. C.
Wallace
> 1996   Mitochondrial DNA Variation in Native Siberians,
> with Special Reference to the Evolutionary His-
> tory of American Indians: Studies on Restriction
> Endonuclease Polymorphism. *Genetika* 32:432–439.

Surovell, T.
> 1999   Can a Coastal Migration Explain Monte Verde?
> Paper presented at the Pioneers on the Land: How
> America Got Its People Conference, Arizona State
> University, Tempe.

Surovell, T. A.
> 2000   Early Paleoindian Women, Children, Mobility, and
> Fertility. *American Antiquity* 65(3):493–508.

Svendsen, J. I., V. I. Astakhov, D. Y. Bolshiyanov, I. Demidov,
J. A. Dowdeswell, V. Gataullin, C. Hjort, H. W. Hubberten,
E. Larsen, J. Mangerud, M. Melles, P. Möller, M. Saarnisto, and
M. J. Siegert
> 1999   Maximum Extent of the Eurasian Ice Sheets in the
> Barents and Kara Sea Region during the Weich-
> selian. *Boreas* 28:234–242.

Swadesh, M.
> 1971   *The Origin and Diversification of Languages*. Aldine-
> Atherton, Chicago.

Swauger, J. L., and W. J. Mayer-Oakes
> 1952   A Fluted Point from Costa Rica. *American Antiquity*
> 17:264–265.

Szathmáry, E. J.
> 1986   Comments. *Current Anthropology* 27:490.

Szathmáry, E. J., and N. S. Ossenberg
> 1978   Are the Biological Differences between North
> American Indians and Eskimos Truly Profound?
> *Current Anthropology* 19:673–701.

Szathmáry, E. J. E.
> 1994   Modeling Ancient Population Relationships from
> Modern Population Genetics. In *Method and Theory*
> *for Investigating the Peopling of the Americas*, edited
> by R. Bonnichsen and D. G. Steele, pp. 117–130.
> Center for the Study of the First Americans, Oregon
> State University, Corvallis.

Tankersley, K. B.
> 1985   The Potential for Early Man Sites at Big Bone Lick,
> Kentucky. *Tennessee Anthropologist* 10:27–49.
> 1989a   A Close Look at the Big Picture: Early Paleoindian
> Lithic Procurement in the Midwestern United
> States. In *Paleoindian Lithic Resource Use*, edited
> by C. Ellis and J. Lathrop, pp. 259–292. Westview
> Press, Boulder, Colo.
> 1989b   Late Pleistocene Lithic Exploitation and Human
> Settlement Patterns in the Midwestern United
> States. Ph.D. dissertation, Indiana University,
> Bloomington.
> 1990a   Late Pleistocene Lithic Exploitation in the Mid-
> west and Midsouth: Indiana, Ohio, and Kentucky.
> In *Early Paleoindian Economies of Eastern North*
> *America*, edited by K. B. Tankersley and B. L. Isaac,
> pp. 259–299. Research in Economic Anthropology
> Supplement, No. 5. JAI Press, Greenwich, Conn.
> 1990b   Paleoindian Period. In *The Archaeology of Ken-*
> *tucky: Past Accomplishments and Future Directions*,
> edited by D. Pollack, pp. 73–142. Kentucky Heritage
> Council, Frankfort.
> 1991   A Geoarchaeological Investigation of Distribution
> and Exchange in the Raw Material Economies
> of Clovis Groups in Eastern North America. In
> *Raw Material Economies among Prehistoric Hunter-*
> *Gatherers*, edited by A. Montet-White and S. Holen,
> pp. 285–303. Publications in Anthropology, No. 19.
> University of Kansas Press, Lawrence.
> 1994a   The Effects of Stone and Technology on Fluted-
> Point Morphometry. *American Antiquity* 59:498–510.
> 1994b   Was Clovis a Colonizing Population in Eastern North
> America? In *The First Discovery of America*, edited by
> W. Dancey, pp. 95–116. Ohio Archaeological Council,
> Columbus.
> 1995   Paleoindian Contexts and Artifact Distribution Pat-
> terns at the Bostrom Site, St. Clair County, Illinois.
> *Midcontinental Journal of Archaeology* 20:40–61.
> 1996   Ice Age Hunters and Gatherers. In *The Prehis-*
> *tory of Kentucky*, edited by R. B. Lewis, pp. 21–38.
> University of Kentucky Press, Lexington.
> 1997   Sheriden: A Clovis Cave Site in Eastern North
> America. *Geoarchaeology* 12(6):713–724.
> 1998a   Clovis Cultural Complex. In *Archaeology of Pre-*
> *historic Native America: An Encyclopedia*, edited by
> G. Gibbon, pp. 161–163. Garland Publishing, New
> York.
> 1998b   The Crook County Cache. *Current Research in the*
> *Pleistocene* 15:86–88.
> 1998c   Variation in the Early Paleoindian Economies of
> Late Pleistocene Eastern North America. *American*
> *Antiquity* 63(1):7–20.

Tankersley, K. B., K. M. Ford, H. G. McDonald, R. A. Genheimer,
and R. Hendricks
> 1997   Late-Pleistocene Archaeology of Sheriden Cave,
> Wyandot County, Ohio. *Current Research in the*
> *Pleistocene* 14:81–83.

Tankersley, K. B., and J. D. Holland
> 1994   Lithic Procurement Patterns at the Paleo-Crossing

Site, Medina County, Ohio. *Current Research in the Pleistocene* 11:61–63.

Tankersley, K. B., and B. L. Isaac

1990a Concluding Remarks on Paleoecology and Paleoeconomy. In *Early Paleoindian Economies of Eastern North America*, edited by K. B. Tankersley and B. L. Isaac, pp. 337–355. Research in Economic Anthropology Supplement, No. 5. JAI Press, Greenwich, Conn.

1990b Introduction. In *Early Paleoindian Economies of Eastern North America*, edited by K. B. Tankersley and B. L. Isaac, pp. xi–xv. Research in Economic Anthropology Supplement, No. 5. JAI Press, Greenwich, Conn.

Tankersley, K. B., B. Koldehoff, and E. Hajic

1993 The Bostrom Site: A Paleo-Indian Habitation in Southwestern Illinois. *North American Archaeologist* 14:43–70.

Tankersley, K. B., and C. S. Landefeld

1998 Geochronology of Sheriden Cave, Ohio: The 1997 Field Season. *Current Research in the Pleistocene* 15:136–138.

Tankersley, K. B., and J. E. Morrow

1993 Clovis Procurement and Land-Use Patterns in the Confluence Region of the Mississippi, Missouri, and Illinois River Valleys. In *Highways to the Past*, edited by T. Emerson, A. Fortier, and D. McElrath, pp. 119–129. Illinois Archaeological Survey, Champaign.

Tankersley, K. B., and B. G. Redmond

1999 Radiocarbon Dating of a Paleoindian Projectile Point from Sheriden Cave, Ohio. *Current Research in the Pleistocene* 16:76–77.

Tankersley, K. B., and E. E. Smith

1992 Clovis in Kaintuckee. In *Paleoindian and Early Archaic Period Research in the Lower Southeast: A South Carolina Perspective*, edited by D. G. Anderson, K. E. Sassaman, and C. Judge, pp. 322–329. Council of South Carolina Professional Archaeologists, Columbia.

Tankersley, K. B., K. O. Tankersley, N. R. Shaffer, M. D. Hess, J. S. Benz, F. R. Turner, M. D. Stafford, G. M. Zeimens, and G. C. Frison

1999 They Have a Rock That Bleeds: Sunrise Red Ochre and Its Early Paleoindian Occurrence at the Hell Gap Site, Wyoming. *Plains Anthropologist* 40:185–194.

Taylor, K.

1999 Rapid Climate Change. *American Scientist* 87:320–327.

Taylor, R. E., C. V. Haynes Jr., and M. Stuiver

1996 Clovis and Folsom Age Estimates: Stratigraphic Context and Radiocarbon Calibration. *Antiquity* 70:515–525.

Taylor, R. E., L. A. Payen, C. A. Prior, P. J. Slota Jr., R. Gillespie, J. A. J. Gowlett, R. E. M. Hedges, A. J. T. Jull, T. H. Zabel, D. J. Donahue, and R. Berger

1985 Major Revisions in the Pleistocene Age Assignments for North American Human Skeletons by C-14 Accelerator Mass Spectrometry: None Older Than 11,000 Years B.P. *American Antiquity* 50(1):136–140.

Terrell, J.

1990 Storytelling and Prehistory. In *Archaeological Method and Theory*, Vol. 2, edited by M. B. Schiffer, pp. 1–29. University of Arizona Press, Tucson.

Tesar, L. D.

2000 *Comments on Earliest American Theme Study*. Division of Historical Resources, Florida Department of State, Tallahassee.

Thompson, W.

1993 Where Have All the Mammoths Gone? *Patina* 1:1–23.

Thomson, R., J. K. Pritchard, P. Shen, P. J. Oefner, and M. W. Feldman

2000 Recent Common Ancestry of Human Y Chromosomes: Evidence from DNA Sequence Data. *Proceedings of the National Academy of Sciences of the United States of America* 97:7360–7365.

Thornhill, N. W.

1990 The Evolutionary Significance of Incest Rules. *Ethology and Sociobiology* 11:113–129.

Thorpe, I. J.

1996 *The Origins of Agriculture in Europe*. Routlege, New York.

Tilley, C.

1989 Archaeology as Socio-political Action in the Present. In *Critical Traditions in Contemporary Archaeology: Essays in the Philosophy, History, and Socio-politics of Archaeology*, edited by V. Pinsky and A. Wylie, pp. 104–116. Cambridge University Press, Cambridge.

1990 On Modernity and Archaeological Discourse. In *Archaeology after Structuralism. Post-structuralism and the Practice of Archaeology*, edited by I. Bapty and T. Yates, pp. 128–152. Routledge, London.

Titmus, G. L., and J. C. Woods

1991 Fluted Points from the Snake River Plain. In *Clovis: Origins and Adaptations*, edited by R. Bonnichsen and K. L. Turnmire, pp. 119–131. Center for the Study of the First Americans, Oregon State University, Corvallis.

Todd, L. C., D. J. Rapson, and J. L. Hofman

1996 Dentition Studies of the Mill Iron Site and Other Early Paleoindian Bison Bonebed Sites. In *The Mill Iron Site*, edited by G. C. Frison, pp. 145–175. University of New Mexico Press, Albuquerque.

Tokunaga, K., and T. Juji

1993 Genetic Link between East Asians and Amerindians: Evidence from HLA Haplotypes. *Current Research in the Pleistocene* 10:46–47.

Tomenchuk, J., and P. L. Storck

1997 Two Newly Recognized Paleoindian Tool Types: Single- and Double-Scribe Compass Gravers and Coring Gravers. *American Antiquity* 62(3):508–522.

Tompkins, C. N.

1993 Classifying Clovis Points: A Study in Metric Variability. M.A. thesis, University of Arizona, Tucson.

Torrence, R.
1989   Retooling: Towards a Behavioral Theory of Stone Tools. In *Time Energy and Stone Tools*, edited by R. Torrence, pp. 57–66. Cambridge University Press, Cambridge.

Torroni, A., H.-J. Bandelt, L. D'Urbano, P. Lahermo, P. Moral, D. Sellitto, C. Rengo, P. Forster, M.-L. Savontaus, B. Bonné-Tamir, and R. Scozzari
1998   mtDNA Analysis Reveals a Major Late Paleolithic Population Expansion from Southwestern to Northwestern Europe. *American Journal of Human Genetics* 62:1137–1152.

Torroni, A., M. D. Brown, M. T. Lott, N. J. Newman, and D. C. Wallace
1995   African, Native American, and European Mitochondrial DNAs in Cubans from the Pinar del Río Province and Implications for the Recent Epidemic Neuropathy in Cuba. *Human Mutation* 5:310–317.

Torroni, A., Y. S. Chen, O. Semino, A. S. Santachiara-Benerecetti, C. R. Scott, M. T. Lott, M. Winter, and D. C. Wallace
1994a   mtDNA and Y-Chromosome Polymorphisms in Four Native American Populations from Southern Mexico. *American Journal of Human Genetics* 54:303–318.

Torroni, A., K. Huoponen, P. Francalacci, M. Petrozzi, L. Morelli, R. Scozzari, D. Obinu, M.-L. Savontaus, and D. C. Wallace
1996   Classification of European mtDNAs from an Analysis of Three European Populations. *Genetics* 144:1835–1850.

Torroni, A., M. T. Lott, M. F. Cabell, Y. S. Chen, L. Lavergne, and D. C. Wallace
1994b   mtDNA and the Origin of Caucasians: Identification of Ancient Caucasian-Specific Haplogroups, One of Which Is Prone to a Recurrent Somatic Duplication in the D-Loop Region. *American Journal of Human Genetics* 55:760–776.

Torroni, A., J. A. Miller, L. G. Moore, S. Zamudio, J. Zhuang, T. Droma, and D. C. Wallace
1994c   Mitochondrial DNA Analysis in Tibet: Implications for the Origin of the Tibetan Population and Its Adaptation to High Altitude. *American Journal of Physical Anthropology* 93:189–199.

Torroni, A., J. V. Neel, R. Barrantes, T. G. Schurr, and D. C. Wallace
1994d   A Mitochondrial DNA "Clock" for the Amerinds and Its Implications for Timing Their Entry into North America. *Proceedings of the National Academy of Sciences of the United States of America* 91:1158–1162.

Torroni, A., T. G. Schurr, M. F. Cabell, M. D. Brown, J. V. Neel, M. Larsen, D. G. Smith, C. M. Vullo, and D. C. Wallace
1993a   Asian Affinities and the Continental Radiation of the Four Founding Native American mtDNAs. *American Journal of Human Genetics* 53:563–590.

Torroni, A., T. G. Schurr, C. C. Yang, E. J. Szathmáry, R. C. Williams, M. S. Schanfield, G. A. Troup, W. C. Knowler, D. N. Lawrence, and K. M. Weiss
1992   Native American Mitochondrial DNA Analysis Indicates That the Amerind and the Na-Dene Populations Were Founded by Two Independent Migrations. *Genetics* 130:153–162.

Torroni, A., R. I. Sukernik, T. G. Schurr, Y. B. Starikovskaya, M. F. Cabell, M. H. Crawford, A. G. Comuzzie, and D. C. Wallace
1993b   mtDNA Variation of Aboriginal Siberians Reveals Distinct Genetic Affinities with Native Americans. *American Journal of Human Genetics* 53:591–608.

Trigger, B. G.
1986   Prospects for a World Archaeology. *World Archaeology* 18(1):1–20.
1989   History and Contemporary American Archaeology: A Critical Analysis. In *Archaeological Thought in America*, edited by G. G. Lamberg-Karlovsky, pp. 19–34. Cambridge University Press, Cambridge.

Tuck, J. A.
1976   *Ancient People of Port au Choix: The Excavation of an Archaic Indian Cemetery in Newfoundland*. Social and Economic Studies, No. 17. Memorial University of Newfoundland, St. Johns.

Tumen, D.
1994   *Proceedings of the Korean-Mongolian Joint Research Project "Eastern Mongolia."* Seoul University Press, Seoul.

Turnbull, C. M.
1981   Mbuti Womanhood. In *Woman the Gatherer*, edited by F. Dahlberg, pp. 205–219. Yale University Press, New Haven, Conn.

Turner, C. G., II
1971   Three-Rooted Mandibular First Permanent Molars and the Question of American Indian Origins. *American Journal of Physical Anthropology* 34:229–241.
1983   Dental Evidence for the Peopling of the Americas. In *Early Man in the New World*, edited by R. Shutler, pp. 147–157. Sage Publications, Beverly Hills, Calif.
1985   The Dental Search for Native American Origins. In *Out of Asia*, edited by R. Kirk and E. Szathmáry, pp. 31–78. Journal of Pacific History, Inc., Australian National University, Canberra.
1986   The First Americans: The Dental Evidence. *National Geographic Research* 2(1):37–46.
1988   Teeth and Prehistory in Asia. *Scientific American* 260:88–96.
1994a   Dental and Archaeological Evidence for the Peopling of the Americas: An Intercontinental Perspective. Paper presented at the Joseph Greenberg Conference, University of Colorado, Boulder.
1994b   New Dental Anthropological Observations Relevant to the Human Population System of the Greater Beringian Realm. In *Anthropology of the North Pacific Rim*, edited by W. W. Fitzhugh and V. Chaussonnet, pp. 97–106. Smithsonian Institution Press, Washington, D.C.
1998   An Update on the Dental Anthropological Interpretation of the Peopling of Siberia and the Americas. In *International Symposium: Siberian Panorama through Millennia, Vol. 2*, edited by A. P. Derevyanko, pp. 180–188. Institute of Archaeology and Ethnography, Russian Academy of Science, Siberian Branch, Novosibirsk.

1999 Teeth, Needles, Dogs, and Siberia: Bioarchaeo-logical Evidence for the Colonization of the New World. Paper presented at the California Academy of Sciences Watts Symposium, San Francisco.

2002 Teeth, Needles, Dogs, and Siberia: Bioarchaeological Evidence for the Colonization of the New World. In *The First Americans: The Pleistocene Colonization of the New World*, edited by N. G. Jablonski, pp. 123–158. Memoirs of the California Academy of Sciences, No. 27. San Francisco.

Turner, C. G., II, Y. Manabe, and D. Hawkey
2000 The Zhoukoudian Upper Cave Dentition. *Acta Anthropologica Sinica* 19(4):253–268.

Turner, F. J.
1893 *The Significance of the Frontier in American History*. State Historical Society of Wisconsin, Madison.

Underhill, P. A., L. Jin, A. A. Lin, S. Q. Mehdi, T. Jenkins, D. Vollrath, R. W. Davis, L. L. Cavalli-Sforza, and P. J. Oefner
1997 Detection of Numerous Y Chromosome Biallelic Polymorphisms by Denaturing High Performance Liquid Chromatography. *Genome Research* 7:996–1005.

Underhill, P. A., L. Jin, R. Zemans, P. J. Oefner, and L. L. Cavalli-Sforza
1996 A Pre-Columbian Y Chromosome-Specific Transition and Its Implications for Human Evolutionary History. *Proceedings of the National Academy of Sciences of the United States of America* 93:196–200.

Underhill, P. A., P. Shen, A. A. Lin, L. Jin, G. Passarino. W. H. Yang, E. Kauffman, B. Bonné-Tamir, J. Bertranpetit, P. Francalacci, M. Ibrahim, T. Jenkins, J. R. Kidd, S. Q. Mehdi, M. T. Seielstad, R. S. Wells, A. Piazza, R. W. Davis, M. W. Feldman, L. L. Cavalli-Sforza, and P. Oefner
2000 Y Chromosome Sequence Variation and the History of Human Populations. *Nature Genetics* 26:358–361.

van Andel, T. H.
2002 The Climate and Landscape of the Middle Part of the Weichselian Glaciation in Europe: The Stage 3 Project. *Quaternary Research* 57(1):2–8.

Vanders, I., and P. F. Kerr
1967 *Mineral Recognition*. Wiley & Sons, New York.

van Dyne, G. M., N. Brockington, Z. Szocs, J. Duek, and C. Ribic
1980 Large Herbivore System. In *Grasslands, Systems Analysis, and Man*, edited by A. I. Breymeyer and G. M. van Dyne, pp. 269–537. Cambridge University Press, Cambridge.

Vansina, J.
1995 New Linguistic Evidence and the Bantu Expansion. *Journal of African History* 36(2):173–195.

van Wyk, P., and N. Fairfall
1969 The Influence of the African Elephant on the Vegetation of the Kruger National Park. *Keodoe* 12:57–89.

Vekua, A., D. Lordkipanidze, G. P. Rightmire, J. Agusti, R. Ferring, G. Maisuradze, A. Mouskhelishvili, M. Nioradze, M. Ponce de Leon, M. Tappen, M. Tvalchrelidze, and C. Zollikofer
2002 A New Skull of Early *Homo* from Dmanisi, Georgia. *Science* 297:85–89.

Versteeg, A. H.
1998 Peuplements et environnements dans les Guyanes entre 10.000 et 1.000 BP. Paper presented at the Seminaire Atelier Peuplement Anciens et Actuels des Forêts Tropicales, Orléans, France.

Vigilant, L., M. Stoneking, H. Harpending, K. Hawkes, and A. C. Wilson
1991 African Populations and the Evolution of Human Mitochondrial DNA. *Science* 253:1503–1513.

Vila, C., P. Savolainen, J. E. Maldonado, I. R. Amorim, J. E. Rice, R. L. Honeycutt, K. A. Crandall, J. Lundeberg, and R. K. Wayne
1997 Multiple and Ancient Origins of the Domestic Dog. *Science* 276:1687–1689.

Wadley, L.
1998 The Invisible Meat Providers. In *Gender in African Prehistory*, edited by S. Kent, pp. 69–81. AltaMira Press, Walnut Creek, Calif.

Wakeley, J.
1993 Substitution Rate Variation among Sites in Hypervariable Region I of Human Mitochondrial DNA. *Journal of Molecular Evolution* 37:613–623.

Walde, D., and N. Willows (editors)
1991 *The Archaeology of Gender: Proceedings of the Twenty-Second Annual Conference of the Archaeological Association of the University of Calgary*. University of Calgary Archaeological Association, Calgary, Alberta.

Walker, B. H., R. H. Emslie, N. Owen-Smith, and R. J. Scholes
1987 To Cull or Not to Cull: Lessons from a Southern African Drought. *Journal of Applied Ecology* 24:381–401.

Walker, D. N.
1982 Early Holocene Vertebrate Fauna. In *The Agate Basin Site: A Record of the Paleoindian Occupation of the Northwestern High Plains*, edited by G. C. Frison and D. J. Stanford, pp. 274–308. Academic Press, New York.

Walker, D. N., and G. C. Frison
1986 The Late Pleistocene Mammalian Fauna from the Colby Mammoth Kill Site, Wyoming. In *The Colby Mammoth Site: Taphonomy and Archaeology of a Clovis Kill in Northern Wyoming*, edited by L. C. Todd, pp. 191–205. University of New Mexico Press, Albuquerque.

Wallace, D. C., M. D. Brown, and M. T. Lott
1999 Mitochondrial DNA Variation in Human Evolution and Disease. *Gene* 238:211–230.

Wallace, D. C., K. Garrison, and W. C. Knowler
1985 Dramatic Founder Effects in Amerindian Mitochondrial DNAs. *American Journal of Physical Anthropology* 68:149–155.

Wallace, D. C., and A. Torroni
1992 American Indian Prehistory as Written in the Mitochondrial DNA: A Review. *Human Biology* 64:403–416.

Ward, J. H., Jr.
1963 Hierarchical Grouping to Optimize an Objective Function. *Journal of the American Statistical Association* 58:236–244.

Ward, R. H.
  1996   Linguistic Divergence and Genetic Evolution: A Molecular Perspective from the New World. In *Molecular Biology and Human Diversity*, edited by A. J. Boyce and C. G. N. Mascie-Taylor, pp. 205–223. Cambridge University Press, Cambridge.

Ward, R. H., B. L. Frazier, K. Dew-Jager, and S. Pääbo
  1991   Extensive Mitochondrial Diversity within a Single Amerindian Tribe. *Proceedings of the National Academy of Sciences of the United States of America* 88: 8720–8724.

Ward, R. H., A. Redd, D. Valencia, B. Frazier, and S. Pääbo
  1993   Genetic and Linguistic Differentiation in the Americas. *Proceedings of the National Academy of Sciences of the United States of America* 90:10063–10067.

Ward, R. H., F. M. Salzano, S. L. Bonatto, M. H. Hutz, C. E. A. Coimbra Jr., and R. V. Santos
  1996   Mitochondrial DNA Polymorphism in Three Brazilian Indian Tribes. *American Journal of Human Biology* 8:317–323.

Warnica, J. M.
  1966   New Discoveries at the Clovis Site. *American Antiquity* 31:345–357.

Watkins, J.
  1998   At What Point "Ours," at What Point "Yours." Paper presented at the 31st Annual Chacmool Conference, University of Calgary, Calgary, Alberta.

Waur, R. H.
  1965   *Pictograph Site in Cave Valley, Zion National Park, Utah*. Anthropological Papers, No. 75. University of Utah, Salt Lake City.

Webb, E., and D. Rindos
  1997   The Mode and Tempo of the Initial Colonization of Empty Landmasses: Sahul and the Americas Compared. In *Rediscovering Darwin: Evolutionary Theory in Archeological Explanation*, edited by C. M. Barton and G. A. Clark, pp. 233–250. Archeological Papers of the American Anthropological Association, No. 7. Washington, D.C.

Webb, R. E.
  1998   Megamarsupial Extinction: The Carrying Capacity Argument. *Antiquity* 72(275):46–55.

Webb, W. S.
  1931   *The Great Plains*. Ginn and Company, Boston.
  1946   *Indian Knoll, Site OH2, Ohio County, Kentucky*. Publications of the Department of Anthropology and Archaeology, No. 4. University of Kentucky Press, Lexington.

Weber, J. L., and C. Wong
  1993   Mutation of Human Short Tandem Repeats. *Human Molecular Genetics* 2:1123–1128.

Webster, D.
  1981   Late Pleistocene Extinction and Human Predation: A Critical Overview. In *Omnivorous Primates: Gathering and Hunting in Human Evolution*, edited by R. S. O. Harding and G. Teleki, pp. 53–74. Columbia University Press, New York.

Weiss, K. M., and E. Woolford
  1986   Comments. *Current Anthropology* 27:491–492.

Wendorf, M.
  1989   Diabetes, the Ice-Free Corridor, and the Paleoindian Settlement of North America. *American Journal of Physical Anthropology* 79:503–520.

Wenke, R. J.
  1989   Comments on "Archaeology into the 1990's." *Norwegian Archaeological Review* 22:31–33.

West, F. H.
  1975   Dating the Denali Complex. *Arctic Anthropology* 12(1):76–81.
  1983   The Antiquity of Man in America. In *Late-Quaternary Environments of the United States*, edited by H. E. Wright, pp. 364–384. University of Minnesota Press, Minneapolis.
  1996a   Beringia and New World Origins: The Archaeological Evidence. In *American Beginnings: The Prehistory and Palaeoecology of Beringia*, edited by F. H. West, pp. 537–559. University of Chicago Press, Chicago.

West, F. H. (editor)
  1996b   *American Beginnings: The Prehistory and Paleoecology of Beringia*. University of Chicago Press, Chicago.

Whallon, R.
  1989   Elements of Culture Change in the Later Palaeolithic. In *The Human Revolution: Behavioral and Biological Perspectives on the Origins of Modern Humans*, edited by P. Mellars and C. Stringer, pp. 433–454. Princeton University Press, Princeton, N.J.

White, J.
  2000   Ice Core Records of Rapid and Abrupt Climate Change: Data and Theory. Paper presented at the Climate Change and Human Responses Conference, Fort Burgwin Research Center, Ranchos de Taos, N.Mex.

Whitley, D. S., and R. I. Dorn
  1993   New Perspectives on the Clovis vs. Pre-Clovis Controversy. *American Antiquity* 58(4):626–647.

Whitlock, C., and L. Grigg
  1999   Paleoecological Evidence of Milankovitch Climate Variations in the Western U.S. during the Late Quaternary. In *Mechanisms of Global Climate Change at Millennial Time Scales*, edited by P. Clark, R. S. Webb, and L. Keigwin, pp. 227–241. American Geophysical Union, Washington, D.C.

Whitney-Smith, E.
  1996   War, Information, and History: Changing Paradigms. In *Cyberwar: Security and Conflict in the Information Age*, edited by A. D. Campen, D. H. Dearth, and R. T. Goodden, pp. 53–71. Armed Forces Communications and Electronics Association (AFCEA), Fairfax, Va.
  2001   Second Order Predation and Pleistocene Extinctions: A System Dynamics Model. Ph.D. dissertation, Harvard University, Cambridge.

Whitridge, P. J.
  2001   Zen Fish: A Consideration of the Discordance between Zooarchaeological and Artifactual Indicators

of Thule Inuit Fish Use. *Journal of Anthropological Archaeology* 20(1):3–72.

Whitthoft, J.
1952 A Paleo-Indian Site in Eastern Pennsylvania: An Early Hunting Culture. *Proceedings of the American Philosophical Society* 96:1–32.

Whittington, S. L., and B. Dyke
1984 Simulating Overkill: Experiments with the Mosimann and Martin Model. In *Quaternary Extinctions: A Prehistoric Revolution*, edited by P. S. Martin and R. G. Klein, pp. 451–466. University of Arizona Press, Tucson.

Whittle, A. W. R.
1996 *Europe in the Neolithic: The Creation of New Worlds.* Cambridge University Press, Cambridge.

Wiessner, P.
1982 Risk, Reciprocity, and Social Influences on !Kung San Economics. In *Politics and History in Band Societies*, edited by E. Leacock and R. B. Lee, pp. 61–84. Cambridge University Press, London.

Wilford, J.
1999 New Answers to an Old Question: Who Got Here First? *New York Times* November 9:F1.

Wilke, P. J., J. J. Flenniken, and T. L. Ozbun
1991 Clovis Technology at the Anzick Site, Montana. *Journal of California and Great Basin Anthropology* 13: 242–272.

Williams, D.
1998 The Archaic Colonization of the Western Guiana Littoral and Its Aftermath. *Archaeology and Anthropology* 12:22–41.

Williams, R. C.
1999 Molecular Variation at the HLA Loci in American Indians: Implications for Population History. Paper presented at the Pioneers on the Land: How America Got Its People Conference, Arizona State University, Tempe.

Williams, R. C., A. G. Steinberg, H. Gershowitz, P. H. Bennett, W. C. Knowler, D. J. Pettitt, W. Butler, R. Baird, L. Dowda-Rea, T. A. Burch, H. G. Morse, and G. S. Charline
1985 GM Allotypes in Native Americans: Evidence for Three Distinct Migrations across the Bering Land Bridge. *American Journal of Physical Anthropology* 66:1–19.

Williams, S., and J. B. Stoltman
1965 An Outline of Southeastern United States Prehistory with Particular Emphasis on the Paleoindian Era. In *The Quaternary of the United States*, edited by H. E. Wright and D. G. Frey, pp. 669–683. Princeton University Press, Princeton, N.J.

Willig, J. A.
1990 Western Clovis Occupation at the Dietz Site, Northern Alkali Lake Basin, Oregon. *Current Research in the Pleistocene* 7:52–56.
1991 Clovis Technology and Adaptation in Far Western North America: Regional Pattern and Environmental Context. In *Clovis: Origins and Adaptations*, edited by R. Bonnichsen and K. L. Turnmire, pp.

91–118. Center for the Study of the First Americans, Oregon State University, Corvallis.
1996 Environmental Context for Early Human Occupation in Western North America. In *Prehistoric Mongoloid Dispersals*, edited by T. Akazawa and E. J. E. Szathmáry, pp. 241–253. Oxford University Press, Oxford.

Willig, J. A., and C. M. Aikens
1988 The Clovis-Archaic Interface in Far Western North America. In *Early Human Occupation in Far Western North America: The Clovis-Archaic Interface*, edited by J. L. Fagan, pp. 1–40. Anthropological Papers, No. 21. Nevada State Museum, Carson City.

Wilmeth, R.
1968 A Fossilized Bone Artifact from Southern Saskatchewan. *American Antiquity* 33:100–101.
1978 *Canadian Archaeological Radiocarbon Dates (Revised Version).* Archaeological Survey of Canada, Mercury Series Paper, No. 77. National Museum of Man, Ottawa.

Wilmsen, E. N.
1973 Interaction, Spacing Behavior, and the Organization of Hunting Bands. *Journal of Anthropological Research* 29:1–31.

Wilmsen, E. N., and F. H. H. Roberts Jr.
1978 *Lindenmeier, 1934–1974: Concluding Report on Investigations.* Smithsonian Contributions to Anthropology, No. 24. Smithsonian Institution Press, Washington, D.C.

Wilson, E. O.
1975 *Sociobiology: The New Synthesis.* Belknap Press, Cambridge, Mass.
1998 *Consilience: The Unity of Knowledge.* Alfred Knopf, New York.

Wilson, M. C.
1996 Late Quaternary Vertebrates and the Opening of the Ice-Free Corridor, with Special Reference to the Genus Bison. *Quaternary International* 32:97–105.

Winkler, M. G.
1997 Late Quaternary Climate, Fire, and Vegetation Dynamics. In *Sediment Records of Biomass Burning and Global Change*, edited by B. Stocks, pp. 329–346. Springer-Verlag, Berlin.

Winterhalder, B., W. Baillargeon, F. Cappalleto, R. Daniel, and C. Prescott
1988 The Population Dynamics of Hunter-Gatherers and Their Prey. *Journal of Anthropological Archaeology* 7: 289–328.

Winterhalder, B., and C. Goland
1997 An Evolutionary Ecology Perspective on Diet Choice, Risk, and Plant Domestication. In *People, Plants, and Landscapes: Studies in Paleoethnobotany*, edited by K. Gremillion, pp. 123–160. University of Alabama Press, Tuscaloosa.

Winterhalder, B., and E. A. Smith
2000 Analyzing Adaptive Strategies: Human Behavioral Ecology at Twenty-Five. *Evolutionary Anthropology* 9(2):51–72.

Winters, H.
1968   Value Systems and Trade Cycles of the Late Archaic in the Midwest. In *New Perspectives in Archaeology*, edited by S. R. Binford and L. R. Binford, pp. 175–222. Aldine, Chicago.

Wisner, G.
1999   Channel Island Woman May Be Oldest Yet: Bones Archived within Sediments Yield New Dates. *Mammoth Trumpet* 14:1, 16–18.

Wobst, H. M.
1974   Boundary Conditions for Paleolithic Social Systems: A Simulation Approach. *American Antiquity* 39(2): 147–178.
1975   The Demography of Finite Populations and the Origins of the Incest Taboo. In *Population Studies in Archaeology and Biological Anthropology: A Symposium*, edited by A. C. Swedlund, pp. 75–81. Memoirs of the Society for American Archaeology, No. 30. Washington, D.C.

Woods, J. C., and G. L. Titmus
1985   A Review of the Simon Clovis Collection. *Idaho Archaeologist* 8:3–8.

Wormington, H. M.
1949   *Ancient Man in North America*. 3rd ed. Popular Series, No. 4. Denver Museum of Natural History, Denver.
1957   *Ancient Man in North America*. 4th ed. Popular Series, No. 4. Denver Museum of Natural History, Denver.

Wright, H. E., Jr.
1991   Environmental Conditions for Paleoindian Immigration. In *The First Americans: Search and Research*, edited by T. D. Dillehay and D. J. Meltzer, pp. 113–135. CRC Press, Boca Raton, Fla.

Wright, H. T.
1996   Comments. In *The Paleoindian and Early Archaic Southeast*, edited by D. G. Anderson and K. E. Sassaman, pp. 430–433. University of Alabama Press, Tuscaloosa.

Wright, R. P. (editor)
1996   *Gender and Archaeology*. University of Pennsylvania Press, Philadelphia.

Wylie, A.
1989   Introduction: Socio-political Context. In *Critical Traditions in Contemporary Archaeology: Essays in the Philosophy, History, and Socio-politics of Archaeology*, edited by V. Pinsky and A. Wylie, pp. 93–95. Cambridge University Press, Cambridge.
2000   Questions of Evidence, Legitimacy, and the (Dis)-union of Science. *American Antiquity* 65:227–238.

Y Chromosome Consortium
2002   A Nomenclature System for the Tree of Human Y-Chromosomal Binary Haplogroups. *Genome Research* 12:339–348.

Yellen, J. E.
1976   Long-Term Hunter-Gatherer Adaptation to Desert Environments: A Biogeographical Perspective. *World Archaeology* 8:262–274.
1977   *Archaeological Approaches to the Present: Models for Reconstructing the Past*. Academic Press, New York.

Yellen, J. E., and H. Harpending
1972   Hunter-Gatherer Populations and Archaeological Inference. *World Archaeology* 4:244–253.

Yengoyan, A. A.
1968   Demographic and Ecological Influences on Aboriginal Australian Marriage Sections. In *Man the Hunter*, edited by R. B. Lee and I. Devore, pp. 185–199. Aldine, New York.

Yesner, D. R.
1980   Maritime Hunter-Gatherers: Ecology and Prehistory. *Current Anthropology* 21:727–750.
1994   Subsistence Diversity and Hunter-Gatherer Strategies in Late Pleistocene/Early Holocene Beringia: Evidence from the Broken Mammoth Site, Big Delta, Alaska. *Current Research in the Pleistocene* 11: 154–156.
1996a   Environments and Peoples at the Pleistocene-Holocene Boundary in the Americas. In *Humans at the End of the Ice Age: The Archaeology of the Pleistocene-Holocene Transition*, edited by L. G. Straus, B. V. Eriksen, J. M. Erlandson, and D. R. Yesner, pp. 243–254. Plenum Press, New York.
1996b   Human Adaptation at the Pleistocene-Holocene Boundary in Eastern Beringia. In *Humans at the End of the Ice Age: The Archaeology of the Pleistocene-Holocene Transition*, edited by L. G. Straus, B. V. Eriksen, J. M. Erlandson, and D. R. Yesner, pp. 255–272. Plenum Press, New York.
1998   Origins and Development of Maritime Adaptations in the Northwest Pacific Region of North America: A Zooarchaeological Perspective. *Arctic Anthropology* 35(1):204–222.
2000   Human Colonization of Eastern Beringia and the Question of Mammoth Hunting. In *Mammoth Site Studies*, edited by D. L. West, pp. 69–84. Publications in Anthropology, No. 22. University of Kansas, Lawrence.
2001   Human Dispersal into Interior Alaska: Antecedent Conditions, Mode of Colonization, and Adaptations. *Quaternary Science Reviews* 20:315–327.
2004   *The Nenana Complex and the Colonization of Interior Alaska*. Anthropological Papers, New Series. University of Alaska, Fairbanks, in press.

Yesner, D. R., N. D. Hamilton, and R. A. Doyle
1983   "Landlocked" Salmon and Early Holocene Lacustrine Adaptations in Southwestern Maine. *North American Archaeologist* 4:307–319.

Yesner, D. R., C. E. Holmes, and K. J. Crossen
1992   Archaeology and Paleoecology of the Broken Mammoth Site, Central Tanana Valley, Interior Alaska. *Current Research in the Pleistocene* 9:1–12.

Yesner, D. R., and G. A. Pearson
2002   Microblades and Migrations: Ethnic and Economic Models in the Peopling of the Americas. In *Thinking Small: Global Perspectives on Microlithization*, edited by R. G. Elston and S. L. Kuhn, pp. 133–162.

Archeological Papers of the American Anthropological Association, No. 12. American Anthropological Association, Arlington, Va.

Yesner, D. R., G. A. Pearson, and D. E. Stone
2000 Additional Organic Artifacts from the Broken Mammoth Site, Big Delta, Alaska. *Current Research in the Pleistocene* 17:87–89.

Yi, S., and G. A. Clark
1983 Observations on the Lower Paleolithic of China. *Current Anthropology* 24(2):181–190, 196–202.
1985 The "Dyuktai Culture" and New World Origins. *Current Anthropology* 26:1–20.

Yoaciel, S. M.
1981 Change in the Populations of Large Herbivores and in the Vegetation Community in Meywa Peninsula, Rwenzori National Park, Uganda. *African Journal of Ecology* 19:303–312.

York, R.
1990 Evidence for Paleoindians on the San Juan National Forest, Southwest Colorado. Manuscript on file, U.S. Department of Agriculture, Forest Service, San Juan National Forest, Durango, Colo.

Young, B., and M. B. Collins
1989 A Cache of Blades with Clovis Affinities from Northeastern Texas. *Current Research in the Pleistocene* 6: 26–28.

Young, D. A., and R. L. Bettinger
1995 Simulating the Global Human Expansion in the Late Pleistocene. *Journal of Archaeological Science* 22: 89–92.

Young, D. A., and R. Bonnichsen
1984 *Understanding Stone Tools: A Cognitive Approach.* Center for the Study of Early Man, University of Maine, Orono.

Yu, P. L.
1996 Solo Cazando o Todo Recollectando? An Examination of South American Paleoindian Immigration and Colonization. Paper presented at the 63rd Annual Meeting of the Society for American Archaeology, Seattle.

Zeder, M. A.
1997 *The American Archaeologist: A Profile.* AltaMira Press, Walnut Creek, Calif.

Zegura, S.
1999 Boys and Girls, Stones and Bones, Sources and Trails, Words and Dates: Disparate Clues, Different Stories. Paper presented at the Pioneers on the Land: How America Got Its People Conference, Arizona State University, Tempe.

Zeimens, G. M.
1982 Analysis of Postcranial Bison Remains. In *The Agate Basin Site: A Record of the Paleoindian Occupation of the Northwestern High Plains*, edited by G. C. Frison and D. J. Stanford, pp. 213–240. Academic Press, New York.

Zeitlin, R. N.
1984 A Summary Report on Three Seasons of Field Investigations into the Archaic Period Prehistory of Lowland Belize. *American Anthropologist* 86: 358–368.

Zerjal, T., B. Dashnyam, A. Pandya, M. Kayser, L. Roewer, F. R. Santos, W. Schiefenhövel, N. Fretwell, M. A. Jobling, S. Harihara, K. Shimizu, D. Semjidmaa, A. Sajantila, P. Salo, M. H. Crawford, E. K. Ginter, O. V. Evgrafov, and C. Tyler-Smith
1997 Genetic Relationships of Asians and Northern Europeans Revealed by Y-Chromosomal DNA Analysis. *American Journal of Human Genetics* 60:1174–1183.

Zilhão, J., and F. d'Errico
1999 The Chronology and Taphonomy of the Earliest Aurignacian and Its Implications for Understanding Neandertal Extinction. *Journal of World Prehistory* 13:1–68.

Zimmerer, K. S.
1994 Human Geography and the "New Ecology": The Prospect and Promise of Integration. *Annals of the Association of American Geographers* 84(1):108–125.

Zubov, A. A., and N. I. Khaldeeva
1979 *Ethnic Odontology of the USSR.* Nauka, Moscow.

Zutter, C.
1989 Predicting North American Late Pleistocene Archaeology Using an Optimal Foraging Model. *Canadian Journal of Archaeology* 13:69–96.

ABOUT THE EDITORS

C. Michael Barton is Professor of Anthropology at Arizona State University in Tempe. He received his Ph.D. degree from the University of Arizona in 1987. Dr. Barton's research interests center around human ecology and the dynamics of Quaternary landscapes. He has long-term projects in the western Mediterranean and American Southwest, where he heads an international, multidisciplinary team studying the socioecology of prehistoric hunter-gatherers and the beginnings of agriculture. A Fulbright Senior Fellow, Dr. Barton is active in the application of quantitative techniques and computer technology in archaeology, especially GIS and remote sensing. His publications, which include nearly 40 papers and six books and monographs, deal with prehistoric technology, land use, and ecology; geoarchaeology; Darwinian theory; prehistoric rock art; and the peopling of the Americas.

Geoffrey A. Clark is the author, coauthor, or editor of more than 200 articles, notes, and comments as well as eight monographs and books on human biological and cultural evolution in "deep time": the past 4 million years. He received his Ph.D. degree from the University of Chicago in 1971. Dr. Clark's current interests involve the logic of inference in modern human origins research and the applications of neo-Darwinian evolutionary theory in archaeology and human paleontology. Recent publications include *Conceptual Issues in Modern Human Origins Research* (coedited with Cathy Willermet, Aldine de Gruyter, 1997) and *Rediscovering Darwin: Evolutionary Theory in Archaeological Explanation* (coedited with C. Michael Barton, American Anthropological Association, 1997). A Regents' Professor in the Department of Anthropology at Arizona State University in Tempe, Dr. Clark has chaired the American Anthropological Association's Archeology Division and the Anthropology Section of the American Association for the Advancement of Science. He lectures on race, racism, and ethnic conflict; the evolution of human mating practices; the conflict between religion and science; human evolution; and modern human origins. A materialist and evolutionist, he has lately been concerned with promoting Western science as a conceptual framework for describing and explaining the experiential world and with contesting the claims of the anti- and pseudoscience constituencies arrayed against it.

Georges A. Pearson is Professor of Anthropology at the University of Kansas in Lawrence, where he received his Ph.D. degree in 2002. His investigations have focused on late Pleistocene cultural exchanges and relationships across the Beringian and Panamanian land bridges. His interest in the peopling of the Americas began in Quebec and eventually led him to the Bering Land Bridge and the Ice Age landscapes of central Alaska, where he directed excavations at late Pleistocene–early Holocene sites (Moose Creek and Campus) and where he worked with David Yesner at the Broken Mammoth site. Following in the footsteps of the first Americans, Dr. Pearson then traveled south to another important land bridge—the Isthmus of Panama—to pursue investigations as a Predoctoral Fellow at the Smithsonian Tropical Research Institute. His survey project in Panama led to the discovery of several Paleoindian sites, including Vampiros Cave, the third locality in Central America and Mexico where fluted points have been found in a buried datable context. With his current work in Central America, Dr. Pearson hopes to link the early records of North and South America and help anthropologists formulate pan-continental colonization models.

David R. Yesner is Professor of Anthropology and Director of the Graduate Program in Anthropology at the University of Alaska in Anchorage. He received his Ph.D. degree from the University of Connecticut in 1977. Dr. Yesner's main interests are in environmental archaeology, especially zooarchaeology, and in ecological anthropology, especially the ecology of hunting and gathering societies. He has worked in various areas of North America and in Cyprus. His main areas of interest, however, include the circumpolar region—especially Alaska, Siberia, and the Russian Far East—and southern South America. Recent projects have included archaeological excavations in south-central Alaska and in Argentine Tierra del Fuego. Dr. Yesner is currently involved in three major projects. The first involves directing the excavation of the 12,000-year-old Broken Mammoth site near Big Delta, Alaska, a project that has been ongoing since 1989. The second entails excavating the historical Knik town site near Wasilla, Alaska, a gold rush community that was composed of both Euramerican settlers and Dena'ina Athabaskans (Alaskan Natives). The third is a collaborative investigation (with Alexander Popov of the Russian Far East National University Museum) of the Boisman II site near Vladivostok, an early Neolithic (4500 B.C.) coastal site that has produced a series of elaborate human burials with Paleoasiatic affinities, as well as faunal remains demonstrating the earliest maritime subsistence in the Russian Far East.

ABOUT THE CONTRIBUTORS

Larry D. Agenbroad is Professor of Geology and former Director of the Quaternary Studies Graduate Program at Northern Arizona University in Flagstaff. His is also Site Director at the Mammoth Site of Hot Springs, South Dakota, Inc. Dr. Agenbroad has conducted research investigations on the Colorado Plateau, in the American West, and in the desert Southwest for more than 30 years, with a special focus on Pleistocene megafauna and the people who hunted them.

C. Loring Brace earned his Ph.D. degree in biological anthropology from Harvard University in 1962. For more than a third of a century he has been Curator of Biological Anthropology at the University of Michigan Museum of Anthropology. He is also Professor of Anthropology at the University of Michigan in Ann Arbor. Dr. Brace has collected and analyzed dental and craniometric measurements from samples representing all the major regions of the world past and present.

Elizabeth S. Chilton is Assistant Professor of Anthropology at the University of Massachusetts in Amherst. Her research focus is the archaeological analysis of subsistence and settlement diversity among Native peoples of eastern North America. Dr. Chilton's recent publications include "Towns They Have None: Diverse Subsistence and Settlement Strategies in Native New England" (in *Northeast Subsistence-Settlement Change: A.D. 700–A.D. 1300*, New York State Museum, 2002).

Stuart J. Fiedel is Senior Archaeologist with the Louis Berger Group, an international consulting firm in Washington, D.C. He specializes in the archaeology of the Northeast and Mid-Atlantic regions. Dr. Fiedel is the author of *Prehistory of the Americas* (Cambridge University Press, 1987; second edition, 1992). He received his Ph.D. degree in anthropology from the University of Pennsylvania in 1979.

India S. Hesse completed her Ph.D. course work in anthropology at the University of Kansas. Since 1998 she has been an archaeological project manager and lithic analyst at SWCA, Inc. Environmental Consultants in Tucson. Her research interests include late Pleistocene and early Holocene hunter-gatherer campsite organization and lithic technology, as well as early agricultural development and sedentism in the American Southwest.

Jane H. Hill is Regents' Professor of Anthropology and Linguistics at the University of Arizona in Tucson. Her research interests include Native American languages, with a special focus on languages of the Uto-Aztecan family. Dr. Hill has conducted research on the structure, use, history, and prehistory of these languages.

Steven R. James is Assistant Professor of Anthropology at California State University in Fullerton. An archaeologist for more than 25 years, he has done fieldwork in California, the Great Basin, and the American Southwest. His research interests include zooarchaeology, prehistoric human impact on the environment, Paleoindians, historical archaeology in the West, pueblo architecture, and hominid evolution. Dr. James has authored more than 50 articles and 175 technical reports on archaeology and cultural resource management.

Douglas H. MacDonald received his Ph.D. degree in anthropology from Washington State University in 1998. He is Principal Investigator for archaeological projects at GAI Consultants, Inc. in Pittsburgh. Dr. MacDonald's research interests include the role of evolutionary theory in interpreting archaeological remains, lithic technological organization, Paleoindian colonization, hunter-gatherer subsistence and settlement systems, and cultural resource management.

Carole A. S. Mandryk received her Ph.D. degree in anthropology and Quaternary studies from the University of Alberta in 1992. She has been a member of Harvard University's Anthropology Department since 1993 and has done fieldwork in Canada, the United States, and the Russian Far East. Dr. Mandryk's research involves reconstructing past environments and analyzing the interactions between humans and the landscapes they inhabit, with a special focus on the rapidly changing environments of the last interglacial transition and its impact on the initial peopling of the Americas.

David J. Meltzer received his Ph.D. degree from the University of Washington in 1984 and immediately joined the faculty at Southern Methodist University in Dallas, where he is now Henderson-Morrison Professor of Prehistory and Director of the Quest Archaeological Research Program. His research interests include the peopling of the Americas, Paleoindians, Quaternary environments, and the history of American archaeology. He has done fieldwork throughout North America, especially in the Great Plains. Dr. Meltzer has published more than 100 articles and has authored or edited half a dozen volumes.

A. Russell Nelson is Adjunct Professor in the Department of Anthropology at the University of Wyoming in Laramie. He earned his Ph.D. degree from the University of Michigan in 1998 and has worked on field projects in Mongolia, Guam, Italy, Albania, and Brazil. Dr. Nelson's major research interests include the biological evidence regarding the peopling of the New World as well as the population distribution and relationships in the Classical World.

Pan Qifeng was trained at Beijing University and has recently retired from the Institute of Archaeology of the Chinese Academy of Social Sciences in Beijing, where he worked for years as an archaeologist. He learned craniometrics from his colleague Han Kangxin, who had studied under Karl Pearson's protégé, Woo Ting-Liang, at Fudan University in Shanghai. Together they have done extensive craniometric work on Chinese Neolithic, Bronze Age, and recent samples.

Steven Schmich is pursuing graduate studies in the Department of Anthropology at Arizona State University in Tempe. His research interests include the long-term dynamics between humans and the landscapes they inhabit. Current projects focus on late Pleistocene hunter-gatherers in southeastern Spain and their use of natural corridors for travel and exchange and on hunter-gatherers in the American Southwest. He has done fieldwork in Germany, Jordan, Spain, and the United States.

Kamille R. Schmitz was a graduate student in bioarchaeology at Arizona State University in Tempe. She currently resides in Oklahoma City, where she is pursuing a degree as a Physician's Assistant.

Theodore G. Schurr has spent the last 15 years investigating the genetic prehistory of Asia and the Americas through both laboratory research and field studies in Siberia. He is currently Assistant Professor in the Department of Anthropology at the University of Pennsylvania in Philadelphia. Dr. Schurr is also Consulting Curator of the Physical Anthropology Section at the University Museum.

Kenneth B. Tankersley earned his Ph.D. degree at Indiana University. His research has been featured on *National Geographic Explorer*, the Discovery Channel International, *All Things Considered*, and the BBC's *Nature*, with funding from the National Science Foundation, the National Academy of Science, and the L.S.B. Leakey Foundation. Dr. Tankersley's current academic affiliations include Northern Kentucky University, Augustana College, and the Cleveland Museum of Natural History. His latest book with Douglas Preston is *In Search of Ice Age Americans* (Gibbs Smith Publishers, 2002).

Elin Whitney-Smith is President of Netalyst in Washington, D.C. Netalyst designs, manages, and maintains large databases, websites, and search engines and does ecological systems modeling for conflict resolution. Dr. Whitney-Smith earned Ph.D. degrees in engineering management from Old Dominion University and in geobiology from George Washington University. She has presented her work on Pleistocene extinctions to the SAA, CANQUA, and AMQUA and on societal change during information revolutions to the U.S. Marine Corps and the U.S. Navy. She has published numerous articles and papers on both topics.

INDEX